4/3b

299

THE WISDEN PAPERS

1947 – 1968

THE WISDEN PAPERS

PAPERS

1947 – 1968

RISE AND FALL

EDITED BY BENNY GREEN

Stanley Paul

LONDON SYDNEY AUCKLAND
JOHANNESBURG

Stanley Paul & Co. Ltd

An imprint of Century Hutchinson Ltd
20 Vauxhall Bridge Road, London SW1V 2SA

Century Hutchinson Australia (Pty) Ltd
20 Alfred Street, Milsons Point, Sydney 2061

Century Hutchinson New Zealand Limited
PO Box 40–086, Glenfield, Auckland 10

Century Hutchinson South Africa (Pty) Ltd
PO Box 337, Bergvlei 2012, South Africa

First published 1990

Set in Times

Photoset by Deltatype Ltd, Ellesmere Port, Cheshire
Printed and bound in Great Britain by
Mackays of Chatham PLC, Chatham, Kent

British Library Cataloguing in Publication Data
The Wisden papers 1947 – 1968.
1. Cricket, 1938 – 1985
I. Green, Benny, 1927 –
796.35'8'0904
ISBN 0 09 1739519

Photo acknowledgement

The author and publishers would like to thank Hutton-Deutsch and Sport & General Press
Agency for allowing them to reproduce their copyright photographs in this book.

CONTENTS

'To glance through Wisden's Obituary pages is not morbid; you may learn something of value, if only that man is mortal.'

A.A. THOMSON.

INTRODUCTION

For the bookish element there were two heartening events in the publishing world of 1888, each connected in its own very different way with the concept of Empire. Rudyard Kipling introduced himself to the English reading public with 'Plain Tales from the Hills', and the editor of Wisden's Cricketers' Almanack acknowledged that even the most statistically minded of his patrons might enjoy reading something. In the 1888 edition of the Almanack there appeared an exhaustive, not to say exhausting, account of a meeting at Lord's to do with 'The Formation of a County Cricket Council'. The report was less a descriptive essay than a set of minutes of some learned society and was certainly not published with a view towards imparting any aesthetic pleasure any more than a volume of Hansard aspires to tempt the reader to keep turning the page in the hope of finding out what happened next. In Hansard nothing ever happens next and in the sporting annuals of the 1880s the same can be said, artistically speaking. But the departure of 1888 led in time to the compilation of a body of cricket literature considerable in quality as well as in sheer bulk. From the moment that Allan Gibson Steel made his star appearance in the 1890 edition, under the editorship of the newly appointed Sydney Pardon, the future of the Wisden essay was assured. In his opening gambit Steel soars far above the world of dusty statistics, offering us a late Victorian tableau so typical of its day as to be unwittingly funny:

> I was sitting in the smoking-room of a country house one night last autumn, thoroughly tired out after a long day's shooting. I felt perfectly comfortable in my large armchair watching the smoke slowly ascend from my briar.

This might be the overture to a comedy of manners in 'The Strand', or, with a few modest adjustments, to the kind of parody of which Stephen Leacock was such a master. But Steel is being perfectly serious and goes on to compile a rather good essay called 'Cambridge Memories', which ends as it starts with a modulation from the general to the particular and a kindly word for the remedial virtues of what he describes as 'the presidential Bollinger'.

The perceptive Pardon, realising the worth of what he had inaugurated, took care to ensure that Steel was followed by all manner of celebrities and functionaries, from the poet-cricketer D. L. A. Jephson to the autocratic crypto-professional A. C. MacLaren; later successors of Pardon observed the tradition and recruited essayists of every type, from the innocently devious B. J. T. Bosanquet to the affable G. H. Longman, from fearless A. E. R. Gilligan to peerless Jack Hobbs, from the larky Patsy Hendren to the magisterial G. O. Allen, from Lord Harris the blimp to H. D. G. Leveson-

Gower the shrimp. All of them and dozens of others contributed to the Almanack a variety of prose statements which were either erudite or amusing or both. By the end of the Second World War it could fairly be claimed that the annual reflective essay was among the most eagerly received features of each new Wisden. For in some charming and perhaps indefinable way the vast dish of small print was often rendered infinitely more palatable by the occasional felicity of a turn of phrase or random thought.

With the return to peace the essay not only maintained its place in Wisden but began to flourish to a degree which would have stupefied old John Wisden. In more recent years it has been not at all unusual for the Almanack to include two, three, or occasionally as many as four specially commissioned essays by figures connected to the game either by achievement or esteem. Very often these contributors have been men who might not otherwise have found the time or the opportunity to appear in print; consequently, over the years the Wisden essay has acquired a sort of rarity value in a world bursting with books about cricket. Where else but in Wisden, for instance, could Grahame Parker, sometime secretary of the Gloucestershire County Cricket Club, have found a home for his revealing account of the Midwinter affair? Who else but the editor of Wisden would have had the bright idea of inviting Sir Compton Mackenzie to give an account of his schoolboy idolatry of W. G. Grace? Through the agency of which other editorial board would Basil Easterbrook have been able to publish his fascinating review of the first-class cricket grounds of England? It is certainly true that right down the century opportunities were lost to incorporate into the Almanack contributions which would have enriched immeasurably the stockpot of cricket literature. In retrospect it seems incredible as well as tragic that Sir Arthur Conan Doyle was never asked to compile a piece on his considerable cricket career, that J. M. Barrie was never approached with a view to contributing a definitive essay on his cricketing affairs from the formation of the Allahakbarries to his improbable alignments with C. G. Macartney and Neville Cardus, that P. G. Wodehouse was never offered the opportunity to reminisce about the opening bowling partnership between himself and N. A. Knox at Dulwich College at the turn of the century, that it occurred to nobody to invite H. G. Wells to pluck the cricketing exploits of his father from the Records Section of the Almanack into the realms of pure prose, that neither Edmund Blunden nor Siegfried Sassoon nor Alec Waugh ever became contributors to the Almanack. Even so, the modern reader must be thankful for the rather more than small mercies that Wisden is able to provide in this regard.

When the post-war game resumed, there came the illusion of a false dawn. After a pedestrian 1946 season in which England defeated the visiting Indians and Yorkshire won the county championship for the umpteenth time, there followed the debacle of the 1946–47 tour of Australia which saw the annihilation of the visitors and the sad, anti-climactic end of the great career of Walter Hammond. Then came the miraculous doings of

1947 in which the English, half-frozen by a savage winter of blizzards and fuel shortages, emerged blinking into the benign sunlight of a vintage summer lit with the fires of Denis Compton's genius. He and his partner Bill Edrich left records strewn on the grass all over England. That one man might one day surpass Tom Hayward's record number of runs in a season was a theoretical possibility. That two men should surpass it in the same season sounded too fanciful for words. That two men from the same side should perform this dual miracle sounded less like the real world than the heightened melodramatics of the tuppenny bloods. Yet Compton and Edrich lived charmed lives that summer, as did English cricket generally. The South African tourists were put to the sword more or less single-handedly by Compton. More significantly, attendances at championship matches reached new heights. By the time Compton had scored his double century for Middlesex against the Rest of England while batting on one leg, more than two million fanciers of cricket had passed through the turnstiles. Who could doubt that the future of the game was assured? It was to prove the cruellest of illusions. After the highwatermark of 1947, attendances began falling away. The fall was never arrested and only the drastic restructuring of the first-class game in the 1960s saved it from total collapse. Yet there was not one reader of Wisden, as he settled down to the account of the exploits of the Middlesex Twins in the spring of 1948, who would have believed a word of it.

BENNY GREEN

PART ONE

1947 – 1956
Rise

COMPTON AND EDRICH [1948]

BY R. C. ROBERTSON-GLASGOW

Long before their annus mirabilis, Compton and Edrich had served notice of their potential. Edrich was 31 when the season started, Compton two years younger. Both were at the peak of their powers and each intimately familiar with the batting approach of the other, for their careers with Middlesex and England had run virtually parallel. Edrich made his debut for Middlesex in 1934 and scored his first century two years later, the same season in which Compton made his debut and scored his maiden century. In 1937 Compton had scored 65 against New Zealand in his Test debut; a year later he joined the select band of players who have scored a century on their debut against Australia, with 102 at Nottingham. Edrich had to wait till 1939 before making his international mark – 219 against South Africa in the timeless Test at Durban. In the 1946–47 tour of Australia, Edrich scored a hundred at Sydney and Compton two in the same match at Adelaide. Even so, nobody was prepared for the astonishing torrent of runs which poured from the two Middlesex stars in 1947. At first it was Edrich who made the pace, but from the middle of July, Compton entered into an enchanted phase which ended only when the season ended. Between July 12 and September 17 he scored 2017 runs, including twelve centuries, for an average of 109.01. To crown the joke, there was the Middlesex-Surrey match at The Oval just after the August Bank Holiday in which Denis bowled so eccentric a compendium of the left-hand spinning arts as to take 6 for 94 and 6 for 80, swelling his figures for the season to 73 wickets at just over 28 runs each. Edrich too performed like an authentic all-rounder, taking 67 wickets at 22.58 each.

But it was their batting and, in Compton's case, the style of the batsmanship, which fired the national imagination. Not since 1925 when Jack Hobbs passed Dr Grace's tally of first-class hundreds or perhaps Len Hutton's celebrated treble century against the Australians at The Oval in 1938, had the feats of any English cricketer transcended the merely sporting and crashed the front pages of the press. It seemed that nothing could ever stem Compton's flow. Yet the signs were there in the last and most extraordinary of all the 30 centuries rattled up by the two partners in the season. In the match between Champion County and the Rest of England, played at The Oval even as the autumn shadows advanced across the grass, Compton's knee, beginning to buckle under the strain of constant football every winter and cricket every summer, caused him to retire in mid-innings. On the second day's play, Monday, he resumed his innings with his knee strapped and, despite batting virtually on one leg, took his score to 246 before being stumped by Evans off Tom Goddard. Edrich made 180 before being dismissed in identical fashion and Middlesex ran out easy winners. But the knee, which newspapers quickly learned to refer to as The Knee, was to curtail Compton's career and reduce, though not destroy, the effect of his genius.

THEY go together in English cricket, as Gilbert and Sullivan go together in English opera. Nor is the analogy so careless as you might suppose. It may be allowable that each or any of these four has been surpassed in his own sphere; that would develop an argument to make any Paper Controller clutch his scanty reserves. But it should not be doubted that, in the art of giving pleasure to an English audience, both pairs lack rival.

In cricket of the first class both D. C. S. Compton and W. J. Edrich have, Providence favouring, at least ten years to go of play and struggle and alliance. As a pair they have yet, at the hour of writing, to quell the fiercest Test attack, in the sense that Hobbs and Sutcliffe quelled it; or as Bradman and Ponsford lorded it over English bowlers here in 1934. In summer, 1947, they scored between them over 2,000 runs against South Africa. To Tuckett and his fellow-bowlers, Compton and Edrich became the daily task and, maybe, the nightly vision. In the matter of Australia, fulfilment is awaited.

But, in that territory which lies outside the microcosm of numerals, already they are kings; benevolent kings appointed and acclaimed by like-minded subjects; champions in the fight against dullness and the commercial standard. In their cricket, it is what they are that matters far more than what they have done. They stand, in these eyes at least, for something which has no place prepared in the books of score and record. They are the mirror of hope and freedom and gaiety; heroic in the manner of the heroes of school stories; the inspiration, and quarry, of the young, because, in a game that threatens to become old in the saddest sense, they do not outgrow the habit, the ideals, the very mistakes of youth.

Most cricketers enjoy doing well, though I could name great ones who had a queer way of showing their enjoyment. But Compton and Edrich are of that happy philosophy which keeps failure in its place by laughter, like boys who fall on an ice-slide and rush back to try it again. They gave the impression, whether batting, bowling or fielding, that they are glad enough merely to be cricketing for Middlesex or England—'Fate cannot harm me, I have played today.' And they seem to be playing not only in front of us and for us, but almost literally with us. Their cricket is communicative. We are almost out of breath at the end of an over by Edrich. We scratch our heads perplexedly at a googly from Compton which refuses to work. We smile with something near to self-satisfaction when, with easy vehemence, he persuades a length-ball from the leg stump to the extra-cover boundary.

That such players should break records is inevitable rather than relevant. Numbers can be such silly things. They excite many and prove nothing, or nothing that matters. Sinatra has had more listeners than Caruso, Clark Gable more letters of homage than Sir Henry Irving. But *homo*, however *sapiens*, cannot feed on artistry alone, and, in cricket, the record-hunt inspires us with as pleasing an insanity as ever took John Peel from the first view-halloo to a death in the morning.

In summer, 1947, records made by the great Surrey and England pair, T. Hayward and J. B. Hobbs, were knocked down. Compton's 18 centuries in a season beat Hobbs's 16 centuries in a season of twenty-two years before; his 3,816 aggregate beat Hayward's 3,518 scored in 1906. And Hayward was also beaten by Edrich with 3,539. Very well done, too. But let us not therefrom deduce comparisons of skill; for, if we were to try anything in this line, we should have to bring up the subject of modern and ancient bowling, and that would lead us not only far from our brief but also to an inescapable, if unpalatable, conclusion. Let us, rather, flatter by inconclusiveness, and meditate on the analogy that Blackpool with 2,000,000 holiday-makers would not necessarily be an improvement upon Blackpool with 1,468,749.

Touching upon this question of records, I received at the end of summer, 1947, a letter from an Australian, a friend of cricket and of mine. 'As one of Compton's admirers,' he wrote, 'and doubtless all who see or meet him get that way, I hardly expected him to score 18 hundreds in a season. I thought him too good a player for that sort of thing. Am I right in assuming that Denis played his usual cricket and the 18 hundreds just happened in the process?' Well, my Sydney friend *is* right, or very nearly.

Compton cannot help it. He has the habit of batting, as the sun has the habit of journeying from east to west; and the fielders are his satellites. Hardest-worked of them, and most perplexed, is cover-point. Other batsmen of our time have been severer on the stroke. Walter Hammond could leave the nimblest cover motionless or just flickering as by token, could use cover's toecaps as an echoing junction for the boundary; but Compton uses cover-point as a game within a game, tantalises him with delayed direction and vexes him with variety. He is for ever seeking fresh by-products of the old forward stroke and has not yet, I fancy, come to the end of experiment. He finds it so amusing and so profitable. He outruns the traditional and discovers new truth. Compton is the axiom of tomorrow.

They say his feet are wrong. So, once, were Whistler's hands. They turn up the diagrams and manuals and grumble about the direction of his left leg. But why legs and feet only? I saw him, last summer at Lord's, playing strokes to Kent's Douglas Wright, when his body went one way, his arms the other way, and the ball the same way, past the fielders. It was genius; also contortionism. Dan Leno should have been batting at the other end, Nervo and Knox should have been in the umpires' coats, and Cinquevalli in the scorers' hutch. But, praise be, Compton has limitations, or pretends to have them. He uses the straight and near-straight drive less than most masters. Perhaps such strokes are too obvious; too easy, almost. They interfere with the jokes he hurls round cover-point. Again, he has a playful weakness for the short-arm sweep of the slow leg-break towards square-leg and long-leg, leading the bowler on to not always frustrated hope of timing error from inconsistency of bounce.

Compton has genius, and, if he knows it, he doesn't care. Edrich has talent; or, more truly, he started with a number of talents and has increased them into riches. Compton, in essence, has not altered from the lad of just eighteen who scored 100 not out at Northampton in 1936 while numbers ten and eleven, Sims and Peebles, admired and defended at the other end. His whereabouts in artistry cannot be doubted. His effect silences question. But Edrich has, as they say, gone through it. He rose, half fell, and rose again, to a place higher and less slippery. The cost and the lesson are expressed in his concentration. With bat and ball he is an all-in cricketer; no funny stuff here; no holidays of mind or body. Compton is poetry; Edrich is prose, robust and clear. Far more than Compton, Edrich uses the practical and old-fashioned methods and areas of attack. He likes the straight hit, and that pull-drive which gave old E. M. Grace so many runs and 'W. G.' so many moments of reflective beard-stroking. Old-fashioned, too, is Edrich's high back-lift in preparation for stroke. He gives the idea of a height and a reach beyond fact. But also he is a hooker, nearly as vicious as his great forerunner, Pat Hendren.

In bowling, though Compton uses the left arm and Edrich the right, they are alike in improvement by use. Edrich began as a muscular slinger, as a but moderate advance on village heroics; then he grew into knowledge of swerve and variety. He is never done with. Others of his kind blaze away for an hour or two, then die into ashes or a mere harmless flicker; but Edrich, near the end of an else fruitless day, flies flat into the attack and unlooses the unanswerable ball. Compton's slow left-hand bowling has about it a certain casual humour. He brings unrehearsed jokes on to the legitimate stage. He can bowl in a Test as if he were trying things out on a friend in the nets. He is still among the joys and errors of experiment. Anything may yet happen.

Both are magnificent fielders and throwers. Edrich has been allotted specialist work in the slips; Compton more often ranges the boundaries, where he may join, for moments of leisure, in that talk which is the salt and salad of cricket.

Both are fitting adornments and exponents of a game that was meant not as an imitation of, but as a refreshment from, the worldly struggle.

NO MAGIC IN FAST BOWLING [1948]

Honest Toil the Key to Success

BY C. J. KORTRIGHT

(IN AN INTERVIEW)

Like a giant shadow from the golden age there loomed in the 1948 edition the figure of Charles Jesse Kortright (1871–1952), nominated by more than one great batsman as the fastest bowler of all time. Kortright, six feet tall and an imposing specimen with an elegantly ferocious moustache, appeared in the Tonbridge side in 1887–88 and in the following season took his place in the

Essex side, where he stayed until the end of his career in 1907. He could count himself desperately unlucky never to have played for his country and shares with his teammate Percy Perrin the claim to have been the best cricketer never to have won an England cap. He was contemporaneous with the great Surrey bowlers Richardson, Lockwood and Knox and with the Lancashire pair Brearley and Mold; had the fates been a little kinder, he would surely have become a Test cricketer. It is said that in 1899, with Richardson injured, Lockwood in decline and Knox still a schoolboy, he would have been an automatic choice had injury not eliminated him. Against Surrey at Leyton in 1895 he bowled out six men, including Abel, Hayward and Lohmann, for four runs. Two years earlier, on the same ground in the same fixture, he had taken thirteen wickets. At Leyton in 1900 he ran through the powerful Yorkshire batting and once took seven for 73 for the Gentlemen against the Players at Lord's. But his most memorable feat may well have been the one he took such delight in describing. He closes his essay with his version of events but does not hint that he was also a more than useful batsman who scored some spectacular centuries. In his review of fast bowling he raises some interesting points regarding the advantages held by modern fast bowlers over the men of his own generation.

ONE of the questions my friends most frequently ask me is why there are so few fast bowlers today compared with the start of the century, and why the few there are attain comparatively small success. They seem to think there was some sort of magic about the old-time men of pace, and that I may be able to explain how it was obtained. Let me disillusion them at once. There is no magic in fast bowling; but, on the contrary, much hard work, coupled with intelligent methods, is the key to success.

I have little patience with modern bowlers who condemn 'these shirt-front wickets' and ask how can they be expected to get men out when the pitch will not help. There were many such pitches in my playing days, the sort on which if we could bounce the ball bail high we thought ourselves pretty clever. Yet every county fielded two, sometimes three, genuinely fast bowlers, who were not discouraged by the wickets.

A basic principle of cricket which I feel is sometimes overlooked is that the prime object of a bowler is to get batsmen out. For this reason I do not favour the modern craze for such expressions as 'in-swingers', 'out-swingers', all sorts of 'spins' and 'swerves'. Some bowlers seem to concentrate on these dubious achievements so much that they forget to keep a length and to bowl at the stumps.

A striking sign of this tendency is the present cult of off-spin bowling to a cluster of short-leg fielders, who would not have been allowed to stay in their suicidal positions by some of the old-time batsmen like Gilbert Jessop and Johnny Tyldesley. This style compares very poorly with the methods of Tom Richardson of Surrey, the finest bowler I ever saw. He used only two leg-side men, a mid-on and a deep fine-leg to save snicks, because he bowled consistently on the off-stump to that beautiful length which meant that batsmen could never leave the ball alone.

Richardson's long easy run, fine action, accuracy and speed, coupled with a little break-back from the off, made him a bowler to be feared; and another man I greatly admired was Walter Brearley, who took a much shorter run but achieved real pace through a splendid body action. Such men as these could take seven or eight wickets in an innings on plumb pitches, nearly all clean bowled, because they bowled a length, bowled with their heads, and bowled at the stumps. What is the use of 'swerves' if you beat the batsman, beat the wicket-keeper, and everybody else? Bowlers like Richardson used to move the ball just that vital inch or two off the pitch, and they hit the stumps.

If England can find a real fast bowler who is willing to take a bit of advice from an old-timer, here is a wrinkle he might well remember. He should never forget to try bowling a fast yorker on the leg stump to a newly arrived batsman. It can be a deadly ball to face early in an innings; I have dismissed many top-class batsmen with it. I frequently used to advise the late Kenneth Farnes to pitch the ball farther up to the batsmen, because I considered that he wasted too much energy on pointless short deliveries, like many other modern pace bowlers.

Another encouragement which I would mention to bowlers and those aspiring to success with the ball is that they enjoy many advantages compared with those of the old days. They have a slightly smaller ball—easier to get the hand round—a wider crease, which helps in varying the angle of delivery, bigger stumps at which to aim. There is also the new leg-before-wicket law by which it is possible to get a decision from a ball pitching on the off-side of the wicket, a boon to the modern bowler. Last but by no means least among present-day benefits is the high standard of umpiring in first-class cricket, one respect in which I admit the game has made a great advance since my days.

The umpires of today are very good and impartial. They watch the ball extremely closely and know the game thoroughly, so that any bowler can feel confident that he will get any decisions he has earned.

A young bowler should not be allowed to over-tax his strength and, although there is no reason why he should not bat well, it should always be remembered that his real task is to take wickets. I remember Alfred Shaw of Nottinghamshire telling me when I was a youngster why the best bowlers so seldom make runs. He said: 'After holding a bat for a long time we lose that freshness in ourselves, and that suppleness in the fingers which helps so much in bowling. So it is better not to bat too much when one will soon have to bowl.'

[*Shaw, between 1864 and 1897, took 2,072 wickets for 11.97 runs each, much the lowest figure of the twenty bowlers who have taken over 2,000 wickets in first-class cricket.*—EDITOR.]

Another thing a bowler should always remember is to mark out his run and stick to it, even at practice. Too many no-balls are delivered by men who should know better, and they represent free gifts to the opposing side.

Perhaps one of the greatest differences between modern and old-time bowling lies in the attitude towards the new ball and the method of gripping it. Personally, I didn't worry a great deal about how I held the ball in relation to the seam as long as I got a firm grip on it, and I think most of my contemporaries felt the same. We wanted to be accurate, and to make the ball move a little off the pitch through finger action. For that reason, fast bowlers often roughened a new ball by rubbing it in the dirt, to obtain a good grip. Now bowlers dirty their clothes in efforts to keep the ball shiny, but I feel sure they do not control it so well.

I do not think we shall get a plentiful supply of bowling talent again until the youngsters realise that there is no easy way to become a good bowler, and no secret either. The road to success lies in enthusiasm coupled with patience and willingness to devote as much time as possible to practice. I do not feel that young cricketers today are always prepared to take the trouble over their game that they should, possibly because there are so many counter-attractions.

One of the clearest recollections of my early days is the 'little cricket' we played at Brentwood School. This involved creeping out through a window at four in the morning, with any sort of makeshift gear, to play against the chapel wall until seven o'clock, the official time for rising. If discovered, we were in trouble, but I thought the game well worth the risk, and I was always ready for two and a half hours of compulsory cricket practice when school was over for the day.

In those days almost invariably I was holding something to throw or bowl, if not a ball a sizeable stone, which I would hurl at a convenient tree or post. All this helped to develop a sense of distance and timing, and built up the muscles of hand, arm and shoulder. I was for ever wanting to project things farther or faster than any of my friends, and this I think accounted for the pace I was able to develop later as a bowler.

The present-day lack of enthusiasm for practice, especially in bowling and fielding, was brought home to me a few years ago when I tried to coach two youngsters in whom I was interested. They batted in the nets for about half an hour, then they wanted to be off to knock a ball about at some other game. As for bowling to somebody else or getting fielding practice—that mattered not at all.

Yet I would stress to all cricketers, especially the youngsters, that if we are to develop great bowlers again, and especially fast bowlers, there must be much greater concentration on fielding. Any bowler is so much better with the support of a keen field, and every player in any side should impose an unwritten law on himself to field well even if he can do little else. I used to enjoy Free Foresters cricket immensely because it was played in a really sporting spirit and the standard of fielding was very high.

As a final word to budding fast bowlers, let me again emphasise that you should not be afraid to pitch the ball well up, and remember the value of the yorker on the leg stump against a newcomer. The first time I hit the stumps in county cricket was with that ball, in the Essex and Surrey match at The Oval in 1892. I bowled Billy Brockwell with a fast one which hit the base of the stumps and brought the bails forward, one breaking as it flew over my head. Another of my yorkers which remains in my memory rebounded from the bottom of the stumps and went back past me almost to the boundary.

[*In the match to which C. J. Kortright refers, he took in all five wickets for 71 runs, three of them bowled, but Surrey, for whom Tom Richardson gained match figures of 12 for 100, won by 195 runs.*—EDITOR.]

My favourite story is rather hard to believe, but I vouch for its truth. Playing in a club match at Wallingford on a very small ground with a pitch perhaps best described as 'sporty', I bowled a ball which rose almost straight and went out of the ground, without a second bounce. I suggest that this made me the first man to bowl a six in byes! The ball was pitched right up to the batsman and on the wicket, so that it was undoubtedly within the striker's reach, and there was no question of wides being awarded.

SIR STANLEY JACKSON [1948]

BY H. PRESTON

In that same edition of 1948 the editor, Hubert Preston, commissioned himself to compose a fulsome obituary of Colonel the Honourable Sir Francis Stanley Jackson, P.C., G.C.S.I., G.C.I.E. (1870–1947), a man who really did live up to the claims of so many Victorian dunderheads to have experienced a life full of incident. Jackson began life with Winston Churchill as his fag at Harrow and very nearly ended it at the hands of an assassin. After his playing days were done, he rose to dizzy heights in politics, but in spite of this he seems to have been a likeable sort of chap. One of the great all-rounders of his generation, his feats of 1905, when he led England through an undefeated series against Australia, won all five tosses and finished top of the batting and bowling averages, is never likely to be matched. Considering the social climate of the day, his refusal to allow the colour of Ranjitsinhji's skin to render him persona non grata in the Cambridge side was a noble stance; he once explained that it was his experience of Indian culture under the captaincy of Lord Hawke in the tour of 1892–93 which endowed him with the insight to see through the prejudice which might otherwise have denied Ranji his rightful place.

Outside the world of cricket, Jackson enjoyed equal success. His record in the Boer War and the Great War was distinguished, but there remains one aspect of his political career which has never adequately been explained away. In 1923 he became chairman of the Unionist Party at a particularly scurvy moment in the history of that exotic organisation. When in that year Ramsay Macdonald's minority Labour Government fell, the issue of the General Election which followed was influenced substantially by the Zinoviev Letter, a dubious document purporting to prove that Macdonald and his colleagues were willing tools of the Kremlin. One of the earliest Reds-under-the-bed scares of the century, the Tory campaign featured a document whose authenticity was never subsequently established. 'The Oxford History of England' reminds us that the original was never produced, that its jargon was maladroit, and its definition of various characters at fault. No one has explained how copies of the Letter reached Conservative Central Office and the editor of the 'Daily Mail' before the Foreign Office was informed. Whether the Hon. F. S. Jackson was involved in the manipulation of this trumped-up bugaboo is a question nobody has ever investigated, but if his hands were indeed clean, posterity may be pardoned for wondering precisely what Sir Stanley's duties as Chairman of the party were; the issue certainly casts on the nonpareil Jackson a light rather less flattering than that generated by Preston's obituary and the tributes of friends.

THE passing of Colonel The Honourable Sir Francis Stanley Jackson, P.C., G.C.I.E., on March 9, in his 77th year, came as a shock, not only to all who knew him personally, but also to every lover of cricket who had watched and enjoyed his wonderful prowess on the field of play. From the time that F. S. Jackson at Lord's by his remarkable all-round success helped Harrow gain a victory over Eton by 156 runs in 1888, he went on from strength to strength, until he became one of the finest cricketers ever seen in England. Unfortunately he could not go on any tour to Australia owing to business reasons, and the presence of Lord Hawke in command of Yorkshire until 1910 prevented him from ever being the county captain, though occasionally in charge of the side. He reached the zenith of fame in 1905 when captain of England against Australia. In all five Tests he won the toss; made 492 runs with an average of 70, among his scores being 144 not out at Leeds, 113 at Manchester, 82 not out at Nottingham, 76 and 31 at The Oval; took 13 wickets at 15.46 each, surpassing the efforts of all his colleagues and opponents. Of the five contests, England won that at Nottingham by 213 runs—after declaring with five men out—and that at Manchester by an innings and 80 runs, while they held much the stronger position in each of the three matches left unfinished. By a curious coincidence Stanley Jackson and Joseph Darling, then the Australian captain, were exactly the same age, both having been born on November 21, 1870. That was Darling's third visit as captain and his last tour in England. He died on January 2, 1946, and his obituary in last year's *Wisden* contains some of his experiences in opposition to Jackson.

Regarding his luck in winning the toss in those 1905 tests and as captain of M.C.C., for whom he scored 85 in a rain-ruined match at Lord's, Jackson said at Scarborough, when captain for the seventh time against the Australians: 'I found Darling stripped to the waist. He said, "Now we'll have a proper tossing, and he who gets on top wins the toss." So I said to George Hirst, "Georgie, you come and toss this time." Darling then said, "All right, we'll toss in the old-fashioned way!" ' Again winning the toss, Jackson scored 123 and 31 not out, rain preventing a definite result.

Born at Chapel Allerton, near Leeds, Stanley Jackson showed

remarkable batting ability when at a preparatory school before he went to Harrow, where he was in the eleven for three years, being captain in 1889. He did little on the first occasion, and his father, then the Rt. Hon. W. L. Jackson, a member of the Cabinet in Lord Salisbury's second Government, promised Stanley a sovereign for each wicket he took and a shilling for each run he made. Stanley scored 21 and 59 and took eleven wickets for 68 runs; Harrow won by 156 runs. His father's generosity over cricket ceased with that match. Stanley's only comment was that he was glad he had come off, as it would 'do father so much good'.

Next year, when captain, five wickets fell to him, and his vigorous 68, best score in the match, accounted largely for victory by nine wickets. Proceeding to Cambridge, Jackson gained his Blue as a Freshman, and in 1892 he headed both the batting and bowling averages, and in first-class matches came out third among the amateur bowlers with 80 wickets for less than 19 runs apiece.

Re-elected captain, he led Cambridge to victory by 266 runs in 1893, showing such convincing form that he was given a place in the England team for the first Test at Lord's. He followed a splendid innings of 91 with 103 at The Oval, but when, late in August, the time came for the third Test—at Manchester—he and other Yorkshiremen who might have been included in the side turned out for their county against Sussex at Brighton. He was one of 'Five All-Rounders' given prominence in 1894 *Wisden*.

Describing his first Test innings of 91 in 1893 at Lord's, Sir Stanley smiled and then related that, in the second Test at The Oval, W. G. Grace, the England captain, said, 'With all these batsmen I don't know where to put you.' 'Anywhere will do.' 'Then number seven.' 'Thanks. That's my lucky number; I was the seventh child.' 'And that match brought my first hundred for England. Mold came in last when I was 99. He nearly ran me out, so in desperation I jumped in and drove Giffen high to the seats, reaching 103. Then the bewildered Mold did run me out.'

Jackson figured in all the 1896 Test matches, also in the next visit from Australia when the 'rubber' was extended to five fixtures, being credited with 118 at The Oval in 1899. In the great games of 1902 Jackson was England's best batsman. He did little at Sheffield, but at Birmingham, when three wickets fell for 35, he scored 53 and with J. T. Tyldesley saved England from collapse. At Lord's Fry and Ranjitsinhji were dismissed without a run, but Jackson and A. C. MacLaren, contemporaries at Harrow, raised the total to 102 without being separated before rain washed out the match. In the memorable Manchester struggle, which Australia won by three runs, five England wickets went down for 44 in reply to a total of 299, but Jackson and Braund pulled the game round with a partnership of 141, Jackson himself going on to make 128. At dinner in the evening of that great day a lady sitting next to him said, 'I was so disappointed that Ranjitsinhji failed'—and this remark was made to the man who had played the innings of his life. He was fond of telling this little yarn against himself.

At The Oval Jackson scored 49, sharing in a partnership of 109 with G. L. Jessop, whose wonderful innings of 104 paved the way to England's one-wicket victory. Altogether Jackson scored 1,415 runs in Test matches against Australia—all in this country—with an average of nearly 49, and took 24 wickets at an average of 33.

Jackson played first for Yorkshire in 1890, and his last appearance for the side was in 1907. During that period he scored 10,405 runs for the county, averaging nearly 34 an innings, and dismissed 506 batsmen for 19 runs apiece. In 1898, the only season when he appeared regularly for his county, he scored 1,566 runs and took 104 wickets. His highest scores for Yorkshire were 160 against Gloucestershire, 158 against Surrey, and 155 against Middlesex. He appeared on many occasions for Gentlemen against Players, and in those games made over a thousand runs, average 31.50, and took 50 wickets. His aggregate for all first-class matches was 16,251 runs, average 33, and 834 wickets at 19 runs each.

Among his bowling triumphs were eight Lancashire wickets at Sheffield in 1902 for 13 runs, and the last four Australian wickets in five balls at Leeds in the same year, his analysis being five wickets for 12; he and George Hirst dismissed the Australians for 23. This happened directly after England in a drawn Test match had disposed of Australia for 36; Rhodes, who took seven wickets for 17, did not bowl in the more remarkable collapse of the Australians for the second lowest total ever recorded by an Australian side in England. When in 1896 Harry Trott's team fell for 18 before M.C.C. at Lord's, Jackson scored 51 on a treacherous pitch. In the Gentlemen and Players match at Lord's in 1894 he and S. M. J. Woods bowled unchanged. Jackson took 12 wickets for 77 and, in addition, made 63—the highest score of the match, which the Gentlemen won by an innings and 37 runs before four o'clock on the second day.

Going to India with Lord Hawke's team in the winter of 1892–93, Jackson took 69 wickets at 10.27 runs apiece and tied for first place in the batting averages with A. J. L. Hill, a Cambridge contemporary. When again captain of the Light Blues in 1893, Jackson gave Ranjitsinhji his Blue. At Lord's he instructed C. M. Wells to bowl wides in order to prevent Oxford from getting a desired follow-on, and Cambridge won by 266 runs. This set an example followed by Frank Mitchell three years later, when Oxford won by four wickets, and so primarily led to an alteration in the laws, making the follow-on an optional choice for the side holding the upper hand.

President of the Marylebone Club in 1921, the highest honour that a cricketer can enjoy, Sir Stanley Jackson was chairman of the Test Match Selection Committee in 1934, and in 1943 presided over the special committee appointed by M.C.C. to consider Post-war Cricket.

Well-built and standing nearly six feet high, Stanley Jackson was equipped with special physical advantages for cricket; to these were added fine judgment, perseverance, and, above all, exceptional courage which amounted to belief in his own abilities. Free and stylish in method, he drove splendidly on either side of the wicket and was perhaps the finest forcing on-side batsman of his time. While essentially a forward player on hard wickets, he had at his command on sticky wickets a strength and science of back play to which few men have attained. His great stroke sent a good-length ball through the covers; he cut square or late and turned the ball cleverly on the leg side with similar precision. Nothing was better than the way he jumped in and drove the ball over the bowler's head, as shown in the life-like picture at Lord's, and as I saw at Bradford, where he sent the ball high over the football stand.

A right-handed rather fast-medium bowler with a nice easy action and plenty of spin, he kept a good length and often got on a sharp off-break. On a difficult wicket he was a bowler who might dispose of any side. While always a keen and smart field, especially at cover-point, he was not in his early days a sure catch, but steadily improved in this respect and made himself in every sense a great player.

At Bradford on one occasion he was out to a brilliant catch in the long field, whereupon he tucked his bat under his arm and joined vigorously in the applause which greeted the fieldsman's splendid effort.

On the same ground, where there is a stone wall in front of the pavilion, a ball bowled by Jackson was sent by a low skimming drive with such force that it rolled back from the wall into the middle of the field, coming to rest practically at the bowler's feet. Jackson, in appreciation of the remarkable occurrence, made the ball a dignified bow.

In the South African War Jackson served with the Royal Lancaster Regiment of Militia, and in the first Great War, 1914–18, he was Lieutenant-Colonel of a West Yorkshire Regiment battalion which he raised and commanded. He entered Parliament in 1915 and remained Unionist member for Howdenshire Division of Yorkshire until 1926. One day in the House of Commons dining-room Mr. Winston Churchill, who had been his fag at Harrow, said, 'Let me introduce you to Mr. Lloyd George.' There came a quick exclamation, 'I have been looking all my life for the man who gave Winston Churchill a hiding at school.'

When he wanted to make his maiden speech the debate went unfavourably, and he received a note from the Speaker: 'I have dropped you in the batting order; it's a sticky wicket.' Then, at a better opportunity, he sent this hint: 'Get your pads on; you're next in.'

In 1922 he was appointed Financial Secretary to the War Office, and next year he succeeded Lord Younger as Chairman of the Unionist Party Organisation. In 1927 he went out to India as Governor of Bengal. There he proved equal to the most trying situation, behaving with splendid nerve and authority when he nearly fell a victim to attempted assassination by a Calcutta girl student who fired five shots at close range, narrowly missing Sir Stanley when presiding at a meeting. His London home was bombed in 1940, and in August 1946 he was run over by a taxi, receiving a severe injury to his right leg: a climax to unpleasant experiences which no doubt contributed to his last illness and hastened the end of this very distinguished Englishman.

H. P.

TRIBUTES

In *Wisden*, 1932, Lord Hawke, in an article—'Fifty Years of Yorkshire County'—wrote:—

'Our greatest amateur was undoubtedly Stanley Jackson, who was "Jacker" to everyone from his Harrow days. He was a great batsman, great bowler, fine fielder—a great cricketer to the core. Few who remember him as a batsman know that he was once No. 10 in the batting order for Yorkshire! This is how it happened. Though he had just taken seven for 42 against Middlesex, somebody had run him out for a song and he did not seem keen to play in the next match at Chesterfield.

' "Why," I argued with him, "you've just got seven of 'em out at six apiece! You must come." So he came all right. Next day as I was writing out the order I asked him where he'd like to go in, so he said, "Oh, don't know. Treat me as a bowler." So I wrote him down No. 10. Brown and Tunnicliffe then proceeded to make 554 for the first wicket. I was No. 3 that day in Jackson's place. As they walked out to bat I put on my pads. I took them off for the lunch interval; I put them on again and took them off again for the tea interval. Again I put them on, and sat another couple of hours. Such is cricket!

'I have never seen "Jacker's" equal at bowling for his field. I remember one occasion when we were "in the cart" at Bradford against Surrey how precisely he bowled for his field, and how he apologised to me for having bowled a ball not intended. Though his grand batting for England is probably best remembered, he was a bowler of the very highest class, with a graceful, flowing delivery of a kind but rarely seen nowadays.

'Since those happy days "Jacker" has passed through more serious times in Bengal. There, a couple of years ago, he and I were the guests of honour at the dinner to us of the Calcutta Cricket Club given at the Bengal Club. We both made speeches, and when he got up to speak first he said across the table to me, "I've got first innings today, old man. You bossed me often enough in the past, but I'm boss here!" '

Sir Pelham Warner, in a letter to *The Times*, wrote:—

'I had known Sir Stanley Jackson since 1889, when Harrow met Rugby at Althorp Park. On that evening began a friendship which grew with the years, and which I prized greatly. "He was my friend, faithful and just to me," and though we all have to face the Pale Horseman there is no need to be afraid of him, and I am certain Sir Stanley faced him with the same calm courage as he showed in the great matches of his day. He was a splendid all-round cricketer—one of the finest in the history of cricket—and never was he finer than in a crisis; it was a stirring sight to see him come down the pavilion steps to set right any early failures there may have been; immaculate in his flannels and his beautifully cleaned pads and boots, with his neat trim figure every inch a cricketer. No English cricketer had a finer record in England against Australia. And then, when he gave up, he sat on the Woolsack of Cricket, as President of the M.C.C., and at the time of his death he was a trustee of Lord's, chairman of the Cricket Committee, and president of the Yorkshire C.C.C. To the end he took the greatest possible interest in M.C.C. Never a week passed, even during the winter, that he was not at Lord's, and in the summer he was the best known of all the men who delight in the charm and atmosphere of the famous ground. He was busy with every avenue and aspect of the game and his enthusiasm never flagged. That he had been seriously ill for some time was obvious, but only a few days before he died he telephoned asking me to come to see him. I found him in good spirits, saying that he felt so much better that he had good hopes of coming to Lord's for a committee meeting.

'As a batsman he was soundness itself, with all the strokes—what I call a "complete" batsman. His style was easy and natural and he inspired confidence. Bowling medium pace, with a beautifully easy action, he kept a length. At cover-point, his usual position, he was not a Hobbs or a Jessop, but active and quick, missing few chances. In a gallery of great players it is impossible to have a fixed order of merit, but he was in the first class of an honours school of cricket both as a batsman and an all-rounder. When you have known and been very fond of a man for nearly sixty years it is not easy to write exactly what you feel about him, but this I will say, that his manner was always easy and pleasant, and in the cricket world, by young and old alike, he was welcomed, appreciated and respected. His absence leaves a big void.'

Wilfred Rhodes, now 70 years of age, wrote:—

'In paying a modest tribute to the late Sir Stanley Jackson it is difficult for me to find words that would express my appreciation of such a great cricketer with so fine a personality. From 1898 to the close of his first-class cricket career I was fortunate to play on the same side for Yorkshire and under his captaincy several times for England, chiefly in Tests against Australia, and had a great admiration for his ability. He was one of England's greatest captains and played many splendid innings during this period. It was a pity he never toured Australia, as I think he would have been very successful with his style of play on their fast wickets.

'A model all-round cricketer if ever there was one, he was immaculately dressed, flannels always neat and trim even at the end of a long innings, and whether batting, bowling or in the field, his movements were stylish and graceful. He was a great batsman and possessed the gift of a fine temperament, with plenty of confidence and pluck, and always appeared at his best on great occasions, especially when fighting with his back to the wall. Many times he pulled the game around for England and helped to put them on the way to victory. His batting was stylish, orthodox and very copy-book, with strokes all round the wicket, and particularly strong to the off.

'As a bowler he used spin and variation of pace with a clever slow one. On one occasion, when bowling to G. L. Jessop at Cambridge, he sent up his slower ball, which was hit out of the field over the trees. Schofield Haigh, fielding mid-on, was laughing, and F. S., turning round, said to him, "What are you laughing at?" Haigh replied, "Your slow ball, sir." F. S.: "It was a good one, wasn't it?" '

George Hirst, the famous Yorkshire cricketer, now in his 77th year, wrote at the time of Sir Stanley's death:—

'I am deeply grieved to learn of the death of my friend and colleague. He was one of the most graceful of all cricketers, whether he was batting, bowling or fielding, and he was a perfect gentleman in everything he did, both on and off the field.

'In him young cricketers had a perfect model. Many are the times I have seen him with a beautifully rolled umbrella in his hand demonstrating strokes to schoolboys. He loved to help the youngsters, and that was possibly why he was always so keenly interested in my work as coach to the county club. I have indeed lost a good friend.'

Mr. H. D. G. Leveson Gower said: 'As a Test Match player Sir Stanley never has been excelled in temperament or skill. I served with him on many M.C.C. committees, and his views on the game always commanded attention. I played against him for Oxford in the 'Varsity match of 1893, and consider the Cambridge eleven he captained one of the most powerful to represent that University. His name will always live in the annals of cricket, the game he adorned.'

Mr. Stanley Christopherson, President of M.C.C. for several years until 1946: 'I held the greatest admiration for Sir Stanley both as a cricketer and for his great work for the game; he was most painstaking and did splendid work on many committees and as a selector.'

Mr. T. L. Taylor, an old Cambridge Blue who was elected the new president of Yorkshire in the autumn, a contemporary player with Sir Stanley, described his death as a very serious loss to county and international cricket and the game in general, and said: 'He was one of Yorkshire's greatest all-rounders, and one of England's most redoubtable Test captains.'

The King was represented by Lord Chorley at the London memorial service for Sir Stanley Jackson. Canon F. H. Gillingham, the former Essex cricketer, who conducted the service, said:—

'The first time I ever played with him I was impressed with his strength of character and control. He always seemed to have that extra reserve of strength to compete with any cricket crisis, however severe.

'He was the most honest man I ever met—in fact he was too honest. I never heard him say an unkind word about anyone, and he always had excuses for anyone who spoke an unkind word to him.

'So we say farewell to a great English gentleman, but we will retain with us for ever the remembrance of all that he meant to us and to the country he served so well.'

AUSTRALIA AND ENGLAND [1948]

Sidelights on the Tests

BY V. G. J. JENKINS

The English cricket public had no sooner digested the prodigies of Compton and Edrich than it was confronted yet again by the minatory presence of Don Bradman. The Australian captain, whose retirements were beginning to sound so operatic that he was in danger of becoming the Dame Nellie Melba of cricket, had decided, after a successful if contentious comeback in the rubber of 1946–47, to make one last tour of England. His hosts, pondering the wholesale slaughter of that campaign, became distinctly anxious at the thought of another encounter with substantially the same side. Wisden carried its usual essay of welcome to the visitors and the man commissioned to compile it was the experienced journalist V. G. J. Jenkins. Jenkins had played for Oxford against Cambridge in the low-scoring drawn game of 1933 and later in the decade made occasional appearances in the championship for Glamorgan. But any reputation Jenkins enjoyed in cricket was totally eclipsed by his legendary stature as one of the greatest full-backs ever to represent Wales in Rugby Union. His review of England–Australia struggles is not especially imaginative but it makes much more pleasant reading than the match reports of the Australian Tests which appeared in the next edition.

IT is a truism that you cannot have the best of anything in this life without having the worst of it as well. This applies to the history of England–Australia Test cricket as surely as it does to the freedom of the Press, Elizabethan drama, Aunt Agatha's cooking, or any other institution subject to the whims and caprices of human nature.

For some reason, wherever there have been Tests there has also been Trouble.

Larwood and 'bodyline' we all know, except those fortunates still in their 'teens. More recently the umpiring controversies of the 1946–47 tour 'down under' are too fresh in the memory to need recalling. But these are only the more recent instalments in a serial that has gone on since the earliest days. As far back as 1879 there occurred in Sydney an incident which, if it were repeated today, would call for the combined efforts of U.N.O. to restore order. Lord Harris's XI, beaten in the first Test match, were due to play a return, but it never took place owing to the high feeling caused by some remarkable scenes when the Tourists met New South Wales.

Umpires, even in those days, and an English one in particular, named Coulthard, caused the trouble. So enraged were the crowd by one of his decisions that they invaded the pitch. Those players best tactically situated were able to grab hold of the stumps to defend themselves. Others had to use their fists. Lord Harris was struck by a man with a stick, but A. N. Hornby intervened and carried off the culprit struggling to the pavilion. One can only imagine what repercussions this would have today.

Much the same happened to Sir Pelham Warner's team on the same ground in 1903–4, but this time physical intervention by the onlookers was limited to long-range bombardment with bottles and other missiles. Once again the reason for the outburst had a familiar ring—'Rain stopped play—crowd not agreeing.'

Money, too, has always been a bone of contention. Five of the first nine teams to visit Australia, from 1862 to 1886, were all-professional ones under professional captains; this might surprise many moderns who constantly clamour for this as though it were something new.

Not unnaturally, with cricket not thoroughly established then as now, the financial side was a matter of some hazard. Therefore it came as a shock to Arthur Shrewsbury's team of 1884–85 when they found after their arrival in Australia that their opponents, supposedly amateurs, also wanted a half-share of the gate receipts. This was against W. L. Murdoch's team, recently back from a successful tour of England. They were at last grudgingly offered 30 per cent of the takings for the first Test at Adelaide. This they refused to accept, but after further wrangling finally agreed to take a flat guarantee of £450 from the South Australian Cricket Association.

In the next Test at Melbourne, Murdoch's men withdrew absolutely, and though they came back to the fold by ones and twos for future matches the whole series became a farce. At Adelaide, Murdoch refused to accept James Lillywhite as an umpire, and two local men were brought in with dire results.

Another extraordinary interlude occurred in 1887–88, when two English teams went off to tour Australia concurrently. One under the Hon. M. B. Hawke, who returned to England because of the death of his father; the other under C. Aubrey Smith, now better known in the role of a Bengal Lancer, with variations. They combined for the one Test, W. W. Read being captain.

Not unnaturally both teams suffered a severe financial loss, but provided an all-time deterrent to similar experiments in the future.

In those days Australian teams came to England on a 'share all profits' basis, except for a few junior members, who had to be satisfied with a half-share as compared with their seniors. Victor Trumper was one such, but was so successful on his first tour that he was promoted to 'full-sharing' status at the end of it.

Managers have always been fair game when other means of causing trouble have exhausted themselves. In 1912 six leading Australian players, Trumper, Clem Hill, Warwick Armstrong, Carter, Ransford and Cotter refused to come to England for the Triangular Tournament unless they were allowed to select their own manager.

To the credit of the Australian Board of Control, they stood firm in the matter and sent the team without the six players concerned, even though it caused a tremendous hullabaloo at the time.

For providing the real touch sinister, however, there has never been anything to beat dark hints about betting. We had a faint echo of it at Sydney in 1946–47. Yet it was in 1888 that some errant spirit, possibly no more than a misguided reveller, broke into the Adelaide Oval overnight to water the pitch and hack lumps out of the turf, and George Giffen was impelled to write: 'Whatever his object could have been is a mystery. If he had backed the Englishmen he did not need to damp the pitch, for they had us under the whip already, whilst if he was a South Australian backer he was not likely to improve our chance by watering the wicket.' Presumably this accounts for the armed policemen who now stand guard over the wickets at night in Brisbane and elsewhere.

Not that bets have always been made *sub rosa*. George Bonnor once won a wager of £100 from a fellow-passenger on the ship to England that he would throw a cricket ball 115 yards on his first throw on landing. He did so—119 yards 5 inches—on the parade ground of Raglan Barracks. At once he offered to make it £200 or nothing on the next throw being 125 yards, but the loser was taking no more chances.

Catering deficiencies, very often with good reason, have frequently stirred the public to wrath. Yet it was an alleged excess of catering zeal that caused one of the noisiest scenes ever witnessed at Kennington Oval.

When the Australians, in 1884, needed only 11 runs to win with nine wickets to fall against the Players, lunch was taken for the sole reason, the crowd thought, of 'avoiding the caterer's loss'. Whether rain might or might not have intervened appears not to have concerned them, and it took the united efforts of players and committeemen to restore order.

So it has gone on. Trouble in major or minor degree all along the line. But what of it? These have been but transient murmurings, squawks from the groundlings long since forgotten.

But Trumper is not forgotten. Nor Grace, Lohmann, Jackson, 'Ranji', MacLaren, Fry, Noble, Murdoch, Spofforth, Clem Hill, Joe Darling, Warren Bardsley, and a host of others whose names trip off the tongue more easily than any list of Cabinet Ministers.

Arguments on the respective merits of Hobbs and Bradman, Hammond and Macartney, S. F. Barnes and O'Reilly will continue long after the storms about umpires' decisions have faded as surely as the minor squabbles of Gengis Khan's courtiers.

'Never the best without the worst.' But it is only the best that survives. For what we have received . . .

SIR DONALD BRADMAN [1949]

BY R. C. ROBERTSON-GLASGOW

The thunderbolt duly arrived and again destroyed the England side. Compton played two immortal innings and Godfrey Evans emerged as one of the great wicket-keepers, but there was little else to console the hosts. At the end of the tour Bradman once again retired, this time putting so much conviction into the announcement that Wisden, with an air of finality, published the full figures of the most amazing batting career in the history of the game. A career average of 99.94 smacks less of reality than of the cloudcuckooland of the tuppenny bloods, yet it is arguable that had Bradman not succumbed, most uncharacteristically, to a fit of sentiment on the occasion of his last innings, in which he was dismissed without scoring, he would have returned final career figures of over a hundred. When, needing only four runs to achieve a three-figure average, he misread the spin of the Warwickshire slow bowler Eric Hollies, there was consternation all round the ground and all round the cricket world. Years later Bradman excused his aberration by telling a cricket journalist, 'It's hard to see the ball when your eyes are full of tears.' Whether or not the story is true, the essay rightly draws attention to the streak in Bradman's nature which precluded any show of affection from the ranks. The writer might have thrust the point home more forcibly by daring to mention the refusal of spirits like Sid Barnes and Keith Miller to tread tiptoe before their captain and take him at his own evaluation.

The essay also makes the point that its subject was after all fallible, especially on sticky wickets against a great artist. Again, the writer could have gone further. Another of Bradman's arch-enemies, his one-time colleague Jack Fingleton, has accused Bradman of cowardice in the face of Bodyline, although, as it was Fingleton who most forcibly put the case that Bodyline was a disgraceful instance of cheating, it is not easy to grasp what it was that he expected Bradman to do. Fingleton was on firmer ground in finding fault with Bradman's technique against spin on a turning wicket. Whatever the justice of the plaint, there is no question that Bradman's defence against his lapses against the likes of Hedley Verity verge on the idiotic. He was quoted as saying that batting on a sticky wicket was like being asked to play billiards on a table with a torn cloth, a simile so bereft of all reason that it is hard to believe so shrewd an operator as Bradman could have coined it. That the greatest batsman of the century—on a good wicket—could fail to perceive that while billiards is played under cover, cricket is not, is one of those whimsicalities which make the writing of cricket books such an endless diversion.

The writer of the Bradman sketch was Raymond Robertson-Glasgow, whose amusing and deeply perceptive writing on the game had graced the

*columns of 'The Morning Post' and 'The Daily Telegraph', and later
lightened the gloom of 'The Observer' and 'The Sunday Times'. Robertson-
Glasgow (1902–65) played for Charterhouse, 1918–19, for Oxford
University, 1920–23, and for Somerset, 1920–37, although his first-class
career effectively ended in the later 1920s. Between 1924 and 1935 he
represented the Gentlemen five times. With his swing bowling he took 464
wickets and once took nine for 36 against Middlesex at Lord's. Among the
many indispensable books he published was an autobiography, '46 Not Out'
which ranks among the best of its kind ever written. In it, he describes the end
of his serious cricket in a style at once whimsical and pathetic:*

> I played again for Gentlemen v Players at Scarborough and listened to
> that famous gourmet and hitter and criminologist, C. L. Thornton,
> discoursing on Madame Fahmy and mutton-fat, and I bowled out
> Sutcliffe in a sea-mist. But I had shot one bolt for ever across cricket's
> door. Till now, I had been a practising cricketer. Afterwards, I was but
> an interloper.

*It is no wonder that by the time he wrote his Bradman piece for the 1949
Almanack, Robertson-Glasgow was one of its most regular contributors.*

DON Bradman will bat no more against England, and two contrary
feelings dispute within us: relief, that our bowlers will no longer be
oppressed by this phenomenon; regret, that a miracle has been removed
from among us. So must ancient Italy have felt when she heard of the death
of Hannibal.

For sheer fame, Dr. W. G. Grace and Don Bradman stand apart from all
other cricketers—apart, indeed, from all other games-players. The
villagers used to crowd to their doors when 'W. G.' and his beard drove
through their little main street. Bradman, on his visits to England, could
never live the life of a private citizen. He couldn't stroll from his hotel to
post a letter or buy a collar-stud. The mob wouldn't let him. There had to
be a car waiting with engine running, and he would plunge into it, like a
cork from a bottle. When cricket was on, Bradman had no private life. He
paid for his greatness, and the payment left some mark. The informal
occasion, the casual conversation, the chance and happy acquaintance,
these were very rarely for him, and his life was that of something between
an Emperor and an Ambassador. Yet, for all that, there remained
something of that boy who, thirty years before, had knocked a ball or ball-
like object about in the backyard of a small house in New South Wales. He
never lost a certain primitive and elemental 'cheekiness', and mingled, as it
were, with his exact and scientific calculations, there was the immortal
impudence of the *gamin*.

But, above all, Bradman was a business-cricketer. About his batting
there was to be no style for style's sake. If there was to be any charm, that
was for the spectator to find or miss. It was not Bradman's concern. His aim
was the making of runs, and he made them in staggering and ceaseless
profusion. He seemed to have eliminated error, to have perfected the

mechanism of stroke. Others before him had come near to doing this; but Bradman did it without abating the temperature of his attack. No other batsman, surely, has ever been able to score so fast while at the same time avoiding risk. He was, as near as a man batting may be, the flawless engine. There were critics who found surfeit in watching him. Man, by his nature, cannot bear perfection in his fellow. The very fact that something is being done which had been believed to be impossible goads and irritates. It is but a short step from annoyance to envy, and Bradman has never been free from envy's attacks. So, when, first in 1930, he reeled off the centuries, single, double and treble, there were not wanting those who compared him unfavourably with other great ones—Trumper, Ranjitsinhji, Hobbs, Macartney. And Bradman's answer was more runs. Others, perhaps, *could* have made them, but they didn't. No one before had ever been quite so fit, quite so ruthless.

It was a coolly considered policy. Cricket was not to be his hobby, his off-hours delight. It was to be his life and his living. A few hundreds here and there for Australia and State—what use in that? Others had done it, would do it again. He did not mean to be just one of the stars, but the sun itself. Never was such ambition achieved and sustained. Never was the limelight directed so unwaveringly on one man in one game. To set such a standard was unique. To keep it was a miracle.

But the sun itself has degrees of splendour; and, whatever the numbers may say, Bradman was never again quite so incredible as in England in the summer of 1930. Like all great artists, he knew how to begin. So he made 236 at Worcester and 185 not out at Leicester. Then, with a mere trifle of 78 against Yorkshire he relented into rest. At Nottingham, in the first Test, he was set fair to win the match for Australia when R. W. V. Robins bowled him with a googly. It is a freak of chance that in both his first and last Test matches in England he should have fatally mistaken a googly for a leg-break. It is also reassurring to mere mortality. In that first Test he scored 131. This was a *hors d'oeuvre* of the feast to follow. At Lord's, in the second Test, he made 254, and the innings only ended with one of those catches that set A. P. F. Chapman apart from the other England fieldsmen. Then, at Leeds, he scored 334.

George Duckworth, who was keeping wicket for England, rates this innings as the greatest he ever saw. Archie Jackson, that glorious and ill-fated batsman, had opened the Australian innings with W. M. Woodfull. Off the fifth ball of the second over from Maurice Tate, Jackson was caught at short-leg. Bradman joined his captain. The first ball that he received from Tate whizzed just over his off-stump, and Duckworth, believing that Bradman must be bowled, let it go for byes. Then the show began. Bradman never hit in the air. Boundaries sprang from his bat with murderous precision and calculated profusion. Larwood, Tate and Geary—no mean trio—were helpless. A new machine was at work. A new standard of ambition had been set. At Manchester, Ian Peebles induced Bradman into error to the leg-break. But Bradman returned to himself with 232 at the Oval in the fifth Test. In the five Tests he had scored 974 runs at an average of 139. Statistics cannot record the number of runs he carried with him to each innings. But, in a country of great fieldsmen, he stood out pre-eminent. His gathering and throwing approached perfection. Only in catching, probably owing to the smallness of his hands, he was no better than the next man.

Then, after he had taken his pleasure of the South African bowling in Australia, came the first eclipse. A new style of attack, popularly known as 'Bodyline', with the great fast bowler Larwood as its spearhead, was launched on the Australians in Australia by D. R. Jardine. This is no place for discussing the ethics of the matter. Technically, Bradman found no satisfactory answer. He met it, certainly, with a virtuosity of footwork possible to him alone. But his average in eight Test innings sank to a mere trifle of 57, including a score of 103 not out.

When Bradman next came to England, in 1934, there was no Larwood against him, and no Voce. He resumed his mastery. In the Leeds Test he scored 304; at The Oval 244. But, whereas in 1930 he had annihilated doubt, there were now certain qualifications. He was found to be incomplete against that great left-hand bowler, Hedley Verity, on a sticky wicket. At Lord's, in the second Test, he lost his head, if one may use such a phrase of such a master of calculation and coolness. Perhaps it was attributable to his uncertain health. But too much emphasis has been laid on this failure. Verity himself did not agree with the popular generalisation that Bradman 'couldn't play on the bad ones'. And he knew. But it should be said that, with the exception of Larwood in Australia during the 1932–33 tour, Verity was the one bowler who battled with Bradman on something like level terms, even on the truest of pitches. Besides this failure at Lord's in 1934, another man, one of his own team, contributed to some dimming of the Bradman glory. That was W. H. Ponsford, of Victoria. He was playing in his last Test series against England. Most of his records, once seemingly unassailable, had been stolen by Bradman; but now Ponsford, one of the greatest players of spin bowling that ever batted, ran level with his rival, and actually beat him in the matter of Test average by a decimal point.

Already Bradman had proved his power to live on a pinnacle of success. Now, against G. O. Allen's team in Australia, 1936–37, he was to show that he could return from failure. He started downright badly, and the vultures that await the fall of the great hovered expectantly. But he disappointed them, and, by the end of the tour, he was once more the authentic Bradman. In 1938, his third visit to England, he came as captain. Henceforward, in Tests, except for one innings of 234 at Sydney, he was to deal in single centuries only. It was a concession to old man Time.

Where does Bradman stand as a captain? Such a question opens the way to opinions which, even when gathered from those who played with him from day to day, cannot be reduced to any certain conclusion. On the field he was superb. He had seen and weighed it all. Shrewd and tough, he was not likely to waste anything in dreams or mercy. No one ever saw Bradman not attending. Cricket, to one who made and kept his way from hard beginnings, was a business, not a pastime.

He made mistakes. He took only three regular bowlers on to the field for the last Test at The Oval in 1938. For him, as for Australia, the match was a disaster. Bradman, when bowling, fell and injured his leg. England scored 903 for seven wickets; Hutton 364. Both these totals are Test records. Bradman was unable to bat, and Australia lost by the record margin of an innings and 579. How different from the scene of ten years later, when Lindwall went through the England batting like a steam drill. But, all in all, Bradman was the supreme tactician.

On the personal side, his success was more doubtful. Great captaincy begins off the field. True leadership springs from affection even more than from respect. Bradman certainly earned the respect. But, by his very nature, he was bound to have admirers rather than friends. Stripped to the truth, he was a solitary man with a solitary aim. It was what the man did rather than what he was that invited obedience. There are humorously affectionate stories about most great cricketers; intimate, if somewhat apocryphal tales about them; of what Dr. Grace said when Ernest Jones bowled a ball through his beard; of Patsy Hendren's reply to a criticism from the Sydney 'Hill'; of what Johnny Douglas uttered when second slip floored a catch. But there are no funny stories about the Don. No one ever laughed about Bradman. He was no laughing matter.

During the War, disturbing rumours reached England about his health; and, whatever truth there may have been in them, certainly the England team under W. R. Hammond found Bradman uncommonly near to being a sick man. But, happily, he recovered. So did his batting. Not without luck, surely earned, he first groped, then rushed, his way back to normal. Enough of the old skill returned for him to score 187 at Brisbane and 234 at Sydney.

There followed his last visit as a Test cricketer to England. As a batsman he no longer flamed high above his fellows. He was now no more than a very fine player, and it was arguable that both S. G. Barnes and A. R. Morris were stronger factors in the quelling of bowlers. But Bradman's fame, if possible, increased. Next to Mr. Winston Churchill, he was the most celebrated man in England during the summer of 1948. His appearances throughout the country were like one continuous farewell matinée. At last his batting showed human fallibility. Often, especially at the start of the innings, he played where the ball wasn't, and spectators rubbed their eyes. But such a treasury of skill could spare some gold and still be rich. He scored 138 against England at Nottingham, and, when it much mattered, 173 not out at Leeds.

Most important of all, he steered Australia through some troubled waters and never grounded on the rocks. Returning home, he received the first Knighthood ever given to a playing cricketer.

Bradman's place as a batsman is among the few who have been blessed with genius. He was the most wonderful run-scorer that the game has yet known, and no batsman in our own time has so highly excited expectation and so rarely disappointed it.

W. G. GRACE CENTENARY [1949]

BY THE EDITOR

Predictably the Almanack marked the occasion of the centenary of the birth of William Gilbert Grace, but in the wrong year. The Doctor had been born in 1848, so the appropriate time to publish yet another tribute was the 1948 Almanack. In fact, Hubert Preston's essay was published in the 1949 edition, for reasons nobody has ever explained. The truth is that the 1948 edition was not all it might have been, in respects other than the Grace centenary. For it was the 1948 Wisden which committed the blasphemy of omitting one of its essential sections, Births and Deaths of Cricketers. The slip appears to have gone either unnoticed or uncriticised, but for all that the omission remains regrettable.

An omission of another kind reduces Preston's essay on Grace to the dimensions of a conventional ramble through the water meadows of reminiscence. The same stories, the well-known statistics. Like all the other writers on the theme of W.G., Preston skirts the one aspect of the career which transforms Grace from a plaster saint to an Eminent Victorian – his ambivalence regarding his own status. When Preston says of his hero that 'he insisted on the closest possible adherence to the laws', he is misleading his readers. One of those laws stipulated that no amateur accept money for playing the game; otherwise he would cease to be what the administrators laughingly called a Gentleman and become a Player instead. Though neither a public schoolboy nor a graduate of Oxbridge, Grace assumed Gentlemanly status as any medical practitioner would. The high comedy of his situation resides in the fact that, being of a charitable disposition, he often dispensed medical treatment to the invalids of Bristol free of charge. However, being also of a mercenary disposition, he accepted money for playing cricket. Here we have a beautifully Victorian exposition of the intricacies of the English caste system, of a great public figure who often refused payment for his professional services, but demanded it for performing what was supposed to be his pastime. Apologists for his cricketing morality have reminded us quite rightly that Grace earned every penny ten times over that he extracted from the turnstiles of his epoch and have added, again with full justification, that, but for Grace, half the grounds in England might never have survived. All of these people hopelessly miss the point, or perhaps deliberately evade it. The unique aspect of Grace's case is not that he was a Gentleman who took money. There were numerous other instances of this. Nor was it unusual in any way for a man to take money while clinging to his amateur status. Again, there have been Gentleman-cricketers who were successful in their efforts to keep their financial arrangements covert. What renders Grace gloriously comic, as he seems to have been perfectly well aware, was his refusal to take much trouble to conceal the facts of his case.

Indeed, there are moments when he seems to be laughing in scorn at the entire class structure of English society.

The time was to come when Wisden would openly admit that Grace was the Great Professional. But the time was not yet and the Centenary was certainly too soon. Another generation was to pass before the Almanack contained any hint that the methods of accountancy practised within the Gloucestershire County Cricket Club in the days of the Graces were eccentric to the brink of knockabout farce. This unwillingness of Preston and legions of other cricket historians to face the truth about Grace appears to be founded on a misconception even more crass than their attempts to paste over the gaping holes in the conventional version of Grace's life. All the dissemblers seem to believe that to be frank about Grace implies a lack of affection for the man. On the contrary, only perfect candour regarding Grace reveals that he was indeed a great Englishman, certainly more eminent than many others who found their way into the pantheon. To smudge the facts about Grace is to render him a gross disservice. He was a cricketing genius, a kindly countryman, an inspired comedian, a figure of towering importance in the context of evolving Victorian society. To pretend that he was of the angels is to deprive him of his irresistibly lovable humanity.

WHEN W. G. Grace passed away in 1915, Sydney Pardon, then Editor of *Wisden*, paid the highest eulogy possible to the greatest figure who ever trod the cricket field, and after the centenary of his birth one may assert confidently that no one has risen to equal fame in the world of cricket. As batsman, bowler and fielder he remains supreme, while to those who knew his attributes from watching many of his wonderful performances his position stands out with all the more clearness. My personal knowledge of his greatness by means of eyesight commenced in 1884 at The Oval Test match in which Australia scored 551. How W. G. kept wicket and caught Midwinter off the Hon. Alfred Lyttelton, who, with his pads on, bowled lobs from the Vauxhall end and finished Australia's innings by taking the last four wickets for eight runs, remains a clear picture to me. When England batted, W. L. Murdoch, the Australian captain, tried the experiment of putting on G. J. Bonnor, the six-foot-four giant, to open the bowling with the pavilion behind him. How W. G. calmly played forward and turned the good-length ball to the leg boundary was a matter of perfect timing and subtle wrist work. W. G. made 19 and then was run out. He played a ball to cover-point, and Blackham, the brilliant wicket-keeper, fourth bearded man in the match, receiving a splendid return, whipped off the balls as Grace slid his bat over the crease. It was a sad disappointment when the umpire signalled 'out'. The stubborn Scotton and free-hitting Walter Read in a ninth-wicket stand of 151 saved England.

I can see the bearded giant at a distance two years later making 170 for England against Australia at The Oval on drying turf. He was second out at 216; he hit splendidly, his on-drives over the boundary from Spofforth arousing much delight. And so by various pictures on to 1895 at

Gravesend, where he came to the Press tent during lunch time and wrote a telegram. To my delight, Edgar Pardon, my chief, introduced me to the Doctor, so making the occasion still more memorable to me—though unforgettable for anyone present. That was the match in which W. G. scored 257 out of 443 before being last out on the Saturday. Then after lunch Kent were dismissed for 76. Of the 106 runs which gave Gloucestershire victory by nine wickets W. G. scored 73, while to complete the remarkable three days, during which he was on the field while every ball was bowled, he trotted from the dressing tent in his tweed tail suit and hard felt hat, carrying his heavy cricket bag to a four-wheeled cab which took him to the station. Nothing 'legendary'—a word misapplied to him by some writers who cannot have seen him—about this, but honest fact. This was the first instance in first-class cricket in England of a side winning after facing a total of over 400—Kent began the match with 470. W. G. was then 47.

Next season came another triumph—the last match in which W. G. led England to victory. In this encounter at The Oval in 1896 the dismissal of Australia by Robert Peel and J. T. Hearne for 44 established what is still a Test record for The Oval, eight less than the total for which the home country fell last season on that sad Saturday, August 14. In that innings of 44, nine wickets were down for 25 when M'Kibbin joined Hugh Trumble and hit up 16 before a grand catch at slip by Abel completed the collapse. W. G. scored 33 runs in the match, an aggregate exceeded only by F. S. Jackson, Robert Abel and Joe Darling, the Australian captain, who equalled Jackson's 47.

So we may look back with thanks to W. G. for one Test match record, and remember that when the Australians came in 1878 he decided not to give up all his time to medicine as he had intended, but to continue participation in the game taught him by his father, uncle and other relations from the time that he could run with a bat in his hands. In 1880 I felt surprise when W. L. Murdoch, with 153 not out, just beat W. G.'s score in the first England v. Australia match at The Oval; and then came 'The Ashes' match—a doleful day for a boy worshipper of cricket even at home as I heard the news.

These are merely memories of what I saw, and are small items in his wonderful life. From the many books on 'W. G.' one gathers an amazing panorama of astonishing events. In 1865 he first appeared for Gentlemen against Players at Lord's, and in this connection it is good to quote the Hon. Robert H. Lyttelton, whose tribute hangs at Lord's by the side of a small copy of the W. G. Grace picture, which is placed prominently in the National Portrait Gallery: 'The Champion' in flannels, wearing the M.C.C. red and yellow cap, as he always did on the cricket field.

WILLIAM GILBERT GRACE 1848–1915

'The greatest of the world's cricketers, as a batsman, supreme; as a bowler, great. In his prime he towered above his contemporaries. From 1850 to 1866 the Professionals won 23 out of 26 matches against the Amateurs. In the next series of 26 matches the Amateurs won 19, the Professionals 1. This remarkable change was entirely due to the black-bearded hero "W. G." A terror to bowlers, he was worshipped by the crowd.'

Arranged as customary for the third week in July, the Gentlemen and Players match at Lord's came opportunely for celebrating the Centenary, and M.C.C. appropriately marked the anniversary.

On entering the ground one saw that laurel leaves surrounded the panels on each side of the gates, on which the exact inscription is:—

TO THE

MEMORY OF

WILLIAM GILBERT
GRACE

THE GREAT CRICKETER

1848–1915

THESE GATES WERE

ERECTED BY THE M.C.C.

AND OTHER FRIENDS

AND ADMIRERS

'The *Great* Cricketer' was decided upon as the simplest and best description at the suggestion of Sir Stanley Jackson.

The score card was headed: 'In celebration of the 100th anniversary of the birth of Dr. W. G. Grace,' and on the back was printed:—

DR. W. G. GRACE

'The Great Cricketer'

July 18th, 1848–October 23rd, 1915.

'In 44 seasons of first-class cricket—1865 to 1908—he scored 54,896 runs, took 2,876 wickets, and made 126 centuries.

'When only sixteen years old, he went in first and opened the bowling for the Gentlemen v. Players at Lord's; on his last appearance for the Gentlemen, in 1906, at The Oval, he made 74 on his 58th birthday. In 84 matches against the Players he scored over 6,000 runs and took 271 wickets.

'In 1880 he scored 152 against Australia in the first Test Match played in this country, and was the automatic first choice and opening batsman for England until 1899.

'In 1876 he scored 839 runs in three consecutive innings against Kent, Nottinghamshire and Yorkshire; nineteen years later he made 1,000 runs in May.

'On fourteen occasions he scored a century and took 10 or more wickets in the same match.

'In prowess and personality alike he dominated the cricket field; he was the kindest of men and no Englishman was better known.'

In Wheatstone Hall, Gloucester, Colonel D. C. Robinson, a former captain of the County team, presided at a meeting, and C. L. Townsend, a fine all-rounder, opened an exhibition of trophies used by W. G. and other players in memorable games. Among the company was Paish, another contemporary of Grace. Gilbert Jessop wrote that 'W. G. was his hero as a boy and remained so still.' Walter Hammond sent a menu card of the banquet held in 1895 to celebrate Grace's 100th century, and the Gloucestershire XI, headed by B. O. Allen, signed a letter of good wishes. As 'The Times' correspondent wrote, 'This exhibition shows how W. G. Grace in this century year of his birth is remembered with pride and affection.'

At Bristol, where his old county met Derbyshire, the W. G. centenary was celebrated by the Duke of Beaufort, the Gloucestershire President, unveiling a memorial plaque on the Nevil Road gates, which are known as 'Grace's Gates'.

Interesting Events

W. G. Grace established a name in the West Country before the Gloucestershire County Club was formed, and he first played at Lord's in 1864 for South Wales against M.C.C. Just 16 years of age, he was then, as stated in *Scores and Biographies*, an inch or two taller than six feet and weighed 14 stone 5 lb. He scored 50, a week after making 170 and 56 not out against Gentlemen of Sussex at Brighton. Yet it was as a bowler that he first attracted attention in first-class cricket. In 1865 at The Oval he and I. D. Walker bowled unchanged through both innings of Players of the South; W. G. took 13 wickets for 84 runs.

When 18 years of age he scored 224 not out for England against Surrey at The Oval. On the second afternoon he was allowed by V. E. Walker, the England captain, to go to Crystal Palace for the National Olympian Association 440 yards hurdle race, which he won over twenty hurdles in 70 seconds.

Also in 1866, for Gentlemen of South against Players of South, he scored 173 not out and took nine wickets for 108 runs. These performances earned him the description 'The Champion'.

In August 1868 he scored 130 and 102 not out for South of Thames v. North of Thames at Canterbury—the first instance of two hundreds being made by a batsman in a first-class match. The season of 1871 brought wonderful performances. W. G. scored 2,739 runs in first-class matches when the over was four balls and every stroke run out except a hit out of the ground for six; he made ten centuries and twice passed 200, average 78.25; also he took 79 wickets at a cost of 17.03 each.

Besides his phenomenal batting in August 1876, when he scored consecutive innings of 344 out of 546 in six hours twenty minutes for M.C.C. against Kent at Canterbury, 177 out of 262 in three hours ten minutes for Gloucestershire against Nottinghamshire at Clifton, and 318 not out against Yorkshire at Cheltenham, carrying his bat through the innings of 528, which lasted eight hours, he took four wickets against Kent, nine against Nottinghamshire, eight in the second innings for 69 runs, and two wickets for 48 against Yorkshire. The Sunday intervening between the first two matches was the only break in these stupendous performances.

His aggregate runs for the reason was 2,622, average 62.42, and he took 129 wickets at 19.05 apiece.

Regarding these wonderful innings, the tale has been handed down that the Nottinghamshire team leaving Clifton met the Yorkshiremen on their way to Cheltenham. 'What did the black-bearded blighter do?' asked a Tyke, and, on being told, said, 'Thank goodness we've got a chance.' The reply came next day—318.

Next season, under less favourable batting conditions, he scored 1,474 runs and took 179 wickets at an average of 12.79. At Cheltenham, 17 Nottinghamshire wickets fell to him at a total cost of 89 runs; he finished the second innings by dismissing seven men in the course of 17 balls without conceding a run.

The match at Gravesend, to which I have referred, might be described as an *encore* to what happened ten years before. In August 1885, at Clifton, after sitting up all night in attendance on a difficult maternity case, he carried his bat through an innings of 348, scoring 221; then took six wickets for 45, and in the Middlesex follow-on five for 75.

Although a splendid athlete—he won more than seventy prizes on the track—he gradually put on weight, and was a very heavy man for his age when, in 1880, he played the only three-figure innings against the powerful Australian side captained by W. L. Murdoch in a season when run-getting generally was low.

In May 1899 W. G. left Gloucestershire because of differences with the club committee, and he captained London County at the Crystal Palace, where he scored 166 against M.C.C. on his 56th birthday. That was his last hundred in important cricket, and in that session, 1904, he made his final appearance for M.C.C. at Lord's.

London County Club then ceased first-class cricket, but W. G. played in various club games. It is related that on one occasion when young strangers were in his side he asked one hopeful: 'Where do you go in?' 'I'm always number one.' 'Number eleven today.' 'And you, my lad, where do you go in?' 'Where I'm put, sir.' 'Then come in first with me.'

W. G. was a strict disciplinarian; his presence kept everyone intent on the game, and it would be for the good of cricket if such an example was with us now. He insisted on the closest possible adherence to the laws, so preventing any attempts at sharp practice by fieldsmen to distract the batsman's attention from the bowler.

W. G. Grace, in his last match—Eltham v. Grove Park on July 25, 1914—when 66 years of age, scored 69 not out in a total of 155 for six wickets declared; the next best score was 30 not out by E. F. Tyler. Grove Park lost eight wickets for 99 and the result was a draw.

The figures given are taken from the book by F. S. Ashley-Cooper, published by John Wisden & Co. on July 18, 1916, and these quotations are worthy of inclusion in a lasting memorial of 'The Champion'.

F. R. Spofforth, the Australian 'Demon' bowler, said: 'He seems different from all other cricketers—a king apart. I never see him in the field but I am reminded of my boyish days when our schoolmaster used to join in the game and teach us the way. W. G. Grace is like a master among his pupils; there may arise pupils who will be no less skilful with the bat and ball, but they never will command the permanent and world-wide reputation of the man who first taught us to play.'

Lord Harris, England captain, contemporary with Grace, wrote: 'He was always a most genial, even-tempered, considerate companion, and of all the many cricketers I have known, the kindest as well as the best. He was ever ready with an encouraging word for the novice, and a compassionate one for the man who made a mistake.'

A National Testimonial organised by M.C.C. raised £1,458, besides a handsome clock, and the presentation was made at Lord's during the 'Over 30 v. Under 30' match in 1879. In 1895, as an appreciation of W. G.'s 'rejuvenation', the M.C.C. initiated a 'Grace Testimonial Fund', which amounted to £2,377 2s. 6d., and a National Testimonial organised by the 'Daily Telegraph' produced £5,000 in shilling subscriptions.

GLAMORGAN'S MARCH OF PROGRESS
[1949]

BY J. H. MORGAN

If it was the swansong of Don Bradman which took the headlines of 1948, the great sensation of the year was the eventual result of the County Championship, which went to one of those counties whose fate it seemed to be to languish forever in the lower reaches of the table. Although the Glamorgan County Club was formed in 1888, it was not until 1921 that the club was admitted to first-class status, the last occasion to date on which the Championship was extended to accommodate a newcomer. Wisden received the neophytes with frosty lack of charity, claiming, through the editorial notes of Sydney Pardon:

I have a strong feeling that the time has come when the admission of a county to the first-class should not be determined wholly by the ability to secure the requisite number of fixtures. There ought clearly to be some clear proof of first-rate form. Far be it from me to discourage ambition, but as a matter of fact there was not sufficient justification for the promotion last year of Glamorgan . . . The County Championship must not be a close borough, but there is an obvious danger in treating teams as first-class when they are really nothing of the kind.

Despite Pardon's strictures, by 1926 Glamorgan were strong contenders for the title, until a late collapse caused them to finish in eighth place. In 1937 they finished seventh and for the first time saw one of their professionals, *A. D. G. Matthews, awarded an England cap, in The Oval Test against New Zealand. After the war came further improvement with a sixth place in 1946. Even so, there was no indication that Glamorgan were poised on the brink of any miracles. But the side, which included both the youthful Parkhouse and the greybeard J. C. Clay, also contained several bits-and-pieces players who seemed to do just enough to win matches. The game which clinched the championship was at Bournemouth against Hampshire and by a nice irony it was to be the last game for the great John Clay, who had been there since the beginnings of 1921. He had served three spells as captain and in 1937 took 176 wickets, including seventeen in the match at Swansea against Worcestershire.*

The footnote concerning John Charles Clay (1878–1973) omits to mention that in addition to his usefulness as a player and as an England selector he was probably the most gifted unknown writer among cricketers in this century. Clay chose to hide his literary light under a bushel so impenetrable that it would probably have gone completely unnoticed had it not been for heroic excavations by John Arlott who nominated Clay as his 'favourite off-break bowler but also my favourite cricket writer'. This remarkable tribute seems perfectly well justified when we take into account the Glamorgan County Cricket Club Yearbook to which from 1933 to 1950 an essay by Clay appeared. Here are a few examples for which we have the zealous Arlott to be thankful for rescuing from oblivion:

Footwork is an instinct for having your feet in the right place at the right moment and if you possess this gift, the world is at your feet and I shall certainly not presume to give you advice. Good dancers ought to make good batsmen so if you are in any doubt as to your capabilities, attend a dance. If your partner goes limp in your arms, closes her eyes and breathes deeply, you are pretty good and ought to make a packet of runs.

Should you ever reach the dizzy heights of County cricket always reserve your best efforts for Saturdays. You will then get your name in the papers twice, on Sunday and Monday.

Arrive early if you can, as you will then get the additional thrill of watching the Captains tossing for choice of innings in front of the pavilion. Actually they have in all probability already tossed up in the changing room and are now going through the motions for the benefit of the press photographer. But though the picture you will see in the evening paper of the captains gazing upwards with the bovine expectancy of cattle regarding the hayloft may not be genuine there is always the chance that if you position yourself cleverly you may get into it.

There is no such thing as unfair play provided you do not break the written laws of cricket. In fact, to break the spirit of the game without breaking the laws is termed, nowadays, 'astute captaincy'.

The only sane view of the Amateur or Professional question is the Australian one – 'Call us what you something well like but we want half the gate'.

Keep fairly fit. It is, perhaps, too much to ask you to cut out every one of that seductive trio, wine, women and song. But you can make a good start by giving up singing.

The M.C.C. should appoint a select committee to draw up a list of all the best men and women cricketers and should endeavour to arrange suitable alliances between them. This is putting it very much in a nutshell, as I quite realise that it will be a tricky business and require much knowledge and tact. It may be wrong, for instance, to assume that the union of a male fast and a female googly bowler will produce an unplayable type embodying the pace of one and the finger spin of the other. Breeders of high-class bloodstock will tell you that the mating of two extremes, a stayer and a sprinter, seldom achieves the happy medium. It will therefore be necessary to co-opt one or two members of the Jockey Club on the Committee. . . . Fees of the members of the Committee should be about £500 a year each. I am prepared to serve on it.

In the light of such revelatory material, it seems time for the collected works of J. C. Clay to be made available to a wider public and for the ghost of Sydney Pardon to recant to the extent of an admission that whatever standards the Glamorgan club may have reached at cricket, they have certainly produced one writer who performs better than he ever did.

Cyfarchiad i Morgannwg, y Concwerwyr Cricket Newydd

PROBABLY for the first time Welsh has invaded the pages of *Wisden*. So is history made. 'Hail Glamorgan! The New Cricket Champions'—which is as good a translation as I can think of to the above tribute in their own native tongue.

Cricket, steeped in tradition, has no parallel to compare with Glamorgan's triumph in taking the championship outside England, cradle of the game, for the first time. It was as spectacular as it was romantic; an achievement beyond the most fantastic dream of a Welsh die-hard. Even a month or so after the championship was safe in Glamorgan's keeping and the banqueting and celebrations were over, J. C. Clay, the 'Peter Pan' of Glamorgan cricket, said: 'It seems that I am still in fairyland.' As one who had been closely associated with the club since its entry into first-class cricket—which the *Wisden* of the time laconically commented 'was not justified by results'—John Clay could not believe that Glamorgan had won the championship. He rubbed his eyes and kept his fingers crossed.

To appreciate fully the magnitude of Glamorgan's striking success it is necessary to know the Glamorgan of the early 'twenties as I did. It was my lucky lot to report Glamorgan cricket during those days of anxious adventure, and I have not missed a single home game since 1922. The team at that time was composed in the main of amateurs, well past their best and unable to play regularly. Indeed, it has been said with every truth that Glamorgan had a stronger side in their Minor Counties era than that which bravely, but not too hopefully, embarked on their first-class career in 1921. Of the recognised batsmen who were prolific scorers in the Minor Counties only Norman Riches and Eddie Bates, former Yorkshire professional, made the grade. Occasionally amateurs like George Cording, Billy Spiller, 'Jock' Tait and Harry Symonds gave the batting a sense of respectability, but consistency was not one of Glamorgan's virtues in their early days. Again, it was rather remarkable that in their first season the brunt of Glamorgan's bowling had to be shared by Jack Nash and Harry Creber, who were 48 and 47 years of age respectively. Yet in that first season Nash took over 90 wickets.

Glamorgan had no delusions. It is officially recorded in the annual report of those days: 'In its first few seasons Glamorgan were like no other side; some will say it was not a side at all.' One suspects that J. C. Clay was the author of this bluntness, but if Glamorgan lacked ability comparable with the English counties they had courage and vision. T. A. L. Whittington, who did so much to raise Glamorgan to first-class status, never despaired, but it was an up-hill struggle for the club. Whittington shared the captaincy with Norman Riches in those pioneer days, and again it is written in the history of Glamorgan: 'The club owes a big debt to them for captaining the side under such conditions.' Because so many amateurs had to be played the side was constantly undergoing alterations, and the placing of the field gave endless worry. Slip fielders, with the exception of Cording, did not exist; there was no regular wicket-keeper, and never less than four aged and infirm had to be 'hidden' somewhere. They were described as 'Ragtime Days'; but Harmony was to come.

The big decision was made that until home products developed in fuller bloom players would have to be imported. It was also a courageous decision because of the financial position of the club. It can now be revealed that Glamorgan entered first-class cricket with an adverse balance of £350 from Minor County days. They lost £97 in 1921, £2,813 in 1922, and £2,951 in 1923. At the end of that year Glamorgan were in debt to the extent of £6,212. They were only kept going on faith and good friends. Nevertheless, new players were drafted into the side, amongst them men like Frank Ryan, Jack Mercer, D. Sullivan and T. E. Abel from Surrey, Jack Bell, and a little later that grand stylist Arnold Dyson, to whom the study of cricket on classical lines was a passion.

More important was the fact that Glamorgan began to produce her own players, and it might be said that the introduction of Cyril Walters, Dai Davies and Emrys Davies marked a new era. It was the first glimmer of better things. But the club was still losing money season after season, and in 1932, when Glamorgan had to dispense with the services of Bates, Bell, Ryan and Joe Hills, a public appeal had to be made for £5,500. Otherwise, the Welsh public was frankly told, Glamorgan would have to declare their innings closed.

It was at this critical stage that Maurice Turnbull joined Glamorgan, not only to take over the captaincy but also as secretary, and it is not too much to say that for the next few years he moulded a new Glamorgan. Even when they were losing Glamorgan always played cricket with a sunny nature and a gay abandon, but under Maurice Turnbull's influence they made all-round progress. An astute captain, a grand forcing bat, brilliant close-to-the-wicket field, and a capable administrator, Maurice Turnbull gave Glamorgan cricket a new meaning, and it was tragic that he did not live to see the ultimate triumph of the club for which he had done so much. Similarly with Arthur Brown and George Cording, men who kept the flag flying during the war years and prepared the way for the boom which blossomed fully in 1946–47–48.

Thus it was left to J. C. Clay to hold the honoured place in Glamorgan's championship year, and what a personal triumph it was for this great disciple who has worshipped at the shrine of Glamorgan cricket since 1921. And how fitting that he should play a decisive part in the critical end of the season matches.

One might well ask: How, with such a chequered past, did Glamorgan come to win the 1948 championship? When the war ended they had only half a side, but again they made a bold decision. There were youngsters like Phil Clift, Gilbert Parkhouse and Alun Watkins who were expected to develop because they were such natural cricketers. Of the pre-war side, Emrys Davies and Willie Jones were available, and, of course, there was always J. C. Clay. By securing Len Muncer, Jim Eaglestone and Norman Hever from Middlesex, the new Glamorgan gradually took shape under the dynamic leadership of Wilfred Wooller, who brought something of the fervour of Welsh Rugby to the cricket fields of the country.

Wilfred Wooller had the priceless gift of getting the best out of the players, but let him speak for himself. In a special interview which he gave me for this tribute to Glamorgan, he told me: 'Enough has been said concerning the side this year. We are aware we cannot compete, for instance, with Middlesex in batting or Derbyshire in bowling. But in fielding we give first to no side. We have attempted to make each fielder, be he a deep long-on or a short-leg, an integral part of a machine. Each man came off the field with the knowledge that he had fulfilled his part by saving runs in some way or another. The interest was competitive, and no small measure of praise came from the team itself if one or another player did something spectacular. If a man failed in batting or bowling, he still knew his part in the game as important. Furthermore, his enjoyment of the battle itself was increased. Tactically also it has been a paying policy to encourage each member of the side to study tactics. Cricket is a game requiring thought and brains. Any thinking player may see something a captain has missed. It detracts nothing from a captain's discipline to accept sound advice.'

I asked Wilfred Wooller about the future. 'The side is at its best on a turning wicket,' he replied. 'We need a first-class left-arm bowler to carry the brunt of the attack on good and bad wickets. This need is common to many counties, but we must find one if Glamorgan are to repeat their success of 1948.'

Glamorgan's march of progress in the post-war years is reflected in the greater support for the game. Knowledge and enthusiasm for county cricket in South Wales has grown since the war like Jack's beanstalk. A wavering 2,000 membership has swollen to nearly 6,000, while the 14,000 capacity of the Cardiff ground has been frequently taxed. The crowded ring of spectators formed an appreciative audience which did much to inspire the side, and it can be said that the increased support for cricket in South Wales contributed to the success of the team. Compared with the big losses in the difficult years, profits in 1948 exceeded £10,000.

'The Land of My Fathers' sends her sons and daughters to the four corners of the earth, but their hearts are always in Wales. That is why Glamorgan's championship success of 1948 had a world-wide popularity.

BOWLING OF J. C. CLAY

Some idea of the value to Glamorgan of J. C. Clay as a slow right-arm bowler throughout their first-class County Championship years is shown by an epitome of his achievements. Altogether he took 1,197 wickets at an average cost of 19.26 runs. In 1922 he dismissed 83 batsmen, and surpassed that performance in 1934 when 100 wickets fell to him at 16.55 each. In three seasons when unable to play regularly his wickets cost under 14 runs apiece, but his greatest achievements came in 1937, with 170 dismissals, averaging 17.38, and in 1946 when, with 120 wickets at 12.72 each, he became the most deadly bowler for any county in the country.

M. P. DONNELLY [1950]

BY R. C. ROBERTSON-GLASGOW

By common consent Martin Paterson Donnelly is one of the oustanding left-handed batsmen of the century, to be compared with the very greatest, as Robertson-Glasgow does in the tribute which appeared in the 1950 edition. Donnelly had first attracted attention in 1937 when, as a teenager, he toured England with the New Zealanders. It was, however, not till 1945, that euphoric year in which peace finally broke out, that he became acknowledged as an undisputed master. The essay mentions the innings at Lord's for the Dominions without quite making enough of the impact of Donnelly's batting on spectators. From that day he was bracketed in the minds of those fortunate enough to witness the innings with the great virtuosi of the past. The rest of his brief career only confirmed what had been suspected on that day at Lord's and it must be regarded as one of the saddest deprivations of the postwar years that he should have so soon retired and given his time to his professional duties. Only the brevity of his career explains the modesty of his statistics. He scored only one Test hundred but it is regarded as one of the finest of the century. Perhaps more to the point, C. B. Fry, when asked to assess him, mentioned only Clem Hill and Frank Woolley as his peers.

IT is neither fashionable nor always politic to exalt the individual above the team, but in the Test matches between England and New Zealand here in summer 1949 there was one man above all others who stood between England and victory, and that was the left-handed batsman, Martin Paterson Donnelly. He batted at number five. It is a position where the player must be equally able and ready to arrest a decline or to blaze an attack, to be Fabius or Jehu at need and in turn. In this exacting role Donnelly went from triumph to triumph. He was, as it were, both the gum and the glitter; and he carried his burden like a banner.

He is a master of technique. He is never seen to hurry or labour a stroke. As is the habit of the great batsman, he plays the ball very late yet with time to spare. He shows no obvious preference for one sort of stroke or one sort of bowling above another, but he has one gift peculiar to himself, that of flicking the seemingly accurate ball to the leg boundary wide of mid-on. Not even Don Bradman played this stroke with such impudent certainty. Add to all this a solid defence with much speed of foot to smother spin, and you have the complete equipment. Some great left-handers, such as Francis Ford and Frank Woolley, have been notable for the beauty and ease of their play; others, such as Philip Mead and Warren Bardsley, were famous for their solidity and vigilance. Donnelly comes between and sufficiently shares in the art of both these pairs. Further, he has that delight in the high occasion without which art is not transferable into figures.

Donnelly, born on October 17, 1917, began his cricket at a very early age on the home lawn with two elder brothers and his father, who was a good club player. At thirteen he went to the New Plymouth High School. Here he showed almost equal skill at cricket and lawn tennis, and at one time it was doubtful which of these two games would take first place in his ambition. He also captained the Rugby football team, and was later to show such versatility that he played outside-half for Oxford University and centre-threequarter for England. In his last year at school he played for Taranaki against E. R. T. Holmes's visiting cricketers from England, and helped to save the game with an innings of 49. He was also coached by A. E. Alderman, the Derbyshire professional, and speaks very highly of the encouragement and instruction received. In 1937 he played for Wellington against Auckland in a Plunket Shield match, and soon afterwards was chosen a member of the New Zealand team to tour England under the captaincy of M. L. Page.

It was never the New Zealand way to amass runs for their own sake, but there was something about this nineteen-year-old left-hander that was different. The impetuosity of youth often cost him his wicket, but even in his shorter innings there were already signs of greatness. In the first Test at Lord's he helped J. L. Kerr to save the match, and in an innings of only 21 showed a cool precision in dealing with bumpers. At Old Trafford, where J. Cowie's bowling rattled some of the best England batsmen, Donnelly was unbeaten in defeat with 37 not out. At The Oval he scored 58 in the last Test and a brilliant 144 against Surrey. At Leeds he delighted those most phlegmatic and knowing spectators with 97 against Yorkshire. He also made 94 against Warwickshire, which became his own county. His left-hand bowling, of comfortable pace, gained him a few wickets. His fielding and throwing were of the highest quality.

Back in New Zealand for the 1937–38 season he played for Wellington, and seldom scored less than 50. In the two following years he played for Canterbury, and in the second season he scored 104, 97, 78, 68 and 138 not out in Plunket Shield matches. Meanwhile he had taken his degree at Canterbury University, and soon afterwards went into military camp as a volunteer. He was commissioned in 1941, and went overseas in 1942. In the last gallop to Trieste he commanded a squadron of tanks. His cricket was confined to a 'few cheerful cow-shots in Cairo'.

In May of 1945 Donnelly came to England, and joined the New Zealand Services team under the captaincy of that notable wicket-keeper K. C. James. Matches were played on grounds that varied from the village green to Lord's. Donnelly had now reached the plenitude of his powers. He played an innings of 100 not out for a New Zealand team against W. R. Hammond's XI at Edgbaston. Within a space of ten days he scored 133 for the Dominions against England at Lord's and 100 and 86 for the New Zealanders against H. D. G. Leveson Gower's XI at Scarborough. Such batting as his and that of Keith Miller, the Australian, were a wonderful sight and a refreshment after six years of war.

In October of that year Donnelly went up to Worcester College, Oxford. In the following summer, 1946, he set a new standard of University batting. He played the professional bowling with almost ludicrous ease. He scored 139 and 45 against Lancashire, 124 against Leicestershire, 117 on a difficult pitch against Gloucestershire and Goddard at Bristol, 116 not out against the touring Indian team, and 101 against Middlesex. Nothing quite like it had been seen before; and the only regret, apart from that suffered by bowlers, was that there were no Test matches in which he was eligible to play. With consummate tact he reserved his very best for the match against Cambridge at Lord's. W. H. Griffiths, the Cambridge opening bowler, began with much fire and a circle of close fielders. Donnelly, going in at 47 for two wickets, soon hit him for three boundaries. On the Saturday evening he was 29 not out; on the Monday he went on to give an exhibition of such mastery that the elders had to go back to H. K. Foster's century of forty-one years earlier. He scored 142 in five minutes under three hours, and the pavilion rose to him.

In summer, 1947, he captained Oxford. During the University term he batted as brilliantly as ever, and once more showed his fondness for the Lancashire bowling with an innings of 154 not out. Against Cambridge he played an innings of 81, which was little inferior to his century of the summer before. Ten days later he touched his zenith with 162 not out at Lord's for Gentlemen versus Players, giving one chance, to slip off Wright, when 39. In the following winter he played Rugby for Oxford against Cambridge and for England against Ireland.

In the next summer, 1948, he played in fifteen matches for Warwickshire, but the claims of business seemed to have taken something from his batting, and his highest score for the county was 96. But at the end of the season he showed his familiar powers in a wonderful innings of 208 not out for M.C.C. v. Yorkshire at Scarborough.

The falling away in his skill was only temporary. When W. A. Hadlee brought his New Zealand team to England in 1949, Donnelly joined them for the tour. He was continually in practice, and in the headlines. It is no exaggeration to say that it was Donnelly's batting which enabled New Zealand to hold England—anyhow in the first two Tests. At Leeds, when the other batsmen floundered on a difficult pitch against the admirable bowling of T. E. Bailey, Donnelly played with superb skill for 64. Had he failed, New Zealand might well have been out for less than a hundred. This was well done, but better was to come at Lord's. Here he batted on a true pitch. After a careful start, he steadily but obviously achieved mastery over all the England bowlers, and his 206 must rank among the great Test innings. By this performance he equalled the record of the former Kent and England captain, A. P. F. Chapman. Both these left-handers have scored a century at Lord's in an Oxford v. Cambridge, a Gentlemen v. Players, and a Test match. He followed this performance with 75 and 80 in the Manchester Test, and his Test average was 77.

Like the other famous New Zealand left-hander, B. Sutcliffe, Donnelly fielded brilliantly throughout the season. A comparison between their batting is inevitable. Sutcliffe perhaps, at his best, has a more powerful ease in his strokes to leg. But, in defence, Donnelly always looked the surer, and no left-hander in our time has excited less expectation in the slips. Indeed, Donnelly's equipment is complete, for he has courage against speed and a nimble foot against subtlety. His place is undoubtedly among the few truly great players of the present—a view in which I know that another great batsman, W. R. Hammond, concurs.

Besides his skill, Donnelly has a charm, a modesty and a wit which have not always adorned those who keep the turnstiles and the scorers busy.

WARWICKSHIRE'S UPS AND DOWNS [1950]

BY M. F. K. FRASER

The county lucky enough to acquire Donnelly's services for his few summers in England after graduation was Warwickshire, a side whose fluctuating fortunes are reflected in the title of the account of their history which appeared in the same issue of the annual. The writer understandably makes great play with F. R. Foster and the winning of the 1911 championship and, if there is a hint of general optimism in his tone, it was very soon to be justified for in 1951 the county won the championship for the second time. A third title came in 1972, but then came the nadir of 1981–82, when the county finished bottom of the championship for two successive seasons. Their stalwarts would have taken heart from the precedent of Northamptonshire who, between 1934 and 1948, finished bottom seven times in nine seasons, and one from the bottom in the other two and yet rose during the 1950s and 60s to be one of the strongest and most attractive sides in the championship.

Dedicated students of Wisden down the years must have been surprised by the reference in the Warwickshire essay to the sometime secretary R. V. Ryder as a man 'somewhat aloof and austere'. Aloof and austere Ryder may have been, but his essay, 'Trials of a County Secretary' which appeared in the 1935, Wisden was a delight to read—touching, perceptive, gently sentimental and full of worldly wisdom, a far better performance in fact, than 'Warwickshire's Ups and Downs'. Perhaps in the literary sense Ryder was another J. C. Clay, too bashful to disclose his abilities.

WARWICKSHIRE, who have figured so prominently in the postwar cricketing revival of the Midland counties, have been a properly constituted club for near seventy years, and a first-class county for fifty-five. They owed their beginnings to the enthusiasm of William Ansell (first secretary), Lord Willoughby de Broke (first president), and David Buchanan, a fine left-arm bowler for twenty seasons, who at the outset shared the secretaryship with Ansell.

The Edgbaston ground, most enviable of all urban county grounds, was acquired on generous terms from Lord Calthorpe in 1886. G. H. Cartland (subsequently chairman for a long time), Dudley and Ludford Docker, H. C. Maul, Charles Lawton, H. W. Bainbridge (captain 1894–1902) and J. Ernest Hill were among the eminent amateurs of the early days, with John Shilton, Harry Pallett, John Devey, Sam Hargreave, Arthur ('Dick') Lilley, Edwin Diver, Sydney Santall and the great little Willie Quaife among the leading professionals. Quaife ranks with Lilley, Foster, Dollery and Wyatt among the club's really conspicuous figures.

For some years after their entry into the county championship Warwickshire did nothing exceptional. There were generally plenty of bats in the side, and always one or two good bowlers. Lilley, as the world's greatest wicket-keeper for many years, gave the club an exceptional distinction; but the billiard-table wickets of Edgbaston encouraged drawn games, and Warwickshire gained a reputation for playing safety-first cricket devoid of adventure.

All this was altered when Frank Rowbotham Foster, the most spectacular and dynamic figure in Warwickshire history, became captain in 1911, at the age of 22. No cricketer, I believe, ever had a more meteoric career. He entered the first-class game in 1908; did nothing much until 1910; figured as the world's most successful amateur all-rounder between 1911 and 1914; then passed from the scene, permanently lamed by an accident. He played for England in the triangular Tests of 1912, and, in association with Sydney Barnes, won a Test series in Australia by his venomous left-arm fast bowling. He made Warwickshire's biggest individual score (305 not out). In 1911 he galvanised a hitherto mediocre team into such liveliness and efficiency that Warwickshire won their—so far—

only championship. And as captain he always set a wonderful example. In 1911, for instance, in all matches he scored 1,614 runs, average 42.47, and took 141 wickets for 20.31 runs each. In 1914 his batting average was nearly 35, and his wickets numbered 122 at 18.62 runs each.

Foster's captaincy was as brilliant as his personal performances. Under him in 1911 the championship-winning side comprised mainly Willie Quaife, Sep Kinneir, Crow Charlesworth, Frank Stephens (all of whom averaged better than 30 with the bat), E. J. Smith (who this season finally replaced Lilley as wicket-keeper), J. H. Parsons, C. S. Baker, 'Dick' Lilley, Sydney Santall (an untiring stock bowler who could also stick in), and Frank Field (a real fast bowler who took a few more wickets than Foster at slightly higher cost). George Stephens, W. C. Hands, and Commander (now Captain) C. F. R. Cowan (the present treasurer) were among less frequent performers.

When county cricket was resumed in 1919, Warwickshire shared the common difficulties of the times. Percy Jeeves, a most promising recruit just before the outbreak of war, had been killed. C. K. Langley, a fine medium-fast bowler, was lost to the game owing to war injuries, and thenceforth his great service to the club was to be rendered in committee and as chairman. Foster, Frank Stephens, Kinneir and Santall (who continued his long service as coach) had dropped out. The incomparable Willie Quaife was 47; but he stayed in the game until, at 56, he retired on the grand note with a farewell century. Jack Parsons was still a soldier, and for the next few years was available only spasmodically. There remained Tiger Smith to continue the tradition of international wicket-keeping, Harry Howell, the thick-set fast bowler, Len Bates (now coach at Christ's Hospital), and some occasional amateurs.

George Stephens captained the side in 1919, then yielded place to the Hon. F. S. G. Calthorpe, who came from Repton, Cambridge and Sussex to be captain for ten years. He was a fine aggressive bat and a steady medium-paced bowler. With Howell he shared the burden of the attack for several seasons, during which they received little support apart from Quaife's beguiling donkey-drops.

Again Warwickshire settled to a long spell of undistinguished obscurity. They were never very high in the final table and generally drew more games than they won or lost. In 1930 R. E. S. Wyatt succeeded Calthorpe, and in 1938 Peter Cranmer succeeded Wyatt. The team's performances rarely excited much interest in the Soccer-proud city of Birmingham. R. V. Ryder was secretary. He had been appointed assistant to Ansell in 1895, and served the club with somewhat austere and aloof integrity for fifty years. His whole career was punctuated by financial crises which involved periodical issues of special appeals.

Yet Warwickshire cricket did not lack personality between the wars. Among batsmen: the tall, fierce-driving J. H. Parsons—professional, amateur, professional again, soldier, parson, Player and Gentleman; the graceful, unpredictable Len Bates; the blond, irrepressible Reggie Santall, who was as likely to hit Yorkshire's best bowlers for a century as to make ducks against mediocre stuff; the forthright 'Tiger' Smith (whom Jack Smart followed as wicket-keeper, and who is now the club's invaluable chief coach); the pugnacious Norman Kilner; the thoughtful, precise Arthur Croom; the gallant, erratic Peter Cranmer; and of course Bob Wyatt, than whom no other Warwickshire cricketer, born or adopted before or since, has received so many of the honours of the game. Later, in time to mature before the second great war, came that superb rationalist, H. E. Dollery, that high-powered midget, J. S. Ord, and that confident wicket-keeper batsman, Jack Buckingham.

Among bowlers: Calthorpe, Howell, 'Danny' Mayer, George Paine (who headed the English averages in 1934), and Eric Hollies, who from 1933 has been a power in the attack and for two years after the second war *was* almost literally the entire attack. 'Occasionals' whose help was greatly valued included Norman Partridge, C. A. Fiddian-Green, G. A. Rotherham, D. G. Foster, G. D. Kemp-Welch, T. W. Durnell and the enthusiastic Ivor Scorer.

After the Second World War Warwickshire began once more under difficulties, with Dollery and Hollies to carry the side as batsman and bowler respectively, with Cranmer as captain. In 1946 Dollery actually made nearly a quarter of the total runs, and Hollies surpassed even this feat by taking more than half the total wickets. The fact that he bowled nearly as many overs as all his colleagues combined helped to strengthen the impression that he was often bowling at both ends. His ten for 49 against Nottinghamshire in one innings, without the aid of a fielder, will probably stand for a long time as a record.

The club now had the inestimable advantage of a generous, enthusiastic and universally congenial president in Dr. Harold Thwaite, and a young, pleasant, tactful and completely efficient secretary in Leslie Deakins. The chairman of committee was C. K. Langley, on whose untimely death in 1948 the office fell to C. A. F. Hastilow, one of the most fervent among cricket's devotees in Warwickshire. Thus led, the club's declared intention was to build a team capable of winning the championship. Concurrently, the ambition was to bring Edgbaston up to Test match standard, with adequate accommodation and amenities for 30,000 patrons.

Elaborate plans to implement the latter ambition are being pursued as vigorously as present restrictions permit. The former ambition involves a policy of recruiting talent wherever in the world it can be found. C. S. Dempster and Martin Donnelly of New Zealand, and A. H. Kardar of India, are among the amateurs thus attracted to Edgbaston.

Professional talent has lately come from New Zealand, Australia, the West Indies, and such diverse English counties as Durham and Cornwall.

Under Cranmer the team played lively cricket, and when they could not win (which was fairly often) met defeat with a smile. In 1948 the captaincy was split between the amateur, R. H. Maudsley, and the professional, H. E. Dollery, a curious expedient which failed both practically and psychologically. So for 1949 the committee, for want of an amateur both capable and desirous of leadership, appointed Dollery as the first full-time professional captain in Warwickshire's history.

This move was immensely popular and immensely successful. To his own immaculate 'offensive-defensive' batting and brilliant close-in fielding Dollery added leadership with something of Foster's dynamic inspiration. Last season he became the third Warwickshire cricketer to make 2,000 runs or more in county matches (Kilner and Wyatt being the others) and again took the lion's share of the team's aggregate. For despite the manifold and well-varied excellencies of Ord, Alan Townsend, Derief Taylor, R. T. Spooner (a wicket-keeper batsman of great promise), A. V. Wolton, F. C. Gardner (the soundest opening batsman since Kilner), J. R. Thompson (a brilliant amateur too rarely available) and R. H. Maudsley, the batting in 1949 was still not quite good enough to exploit to the full the deeds of a splendid attack.

At its best, indeed, the bowling was beyond cavil. Hollies and Kardar with their diverse bewilderments of spin and break; T. L. Pritchard and C. W. Grove with their speed and menace; Alan Townsend, always liable to break a stubborn partnership or take a handful of cheap wickets—a battery of all the talents. There are plenty of others already proved or in the course of development.

Warwickshire were persistent challengers for the championship in 1949. The president and committee are confident it can be won—and held—in the near future. With a record membership and record support at the turnstiles, they are willing to back their confidence by outlay wherever it may be made usefully. There are critics of a policy which has turned the Warwickshire staff into a Cricket League of Nations; but the Birmingham public, nurtured on the liberal transfer system of Soccer, will not worry where their cricket favourites come from so long as they play attractively and win matches.

THEN AND NOW [1951]

BY R. C. ROBERTSON-GLASGOW

In 1951 the Almanack included two shortish contributions which still retain their interest. Robertson-Glasgow in 'Then and Now' contrives within the compass of a thousand words to weave so enchanting a spell that we curse our luck that he was not encouraged to go rambling on in the same hypnotic vein for several pages. As it is we have to rest content with a delightful evocation of days long gone, a few choice verbatim quotes and one of the best jokes concerning cricketers' benefits ever cracked. Characteristically, Robertson-Glasgow who by all accounts found the evolving modern world rather less congenial than he might have hoped, ends with a fragment of barefaced nostalgia, evoking the ghost of none other than Mrs. Beeton to make his effect.

*Vivian Jenkins, marking the astonishing achievement of Leslie Ames in
scoring a century of centuries and claiming more than a thousand victims
behind the stumps, is in a strictly functional mood. He has, however, the
unique advantage of having himself been a victim of Ames who dismissed
him in collusion with Tich Freeman, one of the deadliest conspiracies of the
years between the wars. Ames, selected primarily for his wicket-keeping,
scored eight Test centuries, won the 1936 Lawrence Trophy for the fastest
century of the season, won it again three years later and in 1933 became the
first, and surely the last, wicket-keeper to score over 3,000 runs in a season.*

THE title of this short article—'Then and Now'—suggests that someone
of riper years is seizing his pen to tell disbelieving juniors that those,
and some other, were the days. Nothing of the sort. For these are just a few
impressions from one who loves cricket of any age for its own sake and who
can still admire, and even envy, its players both expert and inaccurate.
And, touching on inaccuracy, the writer craves, as a gentler age used to
say, the indulgence of his readers for any slip of memory. At the hour of
composition he was some 14,000 miles from those comfortable books of
reference whose proximity can invest the critic with the agreeable, if
deceptive, appearance of omniscience.

LASTING FRIENDSHIPS

Like Mrs. Malaprop, I shrink from 'caparisons'. They are heating and
delusive. But, to one who looks only a little way back, to the decade
1920–30, two large truths at once present themselves. First there were
more amateurs in the county game then; secondly, how greatly did they
and the professional cricketers enjoy and profit from each other's
company both on and off the field. Certainly the professionals and
amateurs in these times still tended to issue from separate quarters and
different gates on to the field—a slightly feudal proceeding; but, though
our starting points might be some way apart, our hearts were together.
We were united in local patriotism; both the local and the patriotism.
Those friendships have lasted—outlasted, indeed, the bodily presence of
some of the friends; and I still remember the song that our opening
batsman, the Bath professional 'Tom' Young, used to sing in the train
after defeat. After victory, his quixotic nature might decide on silence.
And I remember the curl of Ernest Robson's early Edwardian moustache
when, at a vivid moment of crisis, he said to number eleven down the
pitch, 'You leave this to me, sir.'

FASTER PITCHES

I have a notion that there were more fast and true pitches in the county
game just after the first Great War, to say nothing of fast untrue. A
medium or fast-medium bowler had a reasonable chance of success if he
pitched the ball well up and used slip fielders rather than an agglomeration
of leg-side waiters. Conversely, the batsman, if so minded, could make
strokes, as they say, especially by a bold forward meeting with the ball. In

the days of Maurice Tate, who came faster from the pitch than any bowler of his sort that I've seen, the forward stroke, controlled and immediate, was the best method for those who wished to score and survive. The back-stroke, even as played by eminent practitioners, was apt to lead only to the death rattle. Slower pitches, deadly true, fatally allied to week-long Test matches, have doubtless improved the standard of back-play and the state of the exchequer. But, for many, they have quenched the brighter flame of cricket and substituted competence for *panache*.

But there were plenty of 'stickers' in those years—batsmen who rated the cut as perilous, and the full drive as almost irreligious. There were those who would as willingly have given the bowler a view of their wickets as a Victorian lady would have conceded a glimpse of ankle to her coachman. Once more, I am sure the pitches must have been faster then, or we would never have prised these obstacular masters from what to them was a lair rather than a crease, and sometimes we did.

Their method so far favoured the bowler in that the ball could be pitched almost to a half volley with impunity; but as against this the old l.b.w. law still operated, and no ball pitched—even fractionally it often seemed!—outside the off stump might stir the umpire to say 'out'. Praise be to Mr. R. H. Lyttelton, who, after crusade and brochure, persuaded the law-givers to award the bowler what he had earned. A year or two before this Charter of Liberty was granted, I remember a Somerset bowler saying, with so quiet a voice and smile, to a certain batsman from the North, 'Excuse me, but is there anything in the nature of stumps between you and the wicket-keeper?'

INSWING EXPERTS

Field placements in these years were more 'orthodox'; that is to say, they answered the still current 'orthodoxy' of pitched-up bowling. There were exceptions, notably in the case of Somerset's W. T. Greswell, the best medium inswing bowler I ever saw. For him was placed a field little different from that placed for the modern inswinger; but there was this difference: Greswell swung in very late with his flight, acutely, and he pitched the ball right up. His would-be successors tend to swing, if at all, from near the start of their flight and to bowl just too short. As dangerous as Greswell, at a faster pace, was Fred Root, of Derbyshire, Worcester-shire and England. But a bowler, anyhow in county cricket, gets the sort of field he needs. Field placements are the reflection of the batsman's answer to the bowler's style. Conclusions may therefore be drawn from the recent tendency to crowd the close leg-side positions. How far these conclusions are favourable, and to whom, is a matter that falls beyond the scope of this light article.

Time and a natural desire for novelty have brought in a few new names for fielding positions. 'Leg-slip' is perhaps simpler than 'close fine-leg'. What used to be called 'silly point' is now 'silly mid-off' or 'short mid-off'. Short or silly, long or wise, what's in a name?

In the matter of benefit matches the professional today is far better placed than once he was. Such matches now receive more competent advance publicity and are organised more shrewdly. There is improvement in the timing and frequency of ground collections. There can seldom be occasion for a repetition of a famous West County professional's remark when asked if he would like to receive a second benefit: 'No, thanks; I don't want to be ruined twice.' All this is to the good in days when 'every million pounds count'. But it could go too far. First-class cricket could be spoilt by money as well as by poverty.

Were we happier then than now? Philosophers since the world began have asked and been asked that question in vain. So how can mere cricketers answer it? All I can say is that we *were* happy in our cricket, happy as only those can be who laughed and sweated, loved and strove, quarrelled and were reconciled, got the softest bed and the best breakfast for 10s. 6d., and, at the advice of immortal Mrs. Beeton, ate 'Christmas Pudding (Rich), sufficient for eight to nine persons, at 1s. 10d.'

LESLIE AMES [1951]

A Century of Centuries

BY VIVIAN JENKINS

LESLIE Egbert George Ames has joined the ranks of the immortals. He has scored a hundred centuries, a feat which raises him to the pinnacle tenanted only by the game's master-craftsmen. Craft and art, let it be noted, are indissolubly linked. J. B. Hobbs, E. Hendren, W. R. Hammond, C. P. Mead, H. Sutcliffe, F. E. Woolley, W. G. Grace, D. G. Bradman, A. Sandham, T. Hayward and Ernest Tyldesley, in quantitative if not necessarily qualitative order of priority, were his predecessors. Not that anyone would argue about the No. 1—if all types of wickets be taken into account.

Hobbs still stands alone. Yet even the great Surrey master could not lay claim to the dual combination of talent which makes Ames possibly the foremost all-rounder the game has yet produced. Statistically, at least. Otherwise George Hirst might get some people's vote, and certainly that of all Yorkshiremen, though Hirst's tally of centuries amounted to no more than sixty. His wickets, of course, were innumerable, but in this context that is beside the point. We are dealing primarily with centuries, and even sixty are insufficient. Depressing thought for anyone whose world has taken on a new look after even one three-figure innings.

As for your bowler, whose Valhalla is written in simple 'double figures', all this probably savours of airy fantasy or purely theoretical mathematics. But read on, unless interest in the game's superman is marred by personal shortcomings. I have mentioned Ames as an all-rounder. It will be appreciated, by those old enough to read before the outbreak of the latest world war, that he also kept wicket—superbly well. Well enough, for the benefit of those prepared to argue, to fulfil that role in the most discussed and not least successful team ever to leave England for Australia, Douglas Jardine's 'bodyline buccaneers' of 1932–33.

Jardine was too knowledgeable a captain to include a man in his side for his batting if his wicket-keeping did not fulfil the requisite standards. Ames's records in the stumped and caught department still stand alone as a target for successors to emulate. In 1928 he caught 69 batsmen and stumped 52, setting a new 'high' of 121 for others to follow. Not content with that, he raised the total to 127 in the following year, with 79 stumpings and 48 catches making up the 'bag'.

In all this his arch accomplice was that wiliest of 'googly' bowlers, tiny 'Tich' Freeman of Kent, a gremlin of the greensward if ever there was one. Freeman, with his unique total of 304 wickets in the summer of 1928, owed much to Ames's cool and deft dexterity behind the stumps. That total owed even more to the combined reputation of the two in destruction which had many a batsman dithering with fright before he went in and contributed almost inevitably to his downfall. Ames and Freeman, in fact, became as formidable a combination in their sphere as Hobbs and Sutcliffe in theirs, and as mutually identified as Alec and Eric Bedser.

In the summer of 1932, if a personal note may be introduced, it fell to Glamorgan to be honoured as one of the sides to visit Kent during Canterbury Week. At that time the Welsh county was still something of a novelty, had a reputation for playing attractive, if sometimes eccentric, cricket, and perhaps a sidelong glance was cast on the possibility of this adding to the gate takings. If so, the object was miserably thwarted. Ames and Freeman, assisted by the band of the Buffs, put an end to the matter in two days, to the detriment of the Kent coffers.

Much advice circulated in the visitors' dressing-room on the subject of how to play Freeman. 'Don't play back to him—he'll get you l.b.w. with his top-spinner,' was one item freely quoted. 'Move down the wicket to him,' was another. Hence my acquisition of an appendage not much relished at the time but treasured in retrospect—st Ames b Freeman 3. Admission to an elect freemasonry, as it were.

Annihilation, when it came, was brief and painless; just a quick flick of the bails, a hopeless backward look, and, from Ames, a tolerant, sympathetic smile. All very dignified, like the conferring of an accolade. For Ames behind the stumps was no shrieking dervish. Quiet, almost apologetic destruction was his way, with no frills or fanfares to stir the rustics from their seats; but the record books, unassailable in black and white, bear witness to its effectiveness.

In that same match at Canterbury, Ames rounded off the festive proceedings with a typical century, full of dazzling footwork—no one ever excelled him in quick approach down the wicket to the slow bowler—and punctuated every so often with full-blooded hooks and drives that had finality written on them from the moment the ball left the bat. Movement by the fielders was superfluous, and the umpires worked overtime signalling the fours and sixes. An innings, in fact, worthy of the scene and the occasion, and the crowd loved it.

Ames has made many a hundred at Canterbury since, but, strangely enough, never another one during the 'Week' itself until the crowning effort against Middlesex last summer which occasions this article. It was a single to fine leg off dapper Jack Young which brought him to his goal and broke a tension which had existed over several previous unsuccessful attempts to reach that final century.

Only a few thousand spectators were present on this last day of the match, but Ames has confessed that the reception they gave him more than made up for any lack of numbers. He admits, too, that a cold shiver went up his spine and he felt that catch in the throat that achievement of a supreme ambition brings to anyone. So much so that he broke out into a cold sweat for several seconds.

One can well understand it. Even the most modest men are only human, and Ames is nothing if not modest. Douglas Jardine, introducing him with other members of his team to a packed audience at Adelaide Town Hall in 1932–33, had this to say of him: 'He is a great keeper and a very fine bat, but at the moment has nothing more lethal to offer than a blush.' Jardine, amongst his many other accomplishments as a captain, was an astute judge of men.

Harold Larwood tells a story which illustrates that Ames had that intuition, too, that all great cricketers, and for that matter games-players of any kind, must have to succeed. Fellow battlers on many a field for England, the two became fast friends. Whenever Kent played Nottinghamshire they stayed at one another's homes and spent their leisure hours together. Thus it was that at Trent Bridge, after Ames had defied all the great fast bowler's attempts to shift him, that Larwood, as friends will, decided to have his little joke. Until the last ball before lunch he had been bowling normally on a length to an off-side field with the usual army of slip fielders. Then, for old time's sake or devilment maybe, he decided to let go a 'bumper'—'one of my specials,' as he describes it. Ames, right foot across and in position almost before the ball was bowled, hooked it magnificently over the square-leg boundary for six.

Going in to lunch together, the pair laughed over the incident. 'It was almost as though you knew I was going to bowl it,' said Larwood. 'I did,' replied Ames, 'but don't ask me why—I just did.' Thus can friends come to know one another's innermost thoughts and scoffers at telepathy be held to ransom.

Much can be written about Ames; much has been written already, a century of centuries of superlatives, as well as runs. But one innings he ranks above his others and remembers with special pride. Naturally, for there could have been no more appropriate setting, no doughtier opponents or more valiant cause—England v. Australia at Lord's in 1934. England were up against it; five batsmen, Sutcliffe, C. F. Walters, Hammond, Hendren and R. E. S. Wyatt, had gone for 182 runs when Ames joined Leyland. Grimmett and O'Reilly—could there have been a greater test?—spearheaded the Australian attack, the fielders were on their toes for the kill. Yet the pair put on 229 before they were separated, Leyland 109, Ames 120. England totalled 440, and Australia were beaten by an innings and 38 runs. Hedley Verity completed the rout with his memorable fifteen for 104.

Thus Ames set the most precious jewel in a collector's piece that has brought joy untold to watchers wherever the game is played—in lands across the seas and on county grounds throughout the length and breadth of England. On their behalf as well as our own we salute him, a cricketer now linked with the game's greatest, a sportsman worthy of all that tradition demands, and a man big enough to wear whatever honours have come his way.

NOTES BY THE EDITOR [1951]

There was one other literary fragment in the 1951 edition certainly deserving to be saved from the oblivion of the reference libraries. It is to be found in the editorial notes of Hubert Preston. In reporting the John Wisden Centenary Luncheon, he features the account of a visit to the Soviet Union by the Prime Minister to be, Harold Wilson. Mr. Wilson (as he then was) is of course Yorkshire born and takes some pleasure in confounding cricket specialists by flinging at them the names of the obscurest villages of his native county, each one of which, according to Mr. Wilson, could probably defeat the West Indies. His affection for the game is perfectly genuine and the bizarre nature of his anecdote qualifies it for inclusion, not just in Wisden, but in any worthy anthology of the unexpected elements of cricket's history.

CENTURIES BY LICENCE

Cricket functions are renowned for the high quality of the speeches they usually produce. After spending a lifetime in the game I naturally expect something brilliant and witty, and it was therefore most appropriate from my point of view that the speakers at the John Wisden & Co., Ltd., centenary luncheon in May lived up to the high tradition. This was a memorable occasion. Mr. Oliver Lyttelton, in his happiest vein, when referring to the West Indies team said: 'I have it on the authority of no less a person than Mr. Harold Wilson (President of the Board of Trade) that, if they won too many matches in this country, he would have seriously to consider setting up a working party to examine the low productivity of British batsmen and bowlers. And that might be followed by the setting up of a development council, and even the nationalisation of cricket itself. I warn West Indies that if they come again in a few years time they may find that centuries will only be scored with a licence, and that maidens will only be obtained with a coupon.'

Of this Almanack Mr. Lyttelton said: 'Within *Wisden*'s well-known covers lie the records of our national game; and those who, like myself, turn its pages in a spirit of escapism can see in their mind's eye many of the beautiful grounds, some of them lying below the gleaming spires of our cathedrals or the smoking chimneys of our industrial life. We know that as long as we have the spirit and tradition of this game and allow them to endure, change and decay which we may discern in other nations will touch us only lightly with their dread fingers.'

RUSSIAN STORY

To Mr. Harold Wilson fell the task of proposing the toast of 'This Wonderful Century'. He confessed that he was no cricketer himself, but he remarked: 'I am a Yorkshireman, and cricket is never far from a Yorkshireman's thoughts.' Then he amused us with an account of the last time he played cricket. He said it was in Moscow when he was there for trade talks with the Russians. 'There was one Sunday afternoon, during a lull in the negotiations, when my delegation repaired to some woods not far from Moscow. A few weeks afterwards, following the breakdown of the discussions, the Moscow Press, who seem to have observed our innocent pastime, came out with an account of the "orgies and strange pirouettes by the lakeside of the English delegation".'

Continuing his reminiscence, Mr Wilson told this story: 'My second over was interrupted by a gentleman from the N.K.V.D. or Ogpu, who was appointed to follow us around and see that we came to no harm. He stood in the middle of the pitch and remonstrated with us in a very long Russian speech which I understood came to this—that we could not do that there! He was supported by two men who came up on horseback with rifles. I persuaded him, after some negotiation, to take up his position at square leg, out of the way of even my bowling. The episode closed with the N.K.V.D. man's failure to make any attempt to catch a ball—and after that my opinion of the Russian secret police fell even lower.' Mr. Wilson suggested that the incident should be recorded in *Wisden* as the 'only case of a catch being missed at square leg by a member of the N.K.V.D. off an off-spinner by a visiting British minister.'

MODERN COUNTY CRICKET [1952]

More Enterprise Needed

BY COLONEL R. S. RAIT KERR

The 1952 edition suggested that panic was beginning to spread through the ranks as the statistical truth about the domestic game sank in. Falling crowds, negative captaincy, greater frequency of drawn games, less overs bowled per day, too much coaching, not enough coaching—what was the true cause of the cancer which seemed to be at the heart of English cricket? Different experts had different answers. Within a single edition of Wisden, we find the secretary of the M.C.C. asking for more enterprise on the field of play, Neville Cardus crying out for those manifestations of individual style which he associated with his boyhood, the editor of the Almanack looking to the amateur to restore vitality to the listless body of the game and then citing the allure of modern forms of leisure as a possible reason for the feeling inside cricket that the game was beleaguered by forces far beyond its control.

All these panaceas had their justifications, yet not one on its own could have cured the blight. Colonel Rait Kerr's advocacy of a return to the splendours of offside play was nothing but a fond dream, while his faith in the efficacy of requests to captains from county committees for brighter play was an astonishing example of unworldliness. Cardus, demanding that culture be made manifest once more at the crease, could have answered himself with the wisest of all his aperçus, that nations get the cricket they deserve. Perhaps the most perceptive diagnostician was the editor himself who, having flirted with the notion of the rescue of postwar cricket by the renaissance of the Edwardian beau ideal, got down to hard facts and disclosed a set of figures which should have, but evidently did not, frighten the life out of every one of cricket's wellwishers. The list consists of statistics relating to potential counter-attractions to cricket:

	1900	1951
Baseball Teams	10	952
Lawn Tennis Clubs	320	5,300
Cinemas	12	5,700
Golf Clubs	120	2,100
Civil Flying Clubs and Schools	NIL	175
Dog-racing courses	NIL	257
Ice-rinks	2	82
Sailing and Motor-boat Clubs	125	247
Private cars licensed	4,300	5,200,000
Motor Cycles	3,000	681,000
Speedway Tracks	NIL	43

The deadly implications of this list might have made more impact had they included two factors which were even more relevant: the increase in the number of palais de danses and, most vital of all, differences in the number of English cricket clubs. Had the activities of weekend cricketers declined in the fifty years covered by the survey? The editor does not tell us but it is much to his credit that he was prepared to allow a few beams of light from the outside world to penetrate the buff bastions of the Almanack's pages. His enterprise may have had something to do with the desire for a new broom to sweep clean. In the preface to the 1952 edition there appears a statement from Norman Preston explaining that his father, Hubert, had been advised by his doctors to retire. Norman Preston inherited a contradictory position in which, while the English game seemed to have embarked on a downward path, the health of the Almanack reporting its doings improved year by year. At any rate, in his first edition, the younger Preston made it quite clear that he intended to maintain the tradition of having essays at the front of the Almanack. Colonel Rait Kerr had become Secretary of the M.C.C. in 1936 and his speech to County Secretaries at Lord's in December 1951 marked his retirement. The Colonel, who had bequeathed to cricket a revised code of laws, made one forgiveable error in his speech, which the editor excised, probably because he thought it irrelevant. Rait Kerr believed that the looming shadow of television constituted a serious threat to the popularity of the first-class game because people who saw how dull the average match had become by catching soporific glimpses on the television screen would then stay away from the grounds. Nobody could have guessed that television would be the agent which multiplied the cricket audience tenfold without noticeably increasing ground attendances. The true threat of the small screen was eventually revealed as the factor which created a new audience of what might be called uncricket fanciers, viewers who knew little about the game but acquired pretensions to an expertise imparted by the chatterings of commentators and the meaningless jumble of computerised statistics. The Colonel's anxiety was certainly justified but he was fated to become just one of an army of diagnosticians unable to locate the cause or to suggest an effective cure.

MANY people are highly critical of modern cricket and are asking if all is well with it. Following the First World War cricket boomed only to fall into the doldrums after a few years. This was the reason why, before the Second World War ended, a Select Committee sat to look into the dim future. It might be salutary if we all re-read that report from time to time, and in particular the following section:—

We are agreed that no recommendation in regard to many of the proposals standing on the agenda in connection with the conduct and administration of County Cricket can be fully effective unless the game is played in the best possible manner and spirit. In the few years preceding the outbreak of war cricket was increasing in its appeal, and the credit was due to County Committees, Captains and Players.

We consider that a satisfactory standard was attained in 1939, and we do not believe that any radical changes in the conduct of the game are called for.

In 1937 the report of the Findlay Commission stressed the importance of 'attacking play' and in our view a wholesome rivalry and determination can be demonstrated to the benefit of the game in ways other than 'batting' and 'bowling'. For example, in the past teams who have paid attention to good fielding and efficient running between the wickets have always been attractive. In particular, we wish to stress the importance of avoiding any delay in changing the field. We do not advocate that County Cricket should develop into displays of unskilled hitting, but rather that the batsman's task is to demonstrate the full artistry of the game by his stroke play, and that the bowler's first duty is to take wickets.

We RECOMMEND that Counties before each season should make it clear to their Captains and Players that it remains the policy of their Committee that:—

(i) *The team shall aim for victory from the first ball of a match, and maintain an enterprising attitude towards the game until the last over is bowled.*

(ii) *The players shall adopt a dynamic attitude towards the game, whether batting, bowling or fielding.*

(iii) *The intervals and Hours of Play as provided for in the Laws of Cricket or in Match Regulations must be strictly adhered to. In particular, the two minutes allowed for the incoming batsman to take his place is a generous allowance which should rarely be utilised to the full, and never exceeded.*

That these recommendations were largely taken to heart would certainly seem to be suggested by the verdict of the Editor of *Wisden* on the 1947 season. It read as follows:—

In every way the season of 1947 bears favourable comparison with any year within living memory. Attendances which rose beyond those known in the past, with obvious appreciation by ever-increasing multitudes, clearly demonstrated the great hold the game takes on spectators once they are aware that both sides and every individual mean to expend all their energies striving for a definite result. The fine weather enjoyed, notably in August, might have meant that with batsmen supreme, drawn games would have predominated, but actually about three-quarters of the County Championship matches were won outright.

I can hardly imagine that his view could be so sanguine today especially were he to look at the graphs shown here. The curve for 'finished matches' omits all those in which no decision was reached on the first innings, thus removing one factor which might otherwise have given a distorted picture.

We naturally would all expect 'attendance' figures to reflect the weather conditions experienced during any season, and it has generally been held that in a wet season the percentage of unfinished matches tends to rise. The graph, of course, has eliminated a major weather factor but I have made an

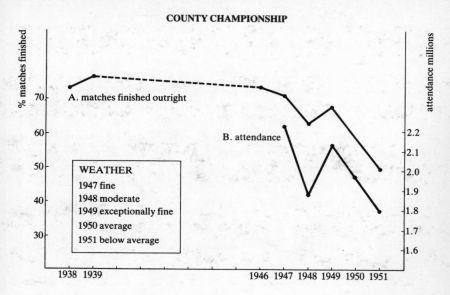

COUNTY CHAMPIONSHIP

N.B. *attendance figures before 1947 not available*

attempt to examine the overall effect of weather in order to ascertain what bearing it has on the incidence of drawn matches.

Before the introduction of the present scoring system in 1938, a correlation between bad weather and a high percentage of drawn matches appears to have existed, and a similar correlation can be seen in the years 1948, 1949 and 1950, but exactly the opposite effect is found in 1938, 1939 and 1947.

I think it is fair to say, therefore, that, after eliminating matches in which no decision was reached on the first innings, the incidence of drawn matches depends by no means entirely on weather.

If you look at the graphs the similarity in the trends of the curves is at once apparent and it is really remarkable how the decrease in matches finished appears to be so closely reflected by a decrease in attendance. The fall in gates is due, besides weather, to a combination of causes, for example, personal incomes, other attractions and the way in which the game is played.

It is surely alarming that the average of 25 per cent of drawn matches in 1938, 1939 and 1946 has steadily risen by the end of the 1951 season to about 50 per cent. The percentage of drawn matches in earlier years was one of the problems specially studied by the Findlay Commission in 1937 and the scoring system for the Championship which they recommended and which was introduced in 1938, was specifically designed to reduce the number of drawn matches. It had an immediate effect and it is therefore all the more disturbing to find that the percentage of 'finished matches' in 1951 was the lowest since 1930.

All of us—and I do not exclude the M.C.C.—are only too keenly aware of our financial problems and if, as I suggest, this marked increase in drawn matches has a powerful bearing on them, surely the cause for such an increase is well worth seeking.

Ultra perfect pitches are often blamed, but this can hardly be the primary cause for the recent increase in drawn matches as they are certainly no more perfect than in 1938 or 1939 and are probably less so in most cases. Much has been written and spoken about the desirability of faster wickets. The dead pitch invites negative cricket. The faster the pitch the more must something happen, runs or wickets. I was interested the other day to hear a very distinguished cricketer repeat in almost identical words what was said by an equally great cricketer many years ago. He said:—

Cricket, to maintain its hold on the national character, must be eager, quick and full of action. Today it is the reverse. . . . Fifty per cent of the matches are drawn and the game itself, becoming listless and dull, is bound to suffer. When cricket ceases to provide excitement for the spectator and player, when it not once but continually allows whole days to be monopolised by two or three batsmen, the rest loafing in the pavilion, then it will cease to attract and spectators and players alike will go elsewhere.

So wrote A. G. Steel in *Wisden* in 1900.

In recent years we have seen the rate of scoring in Test cricket under easy conditions of pitch as low as 40 runs per hour, and if the rate reaches 50 runs per hour it is considered satisfactory. No doubt the bowling is accurate and the fielding splendidly tight, but can the game in this country really survive the emphasis on security first and last?

Modern cricketers have been known to maintain that it is better to be 70 for 0 at lunch on the first day than 120 for 3. I would suggest that a match is often made or marred by tea-time on the first day. 'Made' if a match-winning rate of scoring has been maintained, or 'marred' if the reverse has made it probable that only declarations in the later stages of the game can instil any life into it. Unfortunately, much of the most laborious play is seen on the first day of a match. Saturday is a first day, and Saturday gates are vital to finances.

I know, too, that some players will maintain that modern batting technique has been forced upon them as a result both of the off-side L.B.W. Law and of a definite development in the art of field setting. I would ask them to remember that the present L.B.W. Law has been in existence for sixteen years and whatever truth there may be in these arguments they cannot entirely explain why, when required, batsmen can score quickly on a Tuesday from the same bowling, supported by the same fielding, as had appeared to make the game so difficult on the previous Saturday.

A friend, whose judgment in cricket matters is always balanced, stressed two points, which appeared to him to be fundamental. First, that the technical developments since the war have all been defensive, especially in bowling tactics and field placing—with a leg-side bias. The game must be brought back on to the off-side if we are to recapture its beauty and appeal. Second, that county cricket is now a 'professional' game, but the average professional does not seem to realise that in the long run his livelihood depends on the appeal of the game to the public.

There are no doubt other ills for which cures can be sought, but to me the problem of the drawn match transcends all others. The counties unanimously accepted the Report of the Select Committee in 1944, and as a first step I feel that nothing but good could follow from carrying out the recommendation I have quoted that each season Committees should encourage their captains and players in the belief that cricket must be 'eager, quick and full of action'.

F. R. BROWN: LEADER OF MEN [1952]

BY VIVIAN JENKINS

Much excitement was generated in England, and many hopes raised, in the winter of 1950–51 by the news from Australia, where the visiting English team gave the first clear sign that the vast gulf between them and their opponents was beginning to narrow. In the final Test at Melbourne, England emerged victorious by eight wickets, thanks largely to the batting of Hutton and Simpson and the bowling of Bedser. There were other contributory factors in the improvement in English fortunes. Bailey bowled to better effect than ever before at this level, Evans confirmed his status as the world's best wicket-keeper, and Hutton ended the series with an average twice as high as anyone's on either side. A bonus was the quality of the all-round cricket produced by the surprise choice as captain, Frederick Richard Brown, of Cambridge University, Surrey, the Gentlemen and England, a veteran of Jardine's Bodyline tour of 1932–33, a man whose business commitments and then desperate privation as a prisoner-of-war had eliminated him from the game for many years. Then, in 1949, taking up a business appointment in Northampton, he assumed the captaincy of that ailing county and trans- formed it immediately into one of the stronger sides in the championship. Even so, nobody took him seriously as a candidate for the England captaincy for the very good reason that there were better equipped and markedly younger men available.

The subsequent success, comparatively speaking, of the tourists, was taken to be another indication of Brown's influence. There was some truth in this, for Brown led from the front, endeared himself to the Australian crowds and certainly earned his place in the side on strictly cricketing merits. Indeed, it could be said that but for the freakish failure of Denis Compton to produce in the Tests the brilliance which he showed in the lesser fixtures, England might well have snatched the series. It is also tempting to wonder what might have happened had the selectors behaved with a modicum of sanity and chosen W. R. Edrich instead of consigning him to untima thule for some misdemeanour which has never been specified, could have had nothing to do with his ability, and which was no longer considered a factor when the Australians came to play the 1953 series. But the success of Brown must have brought infinite relief to the selectors who had been so bitterly criticised for appointing him and to the journalistic lobby which had campaigned for him with such devotion. A neutral observer, a Parisian say, or an inhabitant of Tierra del Fuego, would have denied that any controversy existed at all. He would have noted that the selectors had made a controversial choice subsequently justified by events. Although Brown's appointment had been a desperate gamble, even a casual glance at the figures shows that the gamble paid off handsomely. What else need be said? As it happens, a great deal, for the events leading up to the tour of 1950–51 had less to do with cricket than with the inexhaustibly comic spectacle of the English at tribal play.

Nobody who is not a native born Englishman has the remotest chance of grasping the nature of the complexities raised by the selection of Brown as captain of the tourists. The dominant issue, having no faint connection with sport but with social history, remains an impenetrable mystery to all but the English, who have always revelled in the moral contradictions involved in the acquirement of ready money. Ever since Test cricket began, the England side had been captained by a Gentleman, that is, an Amateur, someone who played for sheer love of the game, as distinct from a Player, that is, a Professional, someone who played for money. A riot of syllogistic madness surrounds these propositions, not the most obvious being that very often the Gentlemen took money for loving the game so well and said nothing about it, W. G. Grace and A. C. MacLaren being two well known examples. Yet the differentiation between that commercially-minded pair and the mere players they led on the field of play was, in an odd way, justified after all. The melange of confusion and cant which renders the situation comic is to do with the fact that the differentiation—which dictated that one group be addressed as 'Mister' while the other possessed only surnames, that each group enter and leave the field by separate points of access, that when on tour the Gentlemen slept in one hotel and the hired hands in another—had very little to do with money but everything to do with the gulf between the classes. But, your hypothetical observer may well ask, are not Cash and Class the same thing? Certainly they were not in the heyday of English cricket. The iron curtain which crashed down to sunder the two halves of the cricketing world was there to differentiate, not between financial assets, but between two lifestyles, two sets of hereditary and environmental circumstances. There were various litmus tests to define the middle and working classes of cricket, ranging from style of pronunciation to table manners, from the cut of a man's suit to the degree to which his father had or had not laboured at menial tasks. But the most powerful of all the taboos was to do with education. If a man had attended a public school, if he had enjoyed the amenities of Oxbridge, then assuredly he was a Gentleman. If he had been taught at the local Board School then he was just as indubitably a Player. Of course there was the occasional exception to prove the rule. A. C. MacLaren had attended Harrow but not Oxbridge. W. G. Grace and his brothers had attended neither a public school nor Oxbridge, yet their amateur status was always taken for granted. In the face of this educational and social divide, mere money counted for nothing at all. That paragon of Gentle-men-cricketers, A. G. Steel, was a barrister who left an estate of only £559. The estate of the professional cricketer-footballer William Gunn, who later became a sports outfitter, totalled £57,392, yet Gunn would never have been accepted as the social equal of Steel, and perhaps would never have wished to be. Of the two great Lancastrian cricketers, A. N. Hornby and J. T. Tyldesley, Hornby, who owned a cotton mill, left £6,420, while Tyldesley, who went into the same business as Gunn, left £16,519. Again, the money counted for less than nothing in terms of the great social divide.

What then lay at the heart of the Gentlemen's mystique? It appears to have been one of the fundamentals of Empire. The imperial ethos proclaimed that when a man has been the beneficiary of a costly education, he was all the better equipped to administer the estates of Empire, to show the proper way to lesser breeds who had not the benefit of English law and customs. The tragic comicality of this assumption was exposed once and for all in the mud of Flanders, but it died hard, continuing to flourish in assorted pockets, notably the world of cricket, long after the end of the Great War. In fact, the tradition of Gentlemanly captaincy worked very well, so long as there was a supply of gifted candidates upon whom the selectors could call – men like C. B. Fry, A. P. F. Chapman and G. O. Allen. But by the end of the 1930s the jig was very nearly up. In those harsh times, even the Gentlemen often had to get a job, which meant that playing careers were often blighted. Some of the outstanding amateurs took posts as schoolmasters; the great Essex fast bowler Kenneth Farnes played first-class cricket as a rule only during the summer holidays; as did D. W. Carr, the Kent club cricketer who made his county debut at the age of 37 and within weeks was in the England side. Others, like G. T. S. Stevens and G. O. Allen, might have enjoyed much longer and more regular playing careers but for the demands of business. The domestic history of England in the twentieth century consists of a succession of measures designed to equalise wealth, or at any rate to remove some of the more outrageous disparities. Whether or not the results produced a better England is an issue which falls outside the politics of cricket, but they certainly produced an England unknown to the diehards with the result that even as the 1930s ended, the selectors were finding themselves hard put to find acceptable amateurs worth a place in the national side. In 1938 a desperate situation was remedied only by the cheapskate sorcery of metamorphosing Hammond W. R. into Mr. W. R. Hammond.

In the immediate postwar years, the problem appeared to have eased. After the removal of Hammond, the captaincy devolved on the Yorkshire

Gentleman N. W. D. Yardley, who not only possessed the requisite number of initials to lead a side, but could also claim considerable powers of batsmanship. After Yardley came F. G. Mann, captain of Middlesex and son of a famous club/county-captain. For the 1950 series against the West Indies Yardley resumed command, at which point the tour to Australia loomed. Although Brown had led England against New Zealand in two of the 1949 Tests, nobody so much as considered him as a possible captain in Australia. The first signs of crisis came when on July 10, the secretary of the M.C.C. announced that neither Mann nor Yardley was available for the coming tour. Mann explained with deep regret that he had been 'compelled to turn down the offer purely for business reasons'. Yardley gave as his excuse 'business and family reasons'. From this point, speculation as to the possible identity of the next England captain became a national parlour game. Some touted for G. H. G. Doggart or S. C. Griffith, or D. J. Insole, all varsity men, although Insole was from quite a different social milieu to the other two. Nobody suggested Brown. When the England team was announced for the third Test, Yardley was retained as captain despite already having eliminated himself from the tour of Australia. On that same day, the sides were chosen for the Gentlemen–Players match, and here there seemed to be a hint as to the shape the selectors' thoughts were taking. Yardley, Insole and Doggart were all included, but the captaincy went to Brown. Before anyone could start drawing conclusions, the selectors added a rider to the team lists: 'It is Yardley's wish that as Brown has not before had the honour of captaining the Gentlemen, he should be made captain of this year's team.' This bland evasion further fanned the flames of speculation, which embraced the reputations of certain professional cricketers who might make perfectly servicable captains. Hutton and Compton were spoken of, but the player who now received the widest coverage was Dollery, recognised as a talented batsman and a shrewd captain of Warwickshire. Our hypothetical observer, never having attended an English university and being as a consequence far too coarse a creature to perceive the connection between a man's educational background and his ability to lead a side of cricketers, would probably have named Hutton as captain, Compton as vice-captain and sat back contentedly, wondering what the fuss was about.

Then came the Gentlemen–Players match, one of the more remarkable in the history of the series. Wisden reported:

On the opening day, after his side had been put in, Brown launched a remarkable attack on the bowling. His fierce driving recalled memories of bygone days. So completely was he the master that he scored all but nine of the 131 runs made in the last 110 minutes he had batted. He hit sixteen 4s and celebrated his century with a six into the pavilion.

The prayers of Pelham Warner and his fellow-selectors had been answered at the eleventh hour. Having played a wild card and waited for a miracle, the miracle had duly come. Before the end of the Gentlemen–Players match, Brown had the England captaincy in his pocket. The Australian cricketer-journalist Jack Fingleton later wrote, 'One wonders on whose shoulders the task would have fallen had Brown not succeeded in this Gents–Players game.' The reactions were predictable and once again riotously comic, for a reason best illustrated by the claim of the 'Daily Telegraph' correspondent, E. W. Swanton, who, with reckless abandon, claimed that:

> Brown's runs were a product of a style of play which is essentially that of a cricketer not under the restraint and the taboos of one who plays the game for a living.

Like Denis Compton, presumably. The claim may have had about it a certain rough justice fifty years earlier, but it had long ago ceased to apply, as those thousands of sadder but wiser men knew who naively attended the Oxford–Cambridge matches of the period in the hope of enjoying some of this unrestrained, unpaid cricket only to be confronted by twenty-two young men all playing like insurance brokers.

And so, on the strength of a single brilliant innings, the veteran Brown was chosen to lead England in Australia. 'Cant!', screamed the plebs. 'Nonsense!', hollered the Gents, as accusations of class warfare filled the air. Nor was Brown's elevation the only bone of contention. There was the inexplicable omission of Edrich. What on earth were the selectors thinking of? Not content with favouring a second-rate geriatric as captain, they had omitted one of the five best batsmen in England. But poor Edrich had, it seems, committed some unforgivable sin which put him altogether out of the reckoning. During the tour, when injuries to Hutton and Compton caused speculation about a replacement, Fingleton was 'authoritatively told it would not be Edrich'. It seemed almost as though that man's offence against society was so heinous that the selectors would rather lose the series than call on him. Cries of class preferment were further fuelled when the newsreels showed Brown addressing the cameras and referring to his leading batsman as 'Compton', who responded by addressing 'Mr. Brown'.

Complaints about the Old School Tie eventually died away and the tour proceeded. After the first Test on a freak wicket at Brisbane, where Australia won by only 70 runs, critics of the Selection Committee grew thoughtful. After the second Test, when Australia squeezed home at Melbourne by a mere handful of runs, and where Brown hit top score of 62 in the first innings and led the bowling with four for 26 in the second, the controversial captain had become something of a hero. Long before the end of the tour he was recognised as the dominant personality of the series. Fingleton summed it up as well as anyone:

> The M.C.C. honoured Brown, but it was to prove that the M.C.C. honoured itself and cricket by choosing Brown. Australia was to receive the most popular captain that England had sent us in living memory. Gilligan, Chapman, Johnny Douglas and Gubby Allen had all been outstandingly popular. Brown had some inherent quality that appealed to Australians.

And so the desperate gamble paid off. My Lords Hawke and Harris could rest content in their patrician graves, happy in the knowledge that the evil day of professional captaincy had been staved off at least for the moment. But Brown's selection is an interesting example of how bigotry can turn back on itself, how the prejudice against one class can so easily stand on its head and become prejudice against another. The moment Brown's selection was announced, people smiled knowingly and talked of the Old Boy network. The joke is that very possibly they were right. It may well be that in that late summer of 1950 Warner and company did support the old class system after all when they opted for Brown. If they did, then it was one of the more spectacular cases of the right man being honoured for the wrong reasons. However much truth there may be in that, there is no shadow of a doubt that he was the right man. Ironically, his greatest triumph was still to come. In 1953 he was appointed chairman of the Selection Committee which chose the professional captain Hutton and picked the men who regained the Ashes.

There remains one comment on the apotheosis of F. R. Brown which neither Vivian Jenkins in his Wisden essay nor any of the other writers of the time thought of making. It was to do with the factors which caused England to come so close to bringing off one of the great upsets in international cricket history. The 1950–51 series was the first for twenty-two years in which Bradman made no appearance.

FREDERICK Richard Brown will be remembered in days to come as a great England cricket captain. Even a journalist, shy to a painful degree of the pitfalls of prophecy, can assert as much. It will not be so much for what he and his team accomplished on the 1950–51 tour to Australia—they lost the series, four games to one—but because of what he personally all but inspired them to accomplish, 'e'en in the cannon's mouth' as it were; also because of the place he won in the affections of the Australian public, whose memories, in the cricket sense, are long indeed.

Greatness, we are told, is achieved in one of three ways—by birth, effort, or passive acquiescence in outward circumstance. In this case a combination of all three applies. Brown had the opportunity for greatness thrust upon him, against his better judgment, it was said, after two younger and more fancied candidates in N. W. D. Yardley and F. G. Mann had been obliged to turn it down; he achieved it by a combination of nigh-heroic personal effort and the native qualities for which only his forbears can claim credit.

Rarely has a captain set sail with a sparser degree of public support. 'Too old' was the cry on all sides, even though he had not reached his 40th birthday. Yet Hammond, four years previously, had been 43. When the young and largely untried M.C.C. team touched the depths of indifferent performance in the earlier part of the tour, the gloomiest forebodings of the critics looked like being realised. Then came that glorious, uplifting day at Brisbane, when Australia, opening the batting on the first day of the first Test, on a pitch that was a batsman's paradise, were dismissed by close of play for no more than 228 runs—ignominious failure, compared with the five, six and seven hundred, nay, thousands in some quarters, that had been freely forecast.

If ever I saw resolution writ on a man's face it was on Brown's that morning as he led his team on to the field after losing the toss. That he should win it had been held to be England's only chance—and that a remote one—of offering even token opposition to their hosts. Brown's determination was reflected in the faces of the men under him—Alec Bedser, twirling the ball avidly in his huge hands, Godfrey Evans, all pads and gauntlets and black forearm, and Reg Simpson, slight, but thin-lipped and no less ready to do or die.

I mention these three, and could add Trevor Bailey, for the heroes' parts they played—Bedser, for his great-hearted and unyielding attack throughout the day, Evans, for a superhuman wicket-keeping display—what verve, what acrobatics!—and Simpson, who ran himself to an Olympic athlete's degree of exhaustion on the boundary, and caught two great catches to boot. Cricket memories that can never fade, and all through was Brown, encouraging or reprimanding, not obviously, so that all could see, but with a nod here, a frown or a smile there, or a word dropped casually as the players crossed between the overs.

It was captaincy supreme, and I like to think that here was one instance, at least, where professionals managed to put off the lure of averages, and Press report and transient personal glory. They were playing for England, and their skipper Freddie Brown, and nothing else. To say that we who watched were exhilarated is the palest of understatements.

Rather we were transported to some ecstatic hell of suppressed excitement, where the heart beat louder and louder with increasing hammer-blows as wicket after wicket fell. When Australia were all out by the day's end it was almost too much. We fell back limp and exhausted, and tried to compose our thoughts for the business of letting the folks at home know all about it. The miracle had happened. England had a chance after all. How rain came to make a farce of the match, and how England, foiled by a Brisbane gluepot, lost after all, is now painful history. Australia's 228 had become a winning, not a losing, total. But hope against hope had turned to hope well-founded.

In the end Australia won the series all right, but there was no more complacency. Hassett, as true a sportsman as ever lived, and the fine team he commanded, buckled down to it. In the second Test, at Melbourne, they again emerged victorious, this time by only 28 runs. Soul-rending, but inescapable.

It was here that Brown's stature as a player, quite apart from his captaincy, really began to emerge. In England's first innings, after six wickets had gone for a beggarly 61, he produced a fighting knock of 62 which brought him the most thunderous acclaim I have ever heard when he returned to the dressing rooms. The Australian public by now had detected the man behind the player. They rose to him, over 60,000 of them, and the reception out-Bradmanned, I am told, even those of Bradman, in the Australian's robot prime.

At Sydney, in the third Test, it was much the same. Brown's 79, after Hutton and Compton had both been swept away in one nerve-shattering over from Keith Miller, brought him the ultimate tribute, the approval of the men on the 'Hill', the hardest cricket crowd in the world to please. 'Brownie' became their new god, ruling in a twin firmament with Keith Miller, till then their totem king-of-all. Previously they had seen the England captain bowl himself almost into the ground, for the best part of two days, after injuries had laid Bailey and Wright low.

Came the final scene of all, when victory, long awaited, broke at last. No sooner had Len Hutton—and who more justly?—pushed the winning single in the final Test, at Melbourne, than the crowd flooded over the barriers in a black torrent towards the dressing-rooms. 'We want Brown' went up the cry, and, after what seemed an age, there was England's skipper, high up on a balcony, waving acknowledgment to the very same people who not many weeks before had melted silently away, shunning the obsequies, from an Australian victory on the same ground. That had been a peculiar phenomenon, unique, perhaps, in the history of Anglo-Australian Tests, and, as Brown himself admits, the crowning reward for what had been a singularly amiable series. Feeling between players on either side had been of the friendliest, for which Hasset, no less than Brown, earns credit. The Australian public genuinely wanted England to win at least one Test. Whether that would have applied if it had been equal 2–2 coming to the last one is another matter, but it would have been a poor Australian who wanted to see his own team beaten in that event.

As it was, Brown's personality cast its spell over the whole series. His very appearance was what an Australian expects an Englishman's to be. His pipe and ruddy complexion, blond hair and ample frame, even the comic little hat he wore off duty were all as manna to the hungry caricaturists. They depicted him as John Bull, or Farmer Giles, complete with leggings and gaiters and a straw stuck in his mouth; they might have added Friar Tuck or Little John as well. In the words of the film publicists, he was a smash hit. Added to which the public was well aware that here was a man, not as young as he used to be, who had last appeared among them 20 years since as a member of D. R. Jardine's team in the early 'thirties, and who had only come again because he conceived it his duty to England cricket to do so. His war experiences as a P.O.W. drew sympathy in a country where so many others had known the same rigours. Lest it be thought that I err on the side of over-enthusiasm, let me quote what some of Australia's own writers said about him.

Herewith J. H. Fingleton, opening bat for Australia in the 1931–32 'bodyline' series, in an article in a Melbourne paper: '*This Brown, the most popular English captain with Australian crowds I can remember, is giving us unbelievable stuff. Here he is, at 40 years of age, mark you, calling the tune in innings after innings against the Australians.*'

Or an extract from an Australian weekly magazine, naming Brown as the 'Cricketer of the Year', with a full front-cover picture: '*When he was first chosen to lead England, all of Australia wondered why. Since then he has inspired his team by his own refusal ever to give up a losing fight. That, for our money, is what makes a real cricketer.*'

Finally Ray Robinson, one of the shrewdest Australian critics, in a review of the tour for our own *Cricketer* magazine: '*By determination and deeds for a losing side, Brown soon established himself as the hero of the season, ranking with those fine pre-war captains and popular men, Chapman and Allen, in the estimation of the Australian cricket followers. On top of that, the crowd's admiration for the way he uplifted his side and for his resolute play was heightened by their sympathy for the under-dog, England. . . . In the second and third Tests Brown proved that the ball could be hit hard to the boundary by front-of-the-wicket strokes with a frequency and reasonable safety we had almost forgotten. His drives seemed to be full of red corpuscles, like the ruddy face above the kerchief knotted at his neck.*'

In a success story of this kind, it is appropriate, perhaps, to recall some of Brown's earlier history leading up to the final triumph. Born at Lima, Peru, on December 16, 1910—his father being engaged in an import and export agency business there—he came of cricketing stock. Not many people may be aware that Brown senior, a talented all-round games player, was a good enough cricketer to take five wickets for 60 against Sir Pelham Warner's M.C.C. team out there in 1927. In Liverpool in earlier days he had played Lancashire League cricket in the company of such as Harry Makepeace. So that cricket was in the blood.

One oddity was that as a boy Brown junior was left-handed in everything; batting, bowling, even throwing. His brother, Alec, and sister, Aline (who upheld the family name by appearing for the England Women's XI against Australia), are left-handed to this day. It was Brown senior who made this one son, destined to become England's captain, change to right hand, with the results we now know. That was one strange phase in our hero's development. Another was the process by which he became a leg-break and googly bowler, switching back again to medium-pace swingers in Australia with such marked success that in the five Tests he took 18 wickets for 21.81 runs apiece.

At prep. school a St. Pirans, Maidenhead, where he came under the sway of that magnificent coach, the late Aubrey Faulkner—'the best I've ever known,' says Brown—it was as a straightforward opening seam bowler and batsman that he flourished. When at The Leys School, Cambridge, he continued in the same vein, but learned to bowl the googly and leg-break as a sideline. N. J. Holloway, his cricket master there, an old Cambridge Blue and Sussex fast bowler, used to throw in a slow tweaker at times for the sake of surprise and variety. Brown, as boys will, copied his mentor.

On going up to Cambridge, Faulkner advised him to abandon his first love and concentrate exclusively on spinners—'seamers will be two-a-penny up there,' he told him; 'if you want to get a Blue, go in for the slow stuff.' Thus it was that Brown's propensity for medium-pace accuracy lay hid for years behind a hard-won reputation as a slow bowler who on his day could baffle the best. Events in Australia brought his former talent to light again, but his success was not as surprising as might at first sight have appeared.

Brown soon discovered that accuracy, above all, is the recipe for wicket-taking on Australian pitches, and 'no more tweakers for me' was a remark soon on his lips. Thus the wheel came full circle, and his peak effort, five wickets for 49, in Australia's first innings in the fifth Test, at Melbourne, provided the final justification. In that match he caught and bowled the menacing Keith Miller in both innings, for 7 and 0. It is hard to conceive two better blows struck for England at any time or in any circumstances; and this, of course, was the match which ended the run of Australian postwar successes.

Brown's feats in his earlier career have been fully recorded in the 1933 issue of *Wisden*, when he was one of the 'Five Cricketers of the Year'. His best innings up to then he reckons was his 168 for Surrey against Kent, at Blackheath. Although this was his first encounter with the great 'Tich' Freeman, he hit four 6s and twenty-one 4s in an amazing knock which lasted only two hours ten minutes. Other innings in that year—1932—were 212 (seven 6s, fifteen 4s) in three hours twenty minutes at The Oval, and 135 in two hours at Lord's, both against Middlesex. '*Formidable*', as the Frenchmen say.

Between 1939 and 1948 Brown, reduced from 14½ st. to 10 st. by his prison camp experiences, was not seen in first-class cricket. He played once for Surrey in 1948, which gave little hint of the full re-emergence which was to follow. That came in 1949 when, taking a business appointment in Northampton, he descended in the role of *deus ex machina* to take over the fortunes of the county side and lead it out of the wilderness. Previously the Omega Minus of the county championship and almost invariably at the bottom of the table, they developed in one season into a more than respectable Beta Plus, sixth from the top, and since then have been regarded with new-found respect by their opponents. Brown's part in this was decisive, leading to the final nod of approval from Lord's when he was chosen as England's captain against New Zealand in the same year of 1949.

Even then few people could have considered him a possible for the leadership in Australia, in spite of the crop of 'wise-after-the-event' asseverations which have since appeared.

What clinched matters, when the question mark had swollen beyond the limits of human focus, was a truly patrician innings by Brown in 1950 for the Gentlemen against the Players at Lord's. Girding on a metaphorical sword and buckler he thrashed the opposing bowling to the tune of 122 out of 131 in only 110 minutes. This was after his team had been put in to bat, and, not content with sixteen 4s, he reached his century with the final flourish of a hit into the pavilion for 6. That, in the words of finality, settled it. Brown was 'in', as captain, and it is as well to remember that his doughty batting feats in Australia were not without precedent, even though, as he himself was heard to aver, he may at times have been 'playing from memory'.

His experiences in Australia under D. R. Jardine, when the 'all-speed attack' policy of Larwood, Voce, Allen and Bowes meant his exclusion from all Tests, might have daunted one whose love for the game was less abiding. But even in the prison camps during the war, when he won an M.B.E. for his work in the evacuation of Crete as an R.A.S.C. officer attached to the Guards Brigade, he managed to fit in some cricket.

One story he tells, illustrating his inborn sense of fun—not the least of his attractions—is bound up with another great figure in England cricket of recent years, Bill Bowes, the Yorkshire speed merchant. At one time they were in the same P.O.W. camp together, at Chieti, in Italy. It was only natural that they should start a game of cricket, even though the pads were made of cardboard from Red Cross parcels stuffed with paper, and the pitch the road which went through the middle of the camp. It appears that the Italian guards thought there was something highly suspicious about these unfamiliar proceedings, with possibly an escape tunnel via the batsman's blockhole in contemplation.

When Bowes was half-way through an over, they marched firmly down the road to a position mid-way between the wickets. Bowes, about to commence his run, hesitated. Said Brown, at mid-off: 'Well, what are you waiting for, Bill? Why not let one go?' To which Bowes, with the twinkling eye that belies his otherwise inscrutable appearance, replied in the accent of his native Yorkshire: 'Ah would, but tha never knows, ah might kill b——.' Perhaps it was just as well that discretion prevailed, and that Brown's injunction went unheeded!

All of which may help to explain the character of the man who, for a spell, at least, brought England cricket out of the postwar slough into which it had sunk, and which impelled the famous remark of the quay-side vendor in Sydney. Anxious to promote a quicker side of his wares, he produced his last trump—'Lovely lettuces,' he cried, 'only a shilling and 'earts as big as Freddie Brown's.'

It was worth the journey just to be able to transmit that particular remark to England.

TWENTY YEARS OF INDIAN TEST CRICKET [1952]

BY VIJAY M. MERCHANT

Vijay Madhavji Merchant was one of the outstanding opening batsmen in world cricket between the wars and he did much to raise the image of Indian cricket in his eighteen Test innings. Merchant was born in 1911, not so very long after Lord Harris had poured scorn on the cricketers of India even in the act of encouraging them to improve. In the 1890s Harris had become Governor of Bombay and done all he could to bring on the local cricketers, much to the dismay of the entrenched Raj, who thought that the Governor's place was inside Government House. In helping to lay the foundations of

Indian cricket, Harris occasionally allowed his irascible temperament full flow. In a wonderfully choleric autobiography published in 1921 called 'A Few Short Runs', Harris takes the local cricketers to task for their addiction to the comforts of home and even in paying them a compliment seems to be implying that they are physical freaks:

> When I first went there the amount of time wasted in the calls for, and the drinking of, water by the Parsi batsmen was quite ridiculous, but they got over their weakness, and I suppose are as well able to play a long innings in their own climate without constant resort to drinks as an Englishman. Where I was disappointed with the Parsis was in their fielding. I should have thought that with their activity and what appeared to be rather long arms they would have been specially good fields, but they were not, I consider, as good as Englishmen, and nowhere near as good as Australians.

For all his blimpishness, Harris did a great deal to help make cricket acceptable in India and was prescient enough to insist that 'there cannot be a shadow of doubt that cricket is going to stay in India; it has taken hold all over the country'.

By Merchant's day India was on the brink of the first-class international game. By time time Merchant retired, his nation had split into two Test-playing nations, each of whom proved perfectly capable of defeating any other country. Being a modest man, Merchant was far too self-effacing in his diplomatic account of Indian Test history to make a song and dance about his remarkable achievements. His career batting average was 72.74, and Bradman apart, there is no other batsman who approaches this statistic. Even allowing for the favourable conditions for batting in much of the cricket in which Merchant participated and allowing also that some of the bowling he encountered was first-class in name only, his returns are still outstanding. He scored freely against bowling of the highest class in England, had a Test average of over 47 and remains in the list of the twenty highest individual innings of all time with 359 not out scored in a wartime match for Bombay. Merchant is also too reticent to make any reference to the way in which he became the victim of one of most bizarre methods of dismissal ever seen in a first-class match. There are at least two instances in the modern game and both involve Arsenal wingers. As Wisden disapprovingly described it, in the Test between England and India at The Oval in August 1946:

> Merchant maintained his mastery without ever becoming menacing as a hard hitter, and then lost his wicket unluckily. He started for a short run, was sent back by Mankad but moved too slowly and Compton, running behind the bowler from mid-on, kicked the ball on to the stumps, an incident reminiscent of that by Joe Hulme, another Arsenal and England forward, who in the same way dismissed Iddon of Lancashire in 1938 when Middlesex visited Old Trafford.

In the event, Merchant took no part in the 1952 series.

THE Imperial Cricket Conference gave India Test Match status for their first official tour of England in 1932. That was a red-letter day in the history of Indian cricket and the stepping-stone to the exchange of official visits between India and most of the other cricketing countries. Of the previous visits to England, that of the semi-official side of 1911 was the most notable. Although that team contained some of the finest Indian cricketers, it experienced difficulty in overcoming even the lower-placed counties.

Batting and bowling talent was present, but fielding let India down and the side did not possess the temperament to recover from a difficult situation. In addition, the Maharaja of Patiala, the captain, did not enjoy good health. After playing in the first few matches, he went on a tour of the Continent and took with him Col. K. M. Mistry, his A.D.C. Col. Mistry was the best batsman on the Indian side, and his absence from the remaining fixtures created a gap which was never filled. He had made a big impression on English critics by his 78 against the M.C.C. at Lord's, and the public looked forward to more innings from him.

WONDERFUL HITTING

The next meeting of Indian and English cricketers came in 1926, when a team under Arthur Gilligan visited India. Including as it did such outstanding personalities as Maurice Tate, Andy Sandham, Jack Mercer, George Geary and Bob Wyatt, the M.C.C. side was most successful and provided considerable education to Indian cricketers both old and young. One match on that tour is still talked about by those who saw it. Playing for the M.C.C. against the Hindus at Bombay, Guy Earle, of Somerset, scored 130 in which he hit eight 6s and eleven 4s. People in Bombay had never seen such hitting and never expected to see the like of it again. In the Hindus' innings, however, C. K. Nayudu outshone this performance. He made 153 in 100 minutes by even fiercer hitting. Nayudu's innings contained eleven 6s and thirteen 4s and, in point of merit, was the best I have seen by an Indian cricketer in any land. Although Nayudu never again touched that form, his display will ever be green in the memory of those fortunate enough to be present.

Six years later India fared as well as expected on the 1932 tour of England. Of the twenty-six matches played, they won nine, lost eight and drew nine. Although none of the victories was gained against a leading English county, India did surprisingly well in the only Test match. At Lord's they dismissed Hobbs, Sutcliffe and Woolley cheaply and England were out for 259. India's batsmen did not support the bowlers, but the first innings deficit was not very big. India again got rid of the leading English batsmen cheaply, but Douglas Jardine, the captain, came to the rescue and, with a second sterling innings, paved the way to victory. Had Jardine not played two splendid innings in that match, I wonder if England would have won their first Test against India?

TWO GRAND BOWLERS

Apart from Jardine's batting, features of the game were the fast bowling of Mohamed Nissar and equally fine medium-pace bowling by the late Amar Singh. No better tribute could have been paid to Amar Singh's bowling in England's second innings than the one given to him by *Wisden* itself. 'Better bowling than his in the second innings of the Test mach has not been seen for a long time and more than one famous old cricketer said afterwards that Amar Singh was the best bowler seen in England since the war.'

The M.C.C. returned this visit by sending a strong side to India in 1933–34. They paid Indian cricket a high compliment by appointing Douglas Jardine as captain and sending cricketers like Walters, Bakewell, Nichols, Clark and Hedley Verity. Jardine's was a strong combination in every sense, and apart from defeat by a narrow margin on a matting pitch at Benares, enjoyed uninterrupted success. India was privileged to see some first-rate fast bowling by Nichols and Clark and an exhibition of the art of left-arm slow bowling by Verity. Above all, Jardine's captaincy impressed India more than any single feature or individual performance. His shrewd tactics and ability to get the best out of his men was an object lesson not only to Indian cricketers but to Indian captains as well. He never gave away anything or asked for any concession, and India came to understand how relentlessly he must have pursued his method of attack in Australia in 1932–33. England has possessed few captains with the tenacity and singleness of purpose reflected in Douglas Jardine.

AMARNATH'S DEBUT

In Jardine's tour, India found one player of particular merit, L. Amarnath. In addition, many of the weaknesses which have been the curse of Indian cricket for some years were exposed. The tour showed clearly that India lacked solidity in batting and could not consolidate a good position after a fine start. It also showed that India did not possess the tenacity to turn the tables when odds were against them. Above all it exposed our fielding weakness. Time and again Indian cricket has suffered because of fielding lapses, and even now after nearly twenty years those lapses persist. As for batting, many of our men seem satisfied and content when they reach scores of 50 or thereabouts, and lack the necessary concentration for making big scores in the interest of the side. Of course, there are exceptions like Vijay Hazare, India's present captain, but such per-formances on the part of others are few and far between. There is plenty of batting talent among our batsmen, but few utilise that talent to its fullest extent by making big scores when well set—scores that will help the team out of difficulties or contribute towards making the side's position impregnable.

Against Jardine's team, India lost two Test matches and the other was drawn. In the first Test at Bombay, Amarnath scored a glorious century on his first appearance. Indians had rarely seen such attractive and attacking batsmanship by an Indian cricketer in representative matches. Amarnath looked for runs from the moment he went in and completed a memorable century in two and a quarter hours. Never again did he play such an inspired innings. Another notable achievement was India's score of 249 in the second innings of the Third Test at Madras on a wearing pitch. The previous evening Jack Hobbs (who had come to India to report on the M.C.C. tour) said to me that India would do well to score over 150. The chief credit for this went to the Yuvraj of Patiala who continued to attack the bowling until he made 60.

AN UNHAPPY APPOINTMENT

In 1936 India sent her second official team to England. The tour began with a severe handicap in the captaincy of the Maharaj Kumar of Vizianagram. Originally the Nawab of Pataudi was appointed captain but, because of bad health, he withdrew. Subsequently, Vizianagram was appointed captain. 'Vizzy' had done a great deal for Indian cricket and when in 1931 he invited Hobbs and Sutcliffe to India to play for his team in a series of matches in India and Ceylon, he gave Indian cricketers and public an opportunity to see two of the world's greatest batsmen in action.

The captaincy of India was quite a different matter. On his form he would not have found a place in any good side, but the authorities of India did not seem to realise that captaincy of a country's team on an official tour meant more than individual status or the ability to make good speeches. So far as cricket was concerned, he was a dismal failure. He also made the sad mistake of insisting on playing in as many matches as possible. Neither in the field nor in batting was he an acquisition and, more often than not, the team virtually played with ten men.

The unfortunate Amarnath incident also marred that trip. Similar incidents have occurred in most touring sides, but the drastic action of sending Amarnath home not only was a blot on Indian cricket, but considerably weakened the team in all the Test matches. At the time of his departure Amarnath had made 613 runs, average 32, and had scored two centuries against Essex at Brentwood. He had also taken 32 wickets for 668 runs and proved to be India's most consistent all-rounder. The action against Amarnath seemed to be out of place at the time.

That was proved by the fact that nine years later Amarnath was appointed vice-captain of the Indian team which went to Ceylon; captain of India in Australia in 1947–48 and also captain against the West Indies in 1948–49. If the captain was justified in taking such drastic action in 1936, surely the highest honour that India can bestow on a cricketer should not have been given to Amarnath? And 'Vizzy' has been a Member of the Board for some years now.

TOO MANY PLAYERS

Added unpleasantness on that tour was caused by too many of the team having to sit out from the various matches. India took 18 cricketers on tour and also called upon the services of Amar Singh, Jahangir Khan and Dilawar Hussain, who were in England at the time. C. S. Nayudu was flown to England in June and, in spite of Amarnath's departure, India had 21 cricketers on hand, which meant that from every match ten had to be left out. This naturally led to discontent and unhappiness. The feature of this tour was some grand bowling by Nissar and Amar Singh. My success during a wet summer was beyond my expectations. *Wisden* did me the honour of finding me a place among the 'Five Cricketers of the Year'. How much that meant to me, few will ever realise.

Lord Tennyson brought a team in 1937–38 to India which, in unofficial Tests, won by three matches to two. On paper India were as strong as the visitors, but fielding weakness prevented us from gaining the 'rubber'. It was a happy tour in many ways and the enterprising play of the visitors left a good impression in India. In 1944–45 the Australian Services visited us and India received the opportunity to see that superb cricketer Miller in action. Hassett also entertained us with fine batting. India won the only match of the three representative fixtures which was decided. Although the tour was of short duration, the cricket was enterprising and care-free.

India went to England again in 1946. For the first time we were captained on tour by a man who deserved a place in the team on his merits as a cricketer. The Nawab of Pataudi had achieved notable things in England, and India welcomed his abilities both as captain and batsman. We were fairly and squarely beaten in the first Test match at Lord's and just managed to save ourselves from defeat at Manchester. The Oval Test was a wash-out. India, however, did well against most of the counties and financially the visit proved successful.

Above all, it was a very happy tour and credit for this went to the Nawab of Pataudi. I had the good fortune to make over 2,300 runs and participated in 30 of the 33 matches. During the tour M.C.C. honoured me by inviting me to become a member. Appreciating my difficulty in playing the full number of qualifying matches, they made a special concession—a most generous gesture to a visiting cricketer.

MANKAD'S CONSISTENCY

The highlight of the 1946 tour was the remarkable all-round performance of Vinoo Mankad who scored 1,120 runs and captured 129 wickets. With bat and ball he was consistency personified and, on a pitch which helped him, proved a bowler second to none in the world. He missed only two matches—a tremendous feat for a visiting cricketer playing a season's cricket in England. To our delight *Wisden* honoured Mankad with a place amongst the 'Five Cricketers of the Year'.

India undertook a new venture in 1947–48 when a team was sent to Australia, but with three of the best players staying at home, we could not hold the strong Australians who, under the captaincy of Don Bradman, proved as invincible as they were against W. R. Hammond's M.C.C. team the previous year. Amarnath led India; he batted extremely well in the first-class matches, only to fail in the Tests. The pick of our batsmen were Hazare, Phadkar and Mankad, whose great efforts were spoiled through lack of support.

SLOW BATTING

In 1948–49 the West Indies paid their first visit to India. The first three Tests were drawn and West Indies won at Madras. In the final Test, India narrowly failed to force a victory; only six runs were wanted with one wicket in hand when stumps were drawn on the fifth day. Slow batting that day just before and after lunch prevented India from registering their first success in international cricket. Along with our other weaknesses this has also been a drawback in Indian cricket for the last few years. Some years ago Indian batsmen threw away their wickets for no reason whatsoever. Now some have become too slow and simply cannot force the pace when quick scoring is essential. In 1950–51 against the Second Commonwealth Team, unenterprising batting prevented India from gaining a single victory. Last November also we could not, for the same reason, force a win in the first Test match against England at New Delhi.

While visiting teams average between 50 and 55 runs an hour in representative matches, India have not been able to average more than 35 to 40. Unless, therefore, their fielding—particularly catching—improves considerably and the rate of scoring is speeded up, it will be very difficult for India to go far in international cricket.

That West Indies tour was marked by the consistently brilliant batting of Weekes, who scored four consecutive centuries, and thus set up a record of five centuries in successive Test innings, having made one against England in the West Indies in 1947–48. Hazare and Modi batted magnificently for India. The visits of the two Commonwealth teams to India provided very entertaining cricket. Frank Worrell showed what a great batsman he is and gave us hopes for still better things to come. On the Indian side, Vijay Hazare was a consistent run-getter and proved how difficult it is to dislodge him. He has done more for Indian cricket in the last five years than any other player and, from the point of batting technique and the number of runs scored, should rank amongst the first six in the world at present. Temperamentally he is extremely sound and devoid of nerves. If he can quicken his rate of scoring, few men would be superior to him in contemporary cricket.

EFFECT OF PARTITION

The partition of India has deprived Indian cricket of some outstanding cricketers. Abdul Hafeez Kardar, Fazal Mahommed, Khan Mahommed and Imtiaz Ahmed would have helped considerably to strengthen the Indian team. Today Khan Mahommed is the fastest bowler in this sub-continent and India has no one among the medium-paced bowlers who can be put in the same category as Fazal Mahommed; Kardar is sufficiently well known in England; Nazar Mahommed is a most attractive and dashing opening batsman—India's biggest need today; and Imtiaz Ahmed is an outstanding opening batsman who demonstrated his abilities last year against the Second Commonwealth Team by scoring 300 runs in the last match. That is the highest score made by any Indian or Pakistani cricketer against a visiting team.

Above all, the partition has deprived India of future fast bowlers. In the past, India often relied for fast bowling on the Northern India people who, because of their height and sturdy physique, are better equipped for this kind of bowling than the cricketers of Central India or the South. Now this source of supply has ceased and the gap has not yet been filled. Some time may elapse before India possesses a fast bowler of the calibre of Mahomed Nissar who hailed from the Punjab.

This year India come to England. I sincerely trust we shall show that we have overcome many of the weaknesses which have persisted with Indian cricket in recent years. I am writing several months before the team will be chosen and I hope that Vijay Hazare, who should be an admirable captain, will be given a large proportion of young cricketers. In India too much premium has always been placed on experience and too little faith in youth. Over a period of years this policy has been disastrous. In the Indian team today are men who not only played in 1936 but as far back as 1933–34. Many promising cricketers have had their careers cut short through not receiving opportunities at the right time. Too many have retired soon after returning from a tour. Until and unless the authorities take courage in both hands and give more opportunities to young men, India's inherent weakness will continue and no improvement will be possible. A stage has been reached when it would be better to gamble with youth than to retain faith in older players. Indian cricket needs an injection of youth and I hope that injection will be administered for the 1952 visit to England.

MY RETIREMENT

Originally my intention had been to retire from the game after the 1951–52 tour by M.C.C. Two years ago I informed the Indian Board of Control of this decision and I requested that a younger man might be appointed captain immediately so that he could gain experience to lead India in England in 1952.

Mr. A. S. de Mello, president of the Board of Control until this year, however, insisted that I should carry on until the Indian visits to England and to the West Indies, in 1952–53, had been carried out. I was told that I should place the interests of Indian cricket above my own, and that I should carry on until then at least as a player.

Since it was put to me that way, I felt I had no alternative but to continue temporarily, but I made one proviso. I said that I would go to England if I could more than pull my weight in the side. I did not wish to pay a third visit, at 41, if I was to be merely one of sixteen members of the side. Only if I thought I was likely to be among the first three as a batsman and sufficiently quick in the field to hold my own would I agree to make the trip. I knew also I needed to be exceptionally fit to undertake an English tour, which is always most strenuous, particularly in wet weather. Normally a much younger man would be more useful.

Although I have played for nearly twenty years in India, I spent some of the happiest days of my life on the cricket fields of England. Playing six days a week in different centres, on different pitches, and in different kinds of weather was a unique experience in my life, and something that Indians never do at home. It is truly said that no cricketer's education is complete until he participates in a season in England. If I do not visit England as a member of the 1952 Indian team, I shall be with you to watch the games and see once more the fields on which I have spent so many happy hours.

GROWTH OF HAMPSHIRE CRICKET
[1952]

BY E. D. R. EAGAR

In his review of his beloved county of Hampshire, Edward Desmond Russell Eagar (1917–77) performs a skilful, evasive manoeuvre when dealing with the contentious issue of the Hambledon myth, claiming that 'it is not my purpose to delve into the feats of this great club'. But although Hambledon was certainly not the cradle of the game, it just as certainly was the cradle of the art of writing about it. Cricket literature leapt into being with John Nyren's recollections of the village side his father led, and to this considerable extent historians of the Hampshire club are justified in claiming for it a long and illustrious past. Eagar enjoyed a triple career of player, administrator and historian, being credited as co-author of the official history of the club. Much of his writing is scattered through the pages of that magisterial work, 'The World of Cricket', edited by E. W. Swanton and he could accurately be described as someone who worked literally until death to further the cause of the game in general and of his county in particular.

His note in the 1952 Almanack is informative and well-wrought, but it is a pity that he was not encouraged to wax more eloquent about the towering characters who represented the county at different times. More on Wynyard and Poore would have been especially welcome and the Hon. Lionel Tennyson surely deserved an essay on his own. He might also have been a shade less tight-lipped about C. B. Llewellyn, of whose career he says only that it 'ended, somewhat abruptly, in 1910'. Not half as abruptly as the passage itself, which omits to explain that the reason for Llewellyn's disappearance from the Hampshire ranks was due to a dispute over terms and that after his departure he continued to play in England, in the leagues.

THE history of Hampshire cricket goes back a long way, for it was at a meeting presided over by Mr. Thomas Chamberlayne in 1863 that the County Club was formed. In 1864 there were 140 members who paid a subscription of one guinea; in 1951 it was still possible to become a member for this amount.

Hampshire men claim that the Cricket History of their County started many years before this date. Was not the village of Hambledon the 'Cradle of the Game'? It is not my purpose to delve into the feats of this great club, formed in the middle of the eighteenth century. Hambledon has its own history written by many eminent authorities on the game. Enough to say that little Hambledon could take on and beat the rest of All England in matches often played for large sums of money.

Hambledon played its last recorded match in 1793; it was fitting that the game was played at Lord's, as the M.C.C. was founded in 1787, and from that date took over the leadership of the cricket world from the Hampshire villagers.

The story of Hampshire cricket from 1793 until the county became first-class over 100 years later is one of apathy and constant disappointment. Very few matches are recorded during this period. From time to time hope was raised in the hearts of those few cricket lovers who tried so hard to kindle the flame that would give Hampshire back the cricket glory of earlier years.

SOUTHAMPTON HEADQUARTERS FORMED

In 1842 Daniel Day, an old Surrey professional, took up residence in Southampton, and with the help and encouragement of such patrons as Mr. Thomas Chamberlayne, Sir Frederick Bathurst and Sir J. B. Mill took over the Antelope Cricket Ground, three years after that ground had been opened. Even this venture was not supported, and fixtures were few and far between. From this date Southampton has always been the head-quarters of the County Cricket Club.

The actual formation of the club took place in 1863: yet again the enthusiasts were not supported. We read in the Annual Report for 1872 a motion stating 'that in the hope of enlisting new members, and obtaining further subscriptions, the club be kept on foot. The Committee and Officers remaining the same, but no subscriptions called up, liabilities or expenses incurred, or matches played for the present.'

Momentous decisions were taken at a most successful meeting held at Winchester in 1883. Those who had been working so long and faithfully for their county club at last found their efforts rewarded: one or two county matches were played that year. The county was divided into five districts each with its representative on the full committee. This policy is still in operation today, the county now being divided into fifteen districts, each with its own local sub-committee of the County Cricket Club. At the same meeting steps were taken to secure a permanent home for the club. Colonel James Fellowes, Joint Honorary Secretary with Sir Russell Bencraft, making himself fully responsible for a guarantee fund.

FIRST-CLASS STATUS ATTAINED

The two Honorary Secretaries and the Honorary Treasurer, Mr. J. C. Moberley, were the leading personalities of the club at this time. Due to their tact and perseverance Hampshire became a first-class county twelve years later. Sir Russell Bencraft was the rock on which modern Hampshire cricket was built. In his time he acted as President, Chairman, Honorary

Secretary and captain. No man has ever done more for a cricket club, nor so richly deserved its successful entry into the County Championship.

On January 30, 1884, it was announced that a ground belonging to the Banister estate had been secured on lease for twenty-eight years at an annual rental of £60, on condition that a pavilion be erected. This ground, in Northlands Road, has been the County Cricket Ground ever since, but it was on the old Antelope Ground that F. E. Lacey, later Sir Francis Lacey, Secretary of the M.C.C., in the summer of that year, made Hampshire history with scores of 211 and 92 not out against Kent.

The official opening of the new ground took place on May 8, 1885, with a match between the North and South of Hampshire. The game was ruined by rain and left drawn in favour of the South for whom F. E. Lacey made 181 not out.

In the next ten years famous names began to appear in the few unofficial matches that Hampshire could arrange. Sir Russell Bencraft and Sir Francis Lacey have already been mentioned; to these should be added the amateurs Major E. G. Wynyard, A. J. L. Hill and Charles Robson; and the professionals Harry Baldwin, Tom Soar and Victor Barton.

AUSPICIOUS START

In 1895 Hampshire were admitted to the County Cricket Championship, and signalised their entry by winning their first two matches against Somerset and Derbyshire. At Sheffield in August they beat Yorkshire. In the same year the Hampshire Cricket Ground Company was formed with a nominal capital of £8,000. The company then purchased the ground from Sir Edward Hulse for £5,400.

Hampshire's cricket has always been unpredictable. Never higher than fifth (1914) in the Championship, they have always been liable to spring surprises. Often they have beaten the strongest sides when at their weakest, and lost to weaker opponents when least expected to do so.

BRILLIANT SERVICE CRICKETERS

In the early years, particularly before the 1914–18 war, Hampshire owed much to their cricketers from the Services; for example Major E. G. Wynyard, who played for England against Australia in 1896, and in the same year trounced the Yorkshire attack for 268 runs at Southampton.

General R. M. Poore headed the English batting averages in 1899 with 91.23, his 16 innings for the county giving him an average of 116.58. His 304 in that season against Somerset at Taunton stood as a Hampshire record for thirty-eight years until another Hampshire captain, R. H. Moore, made 316 against Warwickshire at Bournemouth in 1937.

Colonel A. C. Johnston, a splendid batsman, who was second in the English averages for 1912, was so badly wounded that he was lost to county cricket after the First World War. Colonel J. G. Greig served so often overseas that too little was seen of him. He is now Father Greig, and Hampshire remembers with gratitude not only his delightful cricket, but also his time as Honorary Secretary and President of the club. Mr. H. S.

Altham describes him as one of the most beautiful players in the country, and little behind Ranjitsinhji himself as a cutter in the year 1905.

Here then were four great Service players, to whom must be added the names of Captain A. Jaques, a fine bowler, whose career was cut short by his death in action, and Captain E. I. M. Barrett, a most dangerous match-winning batsman. If these players had been available more regularly it would have meant much to Hampshire. In only one season were any of these great players able to play often enough to score more than 1,000 runs for the county.

Finally C. B. Fry, who made his home and his life's work in the Training Ship *Mercury*, could only once spare the time to make over 1,000 runs for the county to which he transferred his allegiance from Sussex in 1909.

As always, the regular nucleus of the side bore the everyday rough and tumble of a cricket season. Led in turn by such fine captains as Sir Russell Bencroft (1895), Major E. G. Wynyard (1896–99), C. Robson (1900–2) and E. M. Sprot (1903–14) Hampshire gradually became a really fine eleven. In 1899 that great South African all-rounder G. C. B. Llewellyn joined Soar, Barton, Baldwin and Webb on the professional staff. He made over 10,000 runs and took over 1,000 wickets before his career ended, somewhat abruptly, in 1910. In 1900 and 1902 Jimmie Stone and Alec Bowell joined the staff. Stone, for long the regular wicket-keeper, scored over 10,000 runs, and Bowell, in his twenty-five years as a player, hit 18,500 runs.

WEAKNESS REMEDIED

For years bowling had been Hampshire's weakness. Llewellyn—the first bowler of the 'Chinaman' and that most dangerous of all balls the left-hander's googly—carried the attack almost unaided from 1899. Now he received some much-needed help. Three successive seasons, 1906, 1907 and 1908, brought a trio of world-famous characters and cricketers to the game in Jack Newman, Alex Kennedy and George Brown.

Kennedy and Newman—what names to conjure with! No pair of bowlers can have performed so often and so well, with so little rest as did these two throughout their long careers. Between them they took just short of 5,000 wickets, and as if this was not enough, the pair found time and strength to score 30,000 runs.

George Brown! Here was further bowling reinforcement of the tearaway variety. Yet George Brown was least known as a bowler, for he kept wicket for England, and was one of the greatest mid-offs who have ever lived. His batting brought him over 25,000 runs, and few men have played really fast bowling with more confidence and courage. Surely the most complete of all-rounders!

FEATS OF MEAD

This almost covers probably the best team ever to represent Hampshire. The decisive addition was one Philip Mead, who arrived at the County Ground, Southampton, in 1905 from Surrey, the county of his birth, where he had been discarded as a left-arm bowler. What can one say about this great player that has not been said already? Figures may be dull reading, but in Mead's case they are worth recording. In twenty-seven consecutive playing seasons from 1906–36 he scored over 1,000 runs, nine times over 2,000 and twice over 3,000. In many of these seasons he carried the Hampshire batting. In all he played 1,335 innings and made 55,060 runs for an average of 47.67 (more even than W. G. Grace). A total which included 153 centuries—138 for his county. That he played only seventeen times for England was due not so much to his own failings as to the tremendous wealth of batting during his own years of greatness. As a bowler he was seldom used, though he managed to take 277 wickets, and despite theories to the contrary, those who knew him best rate him as a fine slip fielder in his prime.

TENNYSON TAKES OVER

After the First World War the captaincy was in the capable hands and cheerful frame of Lionel, Lord Tennyson. He first played with success in 1913. From 1919–33 he led a team which might easily have won the Championship had not war intervened. He led it gallantly as befitted the man who, captaining England in 1921, scored 63 one-handed against the all-conquering Australian pace attack of Gregory and McDonald.

Until 1926 Hampshire were always a force to be reckoned with, and no side could take them lightly. That tireless pair, Kennedy and Newman, shared most of the bowling. In 1921 they took 340 wickets between them in Championship matches, and in 1922 Kennedy had a wonderful season, taking 177 wickets at 16 apiece and scoring 1,000 runs for his county. Hampshire were a remarkable team in those early 'twenties—capable of scoring 392 in the fourth innings of a match against Kent at Southampton in 1922, and yet losing the game. Going one better next year, they defeated Notts and the clock with a fourth innings score of 326.

REMARKABLE WIN

Their most amazing victory occurred in 1922. A game remembered to this day, and possibly the greatest victory from almost certain defeat that has ever occurred. Lord Tennyson asked Warwickshire to bat at Edgbaston. They scored 223, and then proceeded to bowl Hampshire out in half an hour for 15 runs, their lowest total ever. Following on, the captain forecast final victory, and, it is said, was willing to back his fancy! Six wickets went down for 186, but afterwards nothing could stand in their way, and 521 runs were scored in that second innings. George Brown made 172, and Walter Livsey hit 110 not out (his maiden century) in a ninth-wicket partnership of 177. Finally Kennedy and Newman bowled out Warwickshire for 158 and Hampshire were victorious by 155 runs.

From 1927–33, the end of the Tennyson era, age and retirement weakened a side which had depended so much on the 'Four Musketeers', Mead, Brown, Kennedy and Newman, with Livsey quietly active and efficient behind the stumps. Lord Tennyson's courage and cheerfulness remained, and in his last few years Stuart Boyes, who joined the staff in 1921, became an old hand and a very good left-arm slow bowler. A new generation of professionals arrived, Pothecary and Bailey in 1927, Creese in 1928, Arnold and Herman in 1929, and McCorkell and Hill in 1932. Thus Lord Tennyson had the responsibility of shaping and leading the team during the almost complete change-over between the old blood and the new. This he did with inimitable good humour and gusto.

NEW CAPTAINS

After Lionel Tennyson, the captaincy was shared by W. G. Lowndes in 1934–35, R. H. Moore 1936–37, C. G. A. Paris 1938 and G. R. Taylor 1939. Hampshire were lucky in their captains, who had a most difficult task with a newly built and somewhat erratic side. Mead retired in 1936, having passed W. G. Grace's record in scoring his 127th century against Sussex in 1931, but not until 1932 did Mead make a hundred against Derbyshire. This century probably gave him his greatest satisfaction, for he had now scored 100 for his county against all opponents.

If Hampshire's record was not impressive just before the Second World War, the team always played care-free cricket, and the ground fielding, in particular, was a delight. The Second World War, like the first, prevented the further advancement of players all over the country. Hampshire had lost J. P. Blake and Don Walker, both of whom were killed in action, but in 1946 most of the other pre-war players reported, six years older and sadly out of practice. Pothecary soon retired, being followed in the next few seasons by all the pre-war professional staff, till in this year of 1952 Hill alone of the older generation remains.

ENCOURAGING YOUTH

The policy of the committee, under the wise presidency of H. S. Altham—himself a Hampshire player and the Historian of Cricket—has been to train a young side of Hampshire-born cricketers, and import players only when necessary for the efficiency of the team. A new team has been born. It is a very young and inexperienced side, supported by eight younger professionals born and bred in Hampshire, who are learning their trade in the Minor Counties Championship. Players such as the amateur C. J. Knott, and the professionals D. Shackleton and N. H. Rogers have already made names for themselves in postwar cricket, others will surely follow for they are improving each season. Theirs is a rich heritage—they know it—and they will not fail.

[*No review of Hampshire cricket would be complete without reference to the prominent part which Mr. Eagar, the writer of this article, has played in putting the club on its feet since the war. He played for Gloucestershire in 1935 while still at Cheltenham College and gained his Blue at Oxford in 1939. Since 1946 he has captained Hampshire, and besides strengthening the battling has set a fine example by his enthusiasm and leadership both on and off the field.—Editor.*]

A. V. BEDSER: A GIANT AMONG BOWLERS [1953]

BY R. C. ROBERTSON-GLASGOW

One of the more distressing features of English cricket in the immediate postwar seasons was an apparent lack of bowlers with sufficient penetrative power to return matchwinning figures in Test matches. The sole exception seemed to be Alec Victor Bedser of Surrey, whose fast-medium bowling was quickly shown to be capable of turning a series. By the time the country was preparing for the arrival of Hassett's 1953 Australians, Bedser was already accepted as one of the finest bowlers of his style and pace in history and Robertson-Glasgow, in measuring him against Maurice Tate, was by no means overstating the case. His analysis of the similarities and differences between the two is done with such shrewdness and lucidity that we feel thankful that the job was given to a fellow-bowler. In his closing remarks Robertson-Glasgow expresses the hope that when the moment comes to make an assault on the Ashes, Bedser will be at his best. As things turned out, he was better than his best. In the first four Tests, all drawn, he took 36 wickets; it was only in the final, decisive game of the series that part of the burden of sustaining the England attack passed on to younger lions like Trueman, Lock and Laker.

And yet in the very next series Bedser's Test career ended as sensationally as it had begun. Under Hutton's leadership, the England side in Australia in 1954–55 took a Bradmanesque pounding from the home batsmen and lost by an innings, after which Hutton played the pace card comprising Tyson and Statham and swept to a succession of one-sided victories. Bedser's international career ended in the following summer with one cap against South Africa, but he continued to appear for Surrey to great effect, being the inspiration behind the club's record-breaking sequence of seven successive championships from 1952 to 1958. He retired in 1960, after which, in the words of John Warr, 'no one has chosen more Test teams'. (Bedser was prominent as an England selector from 1962 to 1980, including twelve years as chairman.) Since his retirement he has been heard frequently at cricket's social occasions, delivering addresses of endearing gloom and pessimism, insisting that the world is not what it once was, that things are going from bad to worse and that in his day, etc., etc. As a senior citizen he remains what he always was as a player, one of the best-loved men on the world scene.

MANY have bowled for England. Just a few stay in memory's front rank as England's bowlers, and among them, largest and latest, looms Alec Victor Bedser, of Surrey. Already he is an institution in the game, something taken for granted. We do not picture an England attack without him. Since 1946 he has been its spearhead and its stay, its start, middle and finish. Against Australia when Alec Bedser has failed the England bowling has failed.

He is in the succession to S. F. Barnes and M. W. Tate. Only he today can stand comparison with those two masters of the fast-medium method, whatever be the result of the comparing. Perhaps he comes in third on this shortest list. But let us remember, while we compare, the different style of Test game in which Bedser has bowled. Unlike his two great predecessors, he has bowled mostly on pitches dulled by the groundsman's most modern art. And he has bowled to batsmen who, for the most part, have rated survival above stroke-play. Chemistry and the five-day Test have not eased the bowler's task. The business of uprooting is tougher than ever. The methods employed by Bedser have not been unsuccessful.

Alec Bedser and his slightly elder twin brother Eric, were born at Reading on July 4, 1918, American Independence Day. The similarity of the twins in face and stature is so nearly exact that they have been always able to practise jocular deceptions on all but the few. They are not happy when parted for long, and Eric has so far been able to accompany his more distinguished brother on cricket tours abroad. From early boyhood, at Woking, whither the family very soon moved, the twins devoted every possible hour to cricket, and each has done much to develop the ability of the other. At the age of seven they were both members of the All Saints' Choir team at Woodham, Woking. From boyhood their nature has been distinguished by a straightforward simplicity, but not without shrewdness.

Both were determined to stick to cricket; but, when schooldays were done, they seemed to be heading for a legal life with a Lincoln's Inn firm of solicitors and cricket only on Saturdays. Whether they would finally have reached a joint seat on the Woolsack will never be known, because, while they were practising cricket in the nets of a cricket school at Woking, there fell on them the approving eye of Alan Peach, formerly a jocund and skilful all-round cricketer for Surrey. They gave up the Law and, in 1938, became members of the Surrey County cricket staff at The Oval. Originally both twins had been fast-medium bowlers, but they prudently agreed that they were more likely to gain places together in a first-class team if one of them, Eric, developed the off-spinner's art.

World War II came just as they were ready for County cricket. The brothers served in the Royal Air Force Police, took part in the evacuation from Dunkirk and in operations in North Africa, Italy and Austria. They played war-time cricket against the Australians, the West Indies, and the Dominions. In 1946 first-class cricket started again, and at this point we must separate the inseparable twins and concentrate on the career of Alec, very soon to play for England.

Critics are a sceptical bunch, and I doubt whether any at first saw in Alec Bedser's bowling anything more than extreme competence. Yet he began well enough for Surrey. Against India at The Oval he had taken the wicket of V. S. Hazare for 0 and four other wickets fairly cheaply when Sarwate and Banerjee came together and stole the scene with their extraordinary last-wicket stand of 249. A month later, in the Test Trial at Lord's, Alec

Bedser took the wickets of Hutton (82) and Hammond (25). But more interest attached to the bowling and batting of another newcomer to higher cricket, T. J. Ikin of Lancashire. Then came the first Test, at Lord's, between England and India. Of the first five Indian batsmen Bedser ended four, Merchant, Amarnath, Hazare and the Nawab of Pataudi. He also swallowed up the tail, taking in all seven for 49. No other bowler, not even Australia's Clarence Grimmett, had made so startling an entry into Test cricket. In the second innings he took four for 96. A month later, in the second Test at Manchester, Alec Bedser again took eleven Indian wickets. Of course, the batting was blamed. It always is. But the fact was a new 'star' had arrived: one whose light has never since been dimmed for long.

It was natural that Alec Bedser should stand for comparison with M. W. Tate. They have this in common: both have greatness, that quality which can be sensed rather than defined. Both have been willing and, by their strength, able to bowl for a long time at a stretch. Both have used shortish runs to the crease and generated pace and fire by the terrific force of a perfectly timed follow-through. Of the two, I would say that Tate had the more natural genius, Bedser the more invention and variety. In Australia, where both have touched the meridian of their powers, Tate in his prime had the faster, and so the more suitable, pitches to bowl on. He attacked batsmen whose best hope of success lay in the forward stroke. Bedser in Australia has attacked, on slower surfaces, batsmen whose main method has been the back-stroke. Each solved his problem triumphantly. Tate was able to bowl more for the slip catch. Bedser, though his deadliest ball is the one that goes from leg to off, has made far more use of close leg-fielders. But he has used in-swing as a stick, so to speak, not as a prop. He never lulls the batsman by monotony of method.

But both Tate and Bedser suffered from the over-fullness of the first-class programme. They had times of staleness, an occupational affliction that does not attack the less heavily employed Australian bowlers. When W. R. Hammond's England team went to Australia in the winter 1946–47, a severe burden fell on Bedser and Wright. In the Tests each bowled more than twice as many overs as anyone else. Each had to keep going when he should have been resting. On each the strain left its mark. When the South Africans came to England in summer 1947, it was soon evident that even Bedser's tremendous and willing engine needed some rest, and he was omitted from the last three of the five Tests. His rest was to go off and bowl for Surrey.

But in 1948 he came back, to do battle with one of the strongest Australian teams ever to visit England. In that series it was the fast bowling of the two Australians, Lindwall and Miller, that took the headlines. But Bedser's part in the struggle should not be forgotten. He bore the brunt of the work, bowling near 120 overs more than anyone else, and for a time at least he uncovered a weakness in the hitherto flawless batsmanship of Don Bradman. This he did with a ball that dipped in late from the off and caused a catch close on the leg side. Bradman, as he would, recovered from this interlude of perplexity. But it was an achievement. Not since the triumph of Harold Larwood in Australia sixteen years earlier had Bradman looked so fallible. It was in the fourth Test of this series, at Leeds, that Bedser surprised many, but not, I fancy, himself, by playing an innings of 79. He had been sent in at number four to play four balls overnight. But he far exceeded his terms of reference, and gave a notable display of batsmanship off the front foot, using his 75 inches of height and 15 stones of weight to full advantage.

In 1948–49 Bedser went with F. G. Mann's England team to South Africa. He had fair success as a bowler, and was 'in at the death' in that terrific finish of the first Test at Durban. In the next two seasons, 1949 and 1950, Bedser did not add to his reputation as a bowler, his success against the New Zealand and West Indies touring teams being moderate. Indeed, he began to be regarded as reliable rather than penetrative. 'We've seen the best of him,' was the general comment. Yet, at this time of doubt and depreciation, he stood on the threshold of performances that were to raise him to the ledge of immortality as a bowler. F. R. Brown's touring team to Australia, 1950–51, did not set out with a fanfare of trumpets, and its achievements in the early stages were, to put it mildly, meagre.

When Hassett won the toss in the first Test at Brisbane, to take innings on a perfect pitch, a total of about 500 was almost taken for granted. I chanced to be sitting next to a famous Australian bowler of former years when Bedser bowled his first over. 'No good,' he said, 'Bedser's just hitting the bat.' But soon Bedser had Morris l.b.w., bowled Hassett for 8, and stopped Harvey in his dashing journey towards a century. Supported by the fine bowling of Bailey and Brown, and with Evans in his most brilliant form behind the stumps, Bedser took four for 45. This was the start of his domination over Morris, the great left-hander who had averaged over 80 in the Tests here in 1948. Morris did break free at Adelaide, but on a pitch of any pace, as at Melbourne, Bedser was his master. It was in the fifth Test, at Melbourne, that Bedser touched the height of his powers. In each innings he broke through early, and sustained throughout an uncommon intensity of attack. In the match he took ten wickets for 105 runs, a rich contribution to England's first victory over Australia since August 1938. In the whole series he took 30 wickets at 16 each.

Back in England, Bedser played in all five Tests against South Africa. In the first Test, at Trent Bridge, he took six for 37 in the second South African innings, a performance that did not avert defeat. In the third Test, at Manchester, he did much towards winning the match by taking twelve for 112. In the season of 1952 Bedser and the young fast bowler, Trueman, produced an attack to which the Indian batsmen had no effective answer. It was Trueman who stole the story, but those who watched Bedser in action saw very much the same bowler who had troubled in turn such masters as Don Bradman and Arthur Morris. By the end of the season 1952 Bedser had taken 182 wickets in Test matches at 26 each. Only S. F. Barnes, with 189, has taken more for England.

Bedser's bowling for Surrey, Champions in 1952, is a story of continuous excellence and success. A word, too, for his fielding. For a large and heavy man he is unusually quick on his feet. He is a competent fielder anywhere, and at second slip he has made many a fine catch. In bowling he adds to natural gifts a thoughtfulness and sense that are reflections of his character. He is a man of equable and stable temperament, but authentically English in his ironical acceptance of the worst and inward hoping for the best. At 34, he has played in only seven years of first-class cricket. For two or three years yet he may stay at the height of his powers. We shall need them against Australia in summer 1953.

Also we shall be able to show our appreciation of this magnificent cricketer when he takes his benefit for Surrey against Yorkshire at The Oval on July 4, 6, 7. May the sun shine for him.

HISTORY OF DERBYSHIRE CRICKET [1953]

BY W. T. TAYLOR

(COUNTY SECRETARY SINCE 1908)

The 1953 edition included an entertaining account of the history of one of the less fashionable counties which, but for the understandable reticence of the County Secretary, might have been even more entertaining. Mr. Taylor is candid enough to repeat the story of the Notts side which was plied with drink by a Derbyshire supporter to such spectacular effect, but he makes no reference to Spofforth's finest hour as a Derbyshire cricketer. Spofforth performed well enough for his adopted county, but by far his most notable achievement with the club was the hand he played in the curious case of S. Richardson, Assistant Secretary of the club in the 1870s. The county club's dire financial situation during these years was due, it appeared, to the fraudulent activities of Richardson, who may well have got away with his game had it not been for the eagle-eyed Spofforth. The Australian, having married a local girl, attached himself all too briefly to the Derbyshire club and went into business in the district as a tea merchant. Spofforth was as keen a student of commerce as he was of bowling and in his spare time began scrutinising the county books. He soon unmasked Richardson as the cause of the trouble. The culprit was dismissed and adopted a career bizarre even for a cricketer. A list of the subsequent occupations of first-class cricketers represents dizzying variety, from newspaper cartoonist to Acting Governor of Rhodesia, from Librarian of the House of Lords to manager of a greyhound racing stadium. But surely none ever filled a more unexpected post than the felonious Richardson, who fled to Madrid and became Court Tailor to the King of Spain. Posterity assumes he specialised in coats with capacious pockets.

It was during my childhood that the Derbyshire club suddenly vaulted from comparative anonymity to great celebrity as the County Champions. In an epoch dominated by Yorkshire, Derbyshire snatched the Championship in 1936, thanks to the all-round efficiency of a side distinguished for the batting of Worthington and Denis Smith and the bowling of Copson and Mitchell.

Mr. Taylor's readability might have been further enhanced had he made even passing reference to one of the more risible incidents in the postwar affairs of the County, an incident notorious for the wonderful extremes of euphemism to which the 1950 edition of Wisden resorted in an attempt to maintain an air of diocesan calm:

Middlesex v. Derbyshire, Lord's, August 24, 25, 26, 1949
The equanimity of the Lord's Pavilion was disturbed when Gladwin, after being run out by his partner, accidentally put his bat through the dressing-room window.

THE history of Derbyshire cricket is that of a gallant struggle against adversity and financial difficulties. In scarcely one year since the club was formed eighty-two years ago has there been a credit balance. In fact, more than once Derbyshire have carried on only through the generosity of the cricketing public of the county, who have risen nobly to the club's many appeals for monetary assistance.

Derbyshire were formed on November 4, 1870, at a meeting called in the Guildhall, Derby, by an exceptionally enthusiastic cricket-lover, Mr. Walter Boden. A large and influential gathering passed the resolution: 'That a cricket club be formed, representing the whole strength of the county, to be called the Derbyshire County Club.'

Upon the election of a committee and officials, the Earl of Chesterfield, patron of all manly sports, accepted the Presidency. The Hon. W. M. Jervis was asked to be the first Honorary Secretary. Unfortunately for Derbyshire, the Earl died in the first year of the club's existence. The Hon. W. M. Jervis succeeded him as President until 1887, when, on the appointment of Mr. G. H. Strutt to the Presidency, he resumed his secretarial duties.

FINANCIAL CRISIS

In those days the subscription list was small and the loss of a few hundred pounds on the year's working, a matter of much concern. In 1887 the debt was fully £1,000 and the position critical. With the help of Mr. Boden and other friends of the club, the Hon. W. M. Jervis immediately set about removing this burden, and in one year the liabilities were liquidated. This is only one instance of the generosity which has been manifested through the years. Heavy taxation now prevents assistance from those who would wish to give it and the flag is kept flying with the help of receipts from Test Match profits and the organisation of various extraneous forms of raising money.

Although Derbyshire have not the colourful cricket traditions of some counties, the game has always held a warm corner in the hearts of the sports-loving people of the Peak County. Exact details of cricket's origin in Derbyshire are difficult to obtain, but records indicate that games were played in many parts of the county soon after the opening of the nineteenth century. Certainly in 1824 Derby defeated Chesterfield by an innings and 23 runs. One of the leading clubs in Derby at that time was the Derby Old Club and a prominent one in Chesterfield was the North Derbyshire Cricket Club.

Chesterfield continued to be a key point in the early history of Derbyshire. Tom Hunt, one of the most versatile of cricketers, was born there in 1819. He excelled in every phase of the game and, in fact, was so gifted that he became known as the 'Star of the North'. In 1856 he scored 102 for North v. South at Manchester, a tremendous innings in those days.

ALL-ENGLAND BEATEN

Seven years earlier, when twenty of the County beat the famous All-England XI by an innings and seven runs, Hunt had made 61 and John Paxton, a fast bowler from Ilkeston, had taken eleven wickets for 47. Next year, 1850, when the match ended in a draw, the same two players were outstanding. Paxton must have been a bowler of unusual merit. In six matches against the All-England XI he took 40 wickets—no mean feat against batsmen acknowledged to be the best in the land.

One of the most important events leading to the formation of the County Club occurred in 1863 when the South Derbyshire Cricket Club, one of the most prominent in the County, who combined with the Derby Town Club in the use of the Holmes ground in Derby, were given notice to leave. At once they acquired a ground from the Derby Recreation Company which held a lease from the corporation. The new ground was prepared for cricket, and to this day it is the leading headquarters of the game in Derbyshire. For many years the Derby County Football Club used the same ground, and not only played there under the auspices of the Cricket Club, but wore their colours of chocolate, amber and pale blue.

About this period a match is reported as having taken place in front of the Grand Stand on the Race Course, within a short distance of the present match centre. It may be interesting to mention at this stage that the Derbyshire Committee now have a scheme in hand for adopting this site for their matches at Derby and of making use of the Grand Stand with its covered accommodation for considerably more spectators.

LANCASHIRE TO THE RESCUE

The main problem arising from the inaugural meeting in 1870 was that of arranging matches against other counties. For the first three seasons Lancashire alone were willing to make fixtures, a fact that should never be forgotten by Derbyshire cricketers. The first of these games, at Manchester in May 1871, ended in victory for Derbyshire by an innings and eleven runs. Lancashire's first innings total of 25 remains their lowest to this day. The Lancashire batsmen were thrown into confusion by the pace of the

Derbyshire fast bowler, Dove Gregory, who took six wickets for nine runs. In the ensuing years, however, Lancashire gained ample revenge.

Derbyshire's inability to secure any additional county opponents caused a good deal of despondency among officials and supporters, but the turning point came in 1873 when a match was arranged at Wirksworth between sixteen of the County and the Nottinghamshire eleven. Considering that at the time Nottinghamshire were a cricket power, the result was staggering. Derbyshire won by an innings and eight runs. In their first innings Nottinghamshire scored a beggarly 14 runs; Joe Flint took six wickets for seven runs and William Mycroft four for six.

HOSPITALITY

Through the years a tale has been handed down about that batting debacle. The story is that a local Derbyshire celebrity, a keen and generous supporter of the club—and the proprietor of an important wine and spirit business, where he blended an attractive and potent brand of whisky—entertained the visitors lavishly at his establishment on the morning when they were to begin their innings.

Who can say that his fanatical enthusiasm for Derbyshire was responsible for the heaviness of his hand when he poured out refreshment for his guests? Might it not have been just the warmth of his hospitality?

That thrilling victory created intense interest in Derbyshire fortunes during the following season, but no one could have been prepared for the outcome. Derbyshire became Champion County in 1874. Vicissitudes too numerous to record in detail had to be encountered and overcome before that title was theirs again sixty-two years later.

When Derbyshire were first proclaimed Champion County, the smallest number of games lost decided the order of merit. What an inducement to play for draws! Through no fault of their own, however, Derbyshire were able to arrange matches only against Lancashire and Kent, three of which ended in victory and the other in a draw.

In the early days of Derbyshire county cricket the side was graced by many stalwart players, but as a counter came a series of exceptional misfortunes. Dove Gregory, a bowler who enjoyed much success, died in 1873 when only 35; the career of William Mycroft (left-arm fast), whom many considered one of the best bowlers produced by a club renowned for its strength in attack, was interfered with by ill-health, and William Cropper, an all-round cricketer of much merit, met with death on the football field before reaching the zenith of his powers. In addition, Frank Sugg and Frank Shacklock left to assist other counties. Almost inevitably such a sequence of disasters meant a lean period on the field, and in 1888 Derbyshire were relegated to second-class.

'WISDEN' DECIDES

I would point out that the classification of rank was not then decided by the authority of M.C.C. The chief arbiters in this matter were the London sporting Press, who might be said to have ruled supreme in everything appertaining to county cricket. Thus it was, that, after much discussion, Derbyshire's relegation was a decision of the Press rather than of any cricketing body. Incidentally, Mr. Charles F. Pardon, then Editor of *Wisden*, was a leading protagonist in the move. Despite strong Derbyshire protests, the other first-class counties and the cricketing public in general assented to the change.

Derbyshire remained in the wilderness until 1894, when they were again designated first-class. On a motion of the captains of the leading counties, they, together with Essex, Leicestershire and Warwickshire, were given first-class status, but the result of matches did not count in the Championship until 1895, by which time Hampshire had also been admitted. The County Championship was reorganised accordingly.

During Derbyshire's period in exile many fine players wore their colours. Prominent among them was S. H. Evershed, who in later years was knighted for public services to his native town of Burton-on-Trent. He captained the eleven with marked ability for many years. Another was that grand veteran, L. G. Wright, a magnificent batsman and unsurpassed as a fieldsman in the old-fashioned position of square-point. So keen and alert was he in 1952 that at the age of 90 he regularly visited the County Ground to watch the matches and he still played an excellent game of bowls. He died early this year.

Other players of top class were George Davidson, whose 274 against Lancashire at Manchester in 1896 remains a Derbyshire batting record, and who, in 1895, scored 1,296 runs and took 138 wickets, the first professional to accomplish this, and only the second player to do the 'double', the first being W. G. Grace; William Chatterton, a batsman of delightful strokes who toured South Africa with an English team in 1891; and William Storer, a skilled wicket-keeper who played in Tests against Australia both at home and abroad. Against Yorkshire in 1896 Storer hit centuries in each innings—a feat performed previously only by W. G. Grace, A. E. Stoddart and George Brann, all amateurs.

Youthful readers may not be aware that the celebrated Australian, F. R. Spofforth, known always as 'The Demon Bowler', played some cricket for Derbyshire. Spofforth last toured England with an Australian side in 1886, and afterwards, when he set up home in Derbyshire, the County authorities sought to persuade the County Cricket Council to allow him to play without waiting for the usual two years' residential qualification. This application was, quite rightly, refused. Even so, Yorkshire generously offered to waive the point so that Spofforth could turn out against them. He did so in two matches in the 1889 season and, moreover, showed his appreciation of their action so much that in one game he took fifteen of their wickets for 81 runs. Next season Spofforth shared the captaincy with S. H. Evershed and, as might have been expected, headed the bowling averages with 42 wickets at 11.36 runs each. He made one appearance in 1891. That was his last.

For many years Derbyshire's participation in the County Championship was uneventful, but occasionally they accomplished performances to be remembered. The defeat of Essex by nine wickets at Chesterfield in 1904 provided the most notable of these. When Essex made 597 in their first innings (P. A. Perrin 343 not out) they looked safe enough from defeat, but Derbyshire replied with 548 (C. A. Olliviere 229), dismissed Essex for 97 in the second innings, and won the game with 149 for one (Olliviere 92 not out) in the last innings.

WORLD RECORD STAND

Another memorable match was that against Warwickshire at Blackwell in 1910, when J. Chapman (165) and Arnold Warren (123) put on 283 for Derbyshire's ninth wicket. This still stands as a world record in first-class cricket. Then in my third year as Derbyshire Secretary, I remember the occasion well. At lunch-time on the last day Warwickshire looked certain of a comfortable win. Derbyshire, with eight second innings wickets down, were a long way behind Warwickshire's first innings score and, well as Chapman and Warren were batting, few Derbyshire folk could hope that defeat would be avoided.

In view of their strong position, Warwickshire, I knew, were hoping to catch an early afternoon train, and, in conversation during the interval, I remarked to their fast bowler, Frank Field: 'You look like catching your train all right, Frank.' The reply was, 'I'm not so sure about that, Mr. Taylor. These chaps are pretty good bats, you know.' How right he was. Chapman and Warren made their runs in less than three hours and Warwickshire had to be content with a draw.

Another historic Derbyshire achievement was the defeat of the Australian Imperial Forces XI in 1919 by 36 runs. This was the only victory gained by a county side against the Australians during their tour. Furthermore, it was accomplished without that great-hearted fast bowler, William Bestwick, who, at the age of 43, was making his first appearance for the Players against the Gentlemen at Lord's. James Horsley—he did the hat-trick—and Arthur Morton shared nineteen wickets in the two Australian innings.

Because Bestwick's debut for Derbyshire had been as far back as 1898 and he had not played for them since 1909, nearly everyone thought he would be past first-class cricket when he returned to the game in 1919. He surprised them all by his powers. In 1921 Bestwick was fourth in the first-class bowling averages with 147 wickets for less than 17 runs each, including all ten for 40 in an innings against Glamorgan at Cardiff. Not bad for a fast bowler of 45 making a come-back! No county ever had a better servant. The stronger the opposition and the better the pitch the harder he tried. His total of 1,452 wickets is a Derbyshire record. On his only Test appearance, at Leeds against Australia in 1905, Bestwick's contemporary, Arnold Warren, a very fast bowler with a lovely action, took five wickets for 57 runs.

One of the features of Derbyshire's cricket from 1899 to 1914 was the wicket-keeping of Joe Humphries. Surely his stumping of batsmen on the leg side when standing up to the fast bowling of Bestwick and Warren has never been surpassed since the days of Gregor MacGregor of Middlesex fame. He toured Australia with the England side of 1907 and, by scoring 16 at a critical time, assisted materially in the winning of the second Test by one wicket.

BESTWICKS MEET QUAIFES

Those who enjoyed the spectacle regretted that A. E. Lawton and G. Curgenven, both batsmen of tremendous hitting powers, were able to assist only infrequently. Limited as were his appearances, Curgenven rarely lost time playing himself in. At Gloucester, for instance, in 1922, he scored 65 in the first innings at little more than one a minute and his 68 out of 119 in the second took less than twenty-five minutes. That year two Derbyshire players figured in an occurrence considered unique in county cricket. When W. Bestwick and R. Bestwick shared the bowling against W. G. Quaife and B. W. Quaife of Warwickshire, spectators witnessed father and son bowling against batsmen likewise related. Similarly, no history of Derbyshire cricket would be complete without reference to the all-round work of Sam Cadman and Arthur Morton. Over a long period of years they were almost always the chief run-getters and wicket-takers. Too much credit cannot be accorded to them.

County cricket resumed in 1919 only through a big effort by everyone connected with the game. At first matches were restricted to two days, but the experiment was not repeated. Unsatisfactory as the season may have been, it was auspicious for Derbyshire because that year marked the beginning of G. R. Jackson's long association.

In 1920 came the most disastrous season ever experienced by any side since the County Championship came into existence. Of the 18 matches played, Derbyshire lost 17 outright. The other was abandoned without a ball being bowled. The only pleasurable memories for Derbyshire were the first appearances of Harry Elliott and Harry Storer. Elliott could be regarded as a most unfortunate wicket-keeper in that his career coincided with the peak years of Herbert Strudwick of Surrey. His big-match honours were confined to tours of South Africa (1927) and India (1933) and one home Test, at Manchester against West Indies in 1928. In first-class cricket Elliott stumped or caught 1,206 victims, a number exceeded by only three players. His 1,183 dismissals for Derbyshire are easily a county record. Two special feats by him were in not conceding a bye in 25 completed innings in 1936 and in missing only one match through injury from 1920 to 1927. Harry Elliott's nephew, Charles, began to play for Derbyshire in 1932. Twenty years later, when he headed the batting averages, he was still one of the County's most able batsmen. Harry Storer, a nephew of the old wicket-keeper, William Storer, was a most dependable first-wicket batsman, equally at home on fast or slow pitches. But for the claims of first-class football, at which he was capped by England, probably he would have played for his country at cricket as well.

Worried by the appalling results of 1920, G. M. Buckston returned, at 40 years of age, to lead the side next season with the fixed intention of instilling determination into a dispirited eleven. Buckston had not played county cricket since 1907, but a pronounced revival in Derbyshire fortunes coincided with his appointment. Only those who played under him knew how much the team owed to the 'skipper' for his example, cheerfulness and leadership. Having accomplished his mission, Buckston refused to be dissuaded from his intention to retire. Instead, he was elected chairman of the Committee.

G. R. JACKSON ERA

G. R. Jackson took over the captaincy for 1922. Throughout Derbyshire's cricket history no appointment has been followed by such happy results. For nine seasons G. R. Jackson led Derbyshire with masterly judgment. Although a stern disciplinarian, he held the affection and respect of every player. When he retired at the end of the 1930 summer he had laid the foundations of the Championship team six years later. This was *Wisden's* interpretation of G. R. Jackson's effort for Derbyshire cricket: 'For his work in leading and inspiring the team, Jackson deserves immense thanks. He took over control when the fortunes of the county were at a very low ebb, steadily raised the standard of the cricket, and now retires with Derbyshire well established amongst the leading teams of the day.'

During G. R Jackson's captaincy many cricketers destined to give magnificent service over a protracted period entered the county ranks. One was Leslie Townsend (1922), a gifted all-rounder who in 1933 scored 2,268 runs and took 100 wickets. In 1924 that fine aggressive cricketer, Stanley Worthington, embarked upon his county career. He was no mean fast-medium bowler, an attractive batsman on hard pitches and a superb close fielder. A particularly joyous match for Worthington was that against Nottinghamshire at Ilkeston in 1938. Not only did he score two separate centuries, but, in the course of his second innings, he heard of the birth of his only child, a son.

DENIS SMITH ARRIVES

In 1927 Derbyshire were further strengthened by the advent of Denis Smith. At one time this left-hand batsman of beautiful stroke-play was described as a second Frank Woolley. He developed to a high state of efficiency but never quite reached the class expected. Even so, his total of 20,516 runs for Derbyshire constitutes a county record. A year after Worthington came Albert Alderman and Tom Mitchell. Alderman was a steady opening batsman and second to none in the outfield. His catch at The Oval in 1936 when he dismissed Barling is still recalled by those privileged to witness it. When Barling swept a ball from Copson to fine leg the stroke looked certain to produce six runs, but Alderman, sprinting hard for 30 yards, held the ball with his right hand close to the palings.

Mitchell's discovery was unusual and intriguing. With time on his hands during the General Strike of 1926, Mitchell, a miner, practised bowling near the pit-head of the Creswell Colliery at which he normally worked. An old cricketer who saw him turning the ball prodigiously from leg at once recommended him to the local cricket club. They invited Mitchell to play for them. Mitchell not only gathered a harvest of wickets immediately in club cricket, but by 1928 had advanced to the county eleven. Against Leicestershire in 1935 he took all ten for 64 in an innings. Much excellent service was to come also from Alf Pope, a fast-medium bowler and useful batsman who began in county cricket in 1930. Four of Jackson's men, Townsend, Worthington, Denis Smith and Mitchell, played for England and all helped Derbyshire to carry off the Championship in 1936. How lucky were Derbyshire to find so many above average cricketers over so short a period!

Derbyshire were fortunate also in persuading A. W. Richardson to become captain in 1931. Richardson continued as leader until the end of that wonderful 1936 season. Without doubt the chief architects in this glorious episode of Derbyshire cricket were the two captains, G. R. Jackson (1922–30) and A. W. Richardson (1931–36), and the coach, Sam Cadman. By their skill and acumen, Jackson and Richardson gradually moulded Derbyshire into a match-winning combination, and, with the flair for discerning the potentialities of young players, Cadman produced from the cricket nursery no fewer than eight of the Championship team. With Middlesex and Yorkshire issuing late, though strong, challenges, interest in the side was aflame in the closing weeks of the 1936 season and, when he heard the news that the result of the Championship at last had been settled, the Derbyshire President, the Duke of Devonshire, hurriedly left his shooting party at Bolton Abbey to journey to Derby and join the public reception given to the players on their return. The Duke, who had accepted the Presidency in 1909, always showed the deepest interest in the club's affairs. He attended home matches regularly and was always ready to come to the rescue when financial problems presented themselves. When he died in 1938 he was succeeded in the Presidency by his son, who in turn was succeeded by his son, the present eleventh Duke of Devonshire.

DEVASTATING COPSON

Two players of outstanding merit, Bill Copson (1932) and George Pope (1933), began with Derbyshire under A. W. Richardson. Apart from being one of the most likeable fellows who stepped on to a cricket field, Copson was a devastating fast-medium bowler whose gift of making the ball appear to leave the turf faster than he bowled it through the air caused the downfall of scores of first-rate batsmen. Copson did not enjoy the best of health. Nevertheless, he played a vital part in much of Derbyshire's glory. He could not have wished for a better start in big cricket. With the first ball he sent down in a county game, at The Oval in 1932, he dismissed no less a player than Andrew Sandham of Surrey. Copson's most noteworthy feat was that against Warwickshire in the first innings at Derby in 1937. His eight wickets for eleven runs there included four with successive balls. Although Copson did the hat-trick three times, that distinction has been surpassed by the present Derbyshire leg-break bowler, Bert Rhodes (five times). Only three men—D. V. P. Wright (seven), T. W. Goddard (six) and C. W. L. Parker (six)—have exceeded this number.

George Pope was an all-rounder of abundant possibilities whose natural talent should have produced better results than it did. Both he and Copson played for England at home and, along with his county colleague, Worthington, Copson went to Australia in 1936–37 as a member of G. O. Allen's team, but did not make a Test appearance there. R. H. R. Buckston, who followed A. W. Richardson in the leadership, gave every possible encouragement to the younger players. Since the war Buckston has rendered equal aid as captain of the second eleven. His understanding of the 'outlook' of the young cricketer has been valuable in the extreme.

The resumption of county cricket in 1946 presented more problems, the main one affecting Derbyshire being that of finding a regular captain. With the exception of E. J. Gothard, who carried out the duties in 1947 and 1948, no one was available for more than one year. Although no more than a moderate change bowler, Gothard performed a remarkable hat-trick at Derby against Middlesex in their Championship year of 1947 by dismissing A. Fairbairn, W. J. Edrich and R. W. V. Robins. To his credit also went the bowling of Sir Donald Bradman at Derby in 1948.

Luckily for Derbyshire, a regular captain became available from 1951 onwards when G. L. Willatt took over. Under his leadership in 1952 the side finished fourth, their highest position since 1937. Continuity of captaincy is always beneficial to a team, and all followers of Derbyshire cricket must be glad that Willatt signified his ability to continue in 1953. Whenever Willatt was absent in 1952, the side played under the command of D. B. Carr, who, following his tour with the M.C.C. team in India the previous winter, added a balance to the eleven through his all-round skill. Since the Second World War several noteworthy victories have been recorded by Derbyshire. These included the defeat of Somerset in one day in 1947—by an innings and 125 runs.

C. GLADWIN AND L. JACKSON

A further highlight of this period has been the fast-medium bowling of Clifford Gladwin, who, except for 1950 when unfitness kept him out of nearly half the matches, has taken over 100 wickets for Derbyshire in each season. As a fact, Derbyshire are said to have an uncanny facility for producing fast-medium bowlers ('Derbyshire bowlers' they are called). Another of this variety is Leslie Jackson, who came into the side in 1947. At times Jackson is good enough to run through a batting side and even on the hardest pitches he will move the new ball either way. The Australian touring team of 1948 were genuine in their declaration that only two bowlers in England moved the ball away from the bat as much as Jackson. He toured India with the Commonwealth team in the winter of 1950, suffered an injury to his elbow which necessitated his returning to undergo an operation, resumed cricket late in the 1951 season, and returned to his best form in 1952, leading the county bowling with a total of 114 wickets.

PICTURESQUE CHESTERFIELD

Although Derby remains the county ground of the club, it is by no means as pleasing to the eye as the beautiful Queen's Park enclosure at Chesterfield, which Derbyshire first used in 1898 for a match against Surrey. Despite the superb lob bowling of D. L. A. Jephson, who shortened the match by taking nine Derbyshire wickets for 55 runs in the two innings, the size of the crowd at that game made the experiment well worth while and further fixtures were arranged there. In fact Chesterfield became a regular venue for several matches a season. Since those days also the Committee have extended their fixtures to other centres in the county and now no less than five grounds are used. Those responsible for the county's policy believe that they owe a duty to their followers which they can best repay by offering them an opportunity of watching first-class cricket within a reasonable distance of their homes.

The first game at Chesterfield did not pass without incident. Derbyshire supporters were most hostile about Jephson's lobs, against which they protested vigorously, saying that this was 'unfair bowling'. Only a few weeks after that exciting contest Chesterfield was the scene of the establishment of a batting record which stood for thirty-four years. Yorkshire's opening pair, J. T. Brown and J. Tunnicliffe, scored 554 together against Derbyshire in W. Sugg's benefit match before Brown deliberately knocked down his wicket. That partnership was not beaten until two more Yorkshiremen, Percy Holmes and Herbert Sutcliffe, made 555 for the first wicket against Essex at Leyton in 1932.

To record in detail the efforts of all the splendid cricketers who have played for Derbyshire would be quite impossible, but all omissions are regretted. What of the future? Within the next few years some of the present Derbyshire side will finish their careers. Replacements for them have to be found. Many promising young cricketers in the county have been discovered and developed through the medium of the Derbyshire Youth Cricket Advisory Council, who are carrying out the scheme sponsored by the M.C.C. Youth Cricket Association. Properly developed, some of these should mature into top-class players, and I believe that in years ahead Derbyshire will continue to flourish as an attractive county.

*[From 1889 until the present time only three Secretaries have held office for Derbyshire. Mr. W. B. Delacombe did so until his retirement in 1908. He was followed for a few months by Mr. R. S. T. Cochrane. Mr. Taylor, who has been Secretary ever since, is today the longest-serving of the County Secretaries. Although he assisted Derbyshire in a few matches from 1905 onwards, he is better known for his administrative efficiency. In the organisation of special efforts which over the years have raised more than £20,000 for the county club his share has been large—and always unstinted.—*Editor.*]*

SUSSEX THROUGH THE YEARS [1954]

BY A. E. R. GILLIGAN

Arthur Edward Robert Gilligan (1894–1976), of Cambridge, Sussex, the Gentlemen and England, contributed to the eminently readable 1954 edition an account of his native Sussex which informs as well as entertains. But it was not quite his debut as a featured writer in the Almanack. In 1939 he had contributed one of the funniest pieces ever seen in a serious sporting publication with his 'Cricket Conundrums', a series of outré hypothetical situations each with a bizarre solution. The history of Sussex cricket is more sober than the Conundrums piece, but Gilligan clearly had a talent for writing cheery, easily digested potted histories. The great tragedy of his life, to which he never refers, occurred in 1924, the year he captained his country against the visiting South Africans. Batting for the Gentlemen against the Players, he was struck over the heart by the innocuous medium-pace off-spin of the Worcestershire bowler Pearson. Although in great distress, Gilligan foolishly insisted on resuming his innings. He went on to make 112 in the second innings, but his refusal to retire from the match proved disastrous. Later he wrote of his obstinacy: 'That was probably the worst thing I ever did.' Although he played on after the accident, his effectiveness was drastically reduced and he played no more for England. His account of the evolution of the Sussex club is filled with plums which are as educational as they are entertaining—that the club was formed three times, that its ground was a converted barley field, that James Lillywhite never missed a game for twenty years, that Tom Box never missed one for twenty-four and, most extraordinary of all, that there was once a game in which there appeared grandfather William Lillywhite, father James, and a son of James. Gilligan's own dynasty had nothing to match this, but he did become father-in-law to the England captain of a later age, Peter May.

Sussex , my own county, have never been Champions, but no one will deny that they have played an historic part in the development of our great game. Their achievements on the field as a team may have been bettered by many sides, but individually their famous figures of the past who have seen the county through the years compare favourably with any. I will recall the great ones of Sussex as I go back through the annals of the oldest county club.

DUKE VERSUS KNIGHT IN 1728

Sussex cricket goes back over 300 years, in fact to 1622 when at Boxmoor six parishioners were prosecuted for playing cricket in the Churchyard on Sunday. The first known reference to a match of any kind was in the *Foreign Post* of July 7, 1697, to 'Eleven a side in Sussex'. In those days, cricket was a popular pastime in many villages, and we have another game recorded as taking place in 1728 when the Duke of Richmond's XI met a team raised by Sir William Gage. The first inter-county match which I believe to be authentic was staged in August 1735 at Sevenoaks, Kent, where, history tells, 'a great cricket match was played between Sir William Gage, of Firle, and ten other gentlemen of Sussex, and the Earl of Middlesex, the Lord John Sackville and nine other gentlemen of Kent'.

Sussex cricket progressed on an ever-widening basis for the next fifty years, and an enormous fillip was given to the game when, in 1791, the Prince of Wales, afterwards George the Fourth, presented Brighton with a ground situated at the northern end of the town. About this time we find the first Sussex cricketer to make a name for himself—one John Hammond, of Storrington. He was a versatile player, skilled in batting, bowling and wicket-keeping. Batting was probably his forte, for he was known as a terror to slow bowlers because he used his feet and went out to drive them in menacing fashion. (Our present-day county batsmen might make a note of this point.)

THE ROUND-ARM EXPERIMENT

In 1827 came the three experimental matches between Sussex and England to try out the new round-arm bowling of which William Lillywhite and James Broadbridge, of Sussex, were to become noted exponents. The matches were played at Sheffield, Lord's and Brighton. Sussex won the first two contests with some ease and, in consequence, large wagers were laid on Sussex for the third match. Sussex lost. Broadbridge, foolishly throwing his bat at a very wide ball, gave a catch to Mr. Ward at point, and this unexpected reverse of their best batsman so upset the rest of the side that they were beaten by 24 runs. Interest in the match was tremendous, and it is on record that over £300 was taken at the gate in sixpences alone!

All these happenings, so keenly followed by Sussex enthusiasts, led to the formation of the Sussex County Cricket Club in 1836. (It was, by the way, re-formed in 1839 and again in 1857.) Twelve years after its formation, the club acquired the celebrated Royal Brunswick ground on the sea front at Hove, and people came from miles away to see the beautiful turf on wicket and outfield. No other ground could compare with it. Matches against Kent and Surrey were played there, and even at that period inter-county struggles formed the back-bone of the noble game. The 1857 reorganisation, carried out by four gentlemen—Messrs. Stocken, Cooke, Stent and Ashley—put the club on more popular lines, with representatives from different parts of the county to serve on the Committee.

THE LAST GROUND

The year 1871 saw Sussex procure the present County Ground in Hove. The generosity of Mr. Fane Bennett Stanford and the efforts of the Trustees of the Stanford estate had much to do with it. The plot of ground, of about nine acres—all covered with a good crop of barley—was selected, and purchased on a lease of twenty-one years at an annual rental of £100. The first ball in the first county match on the new ground was bowled on June 6, 1872, and two years later the first century for Sussex on the Hove ground came from the bat of R. Fillery, who hit 105 off Surrey. I should mention here that as far back as 1844, C. J. Taylor took a hundred off the M.C.C. bowlers at Brighton. About this time James Lillywhite took fourteen wickets on his first appearance for Sussex, and he went on to play for twenty years without missing a match! Lillywhite was captain in the first two matches ever played in the Antipodes between England and Australia. A family record was created when William Lillywhite, aged 61, James Lillywhite and his son (grandfather, father and son) played together in one match.

WISDEN BOWLS ALL TEN

Then there were John Wisden, Tom Box and H. Phillips. John Wisden, 'The Little Wonder'—so called because he was hardly five feet four in height—played regularly for Sussex from 1846 to 1863 and his 'very fast and ripping deliveries' (as *Scores and Biographies* describes his bowling) made batsmen of all types fear him. His greatest performance was the clean-bowling of all ten wickets for North against South at Lord's in 1850—a unique feat achieved, so it is said, at a cost of 'scarcely 30 runs out of a total of 76'. Wisden bowled true round-arm as did William Lillywhite. As for wicket-keeper Tom Box he helped Sussex from 1832 till 1856 without missing a game.

There were many other fine players before the turn of the century, among them Sir Aubrey Smith, who carried English tradition and cricket to Hollywood, and C. H. G. Bland, who took all ten Kent wickets for 48 in 1899. We remember the free hitting of F. M. Lucas who struck the first double-century for Sussex—215 not out against Gloucestershire at Hove in 1885. George Bean, eight years later, enjoyed the distinction of being the first batsman to score 1,000 runs in a season. In that year, too, Walter Humphreys, a lob bowler, became the first Sussex bowler to take 100 wickets. His full bag for the county that year was 148. Naturally there was the reverse side of the picture. W. L. Murdoch, Sussex captain in the 1890s, watched helplessly while Victor Trumper hammered 300 not out for the Australians against his side in 1899—still the highest score by a touring team against Sussex.

THE GOLDEN AGE

A glorious era for Sussex unfolded with the advent of a young Indian cricketer and Cambridge Blue—one K. S. Ranjitsinhji—and an Oxford Blue named C. B. Fry. Before long Sussex, largely through their efforts, were almost on top of the world. In successive years—1902 and 1903—they finished second in the Championship.

'Ranji', as everyone soon called him, and Fry became famous for their remarkable batting performances—and they were truly amazing. In 1900, in county matches alone, they scored between them 4,393 runs—'Ranji'

2,563, average 85, and Fry 1,830, average 63. 'C. B.' opened for Sussex with Joe Vine and they scored over one hundred for the first wicket thirty-three times. The early years of the twentieth century brought many other players to the fore for Sussex, including such personalities as A. E. Relf, C. L. A. Smith, E. H. Killick, G. Leach, W. Newham, G. Brann, F. W. Tate (father of Maurice), G. Cox and H. R. Butt. A little later R. R. Relf, H. L. Simms and V. W. C. Jupp played prominent parts in Sussex cricket. Jupp went on to give good service to Northamptonshire and, talking of men of two counties, it is interesting to note that P. G. H. Fender, afterwards Surrey captain, turned out for Sussex before the First World War. I must mention that 'Billy' Newham, in various capacities, assisted Sussex for sixty-three years—a proud record. Killick will be remembered in one unhappy connection for in 1911 Alletson, of Notts, hit him for 34 in one over which included two no-balls. Alletson's scoring strokes in this historic over were: 4, 6, 6, 4, 4, 4, 6.

SOME SUSSEX CAPTAINS

From 1900 to the outbreak of war in 1914, Sussex had four captains—'Ranji', C. B. Fry, C. L. A. Smith and H. P. Chaplin. When cricket was resumed in 1919, H. L. Wilson did a useful job as skipper in a team-building period, and when I took over in 1922 I had the good fortune to have at my command players like Ted Bowley, Maurice Tate, George Cox senior, Tom Cook, George Street and Bert Wensley.

TATE BEST SUSSEX BOWLER

Tate, I must say at once, was the greatest bowler our county has produced. Curiously, when I first played for Sussex Maurice used the same run-up and style of delivery as his father—a slow bowler! A sheer piece of luck caused Maurice to change his methods. Sussex had batted very badly in 1922, and when we had a day off the whole team practised at the nets. Maurice Tate bowled me several of his slow deliveries, then down came a quick one which spreadeagled my stumps. He did this three times. I went up to him and said: 'Maurice, you must change your style of bowling immediately.' My hunch paid. In the next match, against Kent at Tunbridge Wells, Maurice, in his new style as a quick bowler, was unplayable. He took three wickets in four balls and eight in the innings for 67. That was the turning point in his career.

In the Test Trial Match at Lord's in 1923, he took five wickets without a run being scored from him after the Rest had made 200 for four wickets. They were out for 205. The following year Maurice and I bowled out South Africa at Birmingham for 30—a day neither of us will ever forget. I was fortunate to take six for seven runs, and Maurice captured the other four for 12. In the second innings we shared nine wickets and England won by an innings. The tide flowed for Sussex bowlers about that time, for we had previously dismissed Surrey for 53 at The Oval, and in the Whitsuntide match at Lord's had disposed of Middlesex, in their second innings, for 41.

COMPARISON WITH BEDSER

Maurice was a member of my 1924–25 M.C.C. Team to Australia and on this tour he beat Arthur Mailey's record of 36 wickets in a Test series by taking 38. He bowled Mailey out to gain his 37th success! Beside being a great bowler, Maurice was a hard-hitting batsman with a wealth of strokes. He scored 17,518 runs for the county, and took 2,223 wickets. For seven consecutive seasons he did the 'double', and in 1929 he took over 100 wickets for the county alone and scored more than 1,000 runs in first-class cricket. In fact, with the exception of 1933 when a damaged foot kept him out of the last three matches (he had taken 99 wickets) he never failed to take over 100 wickets for Sussex.

In 1953 Alec Bedser beat Tate's Test record by taking 39 wickets in a series, and many times since I have been asked how I compare Bedser with Maurice. My answer is: 'They are two very great bowlers.' Having said that I still think that Maurice Tate just stands out as the superior bowler of the two, bearing in mind the strength of the Australian batting in the 1924–25 series. But it is a very close thing indeed and one must not forget that Bedser had to contend with Bradman between 1946 and 1948.

'DULEEP'S' DAYS

Sussex cricket has never lacked cricketers of note. There came the Parks brothers—Jim and Harry, the Langridges—James and John, and K. S. Duleepsinhji, nephew of 'Ranji', before I handed over the captaincy to my brother, Harold, in 1930. 'Duleep' played some wonderful innings during his short career, with his magnificent scores of 115 and 246 in the match against Kent at Hastings in 1929 as probably his supreme effort. He was a joy to watch. Another historic day came in May 1930 when against Northamptonshire at Hove 'Duleep' hit the record Sussex individual score, 333, beating his uncle's 285 not out against Somerset at Taunton in 1901. Duleepsinhji and my brother suffered in health, but 'Duleep' helped Sussex finish second in 1932, a position they kept in the two following years under R. S. G. Scott and Alan Melville, afterwards captain of South Africa. A. J. Holmes took over the leadership of the county in 1936 and carried on until the outbreak of World War II.

UNIQUE DOUBLE

A red-letter day in Sussex history, and indeed in first-class cricket, occurred in 1937, when J. H. Parks achieved the unique feat of having taken 100 wickets and scored 3,000 runs. His full figures for a memorable season were 3,003 runs, average 50.89, and 101 wickets, average 25.83.

I would like to record here that I am much obliged to Sir Home Gordon, Bart., for many facts of interest concerning Sussex. A good friend to Sussex cricket since 1919, he was President of the County Cricket Club in 1948 and, now in his 82nd year, he is still one of the keenest supporters of the game.

AFTER THE WAR

When cricket recommenced in 1946, S. C. Griffith captained Sussex. H. T. Bartlett took over in 1947 and was followed in 1950 by James Langridge, the first professional captain to lead the county team. He held the post for three years until D. S. Sheppard, captain of Cambridge in 1952, was appointed in his place. Last season brought a personal triumph for Sheppard, and I think it only right for the satisfaction of present-day well-wishers of my county, that I should enlarge on their performances under his captaincy. Sheppard put Sussex back into the limelight, and for the first time since 1934 the county finished second and were serious challengers to Surrey for the Championship title right until the last week of the season. Sheppard set a magnificent example at all times and moulded Sussex into a grand team showing a tremendous improvement in fielding. Sheppard batted in top-class style, and he scored 2,048 runs for an average of 52.51. John Langridge opened with him and a fine pair they were. Young George Cox, son of George Cox senior, who was my leading professional, had a splendid season. He played several of his audacious knocks and rescued the side when they were in trouble. James Langridge retired from first-class cricket after the Australian match—a fitting end to his career embracing thirty years of the most valuable service to the club. He was appointed coach.

PROMISING YOUNGSTERS

Quite one of the most encouraging features of 1953 was the progress made by the young brigade, particularly K. G. Suttle and N. L. Thomson. Suttle, a left-handed bat, scored 1,377 runs and was always ready to use his feet and attack the bowling. At all times his fielding was brilliant. He was rewarded with an invitation to tour West Indies with the M.C.C. team. Thomson took 101 wickets in his first season as a professional, and was a fine replacement for the faithful Jim Cornford who has gone to live in Rhodesia. A. E. James took 104 wickets with his good length bowling, while Oakman, until he broke a finger at the end of July, put up some fine performances with his spin bowling. Young Jim Parks, son of J. H., returned from service in the R.A.F. and scored 1,277 runs, but he did not get going as well as many had hoped. However, there is a great future, I am sure, for this young player.

Nor must Jim Wood be forgotten. Although not as successful as in previous years he was always one of the hardest triers in the team. The end of the school term brought this year's captain, Hubert Doggart, into the side and with Robin Marlar, the 1953 Cambridge captain, bowling magnificently, Sheppard was able to captain a great match-winning side.

PRESIDENT'S INSPIRATION

Our President, the Duke of Norfolk, has taken a real and lively interest in all the county games. He has given a lead that puts inspiration and stimulation into the hearts of all keen Sussex cricket lovers. Arrangements for the Coronation occupied a tremendous amount of His Grace's time, but he managed to see many of our county games. His own match at the beautiful Arundel Park ground against H.R.H. the Duke of Edinburgh's XI attracted over 30,000 people and renewed memories of that match of 1728. The Chairman of the Sussex Committee, Mr. A. K. Wilson, is another enthusiast to whom the county owes a great deal, and Lieut.-Col. G. S. Grimston, our energetic Secretary, hopes to have his reward in seeing Sussex go from strength to strength.

THIRTY YEARS AN UMPIRE [1955]

Chester's Unique Place in Cricket

BY VIVIAN JENKINS

By now it hardly seemed like Wisden at all if there was no essay by Vivian Jenkins. In 1955 he contributed one of his happiest compositions, a tribute to the great umpire, Frank Chester. Most of the facts of Chester's tragic but ultimately triumphant career were familiar enough to readers, his precocious brilliance as an all-rounder with Worcestershire in the days before the Great War, the wound at Salonika followed by the loss of his right hand, then the equally precocious debut as an umpire and the rise to a position of such eminence that Bradman himself was able to find no fault. But the Jenkins piece becomes something more than a conventional tribute with the anecdotal references by Chester, in particular a glimpse of the imperturbable Sutcliffe preparing for an historic innings and a reference to the bowling conditions at Lord's in the famous Test of 1934 which will bring a warm glow to all idolators of Hedley Verity. Chester (1895–1957) stood in 48 Tests between 1924 and his retirement in 1955.

UMPIRES, like weekends off and the water supply, are apt to be taken for granted. Until something goes wrong, that is. Then they assume a vast importance. Indeed, one might go further: it is only when they make a mistake that their talents get the measure of attention they deserve. Homeric nods, as it were, or recognition by way of omission. Then the full blast of publicity sweeps down on their uncovered heads, and doubtless, through sleepless nights, they wish themselves anywhere but where they are. Messrs. Scott and Barlow, who stood—nearly everything—in Australia in 1946–47, could enlarge on this theme.

Never, for instance, can there have been such a hullabaloo about a mere 'mark on the bat' as attended the dismissal of Edrich, l.b.w., in the third Test, at Melbourne; never such world-wide clamour over so infinitesimal a noise. Bradman, Hutton, Bedser, Miller and the rest were swept from the stage. Every headline, every purple outpouring of the more indignant scribes was let loose on the unfortunate official concerned. He became 'front page news'. Indirectly, no greater tribute to umpires and their functions could have been paid.

Infallibility, it seems, and nothing else, is good enough. Even Len Hutton or Alec Bedser is permitted an occasional lapse from grace. But umpires, never. It prompts the paradoxical thought that the Perfect Umpire, assuming that such a one ever existed, has probably never been heard of by the world at large. He made the mistake, in Irish parlance, of never making a mistake.

Of all the umpires of modern times no one has figured more largely, both in print and popular esteem, than Frank Chester. It is safe to assume, then, that he has made his mistakes. But, if so, they have been remarkably few, and have served to accentuate, not minimise, his virtues. If anything, he is the exception that proves the rule. His good points claim more attention than his bad ones.

What umpire, for instance, could hope for a bigger tribute than the following? Sir Donald Bradman, if anyone, should know about umpires— he spent more time than you or I or almost anyone else in their immediate vicinity. In his book *Farewell to Cricket* he has this to say of Chester: 'Without hesitation I rank Frank Chester as the greatest umpire under whom I played. In my four seasons' cricket in England he stood for a large percentage of the matches and seldom made a mistake. On the other hand, he gave some really wonderful decisions. Not only was his judgment sound, but Chester exercised a measure of control over the game which I think was desirable.' From an Australian, and the most famed one, on a topic he could well be forgiven for regarding with a somewhat jaundiced eye, this is praise *par excellence*. It emphasises Bradman's severely analytical approach to the game, with sentiment and prejudice ruthlessly pruned.

Elsewhere in the same book Bradman makes reference to what he described as 'the cleverest decision ever made against me'. At Nottingham in the first Test of 1938, the records show him as having been dismissed in his side's first innings, for 51, c Ames b Sinfield. Says Bradman: 'The ball turned from the off, very faintly touched the inside edge of the bat, then hit my pad, went over the stumps and was caught by Ames whilst all this was happening amidst a jumble of feet, pads and bat. I slightly overbalanced, and Ames whipped off the bails for a possible stumping. There was an instant appeal to the square-leg umpire who gave me not out, whereupon Ames appealed to Chester at the bowler's end, and very calmly, as though it was obvious to all, Chester simply said "Out, caught," and turned his back on the scene. It was one of those remarkable pieces of judgment upon which I base my opinion that Chester was the greatest of all umpires.' No one claiming admission to an umpiring Valhalla could hope to produce a better reference.

Recently there have been one or two dissentients among international cricketers of slightly less imposing stature, but Bradman's opinion is the one likely to last. If there is one small chink in Chester's armour—and recent duodenal trouble has not improved it—it is his disinclination to suffer fools, and more particularly knaves, gladly. He has been known to embellish an answer to an appeal with some forthright comment of his own. 'Not out, and that was a very bad appeal' fell from his lips on one occasion to a very famous bowler on an international occasion at Lord's.

Some may cavil at this, feeling that the umpire's function is discharged by the unadorned yea or nay, and no more. If that is so, the corollary applies, surely, that the players also must behave themselves. Bowlers who throw the ball down in disgust, fielders who appeal for l.b.w. from all points of the compass, batsmen who mutter as they retire to the pavilion cannot go unchecked for ever. It is asking too much of human nature. They, too, transgress the unwritten laws, and any faults they profess to find in the umpire merely mirror their own action. To the young player, by contrast, making his first appearance in the big match Chester could be kindliness itself. I speak here, as many others could, from personal experience.

'Hearing, eyesight and knowledge of the Laws of the game' are laid down by Chester as the three main requisites in an umpire's make-up. Impartiality, of course, he takes for granted. 'You never umpire *for* this team or that,' he says, 'you just umpire.'

Some village green officials of our acquaintance may object to the imputations, but cannot quarrel with the maxim. 'Give the batsman the benefit of the doubt' is another catch-phrase with which Chester holds no truck. 'There never should be any doubt,' he says. Wherein he voices a doctrine of perfection beyond most people's scope. 'It's all right for him'—you can hear the objectors massing to their own defence. But to Chester himself the remark comes naturally, and does not offend the hearer familiar at first hand with his talents.

What manner of man is this—the most famous umpire of our time—with 56 Tests behind him, a record unapproached and, unless infants in arms take on the job, unapproachable? Tallish, but sparely built, with a slight stoop when at the wicket—occupational perhaps, in quest for eternal no-balls—he might easily be taken for a Cockney, but for his accent and the certain fact that he was born in Hertfordshire. He has, above all, the Londoner's intense awareness of all that is going on around him, and the quick and witty response. His eyes are his most striking feature, quick, alive, ever ready to pounce on the unusual. In another sphere he might have made his mark in the C.I.D.

Umpires, traditionally, are inanimate and, for all one knows, asleep. No one could ever accuse Chester of this. Intensity is the keynote of all he does. It communicates itself even to those outside the boundary—how much more so, then, to the players. As Bradman says, he not only officiates, he takes control, a rare quality among those who too often are content to stand and wait. In the records his date of birth is given as January 20, 1896, and the place—Bushey, Hertfordshire, where he lives to this day.

From early youth he was nurtured in the game. Gilbert Jessop, R. E. Foster and Frank Mason were among those he watched as an eager schoolboy on the local ground. Ambition fired, he made his own debut for Bushey at the age of twelve. At thirteen he topped the club batting averages. At fourteen, on the recommendation of Alec Hearne, of Kent and England, he sallied forth to qualify for Worcestershire. In 1912, when only sixteen and a half—he won his county cap—surely the youngest ever to do so. In that year the Australians and South Africans were here for the Triangular Tournament, and he played against both countries.

In 1913 he scored three centuries. One of them, 128 not out v. Hampshire at Southampton, was coupled with six wickets for 43 runs on the same day. His batting followed the mood of the times. Stroke-play, and if the runs came so much the better. If not, stroke-play just the same. At Coalville, against Leicestershire in 1914, he hit 93 in one hour ten minutes. His highest score was 178 not out against Essex, including four 6s off J. W. H. T. Douglas.

As a bowler he served up a mixture of off and leg breaks, and confesses to a moment of youthful pride when he bowled out Tom Hayward at The Oval for only 59—relative failure for the great man and a feather in the cap of 'the Nipper', as Chester was inevitably nicknamed.

In December, 1914, he joined the Royal Field Artillery, at Lewes. Even in this cricket was behind his choice. Major Allsopp, captain of the Worcestershire Second Eleven, was the battery commander. After surviving the Second Battle of Loos, he moved with his unit to Salonika, and it was there he met with the wound that ended his active playing career. Enemy bombers attacked an ammunition dump he was helping to guard; a splinter of shrapnel led to gangrene and, following many operations, the loss of his right arm. Had penicillin been discovered, we might now be lauding, not an umpire, but a great England batsman.

As it was, he took up the threads again in 1922 by joining the first-class umpires' list. Only 26, he could not have found it an easy decision, and at the end of his first season he nearly abandoned it again. At Northampton he had the disconcerting experience of being refused admission to the ground. One of the gatemen, told that he was one of the umpires, treated it as a joke. 'You've made a mistake,' he said. 'This is a first-class match.' Nor did he relent until the secretary was brought to explain.

At his first county match, Essex v. Somerset at Leyton, young Chester was called on to give decisions against both captains, Johnny Douglas and John Daniell, and did his duty according to his lights. Douglas l.b.w., Daniell stumped. 'You'll be signing your death warrant if you go on like that,' he was warned by his venerable colleague. But Chester has gone on giving captains out ever since, reports to Lord's notwithstanding, and it has increased, not diminished, his stature.

He has seen all the great players of the past thirty years at closer quarters than any man living. Hobbs and Hutton, Larwood and Lindwall, Woolley, Worrell, Tate, Bedser, Constantine, Hammond, Duleepsinhji, Macartney, Mankad and the rest—not through the straining binocular or second-hand on T.V., but right at their elbows. No small recompense for the blow of World War I.

His memory, too, is microscopic. Spend an evening in his company and the tales he tells enthrall. Hobbs's century against Australia at The Oval in 1926—'the greatest innings I ever saw and on the worst wicket'; Herbert Sutcliffe, brushing his hair and smoking his pipe before going in to bat on the same day, then making 161 after declaring beforehand, 'I don't think we shall get 70.' 'What a temperament,' says Chester.

Hedley Verity's fourteen wickets in the day at Lord's in 1934—'not a really bad wicket; just a patch as big as a tray where the rain had seeped under the covers, but he kept hitting it all the time'; O'Reilly's bowling at Leeds, five for 66 and five for 56, in 1938—'far from a bowler's paradise, about 50–50 with the batsmen, but what a fighter'; batsmen, bowlers, wicket-keepers, cover-points, outfielders, slips—Chester has a story about them all. A cricketing cavalcade of our time, all in the head of one man.

There have been other umpires, and if we talk so much of one it is because he represents them in the generic sense as surely as Henry Cotton does his fellow golf professionals or Joe Davis the world of snooker. He is the 'Mr. Umpiring' of the brasher columnists, and in more sedate circles the authority supreme. 'Chester says so' has settled as many pavilion bets as the photo-finish on the racecourse.

As long ago as 1888 Robert Thoms, the leading umpire of the day, in reply to a questionnaire from the Editor of *Wisden* about changes in the l.b.w. law, made some trenchant remarks about the new practice of 'padding up' which had crept into the game. 'This very unsightly play cannot be termed batting,' he wrote, ''tis simply scientific legging.' But he hastened to add, 'It makes no difference to me as an "Umpty Dumpty", although I am a great sticker up for everything fair and honourable, how they at length settle the question.'

Therein, surely, lies the germ of an umpire's epitaph through the ages. Umpty Dumpties, Aunt Sallies, call them what you will, there has never been any doubt, in balanced minds, of their being 'fair and honourable', and ready to interpret the laws as they find them. Mortal, perhaps, in that they are subject to error, but the gods, no doubt, would find umpiring a bore, and the players themselves resent their intrusion. It might spoil the fun. Men like Dai Davies, Alec Skelding, Bill Reeves, Dick Burrows, Len Braund and a host of other ex-players turned umpire stretching back to 'Bob' Thoms himself, and beyond, have enriched the game with their personalities as surely as the great batsmen and bowlers.

Father Time, on his pedestal at Lord's, has the last word. He lifts off the bails for the umpires themselves. But cricket goes on, and as long as there are men like Chester to see fair play it will be in safe hands.

THE STORY OF YORKSHIRE [1955]

BY J. M. KILBURN

J. M. Kilburn, in his potted history of his native county shows characteristic candour. For most of his professional life, Kilburn served as the cricket correspondent of 'The Yorkshire Post' and also published several books about cricket in which he treads a tactful middle line between idolatry of the major-generals and derision of their achievements. For example, in approaching the figure of that tiny giant Martin, Lord Hawke, he seems almost to be trying not to laugh as he qualifies every word of praise with the implication of critical disapproval. He was not a handicap in the field, but only in his younger days. He was 'useful' as a batsman but only in the lower half of the order. He was a martinet, he was obstinate and he 'could never be classed as an outstanding player'. To all of this one responds by wondering what he was doing there at all.

Kilburn spares his lordship further exposure by not mentioning three incidents in his career which tell us as much as we need to know about him; the expulsion from cricket of Bobby Peel, the confusions of a tour to the West Indies and the arrangements insisted upon in Yorkshire for matri- monial partnerships. Peel's expulsion was a vicious punishment for a bout of drunkenness, but it was the affair of the West Indies tour of 1894–95 which shows Hawke at his most resplendently fatuous. In fact there were two English touring sides in the West Indies at the same time, a farcical situation best explained not by any committed Yorkshireman but by a choleric realist like Major Bowen:

> Both tours took place through the stubborn and ill-measured mulishness amounting almost to insufferable arrogance on the part of Lord Hawke.

The third of his lordship's immortal innovations moves beyond the realm of sporting altogether and up into the rarified air of cloudcuckooland. It was understood in his day that no Yorkshire professional be permitted to take a wife until Hawke had cast his approving eye over her. Fool or blackguard, noodle or lout? Sadly, Kilburn does not pursue this promising theme. But I must say that writing, as the native born Yorkshireman I am, on the subject of Lord Hawke, who was not, I am constantly amazed that even the most rabid county supporter should take the trouble to defend so monumental a blockhead.

In closing his account, Kilburn understandably asks for a return to the greatness of the old Yorkshire elevens. But again, he excises from his account the disgraceful conduct of the Yorkshire committee of the time in snubbing its greatest player. Why does he make no reference to the fact that there resided within the club a cricketer great enough and a leader astute enough to win the Ashes in England and then retain them in Australia, but

*who was evidently not good enough for the burghers of Yorkshire? In
retrospect it is not hard to see why the club sank lower and still lower in its
administrative ineptitude until at last, by the 1980s, the affairs of Yorkshire
had become the laughing stock of the entire sporting world. This decline,
from paramountcy to pigheadedness, must surely qualify as one of the
saddest spectacles in all the history of English sport.*

THE history of cricket, its records and its honours are bound up with the
deeds of Yorkshire and Yorkshire players. Founded in 1863, Yorkshire
were one of the original nine counties considered first-class when the
Championship was formed in 1873. They took twenty years to win the title
for the first time, since when they have been almost regular contenders.
Twenty-two summers have ended with the White Rose at the top. No other
county can match this tale of success. Here is a tribute to men who have put
Yorkshire in the forefront of the cricket world.

Yorkshire County cricket is not to be identified with any one Yorkshire
centre. The administrative offices are in Leeds and only Headingley of the
Yorkshire grounds is now granted a Test match, but there would be prompt
and fierce protest from every Riding were any individual claims put
forward for distinction as the home of Yorkshire cricket. The county club
owns no ground, though it has financial interest in several. Home fixtures
are spread as widely as circumstances and accommodation allow; playing
resources are discovered and developed everywhere.

SHEFFIELD INFLUENCE

This distribution of favour has its origins in the early history of the county's
cricket when a narrow conception of resources and interests found little
favour. The Kent secretary of 1864 remarked that it was difficult to know
who were the proper parties to get up Yorkshire county matches, and some
years passed after the formal foundation of the county club before its
authority was accepted with much grace, or indeed accepted at all, outside
the Sheffield area. Perhaps the difference of outlook was more an
illustration of characteristic wariness than of protest against local leadership, because the original Sheffield resolution of formation did envisage an
unlimited membership with subscriptions 'to provide funds for the playing
of first-class matches in Sheffield and other centres'. Moreover, when the
first side was chosen it contained cricketers from Huddersfield, Bradford,
Ripon and the North Riding as well as from Sheffield.

Storms soon blew into the life of the young Yorkshire club and in 1865
there was a secession by five of the leading players, less through any quarrel
with their own management than because of personal ill-feeling between
players of the North and the South. Yorkshire, governed wholly from
Sheffield, resolved to play and lose rather than abandon their venture, and
determination preserved existence. Prodigals returned, new talent came
forward and Yorkshire established themselves as a force in the cricketing

land. In 1867 seven engagements were undertaken and in these matches fifty-one wickets went to George Freeman and thirty to Tom Emmett. The highest total of any opposing innings was Lancashire's 159. George Freeman was accounted the finest fast bowler of the day by his contemporaries, who included W. G. Grace and Richard Daft, and though his career was short he left an imperishable name.

Tom Emmett lasted longer, playing from 1866 to 1888, carrying Yorkshire through the period of establishment of the County Championship and holding a principal part in a company that included Alan Hill as Freeman's successor in fast bowling; George Pinder, the wicket-keeper who was beyond compare in his time; Ephraim Lockwood, sturdiest of batsmen whose bucolic appearance belied his talent; George Ulyett, a bowler who fell in love with batting and was indulged in his fancy; and Peate and Peel, leaders of that long line of left-arm slow bowlers giving cause for so much Yorkshire gratitude.

THE DISCIPLINED YORKSHIRE

The potentialities in such a collection of players was beyond doubting. The results were wholly unworthy. The side remained a collection of individuals without common purpose or spur. In 1893 endurance reached its limit, and a complete reorganisation of the Committee was accepted. The change was wise and profitable, though its justice at the particular moment might be questioned. The new Yorkshire, the disciplined Yorkshire, began to satisfy themselves.

There can be no doubt that much of the spirit inculcated into the Yorkshire side during the 1890s came directly from the leadership of Lord Hawke. It was his declared ambition to win for Yorkshire cricket not only admiration but respect, and he took some drastic steps to ensure that his teams became acceptable everywhere for their conduct both on the field and off. Lord Hawke could never be classed as an outstanding player. Experience gave him usefulness as a batsmen in the lower half of the order and in his younger days he was certainly not a handicap to his team in the field, but other qualities than playing ability were needed to raise him to the eminence he attained on the fields and in the councils of cricket.

Those qualities were an abiding affection for his cause, which was Yorkshire cricket, and a happy understanding of the men who played under his captaincy. As a captain Lord Hawke was a martinet; in course of time firmness could have been seen as obstinacy, depending upon the viewpoint, and his major interest tended to become paramount. Yet there can be no denying that in developing Yorkshire cricket Lord Hawke did rare service to cricket in its widest sphere. He set standards that have survived him and he took cricket to Australia, India, Canada, United States, South Africa, West Indies and the Argentine. He was captain of Yorkshire from 1883 to 1910 and President of the club from 1898 until his death in 1938.

By his influence alone Lord Hawke could have changed the character of the Yorkshire team, but he could not have achieved the historic results for ever to be associated with his name without help from players of unimpeachable quality. Lord Hawke's time was the time of George Hirst and Wilfred Rhodes; of Tunnicliffe and Brown and David Denton; of Wainwright and Peel; of F. S. Jackson and T. L. Taylor and Ernest Smith; of Haigh and Hunter. He who gave such memorable service was himself well served.

TRIPLE CHAMPIONS

The peak of Yorkshire playing success under the captaincy of Lord Hawke came in the seasons of 1900–01–02 when the Championship was won so comprehensively that the wonder of the time was not a Yorkshire victory but a Yorkshire failure to complete victory. In those three years only two championship matches were lost, both of them to Somerset, and some of the victories provided staggering figures. Nottinghamshire were dismissed for 13; against Worcestershire, Yorkshire were all out for 99 and still had margin to win by an innings. There seemed no end to the triumphs, and a new conception of cricketing power was created. Yorkshire have had benefit ever since. They have believed in themselves, and they have undoubtedly impressed that belief upon their opponents.

However great a part the determination to win and the strong team-spirit may have played in Yorkshire's establishment as one of the most successful of all cricketing counties, the essential basis of rare technical quality must not be overlooked. Yorkshire have enjoyed the service of a succession of players to be ranked among the very highest, players as familiar by repute in Sydney as in Sheffield. There was never a more dominating cricketer than F. S. Jackson; never a cricketer more respected for his wisdom and skill than Wilfred Rhodes; never a cricketer to capture the heart and the imagination and the affections more firmly than George Herbert Hirst.

Jackson was a player by the light of nature, gifted in the rhythm of movement, scarcely needing practice to attain perfection of form. He bowled with economy of effort and batted with graceful efficiency. He knew his own abilities and was surprised at personal failure because he counted it unreasonable. The more demanding the occasion the more likely his success, and his Test match record against Australia is incomparable.

GENIUS OF RHODES

Wilfred Rhodes has no parallel in cricket, in either the county or the international story. In his first season he established himself as one of the world's leading bowlers; twelve years later he was opening the innings for England; at the age of 48 he was playing again for England, an invaluable all-rounder. He was cricketing genius; as a bowler with the genius that comes as a gift from the gods, and as a batsman with the genius that is the infinite capacity for taking pains. He was born wise in cricketing ways. In more than thirty years on the first-class fields his principles of the game were never outmoded. Whilst Wilfred Rhodes was playing nobody ever ventured the opinion that Rhodes's type of bowling would not take wickets in current conditions. Results spoke only too clearly for themselves throughout a career that linked the batsmanship of Grace with that of Bradman.

HIRST THE WARRIOR

George Hirst became the epitome of Yorkshire cricket, the happy warrior that every Yorkshire cricketing knight-at-arms would wish to be. It was part of Hirst's nature that the greater the need of the occasion the greater the response to be called from him. Often enough his innings was brief or his bowling comparatively unsuccessful when no particular demand was laid upon him, but in time of crisis he was the most trustworthy of all his contemporaries as either batsman or bowler. He seldom failed when a failure would have been fatal to his side, and this fighting spirit, presented always with the broad, bold facets of a noble character, brought him the affection and admiration of the whole county, and, indeed, of all the cricketing world. Yorkshire cricket will always accept George Hirst as its representative, anywhere in any age. His public esteem was reflected in his benefit match which brought him, in 1904, the then enormous return of £3,700. His playing stature rests on the performances of perhaps the most amazing individual feat in cricket history; in 1906 he scored over 2,000 runs and took over 200 wickets in the first-class season. His batting average was 45.86 and his bowling average 16.50.

Hirst and Rhodes remained Yorkshire's leading players for many years after the disintegration of the great side of the early 1900s and they helped the county to Championship victories in 1905, 1908 and 1912. Hirst was still playing—and whenever he played he was a significant force—in the improvisation of 1919, but Rhodes went on alone into the second period of dominance which began in 1922 and persisted for four seasons. In that era Yorkshire played 122 Championship matches, won 81 of them and lost only six. In general the performances were as remarkable as the figures, for Yorkshire were ruthless conquerors crushing their enemies so thoroughly that they came to regard the five-day week as an expectation rather than a privilege. In 1923 they won 25 of their 32 Championship matches, and 13 of the 25 were won with an innings to spare.

Such achievements suggest, and rightly suggest, powerful batting resources, but it was the bowling strength in all conditions that made the side so formidable. Rhodes after his period of concentration upon batsmanship returned to full honour as a bowler; Waddington blazed across the cricketing sky; Macaulay and Emmott Robinson were surprised and disappointed if they did not take 100 wickets in a season; and Roy Kilner rapidly established himself, not as a rival to Rhodes, but complementary to him in the slow left-arm attack. As often as not Kilner bowled over the wicket, where Rhodes invariably bowled round in the classical tradition.

Success did not bring Yorkshire universal popularity. They were acknowledged cricketing masters of the counties, but they were not always on the happiest of terms with some of their rivals. The very fixity of their purpose, the grim determination of their methods cost them some affection, and there were one or two occasions when the pressure in the boiler of neighbourly goodwill ran dangerously high. Naturally enough, the bowling fires were the first to fade. When Lancashire took over the Championship in the late 1920s Yorkshire preserved their formidable batting, but awaited the arrival of new bowling of the necessary vitality. When they found it, the batting of Sutcliffe, Holmes, Oldroyd, Leyland, and their company guaranteed all the scope needed for the winning of more Championships.

HOLMES AND SUTCLIFFE

Holmes and Sutcliffe developed the most successful of all opening partnerships in county cricket. They came together experimentally and began inauspiciously, for the first time they opened the innings together the scoreboard quickly showed 0 for one, but their individual technical skill allied to the indefinable sympathy that grew between them soon made their association safe and their achievements historic. They put up a century partnership 69 times for Yorkshire and 74 times in all, and in 1932 they took the world's record opening partnership from their distinguished predecessors. Tunnicliffe and Brown made 554 against Derbyshire in 1898; Holmes and Sutcliffe made 555 against Essex. Curiously enough both these enormous stands were contrived with one of the batsmen under physical handicap. At Chesterfield, Tunnicliffe chose to sit up all night rather than risk unsatisfactory hotel accommodation, and he batted throughout the next day with a sandwich as his only sustenance because of catering confusion at the ground. At Leyton, Holmes was suffering from lumbago and in obvious pain throughout the long innings.

Holmes played for Yorkshire from 1913 to 1933 and therefore saw the beginning but not the end of the wonders of the 1930s. Sutcliffe's career extended from war to war, and he was a member of the teams that won the Championship seven times in the nine seasons from 1931 to 1939. He was always an outstanding member because he scarcely ever knew a year of personal failure and because his was a personality that could never be overlooked.

Sutcliffe's batsmanship has been accounted of limited range, but no question of its efficiency has been raised. No question could be raised while memories last and scoreboards remain to be read. Sutcliffe's limitations were mainly self-imposed. He restricted himself because restriction best served his purpose. He batted in the light of circumstances. His problems were the problems of the moment, each to be treated as it arose and instantly dismissed upon solution. The sum of his achievements represents the adequacy of his exposition. For Yorkshire, and for England, he rendered imperishable service.

By 1930 Yorkshire had found the bowling they sought as the basis for a great team, and to Bowes and Verity, Wilfred Rhodes and Emmott Robinson hastened to pass on the legacy of accumulated wisdom and intensity of purpose. The training was invaluable, the material for instruction more than adequate. Bowes, Verity and Macaulay, with Smailes and Ellis Robinson in subsequent support, and Sutcliffe, Leyland, Mitchell, Barber and eventually Hutton, brought Yorkshire to glories as great as they had ever known. They became a living legend in all the cricketing lands. They toured Jamaica as a county side, and had Australian wish been granted they would have toured Australia, too.

THE SELLERS ERA

It was not, of course, in the mere possession of individuals beyond the ordinary that Yorkshire found their strength. Great players do not necessarily establish great teams. Yorkshire had great players in the 1930s and they established a great team primarily because they were prepared to devote their special talents to a common cause. The character of the side became something more than the agglomerated characters of the members. Yorkshire cricket given to be the over-riding concern of every player and the personal achievement was the common satisfaction. The origin of this outlook lay far back in history but its development, or its renaissance, at least, was the contribution of A. B. Sellers who took over the captaincy in 1933 and held office for fifteen seasons. Perhaps Lord Hawke did more than Sellers in that there was more to do, but neither Lord Hawke nor any other Yorkshire leader brought greater devotion or persistent efficiency to the task in hand.

Sellers drew loyalty because he gave loyalty. He maintained unswervingly the principle that team interests were paramount, and his principles were so clearly illustrated that they could not escape the notice of established player or newcomer. The Yorkshire of Brian Sellers' time would have been unmistakable in multi-coloured caps and disguised by beards. They carried their character on to every field they visited.

AGGRESSIVE FIELDING

Much was asked. Bowling had to be justifiable in cricket strategy; mere bowling and hoping for the best was not acceptable. Fielding had to be a positive ally to bowling. It was not enough to wait in likely places for catches to come; catches had to be created where none would have existed without courage, and confidence in the ability of colleagues. Yorkshire did not invent the 'aggressive field' in the 1930s but they advanced its position in cricket. Their performances and their principles stood as the standard for the time and it is doubtful if the standard has ever been higher. In the nine seasons between 1931 and 1939 Yorkshire were County Champions seven times and there is no knowing how long their dominance would have continued but for the interruption of the Second World War. When cricket came again the greatness had gone. Sutcliffe and Wood passed into retirement; Bowes was no longer a fast bowler after four years in prison camps; Verity died of wounds in Italy. In 1946 the remainder of the old guard reassembled to win yet another Championship but their success contained the sunset gleam. Leyland and Turner brought their first-class careers to an end, Bowes and Smailes followed in the next season or two and Sellers himself handed on the torch of leadership in 1948, though he gave help when his appointed successor, Norman Yardley, was involved in Test match captaincy and selectorial duties.

Recent years have been spent in reconstruction; and in the inevitable experiment Yorkshire have missed both success and satisfaction. The Championship was shared with Middlesex in 1949 and second position has been attained three times in the past four seasons, but 1953 saw a humiliating descent into the bottom half of the table and the optimism of spring has rarely been matched in the reflections of autumn. Perhaps the essential lack has been a direct link between the old Yorkshire and the new. Players joining the side since 1946 could not acquire tradition by first-hand observation. They knew only their own way of playing cricket, the current way, and time was required for adjustment in a world inclined to be casual in reaction against the taut living of war.

PROBLEMS FOR YARDLEY

Yorkshire made mistakes in selectorial judgment as well as in playing technique and they had therefore to extend the period of experiment beyond the term expected. Yardley found himself with as difficult a task as any current county captain, for he had played long enough to appreciate needs and desires but could find no illustration of intentions for the newcomers.

Young Yorkshiremen did not know quite what was expected of them and were short of a yardstick for comparison. Social circumstances were a handicap to every county and a particular trial to Yorkshire who have long expected their young players to fit into a given pattern, of proven worth. Yardley's success in captaincy has been limited by the lack of understanding and ambition in some of his players, but he has done invaluable work in keeping the good name of Yorkshire cricket at the highest level.

Another era of playing distinction comparable with those of the past still remains speculative. There are players of immense potentiality now wearing the Yorkshire cap and it is to be presumed that Appleyard, Close and Trueman among others have not yet reached the peak of their careers; but character has yet to be confirmed in the side as a whole, and there are obvious shortcomings to be eradicated before a good team can turn itself into a great one. The Yorkshire enthusiasm stands as high as ever; the Yorkshire ambition is in no way diminished. Cricket is an integral part of the Yorkshire scene and the club has never been in more flourishing financial condition. Len Hutton's genius in batsmanship remains a beacon to guide the struggling and a vicarious pride to every compatriot. Yorkshiremen need only be true to their inheritance to find the cricketing satisfactions they desire.

GROWING PAINS OF CRICKET [1956]
Seeking a Remedy

BY W. E. BOWES (YORKSHIRE AND ENGLAND)

As the 1950s proceeded, there became apparent a growing unease in the councils of the game. In spite of the success of the England side, public support for the bread-and-butter fixtures in the County Championship seemed to be falling away. There was a vague nightmarish feeling that no matter what the administrators might do, the tempo of English first-class cricket was slowing down to a point where its rhythms might disintegrate completely. Was the malaise to be located in the law governing l.b.w.? Or was it something to do with the preparation of pitches? Was it the size of the ball? The size of the stumps? The number of stumps? Was it the fault of batsmen for not being more aggressive? Or of the bowlers for being too defensive? Any one of these reasons, and perhaps all of them might be offered in explanation, but nobody seemed sure what to do or even if there was anything to be done. Essays and symposia like the exhaustive 1956 feature were to become familiar in the cricket journals of the epoch but the source of the sickness was never found and indeed remains undetected to this day.

In retrospect, it looks as though something far more obscure, more difficult to identify and virtually impossible to remedy was gnawing away at the vitals of the game, something no less deadly just because it happened to be nebulous.

English cricket was changing because English life was changing. A writer like Neville Cardus was right after all. A society really did get the cricket, and everything else, it deserved and in a climate of post-imperial decline and of a radical contraction of the British role in world affairs, it was inevitable that cricket, along with everything else, should show signs of exhaustion and ennui. It could not be otherwise. The way we play our cricket is an expression of personality, personality is shaped to a great extent by environment, and the environment of British life then and since has been undergoing adjustments as melodramatic as any in world history. To have suggested anything so fanciful as the zeitgeist as the culprit at the time would have been to court the most ribald derision. A generation later, what might once have seemed insufferably pretentious begins to take on the lineaments of truth. It is no wonder that when asked for their views, the great players of the world, past and present, should so emphatically have contradicted each other.

The author of the essay, William Eric Bowes (1908–87) was probably the least likely looking fastish bowler since the tiny John Wisden. Where Wisden seemed too short for his trade, Bowes seemed too skinny. Lacking the pace to be a pure fast bowler, Bowes thought and studied and practised his way to become the most difficult fast-medium bowler in the Championship. Yet Bowes, with his genial, schoolboy-clumsy aspect was not so innocuous as all that. In a county game for Yorkshire against Surrey at The Oval in the late summer of 1932, Bowes had bowled a sort of Bodyline attack at Jack Hobbs, who reacted to the unprecedented tactic by walking down the pitch to remonstrate with the gentle Bowes. 'If this goes on,' Hobbs later remarked, 'someone will get killed.' In June 1933 the Lancashire opener Watson was struck on the head and knocked unconscious by a Bowes delivery amid what Fingleton described as 'uproar'. All this ancient history is relevant only in relation to the evasions of Bowes's moral response to the crisis of the Bodyline tour.

And yet, for a man who could cause even the finest batsmen extreme discomfort with the rearing delivery, Bowes was a frail creature indeed. It is worth quoting one remarkable passage from the exhaustive Wisden obituary which eventually came his way:

There has never been a great cricketer who looked less like one than Bowes. Standing 6ft 4 inches, he was clumsily built and a poor mover. Wearing strong spectacles, he looked far more like a university professor, and indeed batted and fielded like one. However, no side has been so closely welded as Yorkshire in the 1920s and 1930s; every man knew just what he was expected to do, and did it without being told. When Bowes suggested that it might be a good thing if he were taught the rudiments of batting, he was told firmly that his job was to take wickets; he was not to waste his valuable strength on making runs. If he ever showed signs of forgetting this, his partners were expected to run him out. Similarly in the field. He was stationed at mid-on and, if the ball came to him, he was to catch it or stop it as the case might be. But if it passed him, he was not to move; it was someone else's duty to chase it and throw it in. This was fully understood on the Yorkshire side. After all, Bowes was their great opener, and they had no alternative to him.

In 1942, serving as an army officer in the Middle East, Bowes was taken prisoner at Tobruk. Despite the ageing process and the loss of weight, he resumed his first-class career in 1946 and won his last England cap, against India at Lord's. After one more season in which he collected a then record benefit, he retired and spent the rest of his life writing about the game, retaining to the very end, through the homely aspect of his haircut and his giglamps, the intimations of a bygone age.

WHAT is wrong with the modern game of cricket? Anything?

   (a) Are you satisfied with the present l.b.w. rule?
   (b) Is the present trend of leg-theory bowling excessive and, if so, is it for the good of the game?
   (c) Do you agree that there is a general lack of high-class batsmen and that the cover-drive, one of the loveliest strokes in cricket, is disappearing?

Lord Hawke, the autocrat of the county table, personification of Yorkshire cricket. An amateur in more ways than one, ship's prestige can hardly be conceived in these egalitarian times. Not even Bradman or Compton would arrange for a valk a decorous three paces behind him

Left Charles Jessie Kortright, the Essex legend who w
fastest bowler never to play for England. Crowned by
crisp, debonair elegance of the straw boater, he gaze
face at the camera – the paragon of the age, adored
schoolboys, feared by all batsmen. Before he retired
the clean-shaven Victorian upper lip had vanished un
fungoid pretensions of the Edwardians

Top right Charles Parker, the slow left-arm sorcerer w
played for Gloucestershire from 1903 to 1935, who too
3000 wickets at less than 20 apiece, who did the hat-t
twice in the same match, who once hit the stumps with
consecutive deliveries (one no ball) and yet who playe
once for England. Why? Parker was what was
euphemistically known as 'outspoken', and is said to h
consoled himself for victimisation at the hands of fooli
selectors by once meeting Pelham Warner in a lift and
punching him on his patrician nose

Below right A.P. 'Tich' Freeman, the tiny Kentish spin
toyed with batsmen to such devastating effect that in
he became the first and last England bowler to take 3(
wickets in a season. Success did not always smile, ho
and in 1933 he had to be content with 298. On retirem
1936, after taking 3776 wickets, he pointedly called h'
house 'Dunbowlin'

Below In the spring of 1925 Arthur Edward Robert Gi
having led England in an unsuccessful attempt to brir
home the Ashes, arrives home defeated but not disho
In the previous summer, after taking 6 for 7 in a Test a
South Africa, he had been hit over the heart while batt
was never the same man again. He is seen here arrivi
home at Victoria to be ambushed by a doting parent
disguised in one of Florrie Ford's hats. Ivor Novello wa
possibly inspired by this scene when he composed 'A
Mother Came Too'

Left Frank Edward Woolley, the Kentish *beau idéal*, th[e] graceful yet powerful of left-handers, who scored the [v] total of nearly 59,000 runs, took over 2000 wickets and holds the catching record with 1015. In his eighties he [] remarried and emigrated to Canada where he died an[d] folk who must have wondered why he had the quietly confident demeanour of a great man

Top right William Bowes, quiffed and giglamped, pee[rs] sheepishly at the camera followed by an admiring Dar[by and] Joan who know that no matter how frail he may look B[owes] the Yorkshire fast bowler with the schoolmasterish demeanour

Below right It is the sun-drenched summer of 1947, Middlesex *v.* Sussex at Lord's, late in May. The old gentlemen on the pavilion seats awake from their drea[m of] Stoddart and Albert Trott and prepare for fireworks. In [the] event, no more than a fair to middling day – Edrich 10[0] Compton 110. A promising prelude of the most prolific glut in the history of English cricket

Below centre Before the Second World War Learie Constantine graduated to the status of senior West Ind[ies] cricketer, combining his career as a lawyer and his ca[re of] the welfare of fellow islanders, with several appearanc[es at] Lord's, electrifying the crowds who thronged to see hi[m. He] is caught here returning to the pavilion one afternoon i[n] ...

Below Douglas Jardine, captain of England, on board [the] *SS Orontes*, embarked in the ill-starred Australian tour [of] 1932/33. Before he sailed home again, he had succee[ded in] flinging the Empire into turmoil. Yet he looks innocuous enough, less like a malcontent than the ship's barber, enjoying a quiet smoke

eft Martin Donnelly, one of the greatest of all left-handed batsmen, who became one of the few men to score hundreds
~iversity, for the Gentlemen and for his country in a Test match. He is seen here in 1949, the season in which he
~06 against England in the Lord's Test. He remains the only New Zealand Test cricketer to win a Rugby Union cap for
. His career was cut short far too soon by business commitments

ght In 1950 Frank Worrell toured England with the West Indies under J.D. Goddard and covered himself with glory in
~ Test at Nottingham, where he slaughtered a mediocre England attack to the tune of 261. Later he was to return to
~ as the first black West Indian captain, to establish himself as one of the great diplomats of the game, to be knighted,
~e tragically young

~948 Don Bradman performed a ceremonial march around the cricket grounds of England. After one or two retirements
~o be merely operatic, this was his very last tour of England. The crowds rose to him everywhere, nowhere more
~ally charged than at Lord's. Bradman, here seen smacking Coxon to fine leg, made 38 and 89, being dismissed twice
~3edser

In 1950 the West Indians arrived in England to upset the balance of international power thanks to a remarkable 'mystery' spinner, Sonny Ramadhin. His habit of concealing his fingers and bowling with his wrist shrouded in shirt cuff added to t problems of deciphering his spin. In this glimpse of him at Cambridge University he seems almost as fascinated by the eventual drift of the ball as the batsman standing next to him, Peter May

(d) Are you completely satisfied that the present-day pitch is the ideal surface on which to see cricket at its best?

These questions were posed to me by the Editor of *Wisden*. My replies brought an invitation to conduct a thorough investigation into the problems confronting the game at the present time, and to assist in this regard, a letter was sent to prominent personalities in the game, a majority of whom played first-class cricket before and after the l.b.w. law was altered, asking their views.

As one who has always regarded *Wisden* as the Textbook of Cricket, I was delighted to be made responsible for the main inquiry; but let me point out this one important feature at the outset: my own findings are opinion not fact. The replies received from famous personalities in the game were expressions of opinion, nothing more, and in fairness to them, especially where we differ, I have given their comments as received.

It is a remarkable thing that away down the years, prominent writers and cricketers have expressed the view that unless there was a new approach to cricket, unless rules were changed and the game made more attractive to the public, cricket would die a natural death. Very fortunately our administrators have not easily panicked. Changes to the Laws have been made only when, as a general principle, the mass of those playing the game demanded it.

No game can stand still. It must go either backward or forward, and to the everlasting credit of M.C.C., no matter how much the County game today might depend on football pools and the share-out of Tour profits, cricket has progressed. Always it has been allowed to develop easily, naturally. Progress has been maintained in the natural sequence of bowlers finding a method of getting batsmen out, and batsmen then finding the counter. Curved bats, like hockey sticks, were discarded for the straight bat when bowlers began to bounce the ball, or undulations in the pitch caused the ball to bounce over the curve of the bat.

The art of batsmanship improved considerably as the bowlers, continually looking for something new, introduced spin; with the advent of overarm bowling, speed; and, in later years, swerve, the googly, off-theory, leg-theory; and finally to the point where, using one skill or the other, specialist fieldsmen were employed in cleverly thought-out positions, and bowlers learned to bowl accurately to them.

With each skill in bowling came improvement in the art of batsmanship. In the days of W. G. Grace, P. F. Warner and the Palairets, batsmen used the right leg as a pivot. The left foot was put towards the ball and strokes to the covers were made in abundance. Bowlers replied with off-theory. They found that by bowling at the off-stump, and just outside, that the batsmen were not always 'far enough across' to the ball when driving, and slip catches resulted.

The newer school of batsmen, Jack Hobbs, Wilfred Rhodes (with his famous three lines of defence, left foot, bat, right leg swinging across), Mead, Hammond and others came along. Instead of the right foot being used as a pivot, the first movements were to cover up the stumps with the pads. Do you recall that shuffle across of Philip Mead? My own early recollection of first-class cricket, every time I bowled a ball just outside the off-stump, was seeing Jack Hobbs, Sutcliffe and the rest, 'shouldering arms'. Without playing a shot, they put bat above their heads, pads in front of the stumps, and allowed the bowler to waste his energy.

The leg-break bowler, the out-swinger with speed, became vital necessities in any attack, and when groundsmen prepared a pitch of such excellence that swing and spin was impossible, I was advised by every batsman in the country (particularly when playing with him and not against him) to bowl the bouncer. It was bowled not with the intention of hitting the batsman, but in the hope of moving him away from the stumps, or getting a catch to long leg. I know of no batsman who denied the right of the fast bowler to bowl a bouncer.

Particularly do I contend that, from the beginning of cricket until 1932, the game was allowed to develop on natural lines, the bowlers calling the tune and the batsmen evolving methods that were many times beautiful to watch. Then came the fast leg-theory of Harold Larwood in Australia during the tour of 1932–33 which later became known as 'The Bodyline tour of D. R. Jardine'.

It is not for me in the scope of this inquiry to discuss the merits or demerits of the attack used. I can only point out that the world's greatest batsman, Don Bradman, in his book (*Farewell to Cricket*, page 71) states, 'Bodyline was first used against me in a match on the Melbourne Cricket Ground between the M.C.C. and an Australian XI. I reported privately to certain cricket administrators that, in my opinion, there would be serious trouble unless the matter was dealt with quickly.'

I shall always regret that 'The Don', with his great ability, condemned 'Bodyline' from the first moment. The 'swervers' of George Hirst and the 'googlies' invented by Bosanquet had the world's greatest batsmen floundering for a complete season or more, but the batsmen found the answer eventually.

Perhaps the physical danger of 'Bodyline' made it different. Sufficient it is to say that the weight of opinion caused this natural development of cricket theory and tactics to stop. After careful deliberation M.C.C. decided to legislate against Bodyline, and I believe, realising that the bowlers must be given something in return and that pitches were of such perfection that batsmen had all the favours, they made experiments with the l.b.w. law and provided earlier opportunity for the new ball to be taken.

It must be remembered that shortly before the advent of 'Bodyline' more help had been given to bowlers. In 1927 the circumference of the ball was reduced and in 1931 the wicket was enlarged by making the stumps higher and broader.

D. R. Jardine, the England captain, during the 'Bodyline' tour, suggested a yet smaller ball, but this was not tried until last season when it was used in a few non-competitive first-class matches. It did not win much support and has been discarded.

Now, twenty years after the l.b.w. change, we are asked, 'Were the measures taken satisfactory? Did they work towards the betterment of cricket?'

Without hesitation my reply is: No. The new l.b.w. rule, good in theory, has worked badly in practice. I believe, with all my love of the first-class game, that the village green is the real home of cricket. For club cricketers the game was hard enough before. Rules should be kept simple and anything which complicates the game should be avoided. If it is necessary to give the bowlers an advantage, well, go the whole way. Make it so that the Law applies to deliveries pitched on either side of the wickets, or at least, make it so that any ball pitching on the off gains the umpire's verdict of 'out' if the batsman prevents it hitting his stumps with the pads. Let us not complicate the issue by saying the batsman is out 'If, with any part of his person except the hand, which is in a straight line between wicket and wicket, etc. etc.'

But I am moving too fast. If the game is to be played with enjoyment on the village green it should be worth the watching when the finest exponents in the world have the ball and bat. The weight of opinion seems to be that the l.b.w. law has not improved the game either in skill or spectacle.

It is all very well to say that the laws are all right; it is the interpretation by the players that is wrong: to point to the splendid scoring feats that are shown on the third day of a match, after a fancy declaration, and ask, 'Why cannot we have more of that enterprise on the first day?'

To my mind that very argument proves that the attitude of the present-day cricketer is good. When the occasion demands he can set about the bowling without thought of averages and failure. The real question is this: What manner of batsman is it who does not think himself capable of making a century no matter how much the bowler is being favoured?

I have seen those great left-arm bowlers, Rhodes and Verity, achieve some unbelievable performances on 'sticky' wickets. Verity could never have gained an analysis of ten wickets for 10 runs if every batsman in the opposition had gone down the pitch and had a wallop. But, if that had been the attitude of cricketers whenever bowlers were on top, then I would never have seen any magnificent technical fighting innings like those of Hammond, Woolley, Hobbs, Mead, Hearne . . . performances which would send me the length of England if I could see them again.

The Findlay Report of 1937—which is accepted as impartial—suggested that players should have a different approach to the game. No doubt some could adopt a more dynamic attitude, but this in no way changes the argument.

The more help you give the bowler the more defensive must be the attitude of the batsman. It would be wrong otherwise, for no batsman worth his salt would give the bowler best.

The new l.b.w. rule, designed to encourage the batsmen to hit the ball towards the covers, did not do so. Batsmen accepted the extra limitations, and I believe they found that excessive pad-play, or getting pads outside the off-stump, helped them. The need for this exaggerated pad-play, and the necessity of the batsman to play at the ball pitching just outside the off-stump, again in the natural sequence of development, caused the bowlers to search for fresh ideas.

They found that a leg-stump attack to expert short-leg and leg-slip fieldsmen paid dividends. It was discovered that the medium-pace bowlers, swinging or cutting the ball inwards to the batsmen, were as potent as it was hoped Larwood with his extra pace (apart from physical danger) might have been under the old l.b.w. law.

The new l.b.w. rule unwittingly encouraged the use of the leg-stump attack and sent the wheel its full cycle. It was found the nearer you bowl to a batsman's legs—with a well-placed field—the more you limit his scoring strokes. During last summer the South African bowler, Goddard, showed that this type of attack could be extended to well outside the leg-stump and still be successful.

The new rule brought an undesirable trend into the game and from the replies to the questionnaire sent out by the Editor of *Wisden* it is clear that almost every cricketer deplores the l.b.w. law as it is now framed, or its consequences.

Not for a moment am I prepared to admit we have not the batsmen to-day that we had in years gone by. Leg-theory bowling must close up the game. Bradman fell a victim to Bedser's leg-stump attack three times before he accepted the limitations and began to take four instead of two and a half hours for a century. Bailey at Leeds four years ago prevented an Australian victory against the clock by bowling wide of the leg-stump. South Africa with negative bowling against England almost took the rubber. Hutton, May, Cowdrey, Compton and Graveney have cover drives as beautiful as any seen on a cricket ground, but they are seldom permitted to use the stroke. An attack directed at the legs of the batsman will always close the game.

No alteration in rule can make a batsman score freely from the attack directed at the leg-stump, but maybe an alteration in rule can make a bowler want to bowl straighter. On that point I believe everyone is agreed. Suitable pitches, of course, would make any bowler attack the stumps, but such is the variable nature of soils and pitches throughout the world that any legislation is impossible.

By legislation it strikes me there are only four possible methods:

(a)   Scrap the present l.b.w. law and go back to the old.

(b)   Limit the fieldsmen a bowler may use on the leg-side of the field.

(c)   Extend the l.b.w. law further to include both sides of the pitch or provide that any ball pitched between wicket and wicket or to the off is successful if a batsman stops it from hitting the stumps with his pads, etc.

(d)   Make any runs scored on the leg-side count double.

If the old l.b.w. law came back, then, I presume, cricket would soon drift into the type of play which caused the administrators to make changes. The bowlers needed help.

To deny a bowler the right to use his fieldsmen to the best advantage to suit the tactics of the moment or the state of the pitch would, I believe, be another retrograde step, but, just as in football it was necessary to alter the offside law in order to help the attackers, so may it work out in cricket. It would have been interesting to see the results when this idea was first produced by the New South Wales Cricket Association. It was a pity they did not give it a trial.

The extension of the l.b.w. rule to include both sides of the pitch would not be good. I can imagine Tyson, Statham, Trueman and the rest of the fast bowlers moving to round-the-wicket attack.

The physical danger would again become important, and rules would become far more complicated, or the game suffer, if the bowlers' right to deliver over or round-the-wicket was limited. The second alteration of the law seems much more feasible, i.e. to delete the phrase about stopping the ball with a part of the person in a direct line between the stumps.

If the batsman could be out l.b.w. to any ball which, pitching straight or on the off, would hit the stumps, it seems likely that the leg-break-googly bowler would be encouraged, that bowlers would attack, and batsmen would use the bat more. In practice it may well be found that the off-spin bowler would reap tremendous advantage. Certain it is that the batsman scoring a century would deserve his name in the record book! Yet, once accustomed to a new sense of values, it may not be a bad thing to have the run worth more. Good fielding would be most important.

The fourth suggestion about doubling the score would only work if, by trial and error, the bowlers found it was more expensive to attack the batsman's legs. If every run conceded by South Africa's Goddard had been doubled, he would still have been a most economical bowler on last season's performances.

Suggestions that our England cricket suffers because of the staleness of our players through too much cricket, I have ignored. The leg-stump attack is used almost universally now and was not employed by the South Africans because of staleness.

The idea of using a fourth stump similarly does nothing to eliminate bowling at the batsman's legs. It does not follow that the batsman, given more to defend, will take bigger risks. They are likely to be more careful. And bowlers will not change a mode of attack unless in the process of trial and error they find some other type more successful. Time limits and penalties for bowlers or batsmen are a very last resort. Yet something should be tried.

Why not, in the Festival matches at the end of the season, try out the idea of limiting fieldsmen on the leg-side to four? If it makes for better cricket the Festival Committees and the public will be delighted. Why not, in M.C.C. matches at Lord's, try out an extension of the l.b.w. law and make it known that the results do not count in the first-class averages? I am sure the Australian legislators, anxious to brighten and improve the game just as much as we are, would give this idea a trial.

A remedy for the present growing pains of cricket is hard to find.

General opinion points to the latest l.b.w. law as the cause, and if that is so, it should be discarded or widened in scope. It must come sooner or later . . . and the sooner the better.

TWO ERAS OF AUSTRALIAN PACE [1956]

Gregory—McDonald to Lindwall—Miller

BY I. A. R. PEEBLES

Even as Wisden welcomed the 1956 tourists by publishing its review of Australian fast bowling, the second of the two eras to which it referred was about to end. Ray Lindwall and Keith Miller, who had inflicted such deadly damage to England sides since the tour of 1946–47, were coming at last to the final overs of one of the most magnificent pace partnerships in cricket history. Miller was to appear no more for his country after 1956. Lindwall soldiered on until 1959, but some idea of the extent to which his effectiveness had declined can be gathered from the fact that in the historic 1956 series, he took only seven wickets. Ironically, Miller, in his last season as an international player, topped the Australian bowling list with 21 wickets at 22 each. Lindwall, a consummate artist, was a highly popular figure in England, but Miller was as much an idol to the English crowds as he was to his own. A dashing, handsome player who always proceeded on the assumption that when all was said and done, cricket was after all a game, not a form of warfare, always bowled and batted to the limit of his great powers but never giving a thought to statistical considerations. The fact that in his Test career he scored just under 3,000 runs at an average of less than 40 gives not the faintest idea of the spellbinding romanticism of his great innings. During the war, when as a fighter pilot on leave he had first introduced himself to the crowds at Lord's, he had become an instant hero and never forfeited this status even in retirement. Only the mean-spirited imbecilities of cricketing politics deprived him of the captaincy of his country he so richly merited, and posterity will goggle in disbelief at the hard facts of the 1956 selection, which preferred Ian Johnson to Miller as a leader. Miller took 170 Test wickets at 22 each, Lindwall 228 at 23 each.

Their astute chronicler in the 1956 Wisden, Ian Alexander Ross Peebles (1908–80), of Oxford, Middlesex and England, was one of the most courteous and charming of men and one of the best writers on the game of his generation. Blessed with an irrepressible sense of humour and a loyalty to his own past which eventually flowered into a prizewinning autobiography, Peebles was for a time so gifted a slow bowler that only his Wisden obituary does justice to the bare truth:

. . . he was for a short time one of the most formidable bowlers in the world and one of the few who could make Bradman look fallible. A tall man with a beautifully easy run-up and a high action, which gave him a particularly awkward flight, he bowled leg-breaks and googlies, and in an age of fine leg-spinners he was, for a while, the equal of any.

After 1934 injury and the demands of a business career reduced him to the status of a change bowler, and it was not till 1939 that he resumed regular cricket as captain of the Middlesex side. The loss of an eye during the war ended his career which, however, blossomed all over again as he quickly established himself as one of the wisest and wittiest of cricket writers. As the Almanack observed, 'For any student of cricket history over the last 60 years, his many books are compulsory and delightful reading.'

BARRING mishaps, it does seem certain that once again England will see the old firm of Lindwall and Miller in action. In the past there have been premature reports of their impending retirement, and even at the moment of writing when Sheffield Shield cricket in Australia is well under way and the selectors are doubtless studying the individual form of the players with anxious eyes, both have been troubled by injury. Whatever the future may bring, a comparison between Lindwall and Miller and their only rivals as a pair in the present century of Australian cricket, Gregory and McDonald, is fascinating as it is inevitable.

In making any such comparison, it is necessary to recognise that fashions and techniques in cricket, as in other matters, have changed with the passing of the generation which separates two distinct eras. It is a wide subject and, as space will allow only the study of certain aspects, these few reflections are perforce confined to the bowlers' point of view, and again largely to that of the pace bowler.

This will be the third Australian team to visit England since the war, and it will embark on the sixth series since that major interruption. In the number of matches and in actual years this period is almost the exact counterpart of that between the end of the first war and the eve of the 1930 tour. There is also a close parallel in the trend of events. In both cases England were outplayed in the reopening tour and the return visit, achieved a solitary victory in the third series and won the fourth in each case by a final deciding match at The Oval. The succeeding series, those of 1928–29 and 1954–55, saw England once more in the ascendancy by a good margin.

The similarity in result during these decades was reflected by a close resemblance in the actual play. A period of Australian supremacy, achieved by a combination of powerful batting, devastating fast bowling and much superior fielding, was followed by a gradual English resurgence led by an outstanding fast-medium bowler. Finally, there comes a complete reversal of the balance, largely brought about by a counterblast of fast bowling. Certainly there were many other factors which contributed to the ebb and flow of the tide, some alike and some totally dissimilar, but few cricket cycles can have been so alike in broad outline.

BRADMAN INTERVENES

They were divided by the era of Bradman who made his first appearance in the 1928–29 series and led the triumphant teams of 1946–47 and 1948. Despite the overlap, the division may be regarded as fairly clear, for on the one hand, despite early success, he was still something of an unknown quantity and, on the other, although still a tremendous force, he was scarcely the man who changed the character of international cricket in the 'thirties. In comparing the two eras, it is possible to identify several elements which affected tactics and techniques; but to say for how many of these Bradman was directly or indirectly accountable or to estimate his total influence on the game as a whole is very difficult. What is plain is that the game as played in the post second war years differed considerably in form from that of 1921.

To start with cold, impersonal figures—if indeed cricket figures can ever be cold or impersonal—surely the most pertinent item amongst Mr. Roy Webber's exhaustive figures dealing with these years is the fact that in the 1920–21 and 1921 series England, a well-beaten side, scored 49 and 50 runs per hundred balls bowled. Australia were naturally rather more expeditious scoring 53 and 56. In the first two post second war series the rates dropped to 37 and 38 for England and 50 and 46 for Australia. Thereafter the Australian rate dropped farther back. The trend in the intervening years had been a steady decline in the pace of scoring despite a large proportion of runs supplied by Bradman at an exceptionally high personal rate. Even if the 1920–21 and 1921 seasons were abnormal, it hardly calls for the mass of additional evidence available to demonstrate that the play of thirty-five years ago was of a considerably freer character. Whether it was as efficient is another matter.

What is the main reason for this change or deceleration? The broad answer must surely be the transference of the bowlers' focus from the region of the off-stump to that of the leg and the consequent throttling of off-side play but, equally importantly, the denial of the safe deflecting stroke to leg. The causes of this transference are several and complex, and the credit of responsibility must be shared between groundsman, bowler and batsman in what proportion we may later determine. Somewhat unfashionably I am inclined to exculpate the legislators.

In 1921 the spearhead of the Australian attack, the speed of Gregory and McDonald, was directed at the stumps and supported by three slips. The good length ball aimed at the stumps pitched regularly to the off and it was desirable that any error should be further in that direction. If the error was to drop the ball outside the leg-stump the batsman could play boldly in the knowledge that he had free passage to a distant fine-leg who could, at most, rob him of three runs.

When Lindwall and Miller bowled the slips had increased in number and some of them had now migrated to the hitherto uninhabited regions on the leg-side. For England, Bedser, with his sharp in-swerver, had perfected the same technique and the impact on batsmanship must have been as profound as the introduction of the googly. What had been a safe and attractive scoring shot had now elements of suicide, for if the ball 'moved' a little to the on a mishit was almost certain to result in a catch. Indeed, a correctly executed stroke was often fatal, owing to the difficulty of placing and keeping the ball down in this sector. The dangers of this situation were clear when Bradman, who seldom repeated a serious mistake, fell three times in succession to the backward short-leg position during the 1948 series.

The development of this form of attack is, as I have said, attributable to several causes. Most are agreed that the glory of cricket exists on the off-side, the highest art of the bowler to make the ball go away, and the beauty of batsmanship the variety of stroke between third-man and mid-off. But with the undoubted improvement in defensive back-play and the increase of dead, over-prepared pitches the bowler was given little incentive to attack, especially on the off-side.

While the old l.b.w. rule prevailed it was extremely hard to dislodge a batsman who made good use of his pads, for under its terms the ball had to pitch on and hit. Geometrically it is almost impossible for the faster bowler to drop the ball on a good length and comply with these requirements, unless he turns the ball from the leg—a tall order in the circumstances where it is most required. (In passing, it seems strange that those who advocate the reintroduction of the old law, having robbed the bowler of what little opportunity the present rule affords him in that quarter, expect thereby a return to off-side play.)

When the bowler was shorn of practically all means of positive action on the off-side it was not unnatural that he should seek some line of defence, or at least economy, and the on-side offered decided advantages in time of stress. It was seen as an area of attack in the 1932–33 series, a state of affairs largely precipitated by the tremendous off-side attacks of Bradman on the paceless pitches of 1930. At the same time O'Reilly dimmed much of Hammond's brilliance by concentrating on his relatively weaker on-side play. From then on much thought was given to the placing and feeding of the close leg-side field.

In the present age the 'in-coming' form of attack, so to speak, has been brought to a very fine art and one speculates on the reactions of the great stroke players of the past suddenly confronted with Bedser at his best. On the other side one wonders what additional problems Barnes and Tate might have raised by systematic use of the close leg field.

It is important to distinguish between the legitimate leg stump attack and 'leg-theory' applied in a purely negative sense to discourage scoring. That any bowler should be permitted to pack the leg-side field and bowl outside the batsman's legs is deplorable and to be discouraged at all costs. Appeals to the spirit of the game are, to my mind, of dubious value, for the very good reason that the 'spirit' is inclined to vary greatly with circumstances and in interpretation. A clear-cut law operates with certainty in all conditions, but the difficulty in this case is, admittedly, to frame such a law without adding further complication to an already intricate code.

My own suggestion to meet this situation has just that disadvantage but seems to have a basis of justice. If, which is perhaps improbable, this form of bowling should ever become widespread, would it not be possible to say that, when five or more fielders were posted to the on, any ball pitching outside the leg stump should be a no-ball? This may be cumbersome but it would exercise restraint where it is needed without interfering with the honest citizen.

The real answer to all cricket problems is, of course, to give the bowler fair incentive and opportunity to attack at all times. In doing so he will get wickets but will be more prone to make mistakes from which the striker can derive benefit and, indeed, in the absence of any guaranteed security, will be anxious to do so. This is hardly the place in which to reopen the discussion as to the best ways and means of achieving this healthy state of affairs, but, as I have implied, a return to the old l.b.w. law is surely not one of them.

The point of these rather rambling reflections is really to say that could the modern spectator be wafted back thirty-five years he would not only see a faster scoring match but one of largely different character. It might or might not be that he would find them more interesting than the battles of attrition to which he has grown accustomed. It might be more accurate to say 'had grown accustomed', for it must be borne in mind that the recent series in Australia was the most exciting cricket, whatever its standard. But it was also exceptional.

Much of the action and excitement was due to the fact that the pitches gave considerable, and not always fair, help to the prevailing type of bowling. Their inconsistency occasionally gave the proceedings an air of hit or miss which went beyond the bounds of 'glorious uncertainty' and must always detract from an equally balanced and scientific contest. To one who has played on it, the thought constantly recurs that the matting wicket of the old Wanderers ground at Johannesburg, with all its disadvantages, was the one surface which gave both departments full scope for their talents and was at all times a true reflection of merit.

The highlights of each era, Gregory and McDonald attacking Hobbs and Woolley or Lindwall and Miller in action against Compton and Hutton obviously transcended the differences in character to which I have referred and even the one-sided nature of the matches. The chief point in common amongst the batsmen is that they formed a first line of defence with little reserve behind them. The bowlers have much similarity in circumstance and in performance. They reigned supreme at a time when there was a world shortage of fast bowling and batsmen were ill-equipped to meet it.

Which was the finer pair and which the greatest individual must ever be open to argument and is much a matter of opinion. Certainly in span and in the matter of statistics the moderns have a much more impressive record. Gregory and McDonald appeared together in but eleven Test matches, eight against England and three against South Africa. The latter then left the international field at the height of his powers but his senior partner played for another seven years, a total of 24 matches. There is no doubt, however, that his powers declined greatly after the dissolution of the partnership.

COMPARISON OF FIGURES

Up to the present Lindwall and Miller have appeared together on 46 occasions and have played 49 and 47 Test matches respectively. In his Test career Gregory took 75 wickets at 35.30 runs apiece and McDonald 43 at 35.60 each. So far Lindwall has taken 192 wickets for 21.88 apiece and Miller 147 at 22.99 runs each.

There can be little doubt that McDonald was the most graceful of the quartette and possibly the most perfect cricket machine of all time. In the opinion of many well-qualified judges he could produce a faster ball than anyone within living memory. In his county days he seldom exerted himself to the full; only recently I was given an enthralling eye-witness account of one of his latter bursts of speed, occasioned by the appearance of an amateur who had treated him roughly in a previous match. This apparently irritated him out of his customary impassive calm and the results were spectacular. My informant, who has played most of the fast bowlers of the last thirty years, says it was the fastest bowling he has ever seen and only approached by Lindwall's stupendous three-over burst at Manchester in 1948. It was interesting to hear that the only perceptible increase in effort was that he accelerated in the last five yards of the impeccable run up to a swift gallop. His point established he reverted to the normal cruising speed which carried him through many strenuous seasons.

Gregory was to my mind the most inspiring. One might apply to him the words of a motoring critic who said of a famous make of sports car that others might have gone faster but none had achieved the glorious frenzy of its progress. Estimates as to his maximum speed vary, but it must have been extremely swift especially in the opening overs, and his height and very high arm added greatly to the general hostility of the performance. It might also be said of both Gregory and Miller that, in contrast to the polished craftsmanship of their partners, they were both children of nature.

LINDWALL COMES FIRST

A large mass of opinion places Lindwall first of all fast bowlers, a judgement based on pace, variation, control and consummate technique of seam and swerve. In addition he is a wonderfully shrewd and discerning tactician. I have already dwelt on the modern emphasis on the leg stump and the close surrounding field. Lindwall has retained the classical off-side attack but has added to it the cramping assault on the region of the batsman's pads. The so-called 'Carmody field', which consists of a cover-point and a short-leg to the fore and the rest of the field spread on either side of the wicket-keeper like the horns of a Zulu Impi, would doubtless appear monstrous and absurd to an eye reopened after thirty years. In the hands of the master it is in fact a formidable instrument. When it is new, the bowler pitches the ball well up, almost to half-volley length, and invites the batsman to drive him into the untenanted foreground. But swinging bat and very late swinging ball are ill met and the mis-hit from either edge means almost certain disaster with the Australian in-field to hand.

Batsmen have told me that Lindwall's low arm gives the ball an awkward angle of flight in addition to the complication of his late and unpredicted dip in either direction. When, as in the last series, the ball came at varying heights from the pitch the skill demanded of the modern opener is such that it is not surprising that few regularly succeed in such circumstances. It may be observed that doped, paceless wickets kill these dangers just as effectively as they obliterate any other point of interest.

Of Miller it might be said that he is the most mercurial but, in the mood, as deadly as any. His careless, almost casual air bears no relation to the power and fire of his action which seems to develop its maximum effort and weight as the arm comes to the downward sector of its swing so that the ball hits the pitch with a resounding thump. Although it may be with less design than in the case of Lindwall, he makes the ball move sharply in either direction.

MILLER THE MENACE

After the splendid performances of our own fast bowlers in Australia in 1954–55 it may seem almost ungrateful to say so but, with Lindwall in at least a temporary decline, Miller was the most menacing bowler of the series with the new ball. He may have lost something of his stamina but his opening assaults at Brisbane, Melbourne and Adelaide were positively hair-raising as seen through the eyes of a visiting supporter. Three balls at the start of the crucial second innings at Adelaide all but wrecked English hopes and remain vividly in the imagination. First there was a ferocious 'in-dipper', which appeared to affect Edrich's nervous system as violently as it did his middle and leg stumps. This was followed at uncomfortably short intervals by two very fast balls to Hutton and Cowdrey which left the pitch like leg-breaks and resulted in bullet-like catches, both beautifully picked up in the slips. The challenge was met by magnificent batting by May and Compton, but until the first welcome signs of fatigue appeared the final target of 94 runs seemed immeasurably distant.

Miller has the additional virtue of being a most entertaining bowler, and his impish delight in loosing off googlies and round armers without previous notice must be highly disconcerting, if it does not seem to meet with any great material success.

THE COMBINED EFFORT

But when all is said and done, which of these great pairs will be given premier place in Australian cricket history in the years to come is a very open question. Gregory and McDonald have one very special niche in all cricket history. At least so far as international cricket is concerned they were the pioneers of all fast opening attack. Since then it has been regarded as the most effective use that can be made of the new ball, and it can well be argued that two fast bowlers, provided they are of quality, have had more influence on the result of a given series than any other factor, with the possible exception of the phenomenal Bradman. In support of this view I would cite Larwood and Voce; Martindale and Constantine in their own country, Lindwall and Miller and finally Statham and Tyson. There have been many fine individual performers during the same time, but it seems that the combined effort is necessary to derive the fullest service from the individual.

CENTENARY OF FREE FORESTERS [1956]

BY COLONEL K. B. STANLEY
(HONORARY SECRETARY SINCE 1936)

There may be found in the 1956 edition of the Almanack one brief but delightful concession to that eccentric tendency among the Gentlemen-cricketers of the Victorian age to form wandering cricket clubs with bizarre constitutions and vaguely altruistic policies. The most renowned is I Zingari but among that club's distinguished rivals, the Free Foresters stand high. The essay marking the club's centenary, besides speculating on the epitaphs which may have been inspired by the fearsome Goodrich, suddenly exfloriates in its closing paragraph into the higher reaches of scholarship, providing the answer to one of the more inscrutable queries of the student of the game, concerning the physical aspect of the umpire.

CRICKET's famous wandering side, the Free Foresters, celebrate their centenary this summer. Behind this bare announcement lies the story of the rise and progress of a club which has become a by-word of sportsmanship and good company wherever the game is played.

It is fitting that the Free Foresters enjoy such a reputation, for their founder, the Rev. W. K. R. Bedford, always envisaged a club which would embody the highest traditions. Bedford, the local squarson, had his own cricket ground at Sutton Coldfield rectory and was assisted in the formation of the club by a trio of brothers well known at Oxford, W. G., H. S. and J. R. Armitstead, and the families of Charles and Robert Garnett who resided in the neighbourhood of Tamworth.

Recording the purpose of the club, Bedford wrote: 'The composition of the club was intended to have a Midland county character—not to be a provincial I. Zingari, because we did not propose to exact that unlimited fealty to our colours which the queen-mother of amateur wandering elevens so rigidly requires, but to imitate that unrivalled club in dispensing altogether with the hired assistance without which some of the strongest local clubs of gentlemen then imagined themselves unable to play matches.

'This was the meaning of the motto we adopted "United though Untied" which I borrowed from an epigram I met with in some book of the period and adapted it to a heraldic design called the Hastings knot, a cord loosely entwined connecting a sickle and a wheatsheaf for which we substituted two capital Fs. . . .'

The title was derived from the fact that all Bedford's eleven were from the precincts of the Forest of Arden in Warwickshire, or Needwood in Staffordshire.

Yet, as Bedford explained, 'my castles in the air would have been swallowed up by night' had he not renewed acquaintance with the brothers Armitstead. They promised to bring an eleven to inaugurate his new ground at Sutton rectory, and it was on this occasion that the Free Foresters first entered the pages of the sporting chronicles.

The match was played on July 20, 1856, the opposition bearing the picturesque title of the 'Pilgrims of the Dee'. The Free Foresters made scores of 65 and 57 and the Pilgrims obtained totals of 38 and 66. The obvious dominance of ball over bat in the country games of those days was due to a variety of factors, several of which a friend quoted to Bedford when they discussed the matter some forty years later. 'Scores were generally small,' recalled this associate of the sporting parson. 'There were no boundaries, no cane-handled bats and the wicket was mown with a scythe at 3 a.m. on the morning of the match and the rest of the ground only fed sheep.'

The fixture was repeated the following year and the Free Foresters played four other matches at Rugby, Leamington and Manchester. 'The Rubicon then was crossed, but what next and next?' commented the Rev. Bedford when he discussed those early days in a book he published toward the end of the last century. 'Were we to join the "swarm of butterflies, grasshoppers, chrysalis wasps and other ephemeral bodies that quicken in the summer-time under the genial influence of cricket," consider the lawn match our metier, and a pretty ribbon and a pleasant autumn the objects of our ambition; or fling down the gauntlet of higher pretensions in the recognised centres of cricket?

'In either event we required some kind of organisation; so when we met at Oxford on June 1, 1858, we at once proceeded to appoint a secretary and a committee, the first office falling to my share, and four cricketers being selected from our ranks as committee men representing the various interests bound up in our welfare.

'One of the most prominent of these was a man hardly less instrumental in raising our club in the proud position it eventually attained than were Armitstead or Goodrich—Arthur Faber, Fellow of New College, who a few years later became headmaster of the newly founded school at Malvern . . . a player who ought to be remembered as having held the premier place in the batting averages of amateur cricket in the year immediately preceding the rise of Mr. W. G. Grace.'

Goodrich, who first played for the club in 1857 when he took 13 wickets against the Western club, Manchester, had already established such a reputation that it was written of him: 'Over the early grave of many a younger cricketer shall it be written "Frightened to death by the slow bowling of Goodrich".'

At their meeting in Oxford the Free Foresters not only settled upon a motto but also decided that the colours would be crimson, green and white. These colours occasioned some opposition on the part of the older members who recalled that they were similar to those of the Chartists of 1848, but this appears to have been only a passing criticism. The same three shades are still worn today, a living symbol to the influence and standing of the club.

The meeting also decreed that members elected from the families (entail male) of Armitstead, Bedford and Garnett should be honoured with the title of 'Founders' Kin'.

No rules were evolved or printed until 1866. Meanwhile the Rev. Bedford ensured the success of the Free Foresters by the gradual expansion and improvement of fixtures, and the careful selection of promising young players, especially bowlers, from the public schools.

In the rules the club's policy was 'to play against County, University, College, Regimental elevens and with recognised clubs in desirable localities'; except for Counties this policy holds good today, though the club now play cricket wherever the interests of the game can be encouraged and assisted.

With this in mind Free Foresters make tours a feature of their fixture list. They have travelled to Scotland, the Channel Islands, Ireland, Holland, Germany, Egypt, India and Singapore. The list has steadily increased from fifteen matches in 1858, fifty in 1900, to a maximum of one hundred and twelve in 1938. After the Second World War, through force of circumstances, the number of fixtures had to be reduced to between sixty and seventy.

The Free Foresters are perhaps unique in that they have no president or chairman. The affairs of the club remain, as they began, in the hands of a secretary, who is helped by a treasurer, match secretary and fifteen members of committee. An entrance fee of five guineas is the sole subscription. Each match has to pay for itself, the players being responsible for their individual travel and hotel expenses, and they share other costs such as purchase of balls and umpires' fees.

In conclusion, an incident which is responsible for umpires today being supplied with white coats, is worth recording. It occurred during a match at Eccles in 1861 when the United England XI were beaten by Sixteen Free Foresters. W. G. Armitstead, the old Oxford Blue to whom reference was made earlier in this article, complained that he could not see the hand of G. Atkinson, a Yorkshire professional bowler, against the umpire's body. After a short delay a white garment, possibly a night shirt, was produced for the umpire to wear. It was the first time in cricket history that an umpire had been so invested.

Many of the greatest names in cricket have represented the club. All can bear witness to the comradeship which springs from being a Free Forester: 'United though Untied'.

PART TWO

1957 – 1968
Fall

STUART SURRIDGE: SURREY'S INSPIRATION [1957]

BY D. R. JARDINE

The 1957 edition saw a rare public appearance by the most controversial English player of prewar years, Douglas Robert Jardine (1900–58) whose evident inability to place the playing of cricket in its correct order of precedence in the destiny of the universe led to the regrettable squalor of Bodyline. What is doubly remarkable is that a generation later, Jardine was still unable to grasp the proposition that the playing of games is supposed primarily to give pleasure to the practitioner and only secondarily to the spectators. While technique and moral courage, to say nothing of a judicious balance between pugnacity and generosity, are integral elements, cricket nevertheless remains a game; in the last reckoning, dynasties will not crumble nor personal honour be compromised if the game be lost. Having insisted that first-class cricketers are not public entertainers and having conveniently forgotten that by the policies he once pursued he reduced the cricket field to a bear garden, Jardine proceeds with the most distasteful of similes by introducing into the debate those pariahs whose idea of manly sport is to spatter the blood of animals. He even compares the killing of a fox with the defeat of cricket opponents. But if the comparison is revolting, it does go some way to explaining Jardine's intractable stance throughout the shameful episode of the Bodyline tour. All in all, the blandness with which he paints his sunny portrait of cricket in England shows dissimulation brought to a fine art. Nor was it the only example of monumental evasion to be found in the 1957 edition.

*S*URREY, *under the bold leadership of W. S. Surridge, broke all county cricket records by winning the Championship outright for five consecutive years. Here, Douglas Jardine, whom many people regard as England's shrewdest captain since the turn of the century, pays tribute to Surridge. Jardine himself played for Surrey and captained the side for two seasons, 1932–33.*

INSPIRATION is the operative word.

Exactly what inspiration may mean varies too much for exact definition of analysis. Leave it, therefore, that most people would claim to recognise it when they see it, and what is quite as important, everyone appreciates the difference between being at the sending or at the receiving end of inspiration.

Having got his inspiration, Mr. Stuart Surridge was able not only to digest it, but to pass it on to each and every Surrey side from 1952 to 1956. In this, rather than in changing personnel, can be summed up the difference between the sides of 1948 to 1951.

To some extent Surridge's advent as leader may, from his own point of view, be considered to have been fortunately timed. It is no secret that during the years from 1948 to 1951 there was a very general conviction among players and members alike that there was present in the team, in good measure, all the ability and talent needed to win the County Cricket Championship. But the title continued to elude the County's grasp. The ability was never quite harnessed, or the talent fully and firmly exploited.

It is improbable that many recognised Surridge's inspiration for what it was. Few, however, could fail to appreciate his enthusiasm and the tautened determination springing naturally from it. The fielding had never been bad; no Oval crowd would tolerate that. But there was, nevertheless, a world of difference between the good workmanlife stuff served up before Surridge and the dynamic current with which he has charged it for the last five years. 'Don't drop a catch and you won't lost the match' is an old and tried adage. It would be no great exaggeration to say that the majority of catches missed by Surrey were chances only because they were made into 'possibles' by the fieldsmen. Surridge supplied the electricity close in on the off-side, while Lock did as much on the leg-side. To the unfortunate who had made nought in the first innings and was looking for a chance to 'get off the mark' in the second innings, the Surrey in-field must have offered anything but an alluring prospect.

Not long ago a county captain stated, in effect, that he regarded his team as first and foremost public entertainers, and impressed that fact upon them. To an elder generation such a statement strikes an altogether false note. A first invitation to play for a county couched in such terms would hardly appeal to the individual recipient, or be calculated to enhance the best interests of the game. By the same criterion a Master of Foxhounds would be a public entertainer, though both imagination and language might prove quite inadequate to record his reactions to the role suggested.

Yet, to borrow a metaphor from the hunting field, Surridge would have been as popular a Master as he proved himself a successful captain. He showed great sport; he went for and achieved definite results, and the number of his 'kills' was satisfactory to a degree.

In the course of doing this he undoubtedly entertained the public—but only incidentally. One knew that, had the fortunes of Surrey required it, entertainment would have been relegated to limbo.

A word now of Surrey and The Oval. For very many years Surrey has been singularly fortunate in the personalities, and incidentally the prowess, of its senior professionals. The results achieved could not have been compassed without a happy background and really first-class organisation. In all this both Secretaries, B. K. Castor and B. O. Babb, played no small part. Far more than the production of eleven or twelve of the best county cricketers is needed to win the Championship today.

At the start of his tenure of office, Surridge was able to lean on Fishlock and Jack Parker, two first-class men for their side, and Alec Bedser has stepped naturally and easily into their shoes as senior professional. Nor does the story end here, for throughout the period the quiet, albeit humorous, balance forthcoming from the scorer, Herbert Strudwick, was just what was needed in good as in bad times to guide the team to success.

Apart from the side itself, but behind it and reinforcing it, was the singularly fruitful 'nursery' controlled by another great and loyal servant, A. Sandham. With Test Matches, nearly every summer, regularly depleting the First Eleven for more than half a dozen matches of upwards of three of its leading performers, the need for worthy substitutes was vital. The nursery has met all such calls and twice in the past three years won the Minor Counties' Championship into the bargain.

Thus in due course we come to the question of wickets at The Oval, nursed and produced by the most successful groundsman in England, Bert Lock.

From a batsman's point of view no wicket has changed more radically since 1939 than that at Kennington Oval. Before 1939 centuries in the second innings were a commonplace; since then they have been rare indeed. Before 1939 no one could remember when Surrey last had a slow left-hand bowler as a regular member of the team.

It is no phenomenon, but merely natural, that wickets over a period not only tend, but do in fact produce just those bowlers best suited to them.

Australian wickets for years have eliminated the medium-pace bowler, just as The Oval up to 1939 eliminated the slow left-hander.

Lock, at Kennington, has more nearly than anyone else achieved the four-fold ideal facing groundsmen today. That consists of producing a wicket which, while fair to batsmen, lends itself to definite results in three days while encouraging both speedy and spin bowlers. Neither Bedser nor Loader nor Laker nor Lock object to bowling on their home pitch.

In these four bowlers, backed by Surridge himself, lies the mainspring of Surrey's success, for like it or not, it is bowling, not batting which in the main wins championships. Where the majority of county captains were too often wondering whom they could or should put on next, Surridge was faced with the pleasanter but not necessarily easier problem of whom to take off in order to give 'X' a chance.

By contrast with the Surrey bowling, the batting has been all too often unimpressive, to say the least of it. But the change of wickets is accountable for much of this. No side including P. B. H. May, and with a tail whose policy it was to hit and not poke its way out of a mess, could be other than dangerous opponents to tackle.

So let us return to Surridge at the summit of his success. The temptation to go on for 'just one more year' must have been well-nigh irresistible; yet he has resisted it, and we can only applaud his voluntary breaking of his wand as he takes his bow with a peerless record as a county captain.

One may regret that he never had the honour of captaining the Gentlemen against the Players at Lord's; still more that he was never entrusted with the task of taking, and bringing on, an England 'A' Team overseas. But Surridge was ever a county man, first and last, and as such can have few if any regrets.

THE GREAT MEN OF GLOUCESTERSHIRE [1957]

BY H. F. HUTT

No county in the Championship has a more colourful history than Gloucestershire and none can match its succession of batting geniuses with the Graces, Jessop and Hammond, and Tom Graveney maintaining the tradition in the modern age. Naturally any account of the county's affairs must be dominated by the Grace family, of which much remains to be written which is of vital interest both to social historians and to lovers of cricket. The account by Mr. Hutt in the 1957 Wisden does not really satisfy. By bowdlerising the club's history to the point where only a catalogue of names and numbers is left, Mr. Hutt misses a glorious opportunity to write one of the most memorable of the Wisden essays. There is no mention in his version of things of the covert professionalism of the Graces and the ribaldry which accompanied it, no detailed account of one of the most extraordinary figures of the Victorian epoch, the arch-dissimulator Billy Midwinter, no reference to the narrow escape from death experienced by Gilbert Jessop at the hands of the British army, no mention of the wonderfully diverting loathing of Charlie Parker for Pelham Warner and of Warner for Parker, a feud which must have cost the richly endowed Parker a sackful of England caps. There is also no mention of Lord Harris's ignoble victimisation of Walter Hammond over Hammond's disputed birth qualification. Because of these sad omissions, Mr. Hutt's history is as flat as a statement of profit and loss. The time was to come, as we shall see, when the Editor of Wisden was to favour more candid and much more entertaining views of things.

THE date of the formation of Gloucestershire as a county club is given as 1871, but the side, which was purely amateur and remained so until 1876, made a start in the world of fairly important cricket in the early 1860s. A team under the name of Gloucestershire played a fixture against Devon in 1862, and there is a note of a Gloucestershire v. Somerset game in 1863. In 1868, Gloucestershire beat M.C.C. in two days at Lord's, but it was not until 1870 that the enthusiasm of the Grace family—well known as a cricketing family long before 'W. G.' was born at Downend in 1848—put the club on a sound basis and enabled Gloucestershire to play other counties in a more or less settled programme.

The West Country team, soon to be dubbed the 'County of the Graces', engaged in first-class county matches for the first time in 1870. In 1873, Gloucestershire were admitted to the newly-formed County Championship as one of the nine sides considered first-class. Their amateur talent, under the captaincy of 'W. G.', immediately showed their worth in a competition of largely professional strength by sharing the Championship with Nottinghamshire who usually had ten or eleven paid players.

The black-bearded 'W. G.' strode through these early years of Gloucestershire successes like a colossus. He and his brothers—E. M. and G. F.—dominated match after match and in 1876 and 1877 Gloucestershire carried off the Championship on their own. Until beaten by the first Australian Eleven in 1878 the team never lost a match at home. The glory faded after the death of G. F. Grace in 1880, and apart from brief revivals the team over a whole season have not recaptured it.

Second place in 1930, 1931 and 1947 was the nearest the county came to finishing top since the great days of the 1870s. Still, Gloucestershire's valuable contribution to the game cannot be measured by match results.

The feats of 'W. G.', who died in 1915, aged 67, are legendary. He led Gloucestershire from 1870 to 1899 and did more to popularise cricket than anyone else. As a batsman he achieved almost everything of distinction—two centuries in a match, three hundreds in succession, 2,000 runs in a season and three scores of over 300. A bowler of medium pace, with round-arm action and a little break from leg, he took all ten wickets in an innings, and he did the 'Double' on eight occasions. 'W. G.' hit 126 centuries, 51 of them for Gloucestershire, with a highest score for the county of 318 not out, and the remarkable average of 40.80 spread over 30 years with the club. In 1895, when 47 years old, he scored 1,000 runs in May—an amazing performance.

'W. G.' himself gave his recipe for success. 'I aim,' he said, 'at playing every ball, however straight and good the length of it, for that is the only way to score at all rapidly against crack bowlers who can bowl over after over every ball on the wicket.' As a bowler, no one was quicker than the 'Doctor' to find out the weak points of a batsman, and in Gloucestershire's heyday the brilliant fielding of G. F. (Fred) Grace was invaluable to him. 'W. G.' began as an alert outfield, despite his bulk, capable of very long throws, but in later years he fielded near the wicket and only E. M. Grace, his other brother in the Gloucestershire Eleven, was his superior at point.

THE BEARD LEGEND

Inevitably there have been many stories told about 'The Champion', and there are several versions of the one about the bumping ball which flew through his beard. Ernest Jones, the Australian fast bowler, was the man concerned, but Sir Stanley Jackson, who was at the wicket with 'W. G.' when the incident occurred, has put on record that he does not think the ball actually touched Grace's beard. Sir Stanley, who died in 1947, said that he believed he was responsible for the beard-parting story as on his return to the Pavilion he jocularly cried to his team-mates: 'Did you see that one go through "W. G.'s" beard?' So history is written.

There have been many memorials to 'W. G.' and the cradle in which he was rocked in his home at Downend more than one hundred years ago is now in Bristol Museum.

During his years as captain, the great man had the help of such brilliant players as Jessop, C. L. Townsend, F. G. Roberts and J. H. Board. The

'Doctor' also introduced, in 1877, the county's first professional, W. E. Midwinter, a Gloucestershire-born all-rounder, who is the only man ever to play for both countries in the England and Australia series. 'W. G.', while touring with the England team in Australia, offered Midwinter an engagement and he stayed with Gloucestershire until he once more went to Australia in 1882.

Next to the name of 'W. G.', that of Jessop was the magic one. Captain of Gloucestershire from 1900 to 1912, Jessop, like 'W. G.' before him and Hammond after him, had the personality to bring people flocking from homes, offices, factories and shops to see him.

Popularly known as 'The Croucher', 'Jessopus' and 'The Human Catapult', Jessop thrilled the crowds with his tremendous hitting. In an hour he could alter the course of a game. A dynamic driver, he would advance down the pitch, then like a tightly-wound spring snapping open he would unleash his energy and smite the ball with terrific power. Jessop trounced fast as well as medium and slow-paced bowlers, and his severe cutting of the quicker men was a joy to see.

Who of the moderns could equal these prodigious feats—101 out of 118 in 40 minutes (for Gloucestershire against Yorkshire at Harrogate in 1897 with G. H. Hirst playing), or 191 out of 234 in 90 minutes (for Gentlemen of South against The Players of South at Hastings in 1907)?

Like 'W. G.', Jessop was an all-rounder. He bowled aggressively and, possessed of a swift and accurate throw, he fielded magnificently. He did the 'Double' in 1897 and 1900. In his association with Gloucestershire from 1894 to 1914, Jessop scored 18,936 runs, with a highest innings of 286 and average of 32.53, and took 620 wickets at 22.34 runs apiece.

Townsend, who spanned the years 1893 to 1922, first regularly and then irregularly, began with the county as a leg-break bowler before developing into one of the best left-hand bats in the land. His bowling achievements included the taking of 16 wickets against Nottinghamshire at Trent Bridge in 1895 and that unparalleled performance in first-class cricket of a 'hat-trick' by stumpings.

W. H. Brain, who kept wicket for Gloucestershire for only the one season of 1893, shared in that unique feat at the expense of Somerset at Cheltenham. C. L. Townsend scored 7,754 runs for Gloucestershire, with a highest innings of 224 not out, and took 653 wickets. He twice did the 'Double'.

Roberts, a skilful left-arm bowler, and Board, a dependable wicket-keeper-batsman, also blossomed under the leadership of Jessop whose term of captaincy saw such players as C. O. H. Sewell (captain 1913–14), A. E. Dipper, G. Dennett, P. T. Mills and C. W. L. Parker come into prominence or start upon their noted careers. Dennett, master of flight and spin, was the first of Gloucestershire's famous left-arm bowlers, and had he not been contemporary with Rhodes and Blythe he must have gained Test honours. In eleven consecutive seasons to 1914, Dennett averaged nearly 150 wickets for under twenty runs each. In 1906 he took all ten Essex wickets in the first innings at Bristol for 40 runs, and in 1907 at Gloucester he shared with Jessop the distinction of dismissing Northampton for 12 runs—the lowest total recorded in any county match. Dennett took eight wickets for nine runs and Jessop the other two for three runs. Dennett, who played for Gloucestershire from 1903 to 1926, captured 2,082 wickets for the county at 19.88 runs apiece.

Gloucestershire's production of personalities was only temporarily checked by the First World War. Dipper, an opening batsman of the utmost reliability, carried his bat no fewer than 11 times for the county before he retired in 1932. He was the most stubborn and imperturbable of defenders when occasion demanded it, and he hit 53 centuries for the county, with a top score of 252 not out against Glamorgan at Cheltenham in 1923. Dipper's full batting figures for Gloucestershire, between 1908 and 1932, were 27,948 runs, average 35.28.

PARKER'S ENEMIES

Parker, a bowler who regarded batsmen as his natural enemies, developed into the county's greatest left-arm exponent. He spun nearly every ball, and when batsmen heard the snap of his fingers they knew the ball would turn viciously. From 1903 to 1935 he took 3,171 wickets for Gloucestershire at average cost of 19.43 runs—really great bowling. In 16 consecutive seasons between 1920 and 1935 he took over 100 wickets and five times passed 200 in all cricket.

He did the hat-trick six times—including twice in one match—took all ten Somerset wickets for 79 runs at Bristol in 1921, and conceded only 56 runs in both innings while disposing of 17 Essex batsmen at Gloucester in 1925. He may, though, be remembered best of all for his almost unbelievable performance in his own benefit match, against Yorkshire at Bristol in 1922. He hit the stumps with five consecutive deliveries, but unfortunately the second delivery was called 'no ball'. On two occasions Parker bowled unchanged in a match, and both were in 1922 in company with Mills, a fingerspin bowler of the old order who took the last five Somerset wickets at Bristol in 1928 in the course of 40 deliveries without having a run hit off him.

From the resumption of cricket after the First World War until the coming of the adventurous B. H. Lyon in 1929, Gloucestershire were served by four captains—F. G. Robinson, P. F. C. Williams, Lt.-Col. D. C. Robinson and W. H. Rowlands. During their reign a new star appeared in the cricket firmament. Hammond was the name. As 'W. G.' and Jessop had done in the eras before him, Hammond drew cricket lovers as surely as a magnet draws steel. His career—from 1920 to 1947—was full of wonderful achievements. The crowds idolised him, and he responded by giving sheer delight with his artistry of batting. On a hot summer's day, with his silken shirt rippling in the gentle breeze, Hammond looked every inch the greatest cricketer in the world as he scored with freedom, style and assurance against the best that pace or spin bowlers could send down to him. Of strong physique, he excelled with his strokes through the covers, and the perfect timing, power and exquisite grace of his off-driving has never been surpassed.

Hammond's performances for Gloucestershire and England would fill pages. Of his 167 centuries, 113 were for the county, and 24 of them were over 200! He scored more runs for Gloucestershire than any other player—33,664, for the incredible average of 57.05 and his highest score for the county 317. Hammond, true to the tradition of 'W. G.' and Jessop, was an all-rounder. A clever bowler of medium-pace with the old or new ball, he took 504 wickets for Gloucestershire but was never used regularly enough as a bowler to enable him to do the 'double'. For all that he could be counted on to beat the best batsmen in the world.

His other great asset was his fielding. As a slip fielder he was unapproached, and the nonchalant way he used to take the slightest of snicks, especially off the bowling of Parker, was remarkable.

Hammond still heads the list of players, other than wicket-keepers, who have made most catches in a season, for in 1928 he held 78. In that summer, too, he established, against Surrey at Cheltenham, the record of 10 catches in a match—a feat equalled, curiously, by another Gloucestershire man in wicket-keeper A. E. Wilson, against Hampshire at Portsmouth in 1953. No other players anywhere have this distinction to their credit. In 1938, Hammond changed his professional status and as an amateur he captained Gloucestershire in 1939 and 1946.

LYON THE CAVALIER

B. H. Lyon, captain from 1929 to 1934, encouraged the enterprise and showmanship of his players, and in this period, when Gloucestershire cricket was once more a force in the Championship, it was surprising that his team did not carry off top honours. Lyon, a hard-hitting batsman, was an astute captain who knew the weaknesses of his rivals as well as he realised the capabilities of his own men. He did much to brighten cricket and would never let a game peter out into a tame draw.

His unorthodox actions caused consternation among cricket legislators—and an alteration in the Laws. There was the notable match at Sheffield in 1931, when, after delay owing to rain, a result on two innings apiece was impossible, and both the Yorkshire and Gloucestershire first innings were declared closed with four byes from one ball bowled by each side. That action permitted the full points to be available for the winners, and Gloucestershire secured them with victory by 47 runs.

Lyon had a brilliant side at his command, with Hammond, C. J. Barnett, R. A. Sinfield, C. C. Dacre, W. L. Neale, Parker, T. W. Goddard and H. Smith to call upon. In addition to the superlative skill and consistency of Hammond, an attraction for the public was the clean, hard hitting of Barnett whose nature simply compelled him to hit the punishable ball, even if it were the first of the match. He played many magnificent innings, including 38 hundreds for Gloucestershire, and still holds the record for the highest number of sixes in an innings. He hit eleven—besides eighteen 4s—in his 194 against Somerset at Bath in 1934.

Dacre, the New Zealander who came over with the 1927 team and qualified for the county, was another hitter of sixes. He often took a leaf out of Jessop's book by going down the pitch to drive and if he could hit the ball out of the ground so much the better for his mood. Gloucestershire, at this time, were certainly the apostles of the brighter cricket campaign, but they knew they had the solidarity of Sinfield and Neale to stop a gap if their lively methods failed.

In bowling they were as strong as any county and the combination of Parker and the tall Goddard became renowned. Goddard, originally a fast bowler, changed to off-spin bowling with great success. Using his height and keeping an immaculate length, he brought the ball down hard and made it lift. On turf at all helpful he proved unplayable and he achieved phenomenal performances during a long career which began in 1922 and finished only a few seasons ago. His 'bag' for Gloucestershire was 2,862 wickets for 19.58 runs apiece, but these bare figures do not tell of his finest days. He joined the ranks of the cricket immortals in 1939 by taking 17 Kent wickets in a day at Bristol—a world record shared previously by Blythe and H. Verity. Against Worcestershire at Cheltenham in 1937, Goddard took all ten wickets in an innings for 113. Like Parker, he also performed the hat-trick six times.

Sinfield's value was as batsman and bowler. He had the temperament for a crisis and he did the 'double' in 1934 and 1937—the first and only Gloucestershire professional player to reach this standard of all-round excellence. Sinfield hit 16 hundreds for the county, and Smith, an unostentatious yet very effective wicket-keeper, hit ten.

Many were the days of exciting cricket in the early 1930s, but surely none was so breath-taking as the memorable tie with the Australians at Bristol. C. W. Walker, the last Australian man in, took up his stand at the wicket with the tourists needing three runs to win. Hornibrook, at the other end, hit two singles. With the scores level three maiden overs were bowled and Smith kept wicket so coolly and efficiently that not a ball passed him at this vital stage. Then Hornibrook was l.b.w. to Goddard. The crowd's enthusiasm broke loose and they carried Parker, the real hero of the match, shoulder-high to the pavilion in triumph. Parker had taken seven wickets for 54 and bowled unchanged in the innings with Goddard.

A day of tragedy was September 2, 1936, when D. A. C. Page, captain for two years after B. H. Lyon, lost his life in a car crash. Page, only 25, had enthusiastically led Gloucestershire to fourth place in the table, and in all the sorrow which his death caused it must have been a happy memory to his relatives and colleagues that the last thing he did on the field was to make a catch which gave Gloucestershire victory over Nottinghamshire.

B. O. Allen, a stalwart left-hand bat and Cambridge Blue, led Gloucestershire in 1937 and 1938, and after Hammond's single postwar season as captain Allen stepped into the breach again and held control of the team from 1947 to 1950.

An able leader as well as a consistent opening batsman, Allen, in 1947, went close to restoring the old glories of Gloucestershire. A daring and fearless close-in fielder, he inspired his men to great heights and the county finished second in the Championship to Middlesex. Then the pendulum swung back. With Neale and Barnett following Hammond into retirement the county's batting strength was sapped and in 1950 Goddard, in his fiftieth year, at length gave up.

Yet Gloucestershire, in the present decade, have high hopes of the future. In an age when amateur leaders are difficult to find, the county called Sir Derrick Bailey from the Second Eleven to captain them in 1951 and 1952, and since then the captaincy has devolved in turn upon the professionals J. F. Crapp and G. M. Emmett. Crapp's solid left-hand batting has demoralised many attacks, and Emmett, a player of delightful strokes, also has a long list of centuries to his name.

Lambert, one of Gloucestershire's best fast bowlers, has been a mainstay of the team in modern times, and Wilson shone as batsman as well as wicket-keeper. Now there is T. W. Graveney, of the graceful and entertaining stroke-play, C. A. Milton, a brilliant fielder and fine batsman, D. M. Young, a sound opener, C. Cook, who has continued the series of the side's noted left-arm slow bowlers, and a host of youngsters, among them the off-spinners B. D. Wells and J. Mortimore, to keep the flag flying. Another Graveney would have been in the list, but Gloucestershire lost a potentially great all-rounder when J. K., brother of the Test player, had to give up county cricket because of a strained back soon after he took ten Derbyshire wickets in an innings in 1949.

The 'County of the Graces' is sparing no effort to develop Gloucestershire-born talent. 'W. G.' was always pleased to discover a promising cricketer, and those who now direct the county's fortunes feel that the finest tribute they can pay to the memory of their Champion is the encouragement of youthful cricketers raised within its borders.

HOW WEST INDIES CRICKET GREW UP [1957]

BY LEARIE N. CONSTANTINE

Their sensational victories in England in 1950 had provided the West Indies with the right to claim parity with the world's strongest sides. Those triumphs had been achieved, uncharacteristically to modern eyes, through spin, particularly the surprise element of the bowling of the unknown Ramadhin, who now returned for the 1957 campaign with the reputation of an inscrutable enigma. The tourists looked strong enough on paper to justify the optimism of their elder statesman Learie Constantine, although he was shrewd enough to close his essay with the opinion that the odds were on England. Constantine's life is an encapsulation of the gathering maturity of his homeland. His father had figured prominently in the emergent years of West Indian cricket and had played in that freak game at Bristol in 1900 when Gilbert Jessop batted with such extravagant genius to score 157 in an hour, reducing the opposing attack to a disarray which expressed itself in uncontained hilarity. Constantine junior made his Test debut against England in 1928 and won fame as the world's most spectacular all-rounder, a mercurial batsman, a genuinely fast bowler and the most wonderful fielder in living memory. Towards the end of the war he had played innings in the weekend matches at Lord's still talked about by those fortunate enough to have witnessed them.

But the 1957 campaign was destined to be a disaster. Once again spin dominated, but this time it was the hosts who held the trumps. The Surrey pair, Laker and Lock, together with Fred Trueman, took 55 wickets in the series at such little cost that no West Indian batsman averaged 40 in the series. On the other hand, seven home batsmen averaged more than 50, with May, Cowdrey and Graveney especially prolific. The series turned in the second innings of the first Test, when May and Cowdrey, having witnessed the annihilation of their side once again by Ramadhin, deployed the stratagem of playing forward to virtually everything and by smothering the spin, dispensed with the challenge of deciphering its axis. The significance of that record-breaking stand between May and Cowdrey may be gathered from the fact that in the first innings Ramadhin had taken 7 for 49. In the rest of the series his figures were 7 for 498. Among the other problems afflicting the tourists of 1957 were the decline of Weekes and Walcott partly through injury and the lack of a reliable opening batting pair. Yet in retrospect we can see that Constantine's cheeriness about the future was justified. Among the apprentice players in the party were Sobers, Kanhai, Collie Smith and Wes Hall. Smith was to die tragically in a car accident two years later but the promise of the other three was more than fulfilled.

T HE West Indies have been close to England for a long time by virtue of the relationship and status of Colonies. Even at cricket England has stood in the unassailable position of parent and tutor; the fact that the parent can now be beaten at her own game has never altered the relationship. But West Indies cricket has grown up and in the summer of 1950 reached a peak that it has since striven to maintain, but without success.

We like to think in my family that when cricket was born in the West Indies a Constantine was there as chief midwife. Test Match status was not granted to the West Indies until after 1928, but I was included in a West Indies side that toured England in 1923 and my father did the same on two previous occasions many years before that. Trinidad was discovered by Columbus in 1492 and by the M.C.C. in 1895; when I discovered England in 1923 there had already been quite a lot of cricket between the two countries.

In my boyhood there was an enthusiasm for cricket in Trinidad such as I have seldom seen equalled anywhere else in the world. My father set the family to work to make a private pitch from rolled clay covered with matting; it was the fashion everywhere and tremendous cricket battles were fought out between neighbouring families. My mother could keep wicket almost as well as a Test 'keeper; my sister had as much aptitude for batting as I had; one of my uncles was an international player and another was just as skilled. When we small boys were not playing in bigger games, we incessantly opposed each other, using oranges for balls and coconut branches for bats.

Such intense interest bred great young cricketers. I shall always remember watching two famous Trinidad clubs play a match during my boyhood. One of them, Stingo, boasted no less than seven bowlers in the international class. Stingo won the toss, and put in their rivals for the fun of skittling them out. But this time their opponents had prepared a surprise. The name of this rival club was Victoria, for which my father played, so you can guess where my sympathies lay. I could hardly bear to breathe as the Victoria opening pair took their places at the wicket. One was the 'secret weapon', a slim and immature-looking boy called Wilton St. Hill—alas! now no more. He was smoking as he walked out; he took his stance, still smoking, glanced idly round the field, then threw away his cigarette. George John—also now gone to the 'great divide'—one of the most formidable fast bowlers who ever handled a ball, thundered up at the other end and sent down a red lightning flash—atomic if you wish—but the slender boy flicked his wrists and the ball flew to the boundary faster than sound. The next went the same way. The boy batted from his wrists; he never seemed to use any force. I don't believe he had the strength even if he so desired. His was just perfect timing. Wilton St. Hill became famous later, but I never saw him or anyone else play a more heart-lifting innings than he did that day.

I began in club cricket in Trinidad when such men as St. Hill, George Challoner, Pascal, Cumberbatch, Bertie Harragin, John, Small, Dewhurst, Tarilton, Austin, C. R. Browne and my father were the great players of the day. Then came my selection for the 1923 voyage to England.

In the first games in England most of us youngsters found that we could not tell one white player from another. It was bewildering and annoying, especially when, as it seemed to us, people like Jack Hobbs, Andy Sandham, Ernest Tyldesley and Harry Makepeace, having been dismissed and sent back to the pavilion, immediately came walking out to bat again! It was many years after that I learnt that some English players shared the same thoughts and anguish about us.

The last match of that tour was the most exciting of all. At Scarborough, against what was really an All-England XI, we were twice put out for low scores on a nasty wicket and in the final knock our opponents needed only 31 runs to win. Hobbs, Stevens, Tyldesley, Rhodes, Chapman and Mann were sent back by John and Francis for 19 runs, and for a moment it looked as if we had a chance. Then some unfavourable l.b.w. decisions robbed us of our hopes. Sir H. D. G. Leveson Gower stated later that it was mainly because of that terrific game that the West Indies won Test Match status for the next tour in 1928.

1 I was selected for that tour, also. We did not win a Test, but I shall always

remember a match at Lord's against Middlesex. I had torn a muscle just previously and was ordered not to play. But we needed financial help and as our team-manager considered me a 'drawing-card', he asked me if I could possibly manage to turn out. The doctor was very worried and said that if I played I must on no account do any bowling.

Middlesex, batting first, declared at 352 for 6. We began with 79 for 5; then I got 86 in 55 minutes and we managed a total of 230. After that, I *had* to bowl! I took six wickets for 11 in one spell and when we walked in after the innings closed, the members in the pavilion rose for me. Again our first five wickets went down for poor score, but my star was in the skies; I made a century in an hour and we won by three wickets. As we walked in, the members rose for me a second time, as they did for Keith Miller last summer.

I was with the first West Indies side to tour Australia. That was in 1930–31 and I shall never forget it. Being a 'drawing-card' is an exacting business. For example, during this tour of 15 games I played in 14 and rested once. In one big match I took six for 45 and made 59 in 35 minutes including four 6s; and in another a century in 50 minutes. I also had the pleasure of clean-bowling Sir Don Bradman and Stan McCabe on the same day. But far more important to me and to us all was the terrific thrill of beating Australia in the final Test. That, too, made history for my country.

In the autumn of 1934 came one of the happiest events of my life—an invitation to visit India and play in the Gold Cup Tournament. I stayed in a Maharajah's palace for a few days amidst such beauty and luxury as had seemed formerly to belong only to dreams—gold coaches, gold chairs, diamonds, turquoises, sapphires, ivories and silks. I found Indian cricketers equal to the best in the world in technique and invariably sporting and cheerful, however the game went. I was amazed and impressed at the fine condition of many of the Indian cricket grounds, and even more by the magnificent enthusiasm of both players and non-players for their country's fortunes.

I went back to the West Indies for the 1934 Tests against England. Wyatt, the English skipper, said publicly that his side was the strongest ever sent to visit us. It included Hammond, Hendren, Ames, Iddon, Holmes, Leyland, Farnes and others as good; I doubt whether any team as powerful has visited the West Indies since. I did not reach home in time to play in the first Test, which England won, but in the second, bowling the last over of the match, I took the final English wicket with my fifth ball with sixteen seconds to go! For the second time in history, West Indies had beaten England in a Test Match—and my hand had discharged the fatal missile.

The next Test was drawn and the fourth and final one provided another terrific thrill—more than one, in fact. First, Wyatt, the English captain, was knocked out and had to leave the match in the hands of a deputy. Then Grant, our skipper, sprained an ankle at a critical point of the game, and so the Test deputy-captaincy fell on me. But again our fortunes were in the ascendant and once more a ball from me took the last wicket; this time we had won a rubber against England and for the first time.

I was back again in Test Cricket in 1939 just before World War II began. In fact, as an 'old man' (as cricketers go) I made 79 in 55 minutes and took five for 75 beneath the silvery barrage-balloons that were already floating over The Oval ground. Then our team had to cut short its tour and get home as best it could the long way round via Glasgow and Montreal, with the U-boats already hunting the seas for victims.

Big cricket for me ended with the sunny pre-war era when nobody had heard of atom bombs and when cricket could compete for the headlines. But West Indian cricket has gone from strength to strength. Such names as Worrell, Weekes, Ramadhin, Valentine, Walcott, Rae, Stollmeyer and Gomez and many more have rung around the world. Records have been gleefully made in the sunshine on many a green field; Test matches have been doggedly fought; Commonwealth countries have played each other and also challenged on equal terms the might of England and, I think it just to say, covered themselves with honour.

Even as an old man in his fifties I, myself, can go and cheer at such games—and I can add a little more to my store of cricket knowledge. It all comes in useful, especially at such times as three years ago when I went out to Ceylon on a coaching and cricket-lecturing tour. There are some grand young players coming on in Ceylon; they are well worth watching. Some are now engaged in English League cricket, enlarging and cementing the philosophy of Commonwealth solidarity.

Of English cricket I would say that on its showing against Australia and South Africa the standard is improving rapidly. Never let anyone tell you that the heroes of yesterday's English cricket will never be equalled. I know so many of them so well and they are the first to laugh at such a statement and to say that cricket, like other forms of sport, should and will steadily *improve*. We old fellows who set up records made them for youngsters to break, just as we broke our predecessors' records whenever we could.

The West Indies tour of England in 1950 stands out as the finest in our history. Whether we shall be able to repeat the performances and win the rubber again, I have grave doubts. Ramadhin and Valentine, I suspect, will be there. The terrible trio—Worrell, Weekes and Walcott—will also be there. Goddard has accepted the captaincy and will lead the side. His task will not be as simple as in 1950 when English cricket was struggling to shake off the effects of the years the war had eaten. Nevertheless, the material at his disposal will be good and if England maintains its progress under May, a terrific series of Tests should ensue, with the odds in favour of England.

MILESTONES IN WEST INDIES CRICKET

1842	Trinidad C.C. already 'of very long standing'.
1863	Kingston C.C. formed in Jamaica.
1864–65	Barbados and British Guiana met in first representative match.
1887–88	Philadelphians (U.S.A.) first overseas team to tour West Indies.
1891	First Triangular Tournament between Barbados, Trinidad and Demerara.

1894–95   First visit of an English team (captain R. S. Lucas).

1900   First West Indies team toured England.

1901–2   First matches of an English touring team (captain R. A. Bennett) against the combined West Indies.

1906   Second West Indies tour of England. S. G. Smith achieved 'the double'.

1910–11   First M.C.C. team (captain A. F. Somerset) visited West Indies.

1923   Third West Indies team visited England.

1925–26   Second M.C.C. team toured West Indies.

1927–28   G. A. Headley made his debut, scoring 409 runs in five innings, with 211 (made out of 348) his highest, against Lord Tennyson's touring team.

1928   Fourth West Indies team toured England, playing Test matches for first time. England won all three.

1929–30   M.C.C. visited West Indies, playing four Test matches in which G. A. Headley hit 176; 114 and 112 in the third; and 223. In winning at Georgetown, West Indies gained their first Test victory. A. Sandham, with 325 in the last, scored the first treble-century in Test cricket.

1930–31   West Indies toured Australia for first time.

1933   Fifth West Indies team to England.

1934–35   M.C.C. toured West Indies. For first time in history, West Indies won Test rubber.

1939   Sixth West Indies team to England.

1947–48   M.C.C. visited West Indies and did not win any of their first-class engagements.

1950   Seventh West Indies team to England (captain J. D. Goddard). West Indies gained first Test victory in England and won rubber.

1951–52   Second West Indies team to Australia.

1952–53   First Indian team to West Indies.

1953–54   M.C.C. team toured West Indies, drawing rubber. With 681 for eight wickets at Port of Spain, West Indies hit their highest Test total. A. L. Valentine (24) became youngest player to complete 100 Test Match wickets.

1954–55   First Australian team visited West Indies; were first visiting side to win Test rubber in Caribbean.

UPS AND DOWNS OF NORTHAMPTONSHIRE [1958]

BY JAMES D. COLDHAM

The Cinderella saga of Northamptonshire had come so close to a happy ending in 1957 that in the 1958 Almanack there appeared a well-written account of the club's history. Northants had finished second in the Championship, a dizzy height for a club which for so many years had languished in the lower reaches. In fact the county's early history incorporates more triumphs than posterity is inclined to remember. In George Thompson and S. G. Smith they possessed two of the most attractive all-rounders of the Edwardian age. Thompson was the first member of the county side to win England caps, while Smith had been the star of the visiting West Indies side of 1906. When that tour was over he remained in England and qualified by residence to represent the club. It is, then, not altogether surprising that in 1912 the county finished second in the Championship.

Great cricketers came the way of the club from time to time, none more richly gifted than A. H. Bakewell, the victim of a car accident in 1936. So utterly did he vanish from the cricket scene that in later years people assumed that he must have died in the crash; instead he survived until 1983, by which time the makers of fashion had long since forgotten all about him. With his departure, although not as a result of it, the county sank to the foot of the table and stayed there for some seasons. Not until the postwar revival under F. R. Brown did the club once again become worthy opponents to the best sides in the Championship. But it is the early history which makes the best reading. For instance, the county can probably claim a world record in the possession of the prolific brotherhood of the Kingstons, who outfostered the Fosters by having eight of their number as county players. There is a spectacular groundsman story, also the best telegram of its day. We also spare a derisory thought for local gentry of the emergent years who, unlike their co-equals in other counties, refused to take an interest in their local club. In the years following the appearance of Mr. Coldham's essay, the club continued to vacillate between virtuosity and nebulosity, rising once more to the eminence of second place, sinking yet again to the foot of the table. That ignominy reminds me that in my boyhood, when Northants finished seventeenth for five successive years and failed to win a game in the last three of those, there was a cruel joke to the effect that had they sunk any lower they would have been competing in the Sheffield Shield. Happily, their recent history has been much happier. In 1976 the Gillette Cup was theirs and four years later they topped the Benson and Hedges competition.

NORTHAMPTONSHIRE County Cricket Club grew naturally out of the Northampton Town Club which was formed in 1820 and by 1850 was the most powerful in the county. Some of the members were drawn from outlying districts, and in the latter year the local Press began referring loosely to this Town Club as 'Northamptonshire'. The venue was the Northampton Race Course, an expanse of 120 acres and for generations a public right-of-way, jealousy guarded by the Freemen and townspeople.

In the 'seventies representative cricket was at a low ebb and as the outcome of a discussion on July 3, 1878, during the annual North versus South Northants match at Kettering, a Public Meeting at the George Hotel, Kettering, on July 31 considered 'the best means of placing the County Club on a footing of equality with other counties'. As it was realised that 'Northamptonshire' had never been properly organised and was really a town club supported by few of the gentry, a Committee was elected *representing all parts of the County*, the Earl Spencer remaining President. Other notable officials were Sir Herewald Wake, a member of M.C.C., the Hon. and Rev. J. Marsham of the eminent Kent family, and Mr. Fred Tebbutt, proprietor of a shoe business and energetic Honorary Secretary, who arranged more ambitious fixtures.

From 1881 until 1885, of thirty-five matches eighteen were won and eight lost. Essex and M.C.C. were defeated; the first game (in 1884) at Wellingborough School saw Warwickshire worsted by an innings. Eighteen of Northamptonshire met the Australians in 1880 and two years later the County played them (with the aid of Alfred Shaw) on equal terms; both ventures were lost.

Tom Bowley, Joe Potter and Tom Alley secured 458 wickets. A schoolmaster, G. J. Gulliver, hit the first century, 103, off M.C.C. at Lord's in 1884; and five brothers Kingston batted zestfully. Eight of them appeared between 1874 and 1909.

NEW COUNTY GROUND

As a small body of Freemen claimed that they possessed the freehold of the Race Course, the expansion of County Cricket there was impossible. Once a brewer's dray was driven deliberately across the pitch prepared by the Yorkshire-born groundsman, who gave the driver a good thrashing and asked the Committee for a small rise in pay.

In 1885 a ploughed field of ten acres of Abington Parish was purchased from Sir R. Loyd Lindsay (afterwards Lord Wantage) by the new 'Northamptonshire County Cricket and Recreation Grounds Company, Ltd.', Sir Herewald Wake and Mr. Joseph Hill, Squire of Wollaston, advancing £2,000 for the site. The first match at the present County Ground was on May 14, 16, 1886, when Surrey Club and Ground won by six wickets.

Northamptonshire did not flourish as the best professionals were lured to more prosperous counties, Arthur Mold, for instance, joining Lancashire and playing for England; the membership was about 300; the County families remained aloof; finance was always a worry.

Wellingborough School and the local Leagues produced some talented players, and in 1896 a rebuilt side entered the Minor Counties Championship. Between 1899 and 1904 they enjoyed substantial success, twice winning the title outright and twice tying for first place. No matches were lost between July 1898 and July 1901.

The genial Reptonian, Tom Horton, was captain and he was assured of class batting from the impetuous C. J. T. Pool, more solidity from W. H. Kingston, and ballast down to number eleven. Besides scoring prolifically, G. J. Thompson and W. East carried the attack. From 1898 until 1904 ninety-one games brought them 964 wickets. Thompson was the greatest all-rounder ever produced by Northamptonshire; East was a capable and accurate medium pacer and dour batsman.

GEORGE THOMPSON

An Old Wellingburian, George Thompson, first appeared in 1895 at the age of seventeen, and bowled and batted the County into first-class cricket. With his complete double circle of the arm action, he was above medium pace and brought the ball off the ground with plenty of life and spin. His length was superb. As a batsman he tended to be over-cautious, but when conditions warranted he would hit hard and often. Close in he held many catches. In Minor County days he scored 5,174 runs, average 35.93, and took 751 wickets at 14.01 runs each; and from 1905 until 1922 his figures were 8,322 runs, average 23.57, and 1,078 wickets at 18.88 runs each. The first Northants player to represent England against Australia—at Birmingham in 1909—Thompson came second to Hobbs with an average of 33.37 in the Tests in South Africa that winter, besides taking 23 wickets.

Promotion came in 1905, and no one worked harder for it than the open-handed and enthusiastic President, Lord Lilford, and the Honorary Secretary, the gifted Mr. A. J. Darnell, a household name in Law, Politics and Sport.

During the first four seasons irresolute and unenterprising batting were the bane, excepting such as C. J. T. Pool's 166 at Worcester, Dr. H. C. Pretty's 200 in as many minutes at Chesterfield, and Thompson's not out 103 at Fenner's after Cambridge had routed them for 57 and replied with 405, all in 1906. Top-class spinners were specially feared. In 1907 Blythe of Kent took seventeen wickets in one day; and when at Ashley Down the County sank to a new low—12 all out—before Gloucestershire's Dennett, a telegram to the captain, E. M. Crosse, read: 'Bring the Boys Home— Mother.'

Thompson and East virtually monopolised the attack until 1908 when W. 'Bumper' Wells, who could make the ball fly disagreeably, earned a regular place. They commanded respect. At The Oval in 1906 Surrey were dismissed on a plumb pitch for 96; the same year Thompson secured fifteen for 167 against Leicestershire at Northampton. It was heartening to beat Lancashire by one wicket at Northampton; and Northants did *not* finish last in those years.

NEW BLOOD

Composed almost entirely of local men, the team received an enlivening 'shot in the arm' from outside. Fresh natives like the Denton twins, J. S. and W. H., both sound run-getters, F. 'Fanny' Walden, a mighty atom of cricket and soccer, and stout W. A. Buswell, a cheerful 'keeper, were joined by four bold batsmen, R. A. Haywood and C. N. Woolley from Kent, John Seymour from Sussex and versatile S. G. Smith, the outstanding West Indian all-rounder who was, moreover, the first high-class left-hander Northamptonshire possessed.

HALCYON DAYS

After a poor start in 1909, eight of nine consecutive matches were won, the bowling of Smith and Thompson, who each took a hundred wickets and were admirably contrasted, being supported by increasingly offensive batting and lively fielding. Despite a drop from seventh to tenth place in 1910, S. G. Smith notched a thousand runs; at Sheffield, Yorkshire were beaten for the first time by five wickets, G. A. T. Vials contributing a sparkling 100. With Gloucestershire at Northampton 1,391 runs were scored for thirty-six wickets, including a mighty 204 by Smith. At Portsmouth, Northants were in dire straits until Smith and Thompson added 232. In 1911 only once was a total of 300 exceeded against the attack; and the batting advanced in all the rightful qualities. Against Gloucestershire at home Thompson and Haywood hit 222 in two and a half hours; the same pair put on 236 at Dewsbury. East's seven for 11 at the expense of Lancashire compensated somewhat for two collapses. Kent, however, were overcome at Tonbridge by 135 runs, Thompson securing twelve wickets; and everyone pulled well to beat Yorkshire at Northampton by 44 runs.

In the wet 1912 Northants finished a close second to Yorkshire. Ten matches were won and one lost out of eighteen. A reasonable assumption is that if rain had not curtailed play on August 7, Yorkshire (103 and 105 for seven wickets) could have been beaten by Lancashire (347) and Northants (211 for eight wickets declared) could have upset Leicestershire (96 and 96 for six wickets)— and Northamptonshire would have displaced Yorkshire! The success was due to the determination of the captain, Vials, the collective power resulting from constant association—only twelve appeared in the County matches— and excellent, well-varied bowling. Vials headed the batting with an average of 28.26; Smith took 84 wickets at 12.15 runs each and Thompson 106 at 14.59 each.

RUMPUS AT LORD'S

All was not well with County Cricket and early in 1913 A. J. Darnell, a pioneer of the Saturday start, proposed to the Advisory Committee of M.C.C. that matches be restricted to two days and there be a system of promotion and regulation. Lord Hawke, who favoured a smaller Championship, complained that Northamptonshire were taking too much of a lead. After a rumpus at Lord's, Lord Harris stilled the troubled waters and Mr. Darnell apologised for having unintentionally caused antipathy—and a few days later Yorkshire were beaten at Leeds by 20 runs, Smith (the new captain) and Thompson collecting eighteen wickets.

Northants finished fourth, winning thirteen games. Batsmen made great strides, four reaching four figures—Haywood 1,453, Smith 1,424, W. H. Denton 1,055 and J. S. Denton 1,007—and Thompson mustered 902 runs. Between them, Thompson and Smith secured 255 wickets. At Bristol, 516 was compiled in little over five hours, this orgy being led by Smith and Haywood, who in two hours added 216 for the third partnership. At Leyton, W. H. Denton carried out his bat for a solid 230. At Horsham, Thompson and Smith, who each took ten wickets, bowled unchanged.

S. G. Smith's 'swan-song' in 1914 brought him 1,193 runs, average 41.13, and 99 wickets at 16.63 runs apiece. Again, his chief helper was Thompson. Despite a fall to ninth place, the County continued strongly all round. Against Sussex at Brighton their 557 for six wickets, declared, remains the highest ever; Smith stole the honours with 177, adding 180 with Thompson. Fifty-five matches had been won in six great years, but financially the club was as certain of instability as the Liberal Party was of power.

In 1919 S. G. Smith was domiciled in New Zealand and Thompson wounded and ill; the head and the right arm were gone. Under a succession of captains the County struggled. 1921 found Haywood glorious with 1,909 runs, average 42.42, including eight centuries; it was a severe blow when he departed that autumn. Financial losses resulted in two general meetings battling over Reconstruction; V. W. C. Jupp of Sussex and England was appointed Secretary and Stephen Schilizzi emerged as a benefactor of the practical 'Cricket is a business' School.

In February 1923 a prominent local agriculturalist, Alfred Cockerill, who had spent £10,000 in acquiring the County Ground, gave it to the club to be preserved for sport for ever; a unique gift. That year, however, Northants finished last for the first time.

JUPP THE CORNERSTONE

V. W. C. Jupp was qualified in 1924. The following summer he scored 1,143 runs and took 110 wickets; it was the cornerstone of the most successful season between the wars when nine encounters brought victory and eleventh place was attained. The short, broad and increasingly rotund Jupp threw himself into the fight against odds. Secretary for eleven years, captain for six, a nimble-footed batsman on all sorts of wickets and a grand adaptable off- and leg-spinner, he scored 13,635 runs, average 30.44, and collected 1,078 wickets, average 22.31; six times he achieved the 'double' for the County before he gave up in 1938.

In the 'twenties other remarkable exponents included Woolley, by now reliant on economy of effort at number one; 'Fanny' Walden, at his best when the need was greatest; A. P. R. Hawtin, a stylish and confident stroke-maker; Ben Bellamy, second best wicket-keeper-batsman in the country; 'Bumper' Wells, veteran fast bowler and hard hitter; length specialist A. E. Thomas, 'the William Attewell of Northants cricket'; two class batsmen in H. F. Bagnall and W. W. Timms; and E. W. 'Nobby' Clark, a fast left-hander with a beautiful action who touched a peak that few others of his generation reached. Eighteen seasons brought him 1,097 wickets at 21.31 runs apiece, and eight appearances for England.

The measure of the weakness was revealed to the full against Yorkshire, although Jupp, Wells, Thomas and Clark sometimes bowled wonderfully well against the strongest county.

THE ARRIVAL OF BAKEWELL

In 1930 the Australians were spun out at Northampton for 93, but Northants finished at the foot of the table. Things became worse, and although, in September 1931, a Special General Meeting assented to the continuance of the club, thorough-going retrenchment was advocated.

Northants commenced 1933 by overwhelming West Indies by an innings and 62 runs; though they finished disappointingly, A. H. Bakewell shone brightly. He became the first to reach 2,000 in all matches in a season, which included 246 against Nottinghamshire at Northampton and 257 against Glamorgan at Swansea in successive innings. A great future was being forecast for him. Making his debut in 1928, he impressed immediately with his brilliancy at short-leg; later his stroke-play won him his place for England. A better batsman than he looked, in an effort of 30 he would produce every stroke in the game, his off-driving being particularly exhilarating. Returning from Chesterfield after the last match of 1936, in which he batted superbly for 241 not out, Bakewell was injured in a tragic car smash; his career was finished and Northants, who would soon be bereft of Jupp and Clark, could ill-afford to lose him.

SNOWDEN'S FEATS

A. W. Snowden, an amateur opening batsman from Peterborough, made his debut against New Zealand in 1931 at the age of 17; he scored his first fifty against India and his maiden century against Australia. He captained the county at the age of 18 and before he was 21 he and Bakewell achieved a feat which was then without parallel by compiling two opening stands of over 100 on the same day against Warwickshire at Edgbaston. Unfortunately business claimed him soon after he came of age.

Between May 1935 and May 1939, 101 matches failed to produce a victory. It was a shocking patch, but several players epitomised 'Courage': J. E. Timms, a well-equipped and defiant cavalier batsman and relisher of any fight with high-bouncing bowlers; young Dennis Brookes, already looking an England batsman with his upstanding stance and style of purest simplicity; R. J. Partridge, swinging the new ball appreciably and spurred on by his thankless task; New Zealander, K. C. James, maintaining his international reputation behind the stumps; and a born leader, R. P. Nelson, the powerful left-handed Cambridge Blue, taking charge in 1938 and bringing the County finally out of the slough of despond in May 1939, when Leicestershire were vanquished at Northampton by an innings and 193 runs.

R. P. Nelson was killed, alas, in 1940; but Northamptonshire's Elder Statesman, A. P. R. Hawtin, and an enthusiastic captain, P. E. Murray Willis, kept the club in the news. Matches were played each war summer, and this shire which had finished seventeenth eight times between 1919 and 1939 did more for the game than any other.

The opening match in 1946 was appropriately at Lord's with Middlesex; at the close the Middlesex last pair were together and 23 runs were needed. There was a heightened tone about Northamptonshire's cricket; subsequent results disappointed. One recalls pleasurably the opening stands of Brookes and Percy Davis; left-handed Barron, so full of promise; the comeback of 'Nobby' Clark, for five overs the fastest in the land; Timms at cover; and slow left-hander Vincent Broderick, a young England hope; but few matches ended in their favour. A strong leader was required.

F. R. BROWN ERA

In 1949 F. R. Brown of Cambridge, Surrey and England, who was living at Daventry, took the reins, and a 'New Look' transformed the County. He understood the game thoroughly; at his elbow were a revitalised Executive and a playing staff rich in numbers and prowess. Winning ten matches in 1949, Northants jumped to sixth place; in 1952 they finished eighth. Skipper from 1949 to 1953, Brown, when freed from representative calls, scored with his pugnacious approach 4,331 runs, average 30.94, and took 391 wickets, average 23.23, while reshaping the seam, leg-break and googly departments. His right-hand man was the Yorkshireman Brookes; when at Headingly in 1953 Yorkshire were defeated for the first time for forty years, he was both acting-captain and century-maker. These years saw two pre-war Lancastrians in Norman Oldfield, overflowing with neat strokes and scorer in 1949 of 2,192 runs, average 49.81, and Albert Nutter, a hostile opening bowler; F. Jakeman who, by fierce left-handed hitting in 1951, made 558 runs in four consecutive innings before dismissal, including 258 not out off Essex at Northampton; Frank Tyson, the fastest bowler in the country; Australians 'Jock' Livingston, a left-handed batsman and ubiquitous fieldsman of sheer delight, and George Tribe of Herculean all-round feats; and Desmond Barrick, who hits the ball harder than most.

NOTABLE PERSONALITIES

As captain since 1954 the quiet, knowledgeable and shrewd Brookes has proved even more successful than Brown. No longer is the Northampton pitch easy paced and a nightmare to all bowlers alike; decisive results have increased. Since 1955, Surrey have been beaten four times; and Northants rose from seventh in 1954 and 1955 to fourth in 1956, and to second in 1957—the most successful campaign in their history, with 218 points from 28 matches, of which 15 were won. The battery of left-handed spinners, including one Tribe who accomplished the 'double' for the sixth successive year, and the 'Typhoon' that did *not* fizzle out into a gentle zephyr, together with a grand 'keeper in Andrew who created a new Northants record (68 victims), were the men-of-the-season. The potential is tremendous; the best has not yet been seen of the Cambridge Blue, Raman Subba Row, who in 1955 broke fresh ground in hitting 260 not out against Lancashire at Northampton, and several young bowlers who may well beat Tribe's record of 175 wickets taken the same year. Through it all remains Dennis Brookes, who first appeared in 1934, and is the sheet-anchor in a side of quick scorers. No one has amassed more runs for the county: 26,075, average 36.52, which includes 257 off Gloucestershire at Bristol in 1949; or more centuries: 63; or more runs in a season: 2,198, average 51.11 in 1952.

No reference to Northamptonshire cricket would be complete without mention of Leo Bullimer who was for 51 years the county scorer until retiring in 1950. His efforts in raising funds did much to keep Northamptonshire going during some of their worst financial crises.

A CONTROVERSY

Why do Northamptonshire engage so many players from outside (especially from overseas)? The answer is plain. A small county without either the population or resources of Yorkshire, Northamptonshire, nevertheless, possess a public with the palate for good cricket—and cricketers. Therefore, while talent scouts comb the country and trials are held regularly, experts from elsewhere are encouraged to become specially registered. Financial backing? That go-ahead modern firm British Timken is prepared to offer winter employment, something that redounds to the honour and skill of the present-day professional; and there is a football competition, organised by the county's eleven-year-old Supporters' Club which, whatever anyone else may think of it, makes football serve the needs of cricket. The county have 2,000 members; 63,000 odd if one includes those who support this competition.

Heading for the title of 'Champion County', Northamptonshire consider they are doing a real service to English cricket by making so many excellent craftsmen available for our delectation.

STORY OF NEW ZEALAND CRICKET
[1958]

BY CHARLES BRAY

The most interesting aspect of the 1958 essay on the visiting New Zealanders was the career of its author. As to the visitors, they were hardly equipped to cope with the full England side and were duly put to the sword, with their batting proving particularly substandard. At Edgbaston in the first Test they were skittled out by Trueman. At Lord's Laker and Lock ran through them twice, their aggregate of runs in two completed innings being only 121. At Headingly they made a mere 67 in their first innings and never came remotely within distance of their opponents, who three times defeated them by an innings. The decline of Bert Sutcliffe and the premature retirement of Martin Donnelly had much to do with their troubles and it was to be some years yet before they would be able to again match the best sides with confidence. In the account of New Zealand's history, there is no mention of the Canterbury player Daniel Reese, who came to England and played for W. G. Grace's London County side, went on to captain his country and did sterling work in helping to establish the credentials of New Zealand cricket.

The essay was written by Charles Bray, one of the most unusual figures of his time, an amateur who never attended a university and whose subsequent career enabled him to play first-class cricket while observing it from the detachment of the Press Box. Brighton-born, he began his journalistic career in Yorkshire, concurrently representing Bradford in league cricket. When transferred to Belfast he did the same for Ulster. In 1922 he became London editor of a Belfast newspaper and, being a Lobby correspondent, often turned out for Lords and Commons. In the 1920s he played club cricket for Southend before making his debut for Essex in 1927, remaining with the county till 1937 and often captaining the side. In 1931 he scored a century against the visiting New Zealanders. From 1935 to 1964 he wrote on cricket in 'The Daily Herald', played soccer for Leyton and won a Rugby Union cap for Northern Ireland. During the war he was chief P.R.O. to Sir Arthur Tedder, later becoming a war correspondent who covered the D-Day landings and the fall of Berlin. After leaving 'The Daily Herald' he became a freelance writer and published a history of Essex County Cricket Club.

A YORKSHIREMAN, James Cook, discovered New Zealand in 1769, but there is no evidence that this distinguished son of the 'broad acres' was an ardent cricketer or that he introduced the game to the natives of his newly-discovered land. More likely it came with the arrival of the military as it did in South Africa. In 1840 New Zealand was declared a Crown Colony. By that time cricket had made its appearance in both the North and South islands.

Nineteen years passed, however, before any definite competitive spirit appeared. In 1859 Auckland sent by slow coastal steamer (there was no other means of communication) a challenge to Wellington to play a cricket match. It took a long time for the challenge to reach its destination, a long time for Wellington to make up their minds and still more delay for the reply to get back to Auckland. Weeks went by. Then unannounced the Auckland team arrived in Wellington. The local lads were caught on the hop. Some of their best players, so history tells us, were up country and could not be contacted. Yet the match had to be played. Auckland went home cock-a-hoop having won by four wickets.

Three years later Wellington challenged Auckland to a return encounter. The match was duly played and again Wellington lost. But the foundations, upon which New Zealand was to build her Test cricket, had been well and truly laid. It was destined to be a hard uphill fight. There were, however, men of steel in this thinly-populated new country. The greater the difficulties the more determined were these early pioneers to place New Zealand on the cricket map of the world. One called Shadrach Jones of Dunedin took the first step. He was personally responsible for bringing Parr's All-England XI touring Australia in 1864 to New Zealand and it cost him £5,000. He didn't care. The ice was broken.

In 1876 Lillywhite's All-England team played eight matches, winning six and drawing two. In 1881–82 Shaw and Shrewsbury's English XI had seven games, five of which they won. Between those two visits the first Australian team sailed the Tasman sea, and played seven matches before going to England. A tremendous fillip was given to New Zealand cricket when Canterbury beat that side which included such illustrious names as Spofforth, Murdoch, Boyle, Garrett, Bannerman and Horan.

Those sturdy pioneers were now reaping some reward for their labours. Before the end of the century four more representative Australian teams toured New Zealand. Tasmania sent a side. So did Fiji and several came from Australian States. In 1902–3 Sir Pelham Warner skippered a team from England known as Lord Hawke's XI and in 1906–7 came the first M.C.C. side led by Captain Wynyard.

Lord Plunket was Governor of New Zealand at this time and it was in 1906 that he presented a challenge trophy (The Plunket Shield) to be competed for by the provinces. The four major associations are Auckland, Wellington, Canterbury and Otago, and each plays the other usually around Christmas because it is as well to remember that cricket in New Zealand always has been and still is strictly amateur apart from the odd professional coach.

Landmarks in the Dominion's cricket history now became frequent. After the First World War there was a gap, but in 1922–23 A. C. MacLaren led an M.C.C. side which included such brilliant players as A. P. F. Chapman, the Hon. F. S. Calthorpe, Tom Lowry, a New Zealander then up at Cambridge who was later to captain his country on two tours of England, Tich Freeman and Dick Tyldesley. The two professionals were a great success and a great attraction. So was the young Percy Chapman and the burly Tom Lowry who rather indiscreetly hit 130 in the third match at Wellington.

The year 1927 was a red-letter one in New Zealand's cricket history. It saw their first visit to England as a cricketing country. Tom Lowry led the team. They were not accorded Test match status but did sufficiently well to warrant official recognition for the side which followed four years later.

The first Lowry team played 26 first-class matches, won seven, lost five and drew 14. The team included names subsequently to become famous not only in New Zealand but wherever the game was played: C. S. Dempster; Charles Dacre; Roger Blunt; J. E. Mills; M. L. Page, later to captain his country; K. C. James, a great little wicket-keeper; and W. E. Merritt, a spin bowler of international class. Merritt, only 18, took 169 wickets in all matches. At the end of the tour Dacre signed as professional for Gloucestershire. Later Merritt went to Lancashire league, Blunt took up a business appointment in Nottingham, James qualified for Northamptonshire and Dempster for Leicestershire.

In this his first visit, C. S. Dempster showed his remarkable skill with the bat. He made 1,430 runs, average 44.68, and was second in the bowling averages although bowling was not one of his recognised accomplishments. Six of the New Zealanders scored over a thousand runs on that tour. The bowling was weak. The fielding, appalling at first, improved tremendously under the stern direction of the captain.

Harold Gilligan, who has been New Zealand's representative in England for many years, took the next M.C.C. side to the Dominion in the winter of 1929–30. They opened with five matches in Australia, but the main purpose of the tour was to play in New Zealand. This was an even stronger side than the previous one. Gilligan had with him such brilliant amateurs as K. S. Duleepsinhji, E. W. Dawson, G. B. Legge, M. J. Turnbull and M. J. C. Allom and six of the leading professionals of the day—F. E. Woolley, E. H. Bowley, M. S. Nichols, T. S. Worthington, F. Barratt and W. L. Cornford. The three Tests originally arranged were increased to four but only the first produced a definite result, England winning by eight wickets.

This was a famous match. Batting first, New Zealand lost three wickets for 15 runs to Nichols and then Allom, bowling in his first Test, took four wickets in five balls, including a hat-trick. Duleepsinhji, who prior to the first Test could not make a run, suddenly hit form and in six Test innings scored 358 runs, twice not out, for an average of 89.75. In the second Test Dempster and Mills made centuries for New Zealand in the first innings. Frank Woolley achieved the remarkable bowling figures of seven for 76 in an innings of 440 runs.

A year later (1931) New Zealand undertook their second tour of England and this time with Test match status, but only one Test was allotted them. They did so well in their opening matches—a strong M.C.C. team was defeated by an innings and 122 runs—and made such a brilliant recovery to save the first Test at Lord's that two more Tests were arranged. The Lord's game is still regarded as the most famous in New Zealand cricket history. It was their first Test match abroad. It was at headquarters and it ended in New Zealand striving for victory after being 230 runs behind on the first innings. Heroes of the fight-back were Dempster (120), Blunt (96), Page (104) and the skipper Tom Lowry, who made 34 with an injured hand. England, set to get 240 to win in two hours twenty minutes, never tried to get the runs.

In the second Test at The Oval New Zealand took a thrashing, Herbert Sutcliffe, Hammond and Duleepsinhji making hundreds which enabled Jardine to declare at 416 for four wickets. The tourists were unable to reach 200 in either innings. The third Test at Old Trafford was washed out, play being possible only on the third day.

Of the 32 first-class matches, New Zealand won six, lost only three, the other 23 being drawn. The strength of the batting and the comparative weakness of the bowling was undoubtedly the reason for the high number of drawn games. Dempster, Blunt, Mills, Lowry, Vivian and Weir all made over a thousand runs. No bowler took a hundred wickets although Merritt came within one of that feat, but the average cost was 26.48 runs apiece.

I have reason to remember this New Zealand tour. In their first match against Essex, Dempster made a double century. I dropped him in the slips when he was 46. Jack O'Connor made 129 (remember the figure) in our first innings. In the second match against my county Tom Lowry made 129 before he was caught on the boundary by me, a catch which caused some controversy because I could not say whether I was over the boundary line when I caught the ball. The umpire consulted the crowd and eventually gave Lowry out. It has remained a subject of good-natured banter between us ever since. To complete the coincidence of 129 I made exactly that score in our second innings.

The winter of 1932 recorded another landmark in New Zealand cricket history. So impressive had been Tom Lowry's 1931 side that when D. R. Jardine took his famous 'Bodyline' team to Australia, New Zealand was included in the tour; two Tests were played and both drawn. Walter Hammond was then in his prime. He made 227 at Christchurch and 336 not out at Auckland—then the record individual Test score. The precedent established by Jardine's team was continued. It is now the normal practice for the England team to cross to New Zealand after the end of each Australian tour.

G. O. Allen's team of 1936–37 did not play any Tests in New Zealand because the Dominion was sending a team to England the following summer. This time Lowry came as manager but played in a number of matches. M. L. Page was the captain with H. G. Vivian vice-captain.

Three Tests were played and again it was made apparent that three days were not enough to ensure definite results. Two of the three were drawn, England winning the Manchester match by 130 runs. The third Test is historic in that Denis Compton made his debut. He scored 65 before being run out unluckily. A hard drive from Hardstaff cannoned off the bowler's hand into the stumps with Compton out of his ground. The record of M. L. Page's side was on a par with the previous New Zealand touring team. Out of the 32 first-class matches, nine were won, nine were lost and 14 drawn. Again the side was top-heavy in batting. Two brilliant young batsmen made their appearance, W. M. Wallace, aged 20, and M. P. Donnelly, 19. They finished first and second in the team's batting averages. The tall W. A. Hadlee was also a most promising performer. John Cowie was the pick of the bowlers, taking over a hundred wickets, the first New Zealander to accomplish that feat on an England tour.

The Second World War hit this young cricketing country as hard if not harder than any other. But when W. R. Hammond's M.C.C. team returned after playing four matches, including one Test in New Zealand after the 1946–47 Australian tour, they brought back glowing accounts of a young left-hander named Sutcliffe. He had hit two hundreds, 197 and 128, in one match against the tourists for Otago and scored 58 in the only Test.

W. A. Hadlee showed that he had developed into a class batsman and it was no surprise when he was chosen to lead the 1949 team to England.

This was unquestionably New Zealand's best team. They drew all four Tests with England. Thirteen of the 32 first-class matches were won. The only defeat was by Oxford University. Under the genial managership of Mr. J. H. Phillipps and the efficient captaincy of W. A. Hadlee so popular did the tourists become that not only did the receipts cover the £25,000 expenses but a net profit of £15,000 was taken back to New Zealand. Martin Donnelly and Bert Sutcliffe had a superb season both making over 2,000 runs. Sutcliffe scored seven centuries, Donnelly five. V. J. Scott and W. M. Wallace also hit five hundreds each and J. R. Reid four. The batting was immensely strong. A pity the bowling was not as good. Cowie was affected by minor strains and therefore did not repeat his success of 1937. He was now 37. Age was beginning to tell.

A young fast bowler, J. A. Hayes, tore a muscle so badly halfway through the tour that he was unable to play again. The bulk of the bowling fell on the tubby, cheerful T. B. Burtt, slow left-arm immaculate length, good flight, who attacked the off-stump so accurately that he constantly tied down the opposing batsmen. Burtt took 128 wickets for an average of 22.88.

This side did not achieve the long-coveted first victory over England but they did well enough for New Zealand to shed the mantle of 'the poor relation' of international cricket and to warrant a full Test programme with the home country in future.

It was therefore a profound disappointment when Sir Leonard Hutton's Ashes-winning team went on to New Zealand in 1955 to find that first-class cricket in the Dominion had suffered an astonishing set-back. Bert Sutcliffe was only a shadow of his former self. Hadlee, Wallace, Donnelly, Scott, Cowie and Burtt had all left the international arena. None of similar calibre had been discovered to fill the gaps. The result was that the M.C.C. won all four matches. The two Tests must have been bitterly disappointing for New Zealand. The first they lost by eight wickets and the second went against them by an innings and 20 runs in three days. England achieved a world's record by dismissing New Zealand in the second innings for 26, the lowest total in Test cricket.

Since that disaster, however, New Zealand have registered their first Test victory. It was against the West Indies at Auckland in March 1956 by 190 runs. The fact that New Zealand had lost the first three Tests did not lessen the joy in winning their first victory in 26 years of Test cricket.

So to 1958. This will be New Zealand's fifth official visit to England. For the first time they will play five Tests of five days' duration. We look forward to having them here again and wish them a happy and prosperous tour.

THE LOVE OF CRICKET [1958]

BY THE RT. HON. LORD BIRKETT, P.C.

Towering above all else in the 1958 Almanack was an authentic Eng.Lit. essay by the juridical eminence William Norman, First Baron Birkett (1888–1962), vice-president of Lancashire County Cricket Club despite his lifelong idolatry of Surrey, which features in one of his favourite after-dinner jokes. He recalled that as a small boy praying to the deity for each Surrey player individually, beginning with 'God bless Hobbs, God bless Hayward', proceeding down the order and ending with the fine flourish 'and God bless byes, leg-byes and no-balls'. He was a regular turn at the annual Cricket Writers' Club and was often the star speechmaker at cricketing occasions. When not watching cricket, he was one of the nation's most distinguished legal figures, serving as Judge of the King's Bench Division and Lord Justice of Appeal. More important, he was a good judge of a cricketer. In its obituary of Birkett, Wisden described this essay as 'a little gem'. And so it is.

IT is one of life's little ironies that if you would write about the summer game for *Wisden* you must do it in the depth of winter. Your words will not be read until the winter is past and the rain is over and gone and the time of the singing birds is come; but you write them when the winds blow and the rains fall and the clouds lie very near to the earth. It is perhaps just as well that this is so, for in winter the love of cricket can be a rampart to the mind. Memory can bring back the sunlit fields, and Imagination can conjure up in anticipation the joys that belong to the English spring, and cricket played between the showers. At any rate it is so with me, and though the love of cricket has been sung ever since James Love set down his opening line more than two hundred years ago—

'Hail, Cricket! glorious, manly British game!'—

and though the songs and the writings are in four thousand volumes in the British Museum, the theme never grows old, and will no doubt continue to be sung long after we are all gathered to the pavilion of a better world and gaze out on Elysian swards.

I have assumed, of course, that all who read these words are genuine lovers of cricket, for otherwise all that I have written is vanity and vexation of spirit; my words are intended for those who are of the household of faith, and even in that house there are many mansions. The great John Selden who came from the Inner Temple, I am glad to think, and gave us the famous *Table Talk*, reminded us some centuries ago that whilst all men are 'equally given to their pleasures, one man's pleasure lies one way and another's another.' What makes one man a lover of cricket with a passionate intensity, and at the same time makes another equally good man quite indifferent to it, is past all finding out. 'One man's meat is another man's poison' has been true in all ages and is now proverbial. It applies to the major as well as to the minor pleasures of life, and only one thing is certain and that is—

> *'Never lad that trod on leather*
> *Lived to feast his heart with all.'*

But the lovers of cricket make up a very great company, and a delightfully mixed one. Over the past two hundred years the poets and the prose writers have been chanting the love of cricket until there is no human experience, grave or slight, that has gone unrecorded. Think of the ecstasy with which Norman Gale celebrated the feat of bowling three curates with three consecutive balls—

> *'I bowled three sanctified souls*
> *With three consecutive balls!*
> *What do I care if Blondin trod*
> *Over Niagara falls?'*

And think of the grave John Nyren compiling the only true cricket classic we possess, and creating one of the immortal books of the world because of the unquenchable love of cricket it breathes in every word and line.

John Nyren with the help of Cowden Clarke, or Cowden Clarke with the help of John Nyren (the mystery will never be solved), produced *The Cricketers of my Time* but the genius of the book extends far beyond the playing of the game, and makes immortal the men of Hambledon who played at Broadhalfpenny Down and Windmill Down in the remote Hampshire countryside. Because of Nyren, Harris and Beldham are as real as Grace, and with the cheering hosts who watched them play, crying 'Tich and Turn,' as Silver Billy ran, they still stir the imagination with delight.

Today most people love the game of cricket because they play it. Happy indeed are they. They fill the schools, and the Universities and the Clubs, and the Village sides, and even the streets where the three chalk marks on the wall serve as wickets. For the most part they are young men and women rejoicing in their youth; but there are some who no longer can be counted young, who find their names getting nearer and nearer to the Byes in the batting order as the years pass. Saturday afternoon for such as these is still the great day of the week, and the cricket pitch what the Bat and the Ball Inn was to Nyren, 'a little Heaven below'.

After all, the great W. G. made 69 runs in the last match he ever played, and was then not out; and he was 66 years of age. At the age of 48, when playing against Somerset, he was c Palairet b Woods for 186, having batted for four hours fifty minutes, and went on to take six Somerset wickets for 64 runs in 48 overs.

No doubt those who love cricket because they play it love also the setting of the game, and find this particular love to grow and develop with the years. They love their own ground set in our incomparable English countryside; they love the companionship of their fellow players, this, too, growing stronger as time passes, and memories accumulate of fine and gallant stands in critical moments, and of wonderful loyalties displayed; they love the long days in the sun, and the curious charm that belongs to a May day of showers; they love the moments, fielding at the boundary's edge, when they have time to see the great, white clouds overhead as miracles of beauty; and they savour with keen pleasure all the joys that belong to the best months of the year, and which the summer brings to the true cricketer. Cricket has imperishable memories and indestructible traditions, and the lover of cricket enters into them and makes them his own.

The window of the room where I write these words commands a distant view of the Chiltern Hills and the long sweep of the Misbourne valley. Today, as I write, the familiar scene is almost blotted out with dark low-lying ominous clouds, and the rain beats on my roof with a fierce insistence. Yet down there in the valley, lying close to a beautiful old town, is a cricket field of a singular beauty that I know well. It was once part of a vast park and is set amidst noble trees with the Mansion on the hill-top still to be seen. There is a small pavilion with a little white verandah, and a flag pole where the club colours fly when a match is being played, and attractive wooden benches are set at intervals round the lovely turf. It will be a desolate scene this morning, I know, although I cannot see it, yet here in this book-lined room I can recall this ground, sunlit and radiant, as I have so often seen it, and as it will soon be again. But if you would know how deep and universal is the love of cricket you must know that one of the great highways to the north passes the very edge of the ground. From April to October, when matches are being played, and the white figures of the players can be seen through the trees, then the cars come to a stop at the side of the road, and the occupants watch, if only for a few overs, and enjoy a few moments in this essentially English scene.

Farther up the valley is another lovely ground which adjoins the railway. And there, whenever a match is being played, and a train passes, the passengers crowd to the windows in the hope (usually vain!) of seeing at least one ball bowled, or one run made, or a catch taken. (Curious how often when a train passes it is the end of an over or a wicket has fallen a few moments before!)

It was a sure instinct which made J. M. Barrie picture the dead returning to old and familiar scenes, and the Englishmen dropping out on the endless march to lean over the gate to watch the cricket on a village ground. It was the same instinct that led T. C. P. Wilson to write his lovely but little-known verse of the war heroes who were making the same endless and eternal march, who suddenly exclaimed in recognition—

> *'God! but it's England,' then they said,*
> *'And there's a cricket field.'*

But many lovers of cricket turn to the great contests staged at Lord's and The Oval and the great grounds whose names have power to evoke the most fragrant memories. It has long been remarked how certain words can stir the emotions in the most remarkable way. To the cricket lover

LORD'S is such a word. Lord's belongs to the whole cricketing world as does no other place. It is not only filled with memories of Grace and Hobbs and a thousand more, but it belongs to Bradman and Victor Trumper and Learie Constantine and George Headley and Nourse, too, and that great company of men from almost every nation under heaven, where English is spoken.

Lord's holds very special memories for all those who were ever there and in whatever capacity. For myself, I think of Bradman coming out of the shade of the pavilion on a June Saturday night more than twenty years ago, before the applauding thousands, and driving Verity for three successive fours off the first three balls he received. It was thrilling beyond all telling. I have seen Bradman make his double centuries, but that moment of mastery on the greatest ground in the world on that June night remains in the memory for ever. He made 36 runs only, and the experts say that he didn't make them very well; but for me it was an innings of beauty and power in an unforgettable setting. And a hundred great moments come to the mind unbidden when the talk is of the love of cricket.

The first sight of MacLaren at Old Trafford; Hammond and Paynter in their noble stand at Lord's in 1938; Denis Compton coming out of the pavilion to a perfect storm of shrill, schoolboy cheering; Jack Hobbs at the wicket or at cover point; Frank Woolley standing up to the fearsome attack of Gregory and McDonald; the fielding of Jack Fingleton; Pellew racing along the boundary, as Clem Hill must have done when he caught Lilley in the most famous Test match of all; Patsy Hendren running between the wickets with his scampering, twinkling feet; Peter May, Tom Graveney, Colin Cowdrey, all visibly in the great tradition; David Sheppard standing firm in a crisis; and a great host of cricketers of every rank and clime. Some lovers of cricket love to read the annals of the game; and some find pleasure in just watching cricket wherever it is played, with a preference perhaps for the lovely little ground tucked away in the countryside.

But to all lovers of cricket there is a kind of music in the sound of the great names, the sound of Grace and Hobbs, the sound of Trent Bridge and Old Trafford; but the greatest music of all is the sound of the bat against the ball. Mr. Ratcliff Ellis expressed this idea to perfection in his lines—

> *'The merry click of bat against the ball,*
> *The expectant hush, the cheering that proclaims*
> *Skill of the greatest of all English games;*
> *Flutter of flags, the branches of the trees*
> *Swaying beneath the gentle summer breeze;*
> *No sweeter music in the world is found*
> *Than that upon an English cricket ground.'*

FROM DR. GRACE TO PETER MAY [1958]

BY HERBERT STRUDWICK

One of the inestimable advantages of living to a great age is that few of your contemporaries remain to contradict you, so that a magisterial authority attaches to any comparative judgments you may care to make. When Herbert Strudwick (1880–1970) nominates Tom Richardson and Jack Hobbs as the greatest cricketers he knew, who is prepared to argue with someone who saw Grace and Bradman, Lindwall and Larwood? Strudwick enjoyed one of the longest cricket careers in history, joining the Surrey ground staff as a boy, and serving as player and scorer for a total of sixty years, becoming an idol of The Oval crowd. He toured Australia four times. But perhaps most impressive of all is that a man who travelled to the ground in a hansom retained his relevance for long enough to be interviewed on television. In his charming and illuminating retrospective, Strudwick describes his tactic of chasing the ball to the leg boundary if no fielder was available. What he is tactful enough not to add is that effective though this tactic was, its unorthodoxy caused considerable disquiet in the councils of Wisden, whose editor one year suggested that the Surrey club institute a tariff of fines to be imposed on Strudwick until he managed to curb the habit. The suggestion was never taken up, the habit was never curbed and nobody ever complained.

Strudwick was one of that group of pre-Great War players who lived on to a great age. He was ninety when he died; his teammate Andrew Sandham lived to be 91, Sydney Barnes was 94, Wilfred Rhodes 95. Apart from the sentimental pleasure to be derived from the spectacle of famous old men enjoying the fruits of survival, the benefit to posterity was inestimable. To hear any of these men voicing their opinions was like receiving the tablets of the law. This essay by Strudwick was to receive much critical praise.

THEY say that all good things must come to an end. Sad though it is to me, my official connection with Surrey, which began in 1897, finished last season when, after being wicket-keeper for 30 years and scorer for a similar period, I made way for a younger man. In bidding good-bye to The Oval, known the world over for the great cricketers it has produced and the exciting games it has staged, I cannot sufficiently thank the Surrey Club and the committees I have served under for all those years for giving me so much help and showing me so much kindness.

I feel, too, that I owe a debt to a lady, a Miss Wilson, daughter of the Vicar of Mitcham, where I was born on January 28, 1880. She used to supervise the choir-boys' cricket matches in which, when I was about ten years old, I took part. It was my habit to run in from cover to the wicket to take returns from the field and I apparently did this well enough to prompt her to say one day: 'You ought to be a wicket-keeper.' From that time I became a stumper and I was sufficiently good at the job to play for Surrey for 25 years and to keep for England 28 times at a period when Australia and South Africa were our only Test opponents.

I have known nearly all the famous cricketers of the twentieth century, from Dr. W. G. Grace to Peter May, the present Surrey and England captain. One recollection I have of Grace was when I played for Surrey against London County at the Old Crystal Palace ground in 1902. On the day that 'W. G.' bowled me for my second 'duck' of the match, Southampton and Sheffield United were fighting out the F. A. Cup Final, also at the Crystal Palace. As I passed the Doctor on my way out, he said to me: 'Why didn't you tell me you got a duck in the first innings, youngster? I would have give you one to get off the mark.' 'Never mind, sir,' I said. 'I want to see the second-half of that Cup Final.' And away I scampered.

The young professional of today has a much easier time than when I began, of that I am sure. First of all, he has a fixed wage guaranteed all the year round, differing, I presume, according to the ability of the player. My first wage was £1 per week—no match fees—for four months during the summer, expenses, train-fare and 2s. 6d. a day for lunch. Tea was free, and how we enjoyed it. If we could not get lunch on the ground, we went to a pub, for there was always one close by. There we had either arrowroot biscuit and cheese or a large piece of bread and cheese. That cost 9d. or 1s. 0d., so we made 1s. 6d. on our lunch allowance—which was then quite a lot of money.

As there were nearly 40 on the staff and a lot of amateurs came in for the club matches, we had only a few games each summer until we got a place in the Second Eleven. Now the staff numbers only about 24 and it is something of a job to find enough players. We spent most of our time bowling to members. Doing this from half-past eleven till half-past six was a much more tiring job than playing. That is a thing of the past, for now there are very few members who take a net. They used to place coins on top of the stumps, and these went to the bowlers who hit the stumps. Needless to say, the senior professionals took the 'half-crown batsmen', leaving the sixpenny ones to the youngsters.

The chief enjoyment is when a team goes off to play in some club games, and the boys are not only playing most days now, but earning good money because few amateurs are available, more's the pity.

When I went to The Oval for a trial in 1896, I went behind in the nets and received a smack on the head from a fast ball from Len Braund. They told me I was too young to be taken on, but I came back and in the first trial in 1898 Braund, who was bowling slow leg-breaks, suddenly whipped in a very fast ball wide of the off-stump and split the joint of my first finger. I stood close up to the stumps and had never played on so fast a pitch or taken a bowler who did that sort of thing. With three wicket-keepers already on the staff, I thought this might mean the end of my engagement, but H. Wood and C. Marshall were getting on in years and, Fred Stedman being eight years older than I was, I felt there was some hope.

There was no ceremony about the arrival of a new member of the ground staff. I received no introduction to any of the players, just told my duties and where to find the young players' room. I was lucky to find three Mitcham men already there, two brothers, A. and W. Baker, and W. Montgomery, and they took me in hand. All have passed over now, worse luck, for they were charming fellows.

After seeing a few matches, I made up my mind to go all out to get into the county side. The new Pavilion was nearly finished in the year I started, 1898, and there were two large rooms for the players, one upstairs for those who had played in the first and second teams and the other downstairs for the rest. There were also separate doors to get on to the ground. I once went upstairs and ran into Tom Hayward, who demanded: 'Who are you?' I told him and he said: 'You have the advantage of me and your place is downstairs.'

Being very shy, I felt that this was a bad start for me, but it did not break my spirit, and the will to win and get up those stairs was stronger than ever. Little did I then dream that I should be using that room for nearly 60 years.

The great Surrey players of that day were a tough lot and it was hard work to get under their skins. Until you reached their level you were lucky to get an answer if you spoke to them! I played with a number of them before I finished and they were grand chaps. I always used to feel sad when the old ones left and that is why I took on the scoring job when I finished playing in 1927. I did not want to leave the boys; and after 60 years I feel the same.

Certain incidents stick in the mind. I remember once missing Carpenter, of Essex, when he was 29. 'Sorry about that,' said Carpenter sympathetically. So was I, for he was 199 when he gave his next chance—and this time I held it.

Then there was the occasion of my first Gentlemen and Players match when I asked Albert Trott how I could find his fast ball, which he disguised so well. 'You'll soon find it,' Albert told me. It was some time before he bowled it and when he did it just missed the leg-stump and hit me full toss on the left foot. I was hopping round in great pain when Albert came up to me. 'You found it all right then,' he said.

I had just received my invitation to tour Australia with the M.C.C. team of 1911 when I shared a hansom cab with Bill Lockwood to Lord's, where we were to play Middlesex. Bill said to me: 'Matey, I'm going to Australia with you this winter.' I said: 'Are you, Bill? That's good.' He said: 'You watch me bowl today.' At that time we were going over Vauxhall Bridge when the horse stumbled and landed on its knees. Off went the two cricket bags, and I remarked that that was not a good start. However, Bill got nine wickets that day—but he did not go to Australia.

Slow bowlers always employed a deep field, or two if the batsmen were quick on their feet and able to get out to the ball. Nottingham marl spread over the table after the end of each season was taken into the pitches by rain and weather. This made the surface fine in hard weather, but very nasty after rain, and matches were often finished by lunch-time on the second day, for there was then no covering of the pitch and only a bag of sawdust protected the bowlers' footholes.

I remember a match at Packer's Ground at Bristol when we were batting on the second day and, following overnight rain, Charlie Parker, the Gloucestershire left-hander, went on to bowl. The rain had penetrated through the sawdust and as Parker attempted to deliver the ball, he slipped and fell. 'I can't bowl on that,' said Charlie, and the game was held up for twenty minutes while the groundsmen and umpires got to work with rakes and shovels to improve the foothold. At the end of the match Gloucestershire wanted quite a few runs with one wicket to fall. This could have been far different had the pitch been covered.

In my younger days cricket was the only summer sport, except for golf and lawn-tennis, which were too expensive for the average chap. So most people played cricket and the majority of spectators understood the finer points of the game and appreciated good bowling besides good batting and fielding. For that reason crowds of that time showed more patience than those of today. They were content to watch and enjoy cricket, knowing full well that the bowler was doing his best to get the batsman out and not to give him runs. Another thing, cricket received more space in the newspapers and it was given to good news and not to how many 4s a batsman hit and how long he batted. I wish that reporters would be more free with praise instead of finding so much to criticise in the best game in the world.

More amateurs played 60 years ago than now. In 1899 Surrey had seven at different times, Gloucestershire seven, Somerset eight, Middlesex seven, Kent eight, Essex six, Hampshire five, and so on. Now the amateurs cannot spare the time and so have taken up golf. As long as I can remember, Surrey have had an amateur captain and I hope they will always find one good enough to take over. They are lucky to have such a fine player as Mr. May to lead them and to captain England.

I think there were more first-class players in every county in my time than nowadays and the strength of the sides was more equal. One finds it difficult to realise that Nottinghamshire were at the bottom of the Championship table last summer. I did not like to see it, for when I first started they were a very powerful team. Then there are the changes in the Laws—larger stumps, new L.B.W. Law, different scoring of points and the changing of the ball. At one time, no change of the ball was permitted unless it lost its shape. Later a new ball was allowed when 200 runs had been scored, but only in recent years have the number of overs bowled counted as an alternative. It began with experiments in 1947 with 55 overs, later changed to 65 overs and now 75 overs.

I recall Mr. Fender once bowling a ball which went very wide of the leg-stump for four byes. 'What's the idea, skipper?' I asked him. He replied: 'I want to get the new ball.' 'Right,' I said, 'you bowl some long hops and full-pitches and they'll soon get the runs. I'm going to stand back. But,' I added, 'I don't see why they should get 200. Bowl 'em out!'

I was naturally delighted when I got my first game with Surrey's first team, against the West Indies in 1900, though I had the feeling that a better man in Fred Stedman was standing down. Wicket-keepers used to have to put up with a good deal of knocking about then, for it was not always possible to gauge how the ball would come to you and our equipment was not what it is now. Stedman used to protect his chest with a copy of the South Western Railway time-table and on one occasion, after receiving a specially heavy blow, he remarked to a team-mate: 'I shall have to catch a later train tonight. That one knocked off the 7.30!'

I was never at any time nervous on the field and I always did my best. A wicket-keeper needs patience because he cannot make his own chances. He must expect a catch from every ball and not a stumping chance which will make him snatch at it. If he catches the ball, he can soon break the wicket if the batsman is out of his ground. Once when I went out to bat against Somerset their wicket-keeper, W. Hill, said to me: 'I've been out here all day and haven't had a chance of a catch or a stumping.' I said: 'Don't worry, you will.' 'No,' he said, 'I have given it up.' I gave him two chances—and he missed both!

I liked to save every run possible. I often used to chase the ball to the boundary if it were played on the leg-side where no fieldsman was placed. On one occasion when we were playing Kent, Lockwood was standing at point a long way back, so that the batsman, by pushing the ball towards him, was able to steal quite a number of singles. So at length I moved right up to the stumps, and as the bowler delivered the ball, dashed out towards point, picked up the ball and ran out A. P. Day. If the batsman had missed his stroke, the ball would have gone for four byes! Another thing, I often used to take catches in front of the wicket—sometimes almost off the bat—especially when 'Razor' Smith made the ball jump.

Though the performance of winning seven Championships in successive seasons might be considered to give them pride of place, it is an open question whether the present side is the best Surrey have had, for there were some very fine teams in the past. The batting has not been too strong for the last two seasons, and that may have helped them, because they wasted no time over unnecessary runs. I do not think they have ever had a better bowling side. How the 1906 team would have shaped on The Oval pitch today with the larger stumps and the new L.B.W. Law is hard to say. The batsmen were better, but they might not have got so many runs under changed conditions. I think the bowlers would have done better than they used to.

The captain who began this run of Championship successes, Mr. Surridge, did great work in moulding the team to catch and field as he did, especially close in on the leg-side. What a tonic to bowlers that meant. The bowling of Alec Bedser, Jim Laker, Tony Lock and Peter Loader, backed up by such wonderful catching by Mr. Surridge, Michael Stewart, Lock and Ken Barrington has been beyond praise. The last year that Mr. Surridge captained the side, 1956, Surrey looked as if they had no chance of the title and some of the players said as much to the skipper. 'We'll win it yet,' said Mr. Surridge. That is the secret: the will to win. To be without four of your best players, especially bowlers who are hard to find, for ten matches and still finish at the top is a magnificent achievement. Mind you, I don't think Surrey's performance could have been done years ago when there were so many strong counties.

It is difficult to say who is the best batsman I have seen. So many have appealed to me at different times. I feel that I must give first place to Sir Jack Hobbs for his play on all wickets and against all types of bowling. He is the only batsman about whom I felt that he would not get out till he wanted to. Generally he threw his wicket away after scoring a century. I remember G. A. Faulkner after an England tour in South Africa, saying to Jack: 'I only bowled you one googly.' 'Why,' said Jack, 'I didn't know you bowled one.' Faulkner said: 'You hit the first one I bowled for four. If you didn't know it, how did you know it would turn from the off?' 'I didn't,' answered Jack. 'I watched it off the pitch.' Yes, Jack had shots all off the wickets to different parts of the field.

K. S. Ranjitsinhji was the most polished batsman in my experience. His perfect leg-glide was one of his favourite strokes, even off the middle stump. He played fast bowling with the greatest of ease, placing the bowlers to all quarters of the compass. I believe that he could have made as many runs as he wanted to. I remember once when he was plumb l.b.w. to Tom Richardson and given not out, he went on to make 200. Then he deliberately skied a ball from McDonnell for Richardson to catch. During the time he was at Cambridge, he used whenever possible to engage Bill Lockwood and Richardson to bowl to him.

Sir Don Bradman I consider the best run-getter of my time. He never seemed to tire, he had all the other batsmen's shots—and a few of his own. He was also the best fielder I have seen. When he was fielding deep on the leg-side during a Test at The Oval, I did not see any batsman run more than a single from a ball played anywhere near him, and his return to the wicket-keeper was a full toss right over the stumps. There have been lots of great batsmen from Australia, but never one as good.

One of the best forcing batsmen England have ever had was Walter Hammond. He could play strokes all round the wicket, and his favourite drive through the covers was a joy to watch. I recall in 1928, when we were playing Gloucestershire at Cheltenham, that Mr. Fender was forced to place a cover-point, two extra-covers and a mid-off, and still Hammond found a way past them without giving them a chance to stop the ball. In that match he hit 139 in the first innings and 143 in the second and held ten catches. He was also a very fine bowler and could field anywhere. Nobody is taught to hit like him nowadays. I do wish cricket instructors would teach their pupils the way to hit the ball, the way to play back and force it off the back foot, instead of forward, forward and again forward.

Another great batsman was Victor Trumper, a hard hitter who was a delight to watch. How I would have loved to see Bradman and Trumper batting together. Tom Hayward, too, was a demon against fast bowling. He once made four separate centuries in a week. I was lucky enough to be in with him when he made one of them at Nottingham. When I went in he said to me: 'Run for the fifth ball or the sixth.' If it happened to be the fifth ball and I had a chance to get a run, he refused the call. After he got his 100, I was run out! He used to help pick the side and would come down to the Surrey dressing-room and say to Razor Smith: 'I bet you half a crown you are playing.' Although Razor knew he was selected, he always took the bet. I once said to Razor: 'You know you are playing. They can't leave you out.' Razor grinned and said: 'I know when I am well off.' Hayward did the 'double' one year and then gave up bowling when he began to make big scores.

Mr. May is now occupying the place once filled by Jack Hobbs and Tom Hayward and is England's leading batsman with powerful shots all round. When he goes to the wicket he is out to make runs and stands up nearly straight ready to hit the first ball, if it wants hitting, not prepared to play forward for the first few overs. A four off the first ball is the best tonic to make one feel at home and relaxed. Against Nottinghamshire at The Oval last season Jepson, the fast bowler, was bowling when May went in. The first ball he received May hit over the bowler's head for six. There was a look of astonishment on Jepson's face as he watched it go. The next delivery was hit in the same direction for four. Only a class player could do that. Mr. May, besides being a great cricketer, is a most charming man.

Sir Leonard Hutton was another outstanding batsman, though not the dashing player that Bradman was. Hutton had plenty of patience, but never a loose ball passed him and his cover-point shots were perfect.

What a joy to watch was Denis Compton. I wish a few more batsmen would use their feet as he did and play the strokes he did; there would be no half-empty grounds. Edrich and Compton were a great pair and the only two who received constant mention by the Press after the war. 'Patsy' Hendren was another who gave much pleasure to the crowds, whether batting or fielding, and what a lovely companion.

There are so many I would like to mention, worthy men all. Frank Woolley, the best and hardest-hitting of left-handers I have seen. He stood straight up, very seldom playing forward, but his shots off the back foot and his powerful drives delighted everybody except the bowlers. In his day he was among our best all-rounders.

Andy Sandham, Jack Hobbs's opening partner for such a long time, was unlucky in having so great a player at the other end, for no player was more adept at finding an opening for a run off the fifth or sixth ball than Jack. Andy always expected it and was ready to run.

Turning to bowlers, I regard Tom Richardson as the fastest and best of men of pace. Years ago, when Surrey were playing at Nottingham, I saw Bill Lockwood, whom many thought was the best but not the fastest. Bill was sitting in a wheeled chair and I asked him whom he thought was the best and fastest bowler he had seen. 'There's only one in it,' he replied. 'Tom Richardson.' I said: 'What about yourself?' Bill shook his head. 'I wasn't in the same parish as Tom, never mind the same street,' he said. I think J. M. Gregory and E. A. McDonald, the two fastest men from Australia I ever saw, were on a par with Richardson and Lockwood.

Maurice Tate, Alec Bedser, G. G. Macaulay, C. Kelleway and F. R. Foster stand out among fast-medium bowlers. Foster, left-arm, was a bit faster than the others and very quick off the pitch. The first time I kept wicket to him was in a trial match at Lord's. The first ball he bowled swung right across the pitch to outside the leg-stump, turned sharply and went over the top of the off-stump, leaving the batsman and me stone cold and hitting the sight-screen with a bang. James Seymour, the batsman, had half turned to play the ball to leg. I said to him: 'It looks as if there will be 50 byes before lunch, but I'm not going to stand back to him.' Nor did I. In the first match at Sydney in 1911 I gave Foster the signal to bowl one outside the leg-stump for me to try and stump Duff, who I thought might move his right foot in making his shot. Instead of bowling the ball I wanted, Foster sent it very wide outside the off-stump and four byes resulted. The second time I signalled, I made sure he saw what I meant. This time he bowled the ball straight to Frank Woolley at first slip. Then I realised he did not intend to give me the chance which he might have allowed had 'Tiger' Smith, his own county's wicket-keeper, been behind the stumps.

One incident about Maurice Tate lingers in my memory. In his first Australian tour, 1924, Maurice bowled two overs, of eight balls per over, to Ponsford in the opening Test at Sydney. Ponsford tried to play at every ball, but each time he missed. He turned to me and said: 'I've never played against such bowling in all my life.' I said: 'It doesn't look as though you have. You ought to have been out sixteen times!' Then 'Horseshoe' Collins schemed it so that he should face Tate, and defended solidly till the Sussex bowler tired. The tactics worked, for Ponsford went on to get 110.

Sidney Barnes was the best of the medium-pace bowlers in my day, but the Australian W. J. O'Reilly followed him pretty closely. As regards slow bowlers, there were so many as good as each other. There were the left-handers Rhodes, Blythe, Verity, Woolley and Parker and numerous right-handers, with 'Tich' Freeman, of Kent, at the top.

In my day the premier wicket-keepers were A. A. Lilley, G. MacGregor, H. Martin, E. J. Smith, F. H. Huish, D. Hunter, W. Storer, J. C. Hubble, G. Duckworth and L. E. G. Ames. G. J. V. Weigall, the old Cambridge and Kent player, told me one day: 'I have found the best wicket-keeper-batsman England will ever have.' When I asked him the name of this player, he said: 'Leslie Ames.' How right he was. There will never be another like Ames, who during his career hit 37,245 runs in addition to his vast number of victims. Kent have been extremely fortunate in their wicket-keepers, Huish, Hubble, Ames and Godfrey Evans all being in the very top class.

I have never seen a better wicket-keeper than Evans, but I class W. A. Oldfield, the Australian, H. B. Cameron, of South Africa, and Lilley as his equal. These men, who stood close up to the wicket to all bowling, had splendid records and did their work without any fuss. Each was quick in putting down the wicket when the occasion arose and none could be excelled when it came to taking catches. Evans does all these things equally well, and his happy disposition allows him to enjoy every minute on the field. Full of energy and enthusiasm, he makes everything difficult look easy—though he tries to make the easy ones appear difficult! Yes, Evans is a great provider of entertainment for the crowd, and is an inspiration to his team-mates, especially the bowlers, to whom he must give considerable confidence to do their utmost.

It is my opinion that games are won on the field, and not in the dressing-rooms. A captain cannot plan his campaign overnight—how he will use his bowlers and from which end they should operate, and so forth. We hear so much about 'seamers' wickets' nowadays. I don't know what the term means, but I notice that if the wicket is one considered favourable to 'seamers', the fast bowlers keep going till they are dead beat and cannot come back again when wanted. I do not like the captain who looks at the clock when going out to field and says to himself: '11.30. First change 12.30.' It takes two fast bowlers an hour to bowl 16 overs between them, and if one gets a wicket in his seventh or eighth over, he has to send down another three or four.

This is where the good captains make their mark. I name three I consider superior to all others: A. B. Sellers, W. S. Surridge and P. G. H. Fender. Sellers welded his team into the best fielding combination I ever encountered. His placing of the field was wellnigh perfect. Always on the alert himself, he saw that the men under him were constantly on their toes. He changed his bowlers more often than any other captain I have known and with great success. I have seen a bowler get a wicket and be taken off next over, and the man who replaced him would at once succeed in disposing of a batsman. Was it luck? I don't think so. It was the captain's wicket. Sellers's heart and soul were in the game and he was out to win every time. He was a live wire on the field, never giving up, and if a player did not follow his example he was soon out of the side. I like his type, all out till the match is over.

Mr. Surridge possessed the same gifts and drive. This new L.B.W. Law and two of the best slow bowlers of today gave him the opportunity which he took with both hands. He did more than anybody to make Laker and Lock what they are today. His placing of three fieldsmen within a few yards of the bat on the leg-side gave the batsmen little chance against Laker's off-spinner and I believe was the reason why M.C.C. restricted the number of fieldsmen in those positions. There is no doubt that these close-in fieldsmen won matches and the Championship for Surrey.

Mr. Fender was one of the finest captains who never was asked to lead England. A grand all-rounder, he would, I am sure, have won one or two Championships had the pitches been what they are today instead of the cast-iron affairs of his time, coupled with the larger stumps, new L.B.W. Law and the third-day declarations. The rule those days was that if you could not win you must try and save the game. I could not see any county giving Surrey a chance to win if they could avoid it.

Only once can I recall this happening and that was at Leicester. When we were coming in for tea, Mr. Fender asked his rival captain, Major G. H. S. Fowke, if he intended to declare. 'I don't think so,' said the Major.

Returning from tea, he saw Mr. A. Jeacocke sitting at the dressing-room door with his pads on. 'What are you doing?' asked the Major in surprise. 'You have declared, haven't you?' said Jeacocke. 'No,' replied Major Fowke, 'but I suppose I had better do so now.' And Surrey won the match, Mr. Fender's winning hit for 6 sending the ball through the dressing-room door. Many of the Leicestershire members were so annoyed about this that they threatened to resign. I said to one of them: 'Why are you grumbling? You've seen one of the best afternoon's cricket you will ever see. Suppose it had been Leicestershire who had won?' 'Ah, but it wasn't Leicestershire,' he said.

It is nothing in these days for a team to declare in both innings. There was a craze before the war, when rain left only one day for play, for one side to go in, be given four runs and declare. The other side followed suit and the result really depended on the second innings. Surrey did this at Cardiff and lost the match.

There is no reason why a professional should not make an able captain. Alec Bedser, H. E. Dollery and George Emmett all showed their ability in this direction. They knew the game inside out and it was their job. No one talks more about the game than a professional cricketer. At the same time there are certain responsibilities, such as choosing the team. The professional is not a member of the club and therefore has no vote. He will be given the names of twelve or thirteen players and he has to leave out one or two men, a thing he does not like to do because they are all his pals. So he develops a conscience. If he is a bowler, he will choose the worst end to bowl from, probably against the wind. If he over-rides his conscience, he will pick the better end! Temperament plays a big part in cricket. The amateur captain, as a member of the club, has very little to worry about. He can seek the advice of the senior professional, and the odd chat with the players helps to ease the tension of a match. Yes, I am all in favour of the amateur skipper, providing that he has a sound knowledge of the game and is a reasonably good cricketer.

Sometimes I am asked how modern cricket compares with that of those far-off days. Frankly I cannot see much difference except that in my time the batsmen found it easier to score faster. The ball came more quickly on to the bat and got up stump-high from the hard pitches, giving them the chance to make more shots. The bowlers concentrated more on or outside the off-stump and those of fast and fast-medium pace had only two men on the on-side—a mid-on and a deep fine-leg.

The bowlers when I first played always tried to bowl just outside the off-stump. Dick Lilley, the Warwickshire wicket-keeper, used to hold his hands out for the bowler to bowl to in Australia.

THE EARLY COUNTY CHAMPIONS [1959]

BY ROWLAND BOWEN

The 1959 edition carried one of the weightiest essays ever commissioned by Wisden, a display of erudition based on meticulous research by that rogue elephant among cricket historians Major Rowland Bowen (1916–78). A cantankerous man prone to deep distrust of ruling bodies, the Major was given to in-depth investigations into abstruse corners of cricket history which most other researchers shunned. When in 1963 he founded 'The Cricket Quarterly' and edited it for the full length of its eight-year life, he raised scholarship to a level not previously attained, in the process ruffling so many sensibilities that to this day the collection of the Quarterly in the Lord's library is kept under wraps. Bowen was educated at Westminster, which is what he probably had in mind when he claimed to be intimate through association with the devious ways of the Establishment. Decidedly a man who believed in the Conspiracy theory of history rather than the more plausible alternative of the Universal Cock-Up, Bowen always attacked his theme with relish, often in defiance of accepted canons of good taste. His 'Cricket, a History' (Eyre and Spottiswoode; 1970) is an extraordinary, brilliant, heretical work, one of the indispensables of cricket literature. Some of the issues it raises are not so much as mentioned in more polite histories, which means that for a rational discussion of, say, covert professionalism, jingo hysteria or the sudden disappearance from England of W. R. Gilbert, it is a case of Bowen or nobody. In this essay, having placed a bomb under the structure of the County Championship and having been relentless in his exposition, Bowen stands back and defies posterity to argue. It can only be imagined with what apoplectic rage he must have reacted to the timid editorial disclaimer tacked to the base of the monument. Nonetheless, the annals of Wisden are all the richer for the inclusion of Bowen's research and dialectical method.

RECENT controversy has drawn attention to the doubts which have often been expressed down the years on the accepted list of County Champions in the early days of first-class cricket. At the request of the Editor of *Wisden* I have conducted extensive research into contemporary publications to see what light they cast on the early years. The four principal annuals consulted were *Fred Lillywhite's Guide* for seasons from 1854 up to and including 1865 (referred to as the *Guide*): *John and James Lillywhite's Companion* from season 1865 to 1884—it incorporated the *Guide* from season 1866 (referred to as the *Companion*); *James Lillywhite's Annual* from season 1871 till its cessation—it incorporated the *Companion* from season 1885 (referred to as the *Annual*); and, of course, *Wisden* from 1864. A very large number of other annuals—usually individual and often unofficial—and county cricket annuals have also been examined, as well as individual county cricket histories and other publications. They are mentioned by name where necessary.

This examination has led to the following conclusions: (1) there has been an uncritical acceptance and repetition of statements concerning earlier periods, or statistics about earlier cricket, which would horrify a professional historian; (2) the concepts of first-class cricket, and of a county cricket championship *as we know them* were things quite alien to the minds of cricket enthusiasts and writers of 80 and more years ago; (3) there is no evidence that the championship started in 1873; (4) there was no agreement amongst various contemporary publications as to how the championship was to be decided in the early years; (5) the hitherto accepted list of champions is certainly wrong for two of the years given, and in four further years there can be legitimate argument.

The proof of the first conclusion will become obvious during the course of this article.

As regards the second conclusion, there was generally no agreement whether Hampshire and Somerset were to be considered among the 'celebrated' counties; averages often included all county matches even against such teams as Buckinghamshire. For example, W. G. Grace's published records for first-class matches include such games as M.C.C. v. Hertfordshire. Moreover, there seems to be a distinction between the county champions and the county championship. In other words, the county champions were the best county *against all comers*; the idea of restricting the choice of champions by reference only to games against other counties did not appear to exist, certainly in the minds of the editors of the *Companion* or *Annual* until some time in the late 70s or early 80s.

As regards the third conclusion, the *Companion* said of 1865, 'if one county was better than any other, it was Nottinghamshire,' and of 1866, 'Middlesex occupy premier position,' and of 1867, 'Middlesex forfeited the premiership to Yorkshire'; no comment in 1868, but in 1869 'Yorkshire and Nottinghamshire were champion counties'; in 1870 'Yorkshire now fairly champion county'—supported by *Wisden* for that season; in 1871 *Companion* and *Wisden* agreed that Nottinghamshire were champions, but conceded that Sussex were the champions of the south; the *Annual* said 'Nottinghamshire will not be deprived of the championship'; in 1872 *Companion* and *Annual* agreed Nottinghamshire were champions. The only significant thing about 1873 was that for that season, rules governing qualification for counties were agreed—nothing else was decided—certainly not how the championship should be run. The fact that those rules were found necessary indicated clearly that the best county was already being designated champion county, and that it was not right that a county should be so designated when it engaged players who had appeared for some other county that season. There was no organised championship; in fact there was no championship in the strict sense until 1890, when the counties themselves agreed how the championship should be decided; or even until 1894, when M.C.C. were asked in future to designate the county champions.

As regards the fourth conclusion, it was stated (and has been repeated blindly since 1895 so far as I have been able to gather) that the county with the fewest losses were champions up to and including season 1886. This was not so; had it been the *Annual* would scarcely have said of season 1875 that 'the most partial supporter would hardly venture to compare Derbyshire with Gloucestershire' which latter county was stated unequivocally to have been champions. Moreover, *Cricket* for September 21, 1882, used the system not stated to have been adopted until 1887, viz.: one point for a win, half for a draw. Again, between 1873 and 1886 inclusive, the contemporary annuals disagreed with each other on four occasions and they disagreed with the modern list in two further years. Had the champions been designated in the manner stated there could have been no such disagreement. Moreover, in none of those six years was the disagreement affected by the question of whether the two doubtful counties, Hampshire and Somerset, were first-class.

As regards the fifth conclusion, I think it will be conceded that if contemporary publications all agreed that a certain county were champions for a certain year, and if by claiming the championship early histories of that county supported those contemporaries but not the modern list, then the modern list is wrong. Those conditions are fulfilled.

It is worthwhile examining the origins of the present list. It appeared first in Alfred Gibson's *County Cricket Championship* published in 1895—I have not been able to find an earlier list.

The list from 1873 to 1895 is exactly as now accepted. Gibson appears to have been a statistician who tried to read back into the minds of the writers of twenty years earlier his own ideas; hence the faults in the list. It was copied and brought up to date by the Rev. R. S. Holmes in a publication of the same name up to 1896. *Wisden* was the first annual to show the list, in 1901, but omitted 1873 and 1874. It was then copied into various county yearbooks, notably the one printed by Yorkshire, and into other annuals. It was reprinted by *Wisden* in 1907 and again in 1911, when 1873 and 1874 were added as in Gibson's list.

I now propose to examine the situation before 1873, year by year, and from 1873 in the years in which there is any argument. The contemporary annuals are not as helpful as they might be. *Wisden* did not always designate a champion, and did not publish a table until 1888; it published an order of merit for the two previous seasons, however. Earlier, the order in which the counties appeared in *Wisden* is evidence, for Surrey were always shown first, until 1877, and thereafter Middlesex, and the next county shown is usually found to have been considered champions. The *Companion* never published a table, but usually listed the counties in their order of merit. The order of merit in the *Companion* has to be deduced since Surrey were always conventionally shown first, and Middlesex second, until season 1870. The *Annual* first published a table for 1872 (though it included all games), omitted one for 1874, 1887 and 1888 and had a table in purely alphabetical order for 1877 and 1880; from 1873 to 1885 the order in which the counties appeared in the *Annual* was purely alphabetical. It will be seen that something can be disinterred!

Before 1864, the *Guide* does not claim any county as champions.

1864   Surrey had easily the best record, winning seven games and drawing one. They were conventionally placed first in *Wisden*, *Guide* and *Companion*, but there was still no claim made nor implication that they were champions by whatever names designated. This would imply that the concept of champions—or premiers, call it what you will—only came in during the next two or three years.

1865   The *Companion* said 'if one county were better than any other it was Nottinghamshire.' No other publication made this statement; nor do the various orders in which the counties are listed assist us. Nottinghamshire's record was won five, lost two. The *Companion* listed second to Surrey (conventionally first in all three annuals) Middlesex—won three, drawn one, lost one; the *Guide* gave Kent as second—won two, drawn two, lost two. Perhaps Nottinghamshire were best—but *not* on a basis of least lost.

1866   The *Companion* said Middlesex occupied premier position. Their playing record was won seven, drawn one, lost one; and no one else came near them. *Perhaps* it is the statement in the following season that enables us to date the first champion county—though not, perhaps, the county championship—from 1866, for in

1867   The *Companion* said 'Middlesex forfeited the premiership to Yorkshire'. Of this there can be no possible doubt, for Yorkshire won all their seven games, and no other county had even an unbeaten record.

1868   No one was designated champions. Nottinghamshire were listed second by *Wisden* to the conventionally first Surrey. Nottinghamshire had the best record, won four, lost two, but the counties seem to have been even. Probably Nottinghamshire were champions, but I can find no statement or claim to this effect.

1869   The *Companion* unequivocally said 'Yorkshire and Nottinghamshire were champions'—and this was the first use of the term; hereafter it was always used (or implied in years of argument). There can be no doubt then about the propriety of dating back the list of county champions to this season.

1870   The *Companion* said 'Yorkshire are now fairly champion county.' This was supported by the order of counties in *Wisden*, since Yorkshire appeared second to the conventionally first Surrey, by a statement in *Wisden* for that season and also by the *History of Yorkshire County Cricket*, the earliest claim in any individual county history.

1871   The *Companion* said 'Nottinghamshire were champions'; the *Annual* supported this at page 57: 'Nottinghamshire will not be easily deprived of the championship.' *Wisden* agreed about Nottinghamshire. Both the *Companion* and *Wisden* agreed Sussex were champions of the south. The playing records were Nottinghamshire won four, drawn one, lost one; Sussex won four. The orders in which the counties appeared supported the statement that Nottinghamshire were champions. It seems a little hard on Sussex, but the writers of those days were very chary of awarding the championship to counties which had played only a few matches. Anyway, no contemporary put Sussex first and that seems sufficient.

1872   The *Companion* and *Annual* said Nottinghamshire were first; the orders in *Wisden* and *Annual* supported this, Surrey being conventionally first. Nottinghamshire's record was won two, drawn five; Lancashire, however, won all their four games; yet there was no suggestion at all that they were champions. Once more the contemporary judgment of which was the better team must be accepted; this judgment was not based solely on actual results of games, but made some attempt (one cannot help but feeling as one reads those old comments) to take into account how the games actually went, how strong were the opponents and so on. This was the year of the first table, in the *Annual*; it does not help us much since it listed all games played, not only county games. However, F. S. Ashley-Cooper, in his *Nottinghamshire Cricket and Cricketers*, made the claim for Nottinghamshire being champions in 1871 and 1872.

1873 This, the first year now shown in the list of champions, is also the first year in which the statement in that list gives rise to argument. *Wisden*, commenting on the 1873 season, was quite definite that Nottinghamshire were champions. Ashley-Cooper did not make this claim. The *Companion* was unequivocal that Gloucestershire were champions. The *Annual* said at one point when dealing with Gloucestershire that Gloucestershire were champions, but when dealing with Nottinghamshire said that 'Nottinghamshire were co-equal'. There was no claim to the sole championship in the *History of Gloucestershire County Cricket Club*. The playing records of the two counties were Gloucestershire won four, drawn two; Nottinghamshire won five, drawn one. On the face of it, the 1874 *Wisden* would appear to have been correct, but there was no unanimity at the time, and in view of all the statements made, it is probably right to accept what the present list (derived from Alfred Gibson) says, bracketing Gloucestershire and Nottinghamshire as co-equal.

1874 Here again there is grave dispute. The present list shows Derbyshire as champions. The *Annual* I have already quoted—it will bear repetition—'the most partial supporter would hardly venture to compare Derbyshire with Gloucestershire.' Both *Annual* and *Companion* were in no doubt that Gloucestershire were champions, and *Wisden* listed them second to the conventionally placed Surrey (listing Derbyshire last!). *The History of Gloucestershire County Cricket Club* made the definite claim that Gloucestershire were champions in 1874; *Derbyshire County Cricket*, by Piper, published 1897, made no claim for Derbyshire to have been champions in 1874, though it said they were the only unbeaten county, but it is fair to say that the unofficial *Derbyshire Cricket Guide* for 1896 did make the claim (prompted no doubt by A. Gibson). On the other hand 'Feats and Facts of Derbyshire Cricket' in the *Derbyshire Cricket Annual* for 1887, did not mention Derbyshire as champions in 1874—surely it would have if anyone in or out of the county had made the claim? In the face of contemporary unanimity on the subject, there can be no doubt that the present list is wrong, both in supposing that the champions were designated with reference to fewest matches lost, and in designating Derbyshire as champions. At the time, Gloucestershire were accepted as champions, and claimed to be champions; Derbyshire were not, and did not, and the modern list should therefore be corrected. As a matter of interest, Gloucestershire—playing Yorkshire, Surrey and Sussex—won four, drew one and lost one; Derbyshire—playing only Kent and Lancashire, both very weak teams at that time—won three and drew one.

1875 There was no controversy about this season till recently. There need be none, particularly if it is remembered that 'least matches lost' was *not* a rule, but a guide to deciding who were champions. All three annuals were quite positive that Nottinghamshire were champions, and Ashley-Cooper supported this. Sussex made no claim to be champions at the time, nor did they do so until 1958. They did not have an unbeaten record, as they lost to the very weak Hampshire team, in that season reckoned by all three contemporary annuals as among 'the' counties, as they were indeed for the next three seasons. The records were Nottinghamshire won six, drawn three, lost one; Sussex won five, drawn one, lost two. Both *Companion* and *Annual* put Yorkshire (won six, drawn one, lost three) second to Nottinghamshire, as does the *History of Yorkshire County Cricket*—this seems a little unfair to Sussex, but it is clear that they were not even equal first. Both Lillywhites, as well as Wisden, were Sussex men: it is inconceivable that their annuals would have failed to make a claim for Sussex as champions if there had been any sort of justification for such a claim.

1876 and **1877**   Complete agreement with the present list that Gloucestershire were champions.

1878   The present list shows Middlesex. Volume one of the *History of Middlesex C.C.C.* at page 154 did not claim Middlesex as champions, though they had an unbeaten record; it said that 'probably Nottinghamshire, and certainly Yorkshire were stronger'. The records were Middlesex won three, drawn three; Nottinghamshire won seven, drawn four, lost three; Yorkshire won seven, drawn two, lost five. Middlesex drew both games with Nottinghamshire and beat Yorkshire twice. Neither the *History of Yorkshire County Cricket* nor *Nottinghamshire Cricket and Cricketers* made any claim for Yorkshire or Nottinghamshire. The *Companion* twice said that 'no one county were champions' and in a third place, that Nottinghamshire held the leading place amongst counties. The *Annual* did not commit itself. *Wisden* did not help, since it now listed Middlesex first instead of Surrey, but it is clear that the convention changed this season, for from now on Middlesex were listed conventionally first with Surrey often second. The contemporary evidence seems plain, and the correct entry in the list should be 'undecided'.

1879   The present list shows Nottinghamshire and Lancashire bracketed. The *Companion* supported this, more or less, though it rather spoke with two voices. The *Annual* also supported this. *Wisden* listed Nottinghamshire second to the conventionally first Middlesex, with Lancashire eighth. Ashley-Cooper said that Nottinghamshire were agreed to have been the better team, and there were strong implications in *Lancashire County Cricket*, by F. Reynolds (published 1883), that 1881 was the first year in which Lancashire were champions (though this could just be taken as meaning 'sole champions'). It should be added that *Lancashire Cricket Records* 1865–1908 gave Lancashire as champions in 1881, 1897 and 1904 and tied in 1889; it made no claim for 1879, nor 1882. The records were Lancashire won five, drawn four, lost one; Nottinghamshire won five, drawn six, lost one. In all the circumstances, it would seem better to accept the present list, since it is to a great extent supported by contemporary annuals—even if not by *Wisden* of that time.

1880 and **1881**   Complete agreement with the present list that Nottinghamshire in 1880 and Lancashire in 1881 were champions. A recent publication suggests Gloucestershire might be considered as joint champions in 1880. Contemporaries did not support this view. Gloucestershire won four, drew five and lost one against Nottinghamshire's won six, drawn three, lost one—it is clear why contemporaries admitted no argument about Nottinghamshire's supremacy.

1882   The present list shows Nottinghamshire and Lancashire bracketed. The *Companion* at one point said Lancashire had a short-head over Nottinghamshire, at another point an opposite opinion, and at a third that the two counties divided the honours equally. The *Annual* said 'Lancashire and Nottinghamshire were fairly equal'; it published a table showing these two teams first; the table included Hampshire and Somerset which the *Annual* called Minor Counties. This is important as Lancashire beat Somerset twice. *Wisden* said this was Somerset's début amongst the first-class counties; listed Middlesex and Surrey conventionally first and second, Lancashire third and Nottinghamshire fourth; and said: 'In all matches Lancashire lost four games and Nottinghamshire two, therefore Nottinghamshire must be considered champions.' It will be noticed that *Lancashire Cricket Records*, already quoted, made no claim for Lancashire to have been champions, while Ashley-Cooper said Nottinghamshire were surpassed by no other county (which is one way of admitting that they tied!). *Cricket*, however, in its issue for September 21, 1882, awarded one point for a win and a half for a draw, and put Lancashire first. The records were Lancashire won ten, drawn three, lost one against counties, plus won two v. Somerset; Nottinghamshire won eight, drew three, lost one. The matter has been discussed at length (as in the case of season 1879) only because the contemporary *Wisden* gave a different opinion from the present list, and because a Lancashire publication specifically excluded Lancashire from being champions in these two seasons. One finds oneself unable to agree with *Wisden* for 1883 and in view of the two Lillywhite statements, the present list should be accepted as correct.

1883   The present list shows Nottinghamshire as champions. The *Companion* said 'Nottinghamshire were fully entitled to the honours of county champions' but conceded that the difference between them and Yorkshire was minute. The *Annual* said Nottinghamshire were champions under the recognised system of awarding the championship. *Cricket* placed Nottinghamshire first. *Wisden* said that Yorkshire were first and had an undeniable claim, and put Yorkshire third and Nottinghamshire fourth to the conventionally first Middlesex and second Surrey. Ashley-Cooper said that Nottinghamshire were first. *The History of Yorkshire County Cricket* at page 60 gave Yorkshire first. The records were Nottinghamshire won four, drawn seven, lost one (they won one and drew the other game with Yorkshire); Yorkshire won nine, drew five, lost two, and drew two with Leicestershire, not reckoned to be first-class by any contemporary. In the circumstances one can agree with *Wisden* for 1884 that Yorkshire had a claim, but accept the other contemporary evidence that the claim was not conceded.

1884–88   There was complete agreement with the present list in contemporary annuals.

1889   A very minor point. *Wisden* for 1890 bracketed the top three teams in the following order: Nottinghamshire, Lancashire, Surrey. In terms of their records, that was surely correct. Nottinghamshire won nine, drew three, lost two; Lancashire and Surrey won ten, drew one, lost three. From 1887 the custom of awarding one point for a win and a half for a draw had been adopted (as foreseen by *Cricket* five years before), so certainly a triple tie was correct; and equally certain, the *Wisden* order of placing the teams in 1890 was correct. Not until five years later do we find a list which puts them in the order now found, which is neither by merit nor alphabet—Surrey, Lancashire, Nottinghamshire. It is clear that this minor correction should be made in the current list, for the only reason for putting Surrey first among the three is that they were champions in the two previous seasons—even so, Nottinghamshire had a better record than Lancashire.

From 1890 there is no argument about who were first.

We can now sum up with a new list. The only point remaining to be decided is from what date should the list run? It has been clearly shown that one can logically and consistently run the list from 1869, and even from 1865, since that was the first time a county was stated to have been better than any other with gaps in 1868 and 1878. It had been clearly shown that 1873 is not a significant date, except for the one point of qualification. On the other hand, there is a legitimate doubt which counties were first-class, at least until 1886. Cambridge appear from 1863 to 1869. Hampshire were so reckoned in 1863–67 and 1870, but not in 1868 or 1869, nor 1871–73. *Wisden* included them from 1874 to 1878 and again from 1880 to 1885. The *Guide* included them in 1863 and 1864 (in 1854 it said that Hampshire were once, but now no longer). The *Annual* and the *Companion* generally exclude Hampshire except in 1865–67, 1870 and 1874–78. From 1881–85 *Wisden* included Somerset, whereas the others excluded them, save that the *Annual* showed Somerset in its table for 1882. Derbyshire were included from 1872–87 by *Wisden* and *Annual* and by the *Companion* from 1872. Lancashire did not appear until 1867 (though they played Middlesex twice in 1865), and Gloucestershire not until 1870. Surrey, Kent, Sussex, Yorkshire and Nottinghamshire were 'Celebrated counties' from early days, while Middlesex, who were 'creeping along' in 1857 were accepted as 'celebrated' by 1864. The method of reckoning, one point for a win, was introduced in 1887. That would seem, then, to be another suitable date to commence the list. 1890 would be another suitable date; then the counties themselves decided the method of scoring in the championship. The choice is between 1865 and 1859 or between 1887 and 1890. I have selected 1865, merely for the sake of historical completeness.

Period 1865–86. The method of deciding who were county champions was generally by 'fewest losses'. This led to anomalous results and was tempered in several years by a critical judgment of which was the strongest county. The counties most generally selected by contemporaries as champions were:—

1865	Nottinghamshire	1877	Gloucestershire
1866	Middlesex	1878	Undecided
1867	Yorkshire	1879	Nottinghamshire and Lancashire
1868	Undecided (probably Nottinghamshire)	1880	Nottinghamshire
		1881	Lancashire
1869	Nottinghamshire and	1882	Nottinghamshire and Lancashire
1870	Yorkshire	1883	Nottinghamshire
1871	Nottinghamshire	1884	Nottinghamshire
1872	Nottinghamshire	1885	Nottinghamshire
1873	Gloucestershire and Nottinghamshire	1886	Nottinghamshire
1874	Gloucestershire		
1875	Nottinghamshire		
1876	Gloucestershire		

Periods 1887–89. One point for a win, half for a draw.

1887	Surrey		1889	Nottinghamshire,
1888	Surrey			Lancashire, Surrey

Period 1890 to date. As shown in *Wisden* in 1901, 1907 and ever since 1911.

May I conclude by saying that the only evidence that is acceptable from an historical point of view is contemporary evidence even if contemporaries seem, from our point of view, to have been wrong—for they were not wrong from their own point of view; a list of county champions can only name those who were at the time accepted as champions. Critics cannot, twenty, forty or eighty years later, air their views with the same authority.

I have only attempted to decide between the contemporary publications for 1873, 1879, 1882 and 1883 because there is sufficient weight of contemporary opinion and evidence to enable one to do so; and to award the honours equally to the two claimants for three of those years: because it is 75 years after the event I have not inclined to alter the result for 1883. I have had no such doubts for 1874 and 1878 where contemporaries were in complete agreement—nor, of course, for the years 1875 and 1880 which have been the subject of recent discussion, but which presented contemporaries with no problems.

[Editor's Note: Without in any way disputing the conclusions reached by the author, I do not think we can alter the accepted list as regularly published in Wisden for over forty years, even where there are good grounds for disagreeing with it.]

THE STORY OF SOMERSET [1959]

BY ERIC HILL

The opening remark in Eric Hill's history of Somerset may have contained elements of the truth, but it is certainly over-modest. Admittedly the county's performances in the championship were always moderate enough; it took the club more than sixty years of trying before it reached even third place. But the statistics of cricket can be notoriously misleading and few would argue with the proposition that Somerset, winners or no, rank among the most attractive and spectacular sides in history. For no logical reason, unless it is connected in some obscure way with a tendency to rusticity, excitement and laughter have never been very far away and Mr. Hill reminds us that the highest score in the history of first-class cricket in England was made in a match at Taunton, that it was at the same ground that Hobbs equalled and surpassed W. G. Grace's total of first-class centuries, that at Frome in 1935 there took place the most sensational début in all the history of the English game and that although inconsistent, the county has never lost the habit of springing suddenly to the apex of its powers and bringing about the downfall of even the strongest elevens. It is surprising that Mr. Hill, in telling the tale of the defeat of Middlesex at Lord's in 1947, did not make more of the fact that Middlesex were all-conquering throughout the season, that the Middlesex batting order at Lord's began: Robertson, Brown, Edrich, Compton, that in the return at Taunton Somerset again scraped home, and that the side played with such courage and nerve at Lord's that, as Wisden puts it, 'The Middlesex team lined up and cheered as their successful opponents went to the pavilion'.

Very often the championship record of a side gives little impression of the style of cricket it played, nor any hint of the variations in individual virtuosity it offered. A much more reliable guide can sometimes be the hypothetical eleven it could muster from its history. In this regard Somerset instantly rocket from near the bottom of the table to the highest reaches, especially if the years and the players who followed after 1960 are to be included. In batting order, the team would be: L. Palairet, Gimblett, I. V. Richards, Botham, Braund, McCool, Sam Woods, Wellard, Luckes, Garner, J. C. White. Twelfth man and historian, R. C. Robertson-Glasgow.

As this gathering includes the two most consistent hitters of sixes in the history of the championship, the most aggressive of all opening batsmen, as well as two men who were to oppose each other as rival captains in a Test match, it begins to be apparent that Mr. Hill might have boosted the cause a little more recklessly, especially after the enchanting opening flourishes conjuring up visions of a wandering side stoked by the fires of muscular Christianity. No cricket club whose first captain is called the Reverend Stirling Cookesley Voules, of Middle Chinnock, can be all bad. Indeed when the reverend gentleman died in 1923, Sydney Pardon was so preoccupied by the rustic aspects of the case that he devoted three hundred words to the old gentleman without mentioning that he happened to be the inaugural captain of Somerset.

SOMERSET have never been one of the fashionable counties, but from their very beginning they were 'The Team of Surprises'. Even their birth took place away from home, in Devon, for it was immediately after a match between the Gentlemen of Devonshire and the Gentlemen of Somersetshire that a meeting was held at Sidmouth on Wednesday, August 18, 1875, with the Rev. A. C. Ainslie in the chair. Mr. E. Western, of Fullands, Taunton, was requested to act as secretary and he is looked upon as the founder of the now flourishing county club. A circular letter was sent by him from Ilfracombe to likely patrons and included the following four resolutions passed at that inaugural meeting:

1. There shall be no county ground.
2. The club shall depend upon its support by voluntary contributions.
3. County matches shall be played on any ground in the county that may be selected by the Committee.

4. A president, vice-president, treasurer and secretary by nomination, and a committee consisting of nine gentlemen, three from each division of the county, shall be appointed.

FIRST CAPTAIN

The first captain was the Rev. Stirling Cookesley Voules, born at Middle Chinnock, near Crewkerne, an Oxford Blue from 1863 to 1866, who was then Rector of Rise, Hull, in Yorkshire, and formerly a master of Rossall School. The new club experienced various changes of fortune, but progress was made when the freehold of the present ground and headquarters at Taunton was secured in 1886. Down the years many wonderful matches and notable performances in the annals of first-class cricket have been seen there.

It was at Taunton in 1895 that Archie MacLaren hit 424, the highest individual score ever made in England, for Lancashire against Somerset. Previously, in 1892, H. T. Hewett and Lionet Palairet had engaged the then best first-wicket partnership, 346, for Somerset at the expense of Yorkshire. At Taunton, too, in 1925, Jack Hobbs hit two centuries in the same match, to exceed W. G. Grace's record of 126 hundreds.

'SAMMY' WOODS

Through this diverting chronicle of flickering fortune, colourful characters have liberally spread their talents over the pleasant rural grounds that abound in Somerset. From the early days when the lion-hearted S. M. J. Woods, a massive all-rounder from Australia, allied his enormous talents to the graceful attributes of that prince of stylists, the aforesaid L. C. H. Palairet, Somerset's ambition has always been to play cricket for fun. They knew their limitations but from the time of their acceptance as a first-class county in 1891 their form was quite unpredictable.

The first season in the highest grade was a pointer. Quickly, the wisdom of their newly won promotion was held in doubt; the giants, Surrey, bowled them out at The Oval for 37 in each innings to win by the mammoth margin of an innings and 375 runs, but Somerset proceeded to end a long unbeaten run by Kent. They beat Yorkshire at Bradford, avenged the Surrey debacle, and perhaps best of all they succeeded against their neighbouring rivals, Gloucestershire.

Probably what stamped Somerset most as a shock team were their performances at the turn of the century. From 1900 to 1903 they beat Yorkshire three times. In two of those seasons Yorkshire, who were champions, admitted defeat only twice, and each time their colours were lowered by Somerset. The 1901 match at Leeds was the most famous and in fact the score-card still adorns most pavilions Somerset way. At the end of the first day after Rhodes, Haigh and Hirst had skittled Somerset for 87, the story goes that at the Mayoral dinner a civic dignitary offered £100 to the club if Somerset won. L. C. Braund and L. C. H. Palairet, both out for 0 in the first innings, each made 100, putting on 222 in only two hours twenty minutes and the final total reached 630. Then Braund, one of the best all-rounders of all time, joined forces with B. Cranfield and the mighty Northerners were humbled for a paltry total of 130. 'We never got the £100,' said Woods, 'but I won £10 on the game as I took ten to one that Palairet would make a hundred.' Palairet's off-side play was a by-word of the day.

'Sammy' Woods was a real character. As a fast bowler and a hitter he made vivid contributions to the game. Born at Glenfield, near Sydney, and educated at Brighton, he captained Cambridge University in 1890 and had the unusual distinction of playing for Australia against England and for England against South Africa. K. S. Ranjitsinhji, in his Jubilee book, suggested that although Woods's bowling was going off a bit in 1897 it was still good enough to beat the Players for years to come, and added, 'there is no better man to go in when the pitch is bad or things are going wrong, although he does sometimes play forward to a straight ball with his eyes turned full on the square-leg umpire—a stroke he repudiates and never fails to use successfully once or twice an innings.' This remarkable man scored 12,000 runs and took 500 wickets for Somerset. In those days Woods shared most of the Somerset bowling with Braund, one of the first leg-breakers, and E. J. Tyler, a slow left-hander. Besides his prowess as a cricketer, Woods earned equal fame in the Rugby football world. As a forward he gained thirteen caps for England between 1890 and 1895. His quick breaking and relentless tackling set a new style and nowadays he is regarded as the 'Father' of wing-forwards.

From 1901, Braund performed the double three consecutive seasons and played 23 times for England, going on three tours to Australia. Tyler took 869 wickets in his career. He and J. C. White shared the distinction of being the only Somerset bowlers who have taken all ten wickets in an innings. It was in 1895 that his ten for 49 in 35 overs put out Surrey at Taunton.

DIFFICULT YEARS

After their encouraging and spectacular start, Somerset faded as the 1914–18 war approached. The increasing burden began to tell on the old players. Nevertheless, some staunch professional stiffening was forthcoming in the persons of E. Robson and A. E. Lewis, both all-rounders. Robson's fine career spanned thirty years and gave Somerset 12,000 runs and 1,200 wickets. At the age of 51 he gained Somerset the surprise victory of the 1922 season when in the last over of a tense match with Middlesex at Weston-super-Mare he made the winning hit for 6 by lifting the ball clean out of the ground. This feat earned him £50 from an anonymous donor.

We have jumped ahead. Interest waned when the county three times finished last in the Championship between 1910 and 1913, but there were at least two silver linings. W. T. Greswell, a lively pace-bowler who had discovered the knack of the in-swinger, was home from Ceylon and took 100 wickets in 1912; next year came J. C. White, a farmer from Stogumber, who announced his ability to bowl left-arm slow to a perfect length with subtle variation of flight by taking 96 wickets at less than 20 runs each. He was to serve Somerset sublimely.

After the war Somerset, as in the past, relied heavily on an influx of gaily-capped amateurs from the Universities, where John Daniell, the new captain, was always active. Here again was a rumbustious character; an International Rugby forward who became a legend with cricketing beliefs and vocabulary to match. A born leader, Daniell made two centuries in a match with Essex in his 47th year (1925). He is credited with one classic story. When he approached the New Zealander T. C. Lowry about playing for Somerset, he was told that the birthplace was Wellington. Quickly realising there is a town of the same name seven miles from county headquarters, Daniell is said to have closed the deal to the satisfaction of M.C.C.

THE HEYGATE INCIDENT

Somerset were involved in an extraordinary finish with Sussex at Taunton in their very first home match after the war—the experimental two-day season of 1919. Sussex needed a single to win when their ninth wicket fell. Some of the Somerset fielders thought the match was over as H. J. Heygate, the number eleven, was suffering from rheumatism and the effects of a war wound. He had not fielded and was not expected to bat. Indeed, he had not changed, wickets having gone down so suddenly, but wearing a blue lounge suit he limped out to bat. There was a friendly consultation between the captains, H. L. Wilson and J. C. White, but so slow had been his progress that the umpires, A. E. Street and F. G. Roberts, decided he had exceeded his two minutes and pulled up the stumps, declaring the result a tie. This decision was upheld by M.C.C. after widespread comment on the most controversial situation which had occurred since Taunton became a cricket centre.

Somerset finished fifth in 1919, but in the early 'twenties, when White, Robson and J. J. Bridges virtually carried the bowling, amateurs of standing were too often unavailable, but occasionally they strengthened the side, especially in August. Notable performers were four opening batsmen, J. C. W. MacBryan, who played for England in 1924, P. R. Johnson, and the twins A. E. S. and A. D. E. Rippon. M. C. Lyon, another University recruit, was a high-class wicket-keeper and a batsman of decided attacking inclination. His great day came during the 1926 Australian match. Somerset, set to make 302 in three hours forty minutes, began badly, but Lyon, with a burst of sustained hitting, gathered 136 in two and three-quarter hours and took them to within 57 of becoming the only side, other than England, to beat the touring team.

FOUR PLAY FOR GENTLEMEN

From 1924 to 1931 Somerset were never higher than thirteenth in the table, but still the amateur strain was rich. R. C. Robertson-Glasgow, a delightful personality and clever seam bowler from Oxford University, reinforced the attack. Later he gave pleasure to many with his writings on the game. MacBryan, White, Lyon and Robertson-Glasgow all appeared at Lord's in 1924 for the Gentlemen against the Players.

During a long and honourable span—1909 to 1937—White took for his county over 2,000 wickets and scored 11,375 runs, including 100 wickets each season from 1919 to 1932. His effortless bowling played a decisive part in England retaining the Ashes in 1928–29. Carrying on the Somerset tradition of longevity, White was 37 years old during this tour and although by repute his power of spin was slight, this opinion has been repudiated by M. D. Lyon, one of a splendid line of wicket-keepers beginning with the Rev. A. P. Wickham and A. E. Newton. Newton was actually wheeled to the pitch to keep most creditably for Somerset Stragglers on his 75th birthday. Later W. T. Luckes and H. W. Stephenson, from Stockton-on-Tees, shone behind the stumps.

Following J. C. White in the captaincy came R. A. Ingle, who hit two centuries in the same match against Middlesex, and E. F. Longrigg, a talented left-handed batsman. For many years Somerset constantly took the field with nine or ten amateurs, but in the late 'twenties, when fewer of them could afford to spend so much time away from business, the county was compelled to rely more on professionals.

In passing, it is well to note that the increasing emphasis of professional players brought in its train more administrative problems. One of the most successful and highly regarded of Somerset's secretaries was A. F. Davey, who was appointed from seventy-nine applicants in 1923. A happy and useful association with Somerset ended in 1932, when Mr. Davey gave his undoubted organising abilities to Surrey. Two of his early assistants are still intimately connected with the club. They are T. Tout, the present scorer, and E. H. C. Wood, the secretary of the Somerset Supporters' Club.

WELLARD THE HITTER

The county found the schoolboy's dream cricketer when they engaged A. W. Wellard, a Kentish man born at Southfleet. His native county had seen him in action, yet never encouraged him, but for Somerset he made his presence felt as a fast bowler and fearless hitter in his first year, 1929, when his wickets numbered 131. That was the start of a wonderful career which gave him 11,000 runs and over 1,500 wickets. As many as 3,000 of his runs were obtained from 6s. He also developed off-spinners to augment his great-hearted pace-bowling. The brothers Lee, right-handed J. W. and left-handed F. S., now a famous umpire, formed a successful opening partnership with Frank continuing his invaluable contribution after the war. A. (Tom) Young, another doughty performer with a bat and ball and like Wellard a wonderful slip-field, made sure that the years would not find the county wanting for typical Somerset cricketers.

Opening the attack with Wellard was W. H. R. Andrews, a classic type of in-swinger who aims the half-volley at the off-stump and relies on movement not position of delivery from the return crease. With Luckes behind the stumps Somerset could call on a most useful nucleus of professional craftsmen. This team often shocked the big boys. Witness 1936, when having beaten the ultimate champions, Derbyshire, in two days at Ilkeston, they went on to complete an astonishing double at Wells, by a single wicket. In a relatively low-scoring match, Wellard took nine wickets for 136 and scored 103 runs. With Somerset in trouble when they needed 271 to win, Wellard, dropped at one, punished Armstrong for five successive 6s in the same over, hit two more 6s, and ended with 86 out of 102 in sixty-two minutes. Two years later, on the same ground, Wellard repeated his prodigious effort at the expense of the noted Frank Woolley of Kent, off whom he made 31 in an over, again including five consecutive 6s.

When one mentions prolific Somerset hitters the name of G. F. Earle must be included. Tall and proportionately broad, he was not a stylist and came to the fore as a fast bowler for Harrow against Eton in 1908 and three following years, including 'Fowler's match'. He made fleeting appearances for Somerset and no one hit the ball higher or farther. He never wasted time on preliminaries but believed in attacking the bowling.

HAROLD GIMBLETT'S DÉBUT

Somerset were fortunate in having a professional ready to step into J. C. White's shoes in H. L. Hazell of Brislington. He gave many years of splendid service, but the most memorable event of the 1930s as far as this county was concerned was the début of Harold Gimblett—born in a small triangle of West Somerset which includes the birth-places of White and Greswell. Gimblett was a late choice to play against Essex at Frome in 1935. Batting number eight and played mainly as a bowler and lively fielder, he astonished the world and tested credibility by making 123, with three 6s and seventeen 4s, reaching the quickest hundred of the year in sixty-three minutes. It was a début to confound the pundits, and his illustrious career marked by only three international caps and no M.C.C. tour, ended in 1954 when 21,142 runs of the highest calibre had flowed from him at the average rate of 36 an innings.

Gimblett, whom many averred was not a natural opening bat, hit no fewer than 265 sixes, something no other regular number one has ever accomplished. Gimblett holds almost all the Somerset batting records. Among them one finds his 310 against Sussex at Eastbourne in 1948, and a wonderful 184 against Kent on a turning Gravesend pitch which gave Somerset an unexpected win. His uninhibited and powerful shots often gave lustre to many an otherwise dull first day and even first over. Cricket was the poorer for his retirement due to ill-health. His international career hardly started after a characteristic not out 67 against India at Lord's in 1936. The complement to his remarkable first century was the hundred he made in his benefit match against Northamptonshire at Glastonbury in 1952. Gimblett scored forty-nine centuries for the county and one on the Commonwealth tour of India. Twice he hit two hundreds in the same match.

In the period before the last war, Wellard performed the conventional cricketer's double on three occasions and Andrews did it twice, and as war approached, Somerset flickered entertainingly, in tradition, on either side of the middle of the table.

MORE UNIVERSITY INFLUENCE

The 1939 war made few inroads on Somerset's strength. With J. Lawrence, googly bowler and useful batsman from Yorkshire, the only regular addition to the staff, Somerset made full use of their preponderance of skill and experience in 1946. Under E. F. Longrigg, who had been captain since 1938, when another Somerset all-rounder in H. T. F. Buse had joined the staff, the side reached a record fourth position in the table, with twelve Championship victories. The seal was set on a magnificent season of rehabilitation when they scored over 500 in successive innings at Taunton against India, Middlesex and Yorkshire, winning the first two matches with an innings to spare. Also, it was pleasant to note the return of the University influence in the form of M. M. Walford, a triple Blue and batsman whose immaculate technique and temperament made him a leading scorer in August for several seasons. Other gifted amateurs appeared in the team to give occasional strength in R. J. O. Meyer, H. E. Watts, F. Castle. Meyer took over in 1947 when Longrigg retired from the captaincy.

Meyer was another character in the Somerset mould, but unfortunately he had been away during his most productive years. A splendid all-rounder, he had an unhappy season, partly through a series of severe back ailments, and as his side aged, replacements of the necessary calibre were not forthcoming.

True, the nucleus of the professional staff was far from finished, but although G. E. S. Woodhouse, a solid batsman from Dorset, led them to ninth position in 1949 and S. S. Rogers, a Londoner, helped them to seventh in 1950, the old strength was slowly fading away.

TREMLETT'S MATCH

Of the considerable younger brigade given trials, M. F. Tremlett alone had really arrived. Tremlett started work in the county office on leaving school in 1938 and he made a marvellous contribution to winning his first match at Lord's in 1947 by taking eight wickets and making the winning hit with number eleven at the othe end. A natural all-rounder, Tremlett went with M.C.C. to West Indies in 1948 and to South Africa the following winter, but not with the happiest results, especially as far as his bowling was concerned. Efforts of coaches to improve him met with exactly the opposite results.

H. W. Stephenson had also impressed greatly as a wicket-keeper—he narrowly missed the 1950 tour of Australia—but by this time Somerset were becoming woefully weak in fast bowling and class batting. Gimblett compiled 2,063 runs in 1949, a Somerset record which Tremlett took in 1951, but the future looked bleak. In turn S. S. Rogers, B. G. Brocklehurst and G. G. Tordoff were given the captaincy while Somerset collected four consecutive wooden spoons. In 1953, the members of the club were roused into action. After a highly unusual public outcry, a determined effort resulted in numerous players being recruited from far and wide. The critics called Somerset the 'League of Nations', but the policy of going abroad for talent was regarded as a temporary measure while the county was scoured for home-bred material to be developed in the new indoor coaching school at Taunton.

OUT OF THE DOLDRUMS

E. P. Robinson, a very successful off-spinner, whose best years had been spent in the triumphant Yorkshire pre-war side, had come and gone, but B. Langford, a local product, P. B. Wight, J. G. Lomax and J. W. McMahon had all shown considerable potential. At last, in 1956, when the amateur cupboard seemed finally bare of leaders, M. F. Tremlett was appointed the first professional captain. He was lucky enough to have a former Australian Test player, C. L. McCool, in the ranks, and the year was marked by a slight move away from the last position in the table to fifteenth. Bryan Lobb, the rangy pace-bowler from Warwickshire, had come in and J. W. McMahon's two distinctive methods of left-arm slow bowling proved useful. In 1957, with Tremlett striking tremendous form late in the season, and showing untutored but majestic straight hitting to its best advantage, Somerset rose to eighth position in the table. Last summer their monumental effort of resuscitation was rewarded with third place, the best in their history.

This achievement, in contrast to some recoveries of the past, was heightened in value by success of a number of young players who had been on the staff since the stormy controversial days of 1953. Gradually prospects like G. Atkinson, K. Palmer, B. Roe and P. J. Eele were given a taste of cricket at its best in company with the experienced elders. Now there are plenty of contestants eager to show their fitness for the roles filled by their illustrious predecessors.

FINANCIAL AID

One thing has always run true to form in Somerset cricket history. That is the desperate struggle against financial disaster. Nowadays this has been greatly relieved by the activities and energy of an enthusiastic supporters' club. Unlike similar organisations, this one does not give block grants to the county. Instead, money is provided for specific objects, such as players' houses, stands, youth coaching, pitch dryers, local club ground funds and County Second Eleven expenses. In this connection, an example of the increased awareness of the problems of running a first-class team lies in the very successful County 2nd XI. In 1954 only six games were played. In 1959 a schedule of 23 matches has been arranged for them. Meanwhile the County Club continues their strenuous endeavours to balance the working profit and loss account, which it has not done for some years.

HAPPY ATMOSPHERE

Somerset, with a small population and a minimum of industry, cannot call upon many amateurs these days, but the side, with such bright players as W. E. Alley, a left-hander, who made a great mark at the age of 38, with his all-round work in the past two years, Wight, McCool, Tremlett and

Stephenson enables Somerset to live up to and even exceed the reputation gained so long ago. The happy-go-lucky atmosphere of a few years ago is still there, but now it has the essential backing of applied talent. There is plenty of life, both old and new, in Somerset cricket, and one knows that Sammy Woods would chuckle at the help received from three of his countrymen in lifting his old county out of the depths of despair into the sunny heights. And he, who was one of the heroes of Somerset entry into first-class cricket, would indeed be grateful to see at least one of his deathless phrases borne into continual practice by the modern Somerset heroes. 'Draws?' he once muttered mutinously. 'Draws? They're only for bathing in.' This outlook on the game has given Somerset one of the most respected names in county cricket over the past 67 years.

ESSEX—1876 to 1960 [1960]

BY CHARLES BRAY

Charles Bray was back again in 1960 with a potted history of Essex. Surprisingly for so experienced a journalist, Bray makes little attempt to do more than recite a few salient facts, mention a few illustrious names, recall a few memorable games. It might have been worth reminding readers of Fane's unexpected ascent to the captaincy of England in Australia in 1907–8, the achievement of Kenneth Farnes in the last Test of the 1936–37 rubber when he took six for 96 out of an Australian total of 604, the defeat by Yorkshire at Leyton in 1901 when George Hirst took twelve wickets for 29 runs, the financial crisis of 1912 when the club very nearly went under, the Yorkshire game at Leyton in 1933 when Verity took seventeen wickets in a day, Kent's 803 for four at Brentwood in the following year and Arthur Fagg's two double-centuries for the same county at Colchester in 1938. Instead, we read a sudden attack on the England selectors for dropping Trevor Bailey and an assessment of Nichols and Douglas which perhaps verges on the chauvinistic. Most surprising of all, Bray makes no reference to the unique pleasure experienced by Fane when he picked up the 1955 Almanack and read his own elaborate obituary. He lived on until November 1960 and ranks among the distinguished group of cricketers who have been accorded two obituaries.

WHILE there is evidence to show cricket was played in Essex as long ago as 1776, the county club was not formed until one hundred years later. It was on January 7, 1876, that a notice appeared in the 'Chelmsford Chronicle' under the names of I. E. Perry Wallington and James Round calling a public meeting at the Shire Hall on Friday, January 14, to consider the desirability of forming a county cricket club with a ground at Brentwood.

Mr. Round, a Member of Parliament, was a cricket enthusiast. It was he who piloted the new young club through its many teething problems. A ground of some nine and a half acres was rented on the fringe of Brentwood, then, of course, a tiny country town. The rent was £38 a year. The club, however, had the right to sub-let. Ten years went by with the new cricket fledgling growing apace in size, success and ambition.

To become first class, which was the ultimate objective, a new headquarters had to be found. Brentwood was too small. A ground in a thickly populated area was essential and the committee set to work to find one. In 1886, after some delicate negotiation, Leyton was bought for £12,000. It was part of the Lyttelton estate. A local report on the opening of the ground said, 'it gave unwonted loveliness to a district which but for a short while since, presented an appearance of the abomination of desolation.'

LOVABLE LEYTON

Quite obviously there were colourful sports writers in those days too. I played many times at Leyton. Never did I see anything lovely about it or its surroundings but it had character and atmosphere. There was something in its dirtiness, its ramshackle pavilion, its 'cow-shed' along one side and those cold, grim, stone terraces which got under your skin. I don't know any Essex cricketer who played frequently at Leyton who did not come to love it. It was like a dirty urchin—grimy, lovable, but not lovely.

It was the home ground of hallowed names; Charles Kortright, Freddie Fane, Charles McGahey, Walter Mead, John Douglas, Stan Nichols, Father Gillingham, Jack Russell, Jack O'Connor, Percy Perrin, the Ashtons, the fiery moustached Leonard Crawley and many others.

This ground of 'unwonted loveliness' did the trick. Essex were granted first-class status in 1894 and entered the County Championship in 1895.

Their first season was disastrous. Not one of the ten county matches played was won but two years later, in 1897, the county, under the leadership of H. G. Owen, finished third. Undoubtedly Essex had a formidable team at this stage. Charles Kortright and Walter Mead were at their best; Charles McGahey was developing into a fine player; Percy Perrin was a youngster of great promise and F. G. Bull a formidable bowler.

There was a great win over Yorkshire at Leyton in 1897. Charles Kortright and Bull dismissed them for under 200 in each innings. Then Kortright and Mead won the match by hitting off 39 needed to win when Essex had lost seven wickets for 93.

AUSTRALIANS TWICE BEATEN

Two seasons later the county beat the Australians at Leyton by 126 runs. The famous visitors were dismissed in their second innings by 'Sailor' Young and Walter Mead for 73, their lowest total of the tour. Young was chosen for the third and fourth Tests against them.

It was at Leyton that J. W. H. T. Douglas made his first appearance in championship cricket and was bowled by George Hirst in each innings without scoring. Few have got the dreaded 'pair' on their début.

In 1905 the Australians were beaten again. Here are the teams. Essex: F. L. Fane, Carpenter, C. McGahey, the Rev. F. H. Gillingham, G. Tosetti, P. Perrin, Reeves, J. W. H. T. Douglas, Russell (E.), Tremlin and Buckenham. Australia: R. A. Duff, J. Darling, C. Hill. M. A. Noble, C. E. McLeod, S. E. Gregory, A. J. Hopkins, D. R. A. Gehrs, A. Cotter, F. Laver and P. M. Newland. Scores: Essex 118 and 203; Australians 100 and 202.

This was one of Leyton's greatest matches, but not for 'Peter' Perrin. He fell for a duck in each innings. Buckenham and Tremlin shared the wickets in each innings, Buckenham taking six each time and Tremlin four.

In 1911 Douglas became captain. By the time cricket restarted after the First World War the personnel of the Essex team had changed and several old favourites had gone the way all good cricketers go.

Percy Perrin, maker of the Essex record score of 343 not out against Derbyshire at Chesterfield in 1904, and Charles McGahey, the famous Essex 'twins', hung on for a little while but both were rapidly reaching the end of their playing days in first-class cricket. Johnny Douglas, on the other hand, was establishing himself as one of the world's greatest all-rounders. He was the first of an Essex trio, Douglas–Nichols–Bailey, who were to 'hog' the all-rounder position in the England team for almost half a century. Douglas played his first Test in 1911 and his last in 1924—in all he played in twenty-three. Stan Nichols had only fourteen Tests, but what competition there was in his time. I venture to assert that in his prime he would have 'cake-walked' into the present England team. He ranged from 1929 to 1939, and the inimitable Trevor Bailey represented England in sixty-one Tests from 1949 to 1959.

A PROUD RECORD

At the risk of being accused of looking at Essex players through rose-tinted glasses—and why not—I claim this record to be one of which the county has every reason to be very proud.

Of Johnny Douglas I have written much in my time. He nursed me into first-class cricket. He had faith in me as a cricketer when I had lost it in myself. So I'm completely and utterly biassed as far as he is concerned. Yet nobody can deny he was a great cricketer, a great fighter and a grand personality. Stan Nichols, like Douglas and Bailey, was born and bred in Essex. He came from that lovely little village of Stondon Massey, but played most of his early cricket at Wickford. Douglas did the 'double' five times in his career. Trevor Bailey achieved it for the fifth time last season but the big lion-hearted Stan Nichols did it no fewer than eight times, the last five in a row. Yet Nichols played in fourteen Tests compared with Bailey's sixty-one. There are, of course, many more Test matches played nowadays.

Bailey's record is the best. It is a great pity that the dour, tenacious

Trevor was not a contemporary of 'Johnny Won't Hit Today'. How proud
Douglas would have been of Trevor's tremendous fighting spirit which
makes him an infinitely better player when the strain is on and when the
tension is at its greatest.

BAILEY'S GOLDEN YEAR

I'm glad to have it recorded in *Wisden*, for the generations to come, that
the season the selectors decided to 'sack' the man who made a habit of
pulling England 'out of the cart' was Bailey's best. Last season was his
'Golden Year'. He scored 2,011 runs and took 100 wickets, although at the
beginning of the season he could not bowl because of an injury sustained in
Australia the previous winter.

Two people could not look less alike than Bailey and Douglas, yet their
outstanding quality was the same—guts. Throughout his brilliant Test
career—and the more you study the figures the more impressive it
becomes; 2,290 runs, 132 wickets—this great all-rounder, Bailey, played to
win the hard way. He was never the selectors' 'blue-eyed boy'. Far from it.
They took the first opportunity of dropping him on the flimsiest of excuses
or hardly one at all. We will have to dig deep into the records to find a
precedent for sacking a Test player during his best season.

Let us return to Essex between the wars—a colourful period in the
history of the Club. Cricketers good, bad and indifferent appeared and
disappeared, financial crises were as frequent as the flowers in spring, and
the county see-sawed between fourth and sixteenth in the Championship,
only missing the fifth and eleventh positions.

The first sensation of this era was the sacking of John Douglas as captain.
After he underwent an operation for appendicitis in the winter of 1925–26
his cricket skill seemed to desert him. He hung on, tenacious and
determined as ever, but 1927 confirmed the fear that he was past his best.
At the end of the 1928 season, which was my first for the county, the
committee asked Douglas to resign. He refused. The committee appointed
H. M. Morris to succeed him. It was a bad choice. Morris, having accepted
the position, was disinclined to play regularly, which meant somebody else
had to do the job and it frequently fell upon my shoulders.

TOO MANY PLAYERS

Team selection was bad. There was little or no continuity. In 1928 no fewer
than thirty-eight different players were called upon, twenty-six of them
bowlers. In one season seventeen amateurs played. Fortunately there was
a solid professional nucleus of Jim Cutmore, Dudley Pope, Laurie
Eastman, Jack O'Connor, Jack Russell and Stan Nichols. Denis Wilcox
and T. N. Pearce, both to become successful captains, appeared on the
scene and made their mark. The august contingent of amateurs included
Leonard Crawley, Nigel Wykes, Claude and Hubert Ashton, Frank
Gilligan, a most useful wicket-keeper, and, when business permitted,
Harold Palmer, H. T. O. Smith, 'Hopper' Read, and, of course, that
magnificent human specimen and England fast bowler Ken Farnes.

YORKSHIRE'S RECORD 555

Throughout their history, Essex have figured in many remarkable matches far too numerous for me to go into in any detail in this brief review. One, however, must be mentioned for two decisive reasons. First, it still stands as a record and is unlikely ever to be beaten, and second, as Walter Robins once taunted me during a heated discussion, it is one claim to cricket fame . . . I was captain of Essex in the famous match in which Percy Holmes (224 not out) and Herbert Sutcliffe (313) of Yorkshire scored 555 runs for the first wicket.

This match took place in 1932 at Leyton, where the scorers used to sit directly under the scoreboard and consequently could not see when it went wrong. It erred on that fateful morning. With the total 555 Sutcliffe, with the new record achieved, took a terrific swipe at a ball from Laurie Eastman and was clean bowled. The two batsmen posed under the scoreboard for the Press photographers and then the balloon went up. The scorers declared the total to be 554 and not 555.

A very worried Charles McGahey, then Essex scorer, came to me in the dressing room. Would I agree to the total being changed? The umpires (what accommodating people they are) said a no-ball had not been recorded. There was no doubt in Charles's mind an extra run was being 'found'.

I told him I thought the two batsmen had put up a magnificent performance and it would be cruel luck if they were to be deprived of the honour of breaking the record because our scoreboard had gone wrong. If the umpires said a no-ball had not been recorded it was O.K. with me. Charles went away happy.

The Essex bowling figures are worth recalling. Nichols none for 105, Daer none for 106 and Peter Smith, then an up-and-coming spin bowler, none for 128. Even Bray bowled one over.

TOM PEARCE TAKES OVER

The following season (1933) Tom Pearce took over the captaincy until mid-July when he handed over to Denis Wilcox. This arrangement worked admirably for several years. It brought continuity and good captaincy, for both were excellent batsmen and natural leaders. In 1933 Essex finished fourth in the Championship. Thirteen matches were won. O'Connor scored nearly 2,000 runs; Cutmore, Eastman, Nichols, Pope and Taylor all over 1,000. It was the first time six members of the team had topped 1,000. Nichols did the double. Peter Smith obtained his 100 wickets showing that he had become a googly and leg-break bowler of top class.

From 1934 to the outbreak of war few counties could command so many fast bowlers as Essex. I remember going to play Notts when bodyline was very much in the air. When Arthur Carr came into the dressing room for our team, Tom Pearce said with a grin: 'Here it is, Arthur. We've got four fast bowlers. I take it it's going to be a friendly game?' And we did have four good 'uns—Stan Nichols, Ken Farnes, H. T. O. Smith and 'Hopper' Read.

The mercurial and entertaining J. W. A. Stephenson also began to hurl himself about the field in the interests of Essex. His career was all too short. What would we not give for a 'Stevie' these days.

The season of 1934 saw the tragic death of Dudley Pope, killed in a motor accident. In 1935 a game that must go down in Essex history as 'Nichols' Match' took place at Huddersfield. He took four Yorkshire wickets for 17, Read snatched six for 11 and Yorkshire were all out for 31. Then Nichols went on to make 146 out of a total of 334 and took seven for 37 in the second innings. Nichols actually made 16 runs more than Yorkshire did in the match. He put out Len Hutton for a duck in each innings. Essex won by an innings and 204 runs and Nichols sent me a telegram, 'Revenge is sweet.' I did not have to be told to what he referred.

At the end of the 1938 season the county suffered a severe shock for Tom Pearce announced he would not be able to continue as captain the following summer. After much thought and negotiation J. W. A. Stephenson took over, assisted by George Unwin and Denis Wilcox. It was not a good arrangement, but this time the team did not suffer. It was so strong. It had the best opening attack in the country in Farnes, Stephenson and Nichols, with Ray Smith, Peter Smith, Taylor and Laurie Eastman in support. The batting was powerful. The county finished fourth.

KEN FARNES KILLED

The war knocked a nasty hole in the Essex team, as it did in other counties. For one reason or another, half the players who had finished fourth in the Championship in 1939 were unavailable. Ken Farnes had been killed; Laurie Eastman had died; Jack O'Connor had secured the excellent post of coach at Eton; Stan Nichols was in his middle forties and was too old; and Reg Taylor had decided to give up professional cricket for a business career.

On the other side of the balance sheet was the return of Tom Pearce as captain. His value to the county in those difficult seasons following the war cannot be fully assessed. His experience, his unfailing good humour, his batting consistency and his quiet determination to mould a new young side all helped materially at a time when it was not easy to repair the ravages of the war years. His opening attack—almost for the first time in the history of the county—was woefully weak. Ray Smith had to shoulder the brunt of it. His cousin Peter, now an experienced slow bowler, was frequently called upon to bowl for long spells. It did him some good. He was chosen to go to Australia at the end of the 1946 season.

Some good young batsmen began to appear. Dickie Dodds, playing as an amateur, made a thousand runs. Sonny Avery was most consistent and Tom Pearce and Denis Wilcox were always good for runs. Tommy Wade, who first played with me as a bowler, became a wicket-keeper. Ray Smith was a colourful all-rounder who believed in hitting the ball hard and often. Dick Horsfall, a Yorkshireman, became successor to Jack O'Connor, but never lived up to his early promise. Ken Preston was a new, young and most promising fast bowler who unfortunately broke his leg playing football.

When he recovered he found he could not bowl so fast and he had to change to a fast-medium swing bowler. Frank Vigar, an all-rounder of much promise who had made his début in 1938, was a regular member of the side. He never quite made the grade.

BAILEY AND INSOLE ARRIVE

During these troublesome seasons Tom Pearce and the Essex committee had their eyes sharply focused on two Cambridge University undergraduates who looked as if they were right out of the top drawer. They were Trevor Bailey and Doug Insole. Both were in the Light Blues side in 1947 and 1948. Insole was Cambridge captain in 1949, when they won a great victory in the Varsity match.

As Bailey was given a job on the county's administrative staff and Insole, in due course, secured a business appointment which enabled him to play regularly, these two became the back-bone of the Essex team for the next decade. I have already referred to Bailey's brilliant Test career. Insole's does not compare with it but he had played for England nine times and was a highly successful vice-captain to Peter May in South Africa in 1956–57.

Few counties in postwar years have been so fortunate with their captains as Essex. After Tom Pearce's long and successful spell there was Insole to take over in 1950 and carry on where Pearce left off—both fine cricketers, both good, intelligent and popular skippers.

In addition, throughout this period Essex had the best all-rounder in the country in Trevor Bailey. Yet the county finished more frequently in the lower half of the Championship. Only in the last two or three years have the players made their presence felt. In 1957 Essex finished fifth, in 1958 sixth, and last season ninth.

Gordon Barker, who made his début in 1954, continued to improve and became one of the best opening batsmen in the land. Les Savill, having done his national service, is fulfilling early promise and Brian Taylor, a wicket-keeper-batsman who failed to take the golden opportunity offered him by a tour of South Africa in 1956–57, has recaptured his best form.

Bill Greensmith, a leg-break bowler who might easily make the Test grade, and Micky Bear, one of the best fielders in the game today, are other members of the present young Essex team who could hit the headlines, but my eye is on young Barry Knight who came within five runs of doing the 'double' in his first full season with the county.

Will this twenty-two-year-old fast bowler and attractive batsman follow in the footsteps of Trevor Bailey? He could well do it.

In a review so short as this there are bound to be errors of omission both regarding players and matches. I should like to refer to one of two games in recent years. There was that never-to-be-forgotten day at Southend in 1948 when the Australians, led by Don Bradman, hit 721 runs in six hours, a record unlikely to be surpassed in first-class cricket. After Bill Brown and Don Bradman had made hundreds Sam Loxton and Ron Saggers did the same, putting on 219 in ninety minutes.

Then there was the remarkable match against Derbyshire at Chesterfield the previous season, which Essex won by five wickets. Peter Smith, going in last, made 163 and Essex from being 65 for six finished with 417. The Essex batting order is worth recalling. It was Dodds, Cray, Avery, Crabtree, Vigar, Horsfall, Wilcox (captain), Bailey, Insole, Smith, R., Smith, P. No, I have not forgotten the wicket-keeper. He was Doug Insole, who had kept for Cambridge. The last wicket added 218, a record for the county.

THE CHAMPIONS BEATEN

In more recent times an outstanding match was that against Surrey at Clacton in 1957. Surrey had a comfortable first-innings lead of 133, thanks to centuries from Bernard Constable and Ken Barrington. Essex, however, shot out the champions for 119 in the second innings and were set to get 253 in four hours. Insole played what was in truth a 'captain's innings'. He hit sixteen boundaries in making 115 and with help from Savill and Bear won the match with twenty minutes to spare. And Surrey had their full 'England' attack, Alec Bedser, Loader, Laker and Lock, as well as Eric Bedser.

Those who played in the match and those who saw it will not easily forget the victory which came to Essex by two runs over Northamptonshire at Ilford last season with one minute left. Essex, put in, scored 336 for seven, declared, Trevor Bailey and Les Savill making hundreds. Northants were dismissed for 193. Then Essex were bowled out for 127 and Northants wanted 271 in four hours.

The sensations came in the last over for it looked as if Northants were home. They wanted only three more runs and had three wickets left, but lost them all in four balls, Denis Brookes (109) running himself out in his anxiety to win the game.

The return match at Northampton had a similar finish. This time in the last over Northants needed four runs with four wickets in hand. They made only two, lost three wickets and a thrilling contest was left drawn. While such endings to matches continue to occur there is not much to worry about. Mind you, the game would have greater attraction if more of the excitement and sensation could be brought into the first and second days.

NOTES BY THE EDITOR [1960]

The 1960 Almanack also featured analyses of the problems of umpiring and the prevalence among modern bowlers of the arts of 'Throw and Drag'. But of far more interest than either of these features was a small item in the editorial notes which raised one of most notorious ghosts of the past. The antics of the Yorkshire club over the years have given infinite pleasure, off the field as well as on and it is doubtful if any county ever boasted a more eccentric record than Yorkshire when it came to captaincy. Having overlooked Len Hutton as a captain even though he had led his country to first regain and then retain the Ashes, the county then appointed another professional captain, an act which prompted the Editor of the Almanack to raise the comic spectre of Lord Hawke maundering away on the theme of Gentlemanliness. It is revealing that the Editor, Norman Preston, should, as late as 1960, express incredulity that anyone should seriously suggest the abolition of the distinction between amateurs and professionals. His closing remark is perfectly understandable, but it seems surprising that so illustrious a counsellor of the game as the Editor of Wisden should be so out of touch with the world over the hedge. Only three years later he was to write on the same theme in very different terms.

YORKSHIRE'S PROFESSIONAL CAPTAIN

For the first time for many years, Yorkshire now have a professional captain in J. V. Wilson, who has been appointed to succeed J. R. Burnet. Thirty-five years ago the late Lord Hawke said some strong things about professional captains and during the course of time the leadership of Yorkshire has been linked with them, whereas he was expressing his opinion about England.

In the summer of 1924, C. Parkin, then at his zenith, criticised A. E. R. Gilligan, the England captain, for not calling upon him to bowl on the third morning of the Edgbaston Test when South Africa, dismissed by Gilligan and Tate for 30, followed on. Parkin wrote disparagingly about Gilligan's captaincy in general and said he would never play for England again. At the Yorkshire annual meeting in the following January, Lord Hawke touched on this matter and said:

'Pray God no professional will ever captain the England side. I love professionals, every one of them, but we have always had an amateur skipper. If the time comes when we are to have no more amateurs captaining England, well, I don't say England will become exactly like League football, but it will be a thousand pities, and it will not be for the good of the game.'

Lord Hawke did not live to see Leonard Hutton, a Yorkshire professional, restore England's postwar cricket fortunes, nor to learn of the knighthood Hutton received for his services to cricket.

In the early years of his long reign as captain of Yorkshire (1883–1909) Lord Hawke was often helped by Louis Hall, a professional who at one time was termed assistant-captain and led Yorkshire throughout the summer of 1885 when Lord Hawke was away.

I also wonder what Lord Hawke's reaction would have been to recent suggestions that the present time may be the twilight of the amateur. It is seriously suggested that all players should be termed 'Cricketers' and that there should be no distinction between amateur and professional. In the past I may have thought along these lines, but when one remembers the great work done by B. H. Lyon for Gloucestershire, R. W. V. Robins for Middlesex, A. B. Sellers and J. R. Burnet for Yorkshire, and W. S. Surridge and P. B. H. May for Surrey, surely, no matter what the financial set-up, English cricket, and particularly county cricket, cannot afford to lose the amateur. His very independence contributes to the welfare of the game and therefore to the well-being of the professional. Look what M. C. Cowdrey, D. B. Carr, E. R. Dexter, D. J. Insole, T. E. Bailey, M. J. K. Smith, A. C. D. Ingleby-Mackenzie have meant to their sides. True, there are capable professionals who command respect from their men, but I would not like to see the amateur disappear entirely from the English scene.

THE GREATEST TEST MATCH [1961]

Australia and West Indies Tie at Brisbane

BY E. M. WELLINGS

Although nobody seemed to have intended it, least of all the Editor, the theme of the 1961 edition was Contradiction. While Norman Preston brooded over ominous statistics showing a fall in attendances from the 2.3 million of 1947 to just over one million in 1960, Harry Altham made an unconvincing attempt to pass himself off as Dr. Pangloss with a piece called 'Cricket Thrives Here'. Alec Bedser in his valedictory referred to the decline in public support for the first-class game and was already harping on his theme for which he would become renowned in retirement, the tendency of the younger generation to shy away from hard work. In contrast, Jack Fingleton took as his title 'Cricket Alive Again', implying that it had recently suffered from yet another of its periodic death throes. Yet the contents of his essay contradicted its title, for he seemed to have convinced himself that the days of the virtuoso batsman were gone. There was also an exhaustive analysis of the latest campaign to outlaw various forms of illegal bowling, most of which makes rather quaint reading today. The selections for the 'Five Cricketers of the Year' offered a hope for the future with the introduction of E. R. Dexter, but they also included evidence of what Lord Harris would certainly have taken to be the inroads into the game of the dastardly influence of bolshevism—the essay on R. A. McLean opened with a quotation from Bernard Shaw. The 1961 edition also contained an essay entitled 'The Greatest Test Match', a claim by no means inflated and whose contents recorded a contest still remembered for the breathless heights to which cricket can rise in its most exalted moments. The writer was a sporting journalist whose cricket reports were familiar to readers of the London 'Evening News'.

I WAS there. I saw it all. That is something that countless thousands would give much to be able to say. For it was The Greatest Test Match, The Greatest Cricket Match and surely The Greatest Game ever played with a ball. Australia v. West Indies at Brisbane from December 9 to December 14 was already a great match before it bounded explosively to its amazing climax to produce the only tie in the history of Test cricket.

Some time has elapsed since the remarkable events of Hall's last over, in which the final three Australian wickets fell, five runs were made to bring the scores level and one catch dropped. But the picture of those events is more vivid now than it was at the time. Then all was confusion, for so much happened and thrill followed thrill so rapidly that everything became an exciting jumble. Even Meckiff, the last man out, was confused and thought West Indies had won by a run.

THE FINAL OVER

Six runs were wanted by Australia when Hall began what had to be the final over. The first ball hit Grout high on the leg, dropped at his feet, and he and Benaud scampered a single. Now the odds were heavily on Australia for Benaud was 52 and batting in match-winning vein. But immediately the odds were levelled. The next ball was a bouncer and Benaud aimed to hook it, as Davidson a few minutes earlier had superbly hooked a similar ball. He merely nicked it, and every West Indian leapt for joy as Alexander took the catch. So Meckiff arrived to play his first ball quietly back to Hall, and Australia needed a run off each ball.

A bye was run, and Grout skied the fifth ball just out on the leg side. Fielders converged from all directions, but Hall was the tallest and most determined, and he alone put his hands to it as the batsmen were running a single. It bounced out, and the fielders drooped in despair. The next delivery almost completed their despair, for Meckiff courageously clouted it loftily away to leg. He and Grout ran one, then another, and staked all on a third to win the match as Hunte was preparing to throw from the square-leg boundary. It was a glorious low throw, fast and true, and though Grout hurled himself at the line and skidded home on severely grazed forearms he could not counter the speed of the ball.

Umpire Hoy flung his right arm high to announce the decision immediately to everyone anxiously looking towards him, and again the West Indies leapt and flung their arms in triumph. A minute or so later umpire and fielders repeated their actions, only more so. At the fall of the last wicket the joy of the West Indies was so expressed in leaps and bounds and running about that the scene might have served for a ballet of ultramodern abandon. The man who sent them into transports of delight and tied the match was little Solomon when Kline smoothly played the seventh ball of that fateful last over towards square-leg. Meckiff at the other end was well launched on a run, but he never made it. With little more than one stump's width to aim at, Solomon threw the wicket down, as he had done some dozen minutes earlier from farther away to run out Davidson and give his side the chance to save themselves.

THREE RUN OUT

That was not the least remarkable feature of this very remarkable match. Three of the last four batsmen were run out by a fielding side whose throwing often had their wicket-keeper racing yards from the target area to retrieve the ball. At the crisis the throws straightened themselves, or perhaps they were made by the right men, for Hunte and Solomon were not often among the wild throwers.

That final over lasted nine minutes and ended four minutes after the appointed time. Not so long ago it would have been cut short at the dismissal of Grout. But for a comparatively recent law amendment, which provided for the last over being played out whatever the time, we lucky spectators would not have palpitated to the last tremendous thrill of that last tremendous over. Nor perhaps would spectators, bounding with excitement no less than the fielders, have raced across the ground to cheer and call for the heroes of the day, and repeat their cheers again and again in front of the players' pavilion.

UNFORGETTABLE SIGHT

That, like the freely expressed delight of the West Indies fielders, was an unforgettable sight. They were not so numerous as that gathered rapturously in front of The Oval pavilion in 1953, when Hutton's team at last recovered the Ashes from Australia, but the Queenslanders made up for their relative lack of numbers by their enthusiasm. We all recognised that this was more than a tied match. It was tied by teams playing in Homeric manner.

At the climax neither side made the slightest attempt to play for safety. Both were set on winning or perishing in the attempt. With three wickets standing, including that of Benaud, Australia could surely have coasted home to safety, and since they had gallantly pulled themselves up from a position of imminent defeat only two hours earlier, we could hardly have blamed them if they had. On the other side Hall, who had earlier wasted many deliveries barely within the batsman's reach, bowled straight more consistently than at any previous time in the match. Australia and West Indies played out the game in a spirit which should serve as an example to all others.

There have been other Test matches not far removed from being tied. Perhaps the most momentous was that at The Oval in 1902, when Australia were cantering home until Jessop hit a hurricane century and Hirst and Rhodes, the last pair, scored the final runs with typical Yorkshire unconcern in singles to give England the win by one wicket. Now in 1960 the Brisbane Test eclipsed that and all other close and thrilling finishes.

RIGHT EXAMPLE

From first to last the spirit of enterprise was in striking contrast to the play in most other recent Tests. Almost coinciding with it a bitter defensive contest was waged by India and Pakistan without ever any prospect of a definite result. Only two years earlier Brisbane had been the scene of the dullest ever England–Australia Test. England based their sketchy plans entirely on defensive batting and restrictive practices, and there was hardly a hint at batting enterprise until, on the last afternoon, O'Neill hit out for an Australian win. More recently West Indies and England opposed each other with nothing but negative intentions.

Test cricket had come to a sorry pass. Unpalatable though it is to admit, England developed the tight, restrictive tactics. Having then superior forces, they proved victorious for a time. It is not, therefore, surprising that others followed their lead and, in particular, sought to play England at their own game. Hence the tedium of many recent matches. Now Australia and West Indies have given a new lead, which England can neglect to follow only at the risk of grave loss of prestige.

SOBERS' CENTURY

England's recently defensive opponents in the West Indies were very different players against Australia at Brisbane. From the outset their batsmen were attacking, and they hoisted the first 50 off only 58 balls. Their batting attack was somewhat undisciplined and cost wickets, but, in the course of a magnificent stand of 174, Sobers and Worrell proved how fruitful discreet aggression can be. They were superb, and the hundred by Sobers in just over two hours, from no more than 29 overs, was the fastest Test century for many years. Sobers had the glory in his team's innings of 453, which brought runs at the rare average rate of 4.5 per eight-ball over. But Worrell was the man of great cricketing character who imposed discipline on his side's play throughout the match. In this respect Solomon's well-judged batting gave him valuable assistance.

Before the end Hall hit furiously and played amusingly. A partnership between him and Trueman would be enormous fun. Then Australia played an innings of 505 which, by comparison with that of their opponents, did not entirely commend itself to the home critics. Without that comparison, however, it would have been very well received by spectators disillusioned by other Tests. Yet O'Neill's 181, his highest Test score at the time, was not up to the standard of his innings on the same ground in 1958. In the meantime he had apparently fallen into the stultifying groove of current Test cricket.

GREAT PACE

A second West Indies innings of 284, maintained largely by Worrell and Solomon after some of the earlier batsmen had shown suicidal tendencies, left Australia 310 minutes in which to make 233. And so to the final remarkable chapter. It began with Hall, a bowler of great pace and enormous, though sometimes misplaced enthusiasm, bowling now with greater discipline and taking West Indies to the brink of success. Half Australia were out for 57, and Hall had four for 37. Then a sixth wicket fell at 92, and those watchers who lived in Sydney were planning to catch the 5.45 plane. They had to wait until the following morning.

Most batting sides, I think, would have tried to play for a draw in these circumstances. Australia did not. They had their captain at the wicket, and he and Davidson set off for victory. Davidson had already had a great match. He had taken 11 wickets and scored 44. Moreover, while the general standard of Australia's fielding was below their best standards, his own work in the field had been flawless. Now he added 80 more vigorous runs to his fine record and, after playing himself through a sticky period at the start, earned every single of them. Such was his all-round success that in normal circumstances the Test would rightly go down in history as Davidson's Match. As it is, this is to be known as The Greatest Test Match, but it was big enough to carry also a sub-title recognising Davidson's performance.

UP WITH THE CLOCK

He and Benaud batted with outstanding judgment. They played the bowling strictly on its merits and brought off some sterling strokes, among which Davidson's hook off a head-high bumper from Hall stands out as a vivid memory. And they ran like whippets. Time after time they had the West Indies hurling fiercely at their stumps and missing. It would not have mattered if the stumps had been hit, for their judgment was splendid and their understanding perfect. It was astonishing that, after all the hard work Davidson had done, he was running as keenly and as rapidly at the end as at the start. He was tremendously fit.

After tea Australia had to score just above one run a minute, which was not easy when the average tally of overs per two-hour session was around 27. But they kept well up with the clock, and with 12 minutes to go only seven were needed. The story seemed cut and dried. Australia were going to win, and Worrell would perhaps regret not having used the left-arm off-breaks and googlies of Sobers earlier. When Sobers did arrive to use spin after a spell at medium pace, Davidson and Benaud were in full blast and he could not part them.

DEADLY AIM

It was Solomon who did that when 12 minutes remained. Davidson went for an extra run. Perhaps this was the one and only time during the partnership when a direct hit by a fielder could have been effective. Solomon achieved the direct hit from some 25 yards and square with the wicket on the leg side. There followed the two other run-out wickets, and when the dust of excitement had settled there was some talk that Australia had only themselves to blame for faulty running. That is ungenerous to both sides and takes no account of the daring running of Benaud and Davidson, without which they could not have levelled the scores. The attempted runs by Grout and Meckiff in the last over were fully justified.

Post-mortems on such a match are out of place. I am happily content to have been one of the company of 4,100 who saw the thrilling and inspiring end of this greatest match. It serves as a challenge to all cricketers and calls to them to tackle their matches in the same spirit of sporting enterprise. This was essentially a sporting game, as the crowd recognised when they called for the 22 victors in the cause of cricket to show themselves on the patio of their pavilion. Score:

AUSTRALIA v. WEST INDIES

At Brisbane, December 9, 10, 12, 13, 14, 1960. A tie.

West Indies

C. C. Hunte c Benaud b Davidson	24 — c Simpson b Mackay	39
C. Smith c Grout b Davidson	7 — c O'Neill b Davidson	6
R. Kanhai c Grout b Davidson	15 — c Grout b Davidson	54
G. Sobers c Kline b Meckiff	132 — b Davidson	14
*F. M. Worrell c Grout b Davidson	65 — c Grout b Davidson	65
J. S. Solomon hit wkt b Simpson	65 — lbw b Simpson	47
P. Lashley c Grout b Kline	19 — b Davidson	0
†F. C. M. Alexander c Davidson b Kline	60 — b Benaud	5
S. Ramadhin c Harvey b Davidson	12 — c Harvey b Simpson	6
W. Hall st Grout b Kline	50 — b Davidson	18
A. L. Valentine not out	0 — not out	7
L-b 3, w 1	4 B 14, 1-b 7, w 2	23

1/23 2/42 3/65 4/239 5/243 6/283   453   1/13 2/88 3/114 4/127   284
7/347 8/366 9/452   5/210 6/210 7/241 8/250
                                                            9/253

Bowling: *First Innings*— Davidson 30—2—135—5; Meckiff 18—0—129—1; Mackay 3—0—15—0; Benaud 24—3—93—0; Simpson 8—0—25—1; Kline 17.6—6—52—3. *Second Innings*—Davidson 24.6—4—87—6; Meckiff 4—1—19—0; Benaud 31—6—69—1; Mackay 21—7—52—1; Kline 4—0—14—0; Simpson 7—2—18—2; O'Neill 1—0—2—0.

Australia

C. C. McDonald c Hunte b Sobers	57 — b Worrell	16
R. B. Simpson b Ramadhin	92 — c sub b Hall	0
R. N. Harvey b Valentine	15 — c Sobers b Hall	5
N. O'Neill c Valentine b Hall	181 — c Alexander b Hall	26
L. Favell run out	45 — c Solomon b Hall	7
K. Mackay b Sobers	35 — b Ramadhin	28
A. K. Davidson c Alexander b Hall	44 — run out	80
*R. Benaud lbw b Hall	10 — c Alexander b Hall	52
†W. Grout lbw b Hall	4 — run out	2
I. Meckiff run out	4 — run out	2
L. Kline not out	3 — not out	0
B 2, 1-b 8, w 1, n-b 4	15 B 2, 1-b 9, n-b 3	14

1/84 2/138 3/194 4/278 5/381   505   1/1 2/7 3/49 4/49 5/57   232
6/469 7/484 8/489 9/496   6/92 7/226 8/228 9/232

Bowling: *First Innings*—Hall 29.3—1—140—4; Worrell 30—0—93—0; Sobers 32—0—115—2; Valentine 24—6—82—1; Ramadhin 15—1—60—1. *Second Innings*—Hall 17.7—3—63—5; Worrell 16—3—41—1; Sobers 8—0—30—0; Valentine 10—4—27—0; Ramadhin 17—3—57—1.

Umpires: C. Hoy and C. J. Egar.

HAPPY HAMPSHIRE [1961]

BY H. L. V. DAY

The great sensation of 1961 was the triumph of Hampshire who, after a long history of spectacular doings and moderate results, won their first County Championship. Their captain, Colin Ingleby-Mackenzie, was one of cricket's hearties, a man often said to have believed in the superiority of champagne over roadwork as a bucker-up of spirits and who may well have been right. To mark the occasion Wisden had the happy thought of inviting an old Hampshire player to recall memories of the club in less exalted but no less enjoyable times. No better choice could have been made than Harold Lindsay Vernon Day (1899–1972) who appeared for the county between 1922 and 1931; much of the seriousness of his career was dissipated by the distinctly Wodehousean bearing of his captain, Lionel Tennyson. Day gives a vivid impression of a muscular eccentric whose natural inclination it was to approach life as a phenomenon demanding a wild cavalry charge. Day's account is actually a mite too sober to do full justice to the extraordinary Tennyson. Readers may derive enhanced pleasure from their awareness that Walter Livsey was not only the side's wicket-keeper but also valet/chauffeur to his lordship and often advanced loans to him to subsidise pavilion card games, that Lionel's only recollection of his eminently Victorian grandfather was of 'a beard at the end of the bed', that he was adamant that the Poet Laureate had been responsible for 'Hiawatha' and that he emulated the old boy by publishing his own poetic effusions in the form of a volume with the likely title of 'From Bed to Verse'. The author of the essay won four England caps as a Rugby Union wing three-quarter and after retirement won high praise as a referee and finally as a writer on both games for the daily press. He died just too soon to see his county repeat their 1961 success in the 1973 Championship.

CRICKET is a glorious game chiefly because such a vast amount of fun can be derived from it by all and sundry, except apparently by that tiny fraction of the playing fraternity who engage in county cricket. The fun seems to have gone out of that. Since the war, whatever the reason, there has been an increasing amount of abominably dull stuff served up as entertainment by first-class counties, otherwise why all these proposals to ginger up the players, almost all professionals, and the proceedings?

Much of the blame can be laid at the door of the captains. The difference a lively, gay, adventurous captain can make has been well and truly underlined by A. C. D. Ingleby-Mackenzie. He accepted the challenge between bat and ball which is the essence of cricket, and was rewarded by leading Hampshire to their first Championship.

The full details of that commendable achievement are recorded elsewhere, and it is not my province to comment on it, except perhaps to say that it was accomplished without the doubtful bolstering of pools. Surely it is a bad thing for cricket to be dependent for its very existence on other than its own attractions.

LIVELY SPARKS

I have been asked to recall some of the Hampshire cricketers as I knew them. Cricket for me was a huge lark. How could it have been otherwise with Lionel, Baron Tennyson to cajole, harangue, curse or applaud us as the fancy took him? But he did not by any means have it all his own way. We had some lively sparks like T. O. Jameson, C. P. Brutton, W. R. Shirley, R. Aird and R. P. H. Utley among the amateurs. And no game could ever be insipid with George Brown in action with his antics and mimicry.

There is nothing new under the sun according to Holy Writ. I could not help thinking of this as I listened to the answers of the present Hampshire captain, given doubtless with his tongue well up in his cheek, on his training schedule for his team—wine, women and song, and bed before breakfast.

Forty years ago his predecessor in the captaincy followed the same programme but only for himself, and with the proviso that he frequently never went to bed at all. But he would kick up an unholy stink if he caught any of his young amateurs up after midnight, unless he wanted them for some ploy of his own.

They evidently enjoyed themselves in the dim ages of Hampshire cricket on Broad Halfpenny Down whether victors or vanquished. John Nyren records that they drank punch, 'not your modern cat-lap milk punch, but good unsophisticated John Bull stuff that would make a cat speak! Sixpence a bottle!'

Captaincy of any county, never a tea-party, became increasingly complicated. Lionel's leadership was based on unhesitating obedience. He had no intention of humouring anyone. The choice of his team, its strategy and tactics, if any, were his affair. He would allow no interference. He might or might not accept advice from the Committee, or from our tactful and persuasive secretary, Colonel J. G. Greig, but orders never. When there seemed a singular lack of originality in the management of his bowling I felt like the old pastor who, before setting forth on his visiting rounds, would pray 'O, Lord use me if only in an advisory capacity.'

KENNEDY AND NEWMAN

In match after match he would start with Kennedy and Newman, leaving them on until they were fit to drop. How they kept up their inexhaustible persistence and accuracy through a whole season was a mystery. Kennedy with his beautifully smooth action and his ability to move the ball late in its flight, and off the ground, supported by Newman with his vicious off-break, formed as good an opening attack as any county could then boast. What a harvest of wickets Newman would have reaped under the new l.b.w. rule! Furthermore, they could be relied upon for runs. Look at their figures, 4,926 wickets and 31,829 runs.

George Brown could swing the ball amazingly, but Lionel never dreamt of opening the proceedings with him. I did one day at Worcester and received a blistering telling-off for exercising my initiative. Brown bid fair to be the most accomplished all-rounder of all time. Has any other cricketer ever opened the bowling and the batting, and kept wicket with such mastery? He was unsurpassed, too, as a silly mid-off. As a batsman he pricked the bubble of solemnity if the spirit moved him. He could mix barn-door defence with fierce aggression, and village buffoonery with majestic strokes.

Then there was Philip Mead whose appearance as he came waddling to the wicket caused more bad language among bowlers in my hearing than any other batsman. For a man of his build he was impressively quick on his feet, making him a real joy to watch against slow spinners. It has often been stated that he was dull. Nothing of the sort. He got his hundred before lunch, and once 280 in a day. He never gave his wicket away. After collecting one hundred, you could see him settling down for the next. He had a prejudice against getting out.

OXFORDSHIRE RECRUITS

One whose praises went unsung was A. Bowell. The name may mean very little except to old Hampshire cricketers, but this ginger headed, bowed legged, squat figure, who looked anything but an alert and agile cover-point, was also a very useful opening bat, with every stroke in the book, made from a pronounced two-eyed stance.

He joined the county in 1902 so that, presumably, he must have been past his best when I began to play, but he continued to collect and save runs with great consistency. He was the first of a number of valuable recruits obtained from Oxfordshire including the two Rogers, Brown, Arnold and Herman.

By the time he retired in 1927, Bowell had scored more runs for the county than anyone else except Mead, though Brown and Arnold, who came after him, exceeded his total of 18,510. He rarely failed to gather his thousand runs in a season. His most profitable shot was the square cut. Very quick on his feet, he played spin bowling extremely well, a necessary accomplishment in those days, since every county had one or more good slow spinners.

We had two who might have achieved much greater distinction with any other captain than Lionel. They were T. O. Jameson and Boyes. Jameson, like me, was a regular soldier, and his opportunities were strictly limited.

But whenever he played, or rather was allowed to bowl before batsmen had got dug in, Jameson always looked likely to get wickets. The tragedy was that here was a wonderful support for Kennedy and Newman, if used judiciously, but he was so often wasted. He bowled slow right-arm from an enormous height, he stood six feet four, which appeared absolute jam from the ringside but had even the best batsmen in a pother. He was not merely a technically perfect bowler, he was a schemer, constantly probing a batsman's weakness, or playing upon his indulgence. In addition, he became a very stylish batsman with immense wristy power as befitted an amateur rackets champion. A great pity he could not play more frequently.

The other spinner was Stuart Boyes, taken on the ground staff on the recommendation of Bowell. A slow left-arm bowler, he had a beautifully smooth action, turned the ball on any wicket and appreciated the value of flight. Also a very fine fielder close in. Here again was a bowler who could have been a great foil for Kennedy and Newman, if only he had been used with discretion.

TENNYSON'S AVERSION

It may be that Lionel had an aversion to slow bowlers. They made him look rather foolish, especially Tich Freeman. He would, or could, not shift his bulky frame down the pitch. Crease bound, he had to let fly from where he stood, and leg-break bowlers like Freeman had him expending a vast amount of energy thrashing the air.

He came in to join me one day at Bath as I strove to get runs off Jack White's impeccable length. After taking guard, he summoned me to a mid-wicket conference. 'You've been in an hour, and look at the damned score. You get a move on or else I'll run you out.' I tried to explain that I was baffled by the flight, and would like to see how it should be done. 'Flight!' thundered Lionel. 'I'll give him flight.' He scythed and swished for two overs, but somehow the ball had either not arrived or had gone. At any rate, he departed breathing heavily without disturbing Jack White or the fieldsmen, but to the huge disappointment of the onlookers at the quick end to a knock-about turn.

Against fast bowling it was a very different matter. From his semi-crouching stance which combined the comical with the aggressive, he seemed able to deal effectively with the fast men. Had he not been so impetuous he might have ranked with A. W. Carr and F. T. Mann, among the greatest of firm-footed hitters. Playing against Kent on Whit Monday 1920, he carted a ball into the Bannister club's tennis courts, a distance from hit to pitch of 139 yards, 1 foot, 8 inches. Who can ever forget his heroic 63 one-handed against Gregory and McDonald in the 1921 Test match at Leeds?

He had more than his fair share of luck in the matter of being dropped by fieldsmen. In a match against Essex, J. W. H. T. Douglas must have had him missed half a dozen times, and became so exasperated he informed Lionel in his most endearing manner: 'If I had your —— luck, I'd make a thousand every May.' But those sort of digs left him cold. If success attended his efforts, he rejoiced with undisguised delight, for there was none of that reticence that ties the tongue of the diffident English sportsman.

THOSE TELEGRAMS

One of his pleasant little habits was to send telegrams to his batsmen on the field. One day at Trent Bridge I was trying to cope with the Notts fast bowlers. I failed completely to connect with a very short long hop and duly received it around the heart. It flattened me. As I sat on the ground recovering my composure, I got a telegram which read, 'What do you think your —— bat is for,' signed Lionel. Another young amateur, striving to find his touch, received this encouraging message: 'For God's sake get out and let someone else take a hundred off this jam.'

That same young amateur, not a bad bowler, had the temerity to suggest a change in the bowling. Lionel demanded to know with some heat: 'Who's captain of this outfit?' And the poor chap was banished to the deep—at both ends.

Field placing did not worry Lionel unduly. He made up his mind that you were no good in certain positions and nothing could persuade him otherwise, though he used the most horrific language if a catch was put on the floor, or a boundary let through. An amateur, usually distinguished for his fielding near the wicket, happened to be stationed in the deep on the Portsmouth ground, which was not exactly a billiard table since it overlapped the Rugby pitch. He began by putting down a gaper, and followed this by being deceived by three successive drives bouncing very awkwardly. They all went for four. Lionel then decided to change the bowling, and this unfortunate amateur, cupping his hands to his mouth, shouted: 'Where shall I go, Lionel?' And before word could come back from an irate skipper, a broad Yorkshire voice roared: 'Home, guv'nor, home.'

HISTORIC VICTORY

Lionel had no distorted notions that honour or prestige was dependent upon success. He played with the firm conviction that the principal object was to enjoy oneself. This he certainly never failed to do. It was due to this combination of courage and gaiety that Hampshire won the historic match against Warwickshire at Edgbaston in 1922 after being diddled out for 15 by F. S. G. Calthorpe and Harry Howell in the first innings.

As the match against Leicestershire at Southampton ended early the previous day, Lionel ordered me to accompany him in his car to Edgbaston, which I agreed to do provided he got me there at a reasonable hour. But I reckoned without my Lionel. We made lengthy calls at several country houses and did not get to bed until dawn was breaking. When I tried to remonstrate with him he told me not to worry he would win the toss. Imagine his disgust when Calthorpe called correctly and, of course, batted. We did well to get rid of Warwickshire for 223, and in I went for a much needed rest.

Hardly had I settled to a comfortable snooze than Lionel informed me I was to go in first wicket down. I tried to persuade him to put me in lower. A shout announced that one of our opening pair had been removed. It must have been one of the longest two minutes between the outgoing and incoming batsmen. I eventually reached the crease to be greeted by Tiger Smith's enquiry: 'Did you have a nice nap, sir?' Little did he guess—I was hardly awake. Calthorpe swung the ball prodigiously that day. He sent me one that seemed to start from mid-on and was destined to finish at third slip. I made no effort to impede it, but there was a rattle of bails. The extraordinary procession continued and only Philip Mead, six not out, looked as if any of us had ever held a bat before.

BROWN'S GREAT INNINGS

Before our second innings started Calthorpe suggested that the amateurs should play golf at Stourbridge on the following afternoon, as the match would be over in the morning. This brought forth an immediate flow of good Anglo-Saxon from Lionel, who without a quiver of an eyelid announced that Hampshire would be batting until lunch time on the third day. Naturally this was greeted with howls of derision, and there were some substantial bets at long odds against us even drawing, let alone winning, in which I was a party.

Well, as the record shows, Hampshire made 521, chiefly thanks to a magnificent knock by George Brown who, despite six wickets falling for 186, attacked the bowling from the moment he went in and made 172. He received valuable support from Walter Livsey, the number ten, who had the enormous satisfaction of playing a great part in this miraculous recovery and at the same time hitting his first hundred in county cricket. Once again our two imcomparable bowlers, Kennedy and Newman, carried us to victory by 155 runs. Kennedy took five for 53 and Newman four for 47.

At the end of the match Lionel gave a passable imitation of a Highland fling under the shower baths, and both teams retired to the Queen's Hotel as his guests. What a cricket match! It bore out his whole approach to the game which made it such fun.

If only present-day county players would realise that it matters enormously who is going to win; it does not matter a hoot in hell who has won.

AN ENJOYABLE VISIT TO BRITAIN [1962]
But Bring Back the Old L.B.W. Law

BY JACK FINGLETON

The visit of the 1961 Australians produced a series fought in a good spirit and dominated by the feats of two charistmatic captains in Dexter and Benaud. Both men resolved the eventual destination of the pivotal fourth Test in which, with the score at one-all and one drawn, England were left to make 256 to win. Dexter's masterly attacking innings of 76 took the score to 150 for one, with enough time to win and plenty of batting to come. At this point Benaud brought himself on and totally destroyed the England batting. With the final Test drawn, Australia had won both the Series and the Ashes and the account by Jack Fingleton of Benaud's triumph which appeared in the 1962 Wisden takes a seemingly eccentric but shrewdly informed and closely reasoned view of the melodramatic change of fortunes at Old Trafford. Fred Trueman, who had won the Leeds Test with figures of eleven for 88, was now cast as the unwitting villain in Fingleton's version of things; so persuasive is this account that it is difficult to disagree with it. The essay is substantially a medal pinned on the breast of Benaud, who so endeared himself to English crowds and later built on that popularity as an outstanding commentator that he even managed to survive the storms following his involvement in the Packer Circus, one of the less savoury episodes in the history of cricket.

'—and, departing, leave behind us
    Footprints on the sands of time.'

HENRY Longfellow himself departed long before Old Trafford became famous. He died in 1882 (in which year, incidentally, Sir Jack Hobbs was born) but the poet's lines had some significance at Old Trafford on August 1, 1961, when, in the last tumultuous hour of an exciting Test, Richie Benaud pitched on Trueman's footprints and bowled Australia to the telling victory in the series. It was a famous victory for Australia; on the evidence, it was an infamous defeat for England.

Twice, on that last day, England had merely to close its collective fingers on victory. Australia could make only 190 in the first innings on an immaculate pitch. England hit back with 367, an impressive lead. Had the English fieldsmen held their chances, the game could almost have finished on the Monday evening in England's favour with a day to spare. Lawry, badly missed at 25, made 102. Harvey was missed twice but, good fortune notwithstanding, Australia, 296 for six, led by only 119 runs as the game resumed on the final day.

In the first minutes of the morning, Allen took three wickets and victory, surely, was then in England's grasp. This was the first time of sighting on this day although, in sheer technique and command of a tight situation, there was not in the whole series a better partnership than the last-wicket one that followed between Davidson and McKenzie. Last-wicket partnerships, if of any duration, are generally good for a laugh. They mainly comprise a comedy of accidents but there was nothing like that about this one: no chances; no mis-hits; no struggling to cope. Had Davidson, in his long, honest and meritorious Test career, not had to spend toiling hours as a fast bowler he would, I am sure, have revived batting memories of Frank Woolley. This is not sacrilege. He drives as Woolley drove—clean, full-blooded strokes of artistry and challenge that cleave the fieldsmen and singe the grass—but long stretches of fast bowling will dim the batting ardour of most. Davidson, this day, came fresh to his batting task. In one over from Allen, he hit two prodigious 6s and two 4s that surged to the boundary. At the other end was the splendidly proportioned McKenzie, turned 20 only a few weeks before yet playing with the cool head of a veteran and a bat as straight as a surveyor's plumbob.

Was Benaud a lucky captain? This will seem a strange question to interpose here (and particularly as I intend to probe later this fascinating person and his well-publicised methods) but as that last-wicket partnership went on and on that sunny Manchester morning I often noticed Davidson glance towards the Australian balcony. What did he want? One experienced in Test cricket knew immediately that Davidson sought instructions. He wanted Benaud to appear and show by actions his wishes: to give a traffic policeman's 'stop' sign to say he wished Davidson to hold on longer and make England's fight against the clock a harder one; to hold up all fingers to suggest that he wanted the Australian innings to end, say, in ten minutes; to swing with his hands to say he wanted more quick runs.

But Benaud didn't appear. He, himself, had been in the midst of the three quick dismissals in early morning. That sickening set-back had upset whatever preconceived plans the Australians might have had and, moreover, it had put them badly on the run. This brilliant last-wicket stand had brought them back into the game but it was most unexpected, naturally, and even the experienced Davidson wanted a skipper's sign as to intentions. For a period the partnership lost character in its indecisiveness and it was fortuitous that McKenzie should have fallen when he did, just on one o'clock. The partnership was 98.

England thus wanted 256 runs in 230 minutes. In mid-afternoon, the game was as good as over. England, 150 for one, needed only 106 runs in as many minutes. Back in Australia, with the hour around midnight, most turned off their radios and went to bed, accepting the seemingly inevitable.

Come weal, come woe, no Test side in such a position should ever have lost this game. Dexter, in one of the great attacking innings of the century, was 76. Benaud didn't seem to have a card to play. Just previously, against the clamour of the crowd, he had called for drinks. On a hot day, perspiring bowlers and batsmen do need a drink but this call by Benaud seemed more, possibly, in the nature of an old soldier's trick—hoping that the break in play and concentration might do what his bowlers so obviously couldn't.

It made no difference. Dexter sailed on and Subba Row sewed up his end more securely. All that England wanted was just ten more minutes of Dexter but, hereabouts, Benaud played absolutely his last card in the pack. He came around the stumps to pitch on Trueman's marks at the other end. He had to bowl around the stumps to hit the marks at such an angle that the batsmen were forced to play at the ball. Had he bowled over the stumps, the batsmen need not have played with the bat the ball off the roughage.

Benaud had discussed the possibilities of this move the night before with Ray Lindwall, the old Australian bowling fox. Lindwall thought there was merit in it although I doubt whether either thought there was victory in it. Had Benaud thought so, surely he would have tried it sooner.

Dexter went and May came. Usually so reliable and capable, the English captain immediately perpetrated two palpable errors. A swing to fine-leg is always risky. It is doubly risky to a ball coming in off the roughage but the biggest error May made was in attempting such a stroke without covering up his line of retreat. His legs didn't protect his stumps—he could not have been l.b.w. at such an angle—and over they went. May hadn't scored. Close came to turn himself and everybody else inside out with some vainglorious swishes to fine leg. He hit Benaud almost straight for six but he swished fine again and was out and then Subba Row fell also. A pall fell over the ground. A game virtually won at twenty minutes to tea was lost by tea and all because Benaud bowled round the stumps to Trueman's marks.

So, then, did Trueman's footprints on the Old Trafford pitch leave their imprint on the sands of cricket time. Thus is history made. A little but an important thing with a man like Benaud about.

Yet was it such a little thing? The Australians met Yorkshire at Bradford in the first week of this tour and I wrote in the current issue of the London *Sunday Times* that Trueman's untrammelled passage down the pitch after delivery could play into the Australian leg-spin of Benaud and Simpson in the Tests. It was a tip untaken. Both Trueman and Lock were heavy invaders of the pitch in England in 1956. The Australians then did not deter them. We went to the other extreme two years later in Australia and made such a speciality of asking them to run off the pitch that some of the M.C.C. men were justified in asking where, exactly, they *could* put their feet after delivery.

My first captain in Sydney was the old Australian wicket-keeper, Hanson Carter. He was a Yorkshireman by birth (he displayed an appreciation for pitch niceties that was noticeably absent in the county of his birth in 1961) and woe betide the fast bowler or batsman who ran down the pitch when Carter was about. The offender didn't do it the second time and this was as it should be because captains, batsmen, wicket-keepers and umpires are all custodians of the pitch. Some bowling wear is unavoidable but a bowler should, in his follow-through, have veered off the pitch by the time he has reached the good-length mark from the other end.

Trueman, a most colourful cricketer of whom I am very fond, had been allowed to develop this bad habit. On the evidence, with Benaud the Prosecutor, the series of 1961 turned on his footprints. Millions throughout the United Kingdom this day saw on television or heard on the wireless as this game dropped right out of England's lap. It must have been a depressing business for them. I seemed to detect next day some suggestion of national gloom.

In no sense is this article meant to deal with one's impressions of the 1961 tour. A book is needed to cover a tour in detail but a book is not for one who had no attendant 'ghost'—as so many nowadays have—and who jumped like a grasshopper to and from the television, wireless and Press boxes. So, then, I am forced to concentrate here upon a few facets of the tour and this much must be said immediately: this was the happiest tour of England I have known. It was almost devoid of 'incidents'. To be true, at times, the standard was not of the highest. I never ceased to wonder how a palpably weak Australian bowling side could escape as it did—let alone triumph—but the Australians had the merit of holding the important catches and also had commendable all-round batting strength in Lawry, Simpson, O'Neill, Harvey, Burge, Booth, Davidson and McKenzie. Benaud was a big disappointment in his own batting but herein was the side's greatest asset. It had batting strength in depth and it possessed a positive approach to the batting job. Lawry was outstanding though not fully probed in his sensitivity to spin and spin, moreover, that made him use restricted footwork. For all that, Lawry was admirable in his concentration and devotion to duty. Harvey, not the dasher of old, was still the most technically correct of all the batsmen in both sides because he never failed to use his feet to advance towards the ball. Burge and O'Neill played several really magnificent innings, notable in any era. Simpson was a reliable Test batsman, a very good one, indeed, for all that he sometimes gave the impression that he placed overmuch value upon figures. One stood down unjustly, as he had reason to believe, sometimes finds difficulty in dislodging the chip from his shoulder but O'Neill also had had a similar reverse in his early career and had dismissed it from his mind.

Nothing on the field, however, surpassed the strength of Benaud's power and influence off the field. Here was his greatest victory. His team pulled solidly behind him for the whole of this long tour and this is noteworthy for inevitably, because of man's nature, cliques, caves and cynicisms form from long association. The sight of the same 17 male faces over the breakfast table for nine months in itself often starts bickering but Benaud, like a good officer, kept his men happy. He was always one of them, never aloof. This was achievement Number One.

This team, too, had a good collective business sense. Where it originated I do not pretend to know but whereas on other tours the leading lights were quick to accept for themselves the glittering opportunities that offered for leading lights, this team worked on a co-operative front. It had its own off-field agent who handled the business activities and the team pooled the quite considerable sums that were offered for individual feats in this series. This could do nothing else but make for happy comradeship. There were a few occasions when I thought these offerings for individual Test feats had suspect value. Grout, who had an outstanding series, sometimes attempted his impossible and slip's possible. There might have been some prize reason, also, why Mackay did such a long bowling stint at The Oval on the final day. I thought, too, that Jarman deserved a place in the final Test. These could be assumptions on my part but if certain firms are to draw their publicity from Test matches by awarding individual prizes, those at the helm must be doubly careful to see that they are kept in perspective.

In one particular respect Benaud stood head and shoulders over any international captain I have known. His public-relations work was simply superb. His stated plan of campaign at the beginning, to make every match as interesting as he could, had an instant appeal and was in contrast to that of the preceding captain, Johnson, who said he would use county games for Test purposes. In all his appearances on television and in his statements, Benaud said the right and the happy thing. He had a flair for it. The year before, when in England as a journalist, he did a course on television and he considered this of immense value. This tremendous medium of publicity he used to great advantage.

And then there was the way in which he handled the Press. He had no favourites. He greeted them all as brothers, as indeed they were professionally. I often smiled at the exodus from the Press box when Benaud came from the field. He was always available for questioning and, one surmised, helped many with suggestions for angles and stories. He was cricket's gift to the Press. Some of my brethren are notorious for getting grouches off their typewriters at the tour's end but, understandably, this time they had nothing but bouquets for Benaud and his team.

In so many ways, then, Benaud did an unsurpassed job for his team and the game. There was a suggestion, early in the tour, that he was treating the Press too liberally. It seemed that the order came on high from Australia that he was to be 'gagged' somewhat but, if he was, it didn't last. It wasn't long before Benaud pursued his bland and helpful way again.

I had one experience with him that impressed me considerably. I was staying with Mr. Joc Lynam, Headmaster of the Dragon School at Oxford. He asked whether I might bring several of the team to meet the boys one day. In my time, I knew this would have been an unpopular request. Players of my generation did not take kindly to outside 'jaw' on cricket. I put the request to Benaud. 'Certainly,' he said, and looked into the dressing-room, 'Brian and Frank. Would you go along to a school, please, for half an hour?' And Booth and Misson came off with me and both spoke to the boys in a most pleasant manner. Benaud was always eager to please. No wonder he was always clapped to the centre of every ground on which he played.

A winning captain must have good fortune and Benaud has had his measure of this yet it could be claimed that he has encouraged fortune to smile upon him. There was one occasion in Sydney in a Test against England, when he adopted delaying tactics as rigid and as dubious as any I have seen but he would prefer to forget this. For the most part, he has thrown out challenges and has always been ready to accept them. On good, true Australian pitches he has gambled to excess by sending England and the West Indians in when he won the toss. He won both matches. His declarations have been sound yet sporting. His field captaincy has been markedly sound.

I have written at length upon this facet of Benaud and the tour because I feel they merit it. They have to be known and understood because of the important part they played in making this such a happy tour, such a pleasant one for everybody. I can't recall a single untoward incident. May, Cowdrey and their English charges played a prime part in this and the Australians selectors also contributed by wisely not choosing a single bowler with a suspect action. That was important. It was also sound policy yet Benaud, aided by a cheerful and genial manager in Mr. S. G. Webb, Q.C., and a capable assistant manager in Mr. Ray Steele, did by far the biggest job of all. I pity the Australian captain to come after him. In the public relations sense, Benaud has set him a nigh impossible task because the next one is not likely to possess the sound Press background that Benaud has.

It is interesting to reflect that Benaud came into the job only because of illness to Ian Craig. Benaud believes that reports to high quarters on his possibilities as an Australian captain were, at one stage, most unfavourable. It is interesting, too, that he served his apprenticeship under Keith Miller, one of similar outlook to Benaud who had outstanding successes with New South Wales teams but never got the call to higher honours.

There was remarkably little between the teams in this series. The Old Trafford result could so easily have gone the other way and then the emphasis in analysis would have been upon May and his men. I daresay that English pens will closely dissect English cricket in this 'Hundred Coming Up' edition of Wisden's so that I need not, necessarily, delve too deep with my impressions but this I must say: English batting will never be true to itself until it rediscovers the art of footwork.

Over all, this Australian attack should have taken many a hammering. Dexter gave it one at Old Trafford—his magnificent innings of another calibre at Birmingham suggests he has the all-round game to have a tremendous series in the next one in Australia—but one seemed to detect mental flaws in the English approach to batting. Every one of England's leading batsmen hug the crease with the back foot as if he expects the bailiff to come at any minute and find him not at home. This is distressing because batting is only seen at its best when it is built on footwork and I cannot recall one stroke by a leading English batsman in which he moved out of his crease in this series. Hobbs and Bradman were the great masters of footwork that I saw. Hammond was not far behind.

As a small boy, I read C. B. Fry on footwork. It sounded most abstruse. It went something like this: the weight sways back to the back foot, allowing the front foot to be free. The front foot moves down the pitch and the weight sways on to it, freeing the back foot. The back foot comes up and crosses behind the front foot, taking the weight and freeing the front foot. The front foot moves down again and the back foot comes up, again, and crosses behind the front foot and thus allows the front foot to be put to the pitch of the ball. C. B. would have used more polished language, of a certainty. It sounded all very difficult but even as small boys we could follow it. Does anybody read Fry these days?

I must be quick to add that it was most unfortunate that Cowdrey, a gifted player, was not well enough to play at Old Trafford. He would have flourished on such a glorious pitch but Cowdrey is one who often denies his better parts. He is one whose footwork goes into reverse because it seems to be used most by many English stars in circumventing that abomination (to me, anyway) of all cricket rules—l.b.w. to a ball breaking in from outside the off-stump. I would not be surprised if the decline in English batsmanship is directly attributable to this innovation of the late 'thirties. I can see nothing to admire in this rule and its effects. It has fostered the in-swingers, the leg-side attack, the leg-field and—in English cricket, at all events—it has killed the art of slow leg-break bowling. The leg-breakers are not wanted. They are cricket's poor relations and so footwork down the pitch goes into desuetude, the game loses its most attractive strokes and all because footwork, now, consists of a defensive prod with the leg to nullify the effect of a ball breaking in from the off.

This l.b.w. rule, as it now stands, has had more effect upon English than upon Australian batting. The mental effects are noticeable every series when the Englishmen come up against almost an unknown variety of bowling. Some seem to be mesmerised before they start.

Footwork, then, is the first prerequisite if English batting is to recover its pristine glory. A batsman must move both out and back if he is to dominate spin. On a few occasions, Cowdrey has forgotten the inhibitions of the l.b.w. rule and we have seen some wondrous innings from him. Peter May (I sincerely hope our Australian Test fields have not seen the last of this cultured batsman, one of the truly great) has played several of the best Test innings I have seen and has the footwork if he will give the order from the bridge. David Sheppard uses his feet but, unfortunately, we didn't see him this series.

It is in order for an Australian to congratulate the umpires who stood in this series and to give high marks to the groundsman and staff at Edgbaston, Old Trafford and The Oval. They made good cricket possible because they provided Test-match pitches. The Lord's one, alas, now wears the furried ridge of age. Like our Melbourne one of a few years back, it has grown tired of life and needs a complete face-lift. I hope it gets it. On our next visit to Leeds, I hope we find, in the words of Mr. Sellers, that they do know how to make Test pitches up that way. They have contrived to conceal the fact for some time.

May I, finally, advance these causes. There has been trouble for far too long over 'dragging'. Surely, this problem could be settled immediately if the law says the front foot, in delivery, shall be behind the batting crease. The batsman is given that advantage in the pitch: I see no reason why the bowler should not have it, also. In New Zealand and in South Africa there has been much no-balling of bowlers for 'dragging'. So many of our great bowlers have 'fudged' over both lines. If the batting crease is made the important line for bowlers with their front foot, I can see this 'dragging' problem solved over-night. A 'dragging' bowler will always have his front foot well over the batting crease.

I would like, too, to see a fast bowler limited in his run to the crease. So many fast bowlers—and many of them are by no means fast, I might add—seem to run from eternity to get to the crease. These provide many of cricket's dullest moments. That long trudge back, the long run up, the long retreat and so on and on all takes up infinite time. Surely the origin of the long run is in one's tender years as a means of scaring the opposition. So many fast bowlers I have watched get little from their run-up. They are running as fast some yards after their take-off as they are 20 yards later. Tyson and Trueman are two who bowled faster when their run was shortened. I would like to see a white line no more than 15 yards back and all bowlers told to fit their run into that. I could never see the point of a man running 37 paces to bowl a ball 22 yards. And it makes for so much tedious watching.

I end this article with a plea. Let English administrators experiment for two seasons with the l.b.w. rule as it was. I found many English internationals of my generation who shared my dislike of this rule. It will be asking much for English batsmanship to recover its footwork in two years but at least it will be a start.

MY SEVEN YEAR 'STRETCH' [1962]

BY G. O. ALLEN

One of the most distinguished player-administrators of the century, George Oswald Allen retired as chairman of the England selectors at the end of the 1961 season. For the Almanack of the following spring he wrote an account of his experiences which, opening with a priceless item of historical arcana, proceeds with a nice blend of candour and counsel. Allen makes no reference to his distinguished career as an all-rounder who captained Middlesex and England, but concentrates on the committee aspect of his work. Of particular interest is his description of the controversial events of the 1956 series, in which time after time the selection committee opted for the most unexpected choices and were brilliantly vindicated. With the first Test drawn and the second lost, drastic measures were called for and drastic measures were what the committee produced by selecting one of its own members, Washbrook, who had last been seen in a Test match five years before. Washbrook made 98 and England won a comfortable victory. The fourth Test is always remembered for Jim Laker's nineteen wickets, but it was also notable for the induction of David Sheppard, who had given up regular cricket to take Holy Orders and who had batted only four times in the season. Sheppard scored a century and England won again. Having made something of a fetish of selecting half-rejected veterans, Allen and his men now performed the hat-trick by calling on Denis Compton, who was recovering from an operation for the removal of a knee-cap. Compton scored more runs than any player on either side and the series was won, largely through the courage and imagination of Allen and his committee. Since his retirement, Allen has occupied every administrative position of importance which the game has to offer, being awarded a knighthood for services to the game and continuing to perform duties best described by Neville Cardus, who saw Sir George as 'altogether a shrewd, not always visible, Grey Eminence at Lord's'.

THE first selector of whom any record can be found appears to have been the Duke of Cumberland, the victor of Culloden. He soon discovered that a selector's role was not without its vicissitudes. Faced with a challenge from another nobleman he 'ordered 22 players to appear before him in order that he might pick the strongest side'. Having chosen his eleven, he was promptly challenged to a match by the rejects, who offered to test his judgment by playing for 'a crown a head out of their own pocket'. The result was a defeat for His Royal Highness and he does not seem to have derived much benefit from this salutary if humiliating experience for, soon afterwards, he also lost the main event. The moral of this story must be that occasionally the selector's lot, like the policeman's, is not a happy one. For my own part I count myself fortunate that challenges of this kind are no longer regarded as quite the thing.

TWO COMMITTEES

In order to understand the workings of the modern selector, it may perhaps be helpful to know something of the organisation within which he operates. There are, of course, two selection committees in this country, one for Test matches at home and one for tours abroad. The 'home' selectors, four in number, are chosen annually in March by the Board of Control, which comprises representatives from each first-class county and M.C.C. and is the body responsible for the management of Test matches in England.

For tours abroad the selectors are appointed by M.C.C. since all official overseas tours are made under the club's auspices. Fortunately, in practice, the personnel of these two committees is much the same, as M.C.C. generally appoint the four 'home' selectors plus one or two of their own members including the chairman of their cricket sub-committee who, by tradition, acts as chairman. Since for the past six years M.C.C. have elected me chairman of their cricket sub-committee I have as a result been chairman of both selection committees.

My own appointment as a selector for Test matches in this country came about in a rather unorthodox way. One of the Board of Control rules relating to the Section Committee is that prior consent of a candidate must be obtained before his name can be put forward. I was in Australia in the winter of 1954–55, yet in my absence and without my knowledge, Middlesex submitted my name. I was highly indignant when I heard of it, and, justifiably so I feel, as those responsible were well aware that since World War II I had on more than one occasion declined to be nominated. Had I thought that my term of office was going to last seven long years, I am certain that no amount of persuasion or flattery would have made me change my mind. Yet, despite the anxieties and a fair amount of toil and sweat, I have no regrets, neither do I bear my friends on the Middlesex C.C.C. committee any ill-will. Indeed, I am grateful to them, for the work of selection can be both fascinating and rewarding.

THE METHOD

Once appointed, the committee's methods must be governed to some extent by the varying composition and personal idiosyncrasies of its members. There are, however, certain fairly well-established customs. The first meeting generally takes place just before the start of the season when such matters as the lessons of the previous season, policy in its broadest terms, the strengths and weaknesses of the tourists so far as they are then known, and the captaincy are discussed; also a list is drawn up of players to be watched during the season.

The second meeting is nearly always held during the M.C.C. match against the tourists at Lord's. This has been found to be a most convenient occasion, since the fixture is late in May and included in the M.C.C. team are generally many contestants for places in the England XI. If it is possible during this match to arrive at a decision about the captaincy for the first Test match, or indeed for the series, the appointment is made so that the captain, who automatically becomes a co-opted member of the committee, may be present and fully consulted when the team is chosen.

For some years now the England team has been picked on the Sunday immediately preceding the Test match. This decision has been dictated by the presence on many recent selection committees of active county cricketers, and, of course, the captain, who are unable through their playing commitments, to attend on any other day. In my time these meetings have generally started with a review of the previous match and the lessons learned both as regards form and tactics. This has been followed by a discussion about the pitch and the characteristics of the ground on which the match is to be played—such as the 'heavy' atmosphere sometimes prevailing in the North and the slope at Lord's.

Selectors must be wary of early-season form which can often be misleading; they must keep an open mind, remembering always their ultimate aim, a balanced side. Ideally, of course, this contains stability and aggression in the batting, variety in the bowling, at least two 'specialist' fieldsmen, and a blend of youth and experience.

CHIEF DIFFICULTY

Generally speaking, it is easy to pick eight or nine players. It is the last two or three, involving perhaps the balance of the side, who present the real problem. Here I would say that, when in doubt, it is sound policy to put faith in character and class if it is within reach rather than in a successful record in county cricket. I can recall several occasions when a good three hours have been spent choosing the last few places, and others when almost as long have been taken over the reserves. In the latter case the reason has generally been doubt about the fitness of one or two players. Sometimes it has been necessary to vote. This may be inevitable, human nature being what it is, but I am sure the selectors should try to arrive at unanimity on all occasions.

I have often been asked whether selection committees are sometimes guided by intuition. I think the answer is that an occasional choice looks strange because all the facts have not been known or the motive behind it has not been fully understood.

The series against Australia in 1956 provided two good examples of this, namely the inclusion of Cyril Washbrook in the third Test match and of David Sheppard in the fourth. But both these selections were, in my opinion, entirely logical. In the case of Washbrook, the batting had failed lamentably in the previous match at Lord's. England were one down in the series and it was therefore no time for further experiments with young or untried players. What was clearly needed was experience and a little aggression in the middle of the batting order. At the meeting the suggestion provoked a fairly lively discussion, mainly because Peter May, the captain, was at first rather luke-warm about bringing back someone who was 41 years of age and had been out of international cricket for a few years; but once Peter said, 'if you're all happy, I am,' the die was cast. True it must have appeared to some a retrograde step, but no other player seemed to fill the bill and it became a case of backing class and character in a crisis.

With one or two exceptions, the Press 'went to town on us' and when, after winning the toss, England's score at the end of the first hour stood at 17 for three and our nap-selection, Washbrook, was advancing to the wicket to a great reception from the Yorkshire crowd, morale, certainly of some of the selectors, was far from high. However, at the close of play the England total was 202 for four with Cyril Washbrook not out 90 and Peter May just out for 101.

GRATITUDE

When I went into the dressing-room to congratulate Peter on his fine fighting innings, he was oblivious to his own achievement and said in his quiet way: 'Wasn't Cyril magnificent? Thank goodness I listened to you on Sunday'—a typically modest and generous comment in a moment of triumph and a wonderful finish to a day I shall not easily forget. The match, too, had a happy ending and as I drove out of the ground with Walter Robins and Ian Peebles the remaining spectators were kind enough to raise a cheer for the selectors. That prompted Walter to remark that it was a bit different from 1948, when he was a selector. 'Then,' he said, 'we waited till after dark and nipped out of the side gate.' He could perhaps take comfort from the report that once when India were beaten at home the crowd surrounded the pavilion and shouted, 'Death to the selectors.'

The case of David Sheppard was rather different. The series was now level at one all and thus there was less need for drastic measures. Here we had a bit of luck: at a chance meeting earlier in London, harassed by the fallibility of the England batting, I had persuaded Sheppard to start his holiday a fortnight sooner than planned. Earlier in the season he had made 97 for Sussex against Australia, but since his return to first-class cricket in the middle of July he had played only three innings, one of which, of 50 odd, I had fortunately seen. Here was a class batsman, full of strokes which we wanted, and a good close-to-the-wicket fieldsman; but had he played enough cricket to have a chance of succeeding in a Test match against Australia?

OPTIMISM FULFILLED

Perhaps our appetite had been whetted by the success of Washbrook; perhaps we again decided to put our faith in class. Anyhow our luck held and he made a fine hundred. As I elbowed my way down the stairs to the dressing-room I found myself next to three parsons to whom I was able to remark: 'It's been a grand day for the Church.' Judging by their smiles, they fully agreed.

Indeed, fortune was so kind to us that season that Wilfred Rhodes, then in his 79th year and blind, yet still a fairly regular attender at Test matches, could not resist saying: 'I wonder who you will pick next time? You're so lucky that if you pick a Chinese he'll make a hundred.' There being no Chinamen to hand, we did the next best thing and chose Denis Compton, well on the way to recovery after a major operation on his knee. *[Compton's scores were 94 and 35 not out.—Editor.]*

If I have dwelt on some of the successes of the past seven years it is but fair to say that there were also some disappointments, failures and errors of judgment. No selection committee can ever hope to be infallible; the best is the one that makes the least mistakes. It is their duty not only to win the current Test match series but, wherever possible, to look to the future, without cheapening the England cap. If they do not, they, or their successors, may well find themselves, through injury or some other eventuality, devoid of a tried replacement for a vital Test match.

CAPTAIN'S VIEW

It has always been debatable whether a captain should have, without qualification, the side he wants and whether he should be given a completely free hand as regards tactics and approach to the game. To my mind, the answer to the first point is quite clear: the selectors are justified in using all their powers of persuasion, but should never finally include a player whom the captain is unwilling to accept. It can be fair neither to the captain nor to the player and is therefore most unlikely to be successful. The answer to the second point is much more difficult; but as the selectors must be responsible in no small degree for the broader issues of policy, they must be justified in bringing pressure to bear on the captain if they think it necessary.

As regards tactics on the field, I am certain that no definite instructions should be given. On the other hand the selectors must discuss tactics with the captain at selection committee meetings, especially when they may have some bearing on the composition of the team. Once a match has started, the chairman may offer an occasional suggestion. I am happy to say that, in my experience, the captain has just as often asked me for my views.

Opinions naturally vary as to what constitutes the best selection committee. To my mind a blend of different generations is of the utmost importance. I do not think there should be a preponderance of active players, because they may be wedded to the prevailing moods and values of county cricket and thus at times unable to see the wood for the trees. For the older members, practical experience of Test match cricket must be a great asset, as they should at least know what it means to 'go through the hoop'. But all must be devoted to the game, reasonably consistent in their views, with minds of their own yet tolerant of those of their colleagues, and be willing, when the moment comes, to make the difficult or unpopular decision.

URGENT PROBLEM

Looking to the future, I believe an urgent problem lies ahead of the selection committee and the captain, a problem which my colleagues and I have failed to solve though not for the want of trying. It is to inculcate a more aggressive approach into the batting. Without it I fear England are unlikely to regain supremacy in the field of international cricket.

In recent years caution too often has prevailed at times when every effort should have been made to exploit a favourable position. Also there has been a strong tendency to fall back on the defensive as soon as something has gone wrong. These tactics are bad enough in themselves, but the most worrying aspect of them to my mind has been the apparent conviction in some quarters that they pay. They have on one or two occasions, but I maintain that they have more often brought disaster—for example, at Leeds in 1953, Barbados in 1954, Lord's in 1956, Durban in 1957 and Brisbane in 1958, to quote but a few. The records surely show that in recent years it has been a fine crop of bowlers who have won us our many victories, certainly not our batsmen when they have been on the defensive.

Strokeless batting can bring little joy or inspiration to the performer, not to mention the luckless spectator. But negative cricket apart, I have frequently had the impression when watching some of our players that they have not been deriving as much enjoyment from Test matches as they might. Cheerfulness and a touch of gaiety is not incompatible with real positive effort and must help to raise morale and with it the standard of play. In fairness, however, it should be recognised that the life of the present-day English Test player is much tougher, in terms of cricket commitments and publicity, than that of his predecessor of pre-war days, or of his contemporary from overseas. I am sure the limelight of T.V., radio and press has been largely responsible for our 'safety-first' tactics and, indeed, for making some of our players all too conscious of their personal performances. Whilst it may thus be more difficult for them to generate and sustain the gusto of, say, the Australians and West Indians at their best, I feel that they could, and should, make a greater effort to do so.

Finally, I wish to express my gratitude to the cricket authorities of this country, to my colleagues on the selection committees and to the captains and players for their co-operation and friendship which has made my seven year 'stretch' seem, at any rate to me, well worth while. To my successor I wish all good fortune and as much happiness as I have derived from an exacting but wholly absorbing occupation.

SELECTION COMMITTEES FOR TESTS AT HOME

1899	Lord Hawke, W. G. Grace, H. W. Bainbridge.
1902	Lord Hawke, H. W. Bainbridge, C. MacGregor.
1905	Lord Hawke, J. A. Dixon, P. F. Warner.
1907	Lord Hawke, H. K. Foster, C. H. B. Marsham.
1909	Lord Hawke, C. B. Fry, H. D. G. Leveson Gower.
1912	J. Shuter, C. B. Fry, H. K. Foster.
1921	H. K. Foster, R. H. Spooner, J. Daniell.
1924	H. D. G. Leveson Gower, J. Sharp, J. Daniell.
1926	P. F. Warner, P. A. Perrin, A. E. R. Gilligan.
1928	H. D. G. Leveson Gower, J. W. H. T. Douglas, A. W. Carr.
1929	H. D. G. Leveson Gower, J. C. White, N. Haig.
1930	H. D. G. Leveson Gower, J. C. White, F. T. Mann.
1931	P. F. Warner, P. A. Perrin, T. A. Higson.
1932	P. F. Warner, P. A. Perrin, T. A. Higson.
1933	Lord Hawke, P. A. Perrin, T. A. Higson.
1934	Sir Stanley Jackson, P. A. Perrin, T. A. Higson.
1935	P. F. Warner, P. A. Perrin, T. A. Higson.
1936	P. F. Warner, P. A. Perrin, T. A. Higson.
1937	Sir Pelham Warner, P. A. Perrin, T. A. Higson.
1938	Sir Pelham Warner, P. A. Perrin, A. B. Sellers, M. J. Turnbull.
1939	P. A. Perrin, M. J. Turnbull, A. B. Sellers, A. J. Holmes.
1946	A. J. Holmes, A. B. Sellers, R. W. V. Robins.
1947	A. J. Holmes, R. W. V. Robins, J. C. Clay.
1948	A. J. Holmes, J. C. Clay, R. W. V. Robins.
1949	A. J. Holmes, A. B. Sellers, R. E. S. Wyatt, T. N. Pearce.
1950	R. E. S. Wyatt, A. B. Sellers, T. N. Pearce, L. E. G. Ames.
1951	N. W. D. Yardley, R. E. S. Wyatt, F. R. Brown, L. E. G. Ames.
1952	N. W. D. Yardley, R. E. S. Wyatt, F. R. Brown, L. E. G. Ames.
1953	F. R. Brown, N. W. D. Yardley, R. E. S. Wyatt, L. E. G. Ames.
1954	H. S. Altham, N. W. D. Yardley, R. W. V. Robins, L. E. G. Ames.
1955	G. O. Allen, L. E. G. Ames, A. B. Sellers, W. Wooller.
1956	G. O. Allen, L. E. G. Ames, W. Wooller, C. Washbrook.
1957	G. O. Allen, W. Wooller, C. Washbrook, H. E. Dollery.
1958	G. O. Allen, W. Wooller, L. E. G. Ames, H. E. Dollery.
1959	G. O. Allen, W. Wooller, D. J. Insole, H. Sutcliffe.

Miller, handsomest of cricketers, gives the ball an airing in the first match of the 1956 campaign against the Duke of
k's XI. It is only a friendly but S.C. Griffith, behind the stumps, looks apprehensive enough for a Test match. This will be
s third and last tour of England

ndwall bowling for Australia in the opening match of the 1956 tour against the Duke of Norfolk's XI. The match is played
the walls of Arundel Castle but although Lindwall is not as old as the background, his course by now is almost run. This
the last tour for one of the greatest fast bowlers ever seen. During this last campaign he will take only 7 wickets while
ning mate, Miller, will capture 21. But it is all academic, for Jim Laker will take 46

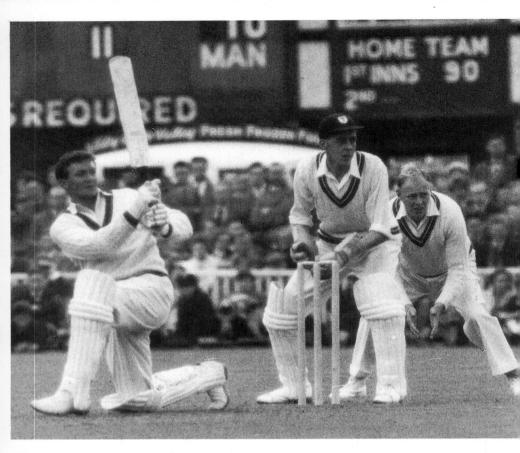

Above Richie Benaud, the young all-rounder, with the 1956 Australian tourists. Benaud is batting against Worcestershire w
the scoreboard tells us, have been put to the sword by Lindwall and Co. In this opening game of the season Benaud score
160, went on to become one of the great Test captains, a broadcasting pundit and an apologist for Kerry Packer. A life fille
with incident

Top right Neville Cardus would surely have captioned this richly comic photograph ''E Dunno Where 'E Are'. The moment
came in the 1964 match between an Old England XI and The Lord's Taverners. W.S. Surridge, attempting to plonk a delive
from his old Surrey colleague Alec Bedser into the crowd at mid wicket, has miscued and sent the ball flying straight at mi
off, who must be asleep because Surridge goes on to make 51 not out

Below right Ever since the mythic days of Hambledon the Hampshire club had combined richness of heritage with modes
performance. Usually an entertaining side, it was not until 1958 that they came within striking distance of the Championshi
finishing second to Surrey. Three years later under the old-style leadership of Colin Ingleby-Mackenzie they took the prize
last. We can only guess how delighted were the shades of that Wodhousian pair, Lord Tennyson and his gentleman's
gentleman-come-wicketkeeper Walter Livsey

Garfield Sobers carves the ball square and pauses in momentary contemplation of his own grace and power. There is no
to run. This is the fourth day of the Lord's Test in 1966 and soon Sobers will declare the innings closed with his own score
163 not out

1960   G. O. Allen, W. Wooller, D. J. Insole, H. Sutcliffe.
1961   G. O. Allen, W. Wooller, D. J. Insole, H. Sutcliffe.

The name of the Chairman of the Committee is placed first.

A HISTORY OF WISDEN [1963]

BY L. E. S. GUTTERIDGE

An air of expectancy hung about the advent of the 1963 edition. It was the hundredth in the series, a miraculous achievement in itself, considering that when John Wisden embarked on the inaugural edition in 1864, it had been in another world, a world in which there was no county structure, no Test match circuit, no real infrastructure at all. Wisden, a shrewd entrepreneur but no editorial giant, was clearly baffled by the sheer nebulosity of his own brainchild and had finally evaded most of the issues by filling the 1864 edition with a gallimaufry of comically irrelevant arcana, from the length of British canals to the dates of the chief battles in the Wars of the Roses. Fortunately, the publication quickly righted itself, doubled in size, doubled again and doubled yet again. Already by the turn of the new century it had become part of cricket's staple diet, its buff-coloured covers as much a part of the English year as the green of the turf and the white of the players' dress.

In a sense the Almanack was fortunate because the phenomenal expansion of cricket into all the great cities of the world meant that some sort of tabulation was required to keep pace with the game's swift advance. The Almanack was fortunate in the way it held the allegiance of a small band of men who joined it as youngsters and stayed for the rest of their lives. A career at Wisden stretching over fifty years was not unknown; its greatest Editor, Sydney Pardon, presided from 1891 to 1925.

Sadly the extent of Wisden's print run for its first 72 years remains unknown and only partial for the next five, but it is heartening to think that since 1946, sales have more than trebled and appear to be still rising. The first edition of more than 500 pages appeared in 1900, the first of more than one thousand by 1950 since when the succession of editors has been hard put to keep the size of the Almanack down to practicable proportions. The Centenary Edition had 1,130 pages which included a comprehensive history of itself.

THE year 1864 was memorable for many reasons. Paraguay was at war with Brazil. Britain was having some trouble with the Bhutanese in India and the Ashantis in West Africa. Charles Dickens produced *Our Mutual Friend*. In Manchester, photographs were taken for the first time by magnesium flashlight; the first stone of the London Embankment was laid; Clifton Suspension Bridge was opened and, after repulsing an attack on Kintang, the great General Gordon exploded 40,000 lb. of powder under the walls of Nanking before recapturing it. Whilst the sound of this explosion was still reverberating, three other earth-shaking events occurred. At fifteen years of age, W. G. Grace scored 170 and 56 not out for the South Wales Cricket Club against the Gentlemen of Sussex at Brighton, over-arm bowling was legalised and, most important of all, *Wisden's Cricketers' Almanack* was born.

A height of five feet four inches and a weight of seven stone is not perhaps the popular image of a fast bowler. Yet, John Wisden, a Brighton builder's son, rightly known as the 'Little Wonder', averaged 225 wickets a season for twelve years, took 455 wickets in 1851, and with a tremendous off-break clean bowled all ten wickets in the second innings for North v. South in 1850. He was largely responsible for the tour—the first by an English team—to Canada and the United States in 1859 where he performed a double hat-trick, actually taking six wickets in six balls. He owned a tobacconist's and sports equipment store in Leicester Square. His chief rival was Lillywhite Brothers & Co. 'dealers in foreign cigars, tobacco etc. (unrivalled shag, highly recommended at 6s. 6d.) and sports equipment', whose premises were at 10, Princes Terrace, Caledonian Road, Islington. Since 1849 they had issued *The Young Cricketer's Guide* at eighteenpence a copy, falling to one shilling for the later issues. It ended in 1866, but *The Cricketer's Companion* had taken its place in 1865. A mind as cogent as John Wisden's realised the value of such a publication as an advertisement and he determined to produce his own. It became a lasting memorial of his fame. It is significant that he played his last first-class match against the M.C.C. and Ground at Brighton in August 1863—exactly one hundred years ago.

Books must not be classified by size and shape alone. They are subject, even as clothes are, to the decrees of fashion. There is a straining after novelty, but always a dislike of breaking with the past. There have been volumes as tall as a man and others as small as a walnut. We confess to a certain dislike of the Elephant folio. At Addison's Banquet of the Books, the folio still takes the top of the table; the twelves are below the salt, and the slim books can hardly find a place at all. *Wisden's Cricketers' Almanack*, having chosen at the outset a most perfect size for its purpose, has retained it through 100 issues, and with age its girth has increased. A natural slimming was evidenced during the lean years of two world wars, but the astonishing and wholly admirable thing is that it continued at all.

In outward appearance, few vital changes can be noticed. The paper covers gave way to a limp-cloth binding in 1938 and an alternative cloth-board edition was commenced in 1896. In 1938 the Wisden *motif* of two top-hatted players at the wicket, appeared on the cover of the limp edition and has continued. In the paper editions 1904–5 the spelling 'Almanac' is employed but this usage does not appear on the front cover nor on the cloth edition, which has 'Almanack'.

The first issue was published for one shilling and was available 'post free for 13 stamps'—obviously penny ones. By 1874 the number of pages had increased from the 112 of 1864 to 208 and a copy was sent post free for 14 stamps. It is curious that the issue for 1875, although 32 pages larger, was available for 13 stamps post free and that this also applied to that for 1876. Changes in postal charges are not unknown today. The post free price for 1878 and 1879 was 1s. 1½d. and that for 1880 (234 pages with the advertisements) was 1s. 2d. The price was increased to 1s. 3d. post free with the issue of 1886 (382 pp.). So size and postage progressed, until today the cheapest way of posting a 1,067-page *Wisden* costs 1s. 3d.

The first advertisement was in 1867 where, on the last page, appears an illustration of John Wisden and Co.'s Patent Catapulta, 'the principle of working which will be shown at 2, New Coventry Street, Leicester Square'. Mr. Wanostrocht, in his *Felix on the Bat* published in 1845, shows a Catapulta which was based on the principle of the siege machine of classical antiquity. Wisden's model was of an entirely different principle, the ball being propelled by a bow-like structure. In 1883, the first advertisement appears in the text and is on the verso of the title-page. Dr. Johnson in 1759 said: 'The trade of advertising is now so near perfection that it is not easy to propose any improvement.' In 1960, Britain spent £456 million on advertising and *Wisden* itself shows a similar evolution of the art to a stage much beyond any that Johnson could have conceived. The earnest desire of the proprietors to keep the cost as low as possible meant that advertisements must increase in quantity and to a very great extent these were banished to the front and end of the actual work itself. The increasing circulation helped to lower the cost of production, but the advertisements were an absolute necessity if the price were to remain at 1s. And so it did for over half its present life, that is for 51 issues until during the First World War in 1915.

With the exception of 1868 there are only three publishers' imprints, with one minor variation. Until 1937 John Wisden and Co. were the publishers (in 1914 it became a limited liability company) and it seems that for a trial period of one year, John Wisden had a partner by name Maynard, and, for the year 1868 only, the imprint was Wisden and Maynard. Research has failed to provide any information on this short partnership. *Wisden*'s publishers were blitzed during the winter of 1940 and all the records were lost, while Wisden's Mortlake factory with other records were destroyed in 1944. H. S. Altham says: 'No doubt the Cabinet was unmoved, but cricketers felt it an almost personal outrage.' Six printers were known to have been concerned with its production and Messrs. Balding and Mansell printed 39 consecutive issues.

A main contributory to *Wisden*'s success was the founding in 1880 of the Cricket Reporting Agency. Begun by Charles Pardon, who, seven years after its foundation first undertook the Editorship of *Wisden*, the editorial work has, since the 1887 edition, been carried through by the Cricket Reporting Agency, and *Wisden*'s Editor has generally been a partner in the firm. Some members of the firm have worked on *Wisden* for long periods, notably Sydney Pardon, from 1887 to 1925, Charles Stewart Cain, 1887 to 1933, S. J. Southerton, 1894 to 1935, and Hubert Preston, 1895 to 1951.

Four current members with long service records are E. Eden, who began in 1922, H. Gee in 1931 and Norman Preston and Leslie Smith in 1933.

Perhaps the greatest of the Editors was S. H. Pardon, who was responsible for the issues from 1891 to 1925. He would have been the first to acknowledge his debt to C. F. Pardon and E. S. Pardon. This was a great and formative period. His first issue had 420 pages and his penultimate one 1,010 pages. Every aspect of the game came under his careful scrutiny. The number of entries under Births and Deaths in 1891 was 753 and in his final issue of 1925, was 6,274. His was a cultured mind. He had definite opinions and was prepared to state them. His editorials make most interesting reading and his influence on the growth of the game throughout the world was immense. Like all great editors, he had the ability to pick the right helpers, and F. S. Ashley-Cooper's meticulously accurate and informed statistical assistance was invaluable. Hubert Preston was in the same tradition and was equally notable in other and different fields.

The present Editor has shown that he too is worthy of the great traditions and has a lively sense of the best interests of the game. He is still fighting space, as all his predecessors have done, but is nevertheless allowing the publication to grow, and even the lesser-known touring teams are allowed their brief mention. At this point it should be stated that the Almanack has attained a most remarkable degree of accuracy. The possibilities of error are incalculable. The fact is that the degree of accuracy attained over the years has been astonishing. The old adage says that there are three kinds of lies. Lies, damned lies and statistics.

Charles Dexter Cleveland in his preface to *A Complete Concordance to the Poetical Works of John Milton* says: 'I had occasion to look at Todd's *Verbal Index* in connection with *Lycidas*. I found 63 mistakes.' This in a poem of 193 lines. Yet, in its day, Todd's *Verbal Index* was considered to be a literary masterpiece. The fact is that in view of the inevitably large content of statistics, *Wisden's Cricketers' Almanack* has performed with very great credit.

Wisden has attained an authoritative position that is now unrivalled. In its earlier days it met and squarely beat its competitors. Captain Bayley produced *The Cricket Chronicle* for the season 1863 which contained full scores of minor as well as important matches and the Lillywhites produced *Guides, Companions* and *Annuals* from 1849 to 1900. *Wisden* appears in the committee rooms of the whole world where cricket is played and is the final arbiter in any matter under dispute. Such is its present authority that I must remind the reader that it is published by a private firm that has no official connection with cricket's rulers. Its success has been due to its manner of presentation and to its emphasis on accuracy and detail. It is a one hundred volume history of the game, a permanent source of information to which many authors have freely admitted their indebtedness and to which many more have not.

The evolution of the growth of overseas cricket is a fascinating study and deserves an article to itself. Even the second issue of 1865 devoted 22 of its 160 pages to the doings of the Twelve in Australia under the captaincy of

George Parr. In 1868, the full scores of a match played by I. Zingari against the Paris Club, which I. Z. won very comfortably, is recorded, and in 1869 both the English Team in America and the results of the visit of the Australian Aboriginals to this country are given ample space. In 1875 an American Baseball team came to this country to demonstrate the virtues of their game and stayed for one month only. The comment generally made was that their fielding was good. Sad to record, they played a number of cricket matches as well and 'the Americans having one or two good bowlers, several plucky hard-hitters, and a team of good fielders, they had the best of every match they played'. When Lillywhite went on his second trip to America in 1868 with Willsher as captain, the team beat the best baseball side that America at that time could produce. In 1887, reference is made to the Tour of the Parsees and also of the visit of the West Indian Gentlemen to Canada and the United States. Australian Inter-Colonial Matches were first recorded in 1891. By 1893 the visit of an Irish team to America, and statistics prepared by Lord Harris of Cricket in India, were considered of sufficient interest to occupy valuable space, and a visit during the month of August by the Gentlemen of Holland was recorded in 1895.

It was nothing less than an editorial stroke of genius when Charles F. Pardon decided that 'to signalise the extraordinary success that bowlers achieved in 1888' he would give 'new portraits, specially photographed by Hawkins of Brighton, of six of the most prominent and skilful of their number'. A proof of its popularity is that the demand for 1889 was so great that for the first time a second edition was necessary. The photograph is still clearly legible and unfaded after over 70 years. (Prints were substituted for actual photographs in 1915.) It became a regular feature thereafter (except for 1916 and 1917, and this for an obvious reason). In 1897, it had developed into that much-loved and delightfully argumentative feature, 'Five Cricketers of the Year'. Why is it that we so rarely guess all the five in advance, and yet agree with the final choice? It was a most happy thought in 1918 to give the 'Five School Bowlers of the Year', and in the following year, the 'Five Public School Cricketers of the Year'. It should be mentioned that one of the latter was A. P. F. Chapman, of Uppingham. 'Though he bowls left-handed with some ability, it is also as a batsman that Chapman is chiefly distinguished . . . he ought to make his mark.' It becomes most impressive on the four occasions that the Five Cricketers of the Year were dropped to find the solitary names of John Wisden, W. G. Grace, P. F. Warner and Jack Hobbs in lonely grandeur.

The beginnings of the important obituary section were in 1872 when 15 cricketers were listed as having died in 1871. These included Mr. Dark, of Lord's, and the father of W. G. Grace. In 1891 a brief obituary notice was given of Charles F. Pardon and this inspired the Editor to do the same for other deaths in the following year and brief biographical notices were added. Since then there have been brief and accurate summaries from various pens. Obituaries of cricketers killed in action were separated from the others during the wars.

I must confess to a certain sadness at the inevitable passing of the almanack that graced the earliest editions. 1864 commences its 12 pages of almanack by informing us that the British Museum closes on January 1st, and amongst other gratuitous information, tells us when carpets were first manufactured in Kidderminster, the date of the Battle of Lodi on the Adda in 1796 and ends with a mention of Thomas Brett, 'the fastest and straightest underhand bowler ever known'. In 1865 the almanack gives more cricket information than other subjects, and in 1870 it is given a new form and has only four pages. This continued until 1879 when a single-page calendar was substituted. Even the calendar disappeared in 1941 and all that is left of the almanack is its mention in the title. (A twelve-page Almanack, extracted from G. D. Martineau's *Cricketer's Historical Calendar* which Sporting Handbooks Ltd. will publish late in 1963, has been included in this edition.) The first issue contained a deal of delightful, but quite extraneous, matter—such as the Rules of Knur and Spell, a brief history of China, the Rules for playing the Game of Bowls, the winners of the Derby, Oaks and St. Leger, and sundry other 'discrete' information on Canals, British Societies, The Wars of the Roses, and Coinage. It ends with a mention of the interesting fact that a brass bell weighing 17 cwt. cast at Woolwich Arsenal in 1699 was cleft by the hammer while ringing from the effect of the severe frost.

The Laws of Cricket have appeared in every edition. In the very earliest editions they followed the almanack, and until 1937 they appeared towards the beginning of the volume. From 1938 to 1947 they were to be found after the statistics and immediately before the details of matches played. From 1948 the Laws have been placed at the end. A study of their variations would in itself provide much of the history of Cricket. The laws governing bets were dropped in 1885.

Women's cricket was honoured by having its first mention in 1938. There is a detailed account with full scores of the first women's Test Match between Australia and England, by Miss V. M. M. Cox, of the Women's Cricket Association.

In later years improvements and additions come thick and fast. Public Schools had space accorded to them as early as the second issue, where a whole page is given to the recording of the Eton v. Harrow match at Lord's when over 9,000 people were present. In 1962 sixty pages are devoted to Public Schools cricket. It is fascinating to notice a C. J. Kortright playing for Tonbridge in 1887 or a T. W. Graveney with 4 innings, twice not out, 27 runs, 10 as the highest innings, and an average of 13.50 for Bristol Grammar School in 1942.

County cricket has always rightly formed a very large part of a year's issue and during the Second World War, when we lacked this important feature of our national life, we were solaced with many details of League cricket and of the Northern Universities. In 1960 room was found for the permanent inclusion of League cricket. Lists of 'Blues' were commenced in 1923 at the suggestion of W. Livingstone Irwin, and Mr. Ashley-Cooper drew up two tables adding the schools of the players. A list of 'Blues' from 1827–1939 appeared in 1940. Statistics of many kinds are provided and the Cricket Records have been amended every year.

The reporting of matches in earlier days was quaint and typical of the period. It was always readable and never descended to the type of journalese provided by Bell's *London Life*. The reporting of matches is now factual and unlike former years, the Test match reports are initialled, thus departing from the strict anonymity that was traditional.

The first article was by W. H. Knight in 1869 and he wrote in a fresh and bright manner on the *Individual Innings of 200 or more Runs*. He is recorded as the Editor in the preface of 1870. Since then, many lesser known and greater names have contributed. The Hon. Mr. Justice Herbert V. Evatt—later the Prime Minister of Australia—contributed an article in 1935, and another celebrated lawyer, Lord Birkett, also appeared in 1958. Among famous cricketers contributing articles are G. O. Allen in 1938 on *A Case for More Natural Wickets*, Sir Jack Hobbs on *The Hobbs Era* and Spofforth on *Schoolboys' Bowling* in 1904. A list of all the special articles appears at the end of the Index which was produced by Mr. Rex Pogson in 1944.

In certain years it was found that an insufficient number of copies of the Almanack had been published. It was decided to issue a second edition and I have seen the issues for each year from 1889 to 1901 except 1896 and 1900. It is always more costly to produce small numbers and the published price in these cases was 2s. for the paper edition and in 1899 3s. for the cloth. A curious situation arose in 1898. The Five Cricketers of the Year appear in one edition on the cover in a pattern of two names with one in the centre and two underneath. But another copy of the same year has a pattern 1 - 2 - 2. Further there is a variation of the same kind that has the name P. F. Warner correctly on the title-page and another that has the misprint W. P. Warner.

A list of cricket books at that time in print was given in 1938 and was dropped in 1943, to reappear in 1950 with a further list of books to be published during the year. A bibliography of cricket was written by that Sussex enthusiast, Alfred J. Gaston, in the editions of 1892, 1894, 1900 and 1923. From 1952, John Arlott has reviewed the books of the previous year except where an item was his own.

Considerable space has always been accorded to the matches of the M.C.C., and all decisions of legislative bodies have been fully covered. Even the dinner following the A.G.M. was reported in 1878 (it must have been a little embarrassing for the retiring President of 1877, Lord Londesborough, to have to record that he had great satisfaction in proposing the Duke of Beaufort as his successor, but that the Duke was not present since he had misinformed him as to the day).

I have frequently been asked why the edition of 1875 is so very scarce and the simple answer can only be that fewer of them were issued. It is always a very difficult problem to estimate circulation and particularly so at the beginning of a new publication's career. The edition of 1873 was a bumper issue for its time and contained the full scores of the visit of the English Twelve to America and Canada. This will have sold well. The issue for 1874 was smaller by 28 pages and may not have had so wide a circulation, although on the basis of the previous year's demand, more copies may have been issued. It would have been normal practice to have reduced the number of copies printed for 1875. It is also interesting to note that at this period, the year of publication was given at the foot of the title-page and that the title-page gave always the same year. This is not true for 1875 which reads 'John Wisden's Cricketers' Almanack for 1875' and had the date at the foot of the title-page as 1874. This implies that 1874 and 1875 were published in the same year, and although this has often been taken for a misprint, it is probably true that 1875 was issued in December 1874.

I have seen a letter addressed to an enquirer by John Wisden & Co., in 1881. It thanked the writer for his letter but regretted that 1875 was not available. It pointed out that they themselves were paying 10s. for a copy, which is the equivalent of paying £10 for a 1962 copy! The 1875 edition is not, however, so scarce as the first issue of 1864. It was a great day for the enthusiast when the present publishers decided to reprint the first fifteen issues in facsimile.

As I have said, Wisden's were their own publishers until 1937. By then, as a result of the years of slump, sales had fallen to such an alarming extent that professional help was called in and the publishing of *Wisden* was passed over to J. Whitaker & Sons, Ltd., publishers of *Whitaker's Almanack*. From the 1938 edition substantial changes were made, designed to make *Wisden* easier to use and understand. The cumbrous 'early Victorian survival' of a division into two parts was discarded, a new cover was designed, a complete index was provided, the Counties were set out in alphabetical order instead of, as previously, in the previous year's County Championship table order, and more illustrations were provided. Sales increased considerably, and immediately.

Whitaker's imprint as publishers stayed until the 1944 edition when the name of the publisher changed to Sporting Handbooks Ltd. (Whitaker's had purchased in 1939 a firm called Sporting Handbooks Ltd. as being a more suitable imprint under which to publish *Wisden*, and Wisden's had taken a share in it, it then being jointly owned by Wisden's and Whitaker's. The change of imprint was made with the 1944 edition, and has remained the same since then. In 1957 Whitaker's bought out the Wisden interest in Sporting Handbooks Ltd. which is now a wholly-owned subsidiary of Whitaker's and continues to publish *Wisden* under agreement with John Wisden & Co. Ltd. who remain the proprietors of the copyright in *Wisden*.)

The quantity printed of the early years would be fascinating to know, but it has proved impossible to trace any printing orders earlier than 1936. The following table shows the number printed in the years from 1936, and the way in which the demand for the cloth boards edition has increased is particularly notable:

Year	Quantity paper		
1936	8,500	(total, no separate cloth boards figure known)	
1937	8,000	(total, no separate cloth boards figure known)	
	limp	*cloth boards*	
1938	12,000	not known	
1939	12,000	not known	
1940	8,000	not known	
1941	3,200	800	(War paper restriction)
1942	4,100	900	"
1943	5,600	1,400	"
1944	5,600	1,400	"
1945	6,500	1,500	"
1946	11,000	5,000	"
1947	14,000	6,000	(Restrictions eased)
1948	14,500	6,500	"
1949	21,500	10,500	(Restriction ended)

1949 was the peak. With other consumer goods in stringently short supply, and sport one of the few outlets, sport and writing about sport boomed as never before. The boom slowly diminished, but even in 1955 the limp edition sold 15,500 copies and the cloth boards edition had increased to 11,000 copies. Today the sale is steady, averaging 11,000 of the limp edition and 10,000 of the cloth boards edition.

What a pity it is that all owners of books do not put their signatures on a fly-leaf! It is far more interesting than a book-plate and takes up less room. It is most interesting to learn who have been the previous owners and to trace them through the relevant volumes. I have, for example, seen the signatures of Haygarth, C. B. Fry, R. Daft and even Horatio Bottomley (once rightly mis-spelled Hotairio) on *Wisdens*, and perhaps even more rewarding are the signatures of such relatively little known players as W. Rashleigh. Perseverance produced the information that he played for Oxford University in 1886 and that he made 21 and 107 against Cambridge University. That he made 49 against a strong M.C.C. side which included Studd, Hearne and Webbe and that in seven matches that year, he had 13 innings and made 343 runs. Did Rashleigh own only the one copy of *Wisden* in which his name appeared to such advantage, or was he a genuine devotee and are the rest of his volumes with his bold signature still in existence somewhere?

I have a catalogue issued by A. J. Gaston in 1899 of the library of T. Padwick. A set (1864–1898) of the Almanack was advertised for £10. One of the best cricket book catalogues ever produced was that of A. Maurice & Co., of Covent Garden. It was issued in 1909 and is itself a rare item. It has no set for sale, but lists the rarer *Wisdens* at 5s. each. Gaston issued a further general catalogue of cricket books in 1925 and has a bound set (1864–1924) available, at fifty guineas. Sotheby's auction in 1937 of the library of J. A. H. Catton had a set (1864–1936) and a further 11 duplicate volumes unspecified. This fetched £33. Messrs. Hodgson & Co., of

Chancery Lane, auctioned a set (1864–1953) in 1954 and the price was £145. The present accepted price for a set in good condition and collated as complete is £250.

Great is bookishness and the charm of books. No doubt there are times in the lives of most reading men when they rebel against the dust of libraries. We all know the 'dark hours' when the vanity of learning and the childishness of merely literary things are brought home to us in such a way as to put the pale student out of conceit with his books, and to make him turn from his best-loved authors as from a friend who has outstayed his welcome. In what a different category are a set or a run of *Wisden*. K. A. Auty, a well known Yorkshireman, who had spent the greater part of a long life in America, and whose obituary appears in *Wisden*, possessed a most notable collection of cricket books. He kept his complete set of *Wisden* under his bed. He could then, having made himself properly comfortable, forget his maturing bills and overdue argosies, dip down and take at random any volume that came to hand. He was often found perusing the same volume hours later.

TABLE I. PAGE NUMBERING

Square brackets denote unnumbered pages. * Denotes largest issue to date.

Year	pages	
1864	[4]+112	(116)
1865	[4]+160	(164)*
1866	[4]+196	(200)*
1867	[4]+159+1	(164)
1868	[4]+112	(116)
1869	[4]+120	(124)
1870	152	
1871	152	
1872	172	
1873	208*	
1874	180	
1875	214+[2]	(216)*
1876	224*	
1877	248*	
1878	250*	
1879	241+[5]	(246)
1880	[2]+216+[18]	(236)
1881	[2]+228+[10]	(240)
1882	[2]+212+[10]	(224)
1883	[2]+284+[18]	(304)*
1884	[2]+268+[18]	(288)
1885	[2]+290+[20]	(312)*
1886	[2]+360+[22]	(384)*
1887	[2]+xx+308+[18]	(348)
1888	[2]+xxviii+362+[20]	(412)*
1889	[2]+xl+356+[22]	(420)*
1890	[2]+lii+301+[21]	(376)
1891	xlvi+354+[20]	(420)

Year	pages	
1892	1xii+330+[20]	(412)
1893	1iv+376+[18]	(448)*
1894	1xxiv+390+[24]	(488)*
1895	1xxviii+386+[14]	(478)
1896	1xxviii+418+[28]	(524)*
1897	1xxxii+416+[30]	(528)*
1898	xciv+428+[24]	(546)*
1899	cxiv+438+[26]	(578)*
1900	cxii+506+[28]	(646)*
1901	cxx×477+[35]	(632)
1902	cxxxviii+536+[38]	(702)*
1903	cx1×532+[42]	(714)*
1904	cx1+492+[50]	(682)
1905	c1xviii+528+[50]	(746)*
1906	cix+602	(762)*
1907	c1xxviii(pt.1)+510 (pt.2)+[36]	(724)
1908	206(pt.1)+574(pt.2)	(780)*
1909	208(pt.1)+562(pt.2)	(770)
1910	212(pt.1)+534(pt.2)	(746)
1911	216(pt.1)+550(pt.2)	(766)
1912	220(pt.1)+566(pt.2)	(786)*
1913	iv+236(pt.1)+607(pt.2)	(847)*
1914	iv+252(pt.1)+543(pt.2)	(799)
1915	iv+252(pt.1)+535(pt.2)	(791)
1916	299	
1917	351	
1918	339	
1919	327	
1920	xii+284(pt.1)+431(pt.2)	(727)
1921	272(pt.1)+523(pt.2)	(795)
1922	1a-c+320(pt.1)+675(pt.2)	(998)*
1923	1a-c+360(pt.1)+607(pt.2)	(970)
1924	328(pt.1)+683(pt.2)	(1011)*
1925	4+336(pt.1)+615(pt.2)	(955)
1926	12+340(pt.1)+679(pt.2)	(1031)*
1927	350(pt.1)+693(pt.2)	(1043)*
1928	352(pt.1)+711(pt.2)	(1063)*
1929	308(pt.1)+707(pt.2)	(1015)
1930	320(pt.1)+739(pt.2)	(1059)
1931	336(pt.1)+730(pt.2)	(1066)*
1932	312(pt.1)+722(pt.2)	(1034)
1933	312(pt.1)+719(pt.2)	(1031)
1934	338(pt.1)+721(pt.2)	(1059)
1935	336(pt.1)+711(pt.2)	(1047)
1936	356(pt.1)+679(pt.2)	(1035)
1937	340(pt.1)+715(pt.2)	(1055)
1938	990+[1]	(991)
1939	958	
1940	871	
1941	426	
1942	391	

1943	403	
1944	343	
1945	367	
1946	xvi+463	(479)
1947	xxxii+715	(747)
1948	xxxii+843	(875)
1949	viii+935	(943)
1950	viii+1003	(1011)
1951	xvi+1019	(1035)
1952	viii+1031	(1039)
1953	xx+1015	(1035)
1954	xx+999	(1019)
1955	xx+1011	(1031)
1956	xxxii+1043	(1075)*
1957	xxxii+1019	(1051)
1958	xxxvi+1035	(1071)
1959	xlviii+1011	(1059)
1960	iv+1023	(1027)
1961	viii+1019	(1027)
1962	iv+1063	(1067)
1963	xlviii+1131	(1179)*

PUBLISHERS

1864–67	John Wisden and Co.
1868	Wisden and Maynard.
1869–1914	John Wisden and Co.
1915–37	John Wisden and Co. Ltd.
1938–43	J. Whitaker and Sons Ltd. for John Wisden and Co. Ltd.
1944–63	Sporting Handbooks Ltd. for John Wisden and Co. Ltd.

COMPILERS AND EDITORS

1864–69	It is likely that W. H. Crockford (S.B. xiv–xxviii) and W. H. Knight were concerned.
1870–79	W. H. Knight
1880–86	George H. West
1887–90	C. F. Pardon
1891–1925	S. H. Pardon
1926–33	C. S. Caine
1934–35	S. J. Southerton
1936–39	W. H. Brookes
1940–43	Haddon Whitaker
1944–51	Hubert Preston
1952–63	Norman Preston

Note: From 1887 to today the material for *Wisden* has been compiled by the staff of the Cricket Reporting Agency, while (except for 1940–43, in the uncertainty of the early war years) the editorial responsibility has been undertaken by one of its partners, usually the senior.

PRINTERS

1864–86	W. H. Crockford	1936–37	S. H. Benson Ltd.
1887–93	Not known	1938–40	Purnell & Sons

1894–96   Wyman & Sons   1941–63   Unwin Brothers Ltd.
1897–1935 Balding & Mansell

No name of a printer is stated from 1887–93. However, there appears to be no difference in the typography between the issues of 1889–93 and those printed by Wyman from 1894–96. It is therefore probable that Wyman were the printers from 1889 onwards. There are only minor differences in the 1887 and 1888 issues and it is possible that these were produced by a different printer. It is also quite conceivable that the printers were again Wyman. The publishers lost all their records of this period during the last war. The printer's name does not appear in the cloth board edition from 1938 onwards, but is given in the limp cloth edition.

PRICE

1864–95	paper	1/-		
1896–1914	"	1/-	cloth boards	2/-
1915–17	"	1/6	"	2/6
1918	"	2/-	"	3/-
1919–20	"	2/6	"	4/-
1921–37	"	5/-	"	7/6
1938–42	limp cloth	5/-	"	7/6
1943–46	"	6/-	"	8/6
1947	"	7/6	"	9/6
1948–50	"	9/6	"	12/-
1951	"	10/6	"	12/6
1952–55	"	12/6	"	15/-
1956	"	15/-	"	17/6
1957–59	"	16/-	"	18/6
1960–61	limp	18/6	"	21/-
1962	"	20/-	"	22/6
1963	"	22/6	"	25/-

No price is given on the title-page from 1891–1938 and therefore nowhere on the 1938 cloth board edition. From 1939 it reappears on the title-page.

ILLUSTRATIONS

Five Cricketers of the Year appeared in the following issues: 1897, 1898, 1902–1908, 1910–11, 1914–15, 1922–23, 1925, 1927–37. From 1939 many other illustrations have been given together with the Five Cricketers of the Year, except in the issues for 1941–46.

In other years before 1938 the following illustrations have appeared:-

1889 6 Great Bowlers
1890 9 Great Batsmen
1891 5 Wicket-keepers
1892 5 Great Bowlers
1893 5 Batsmen of the Year
1894 5 All-round Cricketers
1895 5 Young Batsmen of the Year
1896 W. G. Grace
1899 5 Great Players of the Season
1900 5 Cricketers of the Season
1901 Mr. R. E. Foster and 4
       Yorkshire Cricketers

1909 Lord Hawke and 4 Cricketers of
       the Year
1912 5 Members of M.C.C. to
       Australia
1913 John Wisden
1918 5 School Bowlers of the Year
1919 5 Public School Cricketers of the
       Year
1920 5 Batsmen of the Year
1921 P. F. Warner
1924 5 Bowlers of the Year
1926 J. B. Hobbs

SECOND EDITIONS

Second issues appeared from 1889–1901 except (so far as is at present known) in 1896 and 1900. They are the same as the ordinary issues save only for:-

(i) The additional words on the front cover 'Second Issue'.

(ii) The price 2/- paper (3/- cloth boards from 1898) instead of the normal 1/-.

(iii) The price and words 'Second Issue' on the title pages of the 1889 and 1890 issues. Despite the price announcement for cloth-bound second issues I have been unable to trace any.

STYLE OF FRONT COVER OF PAPER EDITION

1864–1869	First style	(1865 slightly different from 1864)
1870–77	Second style.	Original version
1878–80	Second style.	First variation
1881–84		Second variation
1885	Third style.	Original version
1886		First variation
1887	Fourth style.	Original version
1888		First variation
1889–96		Second variation
1897–1935	Fifth style.	Original version
1936–37		First variation (1937 last paper issue)
1938–62	Sixth style.	(1938 was the first limp cloth issue)

STYLE OF LETTERING ON SPINE OF PAPER EDITION

1887–95	First appearance	
1895–1907	Slightly bolder	
1908–35	Second style	Title vertically reading from
1936–37	Second style. First variation	the bottom
1938–62	Third style	

Some copies of the 1901 first (but not second) issues had 1900 on the spine, covered over with a label bearing the correct date. 1904–1905 paper spines bore the words 'ALMANAC' not the usual 'ALMANACK'. The unusual spelling does not occur on the front cover nor on the spine of the cloth edition.

STYLE OF BRASSES ON FRONT COVER OF CLOTH BOARDS EDITION

1896–1902 First style
1903–28 Second style
1929–37 Second style (Variation due to change of address)
1938–62 Third style

From 1896 to 1937 yellow paper front and back covers were bound in as end papers and faced with yellow advertisement end papers on the insides of the front and back cloth boards.

STYLE OF BRASSES ON SPINE OF CLOTH BOARDS EDITION

1896–1937	First style	Title vertically reading from bottom
1938–40	Second style Original version	Title horizontally; at bottom No. of issue
1941–48	Third style	Title vertically reading from top
1949–62	Second style First variation	Title horizontally; at bottom the publisher's name

COLOUR OF PAPER COVERS

1864–71	Pale buff
1872–77	Pale pink/buff
1878–79	Glossy paper. Pale yellow/buff
1880–82	Pale yellow/buff
1883–86	Pale pink/buff
1887–1937	Bright yellow which fades to buff
1938–62	Limp cloth bright yellow with little or no fading
	Some war issues 1941–45 rather brown

FACSIMILE EDITION

In 1961 a limited facsimile reprint of the issues from 1864 to 1878 was published.

CRICKET—AN ENDURING ART [1963]

BY THE RT. HON. SIR ROBERT MENZIES, K.T., C.H., Q.C.

Prime Minister of Australia

If Mr. Gutteridge provided the hard facts, these were softened by the poetic effusions of the romantics. Neville Cardus's 'Six Giants of the Wisden Century', anthologised elsewhere, was probably the most eagerly read item in the Centenary Edition, but there were two other contemplative essays which embellished the Almanack. Both waxed unashamedly on the matchless pleasures of cricket both as a pastime and as a spectator sport. The then Prime Minister of Australia, Robert Gordon Menzies (1895–1978) had been a dedicated supporter of and lobbyist for the game all his life and in his account of his own cricketing self, reveals to what deep extent love of the game had permeated all levels of Australian life, not excluding the legal. His 'Cricket—An Enduring Art' is paralleled by Robertson-Glasgow's 'The Joy of Cricket', which tells us within a few lines why the flavour of his autobiography, '46 Not Out' (1948) endeared him to so wide an audience. Robertson-Glasgow perpetuated a great many neglected by-ways of cricket life and not the least part of his preservation work was done in the cause of his county captain in Somerset days, John Daniell, who once again strides across the landscape of a Robertson-Glasgow portrait and threatens to steal the show.

FOR me to quote statistics in a contribution to *Wisden* would indeed be to carry coals to Newcastle. I have neither the facilities nor the inclination. To browse through the records in *Wisden*; to snatch down a volume to settle an argument or to be reminded of great feats of the past; to 'revisit the glimpses' of the Five Cricketers; these things are great fun for the cricket-lover. But may I venture upon a heresy? Averages don't prove much, except to more unimaginative selectors. Men are more important than figures. Quality is even more important than quantity. Victor Trumper's batting averages in England in 1899, 1902, 1905 and 1909 were 34.57, 48.49, 36.54 and 33.37. In England–Australia Test Matches his average was 32.79. Yet those who remember him playing cannot speak of him, even now, except with the emotion which is the final tribute to sheer artistry.

For one of the great things about cricket is that it is an art even more than it is a science. The scientific batsman who hits every ball with precision to its appointed place is a great man to have on your side. He will win matches. He will take a high place in the records. But unless he adds art to science, humanity to skill, his glories will soon fade.

For a great artist is not content to move along the orthodox paths. His daemon possesses him. He must experiment. He must essay the unexpected. He must know his medium, but it must be his servant, not his master.

If Trumper's averages were modest by modern and affluent standards, it was largely because of the artistic temperament. To hit the same ball in the same way each time was, for him, tedious. So he hit it to vastly different places, for the fun of it.

If the art of cricket is to survive, many people must contribute to the survival. The spectator naturally loves a good swiping innings, with a few sixes thrown in; but he must also have time and intelligence to admire the artistry of non-scoring defence against aggressive and shrewd bowling.

Cricket-writers also have their part to play. In modern times they have become a numerous brood. They include in their numbers some who are sensitive observers and writers of distinction. But they include far too many who live for sensation and, if possible, scandal; to whom cricket is a sort of warfare to be conducted on and, principally perhaps, off the field; who are incapable of understanding art; who think in headlines.

I sometimes wonder if such onlookers realise what harm they do to cricket. Take an example. The cut, particularly the late cut, is one of the lovely things in cricket. When McCabe made his famous innings at Trent Bridge, I saw him repeatedly late cut lovely out-swingers from Kenneth Farnes. It was sheer ecstasy to see them. But I am sure that there were plenty to say, as I have heard it said of many another batsman, 'That's a dangerous stroke. He should cut it out!' And when fifty or a hundred runs later, that batsman is taken in the slips, they say 'I told you so,' and marvel at their own perspicacity.

If all batsmen had acted on such pusillanimous principles, the loveliest shots would have long since disappeared, and cricket would have died of its own dullness; averages without spirit; performance without pleasure.

My memory of Test Cricket goes back over half of the *Wisden* century. The batsmen who stand out clear in my mind are the artists; the takers of calculated (and sometimes uncalculated) risks; the men of colour and character who have rescued cricket from its occasional and inevitable periods of drabness and decline.

I have no doubt that England–Australia cricket has contributed much to the close association of the two countries in world affairs. There have been, of course, some unhappy experiences, from the 1879 Sydney 'riot', when Lord Harris's team played New South Wales, to the celebrated 'bodyline' controversy of 1932–33. But such matters were eddies on the surface of a broad and flowing river, which, like the Thames in the famous phrase, is 'liquid history'.

Why should I feel able to attach to a game such significance? That question deserves a considered answer.

I will first answer in the broad. Cricket is, as I have said, a great art. It is the mother of great traditions. It dwells in the eye and in the blood. The relative slowness of its tempo induces observation and enables its subtleties to be seen and noted. It has evoked, from writers of talent, a considerable literature.

Let me elaborate a little.

I know that the ancient phrase, that 'art is long', meant that in a short life it was difficult to achieve art. But art is long in another sense. So that it be true art, it has a long life of its own. It dwells on in the eye, in the ear, in the spirit. It perpetuates itself.

When white-haired men like me, during some winter's evening, fall to thinking of cricket and cricketers, what do we remember? Record scores? Averages? Results? Not at all, for these are matters for occasional argument, not reflection. Across the mind's eye passes a panorama of art and artists.

Take the great art of batting, with its infinite complexity. To hit the ball to any one of three hundred and fifty degrees out of the full circle. To accommodate the feel and the stroke to the vagaries of the pitch, and to the pace, length, swing, dip or spin of different bowlers. So far as I know, no mathematician has calculated all the possible permutations and combinations of batsmanship, but the possibilities must be fabulous. It is small wonder that, against the lovely back-drop of the greensward and the white-clad figures, still or swift, the eye of memory sees, as vividly as if it were yesterday, the great batsman as a great artist. It was no mere eccentricity which made Neville Cardus a superb cricket writer and a music critic of eminence. It was, on the contrary, an almost inevitable conjunction of the planets for all save the most narrow-minded of highbrows.

Though possessed myself of no executive cricket competence, but fortunate enough to have a strong visual memory, I could without difficulty describe the great batsmen and bowlers and wicket-keepers and fieldsmen of my half-century, and see them clearly as I described them!

Indeed, the art of cricket, unlike some others, retains its hold upon the art-lover of all generations because its basic elements do not go out of fashion. He does not suffer the puzzlement and frustration of the man who has learned to love and to live with the great works of the impressionist painters and is then called upon to bow (for fashion's sake) before the abstractionists of the modern school.

This conception of cricket as an enduring art is one of the elements we have in common, wherever we may live. In a world in which differences are emphasised and get the headlines, it is more than ever important that we should cherish our unities and keep them in good repair.

I said earlier that cricket is the mother of great traditions. That its history is studded with unsporting incidents cannot be denied. That they are—as I have already said—occasionally magnified into a species of warfare by some press writers must regretfully be admitted. But I have yet to see a match in which the warmest popular approval has not been reserved for the feat of true skill or the honest and sportsmanlike conduct of some player. There is, as one finds in reading them again, a touch of self-conscious pomposity in some of the remarks of schoolboys in the old school stories. Yet Tom Brown was right, when he said at his last school match: 'It's more than a game. It's an institution!'

And, like all great institutions which are part of our inheritance, it gets into the blood, and can even invade the seats of judgment. I will illustrate this by an experience I had in my earlier days at the Victorian Bar. The story will be thought scandalous by some, and perhaps it is. But it is true, and it makes my point.

I had been appearing a good deal before an elderly judge who was not a great lawyer but who had for a brief period been a better than average cricketer. He was somewhat pernickety and abhorred slang expressions, but he was always approachable through his three special hobbies: roses, poultry and cricket. I suppose that purists will say that no advocate should play upon the weaknesses or foibles of a judge. My reply is that any advocate who does not study and know his judge or judges is going to lose many cases, most needlessly.

Anyhow, my story is this. I was for the defendant in a civil action which arose out of events in the neighbourhood of Ballarat, the famous old gold-mining city. My client, as I discovered after a conference with him and his solicitor, was a very decent and honest, but dull man, quite incapable of stating the facts in any coherent or consecutive fashion. Right through the first day of the hearing, the plaintiff and his witnesses were heard. I cross-examined with no particular success. Yet I had a feeling that my bucolic client was right, if he could only register himself with the judge. The plaintiff's case closed just on the adjournment. The judge looked at me, kindly enough (he approved of me because he thought I spoke good English!), and said: 'Mr. Menzies, I think I should tell you that I find the plaintiff's case and witnesses most impressive.' With my usual air of confidence, I replied: 'I would ask Your Honour to suspend judgment until you have heard my client, who will, I am sure impress you very much!'

After the adjournment, I led the solicitor and client (we had no other witness) down to my chambers. All efforts to extract coherence from the client failed. I then produced my cards.

M. 'Mr. X, have you ever grown roses?'
X. 'I think the wife has some in the garden.'
M. 'But can you distinguish a La Belle France from a Frau Carl Drushki?'
X. 'Not a hope!'
M. 'Do you keep fowls?'
X. 'The wife has a few.'

M. 'Can you distinguish between a White Leghorn and an Orpington?'
X. 'Not for the life of me!'
M. 'Have you ever played cricket?'
X. 'Ah! Now you're talking. I played for Ballarat and District against Ivo Bligh's Eleven!'
M. 'Good. Conference ended!'

The next morning I opened my case and called the defendant. He was quite dreadful as a witness. At one stage it became necessary to ask him about a date. Before he could reply I said, in the most helpful manner: 'Take your time, witness. I know that dates are not always easy to remember. Now, if I were to ask you about the date when you played cricket for Ballarat and District against Ivo Bligh's Eleven, that would be much easier!'

The judge, beaming with excitement and delight, switched round in his chair and said 'Is that so? Tell me about the match. Were you a batsman or a bowler?' And at once they were into it. Who was the fast bowler? How many runs did the defendant get? For half an hour we had cricket reminiscences galore. By the time my client, completely relaxed, had returned to and concluded his evidence, the judge turned to the plaintiff's astonished counsel and said: 'Of course, Mr. Y., you may cross-examine if you like. You have a perfect right to do so. But I think I should tell you that in all my years on the bench I have never been more favourably impressed by any witness.'

It is hardly necessary to add that the defendant won and, I think, rightly, on the merits. But it was cricket that did it!

While I am in this mood, I crave leave to record another reminiscence of cricket and the law.

A case had occurred, well over thirty years ago, in the local court at Mildura, the famous irrigation settlement in the far North-West of Victoria, on the River Murray. The Mildura solicitor concerned on the losing side, an old friend of mine, wanted to obtain, in the Supreme Court, an Order Nisi to review the decision. But he overlooked the time factor—the Order had to be applied for within 30 days—and filed his papers and briefed me almost at the last moment. But it was Christmas time, and the Supreme Court was not sitting! But there was a Test Match on at the Melbourne Cricket Ground, and Mr. Justice Cussen was the President of the Club.

I hared off to the ground; it was my only hope. The judge was in the Committee Box. I waited until the end of the over, and then caught the eye of the judge. Happily he was a patient and generous man. I told him the circumstances. He at once caught on. 'I quite see the position. Have I your assurance that the necessary papers are filed?' I assured him that they were. 'Very well,' he said, 'I think the rule is that if you formally apply within the time, and the papers are in order, I can note the fact that you have applied, and adjourn the actual argument to a future date!' I vigorously agreed. He noted the application, turned to the field, and said with a smile: 'That was a fine bit of bowling, wasn't it?'

In my own time I have seen splendid South African teams play in Australia. The first was enriched by such players as Schwartz, Faulkner and Sherwell. The last, under Cheetham, was not so rich in individual stars, but was quite magnificent in the field, and of great team character.

India have played here. The West Indies have been here three times. The last occasion was quite historic. It produced the famous Test Match tie at Brisbane; some fantastic bowling by Wesley Hall; great batting by Kanhai and Sobers; a spirit of dash and attack which seized the Australian imagination and drew large and eager crowds. It must be confessed that the return to Australia in 1961–62 of these three players, added to the new standards of aggressive captaincy set by Benaud, made the Sheffield Shield season the greatest popular success since the days of Bradman.

But in spite of all this, *the* Test Matches are those against England. For England and Australia are 'the founding fathers' of international cricket. Their contests provide the standard of excellence. True they sometimes fall grievously below the standard, when the 'will to win' gives place to the 'will not to be beaten'—a very different and, I fear, a very dull thing.

Yet I would take leave to say that the greatest ambition of every young cricketer in England is to play against Australia; while, for the young Australian, selection against England in a Test Match, and above all selection to tour England, is the ultimate goal. Even the 'statistics' man, now that 'Test matches' are so much more numerous and therefore new overall records are established, will agree that the records of England v. Australia Test performances are in a category of their own.

There are, of course, many reasons for this. There are many new nations in today's world; many forms of government; many historical and intellectual backgrounds; a New Commonwealth which comprises both the old monarchies and the new Republics. But Great Britain and Australia are of the same blood and allegiance and history and instinctive mental processes. We know each other so well, that, thank Heaven, we don't have to be too tactful with each other. If, occasionally, we feel disposed to be polite and formal, some of our more warlike cricket commentators will, like the false doctor in Molière, soon change all that.

Cricket tradition, fashioned over the better part of a century, is a powerful thing. In Australia, in the Sheffield Shield, there is a special flavour about the matches between New South Wales and Victoria. They are the ancient rivals. You have your own wars of the Roses, in which no impertinent outsider can safely intervene. Between us, we have the England v. Australia Test Matches. True, cricket may go through a dull patch; captaincy may become too negative; attendances may fall off for a time; some reformer wants to revive cricket by altering the rules instead of by livening up the players and the play.

And then, a year or so later, great new players emerge, and all is different. We have all seen this; you with the emergence of a Tate, a Larwood, a Hammond, a Compton, a Bedser, a Statham, a Dexter; we with a McDonald, a Mailey, a Bradman, a McCabe, a Grimmett, an O'Reilly, a Harvey, a Lindwall, a Davidson, a Benaud.

The great Test matches have a magnetic attraction which will vary, but will never disappear.

I may be wrong. It is possible that people of my generation tend to be *laudatores temporis acti*. But I believe that the great cricketing names which we have known or read about, are part of our stream of consciousness, which will not, in the minds of our grandchildren, dwindle to a mere trickle.

I remember that, about 25 years ago, I was speaking at Chatham House in London. At question time, a polite but nervous man got up at the back of the hall and asked me—with suitable hesitations and apologies—whether it was true that the earliest settlers in Australia were convicts. I said promptly that many of them were; that he was not hurting my personal feelings, for my own grandparents had gone to Australia of their own accord; but that the records would show that of all the persons convicted of crime in England during the brief period of transportation to Australia, the great majority remained in England! I thought all too late, by a sort of *esprit d'escalier*, that I should have added that cricket was also transported. The regiments stationed in Sydney were playing cricket by 1803!

THE JOY OF CRICKET [1963]

BY R. C. ROBERTSON-GLASGOW

IT was, I think, the Reverend Sydney Smith who said that his height of human happiness would be eating *pâté de foie gras* to the sound of trumpets. This, I admit, might be a pleasurable combination. But, better still, I would like to have bowled the one and only Victor Trumper for 0 in a deciding Test Match.

Cricket has very various meanings and delights. I suppose the most popular dream of boyhood's cricket is to be making a hundred in a Test. The ambition of most young cricketers seems to concern batsmanship. But, myself, I would always rather have sent the stumps than the ball flying. Modesty, no doubt, should forbid mention of any example of such a performance. But the bowler has to work for his great moments, and I don't see why he shouldn't mention some of them, without being condemned as an intolerable bore.

My own moment of greatest joy *should* have been at The Oval in 1920, when, aged eighteen and very absent-minded, I had Jack Hobbs caught at mid-on for 0. But, oddly enough, I didn't believe it at the time, and, in spite of the printed word, I don't believe it yet. At best, it was a fluke.

In a bowler's triumph there should, I feel, be 'an element of violence'. For which reason, the greatest moment in my cricketing life was when I pitched a ball on the middle stump of the left-handed Australian master, Warren Bardsley, and knocked the off-stump past first slip. Perhaps it was his green Australian cap that helped towards the pleasure. Perhaps. But no; most of all, it was the sheer violence of the assassination that thrilled me. It was in 1926, at Taunton. I suppose that the great man, at 42 years, was then 'going over the hill'; but, to borrow Sir Alan Herbert's words, 'This is the day I shall remember the day I am dying'. As a pilgrim of the ball I had travelled far in the wilds before that moment of triumph. Forgive my selfishness.

Cricket, for all its admirers may say, *is* a selfish game. Certainly, bowling is. How often, in my cricketing life, I watched others taking wickets that I regarded as mine by rights. Daylight robbery. There is nothing to equal the joy and sensation of personal triumph. And the nearest that I've been to a heaven on earth was when walking back to the pavilion at Lord's after making a fifty against Cambridge for Oxford, with a borrowed bat.

I fancy that I hear a somewhat pompous voice attacking such heretical views. 'Cricket,' says the voice, 'is, above all, a Team game; a builder of character.' This is not always so. Cricket has murdered many a sunny afternoon for the schoolboy who cannot bat, is not asked to bowl, and does not wish to field. To enjoy cricket, you must be good enough to partake in the ritual. You must be, so to speak, in use.

No; I would not rate Team Spirit as the most ennobling part of cricket. The best part of cricket is the Tour Spirit. No one who has not been on a Cricket Tour, however humble, has tasted the full felicity of the game. The Cricket Tourist can discover the joy of irresponsibility and detachment. If he be wise, no correspondence, threatening or otherwise, will be forwarded to him. If he be wiser still, he will have told his employers and his relatives that the tour is in North Wales, whereas in fact it is in Jersey, perhaps the most hospitable of all European Islands.

In my memory, a little clouded by banquetings, the sun always shone on Jersey. There was magic in its air. However beautiful had been the preceding night, we were always ready to repeat the words of the great Oscar Hammerstein—'Oh, what a beautiful morning!'

In Jersey, too, the newspaper reports of cricket, when they chanced to appear, were full of praise for the visiting team, even if we were all out for 70 and had missed a dozen catches. In which connection I recall a great cricketer who had remarked to a friend, 'Never read newspaper reports of a cricket match unless you've done something very good.' A few days after he'd made this comment, he scored a century on an alien ground, and the local evening paper's sole remark on the feat was, '*How* —— ever makes a century with so peculiar a style must remain a mystery.'

We wander from the title, 'The Joy of Cricket'. My own summit of surprise mingled with pleasure was reached in the Parks at Oxford, 1920. I had not foreseen any chance of playing for a County when the Oxford v. Cambridge match was over. Yet at the end of an exciting game with Somerset, their captain, the inimitable and often unrepeatable John Daniell, asked me to play for Somerset. 'But,' I said, 'I was born and live in Scotland.' 'You mind your own —— business,' replied my benefactor. 'I will,' I said. There was a pause. 'But,' he continued, 'have you no ruddy relations at all around Somerset?' 'Well,' I admitted, 'I have a cousin who is, at the moment, M.P. for Bath.' 'Good enough,' said John D.; and it was.

Somerset have never won the County Championship; but, for the beauty of scenery combined with variety of cricketing styles, Somerset has no equal at all. Win, lose or draw, every day's cricket for Somerset was an indescribable joy. I found myself received with a humorous and unsurprised kindness. Wit and laughter abounded.

The standard of cricketing skill ranged from the highest to the lowest, from Jack White's slow left-hand bowling to . . . well, never mind what. Most particularly do I recall that some of our best batsmen, such as M. D. Lyon and J. C. W. MacBryan, and Tom Young, never *seemed* to practise. There was a tendency to go to bed late and to rise just in time for the resumption of play.

There there was that great all-rounder, Len Braund. In the autumn of his career he still caught catches at slip which others wouldn't have touched. He also missed a fair number; and I remember with pleasure his remark to me after he'd missed a 'sitter'—'Slip fielding's like fishing; let the little ones go.' A philosophy that was not shared by the suffering bowlers.

Humour was, so to speak, both parent and son of Somerset cricket; though I doubt if our captain unreservedly agreed with this view. John Daniell had a most expressive face, as well as vocabulary. He was a magnificent leader, whose team so seldom seemed to come up to his expectations. Perhaps he expected just too much, and was still living in the days of Lionel Palairet and Sammy Woods.

We wouldn't have had him otherwise; fielding brilliantly under a Trilby hat, and scowling at the batsman. Once when the Sussex opening batsman snicked the very first ball of the innings for four past his leg stump, John said to the bowler, 'When the hell are you going to bowl straight?' And the bowler shouted back, 'And when the hell are you going to wear white trousers instead of yellow ones?'

Then there was the beauty of the surrounding country. Mr. Neville Cardus has written memorably on the effect of environmnt upon the type of cricket played, with special reference to Old Trafford. At Taunton, on the horizon rose those lovely hills, the Quantocks; in themselves, surely, a romantic inducement to the cricketer. And the villages around are so aptly named. Combe Florey and Bishop's Lydeard, somehow suggested immortal summers.

Country House cricket abounded; that game of long intervals, variegated blazers, and dubious decisions. The most eccentric match that I ever played in was at a country house, near Maiden Erleigh, in Berkshire, then the home of Mr. Solly Joel. I arrived on a temperamental motorcycle, with my cricket bag precariously strapped on behind. There was an absence of teetotalism. Instead of a tea interval we went off to bathe in a Neronian Swimming-pool, knocked back a drink or two, and returned unpunctually to the fray. When play at length resumed, I recall that Jack White had placed a couple of fielders in an adjoining meadow, to await a catch from that remarkable hitter, P. G. H. Fender.

I never had the luck to play cricket in distant parts of the globe, such as the Antipodes, South Africa, India, Pakistan, and the West Indies, though I do remember that several of us, late one night in our College at Oxford, discussed the possibilities of introducing cricket to China. It remained a possibility. I have always regretted that the Chinaman, who has given his name to a certain type of left-handed delivery, should never have played the game nationally. Today, there seems less chance than ever of his doing so, as Communism and cricket do not seem to be happy bedfellows.

I have played in Portugal, on matting wickets, at Lisbon and Oporto. One of our faster bowlers was erratic both on and off the field, and a source of anxiety to his worthy captain. It was thought that he had missed the ship at the very start, but he was found later playing Jazz on a musical instrument to a partially reluctant audience of fellow-travellers.

On one occasion he did appear, late in our opponents' innings, and bowled one of the fastest, shortest and widest overs that I ever saw. He was, nevertheless, an inimitable champion. He was a scratch golfer; and when, on our overland journey we stopped for a few days to play golf at St. Jean de Luz in the Pyrenean country, he surprised even his elderly and experienced caddie by his skill at improving with the foot the lie of the ball in the rough. He was straight from a P. G. Wodehouse book; and, but for cricket, I would never have known him.

Perhaps the greatest joy in cricket is experienced by the sheer bowler who, by some quirk of providence, finds himself to be an unexpected batsman. I hope I may be acquitted of pride when I say that my most pleasurable times in County cricket were when I was batting around number ten or eleven and achieved success above my station.

As a very late batsman you are welcomed at the crease rather in the same manner as the Walrus and the Carpenter welcomed the Oysters. The bowlers regard you as a benefactor. The umpires smile appreciatively, because soon now they will be able to take the weight off their feet. The wicket-keeper probably asks after your wife and children, if any. You are given 'guard', middle-and-leg, as a formality rather than a convenience.

Your earlier scoring strokes are greeted with tolerance, or even with open laughter. But, after half an hour or so, you become a guest who has outstayed his welcome. The bowlers begin to scowl, and to tire. Yet your performance is not entirely unappreciated; and I remember a fielder, in the West Country, who evidently thought little of the bowler then in use, saying into my ear at the end of an over, 'Good going; now hit the —— for six.'

When fate decides that you've gone far enough, the axe descends. But you are a happy man. And, somehow, you are not at all tired. Within a quarter of an hour of so, you take the new ball and run up to the crease breathing fire and slaughter, and appeal for l.b.w. like a bomb exploding, while the batsman ruefully rubs his thigh.

Then, when playing days are over, dull must be he of soul who cannot derive pleasure and amusement from his fellow-spectators. No other game so richly produces eccentricity among its watchers. Rugger and Soccer crowds tend each to conform to a particular pattern. But, at cricket matches, you find infinite variety and oddity: cabinet-ministers and crossing-sweeps, lunatics, lovers, and poets; men who watch all day through field-glasses and say nothing, female statisticians, who long to be contradicted; odd spectators who keep warm in spite of semi-nudity. All are, in their way, contented; all seem to have absolutely nothing to do in this world except watching cricket.

But, once more, it is the bowler in cricket who knows the deepest joy; because he can hit his victim and pretend to be sorry about it; because he is artist and workman in one; because he can make mistakes and yet suddenly enter the paradise of triumph.

Myself, I go back once more to Taunton in 1926. Clarence Grimmett, who could bowl deadly spinners from somewhere near his right kidney, was at the wicket. Not a great batsman, Clarrie; not even a fairly good one. Never mind. He had raised his bat to cut me square. The ball chose to come in from the off, and it knocked out his middle stump. Leonardo da Vinci should have been there, to paint the incredulity of the batsman, and the unconfined joy of the bowler.

Rejoice then, cricketers; but, most of all, ye bowlers. For, whatever the books may say, yours is the best part in the best play yet invented.

NOTES BY THE EDITOR [1963]

Among the other essays in the 1963 edition, which included an account of the Worcestershire club and a review of Test cricket, there was one section of the editorial notes more important by far, sociologically speaking, than anything to be found in the Almanack's eleven hundred other pages. Norman Preston, who only a season or two earlier, had marvelled that any man could be imperceptive enough to demand the abolition of the distinction between amateurs and professionals, was now obliged to concede to his readers that the distinction had indeed been abolished once and for all. Feeling the hurt deeply, Preston goes on to ask a few rhetorical questions and register a few pleas, all of which show the pathos of the predicament of tens of thousands of men like him, sad at the dumping of a venerable tradition yet still believing that such actions were within the control of the legislators, which of course was quite untrue.

'Is it wise,' asks Preston, 'to throw everything overboard?' The answer is that when the ship has already sunk, there is not much to be gained in pretending it is still afloat. The affluent classes which had once sustained the English first-class game through patronage and participation were now obliged to work like the rest of us. Squeezed by Death Duties, Land Tax,

Income Tax and sundry other delights of the modern world, your gilded Gent found himself no longer gilded. There was nothing for it but to stop playing games and get a job. Preston tells us that 'the amateur has played a very important part'. So had early professionals like George Parr and Fuller Pilch, but there was no point in looking to them for further guidance. Preston professes to be unsure about W. G. Grace's bending of the laws governing payments to amateurs. 'Whether this was true or not. . . .,' he remarks, although if he really was uncertain, then he must have been living in a barrel for the previous fifty years. The real point was not that, as the Editor says, Grace virtually guaranteed the survival of English cricket, but that the rules pertaining to payment turned him into a hypocrite, a man who said one thing and did quite another.

Again, 'the passing of the amateur could have a detrimental effect in the vital matter of captaincy'. Here Preston is being mealy-mouthed. Why only 'could'? Why not the dogmatism of 'would'? Of course the disappearance of the self-appointed leader would have dire effects on the art of leadership. How could it not? A generation later the national side all but disintegrated because no captainlike captain could be found whose cricketing abilities justified his selection. The truth is that it was forces far beyond either the control or the perception of those who controlled the game which pushed the Gentlemen-cricketer into the past. In a sense it was a classic example of the futility of the plea to keep politics out of cricket. A mild form of the legislative class war was being fought out in the streets and the disappearance of the leisured gentleman was one of the results. It was significant that in the very year of Wisden's one hundredth birthday, so profound an acknowledgement of change should be made.

B Y doing away with the amateur, cricket is in danger of losing the spirit of freedom and gaiety which the best amateur players brought to the game.

On the other hand there is at present a source of talent which has been untapped because of the gulf between the amateur and the professional. This comprises the band of cricketers who could get away from business or other activities for periods during the summer to assist their counties if they could receive compensation for loss of salary. In other words, their employers would be willing to release them, but not to pay their salaries during their absence from work.

The passing of the amateur could have a detrimental effect in the vital matter of captaincy both at County and Test level. True, it was under a professional, Sir Leonard Hutton, that England last regained the Ashes in 1953, and men like Tom Dollery (Warwickshire), J. V. Wilson (Yorkshire) and Don Kenyon (Worcestershire) have led their counties with distinction.

Because the amateur possessed independent status, the professionals, generally, preferred to have him as captain. Two of the most popular and most successful captains were A. B. Sellers (Yorkshire) and W. S. Surridge (Surrey). Their gifts of leadership were stronger than their batting or bowling ability. Both were great fielders, but if either had been on equal status as a 'cricketer' with the professional he might well have been passed over.

Under the new set-up, one presumes there will still be players with a full-time contract while others receive match fees and a minority may still prefer to play solely for the love of the game. One can visualise smaller full-time staffs, particularly if, as many reformers desire, there is a reduction in the number of days allotted to county cricket.

Sir John Hobbs, commenting on the change, said: 'It is sad to see the passing of the amateurs because it signals the end of an era in cricket. They were a great asset to the game, much appreciated by all of us because they were able to come in and play freely, whereas many professionals did not feel they could take chances. Now times are different, and I can understand the position of the amateur who has to make his living. You cannot expect him to refuse good offers outside cricket.'

1879 DEFINITION

The difference between the amateur and the professional status is not a modern problem. As far back as 1879 it caused enough controversy in cricket circles for M.C.C. to appoint a sub-committee to inquire into the Definition and Qualification of Amateur Cricketers. Their report, which follows, was adopted unanimously by the General Committee:-

'We have in the first instance referred to the accounts of the last few years, in order to ascertain the amount which has been expended by the club under the long established rule that a gentleman who is invited to play in an M.C.C. match, and would be debarred from playing by the expense to which he would be put, may, on application to the Secretary, receive his reasonable expenses; we find that the total amount paid under this rule is comparatively trifling (under £50 a year in all); that there has been no abuse of this rule, so far as M.C.C. are concerned, at all events since the management of the finances of the club has been in its own hands (1866); and that no gentleman has been retained by the club by extra payment.

'We see no reason for recommending the abolition of the old established rule, but we think it is advisable that the committee should lay down distinctly the principle on which they are prepared to act, especially as regards the match, Gentlemen v. Players.

'We are of the opinion that no Gentlemen ought to make a profit by his service in the cricket field, and that for the future any cricketer taking more than his expenses in any match should not be qualified to play for the Gentlemen against the Players at Lord's but that if any gentleman should feel difficulty in joining in the match without such assistance, he should not be debarred from playing as a Gentleman by having his actual expenses defrayed.

'Whilst expressing our opinion that the payments by the M.C.C. under their rule have been reasonable, we feel that we must notice statements which have been made to us that sums much in excess of actual expenses have been frequently paid to gentlemen by other clubs or individuals.

'We have not thought it desirable to go into this question at any length,

because we hope that if the committee of the M.C.C. should adopt our suggestion as to the above minute, and should make such minute public, that course will have the effect of checking a system which might grow into a serious abuse, and which even as now alleged to be practised is open to grave objection.'

SIR PELHAM WARNER [1964]

BY A. W. T. LANGFORD

The figure of Sir Pelham Warner presents obstacles so insuperable to the chronicler striving for that impartiality said to be so desirable in an annalist that one begins to wonder if it is worth saying anything at all. The problem presented by Warner is that he appears to have been a very slippery customer but because he attended Rugby and Oxford and rose to the presidency of M.C.C. we are not supposed to say so. Anyone tactless enough to ask questions about the peculiar ethical stances adopted by the occasional patrician soon finds himself accused of the most outlandish crimes. So much as hint that Lord Hawke was never likely to be mistaken for Albert Einstein, and you are instantly accused of being the reincarnation of Karl Marx. Express even the slightest misgivings as to Lord Harris's suitability as an ombudsman and the cry of anarchy hangs on the air. Be so bold as to suggest that Douglas Jardine's sense of humour was not quite as ribald as Kierkegaard's and all sorts of frightened folk are convinced they sniff the brimstone of revolution. Silence on all these issues is known as keeping politics out of cricket. But to grant one social group immunity from any blame for anything, so far from keeping politics out of cricket, is to drag it in by the scruff of its neck. Sir Pelham Warner is no more immune from comment than, shall we say, the old Surrey wicket-keeper Ted Pooley, one of the very few cricketers to absent himself from the field of play owing to a prior engagement with the local police.

The obituary of Warner which appeared in the 1964 Wisden is typical of the taxidermist's art which is occasionally deployed in the hope of reshaping the lineaments of some departed hero. Yet the facts of the case are undeniable. Through the long processional of his life, Warner was involved in one fracas in a way which casts grave doubts on his moral integrity. In 1932–33 he was manager of the England tourists to Australia, that party of men led by Jardine into behaviour on the field of play which no sane apologist can ever justify. Jardine disappeared from the game soon after; Warner, who appears to have abrogated all managerial responsibility during the tour, went on to achieve a knighthood for services to cricket and the occupancy of the highest offices of cricketing status. He never adequately answered the charges of negligence and moral cowardice levelled against him, saying in later years that there was no point in raking over old bones. But there surely is a point if you avoided raking them when they were still new. Before the 1932–33 tour Warner announced publicly his distaste for Bodyline. After the tour he again announced publicly his distaste for Bodyline. During the tour he made no attempt to curb Bodyline as being practised by his own charges. Why? Until the questions raised by Warner's passivity in the face of Bodyline are answered adequately, there can be no acceptance of the plaster saint presented by the eulogies, of which the Wisden article is only one among many.

We are told that Warner was a charming man beloved by every dog and baby who crossed his path, which is no doubt true. But even as he pats the dogs and kisses the babies, the vast shadow of Bodyline is always there, darkening the landscape of his reputation. To say as much is to invite the brickbats of his advocates. But it is a curious business. When I confess myself too fastidious to follow the morality of Geoffrey Boycott or regard the gentle art of sledging as half-witted, nobody accuses me of being disloyal to the working classes. As it happens I much prefer, shall we say, Sir Timothy O'Brien to Tony Greig, but I cannot make any sense at all of Mr. Langford's remark that Warner 'never allowed his opposition to interfere with his admiration for Jardine as a man and as a leader. History has of course proved that Sir Pelham was right.' History, it so happens, has proved nothing of the kind and posterity is justified in asking why, if Warner was so much in love with Jardine he ever accepted the managerial hot seat. Answer comes there none. The writer of this fulsome tribute must have known that Warner on his return from that catastrophic tour wrote to the then Governor of South Australia, the future Lord Gowrie: 'Jardine is a queer fellow. When he sees a cricket ground with an Australian on it he goes mad. He rose to his present position on my shoulders and of his attitude to me I do not care to speak.'

The argument has been raging for more than half a century now and seems at this late stage never to be resolved. But those with a taste for the Conspiracy theory of the universe will be intrigued by the item published by Geoffrey Moorhouse in his 1981 publication, 'Lord's':

One of the most arresting features of the whole episode is the dearth of relevant material. As Manager of that tour, Pelham Warner submitted to the M.C.C. Committee a report on all that had happened from the moment the party left home until the day it returned. That document, quite simply, has vanished from the archives at Lord's. So has every letter he wrote from Australia to the M.C.C. secretary Findlay or anyone else in the heirarchy of M.C.C. The protective coating, it seems, has insulated him rather well from historical research.

Posterity's consolation is that at least three good jokes have come out of the Bodyline episode:

'The question was not understood in this country.' Pelham Warner, 'Lord's' (1946).

'I do not propose to discuss it here. It would serve no good purpose.'
Pelham Warner, 'Long Innings' (1951)
'The play's the thing.' Douglas Jardine, 'Cricket' (1936.)

WHEN I was a small boy my father purchased a secondhand copy of *Cricket Across the Seas* by P. F. Warner at the modest price of sixpence.

It was my first cricket book and I devoured every word of it; indeed I almost knew the book by heart. I imagined myself playing Bridge with F. L. Fane on the voyage out to New Zealand—the book was an account of the tour of Lord Hawke's team in New Zealand and Australia—I enjoyed the scenery and I was horrified by A. D. Whatman, one of the wicket-keepers of the team, being so engrossed in a book *The Three Years' War* by Christian de Wet during the match against Otago that he did not watch the cricket at all. A wicket fell, and a companion nudged the bookworm, appraising him of the fact. He sauntered into the pavilion, padded up—and returned to his book. Another wicket fell, another nudge, and Whatman strolled out to the wicket. He played the first ball, but no doubt still thinking of the book he played all over the second one and there was a crash of timber. The book had won! I never forgave Whatman for that episode.

I had entered a new world, but never in my wildest dreams did I think that I was destined to spend well over thirty supremely happy years in the closest possible contact with the author as his assistant on *The Cricketer*.

In the 1921 *Wisden* Sydney Pardon wrote: 'There have been many greater cricketers than Pelham Warner but none more devoted to the game. Nothing has ever damped his enthusiasm. Whether winning or losing he has always been the same.'

With that verdict I imagine few, if any, students of the game will disagree, but in his prime, and in good health, Pelham Warner was a very fine batsman indeed as his record, especially against the redoubtable Yorkshire XIs of his era, testifies.

Pelham Francis Warner was born in the island of Trinidad in the West Indies on October 2, 1873, and he died on January 30, 1963. His father, Charles William Warner, C.B., for many years Attorney General of Trinidad, was born two days before the battle of Trafalgar so father and son between them saw warships develop from the three deckers of Nelson's time to the present day atomic submarine—an astounding thought.

Excluding the handicap of ill health Sir Pelham had a remarkably happy life and received virtually every honour the game has to offer, on and off the field.

He often used to relate that his first recollections of cricket were of batting on a marble gallery at his home, The Hall, Port of Spain, Trinidad, to the bowling of a black boy who rejoiced in the name of Killebree (Humming Bird). At thirteen and a half he came to England, but before that he had three years at Harrison College, Barbados, and at thirteen had gained a place in the first XI.

On May 20, 1887, he paid his first visit to Lord's to see M.C.C. play Sussex. On August Bank Holiday he saw The Oval for the first time, and the following month he entered Whitelaw's House at Rugby where he was in the XI for four years, being captain in 1892. He had the good fortune to be coached by that amusing character Tom Emmett, who taught him to play back in the right way and how to attack the half volley, saying 'if you come to her, come. You may as well be stumped by two feet as by one inch.'

Sir Pelham never tired of recalling his Rugby days, and so vividly did he portray his contemporaries that I almost felt that I knew them personally, particularly a certain Sam Slater, a useful bowler, who laughed his way through five years at Rugby. It was at Rugby that Pelham developed into Plum.

Going up to Oxford, where he was at Oriel, he did not get his Blue until his third year when his captain, G. J. Mordaunt, said to him: 'Plum, I think you would look very nice in a dark blue cap.' Influenza had interfered with his prospects during his first two summers. He was not particularly successful in his two University matches, making 22 and 4 in 1895, and 10 and 17 in 1896, being run out in each innings. The 1896 match was memorable for Cambridge giving away 12 extras to prevent Oxford following on (compulsory in those days) and for G. O. Smith's superb 132 which enabled Oxford to make 330 for six and win by four wickets.

It was in 1894 that Sir Pelham made his début for Middlesex, playing against Somerset at Taunton on August 6, 7 and 8. He scored 6 and 4 and Middlesex won an exciting game by 19 runs. Curiously enough his last innings against Somerset at Taunton was also 6. His next match was against Gloucestershire and W. G. arrived on the ground wearing a morning coat over white flannel trousers and a black hat, half topper and half bowler—a wonderful sartorial effort.

Sir Pelham took his Bar final examination in 1896, and in subsequent years he often stated in his speeches that 'I am by courtesy my learned friend'. It was one of my great privileges to lunch with him on numerous occasions in the Inner Temple and to be fascinated by the brilliant conversation.

The whole course of his life was altered by Lord Hawke's invitation to tour the West Indies, and on January 13, 1897, he began the first of many journeys across the seas. As it happened the opening match was against Trinidad and he had the distinction of scoring 119, the first hundred that had ever been scored in the Island in an important match. Scores of black men rushed across the ground at the end of his innings shouting out 'I taught you, Mr. Pelham. You play well, Sir; we are proud of you.'

On his return from the West Indies, he made his first hundred in a first-class match at his beloved Lord's—108 not out against Yorkshire. This was the first of many fine innings against Yorkshire, and he was justifiably proud of his record against that county; indeed he rarely failed against them as a perusal of the records will show. Furthermore, he had a sincere affection for many of the Yorkshire players, particularly Hirst and Haigh, who were inseparable friends. David Hunter, the old Yorkshire wicket-keeper, paid him a splendid compliment when he said 'Ah, Mr. Warner, you play Wilfred (Rhodes) better than anyone else.' This remark was made when Sir Pelham was batting against Yorkshire on a very false wicket at Bradford. He scored 48 in a total of 87.

Sir Pelham owed a great deal to Lord Hawke and he had an intense admiration and affection for 'The Baron', whose 'Is it quite the same Plum who left us in September? Has England discovered a great leader?' uttered after the triumphant 1903–4 tour, had a life-long influence on him. As Sir Pelham wrote in *Long Innings*, flattery like this is intoxicating wine. I well remember his grief when he learnt of Lord Hawke's death.

The visit to the West Indies with Lord Hawke's team had infected him with the travel bug and in 1897, at the age of 23, he took a side to America. It was on this tour that he first met J. B. King who was the first of the right arm-in-swing bowlers and one of the greatest bowlers of all time. It was also on this tour that the following verses appeared in a long poem about the team:

> At one end stocky Jessop frowned
> The human catapult
> Who wrecks the roofs of distant towns
> When set in his assault
> His mate was that perplexing man
> We know as Looshun Gore
> It isn't spelt at all that way
> We don't know what it's for

In the spring of 1898 he toured Portugal with T. Westray's side. At the end of the season he led another team to America and included Canada, and in December sailed for South Africa as a member of Lord Hawke's team, scoring 132 not out in the first Test match at Johannesburg.

Back from South Africa, and feeling very fit, he played one of the finest innings of his life when he scored 150 against Yorkshire at Lord's and by now had established himself as one of the leading batsmen in the country. He more than maintained his improved form in the 1900 season which he began with 83 and 69 for M.C.C. against Yorkshire, 114 for Middlesex against Sussex and 146 for Middlesex against Lancashire. In this match a nasty blow on the left shin from Mold kept him out of cricket for the next three weeks, and when he went to play for the touring West Indies side against Leicestershire, incidentally making 113, a ball from Woodcock, almost as fast as Mold, struck him on his injured shin and he was laid up once more. But for these injuries he would almost certainly have played for the Gentlemen v. Players at Lord's. As it was he scored five centuries for Middlesex and in 18 matches for the county made 1,335 runs, average 44.50. *Wisden* enthused over his skill in playing fast bowling.

In 1901 Sir Pelham was chosen for the Gentlemen at Lord's—and a successful début it was. He helped C. B. Fry to put on 105 in the first innings for the opening partnership, and in the second innings his 48 was top score for the Gentlemen.

He was a great advocate for the retention of Gentlemen v. Players and in his preface to 'Gentlemen v. Players, 1806–1949' he wrote 'I am indeed fortunate to have lived to attempt to give some sort of history of an historic match which began long before Test matches were dreamed of, and which I pray, and believe, will never die out.' Mercifully he died the day before the decision was made to call all players 'cricketers' which, of course, meant the termination of 'the historic match'.

The year 1902 saw Sir Pelham once more on his travels, this time as captain of Lord Hawke's team to New Zealand and Australia, Lord Hawke himself being unable to go at the last minute owing to the illness of his mother. This tour, although in many ways only of minor importance— many of the New Zealand matches being against odds—was destined to have a far-reaching and historic influence on the future of cricket. While the team were playing in Australia at the conclusion of the New Zealand fixtures it was suggested that he should bring out the next side to Australia (it was the custom in those days for tours to be privately organised). He replied: 'Ask the M.C.C. They are the proper body.' And thus it came about that the M.C.C. took over the organisation of official overseas tours.

When it was announced that Sir Pelham had been appointed captain of the first M.C.C. touring team, F. S. Jackson having stated that he was not available, there was considerable criticism as at the time he had not played in a Test match in England, and A. C. MacLaren was considered by many as the only possible choice. However, all was well in the end, and although MacLaren, Fry, Ranji and Jackson were not available, all the best professionals were able to accept and Sir Pelham had the assistance of the following players: R. E. Foster, B. J. T. Bosanquet, A. A. Lilley, G. H. Hirst, T. Hayward, W. Rhodes, L. C. Braund, J. T. Tyldesley, H. Strudwick, E. G. Arnold, A. E. Relf, A. Fielder and A. E. Knight. One well-known critic of the time wrote that 'when they return beaten five-love they will be more than ever the laughing stock of cricketing England'.

Contrary to this critic's doleful prediction England won the rubber 3–2, Bosanquet's googlies playing a prominent part in the success. Clem Hill went so far as to state that if England had not had Bosanquet Australia would have won the rubber. In the fourth Test, which decided the fate of the Ashes, Bosanquet had a second innings analysis of six for 51. Apart from captaining the side with the greatest possible skill Sir Pelham played his part well as a batsman, helping Hayward in opening stands of 122 at Melbourne and 148 at Adelaide.

On his return from Australia he was honoured with a place on the M.C.C. committee, and a year later he was appointed captain of the first M.C.C. side to tour South Africa. It was a good, but by no means a representative team and South Africa won 4–1 after a titanic struggle in the first Test at Johannesburg where South Africa triumphed by one wicket and beat England for the first time in a Test match. To his dying day I do not think he ever quite forgave that most accurate of bowlers, A. E. Relf, for sending down a full toss to leg to P. W. Sherwell when the scores were level. South Africa had a wonderful array of googly bowlers at that time—

R. O. Schwarz, G. A. Faulkner, A. E. Vogler and J. C. White—and Sir Pelham, as he frankly admitted, was unable to cope with them on the matting wickets.

Back in England, he soon regained his best form, and the following season, the very wet one of 1907, found him missing top place in the averages by only a fraction, C. B. Fry making 1,449 runs, average 46.74 against his 1,891 runs, average 46.12. He considered the best innings he ever played on a good wicket was his 149 against Surrey at The Oval that season, the opposing bowlers being N. A. Knox, W. Lees, J. N. Crawford and T. Rushby. At lunch on the first day he was 115 not out. He and J. Douglas put on 232 for the first wicket in two and a half hours!

He succeeded G. MacGregor in the captaincy of the Middlesex side in 1908 and held the position until his retirement at the end of the 1920 season. The summer of 1908 was an outstanding one for him, his Middlesex record being 1,298 runs, average 54.08, including five centuries, but perhaps his greatest performance that year was his 64 not out in a total of 95 for M.C.C. on a sticky wicket against a Yorkshire attack consisting of Hirst, Rhodes, Haigh and Newstead. He considered this his best innings on a bad wicket, and M.C.C. evidently concurred as they presented him with two bats in appreciation.

Duodenal trouble worried him during the 1909 summer but he was selected for the Old Trafford Test against Australia—his first Test in England—and scored 9 and 25 in a drawn game which was played on a slow wicket.

The summers of 1910 and 1911 were fine ones for Sir Pelham who in the latter year not only scored over 2,000 runs for the first time in his life, but when playing for England against the Champion County, Warwickshire, reached the highest score of his career, 244. He hit thirty-five 4s and batted for five hours and twenty minutes. This great innings was the prelude to his second visit to Australia as captain of an M.C.C. team. This time he had with him J. W. H. T. Douglas, F. R. Foster, W. Rhodes, J. B. Hobbs, H. Strudwick, J. W. Hitch, S. P. Kinneir, E. J. Smith, G. Gunn, J. Iremonger, S. F. Barnes, C. P. Mead, J. Vine, F. E. Woolley and J. W. Hearne. Five of the team were under 25 when they left England and Hitch was only four months over that age.

In the first match of the tour against South Australia he scored 151, but it was, alas, the only innings he played on the tour as he was struck down by a serious illness. England won the series 4–1 with what many people consider the strongest side that has ever visited Australia. Douglas took over the captaincy, but from his sick bed Sir Pelham had considerable influence on the strategy of the campaign.

He had recovered sufficiently from his illness to begin playing in 1912, and on May 23 he scored 126 for the M.C.C. Australian Touring XI against The Rest of England, at Lord's. The Rest, strongly represented, were defeated by an innings and 10 runs which confirmed the strength of the touring side. His early good form gained him a place in the England XIs which met Australia and South Africa in the Lord's Tests—it was the

Triangular Tournament season—but the exertion of his early successes was too much for him, and before the end of June he dropped out of cricket for the rest of the season.

He was able to play fairly regularly in 1913, making 987 runs for Middlesex with an average of 41.12. The county would probably have won the County Championship in 1914 if war had not been declared on August 4. He made no big score that season, but *Wisden* said that 'he played very well in several matches'.

During the Great War he served with the Inns of Court, spent some time at the War Office with the rank of Captain attached General Staff and then in 1916 went into the King Edward VII Hospital for Officers for an operation. After six month's sick leave he served with Col. John Buchan in the Department of Information at the Foreign Office. Another six months and he was again very ill and on March 21, 1918, he had to resign his commission on account of his health.

When county cricket was resumed in 1919 he was then 45 and found the hours of play, 11.30 to 7.30 on the first day, and 11 to 7.30 on the second, too much for him and, as he put it, by the middle of July he was a 'dead dog' and he seriously thought of resigning the Middlesex captaincy, but A. J. Webbe, for whom he had great admiration, persuaded him to continue, and as events proved 1920 was to be his *annus mirabilis*.

At the beginning of the season Middlesex were not rated as very serious contenders for the Championship, and by the end of July were apparently out of the running, but, beginning with the Sussex match at Hove on July 31, they won their last nine matches and the Championship was theirs. Two of the matches were desperately close affairs, Kent being beaten at Canterbury by 5 runs and Yorkshire at Bradford by 4 runs. Surrey were due at Lord's on August 28, 30 and 31, and it was necessary for Middlesex to win to finish as champions.

It was only after a tremendous struggle that Middlesex succeeded by 55 runs. C. H. L. Skeet and H. W. Lee scored hundreds for the winners, and G. T. S. Stevens, then only 19, had a grand match with scores of 53 and 21 not out and five wickets for 61 in Surrey's second innings. But Sir Pelham himself had a rare triumph. He batted for nearly four and a half hours to make 79, top score in the first innings when matters were going none too well for his county, and in his very last innings for Middlesex at Lord's he was 14 not out when he declared, leaving Surrey to make 244 in three hours and seven minutes. Valuable as his batting was, and especially in this match, it was, to quote *Wisden* once again, 'his skill as a captain that made his final season memorable'.

During the whole of his first-class career Sir Pelham scored 29,028 runs with an average of 36.28. He hit sixty centuries and exceeded 1,000 runs in fourteen seasons.

His retirement from first-class cricket did not mean the end of his touring. In 1926–27 he led the M.C.C. team which visited South America, playing seven matches in the Argentine, one at Montevideo, one at Valparaiso and one at Lima. The team included Lord Dunglass, later Lord

Home and now, as I write, Sir Alec Douglas-Home, Prime Minister, and created a tremendous amount of good will. The matches were reported in the South American press, one account saying that the veteran captain was 'eliminado' at slip. As he was fond of saying, there was no disputing that dismissal. A year later he captained M.C.C. for the last time on an overseas tour, taking a strong side to Holland. It was the jubilee of The Hague club, founded in 1878.

In 1932–33 he went to Australia as joint manager with R. C. N. Palairet of the M.C.C. team captained by D. R. Jardine. Bodyline cast a shadow over the tour. He was completely opposed to this type of bowling; indeed he had objected to it as long ago as 1910 when W. B. Burns bowled it for a few overs for Worcestershire against Middlesex at Lord's, but he never allowed his opposition to interfere with his admiration for Jardine as a man and as a leader. History has of course proved that Sir Pelham was right, and in 1937 his outstanding services to cricket, both on and off the field, were recognised by a knighthood.

Shortly before the Second World War started he went to Denmark with an M.C.C. team captained by G. C. Newman, but as he was nearly 66 he naturally took no active part in the cricket.

It has already been stated that he was honoured with a place on the M.C.C. committee in April 1904. He served on and off for virtually the rest of his life. In 1926 he was appointed Chairman of the Selection committee composed of P. Perrin and A. E. R. Gilligan in addition to himself, and to his great delight England regained the Ashes after their memorable win in the fifth Test at The Oval. He was appointed chairman again in 1931, the two other members of the committee being P. Perrin and T. A. Higson. I suppose it would be difficult to think of three men who were so dissimilar in character yet they worked splendidly together even if Higson occasionally 'let fly', and they built up the fine team which won 4–1 in Australia 1932–33.

Sir Pelham was also chairman of the Selectors in 1935, 1936, 1937 and 1938. The South Africans were here in 1935, and for the first time they succeeded in winning a Test match in England, defeating us at Lord's by 157 runs. Sir Pelham that year again had the assistance of Perrin and Higson, with R. E. S. Wyatt, who was appointed captain, co-opted. The selection of the England team for the Lord's Test produced the longest Selection committee meeting of Sir Pelham's long experience. He, Perrin and Higson wanted to play R. W. V. Robins; Wyatt was emphatic in urging T. B. Mitchell of Derbyshire. After an all-day sitting the Selectors with great reluctance gave way to Wyatt and Mitchell played. In a comparatively low scoring match he bowled 53 overs for 164 runs and took only three wickets. It took Sir Pelham a long time to get over that match—if he ever did.

During the Second World War he was appointed Deputy Secretary of M.C.C. He threw himself heart and soul into his work and before long was arranging splendid matches for a harassed public who responded nobly, eagerly seizing the opportunity of seeing some of their favourites playing once again.

He retired from his secretarial duties at Lord's in September 1945 and two years later he sailed with G. O. Allen's M.C.C. side to the West Indies. I do not think it is any secret that some of the younger members of the team were a little apprehensive about having an elderly gentleman touring with them. But his tact, courtly charm and old world manners soon put everyone at their ease, and when the tour was over the players said how pleased they were to have had him with them.

He told me he was fearful that the great honour of being President of M.C.C. might elude him for as he often said 'I'm a delicate old dog and will not be here much longer.' It is therefore not difficult to picture his delight, and relief, when on May 3, 1950, he was nominated President by H.R.H. the Duke of Edinburgh. In point of fact His Royal Highness was unable to be present, and Lord Cornwallis, President in 1947, presided in his absence. When he began to make the announcement he got no farther than 'Sir Pel—' when there was an unprecedented scene, the cheering which followed lasted for several minutes. It was indeed an unforgettable moment. He was 76 years and seven months old when he was nominated, and only one older man has been made President—Stanley Christopherson who beat Sir Pelham by a year. He had been President of Middlesex from 1937 to 1946.

In 1950 he was Chairman of the Committee which selected F. R. Brown's team to tour Australia that winter, and three years later, in November, 1953, the M.C.C. gave a dinner in the Long Room to celebrate his 80th birthday. In 1958 a new grandstand built at Lord's was named after him. There was still one final honour to come to him. In May 1961 he became the first life Vice President of M.C.C.

When Lord Hawke took a team to the West Indies in 1897 he was asked by H. V. L. Stanton ('Wanderer' of 'The Sportsman') if he could arrange for somebody to send back accounts of the matches to be played by his team. Lord Hawke turned to Sir Pelham and said, 'Plummy, you're last from school. Why shouldn't you do it?' He did and that began his career as one of the outstanding writers on the game.

Sir Pelham in fact provided the account of that tour for the *Wisden* of 1898 and in 1911 he contributed a short article for the Almanack entitled 'Our Young Cricketers'. His 'Twilight Reflections', which appeared in the 1955 *Wisden*, was an extensive survey of the game as well as a critical analysis which contained much advice on problems which still confront us.

During his long life he wrote, or edited, the following books: *Cricket in Many Climes*, *Cricket Across the Seas*, *How we recovered the Ashes*, *With M.C.C. in South Africa*, *England v. Australia* (1911–12 Tour) *Cricket Reminiscences*, *Boys' Book of Outdoor Games and Pastimes* (with others), *Imperial Cricket*, *Book of Cricket* (numerous editions), *Cricket* (Badminton Library, revised edition, 1920, with others), *Story of the Ashes* ('Morning Post', 1920), *My Cricketing Life*, *Fight for the Ashes 1926*, *Oxford and Cambridge at the Wicket* (with F. S. Ashley-Cooper), *Cricket Between Two Wars*, *Fight for the Ashes 1930*, *Lord's 1787–1945*, *Gentlemen v. Players 1806–1949*, and *Long Innings*. He was also cricket Correspondent for the *Westminster Gazette*, *The Morning Post* and *The Daily Telegraph*. With his first-class career over, he became Editor of *The Cricketer* when the magazine was founded in 1921, and retained that position until 1962 when he was succeeded by his son, John Warner. I think it is correct to state that when he was appointed it was thought he would be largely a figurehead, but on the contrary he threw himself wholeheartedly into his duties and maintained his enthusiastic interest in the magazine until his death.

In the earlier years he wrote many articles for *The Cricketer*. Often we would discuss a topic, and I would then rough it out. After that we had a session in which we would endeavour to add polish. It was great fun, and I spent many hours with him on this kind of work.

From 1921 to 1932 he wrote regularly for *The Morning Post*. Early in 1933, under the strain of the Bodyline controversy, he cabled the paper and certainly, but quite unwittingly, gave the Editor, H. A. Gwynne, and the Sports Editor, Tom Hodder, the impression that he did not wish to continue as their Cricket Correspondent. There was little time for *The Morning Post* to find another correspondent and they could hardly be blamed for appointing R. C. Robertson-Glasgow—an excellent choice.

Subsequently, Sir Pelham explained that the cable had been misinterpreted, but by then it was too late as *The Morning Post* had committed themselves with Mr. Robertson-Glasgow. Happily the matter ended with Mr. Gwynne and Sir Pelham still the best of friends.

As a result of this unfortunate misunderstanding Sir Pelham was invited to write for *The Daily Telegraph*, and after all these years it may not be out of place to state that he was rather less happy with *The Telegraph* than *The Post*. Possibly they did not quite understand his approach to the game he loved so dearly. For example, when he wrote about Bowes they altered his copy to the 'bespectacled' Bowes, and when Bradman was mobbed by girls at Worcester he received a wire. 'Send 500 words Bradman and the girls.' It would be difficult to imagine anyone less suited to write a 'story' of that nature. He thought the whole thing was a joke, put the wire in his pocket, and took no action. As my boyhood was spent in Sussex I saw very little of Sir Pelham as an active player, and my only real recollection is of seeing him lead Middlesex on to the field at Hove, wearing of course a Harlequin cap which he renewed every two years. As the years passed I got to know him most intimately and to my dying day I shall treasure memories of his great encouragement and countless kindnesses to me. His one fault was that he was far too generous with his praise. Thirty years ago the use of Christian and nicknames was not nearly so common as it is today and therefore I shall always remember with pride the day when he said 'Why don't you call me by my cognomen?'

Until the outbreak of war he visited *The Cricketer* office virtually every morning. His visits did on occasion interfere with work as he delighted in discussing the previous day's play, and if he had been to a show overnight he was quite capable of giving more or less word for word what Harry Lauder, for example, had said at the Palladium—Scottish accent and all.

He was, too, very fond of Western films and I can hear him saying, with a twinkle in his eyes, 'Stick 'em up, Baby'. He was no mean mimic, and he was especially good at imitating Lord Harris, who had a habit of stroking his cheek when a difficult point was being discussed in committee—'We--ll, Warner, there may be something in what you say.' He loved animals, and on one occasion he thought he was paying our then secretary a great compliment when he told her she had eyes just like his spaniel's. She was not amused.

It is, I know, only stating the obvious to say that cricket predominated in Sir Pelham's thoughts, but he was a great patriot, believing passionately in the British way of life and had made a study of Naval and Military history. He delighted in listening to Service debates at Westminster, and one of the happiest experiences of his life was when Admiral Jellicoe asked him to take passage with him in H.M.S. New Zealand to Egypt at the beginning of 1919. But, of course, cricket always came first, and I think this story told to me by Lady Warner was typical of his devotion to the game. Some years ago they, with some friends, were admiring the beauties of a charming little French church. Suddenly, Sir Pelham left the party by the altar and strode off down the aisle towards the West door with a rather grim expression on his face. When he rejoined the party Lady Warner said to him, 'Whatever is the matter, Pelham?' (She never called him Plum.) 'Oh, nothing, it is just as I thought, the length of a cricket pitch.'

He had a great admiration for youth, and he was a remarkably fine judge of a young player, which reminds me of an argument he had with his old friend, the one and only Gerry Weigall, at the Folkestone Festival many years ago. Weigall contended, perhaps with a good deal of reason, that Middlesex were unduly favoured by having the pick of young players at Lord's without any expense to themselves, while Kent had to pay wages to any young cricketer while he was qualifying. To bring home his points Weigall would take off the inevitable straw hat and bang it with his fist before putting it on again. This happened many times as the argument developed to the delight of the rest of us at the tea table. At the end of it all Sir Pelham said, almost with tears in his eyes, 'I can see, my dear Gerry, that you don't want Middlesex to have any young players at all.'

And now a recollection of one of the most entertaining two hours I have ever had in my life. I was at Sir Pelham's flat and just as I was leaving he said, 'Don't go, Charlo (C. B. Fry) is coming.' Well, Fry arrived and for the next two hours I was spellbound. He never ceased talking, he took off his jacket, he played imaginary strokes, he danced about the room, in fact he did everything. Every now and again Sir Pelham tried to get a word in, but every time he did Fry held up his hand in an imperious manner and said 'Plum, be quiet' and off he went again. It was all highly entertaining. The following morning when Sir Pelham came to *The Cricketer* office he said in a most doleful manner: 'Do you know Charlo spoke for forty-five minutes last night before he would let me get a word in', which when one comes to think of it was no mean feat as Sir Pelham was a great talker himself.

On June 7, 1904, he married Agnes Blyth, by whom he had two sons and a daughter, at the Parish Church of St. Marylebone. Lord Hawke was best man, and Field Marshal Lord Roberts signed the register. (Subsequently he was an enthusiastic supporter of Lord Roberts' campaign for National Service.) Many years later as a result of frequent visits to the Warner home I got to know Lady Warner extremely well—and the better I knew her the more I admired her. For the last ten years of her life she was a chronic invalid, being confined to her bed for long periods at a time, but never once did I hear her grumble, and she maintained the keenest possible interest in the events of the day. She was a remarkably brave and patient woman, and I can see her now lying in bed and watching the television, preferably a sporting event. She was a fine judge of cricket, and did not W. H. Patterson once say, 'If you cannot have Warner on the Selection Committee you should ask his wife'?

She was present at the famous Eton and Harrow match of 1910—Fowler's match—and with Eton apparently well beaten she turned to a friend and said 'I shall not send my boy to Eton as they cannot play cricket', and then left Lord's for her home in Kent as the end seemed so near. When she reached Caring she found a telegram awaiting her: 'Better send him Eton won by nine runs'. On another occasion she told me how she used to amuse Sir Pelham when he was recovering from his serious illness in Australia by picking up odd *Wisdens* and asking him what he had scored in a particular match. Almost invariably he answered correctly.

On Friday March 8, 1963, his ashes were scattered at Lord's near the Warner stand close to the spot where he had hit his first 4 for Rugby v. Marlborough in 1889. It was my very great privilege to be present on a most impressive occasion. The wind blew hard during the ceremony, but the sun was shining. Directly we returned to the pavilion it poured with rain. I could not help thinking that dear old Plum had been favoured to the very end.

FOLLOWING LEICESTERSHIRE [1964]

BY BRIAN CHAPMAN

One of the most pleasurable of rituals available to an Englishman in the first half of this century was to wolf his eggs and bacon while studying the contents of the morning newspaper, folded to the desired page and propped up against the tea-cosy. For a mere penny this publication most obligingly reversed the dream of William Morris by bearing news from everywhere, from the plebeian acreage of The Oval, from the train-haunted green at Old Trafford, from the quiet ecclesiastical confidence of Worcester, from the intellectual bluff of Fenner's and the Parks, from wherever the first-class game was proceeding. And although every snippet of news was gratefully received and often relished as though it were part of the meal, rarely did the breakfaster ever stop to ask himself how the cricket correspondent he happened to be reading had gained his entry into the game. Some of these sporting telegraph boys were ex-players, like Fry and Warner, or ex-professionals with extra-terrestrial assistance, like Jack Hobbs. A few, like Cardus and Robertson-Glasgow, were acknowledged as authentic proso-dists. But marching behind these famous men was a small army of scribes whose names were as familiar as their origins were obscure. Wellings, Crawford White, Bannister, Chapman—who were these mysterious entities and how had they reached their enviable eminence? One of them disclosed his roots in the 1964 Alamanck by describing a lifelong allegiance to the county of his birth and reminding us in the process that there is no county in the Championship whose history, especially in its emergent years, does not make entrancing reading.

Brian Chapman mentions in passing several famous men whose distinc-tiveness is perhaps worth expounding in a little more detail, especially the Hon. Charles Edward de Trafford (1864–1951). The Hon. Charles was born at Trafford Park, which incorporated Old Trafford, all of which was a part of his father's garden. Later on the Hon. Charles, a good friend of W. G. Grace, was instrumental in acquiring this as a permanent home for the Lancashire county club. Mr Chapman also recounts the beautifully redolent anecdote of the patriotic default of Aubrey Temple Sharp, who played for the county between 1908 and 1934. The details are that early in August 1914, batting at number five in the match at Northampton, Sharp scored only two runs in the first innings. On the morning of August 5, with Leicestershire requiring only 84 to win in the fourth innings, he packed his bags and left to join his regiment, confident that his side had no urgent need of his services. In the event, George Thompson ran through the Leicestershire batting, Northants scraped home by four runs and the War Office found itself with one more volunteer to cope with. Much to Sharp's credit, he managed to survive the attentions not only of the German army but also of the British General Staff, lived on to his 84th year and was only dismissed at last in a motoring accident.

But the two most noteworthy of Chapman's heroes are Shipman and Knight. Alan Wilfred Shipman (1900–79) won the honour of the following entry in the 1935 edition of Wisden, in which the writer discusses Leicestershire's fortunes in 1934:

The one distressing feature of the season was in the matter of finance. The public demanded brighter cricket and their desires were certainly complied with but even so the gates were extremely disappointing. Indeed, on the occasion of Shipman's benefit the attendances were so poor that the player found himself some £60 out of pocket as a result of the match.

If there was one writer capable of doing justice to this extraordinary statistic, it may well have been the remarkable Albert E. Knight (1874–1946), who represented the county from 1895 to 1912, winning three caps against

Australia in the winter of 1902–3. Knight was a deeply religious man who could carry piety to excess. At least this was the opinion of the Lancashire fast bowler Walter Brearley who took such exception to Knight's habit of requesting the assistance of the Almighty before receiving the first ball of an innings that he lodged an official complaint with the M.C.C. on the grounds that any batsman who consorted so closely with the Creator of the Universe was guilty of ungentlemanly conduct. But Knight's greatest claim to fame and the achievement which will surely render him immortal, is the authorship of one of the most astonishing of all the many thousands of books which have been published about cricket. His 'The Complete Cricketer', which appeared in 1906, is a classic of verbosity, a polysyllabic nightmare, a sesquipedalian masterpiece, a volume so crammed with learning that few professionals and no amateurs could understand it. In its obituary of Knight, Wisden was to sidestep implications of his literary methods by conceding that his only book was 'grandiose in style, containing much startling metaphor'. Presumably what Wisden had in mind was this sort of thing, which finds Knight in one of his less exuberant moments. He is extolling the Oxford–Cambridge fixture. Probably:

> Matthew Arnold, musing o'er the beautiful city which did not appreciate his interpretation of the Faith of the centuries, wrote of Oxford as 'the home of lost causes and forsaken beliefs, of unpopular names and impossible loyalties'. If this were true of theologies, that Oxford bent not her knee to the passing Zeitgeist, but set aloft her lonely light amid the mists of Tubingen criticism, she may do the same for sport.

Looking back on the affair, it seems an awful pity that the Archbishop of Canterbury made no response. After his departure from the first-class game, Knight whiled away many years coaching the young men of Highgate School. No doubt his instruction had a benign influence on their batting but one trembles to think what it did to their prose style.

MY first recollection of Leicestershire cricket still remains one of the most vivid, far back though it is. One morning in the summer of 1911, my father took me to the Aylestone Road ground to watch the County play against Yorkshire—even to a boy of nine renowned as paladins of the game.

We arrived just before lunch to meet the crowd streaming away. The match was over, Yorkshire beaten by an innings and 20 runs. Jack King, with his awesome black moustache the very paragon of an Edwardian professional, had ensnared Yorkshire with his left-arm spinners (ah, bliss of uncovered wickets!), finishing them off with a spell of seven for none.

Much, much later, only half a dozen seasons ago, I sat with Wilfred Rhodes during a Leicestershire–Yorkshire game at Grace Road, he sightlessly 'reading' events in the middle, I an entranced listener.

I asked the great man if he remembered that distant day. Not only did he remember, but he filled in details with fascinating clarity. Then he chuckled: 'I said to Jack King, "I'll give you some stick next time." And I did!' I checked that claim later. Rhodes indeed scored 92 at Bradford and King took 0 for 50.

Is this touch of personal reminiscence out of place in the present brief sketch—a sporting print, as it were—of Leicestershire's history? One hopes not, for if the joy of cricket is not shared intimacy it is a vain thing. To the writer growing up at the time, first-class cricket is impressionably the names of Geary and Astill, those pillars of the temple between two wars. It is sentimentally the delicate tracery of well-loved Aylestone Road pavilion, seen through the sunny haze of youth, with sandwiches and tea in a medicine bottle, the whole washed down with 'giant' cherry ciders.

If you scan tables, or your fancy is to browse upon title-winning statistics, the County whose badge is the golden running fox may not detain you long. Yet it is surely not entirely a rose-coloured view that bestows on them a special quality. They were always a County of character and *characters*. Their ups and downs match the rolling landscape of the Quorn, with perhaps more downs than ups.

About one of the stalwarts, 'Sammy' Coe, a left-hander like King and still holder of the County record with 252 against Northants in 1914, Neville Cardus has written: 'See an innings by Coe, of Leicestershire, and you ought not to be long guessing from the smack of rotund nature about it that he has passed the main portion of his days in the sun on a field with rustic benches running intimately round.'

Another boyhood hero, Albert Knight, of the flashing square drive, the punitive throw-in and the unforgettably blue eyes, seemed somehow remote from other men, yet one of the 'originals' of the game. So, later, was Alec Skelding, whose salty music-hall pronouncements, both as player and umpire, have passed into the folklore of cricket. Once at Lord's, Alec thought a fast bowler was making overmuch fuss in the placing of pyramids of sawdust. At last, after much delay, the bowler was ready for action. Skelding dramatically halted him three parts through his run, walked solemnly to the farthest mound of sawdust, picked up a *PINCH* of it between finger and thumb, minced back to the stumps and deposited it to form his own mock foothold. Then he gravely announced: 'Play!' Knight wrote a sadly neglected masterpiece called 'The Complete Cricketer' which can still be—and ought to be—savoured. The Izaac Walton of cricket writing!

More recently, one of the County's shrewdest captains, C. H. Palmer— he led them briefly to the top—revived the lost art of the donkey drop with results embarrassing for batsmen as distinguished as Worrell and Kanhai. Who could capture, with seeming amiability glinting through rimless spectacles, 8 for 0 against the Surrey Champions and, with Laker's world record of 8 for 2 at his mercy, ignore the frantic advice of the crowd: 'Take yourself off, Charlie!' The queerest quirk was that Palmer intended only one over, to change his bowlers round. But he sent Peter May packing— and persevered!

What is the rarest and maybe least known 'double'? Well, in 1888, Leicestershire won the Second Class Championship and beat Australia.

There's unexpected glory for you! It was with much quiet pride that local enthusiasts noted in last year's Centenary *Wisden* that they shared with Northamptonshire (among Counties now rated first-class) the honour of first forming a 'county organisation' in 1820. Much earlier Leicestershire was stirring and bustling with interest. Sides like Melton Mowbray, Barrow-on-Soar, Mountsorrel and Barwell (where George Geary 'first saw the light') bristled with challenge.

In his admirable *History of Leicestershire* (to which all chroniclers were deeply indebted) Mr. E. E. Snow places 1744 as the earliest Midland mention—lines recited in praise of the game as 'desired by the Gentlemen of Barrow'. By May 1780, ardent spirits met 'to give gentlemen an opportunity of becoming members of a Cricket Club in Leicester founded upon eligible principles'. Three months later comes the first recorded match, Loughborough beating Leicester by more than 50 notches on St. Margaret's Pasture, that 'most kindly nurse' of the County's growth. Right until 1825 most of the big matches were played there.

Those were vigorous masculine times, not less disputatious than some today. Leicester's first encounter with Nottingham in 1781 was a no-decision affair, the umpires (not entirely unprejudiced) falling out on a point of law and calling the whole thing off.

And what a set-to with Coventry, staged half-way between the two towns at Hinckley in 1787. The neutrality of the scene failed to calm passions (there were one hundred guineas at stake). The victorious Leicester players, quaffing and regaling, fell foul of defeated supporters. 'The Hinckley shopkeepers having shut their windows, a scene of bloodshed ensued, scarcely to be credited' (what had become of those gentlemanly 'eligible principles'?).

Leicestershire's fame, and that of neighbouring Rutland, spread abroad, attracting representative sides within their borders. Playing for All-England against Hampshire at Burley-on-the-Hill, near Oakham (one thousand guineas the stake) Silver Billy Beldham collected a 'pair'. After the turn of the century, cricket's hold was established so firmly that public and players looked about for better accommodation. Things started to be organised; the modern era could be dimly descried. 'Leicester New Club' had the temerity to humble Leicestershire Gentlemen in 1829 with scores of 65 and 72 against 61 and 30. In 1825, a new ground was taken over in Wharf Street. It has long since been submerged by repeated waves of builders and 'developers'. Then it was hailed as 'more extensive than any except Lord's'.

Among visiting celebrities was 18-stone Alfred Mynn, who, listed as Number Ten for South against North, managed to hit 21 and 125, both not out. The finish was unhappy. 'Mr. A. Mynn strained his leg (*no wonder!*) and being unable to endure the agony longer, begged Lord Beauclerk to accompany him to one of the marquees, there showing his leg to his Lordship. Lord Frederick instantly sent for a fly to convey him to the stage coach, upon which he proceeded to London.'

That was 1836. As the years rolled past, the cricketing fox found new coverts and hunting grounds. Derbyshire Gentlemen, Birmingham, Manchester, Stamford and Rugby appear in fixture lists. Wharf Street passed under the hammer in 1860. Nobly, its final game drew Daft, Caesar and George Parr. Nobly, 22 of Leicestershire humbled these immortals of All England by an innings. One can imagine the blow dealt by this loss of the centre and being of local cricket, and indeed enthusiasm languished for some time. It was six or seven years before a 'square' (as the moderns say) was levelled in the centre of the old racecourse on windswept Victoria Park (later a turmoil of interlaced club matches on Thursdays and Saturdays, where one cub reporter somehow 'covered' eleven games in the after-noon). As it proved, this was a makeshift arrangement and the next major move was to Aylestone (now Grace Road) in 1878.

What a send-off to be sure! Leicestershire (not yet officially such) went the whole financial hog, being the only club to guarantee Murdoch's Australians a lump sum. They were rewarded with a crowd of 13,000 paying spectators on the second day, which stood as a single day record until Bradman's all-conquering farewell 60 years later.

Bannerman's batting and Spofforth's bowling proved decisive, but a fast left round-armer, Robby Rylott (somehow that name always calls to mind Sherlock Holmes' grim adversary Dr. Roylott), later to do great deeds, proved that home-bred talent was not so homespun. Imagine the spur such crowded scenes afforded to those at the head of affairs in town and county! It must have been a jam of horse brakes hired for family outings, smart dog-carts of the gentry, and the cloth caps of the stockingers mixing with Corinthian bowlers and tie-pinned cravats round embroiled entrance gates.

Little time was wasted. On February 25, 1879, a meeting at the Bulls Head Inn (a recent pious pilgrimage found it, alas! silent and shuttered) was sponsored by the Leicester Cricket Club Company. Preliminaries cleared out of the way, a fully-fledged meeting 'with full powers' took place in Friar Lane. There the Leicestershire County Cricket Club officially came into being. The sixth Earl of Lanesborough, a cricketer in his own not inconsiderable right, was elected President. All officials had one welcome quality in common. They, too, were cricketers, not 'guinea pig' names. Among the committee were W. H. Hay, already a member of county sides; R. W. Gillespie-Stainton, of the Harrow XI; and Canon E. H. L. Willes, of Oxford University, Hampshire and Kent, then vicar at Ashby-de-la-Zouch, on whose rural ground, conjuring up the jousting spirits of 'Ivanhoe', the County still enters the list each season.

It cost one guinea to join and the first match was an Easter friendly against 22 Colts. Wisely guided, the County found favouring winds. They beat Northamptonshire twice by an innings and Sussex twice, Rylott adding to his growing reputation. Stronger opponents were sought and the young County was certainly not discouraged by achieving two draws with Yorkshire in 1883 and beating Surrey by 7 runs. Leaner seasons were in store (as too often in the future), brightened by the emergence of one of the outstanding names in Leicestershire history. This was A. D. (Dick)

Pougher, known to more than Midland fame by his amazing 5 wickets for 0 for M.C.C. against Australia in 1896, when a side boasting S. E. Gregory, Hill, Trumble and Darling was dismissed for 18.

Contemporary pictures suggest a lean, tall figure and a somewhat withdrawn manner (which perhaps explained absent-minded failings in the field). His best ball was a medium pace off-break of high action rising sharply to the bat's shoulder, but he could move the ball from leg as well. Pougher was good enough to trouble the best, no mopper-up of 'nine, ten, jack'. Bobby Abel esteemed him the most difficult of all bowlers, an opinion reinforced when he and Rylott, bowling unchanged throughout, skittled Surrey for 26 and 83. Six times Pougher took 13 or 14 wickets. He died at the cricket ground hotel, Grace Road, in 1926—the year in which his most notable successor, George Geary, was helping England to regain the Ashes and long-lost national pride. ('Woodfull, caught Geary b Larwood 0, Macartney, caught Geary b Larwood 16,' we read gloatingly in the stop press from The Oval. Sheer poetry! The best words in the best order!)

Just over the horizon was that wonder year of 1888. Though mauled by Yorkshire, Leicestershire skittled Australia for 62 and 87 on a bad wicket to win by 20 runs. With 10 for 71 in the match, Pougher began his habit of treating Australians most contemptuously as his 'rabbits'—if that term can be applied to victims like Bannerman (twice), that mighty hitter Bonnor, Turner, Blackham (then opening with Bannerman) and McDonnell.

Leicestershire had to wait seven more years before they were elected to first-class status. They were piloted to promotion chiefly by the inspiring leadership of C. E. de Trafford, who bestrode their fortunes as captain for 16 years from 1890 onwards. Without troubling about the niceties of getting to the ball with his feet, de Trafford certainly got to it with his hands. A huge and unhesitating hitter, he seldom bothered about gloves and once struck a four off his knuckles. Another feat was to break the committee room window at Lord's (what more uncompromising way of 'attracting the attention of the selectors'?). It can be conjectured that Leicestershire did not lack the sort of aggression and vigour that Mr. R. W. V. Robins would heartily applaud. He was fortunate in bringing on men with big reputations to build. Men like Arthur Woodcock (a bowler of almost scaring pace) like King and Knight, and rising batsmen of the class of Coe (firmest of off drivers) and, especially, C. J. B. Wood.

Like Pougher, Woodcock rather fancied himself against Australia and in 1902 dismissed Duff, Hill and Gregory for one run. Still, cricket in the top class was a battle rather than a primrose path and the County usually finished well down in the Championship table.

The new century brought migration to Aylestone Road ('too far for the horse trams' was the verdict on Grace Road) and there Leicestershire remained until 1939. Topping over 2,000 in 1901, Cecil Wood gave a foretaste of the triumphs he was to achieve as possibly the most determined, consistent opening bat in England. He was not exactly graceful to watch, but defence was often enforced in his sheet-anchor role.

We boys found him a figure of fun as a bowler, mimicking an unclassic style with whoops of delight. But he took wickets!

For a dozen years or more, he drove bowlers to near-despair. Proof of his watchful and indestructible technique is that seventeen times he 'carried his bat'. More astonishing—and unlikely ever to be equalled—he brought off this feat twice in one match against Yorkshire—curiously, the occasion of Rhodes' personal tit-for-tat against King. The score card read: Wood not out 107, Wood not out 117. The bowlers? A few trifling tyros, name of Hirst, Booth, Haigh, Rhodes, Bayes. No wonder Hirst, even though he claimed nine wickets all told exclaimed in exasperation: 'Next time, Maister Wood, we'll SHOOT you out with a gun.'

Not until 1904 did Leicestershire really challenge in the Championship race. That season, they stood fourth half-way, but could not quite keep it up and finished seventh. Next year was still better—fifth in the list, a position they were to wait many a long summer to better. Wood was 'in good nick', as they say nowadays, with 1,765 runs, average 43. With their knack for unearthing fast bowlers, the county found still another top performer, Thomas Jayes, born at Ratby, a notable nursery. Jayes would now be compared, in smooth run-up and action, with E. A. Macdonald or R. R. Lindwall. Lung weakness ended his career just short of the heights. Veterans who remember him will not hear of Jayes being rated below England class, but the only time he was picked—against Australia at Lord's—he was the one to be omitted on the eve of the Test.

Unfortunately, the County's high hopes of better things were not sustained and in the nine years until the First World War they never rose above tenth. Standing out like a peak above much that was inclined to be featureless was their record 701 for 4 against Worcestershire in 1906 (Wood 225, Harry Whitehead 174, Knight 97, V. F. S. Crawford 102). Yet they still produced 'characters' like Bill Shipman, swarthy, strong-built fast bowler—again a Ratby man.

Once, at The Oval, Bill was handed a telegram as he went out to field. It announced that he was the proud father of a bouncing boy. He proceeded to clean bowl Hayward, Hobbs and Hayes and capture the first nine Surrey wickets. A stripling called Astill, possibly feeling that parental pride could be carried too far, nipped in with the tenth.

Then there was 'Pecker' Mounteney, mighty if un-Spoonerish hitter. Meeting the powerful Kent team he decided it was impossible to hit the fabled Colin Blythe off his length. But you could, with luck, hit the person of Blythe. He did just that. A slogging straight drive struck Blythe on the thigh, the ball cannoned to MID-OFF, who made the catch! Relating the incident with a raconteur's zest, Aubrey Sharp told me: 'So old Pecker was out, caught Humphreys, bowled Blythe. But so was Blythe. They retired to the pavilion together. If you don't believe me, it's all in *Wisden*' (It is!). See *Wisden* 1913, page 301. But Blythe took 15 for 45 in that very match.

Sharp himself was in the dozen best amateur batsmen of his day and is, besides, in the C. B. Fry class as a demonstrator and critic over coffee and cigars. A solicitor-soldier, he got a summons to join the colours in August

1914, when Leicestershire were playing at Northampton. 'We only wanted 90 to win so I left it to them', he recalls. 'Actually we lost by 4 runs. The point is I left my boots and bat behind. They were handed to me when we went back to Northampton in 1919.'

Now Sharp takes as much pride in following (or presiding over) the fortunes of his village team at Scraptoft as he ever did in leading Leicestershire or hitting 216 against Derbyshire.

One glimmer—perhaps even a dawn—was vouchsafed of fame to come. I still treasure a faded cricket annual that first mentions the names of Astill and Geary. 'William Ewart Astill (so a brief entry runs). There is a Gladstonian ring about his name that alone should spell success.' How true was that prophet in his green covers and yellowed pages! Already, in 1914, Geary captured 117 wickets at 20 and a bit. Fulfilment was postponed; it was not ultimately denied.

From 1919 the County almost WAS Astill and Geary, and Geary and Astill were Leicestershire. Bradman has described the surprise, almost shock, of encountering Geary's leg cutter, then unfamiliar to him, though he later came to think that Alec Bedser's was more deadly. No doubt, it was Geary's most potent ball, but he was armed with all the weapons of medium-fast attack—zip off the pitch, concealed change of pace, perfect and unwearying control. He won England honours both at home and on tour. For his County he took over 100 wickets eleven times, with 10 for 18 against Glamorgan in 1929 his personal best. He was, besides, a very present help when runs were needed, a slip little below the Hammond class, and a willing encourager of young players which Charterhouse—and Peter May—found of inestimable value later on.

Seventy in *Wisden's* centenary year, George was until recently turning his arm over in the winter nets. 'He can still make 'em fizz a bit', the new generation had to acknowledge.

Astill, of the handsome aristocratic looks, possessed an easy, almost lazy approach to the wicket that concealed off-spin wicked on a helpful wicket. Almost, he cajoled batsmen to their downfall. 'Somehow, he wheel's 'em up and wheels 'em out', said one old pro. There was nothing plebeian about his batting; Astill did everything with an air. Yes, 'the lad with the delicate air', the touch that made him superb at billiards. He was Leicestershire's supreme all-rounder. Nine times he accomplished the double, in consecutive seasons from 1921 save for 1927. News of his death, which reached an M.C.C. side touring the West Indies in 1948, came as a real sense of loss.

It was still pretty hard pounding in the Championship. A meritorious ninth in 1919 was followed by uneven standards leading to lowly positions. Tommy Sidwell, a little prince of wicket-keepers in the Strudwick mould and worthy of that comparison, gave stout-hearted support to the two *non-pareils*. Alec Skelding kept up the fast bowling tradition. For half a dozen overs his glasses flashed lightning.

Charles Bray, doyen of cricketer-journalists, recalls opening at Aylestone Road for Essex in his first match. His partner, A. C. Russell, turned to him with words of ghostly advice:

'Mr. Bray, there are two bowlers you are just going to face. One runs a mile and bowls medium. The other takes six strides and let's her go. That's Skelding and he's almighty quick.'

A break-through to seventh enlivened 1927. The attack was varied and E. W. Dawson (a Cambridge acquisition to the batting) and Geary and Astill were all picked to tour South Africa. All three enjoyed repeat performances in 1929—Dawson 1,909 runs, Geary 152 wickets at 19.6 each, Astill 121 wickets at 20.9.

Another prolific batsman, L. G. Berry, advanced to the front with 232 against Sussex in 1930. 'Jinks' Berry, a dedicated cricketer and footballer (he kept goal for Sheffield Wednesday, Bristol Rovers and Swindon Town) claimed a distinguished record both for his County and the R.A.F. For Leicestershire he scored more runs in a season than any other player— 2,446; more centuries—45; more thousands in a season—18 times; and highest career aggregate—30,106.

Perhaps the achievement that gave him most pleasure was batting through the innings against Nottinghamshire at Ashby in 1932 with Larwood and Voce in full flight and winning the match in a last-wicket stand with wicket-keeper Corrall.

Team-wise, old faults crept in and the final indignity—bottom place for the first time—chastened spirits in 1933. It needed the bold step of promoting Astill as first professional captain to send Leicestershire riding high. Under him the side did not lack authority and maturity. That season of 1935 they shot up to sixth, with a record number of 11 matches won.

That season also stands out as the début of C. S. ('Stewie') Dempster, forming with Willie Watson (imported later from Yorkshire) the only couple of genuine world-class batsmen who have won the County's green blazer. Even the New Zealander's accomplished batting (a rippling century at Hove springs delightfully to mind) failed to check a renewed decline which sank Leicestershire to bottom in 1939.

War, and the ugly encroachment of industry, spelt the end of Aylestone Road. The story is told of George Headley affecting to believe that falling smuts were black snow! A return was made to Grace Road, thenceforward the County's headquarters. The fame—and burdens—of Geary and Astill now rested on the broad Australian shoulders of Jack Walsh and Vic Jackson. Berry took over the captaincy and, says *Wisden*, 'his leadership and experience proved of immense value to the younger members of the team'.

In 1947, Berry a hard-hitting opener of unruffled temperament, scored over 1,000 runs for the fifteenth time and Walsh had a magnificent season, taking 152 wickets with his unorthodox left-arm bag of tricks. Better still, this immensely popular player raised the bidding next season to 174. I remember Bill O'Reilly, sitting in the Press box behind Walsh's arm, nominating the wrong 'un with expert infallibility. The batsmen were not always so successful.

Sadly, slipshod fielding and other weaknesses crept in and it was a case of rock bottom again in 1949, a gap of 16 points below the next worst county.

So it was a heavy responsibility that Charles Palmer assumed as captain. Playing many good knocks with the fluent Maurice Tompkin, he just managed to lift the side 'out of the cellar'. That was the rearguard action. They went two better next time, climbed to sixth in 1952. That was the battle course.

They really went 'over the top' in the fine summer of 1953, which suited both the batting and bowling. Leicestershire, in their best-ever season, finished equal third with Lancashire. One splendid weekend in August they led the field, a fact which won Page One prominence in a national newspaper! Palmer gained his place as player-manager of Hutton's tour to the West Indies. Tompkin's cultured driving, beautiful to watch, brought him close on 2,000 runs. But, again to quote *Wisden*, 'excellent team work under Palmer's leadership, which showed itself in many fighting recoveries, was the main factor in the county's success rather than outstanding individual brilliance'.

Dismal weather induced a relapse to sixteenth, but Palmer led his keen side back to sixth the following year. The batting was spiced by the free-scoring style of Maurice Hallam, a fine slip catcher and an opener destined to spread delight across many English fields. Palmer's out-to-win policy led to a spate of close finishes. He and Tompkin each hit a century on opposite sides in the Gentlemen v. Players fixture at Lord's. Palmer, mischievously put on to bowl when his professional colleague was in the nineties, found himself faced with divided loyalties, which he contrived to resolve satisfactorily!

The skipper capped a captivating year with that eight for 7 against Surrey, whose players, notably May, wryly remember Palmer popping his face round their dressing-room door and exclaiming with a cherubic grin, 'Sorry, gentlemen!'

Leicestershire were decidedly no team of 'wet bobs' and dismal summers plummeted them twice to the foot of the chart. Tompkin was pursued by ill health that showed its first symptoms when touring Pakistan for M.C.C. He died, a deeply lamented cavalier of the game, gay as a player, a model of quiet charm as a companion, a perfect ambassador for his country.

With Palmer retiring, and desperate to find extra strength, the Committee called in Watson as captain. His broad, punishing bat provided stiffening urgently needed; too often, however, he received feeble support. Collapses were liable to happen even on good wickets. Leicestershire supporters watching at Lord's in 1960 were exhilarated to see Watson and Hallam put on 196 for the first wicket against Middlesex. Rejoicings were wiped out by a final 214 all out. Nothing more dramatically exposed fatal limitations, and last place was not unexpected or undeserved.

Unremitting search for extra solidity brought Alan Wharton from Lancashire and the attack, getting reasonable targets to bowl at, took heart of grace. The fast men, Brian Boshier (108 wickets at 17.8 each), Terry Spencer (123 at 19.5) and off spinner John Savage, were all grouped near the top of the national averages and consequently Leicestershire rose halfway up the table.

Next season's descent to the depths was hardly deserved. Watson was often away as Test selector and although Jack van Geloven achieved his double 'on the post' luck was unkind. As consolation Leicestershire enjoyed much the better of a last-match draw against Yorkshire, avid for points to clinch the Championship. One Yorkshire player, a trifle shaken, commented: 'Yon lads must be best wooden spooners in ruddy history.'

Now Leicestershire fight under an able and likeable leader in Hallam, one who (perhaps as well) bears adversity stoically and who cannot avoid cheerfulness breaking in. His label, 'the best opener who never played for England', is currently popular and there is some logic in it. His chance seemed to have arrived when he struck tremendously early form in 1959. Had a certain selector prolonged a visit to Grace Road the story might have been different. Hallam went on to hit two quick-time double hundreds. But his eminent audience had departed.

Leicestershire's energetic secretary, Mr. Michael Turner, and assiduous committee keep up the search for new talent. Two newcomers from Ceylon, Stan Jayasinghe and Clive Inman, have already made their mark. If determination—and Hallam—cannot command success it will at least be richly deserved. The County that pioneered Saturday starts and pilot-schemed the Knock-out Cup must, surely, be 'in the hunt'. HARK FORRARD is the cry!

THE PLEASURES OF READING WISDEN
[1964]

BY ROWLAND RYDER

The 1964 Almanack completed a unique family achievement by the Ryders of Warwickshire. In 1936 Rowland Vint Ryder (1873–1949), secretary of the club for nearly fifty years, had written one of the better essays of the period, 'Trials of a County Secretary', in which, among other things, he recalls how Wilfred Rhodes nearly became a Warwickshire player. By composing 'The Pleasures of Reading Wisden', Ryder's son completed a unique family double. Rowland junior maintains and perhaps even surpasses the standards of readability set by his father. Beginning with the heartening flourish of relegating Gladstone and Disraeli in favour of W. G. Grace and Spofforth, he goes on to compare the acquisition of the latest edition of Wisden to the capture of one of the most coveted baubles of Empire, and then presses on to a fascinating theme, The Problem of the Missing Wisden, in which, by offering a broad hint to deductive methodology, he reminds us of what might have been had Sir Arthur Conan Doyle only rectified the gravest of omission of his life and written cricket, and Wisden, into the Sherlockian canon. (The closest Sir Arthur ever came was in 1896 when, for charity, he composed the best of all the Sherlockian lampoons, 'The Field Bazaar', into which he incorporated one of the saddest truisms of the cricketing life: 'My small experience of cricket clubs has taught me that next to churches and cavalry ensigns, they are the most debt-laden things on earth.')

In seeking to mine the rich deposits of nostalgia lying in past editions, Ryder wisely goes for the advertisements, which surely deserve an essay to themselves. There then follows a reference to the most sensational defeat ever sustained by Warwickshire. Only then does he come to his main theme, that curious form of hopscotch with which all dedicated students of the Almanack will be familiar. The chain of reaction from one item to another is endless, but in describing one of ten thousand possible routes through the byways of each edition, Ryder has surely fallen victim to a printer's error. On arrival at 'Test Cricketers', he says, 'You turn to the appropriate section to find how many cricketers have played for their country. The names Clay, Close, Coldwell, Compton, Cook, Copson leap up.' Almost certainly what Ryder actually wrote was: '. . . to see how many cricketers beginning with the letter "C" have played for their country'. If he did, then he was referring to one of the most useful as well as one of the most pleasurable of all cricketing parlour games. The vital ground-rule which he ignores is that in compiling alphabetical Test sides, there must be access to no reference books of any kind. Just to complete Ryder's attractive fantasy, the informed reader who strains for an All-C Test eleven might well arrive at: Challenor, Cowdrey, G. Chappell, Compton, J. N. Crawford, A. P. F. Chapman (capt), Constantine, Cameron, J. C. Clay, D. W. Carr, Cotter. This side has no discernible weaknesses, being well equipped with genuine all-rounders, great fielders, awesome fast bowling, dazzling batsmen, plus Chappell in case Chapman should require someone to roll the ball along the ground and Clay to compose the funniest match report of the year.

As my father was secretary of the Warwickshire County Cricket Club from 1895 to 1944, it is not altogether surprising that the game was a frequent topic of conversation at the family meal table: cricket was our bread and butter.

Reaching double figures in the early 1920s, I naturally heard a good deal about the achievements of Hobbs and Sutcliffe, and, in the cricketless winters, learnt from my father, and from the yellow-backed pages of *Wisden*, about Grace and Spofforth; 'Ranji' and Fry and Jessop; Blackham and Lilley; and, of course, 'My Hornby and my Barlow long ago'. I knew about the cricketing giants of the past before I had learnt about Gladstone and Disraeli, and, looking back on those days of enchantment, and with all respect to those eminent statesmen, I have no regrets.

We had in our living-room a formidable Victorian bookcase, its shelves protected by glass shutters. In one of these shelves, overspilling into a second, were editions of *Wisden*, in strict chronological order—and woe betide anyone who took out a copy and put it back into the wrong place: a bad school report might on some rare occasion be forgiven, but to cause havoc in the thin yellow line of *Wisdens*—that was another matter!

It was always a red letter day for me when our stock was increased by a new volume, and father announced 'I've got the new *Wisden*!' with the same quiet pride that Disraeli—whom I eventually did get to hear about—would have announced that he had secured shares in the Suez Canal. My excited request to peruse the magic pages was always countered by my father with dark allusions to homework; but the reply deceived neither of us, for we both knew that he wanted to read *Wisden* first.

We all have our foibles about the Almanack. For each, of course, his own county. We study our own side's home matches times without number, paying scant attention to the achievements of the other counties. Sir Arthur Conan Doyle, who played for the M.C.C. and for Sussex, who had 'W. G.' as one of his victims, and who wrote *The Missing Three-quarter*, might well have written a cricket detective story, entitled, say, *The Missing Mid-on*. It would go perhaps something like this.

'Did you not observe, my dear Watson, that in the library were 37 editions of *Wisden*?'

This makes Watson forget the Afghan campaign. 'By heavens, Holmes, then the man was possibly interested in cricket?'

'More than that, my dear Watson. I noticed that in all these editions the home matches of Loamshire were heavily thumbed. This put me on the scent of the miscreant.' The possibilities seem endless!

Sherlock Holmes, in any case, is not unconnected with *Wisden*. In the Births and Deaths section of earlier editions will be found the names of Shacklock, F. (Derbyshire, Notts and Otago) and Mycroft, Thomas (Derbyshire), who inspired Conan Doyle to use the names Sherlock and Mycroft Holmes for his detective stories. Perhaps Sir Arthur played against them: certainly the line 'Doyle, Sir A. C. (M.C.C.) b. May 22, 1859' appeared for many years in *Wisden*. Incidentally, could not space be found for the famous though fictitious Raffles in the Births and Deaths? He would enjoy being on the same page as Ranjitsinhji!

For each, too, his favourite editions of *Wisden*. If I were permitted to take eight editions of the Almanack with me to some remote desert island, I would find the task of selection an extremely difficult one. To choose the first half-dozen, recording the most absorbing of the England v. Australia Test match series, would be a tricky enough problem in all conscience.

What of the final pair? The first of all the *Wisdens*?—the current issue?—the copies recounting Warwickshire's Championship triumphs of 1911 and 1951?—the 1915 edition, in which batsmen were laconically recorded as 'Absent' during the fateful first week in August?—how does one choose only a couple from these?

But if on my desert island I could have one *Wisden* and one only, then there be not the faintest tremor of hesitation: I would plump for the issue of 1903, recording that superb vintage year (1902) when the Australians came over with Darling, Trumper, Noble, Clem Hill and Warwick Armstrong, and when, during the course of the series, the English selectors could actually leave out G. L. Jessop, C. B. Fry and Ranjitsinhji, from sides that were to do battle for England.

This, the fortieth edition of *Wisden*, informs us of marquees to be bought for £10, tents for £5, lawn tennis nets for five shillings. Lord Harris eulogises Bartlett's 'Repercussive' cricket bats, on sale at prices varying from nine and six to a guinea. Cricket balls can be bought for tenpence, leg guards for three and six. Peru House Private Hotel, Russell Square (for convenience, quietude, comfort and economy) offers Bedroom and Meat Breakfast for four and six.

The real feast, of course, is provided in the Test match accounts. Of the first Test match, played at Edgbaston, on Thursday, Friday and Saturday, May 29, 30 and 31, the *Wisden* chronicler writes most evocatively, and many authorities have since considered that the team that played for England in this game was the greatest ever to represent the Mother Country—A. C. MacLaren, C. B. Fry, K. S. Ranjitsinhji, F. S. Jackson, J. T. Tyldesley, A. A. Lilley, G. H. Hirst, G. L. Jessop, L. C. Braund, W. H. Lockwood, W. Rhodes.

'A beautiful wicket had been prepared,' says *Wisden*, 'and when MacLaren beat Darling in the toss for innings, it was almost taken for granted that England would make a big score. In the end expectation was realised, but success came only after a deplorable start, and after the Australians had discounted their chances by two or three palpable blunders in the field. Fry was caught by the wicket-keeper standing back in the third over; a misunderstanding, for which Ranjitsinhji considered himself somewhat unjustly blamed, led to MacLaren being run out, and then Ranjitsinhji himself, quite upset by what had happened, was clean bowled, three of the best English wickets being thus down for 35 runs.'

England recovered and finished the day with 351 for 9, Tyldesley scoring 138 and Jackson 53. Owing to rain the game did not commence until 3 o'clock on the second day. 'Some people expected', continues *Wisden*, 'that MacLaren would at once declare the English innings closed, but acting, it was understood, on Lilley's advice, he decided to let his own side go on batting for a time, so that his bowlers might not have to start work on a slippery foothold. He declared when the score had been raised to 376 and then followed one of the chief sensations of the cricket season of 1902, the Australians being got rid of in less than an hour and a half for 36, Trumper, who played fine cricket for seventy minutes, alone making a stand.' Trumper made 18. Wildred Rhodes returned the extraordinary figures:-

O	M	R	W
11	3	17	7

In 1961, when Australia were batting against England once again at Edgbaston, I had the privilege of meeting Wilfred Rhodes, sole survivor of the twenty-two players in that struggle of 1902, and observed that we sorely needed his 7 for 17.

'Ah, yes,' said Wilfred Rhodes reflectively, 'you know how we got them out, don't you? We changed over!' Len Braund, who made an immortal slip catch to dismiss Clem Hill, had bowled one over to allow Hirst (3 for 15) and Rhodes to change ends. Following on, the Australians had scored eight for no wicket at close of play.

Writing in *Wisden*, 1936 (Trials of a County Secretary) the writer's father has this to say about the third day: 'Torrents of rain fell overnight, and at 9 a.m. the ground was a complete lake. Not a square yard of turf was visible and play was, of course, out of the question that day. The head groundsman agreed; I paid off half my gatemen and dispensed with the services of half the police. It proved to be a "penny wise pound foolish" action. The umpires arrived; the players arrived—the captains were there. I have never known any men more patient, more hopeful than those umpires and captains. They just sat still and said nothing most effectively. At two o'clock the sun came out and a great crowd assembled outside the ground. What I hadn't thought of was that two umpires and two captains would sit and wait so long without making a decision. The crowd broke in, and to save our skins we started play at 5.20 on a swamp.' The game ended as a draw with Australia 46 for 2.

The second Test match, says *Wisden*, was 'utterly ruined by rain', the third 'a severe disaster for England' and we lost by 143 runs. Of the last agonising over in the fourth Test, when England had nine wickets down and eight to win, *Wisden* relates: 'Tate got a four on the leg-side from the first ball he received from Saunders, but the fourth, which came a little with the bowler's arm and kept low, hit the wicket and the match was over.'

For the fifth Test match Ranjitsinhji was left out! England, set 263 to win, were saved by G. L. Jessop with possibly the most superb innings of his life. 'He scored', says *Wisden*, 'in just over an hour and a quarter, 104 runs out of 139, his hits being a five in the slips, seventeen 4s, two 3s, four 2s and seventeen singles.' Hirst and Rhodes, the last pair, scored the necessary fifteen runs to win. It was of this occasion that the apocryphal story 'We'll get them in singles, Wilfred!' is told. *Wisden*, preferring accuracy to romance, records 'Rhodes sent a ball from Trumble between the bowler and mid-on, and England won the match by one wicket.'

Yorkshire's victory over the Australians, who were dismissed for 23 in their second innings, is described as 'a big performance'; an Australian victory over Gloucestershire is chronicled in a burst of Edwardian prose—'the Colonials had no great difficulty in beating the western county in a single innings'; and of a match against Surrey we are told 'Trumper and Duff hit up 142 in an hour and a quarter'—this against Richardson and Lockwood! The historian is chatty and informative about the match with Cambridge University. 'So greatly were the Australians weakened by illness that they had to complete their side by playing Dr. R. J. Pope, a cricketer, who it will be remembered, appeared several times for H. J. H. Scott's eleven in 1886. Dr. Pope came over from Australia for a holiday mainly to see the cricket, and was a sort of general medical adviser to the eleven.' Anyway, he made 2 not out!

The 1923 edition contains the saga of the Warwickshire–Hampshire match at Edgbaston; surely the most extraordinary game of county cricket ever played. Warwickshire, batting first, were out for a mediocre 223 on a good wicket. They then proceeded to dismiss their opponents in 53 balls for 15. The analyses of Howell and Calthorpe speak for themselves:

	O	M	R	W
Howell	4.5	2	7	6
Calthorpe	4	3	4	4

Hampshire followed on, and lost 6 wickets for 186. However, as *Wisden* observes, 'Brown batted splendidly for four hours and three-quarters and Livsey made his first hundred without a mistake.' Brown made 172, and Livsey 110 not out; Hampshire made 521, got Warwickshire out for 158 and won by 155 runs. 'The victory, taken as a whole,' says *Wisden*, 'must surely be without precedent in first-class cricket.' And has there been anything like it since?

Not long ago I had the good fortune to discuss the match with the late George Brown in his house at Winchester, where, appropriately enough, a framed score-card of the conflict hung in the hall. He contended that Hampshire should have been out for 7 in their first innings, explaining that 'Tiger' Smith, while unsighted, had let a ball go for four byes, and that Lionel Tennyson was missed at mid-on, the ball then travelling to the boundary.

The chief joy of reading *Wisden* is also the chief snare—once you have picked up a copy you cannot put it down. How many wives have become grass-widowed on account of the limp-covered, yellow-backed magician it is impossible to say.

A teasing problem crops up—when was W. G.'s birthday? Who captained the Australians in 1909? Who won the Championship in 1961? 'I won't be a minute,' says the cricket enthusiast, 'I'll just look it up in *Wisden*'—and he disappears in search of his treasures. And, of course, he isn't a minute: he may be away for an hour or for the rest of the day. He may even never return.

There is one thing that you can be quite certain of in 'looking it up in *Wisden*' and that is that you will pick up a whole miscellany of information before you find the thing you have been looking for.

Suppose, for instance, that you want to look up the match between Kent and Derbyshire at Folkestone in 1963. You pick up your *Wisden* for 1964, open it at random, believing firmly that the problem will be solved in a matter of seconds, and you find yourself confronted with a Lancashire–Yorkshire match at Old Trafford.

The result is a draw. Forgetting now altogether about Kent and Derbyshire at Folkestone, you next turn up the Table of Main Contents to see if you can find out how Yorkshire and Lancashire have fared over the years in their Roses battles. On skimming down the Table of Contents, however, you come across a heading about Test Cricketers (1877–1963). This immediately starts you off on a new track, and you turn to the appropriate section to find how many cricketers have played for their country. The names Clay, Close, Coldwell, Compton, Cook, Copson leap up at you from the printed page: memories of past Test matches dance in bright kaleidoscopic colours before you. *Wisden*, you feel, is as exciting as a Buchan thriller. The word 'Buchan' leads logically enough to Midwinter.

Midwinter—of course!—now, didn't he play for England v. Australia, and also for Australia v. England? Research confirms that such was indeed the case. You look him up in Births and Deaths; but this entails searching an earlier edition. At random you select the issue for 1910; and sailing purposefully past an offer on page 3 of a free sample of Oatine (for Men after Shaving) you find that Midwinter, W. E. was also a regular player for Gloucestershire and for Victoria. Meanwhile, you have hit upon another Test match series.

In the first of this series of Tests England were trying out a twenty-six year old opening batsman named Hobbs (Cambridgeshire and Surrey). He made a 'duck' in his first innings, but did better in the second. 'England wanted 105 to win, and as it happened, Hobbs and Fry hit off the runs in an hour and a half without being separated.'

There are now two tracks that lie ahead. You can follow the Australians on their tour, to find that they won the Ashes but came close to defeat against Sussex and Somerset, and also played some unusual sides—Western Union (Scotland), South Wales, two rain-ridden draws against combined Yorkshire and Lancashire elevens, and, towards the end of the tour, Mr. Bamford's eleven at Uttoxeter.

The other track, of course, is the golden trail of the Master's 197 centuries!

Wisden's attractions are endless. A county cricketer of former days recently told me how much he enjoyed browsing over the Public Schools' averages, 'So that I can see how my friends' sons are getting on.'

Even the briefer obituaries are always interesting to read, and, when occasion demands, amusing—as surely obituaries should be. To return again to the 1903 edition, we read of the Reverend Walter Fellows, described in Scores and Biographies as 'a tremendous fast round-armed bowler'. For Westminster against Rugby (1852) he took nine wickets in the first innings and six in the second. However, in the course of so doing he bowled 30 wides, 'thereby giving away as many runs as Westminster made in their two innings combined'. In 1856 he hit a ball 175 yards 'from hit to pitch. . . . In 1863 he emigrated to Australia, and joined the Melbourne Club the following year. He was interested in the game to the last. Height 5 ft. 11 ins., and playing weight as much as 16 st. 4 lbs.'

And again, in the 1961 edition there is the superb obituary of Alec Skelding. Of the many selected tales *Wisden* recounts of him, perhaps this is the loveliest: 'In a game in 1948 he turned down a strong appeal by the Australian touring team. A little later a dog ran on the field, and one of the Australians captured it, carried it to Skelding and said: "Here you are. All you want now is a white stick!" '

Wisden is indeed better than rubies. *Wisden* is an inexhaustible gold mine in which lies embedded the golden glory of a century of cricketing summers. In the 1964 edition (page 1024) we read the brief statement '*Wisden* for cricket'. I think that sums it up.

A MIDDLESEX CENTURY [1964]

BY I. A. R. PEEBLES

The essay by Ian Peebles on the history of Middlesex is functional rather than literary, brisk rather than discursive and for those reasons a shade disappointing for so entertaining a writer. Several promising issues are shirked and excessive reticence causes the sad ends of Stoddart and Albert Trott never to be mentioned at all. Other omissions are brought about by modesty, especially as there is no mention of the fact that the captain of the highly enterprising 1939 side was Peebles himself. The most painful neglects are of Bosanquet and the splendid Sir Timothy O'Brien. As the great heretic of the golden age, Bosanquet surely deserves a little more attention and it might have been diverting for the author to have discussed a few moments in the glorious career of O'Brien (1861–1948) who, in his 53rd year, scored 90 and 111 in a match against Oxford University and who, to quote the Almanack of 1892, reporting the match against Surrey at The Oval in the previous July, 'was at this period of the season playing under the name of J. E. Johnston'. The optimism of Peebles' review, if not misplaced, took several years to justify itself and it was not till 1976 that the County Championship returned to the tenants of Lord's. They retained the title in the following year, winning again in 1980, 1982 and 1985. The county has also won five assorted one-day trophies, several of which came to them under the astute leadership of J. M. Brearley. But perhaps the most freakish achievement of all, once again unmentioned, occurred during the summer of 1937, in which, in the space of less than four months, the county supplied two England captains. In March G. O. Allen captained the national side against Australia and in June R. W. V. Robins performed the same duties at Lord's against New Zealand.

O N December 15, 1863, a number of gentlemen met in the London Tavern, Bishopsgate, to consider a momentous project. This was the formation of a Middlesex County Cricket Club, and the proceedings were conducted with admirable energy and decision.

Indeed, so assured is the report of the meeting, immediately released to the London newspapers, that it has some resemblance to the announcements following more recent and very much less pleasant events. It opens with a sweeping and surely debatable assumption. 'Sir,' it says, 'Middlesex being the only cricketing county in England that has no County Club'. It proceeds to say that a provisional committee had been formed, and that a general meeting would be held in the London Tavern in February of the following year.

As a result of this benevolent coup d'état events rushed forward. At the promised meeting the secretary, Mr. C. Hillyard, recorded the names of a fair nucleus of members, a regular committee of 16 was appointed, a ground hired in Islington, and four bowlers engaged. The staff was completed by the arrival of a groundsman, happily named George Hearne, and an umpire. A president, in the person of Viscount Enfield, followed soon afterwards.

The Middlesex team burst into action in 1865, with matches against Sussex, Bucks, Hants and M.C.C., with several lesser fixtures. Challenges from the established and powerful counties of Surrey and Lancashire were shrewdly side-stepped for the time being.

Such a dynamic start was not to be maintained. By 1869 Middlesex lost the use of the Islington ground, and could not then afford to accept the M.C.C. terms to play at Lord's. A melancholy two years on the rough Amateur Athletic Association Ground at Lillie Bridge was followed by another abortive tenancy of Prince's ground, near Hyde Park Barracks, which never gave much promise of permanency. At a meeting in 1877 it was decided to take the major step of playing at Lord's, starting the following year with four matches. From this time onwards the fortunes of Middlesex were inevitably bound up with those of M.C.C., yet the tenants have always maintained a sturdy independence in the conduct of their affairs, a state of affairs which exists to this day. From the formation of this partnership starts the real progress of Middlesex as a County Cricket Club.

Many enthusiastic members, players, and administrators had seen the Club through these early vicissitudes. It is not possible to mention many of these deserving names but that of Walker has ever been immortal in Middlesex. 'The Walkers of Southgate' was a brotherly triumvirate whose initials R.D., V.E. and I.D. are still fresh and familiar in the annals of the Club. All were competent administrators as well as being fine cricketers and so contributed to every aspect of the Club's establishment and progress.

The County Championship Birth and Residential qualifications had been introduced in 1873 and Middlesex had competed from that year with varying, but seldom more than modest success except in 1878 when they led the Counties. The start of the new tenancy marked no spectacular advances in these fortunes but very soon some very famous names came to support and perpetuate the foundations laid by the Walkers. In 1876 C. I. Thornton made his first appearance and was soon recognised as a hitter of unprecedented power. A. J. Webbe's active association with the Club began in 1875 and was to last until 1937, as player, captain and President. Webbe played for England but once and his interests were almost entirely focused on Middlesex. In light of this undivided devotion he may justly be described as the greatest figure in the County's hundred years of history. Aided by two Lyttletons and three Studds and, a little later, by Sir Timothy O'Brien, and the great A. E. Stoddart, Middlesex scored more attractively than ever in the 'eighties but, despite G. Burton's consistent slows, were a somewhat ineffective bowling side.

The names of Stoddart and O'Brien were linked as those in later years of Hearne and Hendren, and Compton and Edrich. Stoddart is still regarded by many competent judges as the greatest amateur batsman ever to represent Middlesex. In the course of an outstanding county career he went four times to Australia, twice as captain. His average of 35.57 for 30 innings against Australia was remarkable for the figures of his time. His record on the Rugby football field was no less illustrious.

It was in 1888 that J. T. Hearne made his first appearance, to reach his full powers in 1892, when he took 163 wickets. On the fast side of medium pace he had a beautiful wheeling action, spun the ball sharply from the off, and soon made his mark as the finest bowler of his type in the country. Through the next decade he was the mainstay of the attack with the support of J. T. Rawlin, a serviceable fast bowler. It was not until 1897 that Albert Trott had qualified to spin his leg-breaks from a prodigious hand. (In passing it may be said that this was regarded as the largest hand in cricket until lost in the enveloping grip of A. D. Nourse.)

In the first half of the 'nineties Middlesex with a wealth of amateur batting, and the unflagging talents of J. T. Hearne, kept well to the fore, being third in the table in 1893 and 1894. The names of the amateur batsmen were nigh legion but collectively they had a certain mercurial quality to thwart that consistency which makes for champion counties. Thus, although thrice third and twice runners-up in the 'nineties Middlesex were bested in the first half by neighbouring Surrey and, latterly, by Yorkshire and Lancashire. Surrey were at one time almost invincible with the irresistible force of Richardson and W. H. Lockwood to exploit the performances of a dependable batting order.

Middlesex entered the twentieth century well established as one of the major powers in the County Championship. In the North, Yorkshire always had a slight ascendancy in the struggle for power with their Lancashire neighbours. Nottinghamshire ruled the Midlands. In the South, Middlesex and Surrey dominated the scene. Through the 'nineties Surrey had a great deal the better of the argument but, by the turn of the century, the relative strengths of the rivals had altered so that Yorkshire succeeded as champions in 1900 and 1902 and Middlesex were top in 1903.

Although Middlesex did not again head the table before the outbreak of war, the county prospered greatly under the enlightened captaincy of P. F. Warner who, after a spell during which G. MacGregor led, had succeeded Webbe. In fact, as deputy captain Warner had handled the side frequently during MacGregor's tenure. Warner was very much greater in the international scene than Webbe, but Middlesex was still his first and greatest love. During his term of office he became one of the greatest all-round amateur batsmen in the country if never quite in the same category as C. B. Fry, K. S. Ranjitsinhji and F. S. Jackson. An indomitable defence was allied to sound orthodox scoring strokes, especially to the on, and the whole technique was applied with great intelligence and concentration. Warner brought the same qualities to his captaincy and had, at all times, an observant eye for every detail of the play. He used the extraordinary and occasionally erratic talents of A. E. Trott to best advantage. These consisted of a commendably aggressive attitude to batting, and a great power of leg-spin allied to a remarkably fast and accurate yorker. Many thought the first attribute unduly exaggerated by Trott's determination, on every occasion, to repeat his monumental straight drive which cleared the Lord's Pavilion. All players found it instructive and enormously pleasant to be a member of Warner's side.

The start of the century was quite promising but 1902, a wet season, brought almost unprecedented disaster. Only two matches were won by a Middlesex side which, for one reason or another, was seldom fully represented. It was a surprise to all, including the winners, when Middlesex went to the top of the table in the following year. Warner was now at the height of his powers as a batsman and was well supported by the normal Middlesex reservoir of amateur talent. Trott and Hearne were a formidable pair in this wettest of seasons and had the support of B. J. T. Bosanquet whose 'googlies' had a considerable impact on the game as a whole. Bosanquet, like some other pioneers, never mastered his invention to the extent achieved by many successors but the novelty was too much for many batsmen as the Australians found at Sydney and Trent Bridge. He was in addition a fine batsman with a short pick up but plenty of power.

In 1908 Warner became the official captain of Middlesex. By this time he had wide and varied experience of his craft and got the best out of his side for the next nine playing seasons, culminating in the glorious win of 1920.

Trott's career came to an end in 1909 but F. A. Tarrant had now developed into a splendid all-rounder. A sound and dependable batsman, his left-hand spinners were regarded as being equal to those of Wilfred Rhodes and Colin Blythe in all but accuracy. Further to enhance the County's prospects, J. W. Hearne and E. (Patsy) Hendren had just embarked. Hendren was to take some time to come to full bloom but Hearne's progress was so rapid that within a couple of years he was thought of in the same context as Rhodes and G. H. Hirst. He was a neat, precise batsman who preferred the back foot as a general base of operation. His leg-breaks he spun more than any Englishman within memory, and was only outspun on the arrival of A. A. Mailey. His googly was at least serviceable in an era as yet not wholly familiar with this form of deception. H. R. Murrell, a man of great personality, who was to play a lasting part in Middlesex affairs, kept wicket and batted with great spirit when the occasion demanded.

In an era when County cricket flourished and opposition from the North, Midlands and South bank of the Thames was formidable, Middlesex were always in the first six of the Championship. In 1910 and 1911 they were third and in 1914 ran into second place. With Warner, Tarrant and Hearne at the height of their powers, and Hendren verging on his potential greatness, Middlesex might well have gone further but for the untimely interruption. There were many young men whose names were to become prominent in the 'twenties, F. T. Mann, N. E. Haig, C. N. Bruce, R. H. Twining, S. H. Saville and G. E. V. Crutchley, to name a few, who brought a fine youthful zeal to support the professional skill.

The year of 1919 was an uneasy one for English cricket which, like many

other institutions, was striving to re-organise a wholly disrupted institution. The experiment of three two-day matches a week was found to be a
strenuous and unsatisfactory arrangement. The most pleasing development at Lord's was the batting of Hendren whose form far outstripped any
hope based on pre-war performances.

In the following year P. F. Warner ended his long and brilliant career by
leading his side to the top of the Championship table. His unsurpassed
qualities as captain and tactician made full use of a very talented side.
Hendren and Hearne were the foundation of a very good batting side. G.
T. S. Stevens, largely a protégé of the perspicacious Warner, was a great
amateur addition to the professional core of batsmen, and bowled a
dangerous mixture of leg-breaks and googlies. It was not, however, until
late in the season that the Middlesex challenge became apparent, and not
until the closing moments of the last match of the season that the prize was
finally grasped. Middlesex won a very important toss but were headed by
73 runs on the first innings. Centuries by H. W. Lee and C. H. L. Skeet got
Middlesex well on the way to a good second innings, but time ordained that
Warner should set Surrey, a strong, aggressive batting side, 244 to make in
three hours. At one point Surrey seemed to be well on the way to victory
but, appropriately, a typically shrewd move from Warner turned the day.
Seeing Fender on the balcony give the signal to the batsmen for 'general
chase' he removed Hendren from short leg to deep long-on. Very soon
Shepherd was caught in that position and the spin of Hearne and Stevens
saw Surrey defeated by 55 runs with only ten minutes to spare.

Warner, departing gloriously, handed over to F. T. Mann, who for eight
years led the County with a firm but happy touch which gained him the
lasting affection and admiration of all who played for or against Middlesex.
His reign opened auspiciously when, in 1921, Middlesex again won the
Championship. With T. J. Durston and Haig to open, the bowling was now
a very fair complement to the plentiful batting. Without ever repeating this
success Middlesex were well amongst the leaders for the remainder of the
'twenties. The flow of amateur batting was undiminished with Twining,
Bruce, Crutchley, H. J. Enthoven and H. L. Dales all available for
reasonable periods. Haig, Stevens and G. O. Allen were a tower of all-
round strength and Mann was ever liable to dominate the game with his
explosive hitting powers.

During the season 1929 Mann, although still officially captain, was
prevented by matters of business from playing more than occasional
matches. In his absence Haig took over, and proved himself another most
able captain. The season, with Hearne and Hendren still fine cricketers,
despite the latter's lean patch early on, was brightened by the splendid all-
round cricket and dazzling fielding of R. W. V. Robins. His leg breaks,
bowled at medium pace, were occasionally erratic, but had a most
devastating power of spin and were coupled to a well concealed googly.
Middlesex seemed on the threshold of another splendid decade but, in the
early 'thirties, fortunes declined to a low ebb. As occasionally happens, to
any side, the powers of several important members suffered a sudden

decrease, and others were removed by business calls. It was not until Robins took over in 1935 that once again things got under way.

The side was now largely reconstituted. C. I. J. ('Big Jim') Smith, imported from Wiltshire, had found his best form with the new ball and, employing one basic stroke, hit the ball higher and further than anyone before or since. Soon the great batting partnership of D. C. S. Compton and W. J. Edrich was to take shape whilst J. D. Robertson had developed into a most polished Number One. H. G. O. Owen-Smith and J. H. Human played the same dynamic cricket as their captain and Joe Hulme continued to fly round the deep. J. M. Sims developed into a medium-pace leg-spinner. Only a superb Yorkshire side stood between Middlesex and the Championship. This they succeeded in doing until the war, with Derbyshire at the top in 1936. The season of 1939 saw the retirement of Robins but the momentum he had generated carried the team to second place in the table on the eve of the war, a position they had occupied in the previous three seasons. This was a fine period in Middlesex play, for Robins made the most positive use of the young and energetic talent at his command.

In 1946 Robins returned to the helm and immediately set about reorganising affairs. After a season's effort and experiment Middlesex were poised for the triumph of 1947. The summer was a fine one and the Middlesex batting calculated to make the most of good wickets and bowling which had not yet regained pre-war standards. Robertson and S. M. Brown regularly opened and both scored over 2,000 runs. They were followed by the truly devastating power of Compton and Edrich, both of whom topped the three thousand. This mass of runs was acquired with a speed which gave a good attack, led by L. H. Gray and sustained by J. A. Young, ample time to despatch the opposition. Having won the Championship, Robins retired and F. G. Mann took over. In 1948 the presence of the Australians robbed him of his best players for long periods but, in 1949, he was better served, and Middlesex shared first place with Yorkshire. At this Mann, the only son to succeed a Championship winning father, retired and Middlesex fortunes flagged.

Robins returned for the third time as captain for 1950, before a joint captaincy, shared by Compton and Edrich, fared no better for two years than such compromises incline to do. Edrich took over for five years, but the form of the great fluctuated and little glory came to Lord's.

Compton and Edrich retired in 1957 but J. J. Warr brought a strong reviving influence to bear in 1958, and Middlesex again pushed forward. F. J. Titmus was now a splendid all-rounder and A. E. Moss, who had done so well for almost a decade, still had a fair head of steam to call on. A promising crop of young batsmen, including R. A. Gale, W. E. Russell and P. H. Parfitt helped Middlesex to reach third place in 1960 and when P. I. Bedford succeeded Warr in 1961 he achieved the same success. He, in 1963, gave way to C. D. Drybrough and, whilst the record has been moderate, the prospects are indeed bright at the moment of writing.

Titmus will captain a side which, with himself, includes five of the party that toured South Africa. In addition, Russell has advanced to be a most promising batsman.

After one hundred years of continued existence most institutions, and certainly County Cricket Clubs, take on a distinct character. That of Middlesex is pre-eminently of cheerfulness and enjoyment. These qualities permeate from the players to all associated with the club. Perhaps the best testimony to this spirit was the fact that, after ninety years of harmonious life, it was accidently discovered that, as the original rules had been lost, the club had operated without any written code for almost its entire existence to that date.

Those who have played for Middlesex have known the very best that cricket can offer. It is meet that in so many cases their personal association with the club remains unbroken in the form of service and support. In a comparatively brief survey it has not been possible to pay tribute to more than a few individuals but, in the spirit of the club, those not mentioned would not consider themselves omitted.

The Duke of Edinburgh and the Prime Minister, Sir Alec Douglas-Home, who as Lord Dunglass played a few games for Middlesex, attended the One Hundred Years Celebration dinner at Grosvenor House, Park Lane, on July 20 at which the Middlesex Centenary Youth Campaign was launched. I take this opportunity to extract from the Campaign brochure the full list of:

MIDDLESEX TEST PLAYERS FOR ENGLAND

1878–84	Lucas, A. P.	1898–1912	Warner, P. F.	1935–37	Sims, J. M.
1878–79	Webbe, A. J.	1903–5	Bosanquet, B. J. T.	1937–56	Compton, D. C. S.
1880–84	Lyttleton, Hon. A.	1905–6	Moon, L. J.	1938–55	Edrich, W. J.
1882–83	Leslie, C. F. H.	1911–26	Hearne, J. W.	1938	Price, W. F.
1882–83	Studd, C. T.	1920–35	Hendren, E.	1947–52	Robertson, J. D.
1882–83	Studd, G. B.	1921	Durston, T. J.	1947–49	Young, J. A.
1882–83	Vernon, G. F.	1921–30	Haig, N. E.	1948–51	Dewes, J. G.
1884–96	O'Brien, Sir T. C.	1922–23	Mann, F. T.	1948–49	Mann, F. G.
1887–98	Stoddart, A. E.	1922–30	Stevens, G. T. S.	1950–51	Warr, J. J.
1890–93	MacGregor, G.	1927–31	Peebles, I. A. R.	1953–60	Moss, A. E.
1891–99	Hearne, J. T.	1929	Killick, Rev. E. T.	1955	Titmus, F. J.
1891–95	Philipson, H.	1929–37	Robins, R. W. V.	1961	Murray, J. T.
1894–95	Ford, F. G. T.	1930–48	Allen, G. O.	1961	Parfitt, P. H.
1895–98	Davenport, H. R. Bromley	1930–31	Lee, H. W.	1961	Russell, W. E.
1898–99	Trott, A. E.	1934–37	Smith, C. I. J.	1964	Price, J. S. E.

CRICKET IN THE 17th AND 18th CENTURIES [1965]

BY ROWLAND BOWEN

In 1965 Rowland Bowen made a welcome return to Wisden, once again displaying great power and originality in his approach to the history of cricket. Most modern writers have tended to ignore the mysteries at which Bowen so shrewdly pecks away, preferring instead to celebrate the certitudes of their own age. But it is instructive to point out the extent to which Bowen, by 'thinking' himself into a past epoch, is able to penetrate the mists of confusion, at least to his own satisfaction. His deductions lead him into all sorts of extraneous affairs and he makes a very convincing case for their inclusion in the evolution of the game. So it is that in his intensely erudite and intellectually relentless probe, Bowen asks us to consider such factors as the English Civil War, the East India Company, the deployments of the British Army, the uniqueness of London, the earlier harvests of the rural south, the policies of the Forestry Commission, and the size of a sheep. Five years later Bowen was to correlate all his abstruse knowledge, of affairs peripheral to cricket as well as to the game itself, in the most original cricket history ever written. Much of the flavour of that book, if not its bitter contempt for hypocrisy, is conveyed by his 1965 essay, which presses home one point starkly relevant to the modern world in which Bowen resides. He was always adamant as to the reliance of the first-class game on the patronage of rich friends. To put it another way, cricket has never been self-supporting, which means that with the shrinking of the leisured landowning class, the game would have to find new methods of paying its way. In the same edition which carries Bowen's essay, the reader may find the unfamiliar statistics of the Gillette Cup. Cricket believed that by embracing sponsorship, it had solved its problems. In truth, it had hardly begun to.

By the start of the seventeenth century, cricket exists and is, very shortly afterwards both widespread and popular in parts of South-Eastern England. By the end of the next century, M.C.C. is well established, the game is already being played in many parts of the world, and we are on the threshold of the modern period.

Thus these two hundred years span a most interesting era—one which we can in our ignorance still call the infancy and growth of the game: in our ignorance because we do not know when it is born, or where, or how, or the extent of its development from its birth by the time we reach King James the First's reign.

For the first hundred years we can infer much more about the organisation of the game than about how it was played, and this is true to a lesser extent in the eighteenth century also.

Let us for a moment consider cricket in its very many different guises at the present time: we know all about Test cricket, County cricket, League cricket and Club cricket but how often do we think about playground cricket, street cricket, back-garden cricket, beach cricket? There can be few of us who have not played cricket using no cricket bat, nor any cricket ball, nor stumps, nor bails, let alone pads, gloves and other appurtenances; yet we were never in any doubt that we were playing cricket, nor would any casual bystander have been in any doubt. 'Over the wall, 6 and out', 'broken window, 0 and out, and you'll have to pay for it'—these important local Laws find no mention in any printed Code yet, though oral, they are indisputably part of the indigenous and accepted Laws of the game.

The point we thus make is that there are generally two kinds of cricket, formal cricket which, even if friendly, is competitive, and informal cricket which (often most unfriendly) is play: and these two kinds of cricket exist, and appear always to have existed side by side, following more or less parallel courses but with an undoubted time-lag in informal cricket (under-arm is still not uncommon). Historical and geographical circumstances have sometimes enhanced the differences, and at others have eliminated them. The game which was once played at Stonyhurst was informal cricket of the late sixteenth, and even early seventeenth century, modified for its special environment, and kept as it was by being played by boys, and by boys who were exiles. The game of cricket, known as wicket, which was played in New England even into this century was undoubtedly a perpetuation of informal cricket as it was introduced by the early settlers in North America, but, oddly, maintained in a formal state so that it even caused some students of that game to think it had no relation to cricket at all. However, the word wicket is a good North Country dialect word for cricket, not yet wholly extinct, and there is a further proof that it was cricket from a description of the size of the wicket itself: the wicket was six feet by four inches, and an American visitor to London in 1810 was struck by the difference between 'their' (i.e., English) cricket and 'ours' and went on to say that 'in our cricket, the wickets are only two in number and about three or four inches high'. Moreover, there is a reference to cricket in New York in 1751 being played according to 'the London rules' (doubtless those of 1744) which by implication shows a definite divergence between the American game, and its later development in the country of its birth.

It is that difference in the size of the wicket which is about all we can point to with certainty as an illustration of the way early seventeenth-century cricket differed from ours. It is sometimes said that the original game will have been single wicket, but it is difficult to understand how double wicket could ever have developed from single wicket, whereas single wicket is, from one point of view, merely the informal version of the accepted game. Indeed, one derives strongly the impression from a reading of early eighteenth-century notices of cricket that single-wicket was an innovation of that period, for when such matches are announced they are almost invariably announced as being 'at single wicket' the clear inference being that double wicket would otherwise be expected.

If we could transport ourselves to one of the country districts of Kent (even to 'prophane' Maidstone) towards the end of King James's reign, we would probably see a game which we could readily recognise: the differences would be the wide low wicket, the fast-slung underarm ball, the curved blade of the bat, the necessity to touch the umpire's bat on a completion of a run, the probability (in some games) that one could count a run made from a stroke off which a batsman was out, and the recorder scoring a notch in his tally-pole with a knife. All the rest would be very much as now: a game which then, as now, provided more opportunity for skill and co-ordination of eye and brain and muscle than any other save, perhaps, polo.

It was this which made the game fascinating then, and it is this which still makes it fascinating despite the competition of other games and sports for the attention of the masses. But when, in the early seventeenth century it was not only far and away the most skilful game but also, whether by designed or accidental omission, the only *lawful* game, no wonder that it took root and spread rapidly.

During the first half of that century the game became widespread in Kent, Surrey and Sussex, and in parts of Essex and East Anglia generally. Being widespread it was, therefore, popular amongst a section of the community, but persons of quality had to defend themselves against accusations that cricket was not a proper amusement for a gentleman, or a parson—and this they did with spirit. The game was on its way up the social scale but it was not established when the Civil War commenced. It seems likely that the Interregnum provided both hindrance and encouragement.

Cromwell, we know, forbade the game in Ireland in 1656, but he had himself played the game, when young in Huntingdonshire: if there was, for some reason, a Roundhead antipathy to the game, the Cavaliers, dispersed to their estates from London, may well have found solace in playing the game with their own tenantry—can one imagine any better time possible than having nothing else to do but play cricket? But it is likely that the Restoration was the crucial factor in leading to the social acceptance of the game: 'Old Rowley' himself may even have seen the boys at St. Omer playing their own form of cricket, during his exile in the Spanish Netherlands, and we should not ignore the great part played by his own descendants in the game in the next 200 years or so.

At all events, it was already the accepted thing for English merchants overseas to be found playing cricket during holidays, within half a generation of the Restoration—and it has been ever since. It is intriguing how many of those merchants at Aleppo came from Essex, the Fen country, and Lincolnshire, as well as from Kent. Recalling Cromwell's boyhood, we can muse whether the game was even more widely spread than is generally imagined at that period. Nor is it, perhaps, wholly without significance that William Byrd the younger, of Westover, Virginia, was at Felsted: he may have learnt the game there, though, on balance, the probability is that he had learnt it at home where, years later, a mature man, and a member of the Assembly, he was found playing the game with his friends on near-by estates along the James River.

By the time he wrote of those events, the game was already fashionable and popular in London and the first county game had been played, and the first of the long line of great cricketers had been named—William Bedle, the forerunner of Long Robin, of Minshull, of Small ('makes bat and ball'), of Nyren, of Beldham—we can go no further for we shall be outside our period.

It was at that time, in the first ten or fifteen years of the new century, that we first read of widely advertised matches for considerable sums of money, and though almost our earliest references to the game tell of gambling, it was in this century that it reached what, considering the relative value of money, would now be considered colossal proportions, amounting to thousands of guineas on one match. Indeed, it was not till late Victorian prudery won the ascendancy that bookmakers ceased to shout the odds in front of the Tavern at Lord's: gambling had always been an important part of the game, and there seems good reason to think that many of our earliest detailed records of the game would not have been compiled had not gamblers felt the need to study 'form'.

It was, again, in the first quarter of the eighteenth century that we learn of the great private patrons of the game, Mr. Edwin Stead being perhaps the most notable. Wealthy patrons were to be an important if not essential feature of the game for the next two hundred years, and with the passing of the individual patrons, we find their place taken by commercial organisations. It is often bemoaned that cricket does not pay its way, but it seems rather that the highest form of cricket never, or only rarely, did, from the earliest times: it needed a patron, and wealth, to bring together great cricketers, and it is only by bringing together great cricketers that there can ever be an improvement in the technique of the game.

By the end of that quarter century, we know that county cricket was firmly established. We owe this to a foreign chronicler, M. Cesar de Saussure in June 1728 who writes of county cricket as altogether usual and taken for granted. How much have we lost? We know, in all the years before then, only nine matches which could possibly be called county matches. Moreover, it was in that same period that we first find mention of county clubs. What meaning was then intended is not certain: maybe no more than 'an association of people coming together for a common purpose' or, in other words, club, team or eleven. But later in the century, some 60 or 70 years on, we find mention of a county club (Essex) on which there is just sufficient information to tell us that it hardly differed from the modern pattern of cricket clubs: so it may also be in the earlier period.

Nor had the game only spread to the Americas; as early as 1721, we know that ordinary mariners of the East India Company whiled away their time by playing cricket at Cambay in Gujarat. It is indeed evident that long before the first quarter of the century is over, the game is taken for granted by *all* classes of the population and is no private preserve of a particular locality or sector of society. The numerous references we possess from that time make it clear that they are to ordinary facts, not a chronicling of something unusual. The spread of the game from the south and east was already taking place—we even know of a match so far away as Townham in Gloucestershire in 1729 but, though this is unlikely to be an isolated instance, we find no further mention in that county till 1752. Otherwise, the spread from the homeland seems to have followed the main roads, to Bath and so into the West country, to Newmarket, and the great estates in Norfolk and Suffolk, up the great North Road through Lincolnshire into Yorkshire and beyond. By the middle of the century, the game had spread into Hampshire, to give rise eventually to Hambledon and the many tales that surround that Club and its doings. By the same period, the game was being played by 'red-coats' as far away as Perth.

During the eighteenth century, and for long after, it was the custom for regiments in these islands, with the exception of the Guards and certain others, to recruit in the area where they were garrisoned. If a regiment had been stationed at Chatham for ten or fifteen years, and then been moved to Carlisle, we could expect a strong element of Kentish men in the regiment, and a reasonable certainty that they would have been playing cricket in Carlisle shortly after their arrival there. As the game spread more through the country, we can be sure that red-coats overseas would be found playing the game shortly after disembarkation. It may often be many years later that we find the first actual mention in print and this has led to a serious post-dating of early cricket overseas. However, it has perhaps already been made clear that the cricket played in Royalist New York during the American Rebellion will have owed nothing, beyond the presence of more players, to the arrival of the troops: cricket was widespread in the American colonies long before, and continued after the departure of the British troops.

If we were to consider what was the most significant organisational feature of the game during the first three-quarters of the eighteenth century, it would be the undoubted pre-eminence of the Artillery ground (still thriving in London at Finsbury Square). From 1730 to 1773 we know of no fewer than 206 matches, and other accounts make it clear that it was virtually the Lord's of the period with large crowds in regular attendance. Not that there were not many other good matches elsewhere: there was a great number in the country areas immediately south of London, and we read of journeys by coach, by whole families, with the husband on his horse, to watch great games in Dorking, and at Sevenoaks, and later on at Hambledon. Such journeys would have been arduous, and we know from the bill of fare offered in tents on the grounds that meals were not cheap: it is doubtful whether the modern cricket lover puts up with anything remotely resembling the hardship and discomfort suffered by the fans of those days.

It is interesting to consider what social influences were affecting the game: Stuart blood was prominent amongst the aristocracy who took part, and doubtless the country was well aware that the Pretender was playing cricket in Rome in 1718. No doubt, for similar reasons of courting popularity, we find the Hanoverians taking part in the game as the century rolled on, and, in consequence of the Hanoverian liking for Windsor, we have the rise of Eton and its influence on cricket as on so many other walks of life in this country, and the decline of Westminster, the favoured school of the old Tory aristocracy, which had furnished so many of the founders not only of the Hambledon club but of M.C.C. itself.

The Hambledon Club had arisen around 1767 largely as a result of the decline in importance of the Artillery ground, and within a few years, from the sheer authority of its members, and the ability of its players, had become the game's law-giver. But so remote a country locality could hardly maintain its sway, and it is not surprising that the law-giving power returns to London with the formation of the White Conduit Club in 1782 and of its immediate successor, the Marylebone Cricket Club in 1787. (This is by the way, the conventional date and it is almost certain that the actual year was 1788 but 1787 is generally used as it is the date when the White Conduit Club, or a principle part of its members, removed themselves to Thomas Lord's first ground.)

Throughout the first half of the century, Kent had been the great cricketing county, and its leading town, Dartford: for the rest of the century it was to be Surrey with, for a few years, Hampshire when the Hambledon club founded the county team. But towards the end of the century there seems to have been some falling off in county cricket and we hear more about such leading clubs as the Montpelier, the Homerton, the Brighton and, of course, the Marylebone. It would be interesting to know why this was: the wars with France can have had little to do with it, either then, or till the fall of Napoleon himself, for only an insignificant part of the population, at any level of Society, was directly affected by those wars, and not a very much larger part indirectly. There was, in fact, no parallel with the events of 1914–18 and 1939–45. It is interesting, though, that it was in this period that we first learn of the rise of cricket in three great industrial towns of the Midlands and North. Apart from London (always an exception to every social rule, though often convinced, itself, that it is the norm) cricket was never an urban game: how did it become so popular in those three towns Leicester, Nottingham and Sheffield, when it took little or no root elsewhere till very much later?

The answer is that in each of those towns, trades were practised which gave the opportunity for contract piece work (hose, lace, cutlery) each man working in his own home in his own time, and not regimented into soul-destroying factories. What more natural that, on a sunny day, they should play cricket during the day, and work during the night? (One wonders whether it was the earlier harvests in the south and east which made it possible for cricket to be popular in the rural parts of that area. Elsewhere with very much later harvests, cricket has never been a rural game either, but a game of a limited social class.)

We must retrace our steps again to the middle of the century to pick up some more threads in the game's history. It is well known that the first two full scores date from 1744: it was a quarter of a century later that we know of a score where each batsman's details were written down stroke by stroke—and that score also provides us with the first known century,

Minshull, 107. Now, it is not possible to conceive a mechanism which would provide such details scoring on tally sticks, and it follows that *by that date*, 1769, the practice of keeping the score on paper, much as we do now, was already established (for the match was quite a minor match, and if this was done for a minor match, it can be taken for granted that it had long been the accepted practice in matches of importance). This, of course, raises a problem: for many years after, we find artists showing scorers notching away and it is difficult to explain this. It is possible that 'tally-scorers' were by then honorific and not the effective functionaries: it is possible that the artist was just quite out of date: or it may merely be that, in some cases, the match depicted was in an out-of-the-way country area where the latest innovations were not yet practised. But, recalling that until recently Her Majesty's Stationery Office would supply Government offices with sand for drying ink, we think it most likely that the 'tally-scorers' were redundant.

Certainly by the 1780s we know of match cards which are indistinguishable from those to be had on at least one county ground till shortly before the last war (i.e. they gave no bowling analyses nor falls of wicket) even to the price—2d. By 1792, the averages for the season were being worked out, and though we have, so far, no knowledge of any printed version, yet it is reasonable that such existed. It was in 1791 that Britcher brought out his first annual book of scores, and eight years later, Epps brought out his collection of scores from 1771. All these details point to the need for statistics on the game.

It is also very likely that they met another need, which seems to have existed almost since the game began, of being able to talk with factual knowledge of cricket of the past: always there seems to have been this desire to compare the deeds of today with the deeds of yester-year and cricket lovers seem to have had not only detailed memories, but also lengthy memories: helped no doubt by much printed ephemerides, of which the greater part may well be irretrievably lost to us. (Certainly there is one book of eighteenth-century scores known to Haygarth which is no longer in existence, and even more recently, the first issue of Britcher, known 60 years ago can no longer be traced anywhere.) Because there is so much that we are certain must once have existed, we can always hope for absolutely new and exciting finds to be made.

We have reached the end of the century, and as we indicated, we have reached a state of affairs very similar to our own: cricket annuals, wide coverage in the Press, M.C.C. established. What of the game itself, rather than its organisation and apparatus? We have seen that we knew little of the actual mode of play in the seventeenth century, but there is one matter we do know about, and it must have had a material effect on the mode of play, whether of batsman, bowler, or fielder. It is the size and shape of the wicket. Nyren quoted, and disbelieved, a statement that before 1702, the wicket was two feet wide by one foot high: but we saw that a similarly *shaped* wicket existed in America, though its dimensions were even stranger. If we find a wide low wicket in America, we can be sure there was a wide low wicket in this country, and the actual dimensions are unimportant. But whereas, in America, the wide low wicket persisted, in this country it quickly, after the start of the eighteenth century (though hardly much earlier or a wide low wicket could not have reached America at all), became a tall narrow one. There seem to be certain problems here and it is possible that there were two different shapes and sizes of wicket in this country, one of which was exported, and the other of which gradually became dominant here.

Now, in this connection, it is worth recalling that in the Sussex dialect, stool=stump, and this is almost certainly the real connection of stool-ball with cricket: that stool-ball was, in origin, played with no milkmaid's stool, as has been fancied, but was cricket played in a clearing in a woodland, using the stump of a tree, or stool, as the object to be hit by the bowler. Such an object would have been wider rather than narrow, and lower rather than higher (it should be remembered that the Forestry Commission's conifers are a twentieth-century product). In sheep-rearing areas, a wicket would have been used, and it might well have been a relatively narrow and tall object—enough to admit one sheep in fact! If there is substance in these conjectures, it is indicated that those settlers in America who took cricket with them came from wooded rural areas rather than sheep-rearing areas. Anyway, by 1744, the laws in this country make it clear that the wicket approximated to its modern dimensions, and it can be inferred from the lack of any mention of a change in its shape, that those dimensions obtained at least from 1706 when we have the first full account of a match.

However it may be erroneous to consider the shape and size of the wicket in isolation from the style of bowling, and of batting, which prevailed. It is known that until well after the middle of the eighteenth century, the bat had a curve at the bottom, and this was even more pronounced earlier in the century, to resemble more a hockey stick than a modern bat. By the late 1770s, the bat had assumed the modern shape and appearance. The change in shape can only have been to meet a change in style of bowling, and we can thus be reasonably certain that throughout most of the first half of the century, the ball was in fact bowled, in the sense that we should use the term in the game of Bowling itself. (The rules of 'Stonyhurst cricket'—an evident perpetuation of a much earlier game as we have seen—provided that all bowling should be what we would nowadays call 'sneaks' and this is good confirmation of our assumption, linked as it is, with the old-style shaped bat.)

Certainly this must have been the style of bowling in the celebrated Kent v. England match of 1744. In the next generation it had been transformed, and we find instead the 'length' bowling, the necessity of pitching the ball upon a certain length: this is anything but 'bowling' as strictly understood, and it must have led to a completely different approach to batting, an approach as radically different from what had gone before as was to occur twice in the nineteenth century with the introduction of 'round-arm' and of 'over-arm'. Yet nothing has come down to us of this change, which, however gradual, must surely have excited considerable comment. All we can say is that it is likely that, prior to about 1750, 'bowling' all along the ground was the rule, and that by about 1775 it was largely forsaken: it would never be entirely forsaken till under-arm itself was abandoned.

It seems very likely that just as the new-style bowling will have imposed a new-style bat and approach to batting, it must also have affected the shape of the wicket. It is evident that a 'pitched' ball would not be of much use against a wicket wider than it was high, and if there had been earlier endeavours to 'bowl' the 'pitched' ball, they must have had their part in narrowing the wicket: equally certainly, a low wicket must have seemed intensely unfair to the 'pitch' bowlers who would often have seen a ball bounce over the top though the blade of the bat itself was twice the height of the low wicket. What is difficult to understand in the relative chronology of these changes is that the curved bat should have outlived the taller wicket. Maybe it did not in fact do so by many years, but one would have expected the straighter bat to precede the taller wicket yet, apparently, it did not. We can only await the unearthing of unknown eighteenth-century diaries with possible detailed descriptions of the game to achieve certainty.

We must therefore contrast the start of the century with its termination, as we cannot be sure when these important changes all took place in the middle. At that start we can be tolerably certain that all was indeed true bowling: for this to be effectively met by the old-fashioned bat, little more than a good eye was needed *provided the pitch itself was true*. This was hardly ever the case, and it must have been the irregularity of the early pitches which made the bowler's lot tolerable: nevertheless, we fancy that since only stamina—the necessity to run all hits out—could have limited a batsman's score, there may well have been occasions on relatively good pitches when high scores were made, as relatively boring to spectators of two hundred and more years ago as the Manchester Test of 1964. For, on the whole, scores were very low by our standards, but took often several days to compile: the *art* of the game was the appeal to the spectator, not the breaking of batsman's records. Nor, in those days, can there have been anything resembling stroke-play: only full-blooded hits, 'mows' and deflections.

By the end of the century the picture was quite different: the 'bowler' in the original sense as derived from the game of bowls had almost ceased to be. Indeed, in a few cases, 'jerkers' were recognised, and Hambledon were not ashamed to own one. The pitched ball, with its variety of breaks had come into existence: the bat was now straight, to meet the menace of the new-style of bowling, and was held vertically: all this led to the introduction of a whole family of new strokes, most of which are still with us: for it was the *bounced* ball that made stroke play possible at all, and whether the ball is bounced from an underarm or overarm delivery hardly affects the type of stroke that has to be played, though it very much affects the timing. Once the new style of bowling had been mastered, and the way to play it clearly demonstrated, the way was open to batsmen of the new generation to make higher scores than ever before till, in the next century, a fresh type of 'bowling' appeared, in its turn to be mastered and replaced by yet a fourth style, which too was mastered.

It can perhaps now be seen how very old-fashioned, simple, and even childish, the old game of cricket, as still played in America, must have seemed when compared with the highly sophisticated and developed English cricket when an American traveller compared the two games just after the close of our period. The eighteenth century was what in fact *made* cricket as a spectator sport: not the nineteenth, with its over-arm, and W. G. Grace—they merely added to what had gone before. We can, for example, well imagine ourselves watching, and being enthralled, by a game towards the end of the eighteenth century, but we doubt if we could long have borne the tedium of fast sneaks at the beginning: certainly the people of that time did, but then they did not know what was to follow, and the existence of great bets on the game may well have induced a spurious interest.

We have surveyed two centuries of cricket and we are left at the end with the feeling that, at the commencement of our period, we must have been very near the origins of the game itself. This feeling arises from what we have seen of the development of the game in the second of our two centuries: it does not leave very much to have taken place during the earlier half of our period, and hardly anything at all before then. How then did it arise? We have made no attempt to answer this, but, maybe, before long, we shall know much more about the birth of the game itself. We leave it now, at the start of the nineteenth century, as a lusty young man, having seen to its infancy and upbringing.

THE GREAT YEARS AND THE GREAT PLAYERS OF KENT [1966]

BY R. L. ARROWSMITH

In 1966 came another county history, this time of Kent. In his account of two hundred years of history, Mr. Arrowsmith strives to give the conventional impression of Kentish cricket as something fast and beautiful but, like so many commentators of his period, omits vital details either through an excess of tact, as in the case of Percy Chapman, or through a wrongheaded assessment of what is and what is not important. No account of Colin Blythe, the cockney violinist, should ever fail to mention the supreme irony that a man whose delicacy of temperament inflicted upon him such excrutiating agonies in important matches should have been killed on the Western Front in 1917. There is the predictable leaning over backwards to pay obeisance at the shrine of Lord Harris but sadly there is no attempt to reconcile the claim that his lordship was 'a fine batsman' with the fact that in forty years of first-

class cricket he could manage only ten centuries. The richest joke in the 1966 Almanack is Arrowsmith's claim that Harris was a man 'of absolute fairness', a judgment on which Walter Hammond would have had some interesting things to say. Then there is the business of James Seymour, mentioned only in passing even though there is a sense in which he is one of the significant figures of the century. In 1920 Seymour was awarded the match against Hampshire at Canterbury for his benefit. The subsequent intervention of the Inland Revenue, which demanded a percentage of the tribute, brought about a test case which Seymour fought all the way to the House of Lords, winning his case and establishing the right of a professional cricketer to an untaxed benefit.

T HAT the Kent County Cricket Club was formed in 1842 and re-formed in 1858 and again in 1870 is historically true but for practical purposes irrelevant, as none of these events had any significant effect on the fortunes of the county's cricket. Cricket had indeed flourished in Kent for well over a century before the club was formed. In 1709 we find Kent billed to play Surrey in the first recorded inter-county match and even if, as seems likely, this grandiloquent title conceals a mere club game, we have in the next thirty-five years records of many matches in which one side is styled 'Kent'.

The Kent v. England match in 1744 is remembered not only as the earliest match of which the full score is preserved, but also as having been the occasion of a famous poem by James Love. Throughout the eighteenth century Kent was a notable cricket county, pre-eminent in the first half and in the second disputing the pre-eminence with Hambledon. Those were the days when county cricket depended on patrons and the Kent patrons deserve to be recorded: first Edward Stead, of Harrietsham; then Lord Charles Sackville, later Earl of Middlesex, and his brother, Lord John Philip Sackville; then Lord John Philip's son, the Duke of Dorset; and Sir Horace Mann, on whose ground in Bourne Park many matches were played, and finally Stephen Amherst, of West Farleigh, whom Beldham described as 'the gentleman who made the Kent matches'.

The early years of the nineteenth century are a dim period in the county's history. Few matches were played and the only name that really stands out is that of John Willes, the first militant round-arm bowler. Suddenly in the mid-thirties things sprung to life again and there followed the days of 'the good old Kent eleven' when

> 'with five such mighty cricketers 'twas but natural to win
> As Felix, Wenman, Hillyer, Fuller Pilch and Alfred Mynn.'

Felix, a man of much charm and many talents, was a brilliant left-handed bat; Wenman, the leading wicket-keeper of his day and a noted back-player, was the much-respected captain of the side; Hillyer was a great medium-pace bowler and Fuller Pilch perhaps the finest batsman the world had seen before W. G. But even in this gallery the most commanding figure was Alfred Mynn, a giant of a man, a magnificent and majestic fast bowler, a dangerous forcing batsman and a great slip, who was naturally unbeatable at single-wicket. A kind and generous man, he was universally beloved and inspired the most famous of all cricket poems. With these five, helped by other capable players, Kent frequently played England and frequently proved victorious.

A long period of comparative obscurity followed the break-up of this great eleven. In the 'fifties and 'sixties the county had only one pro of the top class, Edgar Willsher, now remembered chiefly for his part in getting over-arm bowling legalised, but in fact one of the most feared bowlers of his day. A number of good amateurs were qualified but did not apparently care for county cricket, and one senses a general apathy and lack of direction at the top.

In 1870, far more important than the formation of a club, came the first appearance of the man who was destined to change all this, Lord Harris. For almost sixty years he *was* Kent cricket and little could be done without his approval. A fine, attacking batsman and a splendid field, he played for and captained England and was in one season President, Honorary Secretary and Captain of Kent. After his first-class career was over he remained until his death a dominant power behind the scenes both in Kent and at Lord's. A martinet of a type that the present generation has never seen, he was none the less respected for his absolute fairness, his great administrative ability and his whole-hearted love of the game. Moreover, he was a wonderful friend to the pros. Where he was one might be sure that there would never be indiscipline or indecision and his place has never been filled.

Yet even he could not during his own playing days bring the county real success in the field. The amateurs were now willing enough to play, but many of the best could not spare the time to play regularly or for long and there was not a sufficiency of good pros to fill the gaps. Moreover Kent was singularly unlucky at this period in the number of good players lost early from death or injury—Frank and Alfred Penn, C. M. Cunliffe, the Hon. Ivo Bligh, Stanley Christopherson, Herbert, Frank and Walter Hearne and O'Shaughnessy. A further handicap was that throughout the 'eighties and early 'nineties there was no wicket-keeper of any real class regularly available. For professionals the side relied largely on the Hearnes, five of whom got county caps, assisted by a succession of left-hand bowlers, Jimmy Woutton, Walter Wright and 'Nutty' Martin. Martin had the curious distinction of taking twelve for 102 in his only Test against Australia, but neither as a bowler nor as an all-rounder could he expect to be selected when either Peel or Briggs was available. None the less, if Kent did little in the Championship, they could at least beat the Australians, a feat which they accomplished five times between 1884 and 1899 in seven matches and have never accomplished since.

The real turning point in the county's fortunes was the establishment of the Tonbridge Nursery in 1897. Within five or six years this had produced just the nucleus of pros required to form, in combination with an unusually gifted lot of amateurs, a really formidable side. One of its earliest products was 'Charlie' Blythe, who has always been regarded by many as the greatest of all slow left-handers: as difficult as any when the wicket helped him, he stood out head and shoulders above his competitors on plumb wickets, when they must needs bowl defensively and he, with his command of flight and cunning variations of pace, could still attack. So accurate was he that once, when he bowled a full-pitch in Canterbury Week, he remarked, 'There goes the first bad ball I've bowled this season.' A man much loved and the most generous of opponents, he once said to R. H. Spooner, who had just hit him for two or three fours, 'Oh, Mr. Spooner! I'd give all my bowling to be able to bat like that.'

He habitually opened the bowling with Arthur Fielder, a fine fast bowler who played with success for England but lives in cricket history for having taken all ten wickets for the Players at Lord's. Two other early products of the Nursery were Jim Seymour, a brilliant batsman who added to all the orthodox strokes one or two of his own and was perhaps the last man to play the 'dog shot' in county cricket, and 'Punter' Humphreys, who for years opened the batting and, if Blythe was absent, the bowling as well, and who later did splendid work as the county's coach. These two and Fred Huish, a wicket-keeper of the highest class, were with Blythe and Fielder the regular pros of the great side which won the Championship in 1906: Woolley in his first season accomplished some fine performances, but such was the competition that he could not get a place in Canterbury Week.

Of the amateurs the best remembered are Kenneth Hutchings and Jack Mason. Mason was a glorious fast-wicket batsman, a good fast-medium bowler and a great-slip: he had captained the side from 1898 to 1902 and later often did so in August and was probably the best and most popular captain the county ever had. Hutchings was in 1906 and for a few seasons afterwards an exceptionally brilliant batsman and in particular a wonderful driver who hit the ball as hard as anyone ever has. Humphreys, no dodderer himself, once told me that he had made 42 one day when Hutchings came in, 'but Mr. Hutchings got his fifty first'. He was, too, a great fielder anywhere and an astonishingly powerful thrower, who relied entirely on a flick of the wrist. Once in a club match at Canterbury the ball rolled under his deck chair: Hutchings without getting up flicked it up to the wicket, which was pitched right on the farther side of the ground. To support these in 1906 were C. J. Burnup, who actually headed the averages and was also a famous outfield, R. N. R. Blaker, brilliant alike as a hitter and in the field, E. W. Dillon, a most consistent left-hander and Cloudesley Marsham, the captain. Sam Day, as fine a batsman as any of these and the only man who has ever made a hundred for a county the year before he left school, was absent on a football tour, while his younger brother, Arthur, who had made a thousand runs the season before and who later played regularly for the Gentlemen, could not keep his place.

There may have been greater county sides, but there can hardly have been a more attractive batting or fielding side and no county ever had such an array of slips. But indeed for the first forty years of the century Kent hardly had a batsman who was not attractive. In Canterbury Week in 1906 their totals were 568 and 479, both made at over a hundred runs an hour and as far on as 1937 the 219 required to beat Gloucestershire came in seventy-three minutes.

With much of the fast scoring of these thirty years the name of Frank Woolley is inseparably associated. The most graceful and correct of batsmen, playing beautifully straight with a long pendulum swing which seemed to time the ball of itself, he was master of every stroke and bowlers found it impossible to keep him quiet. Indeed, he regarded it as his duty to dictate to them and never to allow them to be on top. A young amateur in his first match for Kent was in difficulties with a fast bowler on a fiery wicket. Woolley simply remarked, 'He wants settling', and lifted the offending bowler twice over the sight-screen. He was also a fine slip and, until he was thirty-five, in the top flight of slow left-handers. On a turning wicket he and Blythe were the Laker and Lock of their day. In Maidstone Week in 1913 Lancashire made 158 and 88 and Middlesex 56 and 86, and first innings totals of 220 and 79 sufficed to bring Kent victories by nine wickets and by seven: Blythe took twenty wickets and Woolley thirteen.

By this time the batting had been reinforced by Wally Hardinge who, if there had been no fast bowlers, might have ranked with the great, and the bowling each August by D. W. Carr, an accurate and deadly googly bowler who had the unique experience of being picked for England in his first season of first-class cricket at the age of thirty-seven before he had ever played in a county match. On that occasion he was left out on the morning of the match: even so, when he played in the final Test, it was only his seventh first-class match. The Championship was won again under the captaincy of Dillon in 1909, 1910 and 1913 and only narrowly missed in 1911.

After the Great War Kent were never quite as good again. They had in 'Tich' Freeman incomparably the most prolific wicket-taker county cricket has ever seen, but he was often poorly supported, and there were apt to be gaps in the batting early in the season before the leading amateurs were available: the solid phalanx of pre-war days, Humphreys, Hardinge, Seymour, Woolley, Hubble, Dillon was missing. Moreover one can't have it both ways: any side that goes for runs as Kent habitually did is bound to take risks and there will be days when things go wrong. Still they were always a menace to the best sides and a delight to watch.

Freeman's regular career began when he was thirty-one and he did not reach his best till he was forty. Yet he took 3,359 wickets for Kent at 14.45. Six years in succession and seven times in all he took 200 wickets for the county: twice he exceeded 250. With a high arm, but owing to his small stature a relatively low trajectory, he was almost impossible to reach full-toss: perhaps only Duleepsinhji succeeded in doing so. He relied mainly on a leg-break pitched on the leg or middle-and-leg, which had therefore to be played, and a top-spinner which was notoriously difficult to spot: the googly he used sparingly. Two lessons he may have for the present generation. In the opinion of those who played with him so far was he from being over-bowled that the enormous amount of bowling he had to do helped him to be always at his best: certainly he hated being taken off.

Secondly, the only players who really mastered him were those who used their feet.

For a few years after the Great War Woolley was still a fine bowler, but otherwise, until the arrival of Doug Wright, the only other bowler of real distinction was that great spinner, 'Father' Marriott, who, like Carr before him, was available only in August.

Batting there was in abundance. Besides Woolley and Hardinge there was for a few years still Seymour, then Ashdown, a beautiful all-round stroke player who twice exceeded 300 in a county match, Todd, who with a different temperament might have been an England all-rounder, and Fagg, whom some at the outset expected to be better than Hutton and who is the only man to have made two scores of over 200 in the same county match. A greater personality than any of these was Les Ames, the best batsman-wicket-keeper that England has ever had. A wonderful runner between the wickets, he was very quick on his feet and a terror to slow bowlers, while acknowledged to be a great player of fast bowling. In his hundredth hundred, made when he was forty-five, he was actually moving down the wicket to drive the fast bowlers. Kent may have had more spectacular keepers but never a safer one and, playing for a side which depended largely on spin, he produced some remarkable records. For several years now he has been Secretary-Manager to the club.

Of amateur batsmen between the wars the supply was unfailing. From pre-war days there survived A. P. Day and C. S. Hurst: then came A. F. Bickmore, C. P. Johnstone, L. P. Hedges, the three Bryans, B. S. Cumberlege, A. J. Evans, C. H. Knott, B. H. Valentine, G. B. Legge, A. M. Crawley, I. Akers-Douglas, J. G. W. Davies and F. G. H. Chalk. Above all there was Percy Chapman. His prime was all too brief and his great years for Kent were 1926 to 1928. After that he became wilder: the head was more in the air, the foot farther from the ball and the incomparable eye was beginning to go. But at Maidstone in 1927 against Lancashire he made 260 in just over three hours, the last 176 of them in one hour fifty minutes: in the last quarter of an hour he made over 50. Never can Macdonald and Dick Tyldesley have received such treatment. Yet even so Chapman is better remembered for his superb fielding and inspiring captaincy: there have been few greater tragedies than the rapid decline of his health and his early death.

The last outstanding cricketer produced by Kent between the wars was Doug Wright, almost as great an enigma as Freeman. Freeman's Test record bears no relation to his county record: Wright's record, whether in Test or county cricket, bears none to his reputation. Yet the truth is that for years he was reckoned to have the best chance of completely defeating a great batsman well set of any bowler in the world. It was this that kept him in Test cricket. Far faster than Freeman and lacking his deadly top-spinner, he relied largely on a leg-break which turned so fiercely and rose so sharply that it tended to beat the wicket as well as the bat. The most charming and modest of men, he was the first professional to be the regularly appointed captain of Kent and is now much valued and greatly loved as coach at Charterhouse.

On Kent cricket since 1946 there is little temptation to dwell. It is not so much the dreary succession of positions well in the lower half of the Championship that discourages one, it is the dreary type of cricket played and played only too often by imported players. Luckily there have been in the last two or three years signs of a revival and in particular the fielding has reached a high standard; yet consistent success still eludes the side.

The twenty years since the war have produced only two players of the highest class, Godfrey Evans and Colin Cowdrey. The experts may argue about Evans's exact place among the great wicket-keepers, but two things are certain: no wicket-keeper has ever so far outstripped his contemporaries and none has contributed so much to keeping alive any game in which he played. There will always, too, be many who believe that he had it in him to be a great batsman had he taken his batting a little more seriously.

Of Cowdrey also there are many who feel that, great as he is, he might be greater. It seems impossible that a bowler should ever keep within bounds one who is so immensely strong whether off his back foot or his front, who plays so straight and so close to his legs and who is such a fine on-side player; and indeed on his great days few bowlers can do so. No bowler likes being dealt with as Cowdrey can deal with him or bowls so well if he is. Alas! too many of his innings both for Kent and England have been played at a time when his failure would mean disaster for the side. How different his approach might have been had he come in after Hardinge and Ashdown, with Woolley, Ames and Chapman to follow! Still, at his best he and he alone of recent Kent players can remind one of the great days of the past.

WELCOME WEST INDIES [1966]

Champions of the World

BY SIR LEARIE CONSTANTINE

The English cricket world looked forward with keen anticipation to the arrival of the 1966 West Indian tourists, accurately described in the essay's sub-title in the Almanack of that spring as champions of the world. The islanders had also made progress of a different but far more significant kind. Since the accession of Frank Worrell, their captains were selected on purely cricketing grounds, a fundamental right which had been denied them down the century by the paternalism of the empire-builders. The essay recites a few comic facts about past anomalies in this connection but its author drops no hint of his own part in the advance of the West Indian cause. And now Worrell was knighted for services to the game as was the author of the essay, the same Constantine who in 1933 had pioneered a well-worn trail when he came to England to combine his law studies with a career as a league professional in Lancashire.

On paper the 1966 tourists looked invincible, with batsmen of the calibre of Butcher, Kanhai and Nurse, an attack led by Hall, Griffith and Lance Gibbs and a captain in Garfield Sobers who may well have been the greatest all-rounder in history. In the event the tourists won easily, playing some brilliant cricket and thrilling the large crowds who flocked to see them. Sobers finished the series with over 700 runs, including three hundreds and an average of 103 and also took twenty wickets. The extent to which the England batsmen fulfilled Constantine's hope was limited. Graveney and Milburn were successful. In retrospect, it can be seen that the dramatic note of the tour was struck when the Worcestershire all-rounder Basil D'Oliveira forced his way into the England side for the second Test at Lord's and held his place for the rest of the series. The cloud was tiny, but it was in time to cast its shadow over the entire cricketing world.

THE West Indies cricket flag flies on high for West Indies are the champions of the cricket world. How has this come about? It was not achieved without hard work and dedication.

The first team to visit West Indies from England went out in 1895, captained by R. Slade Lucus. It could be justly said that this tour evoked such interest and enthusiasm in the West Indies that the ground work was laid for the evolution and progress of cricket in the Caribbean. I remember this well from conversation with my father for he played against that side. West Indies cricket held such promise that they were invited by M.C.C. to tour England in 1900. Aucher Warner, brother of Sir Pelham, was captain and matches were played against the weaker counties with a modicum of success.

The West Indies came again in 1906 with a much better side and two of their cricketers, Sidney Smith and Charlie Ollivierre, remained to qualify for Northamptonshire and Derbyshire respectively. On the 1900 tour, my father, Lebrun, was first wicket-keeper and on the second tour he came as an all-rounder. This tour saw the emergence of George Challenor and it was said that after W. G. Grace had seen him make a few runs he remarked to H. B. G. Austin, 'Keep your eyes on that boy, he is almost certain to do great things in the future.' Challenor was then eighteen years old and how right was W. G. Subsequent performances of George Challenor earned him the reputation of being the West Indies' best ever opening batsman and indicated how knowledgeable was W. G. in the finer arts of cricket.

The 1906 team was captained by H. B. G. Austin who came from Barbados. Aucher Warner, the 1900 captain, hailed from Trinidad. Cricket has always been the game they worshipped in Barbados and since 1895 to the present day top-class batting has constantly flourished in the island. The names Austin, Goodman, Cox, Challenor, Ince, Tarilton Francis, Griffith (H. C.) all adorn the history pages of West Indies cricket. It is no accident that at the present time G. S. Sobers, C. C. Hunte, Sir

Frank Worrell, Clyde Walcott and Everton Weekes are all Barbadians; add to those Wesley Hall, Charlie Griffith, and Seymour Nurse and the strength of Barbados cricket can be seen.

The next visit of M.C.C. in 1912–13 under A. W. F. Somerset brought out some high-class county players: Razor Smith, A. E. Relf, E. Humphreys and Sidney Smith, himself a West Indian, forming the backbone of the team. My own recollections of the visit, I was about eleven, brings back memories of my father's duck. He was bowled down by Sidney Smith first ball which he described to me as an in-swinger; I remember my father saying that he had never received a ball that did so much in the air in the West Indies, but he recalled a similar one bowled to him by George Hirst in 1906 when West Indies played Yorkshire at Harrogate. The gloom which the 1912 duck cast over our home from my mother downwards had to be experienced to be believed.

The 1914–18 war suspended international tours and cricket in the West Indies depended for progress on the inter-colonial tournament between Barbados, Trinidad and British Guiana, the system being that the cup-holders played against the victors of the first match. During those years, Jamaica was too far from the other three cricket centres to participate. This was one of the great handicaps to progress in West Indies cricket.

All the Islands are divided from each other by sea and very often in those far off days the Jamaican players selected to tour the United Kingdom would be unknown to the others until they joined the boat or met each other in England. The introduction of fast ships and the air-liners have happily brought an end to this unsatisfactory state of affairs. The tournament has now been extended to include Jamaica and is called 'Inter-territorial', fitting into an aura of independence and a growing nationalism.

So it was not until 1923 that West Indies again visited England, this time under H. B. G. Austin and including G. Challenor, P. H. Tarilton, H. W. Ince and G. Francis. Austin and Challenor were no strangers to England. From Trinidad there came George Dewhurst, George John, Joe Small, Victor Pascall and myself; from British Guiana, C. R. Browne, C. V. Hunter and Maurice Fernandes; from Jamaica, J. K. Holt, R. K. Nunes and R. L. Phillips.

We were told by our captain that if we played up to our West Indies form there was no county of which we should be afraid. Alas! The cold, plus the strange conditions and the fact that we were not welded into a side played havoc with our chances and we did not live up to those expectations. Austin was away for a long time through illness, and Nunes, who captained the side in his absence, had a pathetic faith in Pascall and Francis, and the performance in the field deteriorated.

We managed to beat Surrey, however, played a great match against Lancashire and finished at Scarborough in fine style against H. D. G. Leveson-Gower's XI. It was this showing which finally brought us Test Match status and is worthy of recapitulation. Leveson Gower had got together J. B. Hobbs, G. T. S. Stevens, Ernest Tyldesley, J. W. H. T.

Douglas, A. P. F. Chapman, Wilfred Rhodes, P. G. H. Fender, F. T. Mann, Cecil Parkin, F. W. Gilligan and himself. The match for us had considerations other than avoiding defeat. Counting preliminary games before we appeared in our first official match at Cambridge, John had taken 94 wickets, Francis 93 and Browne 96 and this was our last match. What a match it turned out to be!

After we had been dismissed for 110, our batting failed as usual, Hobbs and Stevens opened and when Stevens had got off the mark with a single, Francis sent his middle stump somersaulting into the air. All the England XI knew that John and Francis were after their targets and we did well to dismiss this powerful combination for 218. Francis and John each took four wickets so that Francis now had 97 and John 98.

As we could muster only 135 at our second attempt, England needed only 28 runs to win and apart from the fact that this was our last day's cricket in England, Austin had taunted Francis and John about their fast bowling. They were determined to give the batsmen a lively time. Hobbs with his elegance and his vast experience was obviously the danger, but Francis put a little extra pace into one delivery, it kept low and Hobbs, trying to turn it round the corner was l.b.w. with the total three. Next Stevens played a forcing stroke a little bit in the air past the square leg umpire where John threw himself sideways to take Francis to 99.

Soon John went to 99. With the score at 14, Tyldesley edged him into the slips where Browne, throwing himself forward, picked up a catch two inches from the ground. Rhodes had a bad time against the great pace of John before at the other end he edged one to the wicket-keeper, departed for nought, and Francis had got his 100 wickets. Chapman pushed a two past me at cover; then John removed his off stump and he too claimed his 100 wickets.

At this juncture the score-board read 16 for five and we felt that the match was our's. Five wickets remained and the England XI still needed 12 to win. John and Francis, at best, gave nothing away.

Mann, of giant stature, came in and the field spread. He was a terrific hitter and we all knew it. John bowled a full toss when in search of a yorker and Mann put all his power into a cover drive. I was there and it was a certain four if I missed it, so I collected and had it back at Dewhurst, our wicket-keeper, before Mann could move a yard. After the match, Mann asked to look at my hand and it was truly swollen. There was a bump at the back of the right hand where it remained for months.

Mann now faced Francis; he pushed forward and John at short-leg did not have to move: 19 for six. Fender succeeded Mann, joining Douglas who was playing with great assurance, and it was on Fender edging Francis over the slips that this grand match ended with West Indies losing by four wickets. The England XI's final total was 31 for six. The tour was over and our cricket firmly established. When we returned again in 1928, West Indies had joined England, Autralia and South Africa in the upper strata of Test cricket, but we still had much to learn for England won the three Tests by wide margins.

It was in 1935 when R. E. S. Wyatt took the M.C.C. side to the Caribbean that West Indies for the first time emerged triumphant, winning two matches to England's one with one drawn. This series saw E. A. Martindale, who had made his first tour to England in 1933, blossom out into a bowler of terrific speed. I shall never forget seeing Bob Wyatt move into a ball pitched inches outside the off stump which he expected to move away, but this one came in and gave him such a crack on the jaw that it broke it. This was a very strong team with Wally Hammond, Jack Iddon, Leslie Ames, Ken Farnes, W. Farrimond, Patsy Hendren, Eric Hollies, Errol Holmes, Maurice Leyland and big Jim Smith. It could be safely said that the West Indies were on their way to big things.

George Headley, who had a tremendous tour in 1933, maintained his form, and with the fast bowling of L. G. Hylton, Martindale, A. Fuller and myself, and left-hander C. H. Moodie thrown in we proved to be too good for England.

How can one do justice to George Headley, one of the greatest batsmen the world has known? How did he attain his perfection in timing and stroke-making with his ready eagerness to get the ball away, yet never appearing to possess a semblance of rashness? George had a two-eyed stance, or so it seemed, but the intelligent observer could have seen that as the bowler was about to get up to the crease to deliver the ball, George had so adjusted himself that he was standing sideways and ready for all eventualities. He shuffled on his right foot, moving it back, but only just, and was in focus as he used to say. He was ready to hook, drive and cut. Indeed, he employed all the strokes. He used his feet as well as anyone who ever played the game and as far as I could discover J. T. Tyldesley alone stood comparison with him. One thing was outstanding—his absolutely straight bat.

Headley established a standard for balanced West Indies batsmanship which was outstanding for his generation. He was never coached; he copied no one and so was original in every sense. I watched an innings of 61 by George in 1939 against Yorkshire at Harrogate on a rain-affected wicket. Hedley Verity was at his most impish; but George hooked, drove, cut and jumped down the crease in a manner that was thrilling to see. When he was eventually out, caught at extra cover by Maurice Leyland off Verity, the crowd rose to him in tribute to a Master.

Notwithstanding the great success of the three Ws, Worrell, Weekes and Walcott, if I had to pick a batsman to bat for my life on any type of wicket I could not leave it in safer hands than those of Headley. No wonder the uncoached and original Bradman was often labelled the white Headley.

The 1939 tour of England by the West Indies was a big disappointment. R. S. Grant, brother of G. C., led the side. We still had Headley at his best, but he almost carried the batting and on paper our bowling appeared formidable with a fine battery of speed in Hylton, Tyrrel Johnson, Martindale and myself, backed up by C. B. Clarke, J. H. Cameron and Grant himself bowling off-breaks. England won one and two were drawn.

The next tour to the West Indies in 1947–48 found G. O. Allen's team battling to no avail against the powerful West Indies batting and bowling. West Indies won two and two were drawn. M.C.C. for the only time in their history did not win a single match on the whole tour.

West Indies consolidated their gains in their 1950 tour of England. In earlier years the fast bowlers did most of the work and carried the brunt of the attack. This tour saw the emergence of the spin-twins, Sonny Ramadhin and Alf Valentine, and the advent abroad of the three Ws. John Goddard, the captain, had a simple task to perform. All he had to do was find someone to open the bowling, take the gloss off the new ball, and then hand it to the spin-twins. In the only match lost, the first Test at Old Trafford, he directed his wicket-keeper, Walcott, to remove his pads and open the bowling before he gave over to the twins.

The Ws dominated the batting. Openers A. F. Rae and J. B. Stollmeyer did a grand job clearing the way and with the middle order batting of R. J. Christiani, Gerry Gomez and Goddard himself, the superiority of the West Indies could not be denied. Up to this point, four Tests were played; prior and up to 1933 the number was three, but after our success for the first time in England, in 1950, we were brought into line with England and Australia and accorded the honour and right of five Tests.

Sir Leonard Hutton took the 1953–54 side to the West Indies; won two, lost two and drew one. This was a notable performance by England who recovered after losing the first two matches. They won the third, drew the fourth in Trinidad and finally won the fifth in Jamaica. A remarkable tribute to Hutton's leadership.

West Indies were back again in England in 1957 and, alas, Goddard did not have the answer to the new technique the batsmen employed in playing Ramadhin with the pad and front foot. The side were not as well knit as they might have been and these inadequacies were never overcome. England won three Tests and the other two were drawn. Peter May took the 1959–60 M.C.C. side to the West Indies and gained the only victory, four Tests being undecided.

Then came Frank Worrell to England in 1963. No more popular side has ever toured the old country (I quote George Duckworth). With many thousands of the coloured population from the Caribbean having emigrated to the big cities of Great Britain the cricketers received plenty of support from their own people. They flocked to the grounds and their good humour and incessant banter helped to keep the game alive. Garfield Sobers was the leading performer in his all-round capacity and he had plenty of batting help from Conrad Hunte, Rohan Kanhai, Basil Butcher and Joe Solomon. Wesley Hall and Charles Griffith provided the shock pace attack and Lance Gibbs did telling work with his skilful off-spin. With West Indies winning three Tests to England's one, they regained their supremacy and were the first holders of the Wisden Trophy, inaugurated to celebrate the centenary edition of this Almanack. Worrell, the first black man to captain West Indies, received an even higher award in the shape of a knighthood.

The advent of Worrell as captain changed the whole philosophy and structure of West Indies cricket and for the first time in the history of the Tests one resulted in a tie. When R. B. Simpson led the Australians in the West Indies in 1964–65, Sobers, another black man, captained the home team, and the whole story of those encounters can be found in the report of the tour. Suffice here to state that West Indies firmly established themselves as the World's Cricket Champions.

I have always held the view that until 1950 the West Indies rarely played the cricket of which they were capable. Several times in England and Australia we showed our form, and in one or two Tests the potential came to the surface, but never was the consistency equal to the ability our players possessed.

The West Indies player was never a rich person. He was lucky if he had a decent job. Often he was unable to take in the Inter-Colonial tournament because he could not afford it. Consequently, a player owed his selection for an overseas tour to two or three innings, possibly only one. Then, the selection committee did not travel and the judgment of the local pundits had to be accepted, coloured as it might be with local patriotism. I do not exaggerate the difficulties at all.

When in 1930–31 we met the M.C.C. in the West Indies, Headley was the only selection from Jamaica. Neither F. R. Martin nor O. C. Scott made the trip. C. R. Browne played in the first Test but he could not spare the time from his legal practice to travel to Trinidad. In the British Guiana Test, G. N. Francis who had not played either in Trinidad or Barbados came into the side but Herman Griffith could not go. In Jamaica neither Francis, nor C. R. Browne nor I could go. On top of that, E. L. G. Hoad captained the side in the Test in Barbados, N. Betancourt in Trinidad, M. P. Fernandes in British Guiana and R. K. Nunes in Jamaica.

Had we been welded into a team with some spirit we would probably have lost the first Test in Barbados and won the rest. When we went to Australia in 1930–31, Jack Grant came straight from Cambridge to captain West Indies. He did not know our cricket and had not even seen many members of his side. The trouble was not finished there, for when the tour was at an end, Grant went to Rhodesia, L. S. Birkett retired from cricket, I went back to Nelson and Francis to Seaham Harbour. So we never played as a side until the advent of the three Ws and 'those little pals of mine' in 1950.

The question of appointing a captain was a major engagement for the Board of Control. The coloured man was not good enough, and in fact 'no coloured player would play happily under him' it was said. This stupidly went on until the advent of Sir Frank Worrell, and apart from the 1950 side which could almost captain itself, it was under Sir Frank Worrell that West Indies became established.

Two incidents which I shall relate give some idea of the frustration cricket has gone through in the West Indies. In 1925 I had a disagreement with the Queen's Park Cricket Club of Trinidad. Following a bout of illness, I regained fitness and was asked by Barbados would I come, if selected, for the first match against England. I agreed. I never went. I did not receive the final invitation. When H. B. G. Austin came to Trinidad for the second 'Test' he questioned me about my fitness. I answered truthfully and he insisted I should play in the Trinidad matches. I did so and was selected for the 'Tests' thereafter. The story I learned years after was that a telegram was sent from Trinidad to Barbados after the early inquiry: 'If any player invited by you unfit, cable course to follow.' Barbados replied, 'Omit him'. That was the pretext for my missing the first 'Test'.

In 1934–35, the first series won by the West Indies—I was in Nelson and never received an invitation. I went to India and returned two days before Christmas when I got a phone call from Sir Pelham Warner, inviting me to go to the West Indies for the series against England. I agreed and left on Boxing Day by boat, so missing the first Test in Barbados. I was therefore informed that when the West Indies required M.C.C. to forgo some financial loss which might be occasioned on the tour, Sir Pelham refused on the grounds that they had not utilised the services of one of their drawing cards, and he would not agree to write off anything unless they invited me. So in fact M.C.C. invited me and we won the rubber for the first time.

In a sense we have never looked back and good luck to Garfield Sobers and his talented men of 1966. This should be another great series, especially if England attack the bowling like they have just done in Australia.

COUNTIES REJECT THE CLARK PLAN
[1967]

BY CHARLES BRAY

In spite of the tremendous national excitement during the series against the West Indies, an excitement fanned by the rapidly increasing new audience for ball-by-ball television coverage, it was glaringly obvious by 1967 that the bread-and-butter cricket of the English summer was heading towards extinction and bankruptcy at an alarming rate. Gone were the balmy days of 1947, when the sun shone down on more than two million happy heads. Instead, the day-to-day county matches were becoming sporting backwaters, especially during the week, when a nation obliged to earn its living could all too rarely find the time for a day at the cricket. Football had long since usurped the crown of the National Game, especially after the World Cup win of 1966. In the burgeoning industry of advertising it was the star footballers, not their cricketing counterparts, who were in demand.

What to do? Appoint a committee. And what to do then? Reject everything the committee recommended. The truth was that the structure of the game, with its seventeen first-class counties, the two varsities, the annual Test matches, and the winter tours was sanctified by its own antiquity, although in fact Glamorgan had only entered the charmed circle as recently as 1921. Even the really sacrosanct aspects, such as the six-ball over were comparatively modern amendments. The English game had always been alive to the need for adjustment and renovation. But now it seemed as though the very idea of extinction was so horrific that it assumed the shape of nothing more serious than a bad dream. Hypnotised by intimations of their own immortality, the administrators preferred to drift on. The message to the Clark Committee was 'No Change', a response as fatal as it was predictable. Yet again the truth of Rowland Bowen's observation that cricket was not, nor ever had been, self-supporting, was being brought home. The old ways of patronage were drying up. The new ways had not yet been found. As the 1960s drifted to a close, English cricket found itself in the worst economic trough of its history. But no county committee did anything to stop the rot. The number of overs bowled each day continued to fall, the number of substandard pitches continued to rise. The commitment of some professionals seemed at times to be invisible. And the crowds rolled up in their tens of thousands—to other forms of diversion.

And yet the paralysis was perfectly understandable. It may be that the arrangements for English first-class cricket as they stood in the period between the wars were as perfect, or at any rate as little imperfect, as human ingenuity could contrive. Counties were buttressed by private donations and supported by faithful crowds. Test matches were still rare enough to take on the lineaments of homeric encounters. The great milestones all beckoned and were occasionally reached—3,000 runs in a season, 200 wickets in a season, a thousand runs in May. And apart from the physical beauty of the game, there were the statistics, column after column of ravishing figures, percentages, aggregates, analyses, averages. Which sport other than cricket could ever have nurtured a learned society dedicated, not to the study of the game, but to the study of the statistics of the game? If reform were to get out of hand, if the County Championship should be broken up into zones or divisions, if the number of fixtures were to be reduced, not only would the time-honoured statistical landscape be amended beyond recognition, but even the old figures would lose all relevance to what was happening day to day. The administrators desperately needed to embrace drastic reform. And being, contrary to popular rumour, human, they shirked it, waiting like a certain immortal optimist for something to turn up.

THE Clark Committee's bold plan to give the County Championship a new look was killed before it was born. Its main recommendation, which was to alter the existing championship and create an additional one of one-day games, was defeated by 16 votes to 4, a majority so emphatic that the counties may have signed their own death warrant.

Only time will tell. A mountain of labour produced a mouse of achievement. The only change the counties would sanction was a slight alteration in this 1967 season in the points scoring system (eight for a win and four for a first-innings lead) and a reduction in the qualifying period for an overseas player from two years to twelve months.

It would be as well at the outset, to give the reasons for the setting up of the sub-committee. Then to examine its composition, the manner in which it went about its work and finally the two reports which caused such widespread interest and controversy.

In 1950 close on 2,000,000 people paid to see championship cricket in this country. In 1966 the figure had dropped to 513,578. In the early 'fifties the decline was steady but not unduly alarming. Then the tempo increased at an alarming rate until in recent years it became positively frightening. Worse still was the abrupt halt in the overall increase in membership. In 1964 members totalled 141,707. In 1965 139,964 and in 1966 135,045. To combat the double drop in revenue, counties were compelled to increase subscriptions, which in itself caused a drop in membership.

It was then obvious to all, except those with their heads firmly buried in the sand, that first-class cricket in this country was only solvent because of the efforts of supporters' clubs with football pools and Test match profits.

An exhaustive and detailed investigation with perhaps drastic action was imperative, and a committee under the chairmanship of Mr. David Clark was set up. Its terms of reference couldn't have been wider. They were 'to examine the future of County cricket in the widest possible terms and if thought fit to recommend alterations in the structure and playing conditions of the County Championship'.

The sky was the limit and the men chosen to carry out the job combined playing, business and administrative experience. In view of certain criticism made of the Committee and its report, let us examine the respective members' qualifications.

D. G. CLARK, Chairman of the Kent Cricket Committee, former captain of the county. Took M.C.C. team to India in the winter of 1963–64. A successful farmer.

G. O. ALLEN, Treasurer of the M.C.C., who has had more experience of cricket administration than anyone in the world. Former England captain and Test cricketer. A stockbroker.

E. R. DEXTER, former captain of England and Sussex. One of the most dynamic batsmen in English cricket for many years. Several business interests, including close-circuit television.

D. J. INSOLE, Chairman of the England Test Selection Committee, former captain of Essex. Vice-chairman of Essex. Holds important position with well-known firm of contractors and property developers.

A. B. SELLERS, Captain of Yorkshire from 1933 to 1947. A former Test selector. Chairman of Yorkshire Cricket Committee. Runs a printing business in Bradford.

W. S. SURRIDGE, Chairman of Surrey Cricket Committee. A former and highly successful Surrey captain. Head of sports goods manufacturing firm.

E. H. KING, Chairman of Warwickshire. Partner in well-known firm of accountants in Birmingham. Financial adviser to Aston Villa F.C.

O. S. WHEATLEY, The Glamorgan captain.

F. J. TITMUS, Middlesex captain and Test cricketer.

C. G. HOWARD, Manager of several M.C.C. Overseas tours, former secretary of Lancashire. Now Surrey secretary.

K. C. TURNER, Northamptonshire secretary.

F. M. TURNER, Leicestershire secretary.

C. BRAY, Cricket correspondent of a national daily newspaper for 30 years. Played for Essex 1928–38. Reported cricket all over the world. Five tours of Australia, four of West Indies, and three of South Africa.

Ill health prevented Mr. F. M. Turner from attending many meetings and he resigned before the final report was drafted.

The sub-committee held its first meeting in September 1965 and its last in January 1967. Seven meetings were held during the 1965–66 winter. It restarted work in October 1966, met five times and submitted its final report.

To obtain the maximum amount of evidence and data, the sub-committee's first step was to circularise all the counties with a vast questionnaire. This had six main headings: (1) *Pitches*, (2) *Playing conditions*, (3) *Conduct of and approach to the game by players*, (4) *Structure of County cricket*, (5) *Sunday cricket*, (6) *Test matches*. Over thirty pertinent questions were asked and the counties also given the opportunity of offering their own solutions to the various problems.

An analysis of the replies showed that only three counties were satisfied that they had been able to produce fast, true wickets. Only four were entirely satisfied with the approach to the game of their own players and those satisfied with their opponents' approach were two. Seven were in favour of the existing structure. Eight were not satisfied and two were not sure. For Sunday cricket there was an overwhelming majority.

The sub-committee was unanimous in its belief that sub-standard pitches produced sub-standard cricket, a view well supported later by the capped players. Its next step was to call all the county groundsmen to Lord's for a conference. Much opinion and evidence was gathered at this meeting.

Each member of the sub-committee not only answered the questionnaire which had been sent to the counties but also submitted a paper giving in detail his own ideas as to the best way to re-orientate county cricket and put it back on its financial feet, as well as making the game more attractive to the spectator.

It was apparent from these individual papers that there existed in the sub-committee just as wide a divergence of opinion as there was outside. Yet on two major issues—pitches, and the approach to the game by the players—there was complete agreement. It was felt that pitches must be improved and counties should see to it that they were.

To improve the players' approach was a more intricate and delicate matter. The sub-committee, however, was convinced that it was the key factor and in both reports laid great emphasis on the need for an immediate improvement.

Derbyshire in a lengthy statement giving reasons for rejecting the sub-committee's new structure proposals, supported this view in the most forthright terms. 'It is, however, quite clear', the county declared, 'that ultimately an improvement will only follow through very tough action when necessary by County Committees through their captain.'

One does not recall any such action being taken by Derbyshire, or for that matter by any other county with the possible exception of Yorkshire, who on more than one occasion have disciplined a player. Even their action was not directed against the wrong approach to the actual playing of the game but to club discipline off the field rather than on it.

During the summer of 1966 the 'Daily Mail', at the request of the sub-committee, commissioned the National Opinion Polls to carry out a national survey, the object of which was 'to investigate the reasons for the fall in crowds at county grounds and in particular to find out how far the causes of it may be (*a*) counter attractions and present national social habits and (*b*) a feeling that there are defects in the game as a spectator sport on account of the way in which it is played or organised'.

This vast document was of immense value to the sub-committee. In addition, counties were asked to carry out a postal survey of their members, in order to elicit more fully the possible contrast between the opinion of members and that of the cricket-watching public covered in the N.O.P. report.

Still with the object of getting the widest possible evidence and opinion, the sub-committee had a questionnaire sent to all 'capped' players. Well over a hundred replied.

They were almost unanimous that modern pitches were largely to blame for the dull cricket and that modern first-class cricket was not good entertainment. It was significant that of the various suggestions alterations in the structure of the County Championship the players were emphatically against all but the one finally recommended by the Clark committee.

The counties for their part produced some remarkable suggestions. Hampshire were so satisfied with the *status quo* that they didn't want any change for at least three years, despite the state of their finances.

Glamorgan, whose secretary greeted the Clark report with 'it's a lot of tommy rot' were in favour of leaving well alone, although the county lost £10,539 in 1966 and their gate receipts were £6,573 less than in the previous season. They were £5,344, the lowest since the war. A similar reduction this season would see the county paying spectators to watch its cricket.

Sussex went even further than Glamorgan. They suggested even more first-class cricket. In other words they want to give the public more of something of which, by its decreasing support, it has shown that it has too much already.

Gloucestershire put forward an interesting programme, which staggered championship matches to one a week in May, June, and mid-July and then increased the number to two a week until the end of August. They also suggested that the qualification period for one overseas star player should be the period of one playing season, rather than twelve calendar months.

Derbyshire wanted no change and their main reason was that in their opinion they would lose ten per cent of their members. The Northamptonshire chairman put the loss at fifty per cent.

The Clark Committee considered at great length the effect fewer matches might have on membership. It agreed in the end that the loss would not be anything like as big as estimated.

Unless something drastic was done to increase revenue counties would be compelled to go on increasing members' subscriptions. That would have a much greater effect on membership than a reduction in the amount of cricket.

The Clark Committee found overwhelming evidence in favour of Sunday championship cricket. It could and would be a decisive factor in increasing revenue, but it could not be assumed that it would be legalised by 1968, the earliest that any major alteration in the Championship could be made.

At the same time Sunday play was not a complete solution. A serious attempt had to be made: (*a*) to get a more positive and enthusiastic approach by the players, (*b*) to produce a structure that would cause a revival of public interest, and (*c*) to find ways and means of attracting more players into county cricket. In other words to establish a pyramid by which the budding first-class player could graduate from club to county without having to make first-class cricket his sole occupation, as he must do under existing conditions.

The Clark Committee felt that its proposals would be the first definite step towards achieving that end.

The counties have decided otherwise. That was their prerogative, their right. But in doing so they have taken upon their own shoulders the full responsibility of saving our national summer sport.

One may well ask, 'What next?' Few can be so sanguine as to believe that first-class cricket is going to recover on its own. A failure of football pools and most counties would be bankrupt.

Despite the rejection of its report the Clark Committee did not work in vain. It gathered and analysed vital statistics and opinions. It stimulated interest by the controversial nature of its recommendations and it must have awakened the counties to the seriousness of the present situation and their responsibility to do something about it.

NOTTINGHAMSHIRE'S NOTABLE PART IN THE GROWTH OF CRICKET [1967]

BY R. T. SIMPSON

By 1967 the Trent Bridge lobby must have been wondering what it had done to incur the wrath of Wisden which had by now published histories of every county club in the Championship bar the side which had featured George Parr, Alfred Shrewsbury, Richard Daft, the Hardstaffs, the Gunns, Larwood and Voce. The answer is to be found in the arbitrary methods of the county history series, which had begun in the first postwar edition with Surrey. One by one the counties had been honoured, their story described by some distinguished cricket writers, from Cardus and Peebles to Gilligan and Kilburn. The publication of Mr. Arrowsmith's Kent memoir in 1966 had left Nottinghamshire in something less than splendid isolation, so it was a welcome sight to pick up the 1967 Almanack and find there a comprehensive history of the county, compiled by one of its greatest postwar players. In approaching the history of his club, R. T. Simpson was undoubtedly haunted by the ghost of the essayist-critic Edward Verrall Lucas (1868–1938), whose copious writings on the same theme made him the unofficial historian of the club. Perhaps also Simpson recalled one of the great Cardusian flourishes in describing Trent Bridge as 'a Lotos-land for batsmen, a place where it was always afternoon and 360 for two wickets'.

It is perhaps worth paying a slightly more fulsome tribute than Simpson's to the fast bowler Fred Morley, who died at the age of 33. At the end of the 1882 season Morley was among the party led by the Hon. Ivo Bligh which set sail for Australia on board the S.S. 'Peshawur' with the intention of regaining the Ashes. Off Colombo the 'Peshawur' collided with the barque 'Conroy', and Morley suffered serious damage to his ribs. Although he played on the tour he never recovered from his injuries and died from them within a year. Another annotation concerns William Gunn (1858–1921), one of the first double internationals, whose play as a forward with Notts County earned him two England caps.

A LTHOUGH it is not known when cricket was first played in Nottinghamshire there are records of a match in 1771 between Nottingham and Sheffield, which suggests that the game had already flourished in the county for many years. Between 1771 and 1867 twenty-eight matches are known to have taken place between the two towns, Nottingham winning 17, Sheffield eight and the remaining three drawn. Unfortunately, it cannot be said that the spirit of the game was high in the list of priorities in these matches, many of which were played for money and the rivalry being keen, bad blood and ill feeling often resulted.

M.C.C. COME TO NOTTINGHAM

Not even the dates of the inauguration or disbandment of the Nottingham Old Club have survived, but in 1791 an event occurred which must be regarded as a red-letter mark in the county's history for in August of that year they were visited by the M.C.C. Although this now famous club had been in existence for only four years its fame had spread from one end of the country to the other, and even then its position as the recognised head of the game was firmly established. On this occasion, although the play of the Nottinghamshire cricketers excited the admiration and applause of their opponents they were nevertheless defeated by ten wickets, being unacquainted with the system of playing adopted by the Marylebone Club.

The first captain of the Nottingham club was J. Gilbert and perhaps one of the first of a long line of outstanding players was Thomas Warsop, an under-hand bowler, who continued for many years.

THE FATHER OF NOTTINGHAMSHIRE CRICKET

It was not until 1817, in June, that Nottinghamshire had another great day in cricket. This was when the M.C.C. sent eleven players to play Twenty-Two of Nottingham. This match aroused tremendous interest and was witnessed by 12,000 to 14,000 spectators, who paid admission charges of 2s. 6d. per day. The game was again won by the M.C.C., by 30 runs. Making his second appearance for Nottinghamshire was a young player named William Clarke, then 18 years of age, and destined to become one of the outstanding personalities of Nottinghamshire and English cricket. In this particular game he scored 1 and 0 and as far as can be judged did not bowl. However, no one in the history of Nottinghamshire cricket has stood out more prominently than William Clarke, the celebrated slow bowler, who captained the Nottingham team and, practically unaided, for many years conducted all affairs respecting the county's cricket.

He established the Trent Bridge ground, and lastly, founded and led the All England Eleven which did so much missionary work for the game. There is no doubt that he will always be recalled as one of the game's chief characters and exponents, and his career was an unusually long and busy one. He was actually 37 when he first played at Lord's and it was not until he was 47 that he was chosen for the Players. That was in the year 1846, but all in all for 30 years he was a terror to batsmen.

Near the main gates erected in 1933 to the memory of J. A. Dixon, captain of Nottinghamshire for many years, is this inscription:

'THIS THE COUNTY GROUND OF THE NOTTINGHAMSHIRE CRICKET CLUB, FAMOUS THROUGHOUT THE WORLD AS "TRENT BRIDGE", WAS ORIGINALLY A MEADOW ADJOINING THE OLD TRENT BRIDGE INN AT THE TIME WHEN ITS LANDLORD WAS WILLIAM CLARKE, THE INCOMPARABLE SLOW BOWLER, LATER TO EARN THE HONOURED TITLE OF "FATHER OF NOTTINGHAMSHIRE CRICKET". THE GROUND, PREPARED BY HIM, WAS OPENED ON MAY 28, 1838. THE FIRST INTER-COUNTY CONTEST TO BE FOUGHT HERE BEING BETWEEN NOTTINGHAM-SHIRE AND SUSSEX ON JULY 27 AND 28, 1840. SINCE WHEN AS THE SCENE OF

NOTTINGHAMSHIRE MATCHES AND TEST MATCHES ITS HISTORY HAS BEEN STEADILY ILLUSTRIOUS.'

During Clarke's reign another great Notts player emerged, Tom Barker, one of the first of a line of fast bowlers produced by Nottinghamshire. In 1834 he had the distinction of being the first Nottinghamshire man to play in the Gentlemen v. Players match, and continued to represent the latter until 1845.

According to available records the first match to be played at Trent Bridge was on May 28, 1838, between The Forest Club and the South of the Trent; the spectators were charged an admission fee of sixpence, which was much resented by the Forest Club whose spectators were allowed to watch them on the Forest free.

THE LION OF THE NORTH

After William Clarke's death the All England Eleven was managed by George Parr, who next to Clarke was one of the greatest influences in Nottinghamshire cricket and was sometimes referred to as 'The Lion of the North'. He is immortal by reason of his leg-side hitting, which often landed the ball out of the ground, but more often than not in an elm which still stands at Trent Bridge and is affectionately known as Parr's Tree.

Next to Parr as an outstanding personality in those early days was Richard Daft, who was considered a model for the young cricketers. He was an outstanding fielder, and athlete, and a leading batsman of the time, but the actual successor to William Clarke in the bowling line was considered to be Alfred Shaw, who first played for Nottinghamshire in 1864 and whose chief asset was his great control of length and pace. Apparently he had no superior in the way of stamina and accuracy. Like many opening bowlers a large number of his great feats were accomplished with another great bowler of his day, Fred Morley, one of the mainstays of Nottinghamshire until 1884, when he died at the early age of 33, not long after touring Australia.

Morley had no successor as a fast bowler until the arrival of Tom Wass in 1896, except for the brief appearance of Frank Shacklock who made a name for himself by bowling out Surrey at The Oval in 1892 when Nottinghamshire won. To mark this shining event everyone on the winning side was given a medal and each of the professionals twenty guineas. Over 60,000 people watched this match on the first two days.

HALLAM AND WASS

Tom Wass, on his day, was considered to be the most deadly bowler in England and during his career took more wickets than any one else in the county's history, 1,679. During most of his illustrious reign the bowler at the other end was Hallam, who, with his gentle pace, provided the contrast, and the combination of Hallam and Wass became a byword with the cricketers of Nottinghamshire.

WILLIAM GUNN AND SHREWSBURY

Returning to batsmen, one of the most famous of an impressive list of great Nottinghamshire cricketers was Arthur Shrewsbury, who came into the side in 1875 at the age of 19 and continued to play until 1902. It was said that 'W. G.' was his only superior, which gives some idea of his fame in those distant years. Soon the famous partnership of Gunn and Shrewsbury was formed, and they still hold the record for the highest opening partnership for Nottinghamshire; 398 against Sussex at Trent Bridge in 1890. Shrewsbury's partner, the giant William Gunn, played for his county from 1880 to 1905, when he was succeeded by his nephew, John Gunn, the slow bowler and left-handed all-rounder, and George Gunn, his brother. Between 1895 and 1925, John Gunn made 24,601 runs, took 1,243 wickets and held 233 catches, and like many great bowlers it was said of him that on grounds which helped him he was unplayable.

GEORGE GUNN'S WONDERFUL RECORD

George Gunn, perhaps the most famous of all the Nottinghamshire batsmen, made 35,190 runs, the highest number ever reached by a Nottinghamshire cricketer and one that may well stand for all time. He was everything a batsman could be and simply played as the mood took him. Sometimes a stone-waller, sometimes pure virtuoso and sometimes, as one umpire said, he would go to sleep. Typical of the man was the occasion when the lunch hour at Trent Bridge was changed from 1.30 p.m. to 2 p.m. Almost the first time the new hours were used George happened to be still batting at 1.30 p.m. and when he saw the clock immediately started to walk towards the pavilion at the end of the appropriate over. When it was pointed out to him that lunch was 2 p.m., he returned to the crease, gave a dolly of a catch, and walked out with the remark, 'I always take my lunch at 1.30 p.m.', and this when his score was in the 90s.

Returning for a moment to the combination of William Gunn and Shrewsbury, their partnerships were particularly fruitful at Hove, where it used to be said that if Nottinghamshire won the toss all except the first four players felt free to go down to the sea to bathe. Shrewsbury's defensive powers, coupled with his inexhaustible patience, were undoubtedly the chief factors of his greatness, although his late cutting and back play were considered as near perfection as possible, and he had a favourite lofting stroke over mid-off's head which frequently brought him a couple of runs.

It was considered that because of the tactics used against him by the bowlers of his day, who apparently acknowledged him as their master, he was regarded as a slow player. Here it is interesting to note, bearing in mind the present-day theories for the causes of slow play, that it was stated in an article in 1892 regarding Shrewsbury's slow play 'That runs are much more difficult to obtain now than formerly on account of the bowlers' off theory (note 'off' theory) . . . more attractive and all-round cricket would be seen if bowlers would try and hit the wicket, instead of deliberately trying to miss it.'

ALFRED SHAW

It was also said at that time that the critics quite overlooked the fact that bowlers, just as readily as batsmen, can make play dull and uninteresting (modern captains and bowlers please note). It is interesting also to dwell on the remarks of Alfred Shaw that same year. This wise old player believed that the loss of appreciation of good play was due in part to the excitement provided for spectators at football matches and he commented, 'It will not be a good day for English cricket when batsmen are required to assimilate their style to the aspirations of the ignoramus who thinks the higher the hit the better the cricket, and who yells his approval or boos his discontent accordingly.' Interesting to know that cricket had such difficulties in 1892 and that comments such as this had to be made.

Alfred Shaw, who first played for Nottinghamshire in 1864 and continued for 23 years, was one of the greatest of all Nottinghamshire bowlers. He bowled medium pace and could turn the ball either way. Throughout his career he never sent down a wide, over half the number of overs he bowled were maidens and he accomplished the unique feat of bowling more overs to batsmen than they took runs off him. He set up a record by clean bowling 'W. G.' twenty times and was the first captain to lead a county in four successive years to the top of the Championship, 1883–86.

As Nottinghamshire's cricket is at the moment in the doldrums it is interesting to read an article written by the Editor of this illustrious Almanack in 1901, 'The outlook for Notts in the future is not hopeful and the committee must use every possible effort to discover fresh talent. For the decreased skill amongst the young players all over the county it is thought that the immense popularity of football is in some measure responsible. Cricket is now being played in the various villages and small towns with less eagerness and enthusiasm than was once the case.' The present Nottinghamshire committee should take heart from this because after that was written Nottinghamshire had some of their greatest years.

A player who should be mentioned along with William Gunn and Shrewsbury and who performed many great batting feats with this celebrated pair was William Barnes, also a fine bowler, who toured Australia three times, and who in his day was considered probably the best player of fast bowling on a hard wicket.

THE FIRST NOTED LEFT-HANDER

The first left-handed batsman of note to play for Nottinghamshire was William Henry Scotton. After starting his career as a fast scorer and hard hitter, he became the most pronounced stone-waller of his day. On one occasion in 1885 when playing for Nottinghamshire against Gloucestershire he batted for sixty minutes without scoring and in his side's innings of 291 there were 165 maidens. Nevertheless he visited Australia three times.

In 1887 and 1888 Nottinghamshire were captained by that famous wicket-keeper, Mordecai Sherwin, the last professional to do so for over 70 years. The first amateur to take control, in 1889, was J. A. Dixon, who led the team for the following ten years and in whose commemoration, as I have already mentioned, the main gates at Trent Bridge were built. In 1892 one of the most famous amateurs in the history of the game came into the side. That was A. O. Jones, who eventually formed another of those renowned opening partnerships with James Iremonger, and they proceeded to reach the hundred on no fewer than 24 occasions. Jones was a fine fielder, particularly in the gully, and his tally of catches for Nottinghamshire was over 500. His top score was 296. Iremonger played for the county from 1897 until 1921, when he became the coach until the late 'thirties, a position he held with great distinction, being recognised as the finest coach the county have ever had.

SPIRIT OF THE GAME

It is interesting to note the philosophy regarding Nottinghamshire cricket in the period between 1890 and 1900. The side ran into rather lean times and many people boldly asserted that unenterprising tactics were responsible for the lack of public support. Nevertheless, it was agreed that if a team had to choose between losing prettily and endeavouring to avoid defeat by painstaking play, the captain was thoroughly justified in adopting the latter course. So much for the spirit of the game in those days!

A most disheartening year for Nottinghamshire was 1895 when the team sank to a lower level than at any previous period in the club's history; the cricket shown was considered utterly unworthy of a side with such great traditions. Between 1873 and 1889 Nottinghamshire won the County Championship six times and shared the Championship on four other occasions. In March 1895, the club made an important appointment when they secured the services of Mr. H. Turner as secretary. He displayed much energy and under his skilful guidance the club's position improved in every respect, and apart from an increased membership and a healthier financial state, he was mainly responsible for an innovation in April 1897 that had a considerable bearing on cricket itself. An attempt was made to train young players. A staff of bowlers was attached to the ground and coached by Mr. Walter Marshall—a policy which proved most gratifying in its success almost from the moment of its inception.

One of the leading bowlers during this depressing period of Nottinghamshire's cricket was William Attewell. He alone was really reliable and did a tremendous amount of work, often taking twice as many wickets as any other bowler and at a smaller cost. Shortly after the turn of the century there appeared two more players destined to join the ranks of the more famous Nottinghamshire cricketers, Thomas William Oates, the wicket-keeper, and Joseph Hardstaff, father of perhaps an even more famous Hardstaff, young Joe. For some time it was assumed that Hardstaff senior's short stature would prevent him from developing into a first-rate player, but fortunately he was persevered with and consequently served his county and country for many years, later becoming a famous umpire.

ALLETSON'S FAMOUS INNINGS

Other names to hit the headlines before World War I were Wilfred Payton, an extremely sound player for the county for very many years, and, in particular, Edward Alletson. He achieved renown as one of the most vigorous hitters in the game and became nationally famous in 1911 for his innings of 189 out of 227 runs against Sussex at Hove in only ninety minutes. During this innings he took 34 runs off E. H. Killick in one over. Unfortunately, his successes with the bat were very rare and he lasted for only about seven seasons. Still he had been connected with the side that won the Championship again in 1907, but success on this occasion was entirely the result of the tremendous bowling of Hallam and Wass. Hallam took 156 wickets at 12.18 apiece, and Wass 163 at 14.28 apiece.

IMMENSE BATTING POWER

For sixteen years after World War I, Nottinghamshire were always well placed in the County Championship, which they won in 1929. In the early 'twenties they had a very strong batting side, including Arthur Carr, the captain, Whysall, Walker, George and John Gunn, Payton and Hardstaff senior. The chief bowlers at that time were burly Fred Barratt, Matthews, Sam Staples, the great off-spin bowler, and 'Tich' Richmond, the leg-break bowler who season after season took his hundred wickets and held the record for the greatest number of wickets in a season for the county until the advent of Bruce Dooland.

LARWOOD AND VOCE

During this period the groundsman was Walter Marshall, a character, who created pitches that were very fast and very true, the back-cloth for great fast bowlers, which were of tremendous assistance to one of the finest and perhaps easily the most famous of Nottinghamshire fast bowlers, Harold Larwood, who made his first appearance in 1925. Not long afterwards he was joined by Bill Voce, a devastating fast left-arm bowler, and with such a combination Nottinghamshire simply had to win the Championship sooner or later. It was, indeed, surprising that it happened only once whilst Nottinghamshire had this very great side. Eventually the acrimonious bodyline controversy led to the retirement of Arthur Carr and had much to do with Larwood leaving first-class cricket when he did.

In 1935 Nottinghamshire were jointly led by S. D. Rhodes and G. F. H. Heane, but thereafter the latter captained them until 1947, when he was superseded by W. A. Sime. After winning the Championship in 1929 Nottinghamshire suffered a gradual decline in their fortunes, due to a very noticeable falling off in the standard of bowling, and although the batting was still well above average with the great success of a new generation of batsmen in Keeton and Harris, who made a fine opening pair, and the beautifully upright, straight-hitting Joe Hardstaff, no new bowlers could be found apart from Harold Butler. Hardstaff could not help but enthrall anyone who watched him play. His record but for the War would have been tremendous, and as it was he scored 31,841 runs, made 83 centuries, averaged 44.34 and played in 23 Test matches—a wonderful record.

Harold Butler did sterling work for Nottinghamshire but apart from Test matches against South Africa in this country and the ill-fated tour of the West Indies in 1947, he never received the recognition that his bowling really warranted. Probably doubts regarding his fitness were the major factors. The combination of Butler and Jepson served Nottinghamshire well for many years but their bowling, particularly that of the latter, had not really the penetration to raise the side from the lower rungs of the table, and it was not until the advent of Bruce Dooland, from Australia, that this occurred.

DOOLAND'S INFLUENCE

This was the first time Nottinghamshire had broken with tradition and engaged a player from overseas. However, with his extremely accurate leg-spin bowling, coupled with his wrong 'un and 'flipper' he completely mesmerised the majority of batsmen in this country—in fact all of them in his first two years—with the result that Notts jumped from next to the bottom in the Championship to eighth place in his first year and in his second year there was a further improvement. Dooland achieved the double in 1955 and 1957, and created a Nottinghamshire record of 181 wickets in a season. His decision to return to Australia at the end of the 1957 season was a very big blow to the club, and the following years were mostly a time of lamentation and woe, the biggest disappointment to many being the fact that no young players from the county itself were showing promise.

The only bright spot in recent years was the success of Brian Bolus, obtained under special registration from Yorkshire, who scored 2,190 runs and was selected for the last two Test matches against the West Indies in 1963. His fine attacking batsmanship had a wonderful tonic effect on the side and they finished ninth in the Championship. Unfortunately this improvement has not been maintained and Nottinghamshire are once again in the throes of team building for there is still great faith in the future of Nottinghamshire cricket.

Finally, some words on Trent Bridge. It is the considered opinion of many lovers of cricket that no great cricket ground in these islands has a more charming situation than that of Trent Bridge. The accommodation and amenities for public and players alike are more than ample. The playing area exceeds six and a half acres and the wicket is one of the best, if not the best, in the country. During its existence the ground has been the scene of many very stern and heroic contests, helping to make cricket history. A match which provided a perfect example of the fact that the wicket is not so entirely one-sided as some would have us believe was the match played against the Australians in 1921. Nottinghamshire were bowled out for scores of 58 and 100, whilst Australia, thanks to a famous innings of 345 scored in four hours by Macartney, amassed the huge total of 675.

Ever since the ground was established Nottinghamshire players have been extremely fortunate in having had the opportunity to play their cricket on such a wonderful piece of turf. There was actually a period shortly after the last war when the label 'featherbed' was attached to the wicket, but that was often proved erroneous by the outstanding performance of many bowlers, especially from overseas. However, since the re-turfing took place in the late 'fifties to dispense with the marl, it has proved to be an excellent cricket wicket, culminating in the fact that in 1966 it was considered by all to be the best in the country.

MY FAVOURITE SUMMER [1967]

BY A. A. THOMSON

Arthur Alexander Thomson (1894–1968) was one of the most popular cricket writers of his day, even though of his output of more than fifty books, only a few were about his favourite game. Born in Harrogate, Thomson remained all his life an enthusiastic Yorkshireman whose passionate allegiance to his native county sometimes tempted him to dithyrambic excess when it came to the heroes of his boyhood, especially George Hirst. His love of the game was nevertheless so transparent that he was always readable, especially as a retrospective essayist rather than as a commentator on the contemporary game. His essay 'My Step-Uncle Walter' ranks among the most evocative family portraits of the modern game and if Uncle Walter never quite aspires to the Olympian heights of Neville Cardus's Aunt Beatrice, he still remains memorable. Thomson wrote under more than one name on more than one subject; apart from a series of cricket books published in his later years, he will be remembered for an outstanding autobiographical novel published in 1935 called 'The Exquisite Burden'. In 1966 he was awarded the MBE for services to sports writing.

Thomson cannot keep Uncle Walter out of his Wisden essay and clearly delights in a closing passage evoking another of his heroes, one of those men who combined a distinguished literary career with participation in cricket at all but its highest level. Not the least enjoyable aspect of 'My Favourite Summer' is the nature of the surrounding countryside. Hemmed in by controversial reviews of the Clark Report, discussions about the prevalence of illegal bowling deliveries and the problems of Indian cricket, Thomson's gentle retrospections come as a relief as well as a pleasure.

My favourite summer is 1902. I had not then played any cricket, except in the back garden, and I had never seen a first-class match. I was eight years old at the time, but my knowledge of the season was, and remains, considerable. My information came from two main sources: my step-Uncle Walter and *Wisden Cricketers' Almanack* for 1903. I learned, as history students must, partly from patriotic narrative and partly from sober factual report.

Uncle Walter, now in heaven, departed this life in 1935, not long after Yorkshire's innings defeat by Essex at Huddersfield. (At 87 he should have been sheltered from such shocks.) *Wisden* for 1903 happily sits in front of me. If the B.B.C. were to maroon me on a desert island and, according to their pleasant custom, demand to know what book I should like to take with me, there would be no difficulty. *Pickwick* I know by heart and, though I revere Tolstoi, to read *War and Peace* under the breadfruit trees would be too much like starting to watch an innings by J. W. H. T. Douglas and waking up to find that Trevor Bailey was still batting. But *Wisden* for 1903 is the perfect companion. It has almost everything the heart of man could desire.

I doubt, of course, if any historian between Macaulay and Churchill could have produced so glowing, so romantic a tale as Uncle Walter's account of the game at Headingley on June 2 and 3, 1902, in which Hirst and Rhodes dismissed the mighty Australians for 23 and Yorkshire struggled desperately towards the 48 runs needed for victory until Irving Washington, with a cannon-shot clear of mid-on, made it 50. 'Finest innings of Irving's life', Uncle Walter would conclude, 'and would you believe me if I told you he didn't even get double figures?'

Naturally I believed him, just as I believed what he told me about the Spanish Armada, the Death of Nelson, and Jessop's 101 in forty minutes, scored on our own town ground, to Uncle Walter's mingled horror and delight. One at least of these stories was an eye-witness account. Nevertheless it is arguable that *Wisden's* unemotional version may have given an even vivider picture:

	Overs	Mdns	Runs	Wkts.
Hirst	7	4	9	5
Jackson	7	1	12	5

As for Washington's titanic battle with fate, *Wisden* rightly leaves its heights and depths to our imaginations:

I. Washington not out 9

One of the human things about cricket is that it changes continually, but does not change very much. The features that I instinctively look for in *Wisden* today—the Five Cricketers of the Year, the Notes by the Editor, the complete first-class results and averages, the Births and Deaths and the Obituaries—are all to be found in the older Almanack. The 40th volume, containing 672 pages, is a little smaller than the 103rd, which takes up 1,084. I think myself that 672 pages make a tidy book and I sadly sympathise with the Editor whose 'only difficulty is to deal with the immense number of matches crowded into a season within the limits of a volume published at a shilling'.

In the matter of illustrations *Wisden* today, with its wealth of photographs, scores heavily over 'my' *Wisden* which, apart from some sketches of austere-looking stumping gloves in the advertisements, has no pictures except those of the Five Cricketers, which look as though they had come out of a family album with brass clasps. Since this was an Australian summer, three of the Cricketers are Australians. The two Englishmen are C. J. Burnup of Kent and J. Iremonger of Nottinghamshire. Burnup was one of those players who, like the Fosters, the Days and D. J. Knight, were brought up in the graceful batting tradition of Malvern. His best year was 1902, and it was only the immense strength of England's batting in that deplorably wet summer that robbed him of an England cap. The brightest of his hundreds was scored at Tunbridge Wells, a ground which I now associate with its blaze of rhododendrons in June and the spiral stairway which eternally obtrudes the horrors of vertigo between the correspondent and the Press box.

Iremonger, who played full-back for Nottingham Forest, was a sturdy, if rather stiff, batsman who, though no aristocrat, held his own among such masters as Shrewsbury, William Gunn and A. O. Jones. Playing up to the outbreak of the first war, he toured Australia without appearing in a Test, and scored 32 centuries, the oddest of which included one of 1902's oddest incidents. In the Notts game against M.C.C. at Lord's, enamelled stumps were used with the enamel still wet, and when a ball moved one of his stumps, the bail remained faithful. From that moment nothing stopped Iremonger from going ahead to his hundred.

The three Australians were perhaps of heavier metal. Australia has never lacked wicket-keepers and J. J. Kelly, with 36 caps, was the most eminent, I think, between Blackham (35 caps) and Oldfield (54). His reserve wicket-keeper on this tour was Hanson Carter, by profession an undertaker, but Kelly himself presided at the obsequies of 35 victims (23 caught and 12 stumped). His is the most striking of my five faded photographs, because his face was adorned by the most luxurious moustache in cricket history. Like tropical foliage, it cascaded down from his upper lip and I cannot imagine how, as he crouched on duty, he managed to avoid contravening Law 43, which decrees that no part of the wicket-keeper's person shall advance in front of the wicket before the ball arrives, or words to that effect.

Those who saw the gargantuan Warwick Armstrong, when his hard-bitten warriors crushingly defeated England in 1921, might not have recognised the slim boyish figure of the 1902 tour's most gifted all-rounder, who scored 1,087 runs and captured 81 wickets, mainly with deliveries so far outside the leg-stump that the batsmen would get themselves out chasing them in sheer exasperation. This was the first of his four visits and, when *Wisden* said 'It is not unreasonable to expect a great future for him', an understatement was being released that was virtually to become a curse upon our country.

Some cricketers may be judged by statistics; some by eccentricity and some by massive achievement. A rare and enchanted few are remembered for the sheer beauty they brought to the game. Victor Trumper was a superb batsman with, as was said, three strokes for every ball; a vivid fielder and a personality of compelling charm. He did not, in the foolish phrase, 'hate' the bowler; he merely thought the poor fellow couldn't bowl. In that desolate summer Trumper made more runs than anybody else, English or Australian, and every one of his 2,570 runs bore the hallmark of supreme artistry. It is one of *Wisden*'s steadfast virtues to be soberly discriminating; this enables it to reserve its highest praise for the noblest and best.

With Trumper it could go to town: 'No one has been at once so brilliant and so consistent since W. G. Grace was at his best. . . . He seemed independent of varying conditions, being able to play just as dazzling a game after a night's rain as when the wickets were hard and true. All bowling came alike to him . . . in the Tests at Sheffield and Manchester he reduced our best bowlers to the level of the village green. . . . The way in which he took good-length balls off the middle stump and sent them to the boundary, had to be seen to be believed. . . . For the moment he is unapproachable.'

Who were the batsmen of 1902 who could not approach him? The first-class averages mention them: Shrewsbury, Ranjitsinhji, Abel, Grace, R. E. Foster, Fry, Jessop, Jackson, MacLaren, Warner, Palairet and Hayward, to name but a dozen. And who were the village green trundlers whom he cut to ribbons? They were Hirst, Rhodes, Braund, Barnes, Jackson, Lockwood, Cranfield, Trott and Tate who, perhaps as a consolation for his nightmare Test at Old Trafford, finished the season with 180 wickets at 15 runs apiece. In 1902 those nine bowlers took over 1,200 wickets between them and Trumper just felt sorry for them.

The Australian tour of 1902 produced a rubber more exciting than any in history except, and until, the electrifying series between Australia and the West Indies of 1960–61 which began with the fantastic tied match at Brisbane and ended with Australia's heart-hammering victory by two wickets at Melbourne. The 1902 rubber began at Edgbaston with a rain-wrecked game, which England must have won if a full third day's play had been possible. This match had everything except a positive ending. It had what was reckoned the best integrated side that England ever put into the field: MacLaren, Fry, Tyldesley, Ranjitsinhji, Jackson, Braund, Jessop, Hirst, Lilley, Lockwood and Rhodes. It saw a swordsman's century by Tyldesley which dragged England's batting back from the abyss; it staged Australia's dismissal for 36 (Hirst, three for 15 and Rhodes, seven for 17) of which total Trumper magnificently scored half; it then alas, suffered an almost empty last day. (C. B. Fry told me long afterwards that, though Rhodes took seven wickets, it was Hirst who broke the batting's back.) For full measure the score card carried a classic misprint which sets down the extras as three wides. There were, of course, really three byes, probably due to Hirst's terrific swerve. I doubt if Hirst ever bowled three wides in a season or Rhodes three wides in his whole career.

The second match, at Lord's, began sensationally and ended, after less than two hours, in torrential rain. By the end of the fourth over, Fry and Ranjitsinhji were out for ducks, and after 19 runs had been scored, 15 of them by Jackson, rain drove the players off. When they returned MacLaren and Jackson hit 83 more at a run a minute. After that the deluge. The Australians were unlucky in that our abominable climate had hit half of them with influenza; in a minor sense, on the other hand, they were lucky not to have to play out the game in that state.

It was the third Test, at Bramall Lane, that gave Australia victory by 143, and a grip on the rubber they never relaxed. 'They played the finer all-round cricket,' said *Wisden* judicially, 'and fully deserved their victory, but it is no more than the truth to say that all the luck of the game went their way.' They owed their win to superlative batting by Trumper and Hill and equally splendid bowling by Noble. England endured the worst of the wicket, the worst of the light, the worst of the decision to leave out Lockwood, and the worst of Barnes's ineffectiveness in the second innings after he had bowled like an angel in the first. On England's side MacLaren and Jessop batted heroically and Rhodes finished Australia's second innings by taking four wickets in 19 balls. As he said of The Oval Test twenty-four years later: 'They should have put me on sooner. . . .'

The fourth and fifth games of the rubber were, always excepting the 1960–61 tie at 'the Gabba', the most dramatic in Test history. Both have been celebrated in nobler prose than mine and it is not for me to paint the lily in recalling the wonder of Trumper, whose pulling on a fast drying wicket was 'a marvel of ease and certainty'; or the bowling of Lockwood, recalled after the Sheffield *débâcle*, who took six for 48 and five for 28; or Jackson's defiant hundred, practically unsupported, or the torments inflicted on the hapless Tate, who missed a vital catch and, after nerve-racking suspense, was bowled, attempting to batter the four which would have won the match. I will only quote, not *Wisden*, but Uncle Walter who, to his dying day, believed England's defeat to be a dreadful retribution from on high for leaving out George Hirst. 'I knew it would happen,' he said. '*Things can only go so far. . . .*'

The fifth Test at the Oval was Jessop's and only one game in history has been more memorable. Australia's first innings total of 324 looked high enough to win and, when England had six down for 83, it looked higher still. Hirst and Braund rallied the broken ranks and when Hirst, driving furiously, was caught and bowled, England still needed 38 to save the follow-on. It was Lockwood who saved it, with a mixture of fortitude and fortune, by a mere ten runs, and when Australia batted again, it was Lockwood, whose deadly bowling, backed by grand fielding, pulled the game round. Everybody knows how England lost MacLaren, Palairet, Tyldesley, Hayward and Braund for 48; how Jessop, joining Jackson, played his early overs quietly and then, first with Jackson and afterwards with Hirst he burst forth in any apocalyptic blend of high art and controlled violence. In an hour and a quarter his score, enriched by a 5 and seventeen 4s, leaped to 104 out of 139.

'. . . A more astonishing display', says the temperate chronicler, 'has never been seen. What he did would have been scarcely possible under the same circumstances to any other living batsman. The rest of the match was simply one crescendo of excitement. . . .'

Everybody knows, too, how when Rhodes joined Hirst 15 runs were still wanted and how Hirst said, or did not say: 'We'll get 'em in singles.' Fifty years later Rhodes told me it was only a tale and Hirst said: 'At a time like that you don't remember *what* you say.' They did not in fact get them in singles but get them they did in their own good time. This was without question Jessop's match, but close to Jessop came Hirst, bold, imperturbable, the symbol of the bonnie fighter. Scoring 101 for once out, he twice saved the day and the myth that he was no more than a good county player should have lain down and died at The Oval that day.

With so fierce a Test series, you might have imagined the county season to be comparatively dull. Not so. For the third successive time Yorkshire headed the table with three times as many points as Sussex, the runners-up. The method of reckoning was one point for a win, minus one for a loss and nothing for a draw, but no system could have been devised by human brain that would have dislodged Yorkshire from the top. Systems of rewarding excellence, or indeed of assessing any form of merit, are frequently changed on the grounds that they are unjust to somebody. True, but, in an unjust world, the well-meant changes merely transfer the injustice to someone else. The best teams will still come out on top, the least talented at the bottom, and minor variations will occur only in the middle.

That Yorkshire side which beat the Australians were probably as well equipped as any county team have ever been. With an attack which consisted of Hirst, Rhodes, Haigh and Jackson, nothing could compare with it until the Yorkshire bowling of the 1920s and Surrey's in the 1950s. Their early batting—Brown, Tunnicliffe, Jackson and Taylor—was not quite as strong as that of Sussex—Fry, Vine, Killick and Ranjitsinhji—but it was powerful enough for all practical purposes. Denton was developing that cavalier approach which later made him Tyldesley's most dashing rival for the post of England's No. 3; Washington, a maternal uncle of the Kilners, played for Yorkshire and, had illness not shortened his career, would have played for England the left-handed part which Leyland played later with rugged resolution. Hunter, whose luxuriant moustache challenged even J. J. Kelly's, might well have worn England's gloves, but for Arthur Augustus Lilley, of Warwickshire, who appeared to occupy the place behind the stumps on a long lease. T. L. Taylor (1,517 runs) and Haigh (158 wickets) both had their turn as England's twelfth man and Lord Hawke, then a young 41, was the shrewdest of contemporary captains. I would not argue with anyone who denied that Rhodes was England's best bowler.

Could such a side be beaten? Yes, they could. In their three seasons' triumph Yorkshire lost only two matches, both to Somerset who, under the volatile and exuberant leadership of S. M. J. (Sammy) Woods showed time and again a remarkable talent for the unexpected. Sammy, an Australian by birth and an England rugby forward by inclination, radiated such elemental force in hard hitting, fast bowling and electrical fielding that he might have been the forerunner of Sir Learie Constantine. His team had, in L. C. H. Palairet, the most purely graceful batsman in the country, who even today is looked back on as the epitome of elegance; in Leonard Braund they had a batsman-bowler who, even with Hirst, Lockwood and F. S. Jackson in the reckoning, was often deemed the finest all-rounder of the day.

Yorkshire's progress in 1902 was hard to hinder. On Whit Monday, mainly through the bowling of Sydney Barnes, they were put out by Lancashire for 148 and yet this scanty total gave them an innings win, Jackson taking eight for 13. They beat Warwickshire, Kent, Gloucestershire and Middlesex twice; Nottinghamshire by 227 and Surrey by an innings and 102. The second Middlesex game was almost a recording of the first Roses match. Yorkshire made well under 200, but easily won by an innings. (Rhodes, ten for 56, Haigh, nine for 53.) Immediately after this they met Somerset, on a fiendish wicket at Bramall Lane. Somerset, for whom Palairet and Braund scored 44 for the first wicket, scarcely realised that this would be the best stand of the match. Yorkshire were all at sea with the bowling of Braund and Robson and then, after another bold stand by Palairet and Braund and some furious hitting by Gill, Somerset meekly gave in to Haigh who, taking six for 19, hit the stumps five times, three of them for a hat-trick. Asked to make a mere 119, Yorkshire were doomed from the start and Braund (nine for 41) demolished them with his whippy leg-breaks. Altogether, he took fifteen for 71 and hit 65. Very few among the other twenty-one players scored 20 for twice out. It was the one occasion of the season when Yorkshire lost their grip on a game and it was Braund who prised it loose.

You could not say there was a dull county. Sussex, the runners-up, could never be tedious with Fry and Ranjitsinhji on their strength, while Nottinghamshire, who came third, leaned a little on the over-forties, as represented by Shrewbury and William Gunn, but had a fast bowler, Wass, who took 140 wickets and was faster than he looked, which was a feat in itself; this for a county in which Larwood was not to be born for a further two years and Voce for another seven.

Surrey before Hobbs was not necessarily drama before Shakespeare. There have always been outstanding batsmen under the shadow of the gasometers. The firm of Brockwell and Abel was to change to Abel and Hayward before it changed to Hayward and Hobbs. In Hayward's benefit match at The Oval a total of 1,427 runs were scored for 24 wickets and, though the game ended in a draw, it never grew wearisome. The wicket was good and the batsmen were good; could it be that the bowling was feeble? As the bowlers included Hirst, Rhodes, Haigh, Jackson, Richardson and Lockwood (who took seven for 159) I should say not. Perhaps—this is a daring suggestion—they were all enjoying themselves.

In the rest of the 15 counties—Northamptonshire and Glamorgan were not yet with them—were many who today are freshly remembered. Lancashire's MacLaren was England's captain and Tyldesley England's most dashing professional batsman; Warwickshire gave England in Lilley an almost irreplaceable wicket-keeper; Kent had Blythe, next in prestige to Rhodes; Worcestershire boasted a 'pride' of Fosters, of whom R. E. was the most brilliant; Warren and Bestwick were neither the first nor the last of Derbyshire's dreaded pairs of fast bowlers; Leicestershire had C. J. B. Wood, King and Knight, all more than locally famous; Middlesex glittered almost too brightly for their collective success with such names as P. F. Warner, C. M. Wells, Trott, Hearne (J. T.) and the only begetter of the googly, B. J. T. Bosanquet. Essex had their twins, Perrin and McGahey; Gloucestershire, though modestly placed, owned the magnificent Jessop, and Hampshire at the bottom of the table, could be proud of the tireless all-rounder, C. B. Llewellyn, who scored nearly 1,000 runs, took 170 wickets and was in the 14 from whom England's most illustrious eleven were chosen at Edgbaston.

Besides the first-class counties there was London County, captain and secretary, W. G. Grace. This club, founded by W. G. after leaving Gloucestershire under a cloud—the cloud was the county's, not W. G.'s— was presided over by the Old Man himself and his friend, W. L. (Billy) Murdoch. The two, nicknaming each other Father and Muvver, rollicked through the season like schoolboys. At W. G.'s command the club could conscript virtually any cricketer in the land, so that often they could field something like a Test team. In one of their matches at the Crystal Palace against M.C.C. there was a global total of well over 1,000 runs for 30 wickets, garnished with hundreds by C. J. B. Wood, L. O. S. Poidevin and, need you ask, W. G. In this game played Mr. J. Gilman who, still youthful at 88, has recently told delightful stories of those days, including one of W. G. and Murdoch, who in attempting to alight from a hansom, so vied with each other in elephantine politeness—'After you, Father.' 'No, after you, Muvver.'—that their combined thirty-five stone or so went slap through the bottom of the cab.

In the same match appeared the man who, apart from the Graces, was the most celebrated of cricketing doctors, a brisk batsman stumped on his way to a lively 50. There is a legend that, while entering the pavilion at the start of this match, he was accosted by a small autograph-hunting boy.

'Please, sir, is your name Conan Doyle?'

'Yes, sonny. How did you guess?'

'Elementary, my dear Sir Arthur,' said the lad. 'I saw it on your cricket bag.'

So we bid farewell to my favourite summer, with a nostalgic glance at the advertisements in my favourite *Wisden*. You could buy men's white buck leg-guards for 5s. 11d. and guaranteed Australian catgut-sewn cricket balls for 5s. Best of all there were bats with specially selected blades and handles (I quote) *of a particularly resilient nature*, price, with double splice, 18s. 6d. That I have survived those golden days so long does not argue any virtue in me, but it does prove one thing.

I am of a particularly resilient nature.

SIR FRANK WORRELL [1968]

Born in Barbados, August 1, 1924

Died in Jamaica, March 13, 1967

Knighted for his Services to Cricket, 1964

BY SIR LEARIE CONSTANTINE

Every so often a cricketer dies whose life looms so large in the context of his times that Wisden elevates his death notice from the obituary columns to the essays section. In 1968 this posthumous honour came the way of Frank Worrell who, in the previous spring, had died at the tragically premature age of 42. Worrell (1924–67) was one of the greatest all-round stylists of his generation, one of the most beautifully elegant batsmen to watch and among the three or four most inspiring captains of the century. Yet it may well be that his real significance lies beyond the bounds of cricket. The best way to take his measure is to read C. L. R. James's 'Beyond a Boundary', in which the author, weaving an intricate tapestry of polemics and autobiography, explains the two great missions of his life, to live to see West Indian independence and to live to see a West Indies side led by a black cricketer. His story begins in childhood in Trinidad, moves into its second act when in 1933 he arrives in England at the invitation of the author of the forgoing essay, Learie Constantine, who was then blazing the West Indies trail into league cricket by becoming a professional with the Nelson club in Lancashire, and moves into its dénouement with James' return to his homeland and his ceaseless campaigning in the island press on behalf of the two great causes of his life. At which point he achieves the simple yet profound perception that these two great missions which have animated his life, these two apparently disparate themes of cricket and political autonomy are after all the same cause, the same issue, the same crusade. All at once the islands are granted independence and Frank Worrell ascends to his rightful place as leader of the West Indies side.

It goes without saying that Worrell's effect on his teammates was both benign and instantaneous. Few better all-round sides have ever been seen, but more important even than the style and the virtuosity of the cricketers was the spirit in which, under Worrell's cool tutelage, they played the game. Courtesy and friendliness were the order of the day and because it just so happened that Australia too was being led at the time by one of the greatest of all its captains, the series between them is widely regarded as perhaps the most memorable of the century. At the time of his death, Worrell was already starting to move into the political arena, just as Constantine, Wesley Hall and the champion Olympic athlete Arthur Wint were to do. In 1963 Worrell retired from the game; a year later he was knighted and a year after that he was appointed manager of the national side. A great player, a gracious captain and, as Constantine reminds us, a pioneer for the federalist cause.

SIR Frank Worrell once wrote that the island of Barbados, his birthplace, lacked a hero. As usual, he was under-playing himself. Frank Maglinne Worrell was the first hero of the new nation of Barbados and anyone who doubted that had only to be in the island when his body was brought home in mid-March of 1967.

Or in Westminster Abbey when West Indians of all backgrounds and shades of opinion paid their last respects to a man who had done more than any other of their countrymen to bind together the new nations of the Caribbean and established a reputation for fair play throughout the world. Never before had a cricketer been honoured with a memorial service in Westminster Abbey.

Sir Frank was a man of strong convictions, a brave man and it goes without saying, a great cricketer. Though he made his name as a player his greatest contribution was to destroy for ever the myth that a coloured cricketer was not fit to lead a team. Once appointed, he ended the cliques and rivalries between the players of various islands to weld together a team which in the space of five years became the champions of the world.

He was a man of true political sense and feeling, a federalist who surely would have made even greater contributions to the history of the West Indies had he not died so tragically in hospital of leukaemia at the early age of 42, a month after returning from India.

People in England can have little idea of the problems of West Indian cricket. It is not a question of a few countries bordering each other coming together in a joint team. Jamaica is 1,296 flying miles from Barbados and Georgetown in Guyana 462 miles from Bridgetown in Barbados.

Before that wonderful tour of Australia in 1960–61, Barbadians would tend to stick together and so would the Trinidadians, Jamaicans and Guyanans. Worrell cut across all that. Soon there were no groups. Just one team.

He told his batsmen to walk if they were given out. When Gary Sobers appeared to show his dissent with a decision, he reprimanded him. After that, everyone walked as soon as the umpire's finger went up.

So when half a million Australians lined the streets of Melbourne in their ticker tape farewell to Worrell and his men, they were not only paying a final tribute to the team's great achievements, they were recognising the capacity and potential of equals both on and off the turf.

Sir Frank started life in Barbados, worked and lived in Trinidad and died in Jamaica after doing much useful work at the University of the West Indies there. He incurred enmity by leaving his birthplace but he did not care much for insularity, cant and humbug.

He saw the many diverse elements of the West Indies as a whole, a common culture and outlook separated only by the Caribbean Sea. This is why he upset certain people in Barbados when he wrote to a newspaper there criticising the island for having the cheek to challenge the rest of the world to celebrate independence.

Worrell was strongly criticised for this action, bitterly in fact in some quarters. But being attacked did not worry him. He always had the courage to say what he felt about every issue he thought vital to the well-being of the islands.

Sadly, the news that he was dying came through as Barbados played the Rest of the World XI. But Worrell held no rancour against his homeland. He had bought a piece of land there and had intended to retire there eventually.

This willingness to speak out often got him into trouble, even at school. Cricket had come naturally to him as it does to most youngsters in the West Indies, particularly Barbados. More so with him because he was born in a house only a few yards away from the Empire cricket ground. He and his friends used to set up stumps on the outfield and play nearly all day in the holidays.

At Combermere School he fell foul of a master who accused him of hogging the crease and not letting his colleagues bat.

He was to write later: 'I was unfortunate enough to have been under an endemic psychological and mental strain throughout my school days. So much so that by the time I reached the fourth form I was suffering from a persecution complex.

'These were the days when child psychology was not a subject demanded of applicants to teachers' posts. Indeed, the majority of masters did not have the experience of raising families of their own. There was no allowance for the original point of view.'

Worrell was a pupil who always had an original point of view. Also, as it was becoming clear at this time, he was a cricketer with an original talent. He soon made the Barbados team and records began to flow from his bat as he moved up the order from number eleven (yes, that is where he began his career!).

He shared a partnership of 502 with John Goddard in 1943–44 and an unfinished 574 with Clyde Walcott in 1945–46. Typically he dismissed both. 'The conditions were loaded in our favour,' he said. 'I wasn't all that delighted about it.'

In 1947 he tired of living in Barbados. His mother had moved to New York and his father was away at sea most of the time so he moved to Jamaica. English people will be surprised to learn that many of Worrell's fellow Bajans have never forgiven him for this 'betrayal'. When will they ever learn?

He established an international reputation against the 1947–48 England touring side and at the end of that tour took the step that made him a batsman for all seasons and all wickets. He signed as professional for the Central Lancashire League side Radcliffe for a fee of £500 a year.

It was a good year to enter League cricket. The Central Lancashire League was a cricket academy and the young, talented player was bound to improve by the experience. Playing in neighbouring clubs were Bill Alley, Jock Livingston, Ray Lindwall, Cecil Pepper, Clyde Walcott, Everton Weekes, Vinoo Mankad and Dattu Phadkar.

I have always held that League cricket makes a cricketer, not only as a player but as a man. There is much to learn in the field of human relations from the kind, friendly and warm people of the North of England. Frank brought his fiancée, Velda, over and their marriage was another settling influence on him.

Worrell was not just living for the present—as I regret is the case with some of our cricketers—but he was thinking of the future. He took a course at Manchester University and qualified in economics, his chosen subject.

The flag on Radcliffe Town Hall was at half mast on the day of his death. He married his wife, Velda, at Radcliffe, and their daughter was born there. Such was the esteem in which he was held by Radcliffe that in 1964 a street near the cricket ground was named Worrell Close.

The 1950 tour of England was a triumph for him and he topped the Test batting averages with 539 runs at an average of 89.83. His best Test score of 261 was made in this season, at Trent Bridge.

Norman Yardley, the England captain of the time, told me it was impossible to set a field to him. Place the fieldsmen straight and he beat them on the wide. Place them wide and he would beat them straight.

I am not one for averages myself. I am more concerned with how a batsman made his runs and not what his average was at the end of the series. Sir Neville Cardus has written of Sir Frank that he never made a crude or an ungrammatical stroke. I agree with that. Worrell was poetry.

While Walcott bludgeoned the bowlers and Weekes dominated them, the stylist Worrell waved them away. There was none of the savage aggression of a Sobers in his batting. He was the artist. All three 'Ws' were geniuses but Worrell was my favourite because he had more style and elegance. He had all the strokes and the time and capacity to use them without offence to the eye, without ever being hurried.

He was never seen playing across the line. That is why he never hooked. Players and Pressmen agreed that even when he ducked beneath a bouncer, he did so with a lack of panic and great dignity. And remember he had Lindwall and Miller to contend with!

The tour to Australia in 1951–52 was not such a success as the 1950 tour of England. Worrell himself said this was because there were too many factions in the side and John Goddard, previously showered with advice, was not helped this time by the seniors.

When Worrell took over the captaincy nine years later, he was to heed the lessons of this dismal tour. The return series in the West Indies in 1955 was again a disappointment for Worrell; he scored only 206 runs. The 1957 tour of England was a further let down. Clearly the West Indies authorities had to change their policy of always appointing a white man to captain the side.

The break was made in 1960 when Worrell, the only candidate with the outstanding qualities to do this gigantic repair job, was asked to lead the side in Australia. Everyone knows the story of that tour and how much it did to restore the good name of cricket after the 'bumper' rows, 'slow over rates' disputes and other ills which had been afflicting the international game.

Back in Jamaica, Worrell was acclaimed and rightly so. He was appointed Warden of the University College of the West Indies and also a Senator in Parliament.

The Indians were the next tourists to the West Indies and it was typical of the man that when their captain, Nari Contractor, was seriously injured by a blow on the head, Worrell was one of the donors of blood which saved his life.

It was not generally known that Worrell, the thirteenth West Indies captain, was a superstitious man. During the 1951 tour of Australia he was bowled first ball by Geoff Noblet. Determined to make a fresh start in the second innings, he changed every stitch of clothing, fitting himself out in a completely new gear and walked to the wicket hoping that by discarding his old clothes he would change his luck. Not a bit of it! He was out for another first baller!

As he came in, crestfallen, Clyde Walcott, the next batsman, said with a laugh: 'Why do I have to face a hat-trick every time I follow you?'

His finest hours in England came in 1963 when he led the West Indies to more glory. By this time he had slowed up in the field and his figure was well in excess of Miss World proportions. He was 38 (age I mean) and no longer the player he had been. He was a tired man and often told me so.

But his influence over the side as captain was such that it was unthinkable to rest him in any of the Tests. He bowled a few shrewd medium pacers with his deceptively easy delivery and when the crisis was on in the Lord's Test, the greatest Test of all time as it was called by the critics, he helped Butcher to add 110 on the Saturday afternoon. The following Monday morning the second innings collapsed.

Asked if Worrell was worried about this, another player replied: 'No, he is asleep.' Sir Frank had this ability to drop off at any time, particularly when there was a batting collapse. After his death, I wondered whether this had something to do with his illness which was obviously affecting him at this time, though no one knew that he was not a fit man.

As Wes Hall prepared for the final over which could have won or lost the Lord's Test, Worrell went to him with some advice. What was he saying? Bounce them? Bowl 'em straight? No, none of the obvious things. Sir Frank said calmly: 'Make sure you don't give it to them by bowling no balls.' Worrell was the calmest man at Lord's that day and trust him to think of a highly pertinent point which Hall, in his excitement, may have overlooked!

He announced his retirement at the end of this tour which was a triumph of leadership, technical skill and adaptability. The following year Her Majesty the Queen knighted this complete Cricketer, Philosopher and Captain. It was a fitting end to an unforgettable career but there was one more job for him to do—manage the West Indies side against the 1965 Australian tourists.

He had groomed Sobers well for the captaincy and theirs was an unbeatable partnership. At last the West Indies were the undisputed champions in their truly national sport.

Throughout his life, Sir Frank never lost his sense of humour or his sense of dignity. Some nasty things were said and written during that 1965 tour but Sir Frank was ever the diplomat. He lost no friends, made no enemies yet won more respect. He would always come up with a smile and a loud laugh. West Indians really laugh their laughs. And Sir Frank laughed louder than most of us.

He was a happy man, a good man and a great man. The really tragic thing about his death at the age of 42 was that it cut him off from life when he still had plenty to offer the islands he loved. He was only at the beginning. Or was it that the opportunity came to him a bit too late?

OTHER TRIBUTES:

S. C. Griffith (Secretary, M.C.C.): Ever since I first saw him play during the M.C.C. tour of the West Indies, I have thought of Frank Worrell as a great and impressive batsman and a very useful bowler. Even more than that, I have been impressed by his ever growing stature as leader of cricketers, by his tolerance and understanding and by the contribution he was making to the game. He was a great friend of mine and like countless other cricketers I shall miss him more than I can say.

P. B. H. May: The game has lost a personality we all admired. He was one of the greatest of the long line of Barbadian cricketers. One associated him with his two colleagues, Weekes and Walcott, but I regard him as the most accomplished of the trio.

Sir Donald Bradman: His name is for ever enshrined on the Frank Worrell Trophy which Australia is proud to have created for permanent competition between our two countries. Players of his calibre are rare. Not only was he a truly great and stylish batsman, he was also a fine thinker with a broad outlook.

Richie Benaud: He was a great leader of men and one of the finest cricketers on and off the field in the history of the game. It is difficult to realise that the indolent drawl, the feline grace known all over the world are no more. Few men have had a better influence on cricket.

Ian Johnson: He was easily the greatest captain of modern times. He brought West Indies cricket to the top and set a wonderful example to world cricket.

Alan Barnes (Secretary, Australian Board of Control): His name is indelibly linked with the finest traditions of cricket throughout the world and particularly in the hearts of all Australian cricket lovers.

E. R. Dexter: His reputation as a cricketer is beyond dispute. I found him one of the best captains I have seen or played against.

F. S. Trueman: He was one of the nicest people I ever played against.

J. M. Kilburn: Cricket was always distinguished in the presence of Worrell—Sir Frank. His knighthood was a personal honour to a cricketer of rare quality and an acknowledgement that West Indian cricket had reached the highest level in the world. In his captaincy he won esteem and affection by the calm demeanour in which he cloaked firmness and shrewd tactics. His serenity smoothed ruffled feathers and diminished crises.

BATSMEN MUST HIT THE BALL AGAIN [1968]

BY DENIS COMPTON

Someone who knew of Worrell's prowess at first hand was Denis Compton who, since his retirement in 1958, had become prominent as a commentator in the Press and on television. Like most of the players of his generation, Compton was not happy with what he saw on the county grounds but, unlike his contemporaries, he spoke out against what he took, rightly as it happened, to be policies fatal to the future of the game. It was and still is very rare for an ex-player to pitch into the guilty parties as strongly as Compton does in his comments on the notorious Middlesex–Hampshire match at Lord's. The strictures are doubly commendable in view of the fact that it is his own county playing at home which comes in for the brickbats. Compton goes on to talk of 'the depths to which the game has sunk' and expresses the hope that the young generation, victimised by coaching, will have the gumption not to learn undesirable methods. One of the memorable justifications for the empirical view then follows, in a passage concerned with the right or the wrong way to hold a cricket bat. By 1968, too many cricketers had reduced themselves to the indisposition experienced by golfers, who have been known to pay large sums of money to professionals in the hope of acquiring the 'right' grip and the 'right' stance. Compton is almost certainly being perfectly honest when he claims not to recall how he gripped the bat: 'I held it the way it felt most comfortable.'

He then recalls an extraordinary superstition observed by his brother Leslie and nominates as his great hope for the future a younger batsman who was soon to suffer a tragic accident which was to eliminate him from the game. Compton's appeal for brighter, bolder, more imaginative players was timely and perfectly justified and was also totally ignored. In later years he carried the same forthright candour on to the television screen, haranguing his own countrymen as well as the opposition whenever he considered that the play had plumbed the depths, time and again asking the rhetorical question, 'Who wants to see this sort of thing?'. The time came when he disappeared from the TV panels and it would be instructive to know whether this eclipse was connected in any way with his refusal to be mealymouthed.

IN my opinion there is nothing wrong with cricket; it is the attitude of so many first-class players that has gone awry. Cricket is still a wonderful game as played in the schools and at club level but so much big cricket is no longer the spectacle it used to be, and, in particular, the County Championship, which provided me with so much fun, no longer attracts huge crowds. Modern trends, like the family car and the thirst for excitement the whole time, now challenge cricket probably more than any other spectator sport. The safety-first outlook has bedevilled professional cricket far too long and like our traffic in the big cities the three-day game has come almost to a full stop.

We still enjoy the occasional breath-taking displays by such cricketers as Gary Sobers, Tom Graveney, Graeme Pollock, Colin Bland, Denis Lindsay, Bob Barber, Jim Parks and, when in the mood, Ken Barrington. But is not Ken one of the culprits who can be so infuriatingly dull?

A typical example of the way the English first-class cricketer has driven the crowds to seek other amusement occurred in the game between Middlesex and Hampshire which heralded the month of July at Lord's last summer. That contest must go down in County Championship history as the one that touched rock bottom. Three days' cricket on a near-perfect wicket seemed to me so full of promise of good things to enjoy, but everything was ruined as a spectacle by the inability of two teams of professional cricketers even to settle the issue of first-innings points. How the cricketing public suffered!

Hampshire came close to completing an unfortunate double a fortnight later when they played Kent on their own Southampton wicket. It was not until late on the third day that the first-innings points issue was resolved. Again there had been a minimum of interruptions.

These two examples, which are characteristic of Championship cricket today, illustrate the depths to which the game has sunk in recent seasons. Time softens the memory, but I am convinced that we would not have been allowed to get away with such meaningless cricket, either by the crowds or the county committees, in the late 1940s and early 1950s.

It is true that wickets have deteriorated in recent years, although there was encouraging evidence last summer of an improvement in the general standard of pitch preparation. Yet in my day we faced the problem of uncovered wickets exposed to the elements, which resulted in some remarkable surfaces on which any kind of confident stroke play was virtually impossible.

Far from providing an excuse to resort to some of the laboured cricket we have witnessed in recent seasons, such wickets presented a challenge to do the next best thing and throw the bat at the ball. As Leslie Ames, the Kent secretary and manager of the M.C.C. side in the West Indies, says: 'When the wicket is bad there is only one way for a batsman to play, knowing he is not likely to remain at the crease for any length of time. That is to have a go! It is better to chance the arm and make 30 runs quickly than spend an hour of agony collecting the same number of runs.'

Naturally, it must be difficult to work up enthusiasm playing in front of deserted stands and terraces for six days a week. The right atmosphere can make all the difference. I was lucky playing soon after the war before enthusiastic onlookers who had been starved of sporting entertainment.

Because of the absence of crowds at county games in the past few seasons, some cricketers advance the argument that it is difficult to provide entertaining play in such an unreal atmosphere. What they fail to realise is that nobody can be drawn back to the game unless the players—and, in effect, committees—change their attitude. People ARE prepared to watch if the right spirit is adopted. They have shown this to be true by flocking to the Gillette Cup matches. Association football has proved that, with the raising of professional standards, the missing spectators can be lured back.

As a former player and now a devoted cricket watcher, it is the fact that a majority of players seem to have resigned themselves to playing unenterprising cricket that concerns me. So many of them go to considerable lengths to complain about the apparently never-ending stream of medium paced short of a length bowlers who have proved a curse on the game.

Yet nothing, it seems, is done by the batsmen to remove these medium pacers—little phantoms as Brian Statham describes them—from the firing line. The attitude of the batsman is to play back to all the deliveries on a line with the stumps and wait for the loose ball to punish. Against such specialists as Cartwright, Bannister, Alley, Crump, Nicholson, Hooker and Shackleton, such waiting can take a lifetime.

Knock-out cricket has shown that these stock bowlers can be hit. Nobody is going to tell me that Hutton, Washbrook, Bill Edrich, Hardstaff and others like them twenty years ago would not have found a way. I certainly could not have stayed at the crease without making some attempt at attacking them. It would have meant taking risks, using my feet and moving down the wicket. Anything, in fact, which was likely to disturb the bowler's concentration and force him to change his length and direction. With the majority of wicket-keepers standing back these days, it is easier to leave the crease than when there was a Godfrey Evans breathing down a batsman's neck!

Let me stress that such bowling tactics are not new. They have been mastered and, by sensible application, they can be again. I recall a confrontation in the middle between Norman Yardley and Don Bradman during the Test match at Nottingham in 1948 in the days when the new ball was taken after 55 overs. Bradman's tactics were to use Lindwall and Miller for as long as possible and then bring on Toshack bowling on the leg stump to stop the runs until the next new ball was due. Yardley replied by bowling Shackleton-style when the Australians batted, much to Bradman's discomfort.

Eventually Bradman faced an entire over from Yardley without once offering a stroke as the ball went down the leg side. At the end of the over Bradman walked up to Yardley and said: 'If we are all going to continue playing cricket this way we might as well give up the game.' He changed his attitude, Yardley responded and the rest of the series was played at the right tempo.

I was encouraged last season when I heard that Stuart Surridge, in his first season as chairman of Surrey's cricket committee, made his own stand during a second eleven match at The Oval when he saw a Surrey batsman who has had considerable first team experience, playing without any sign of aggression. Surridge squirmed in his seat until he could stand it no longer and asked the Surrey coach, Arthur McIntyre, to go out to the middle and instruct the batsman to play the game the right way or get out!

Too much of the modern game seems to be complicated by theory and the shutting out of natural talent by coaches who insist that all players should be of the same mould as laid down in the coaching manuals. The younger of the overseas cricketers who have been signed up by the counties during the winter will undoubtedly find some of their methods frowned upon by coaches when they first enter county cricket. *I very much hope they will have enough strength of character to resist the attempts to turn them into the factory models filling our county sides.*

Last summer I was surprised when one of our leading batsmen, with many overseas tours behind him, told me he was not happy with the way he was holding the bat. He asked how I held mine. 'I've not the slightest idea,' I replied. 'I never paid any attention to any special grip. I held it the way it felt most comfortable.' So, I should have thought, would any batsman. Of course, a player trying to influence younger and less experienced batsmen to copy his own style is nothing new in the game.

It happened to me in Australia in 1946–47 when Wally Hammond, the greatest batsman I saw, offered his advice on how to deal with the spin of Tribe, Dooland and McCool. 'Play from the crease, Denis. Whatever happens don't be lured from your ground.' It was against my nature but I followed his instructions with disastrous results in the first three Tests. Finally I decided to play my own game and scored 147 and 103 not out in the fourth Test at Adelaide. What may suit one batsman does not necessarily suit another.

Len Hutton issued similar instructions during the West Indies tour in 1953–54 to counter the spin of Ramadhin and Valentine, with a particular warning to Tom Graveney, although Graveney is essentially a front foot player. It was asking him to play an entirely different role to stay on his back foot in the crease instead of using his height and reach. For two Tests we batted the Hutton way and lost both of them. Things came to a head on the third day of the second Test when England scored only 128 runs from 114 overs. Eventually all the batsmen put their point of view to Hutton. He agreed to allow us to play our natural game with the result that we squared the series by winning two of the last three Tests.

One of the main results of coaching has been the steady decline of the hook shot favoured by the Australians and one of the most effective scoring strokes in a batsman's armoury. Today it is frowned upon because of the great element of risk involved, yet Bradman employed it and he was not a player to take outside gambles. Bradman was also an expert in setting fields to try and curb a batsman's use of the hook shot, but I remember Bill Edrich using it repeatedly in a superb exhibition of hooking when scoring a century against Australia at Sydney during the 1946–47 tour. Cyril Washbrook and Joe Hardstaff could also teach some of our young players how to hook with safety.

Humour, too, has faded from the field. Gone are the days when Keith Miller would open the bowling with a ping pong ball as he did against Jack Robertson when the Australians played Middlesex at Lord's, or when my brother Leslie was able to stick the bails on with chewing gum while batting during his benefit match against Sussex in 1954.

I remember also the occasion when a dog held up play during the Surrey and Australians match at The Oval in 1948. Syd Barnes promptly gathered up the dog and presented it to umpire Alex Skelding who had turned down a leg before appeal by Ray Lindwall only moments before! 'All you want now is the white stick', said Barnes. Nor have I forgotten the time Leslie rushed off the field at Lord's after lunch as he was about to continue his innings. Leslie had developed a superstitious habit of bowing to a portrait of Gregor MacGregor, a Middlesex wicket-keeper of the last century, which hangs in the Lord's pavilion. On this occasion his batting partner, Jack Robertson, had deliberately kept Leslie talking all the way to the wicket and it was only as he shaped to face the bowling that Leslie remembered he had forgotten to bow. This was all harmless fun which spectators enjoyed because it made them feel part of the game—and they came again.

Still, I believe there are signs of brighter times ahead. In Colin Milburn we have a batsman of character who is willing to hook, Alan Knott, a wicket-keeper who believes it is part of his job to entertain and Robin Hobbs, who is able to clown in the field without detracting from his ability. Such personalities should be encouraged. If more players were allowed to express themselves naturally, our legislators would find half their problems on the way to being solved. Cricket is too splendid a game to be muted by dull attitudes.

THE GOOGLY SUMMER [1968]

BY A. A. THOMSON

There has usually been a nice balance in the Almanack between contemporary concern and the unabashed sweetness of fond recollection. In 1968 the death of Sir Frank Worrell and Denis Compton's diagnosis of the sickness afflicting modern cricket were in striking contrast to more memories recalled by A. A. Thomson who, once again, selected as his theme for an essay the idyll of a long-vanished summer. Having exhausted the possibilities of the season of Jessop's immortal century against Australia, Thomson now turned to a Wisden of sixty years before and an essay in that edition by the ill-fated virtuoso Reginald Erskine Foster (1878–1914). Foster had been one of the batsmen obliged to face the challenge of a still novel form of bowling when the South African tourists arrived with their ranks positively congested with disciples of great Edwardian heretic B. J. T. Bosanquet. Unlike Thomson, Foster in his shrewdly analytic account makes careful differentiation between the South African spinners; where Thomson tells us that there were unalike, Foster explained exactly how they were unalike:

> Schwarz only breaks the ball from the off, but always with a leg-break action. . . . Vogler's usual ball is the leg-break, but once in two overs perhaps he will bowl 'the wrong 'un'. . . . Faulkner and White are to all intents and purposes the same bowler. . . . Faulkner makes the ball break quite a lot from the off. . . . White on the other hand very often comes straight through.

Being a professional novelist and sometime poet, Thomson prefers, much to the reader's delight, the discursive approach, talking wittily of Lord Chancellors and the price of light refreshments at Lord's, besides offering a few scintillating specimens of phrase-making, putting into the mouth of the ubiquitous Uncle Walter a sparkling simile for the batting of Gilbert Jessop, saying one of the most profound truths ever uttered about the study of Wisden relating to mortality and adding to the list of epigrams relating to Charles Burgess Fry. Not even Cardus ever did much better than Thomson's recollection of something Fry once said 'with a genuine modesty indistinguishable from arrogance'. Encountering such literary felicities, the reader suddenly realises that after a century in the marketplace, Wisden has evolved so far that it is no longer a repository of facts and figures, but a vast pot-pourri into which are often flung the graceful examples of true art.

Sɪʀ Walter Scott, from whose part of the world my family came, began his anonymous career as a novelist with a fictional work called *Waverley* or *'Tis Sixty Years Since*. That sub-title, for no special reason, has always fascinated me. It is not so much that things which happened sixty years ago were more interesting than what happens now; indeed, I hope that as long as I retain a faculty or two, I shall be interested in most things. But, sixty years since, life was less like a ball of string the cat has done its worst with and, if you had a favourite interest, you were at liberty to pursue it without a million distractions. And if you had just passed your thirteenth birthday, and rather liked cricket, it was a wonderful world.

Not many people, especially historians, remember who was Lord Chancellor in 1908. I do. It was Lord Loreburn and I know because *John Wisden's Cricketers' Almanack* for that year tells me he was also President of the Marylebone Cricket Club, whose annual subscription, if you were allowed the privilege of paying it, appears to have been £1 10s. and whose refreshment department showed a profit of £463 15s. 9d. 'In consequence of this satisfactory position', says the report, 'it is proposed to make certain reductions in the charges.' Such sublime words have never been repeated in the 1960s by anybody about the price of anything.

By 1907, about which *Wisden 1908* so richly informs us, my folk had long been settled in Yorkshire, reserving our nostalgic winter allegiance for Border rugby, but for cricket the county of our adoption was fairly satisfactory. We, in fact, felt that the only unsatisfactory item in *Wisden 1908* was that it could not record one of Yorkshire's 30 championships in 1907. The prize had gone to Nottinghamshire and, as I now look back with only mild prejudice, it had gone most deservedly. Yorkshire and a lively Worcestershire, stuffed with Fosters, tied for second place.

It was a horribly wet summer and, trust me, any man with sixty *Wisdens* on his shelves is bound to know more about the English climate than the B.B.C. weather boys with their chatter about weak fronts and troughs of low pressure. (I have in recent seasons watched dreary pairs of opening batsmen whom the phrase 'associated troughs of low pressure' would exactly fit.) So gruesome was the weather that in the Champions' two fixtures with Yorkshire only an hour and a quarter's play could be salvaged from six days. It was, as you would imagine, a bowler's, not a batsman's, year. Only three made 2,000 runs and these were Hayward, Hobbs and Johnny Tyldesley, all batsmen with reasonable claims to places in an all-time world eleven. Notts, the champions, did not boast a single batsman who made 1,000, though, to be fair, both Jack and George Gunn reached the 900s.

On the other hand 19 bowlers took 100 wickets, nine took 150, and one, George Dennett of Gloucestershire, whom I saw capture twelve in a match against my own county, took 201. The Five Cricketers of the Year were all bowlers—is this a record?—though, again to be fair, one of them, Frank Tarrant, the Middlesex Australian, batted enterprisingly enough to do the double, a feat he was to repeat seven times.

The landmark in bowling, of course, was the visit of a South African team which lost the rubber in the only Test which the rain allowed to be finished, but otherwise cantered brilliantly through a long fixture list and undoubtedly earned a reputation as the most richly versatile bowling side that ever went on tour. Their four googly bowlers, R. O. Schwarz, A. E. E. Vogler, G. A. Faulkner and G. C. White, were the most formidable, the first two being chosen as *Wisden*'s Cricketers of the Year, but they had four more, all exceptionally gifted, including J. H. Sinclair, medium fast, and J. J. Kotze, who bowled at terrifying speed and devoutly murmured as he galloped towards you: 'O Lord, shiver his timbers.' In a drier season he might have shivered more timbers than he actually did.

But it was the googly men who took the season by storm and the most intimidating thing about them was their pace off the pitch on the slow wickets of 1907. It was said that they were 'like Briggs in the air and Tom Richardson off the ground'. Or, in more modern terms, you must imagine, say, a West Indian bowler with an action like Lance Gibbs who could make the ball leap at your stumps like Wesley Hall. Now we know that the original inventor of the googly—why doesn't the Post Office issue a stamp?—was B. J. T. Bosanquet of Middlesex, who had exploited it with fearful success three years before in Australia, but the South African quartet were its devoted foster-parents. Bosanquet taught it to Schwartz, who also played for Middlesex, and Schwartz taught it to the others. Some of the others were cleverer still, though, so bewildering was the variety of their attack that English batsmen were never sure whether A, B, C or D gave them the most sleepless nights.

They all bowled with an action which promised a leg-break, but could make the ball whip in from the off. Schwartz was the most successful throughout the tour with 137 wickets, but Vogler, who took 119, was reckoned by the England captain, R. E. Foster, the best in the world. Schwartz on a sticky wicket was capable of breaking a yard and the batsman only had the slightest respite when the ball broke far too much. Vogler, after a short, apologetic run, would bowl with diabolically deceptive variations of flight and pace and every couple of overs would deliver a 'wrong 'un' that fizzed like a Chinese cracker. He twice bowled C. B. Fry, the master of scientific batting, with a slow yorker and he did not so much swing the ball as make it quiver like a bird on the wing. Gordon White and Aubrey Faulkner were not so clever; they merely had their days of devastation, as when Faulkner took six for 17 when England were all out at Headingley for 76.

England won this match, but only after a nerve-racking struggle. The wicket was wet all through and it was a strategic error to play N. A. Knox, a slow bowler as timber-shivering as Kotze, but a mere passenger on so soft a pitch. Starting between showers, England scored 34 for one before lunch and then the rest of the side disintegrated before Faulkner. Breaking both ways, he completely bamboozled every batsman except Hayward, who defended imperturbably, and Hirst, who, knowing all about wet wickets at Leeds, went out and clobbered him.

South Africa did not do much better against the superb slow left-hand bowling of Colin Blythe who, like the violinist he was, played on the batsmen's hesitations with the skill of a virtuoso. Blythe had been preferred to Rhodes, who, though he took 177 wickets that year, was rightly suspected of batting too well. Two years later he was to go in first for England. This was Blythe's finest hour, even though two months before he had taken all ten wickets in Northamptonshire's first innings, and seven in the second, making 17 for 48 in a single day. Nevertheless, the reason why I still count Rhodes the greatest of all bowlers is that he returned after the war to increase his career's bag of wickets to 4,187 and to play a vital part in England's recovery of the Ashes at the age of 48 years 10 months. Blythe, alas, alas, did not come back.

In spite of Blythe, South Africa struggled along and, with the comfort of some flabby fielding and a bit of brave banging about for the eighth wicket, they established a lead of 34. Now England were in disarray. There remained three frightful quarters of an hour before close of play and Fry had to use all his compelling charm—I can just hear him using it—to persuade his captain not to fritter away the evening with ineffective night watchmen. Fry himself and Hayward went in and survived the twilight till six-thirty. The captain almost shed tears of gratitude.

The next day the weather was worse, the wicket was vile and there were four interruptions before lunch. Fry, who made 54, was second out at 100. In his career he made 94 hundreds, six of them in succession, but none better, as he admitted to me many years later, than that 54 at Headingley. 'I choose to flatter myself', he said, with a genuine modesty indistinguishable from arrogance, 'that this was a good innings'. The rain that ended the second day was so intense that there seemed no hope for the third day, but a windy night made play possible and the South African bowlers, especially White, made mincemeat of the rest of England's innings. They were, therefore, set only 139 to win, which hardly seemed impossible, but they lost two wickets for three, survived a slip-chance and then fled from the rain.

Both sides were gluttons for punishment and, when they went out again, a pitched battle was fought for every run. Hirst and then Arnold bowled tightly at one end and Blythe, at the other, bowled even better than in the first innings. Wickets fell: three for 10, four for 16, five for 18. Faulkner and Snooke dug in, defending in a manner foreign to their lively natures, and held the broken line for an hour, but temptation became irresistible and Faulkner hit up a high catch to Foster at point. Resistance was broken, Blythe was unplayable, the end was in sight. Nineteen runs were more or less blindly hit for the ninth and tenth wickets and then Vogler sent up a towering skyer which seemed to hang aloft interminably as Johnny Tyldesley tore round the boundary. As it fell, he made a final leap, rolled over and came up, like a diver, with the ball in one hand.

With the match won, Blythe had to be helped to the pavilion. Immense concentration on every ball of 22.4 beautiful overs had drained every drop of his quivering nervous energy. Years later, Fry recalled the scene: 'It wasn't so much that he took fifteen wickets in the match; it was that in 136 balls he never bowled a single one that was of less than perfect length, knowing, as we all knew, that three bad overs at any time in that innings could have lost us the match.'

Of the other Cricketers of the Year two were the Notts bowlers, Hallam and Wass, whose strongly contrasted talents formed the main reason for their country's first clear triumph in twenty-one years. Hallam was slow and Wass was fast and between them they took 319 wickets (298 in county games); twice they bowled right through a match and eight times right through an innings, and the next bowler to them in the county tables was John Gunn, each of whose 37 wickets cost more than twice as much as any of Hallam's or Wass's. Nobody else in the wicket-taking line seems to have reached double figures. So much for the modern theory that you must start with three pairs of 'seam' bowlers in turn, all almost exactly alike and all entitled to a stint by the clock before you put on a slow bowler to give the batsmen a chance. Imagine putting on Rhodes, Blythe or Dennett for that purpose. . . .

Hallam, a Nottinghamshire lad, had wandered a bit, first with Leicestershire and then, for six seasons, with Lancashire, but when he settled in his native shire he took on the mantle of 'Dick' Attewell. He was the sort of bowler who looked easy to play from the Press box, but he made the batsman play every ball and, as P. F. Warner said, if you made a good score against Hallam, you were apt to feel a better batsman than you had ever thought you were. When chosen as a Cricketer of the Year, he was thirty-five, a pretty advanced age for the honour.

Tom Wass, also around thirty-five, was a different cup of tea, if that is the right expression. He was born at Sutton-in-Ashfield, where practically every baby born had the chance of growing up a famous cricketer. As Lascelles Hall was to Yorkshire cricketers, so Sutton-in-Ashfield was a nursery, not only for Notts men, but for cricketers everywhere. It would have been possible to raise a formidable team of Sutton-in-Ashfield exiles scattered round the counties and, in fact, an ill-natured joke in the form of a satirical greeting card, which suggested that Sutton-in-Ashfield merely existed to be raided for players, almost caused an embittered quarrel between Notts and Lancashire.

Tom Wass was a character. There has been in every age a fast bowler who was a rough diamond and this phenomenon is more frequently found in the north where they suspect the genuineness of their diamonds unless they are rough. His forthright comments were quoted with shocked glee round the dressing-rooms. Once when Gloucestershire scored nearly 700 against his side, he exclaimed: 'If they'd only turn this flamin' wicket upside down, I'd . . . show 'em.'

Tom was a grand bowler. That year he had taken six for 3 against M.C.C. at Lord's and twice in his career he took 16 wickets in a day. On the other hand, he was neither a master-batsman nor a hawk-eyed fielder and *Wisden*, in one of its classic understatements, says that 'when an easy catch goes his way the batsman has a feeling of hopefulness. . . .'

Once when playing at The Oval, he arrived at the gate, accompanied by his wife, and was told by the attendant that the lady could not be admitted free. 'Right,' said Tom, 'if this so-and-so don't come in, then this so-and-so'—he thumped his chest—'don't play neither!' Take him for all in all, he was a cricketing character of the old school and a main reason for Nottinghamshire's well deserved victory.

Besides their two master bowlers, they had enough batting to overhaul any score the enemy might put up without being top-heavy. John Gunn, who had played for England half a dozen times, and his brother, George, that wayward genius whose playing life was to last 30 years and bring him 35,000 runs, headed the batting along with their captain, A. O. Jones, a forceful leader, an entertaining bat and one of the best three slip-fielders in the country, the other two being Braund and Tunnicliffe. The all-round fielding had no superior among the counties with the skipper at slip, John Gunn at cover, and Hardstaff (old Joe, father of the more brilliant young Joe) in the deep. Four members of this businesslike eleven, George Gunn, Jack Gunn, Hardstaff and Jones, who captained M.C.C.'s 1907–8 team in Australia, were to have 38 England caps between them. Their secret was team-work, in the sense that in match after match they were able to put the same eleven into the field and their only serious setback occurred when Oates, their wicket-keeper, who had injured a hand, was replaced (for two matches only) by a capable deputy.

Remember, we were still in the Golden Age, which, when you think of Hallam and Wass and consider the figures of Haigh, whose average was only a decimal point above Hallam's, Hirst (188 wickets), Blythe (183), Tarrant (177) and Dennett (201), was, that year at any rate, a golden age of bowling. Yet there were classic batsmen in every county. Worcestershire, who shared second place with Yorkshire, had three members of the famous Foster family; H. K., G. N. and R. E., England's Test captain for the season; Surrey had Hayward, Hobbs and Hayes (who scored nearly 2,000 runs), just as Lancashire had MacLaren, Spooner and Johnnie Tyldesley. Kent, who had splendidly headed the table the year before, had a poor season, in spite of the fine bowling of Blythe and Fielder, mainly owing to an accident to K. L. Hutchings; this came from a terrific blow on the hand from J. J. Kotze, which kept him from the crease for five vital weeks.

You could go right down the county table and find players of England quality: Sussex, thirteenth, had C. B. Fry, head of the first class (and Test) averages and George Cox (senior), who took 164 wickets, while Derbyshire, the bottom county, provided in the sterling Joe Humphries, a wicket-keeper for the M.C.C.'s Australian tour. Gloucestershire, parked somewhere near the top of the table's bottom half, had the most exciting batsman in England, probably the most exciting in the game's history.

We know broadly who have impressed us with their soundness, their artistry, their elegance, or, possibly, with their combination of the excellences. But excitement? Bradman, obviously, but who today excites? The last England batsman to set the pulses wildly beating was E. R. Dexter. Colin Milburn excites *hopes* of excitement and I should hate to miss Roy Marshall when in town. There are others—Sobers, Kanhai, Graeme Pollock, Majid—who are exciting enough, but they are not for us every day.

In 1907 there was no argument. The most exciting batsman in the world was G. L. Jessop, captain of Gloucestershire. I had never seen him till that year, but his reputation, even among Yorkshire schoolboys, was stupendous. He had on our own ground, ten years before, hit 43 out of 54 before lunch and then, off another eight overs, taken another 58 out of 64 in a further 19 minutes. My step-Uncle Walter, who had seen every ball of this innings, recalled it as magnificent, but as also a kind of impiety, like brawling in church, because the outrage was committed against such eminent bowlers as George Hirst, Ted Wainwright, F. W. Milligan and (how dare he?) F. S. Jackson.

In the match I saw he scored at almost the same pace. From the first moment there was tension. Yorkshire began with a feeble first innings, of which Rhodes, batting at No. 1, made more than half. In their reply Gloucestershire led by only three runs, in spite of masterly batting by C. L. Townsend, making his one appearance of the summer. Then Yorkshire lost six wickets quickly and were only saved by a long stand, running into the next day, between two colts, Hubert Myers and Bates, son of the more famous 'Billy' Bates. Between them they also contributed more than half of the total and, with some honest thumping by Haigh, Yorkshire were able to ask Gloucestershire to make 234 to win. Three wickets fell to Hirst and then Jessop came in. He was no physical giant, but, like Bradman, short, compact and finely proportioned. What astonished us most was his stance, for he bent low to take guard; then, as the ball was delivered, he straightened . . . and struck. It is hard to describe, but it seemed like an artillery barrage. His square-cutting was as ferocious as his driving and his drives seemed propelled by a howitzer. When his successive partners had the strike, the fielders crept in; when Jessop was receiving, they retreated as from the wrath to come. Boundary followed boundary and the only time the scoring slackened was when Jessop with a hurricane sweep, sent the ball flying over the stand beyond the mid-wicket boundary and out of our ken for ever. In half an hour by my five shilling Ingersoll watch he scored 74 and when he got 15 more off four further strokes, Schofield Haigh bowled him an apocalyptic breakback. Everybody stood up on their seats and shouted, as though Mafeking had been relieved all over again. This was the beginning of the end and Rhodes easily polished off the rest.

I have two further memories of this match: one is of the heavily moustached George Dennett, who captured a dozen Yorkshire wickets with his easy rhythmic stuff. In his career he took 2,147 wickets, but never played for England, for the true but cruel reason that he was only the third best of his kind at the time. Even in this wet summer, which gave him more than 200 wickets, Blythe was preferred and, on Test performance, rightly. But I will swear that, if George was not good enough for England, the standard was incredibly high.

The other point was personal. Early the first morning I stood, gaping, with two school friends, waiting for the odd player to come out to the nets. The enemy were mostly anonymous, but . . . *him* we recognised from countless photographs and a certain impatience of step. He had a bat under his arm and, by some conjuring trick, produced three cricket balls. 'Come on, boys,' he said, 'bowl me out.'

Friend A bowled and the ball soared straight across the ground, hitting the entrance gate with a bang. Friend B, whoever he was, bowled and the ball rose, across the ground again, but higher. Then, while the batsman scanned the horizon to see where it had gone, the third bowler, unable to control a reflex action, bowled and hit G. L. Jessop's off-stump. I did not feel, as did Arthur Mailey on a similar occasion, 'like a boy who had shot a dove'. I was numbed. We went on bowling, if I remember rightly, till all the balls had disappeared, but the numbness, as you may perceive, has not worn off yet.

I did not need my precious 1908 *Wisden* to remind me of Jessop's vengeance. It is now regularly recorded in every *Wisden*. At Hastings Festival, playing for Gentlemen of the South against Players of the South, whose bowlers included Woolley, Fairservice, Vine, Humphreys, Albert Relf and our old friend, George Dennett, Jessop hit 191 in an hour and a half; the first 50 in 24 minutes, the second in 18 and the third in 21. And if you think his last 41 runs took a long time, you must remember that, besides his 30 fours, he hammered the ball out of the ground so often and so dangerously that the citizens must have thought it was 1066 all over again. This slowed his scoring rate and slightly spoiled his figures.

To glance through *Wisden*'s Obituary pages is not morbid; you may learn something of value, if only that man is mortal. In this year, among other good men, died H. F. Boyle, the Australian bowler who helped Spofforth to destroy England in the original Ashes match of 1882; and Harvey Fellows, who, sixty years before, bowled so fast in the Eton v. Harrow match that there were 38 byes and 15 wides in the first innings and 28 byes and 4 wides in the second.

Alfred Shaw in a career of over 30 seasons took over 2,000 wickets, did the hat-trick three times, including a double one and once captured seven for 7 against M.C.C. in 41 overs, of which 36 were maidens. His chief assets were his steely accuracy and the benevolently bearded aspect which masked his guile. He never bowled a wide in his life.

Lastly, poor Ted Pooley, the Surrey stumper who did not keep wicket in the first of all Tests, because he happened to be languishing in gaol, through no particular fault of his own, 1,200 miles away. But that is too long a story. . . . The highest compliment ever paid him came from the tough old bruiser, Jem Mace. 'Pooley,' he said, 'I'd rather stand up against any man in England for an hour than stand behind those stumps for five minutes. When that ball hits you, it's like hitting a brick wall.'

Wisden's last words on Pooley were exquisitely compassionate: 'He was in many ways his own enemy, but even to the last he had a geniality and sense of humour that to a certain extent condoned his weakness. . . .'

May heaven grant me so kindly an epitaph.

WARWICKSHIRE THE UNPREDICTABLE [1968]

BY ROWLAND RYDER

A few pages away from Thomson's sparkling entertainment, young Rowland Ryder—to distinguish him from the old one—resorted to identical tactics in setting his scene for an account of the history of the Warwickshire club, swiftly evoking the death of General Gordon, the Transvaal Gold Rush and the Aston Villa of Vaughton and Hodgetts, before arriving at the first authentic epigram in the club's history, delivered by an otherwise forgotten trundler called Jack Shilton. There follows a succession of anecdotes and recollections, a very faintly partisan claim on behalf of Tom Dollery, an amazing statistic concerning the batting of Reggie Santall and the obligatory reference to the county's outstanding professional, Shakespeare, W.

One very famous affair, no more than peripheral to the county's fortunes but beloved of all students of arcana, whether sporting or dramatic, deserves rather more attention than Mr. Ryder is able to give to it. In 1915, married for less than two years and still struggling to master the elusive trick of developing a mid-Atlantic style calculated to rest as easily with New Yorkers as with Londoners, Pelham Grenville Wodehouse (1881–1975), set to work on a short story called 'Extricating Young Gussie'. This brief tale tells how Gussie Fink-Nottle, in an attempt to win the love of a vaudevillean, takes to the stage with predictably idiotic results. A few months later, Wodehouse published a novel called 'Something Fresh', which did indeed contain something fresh, the figure of Clarence, ninth Earl of Emsworth. And as 'Extricating Young Gussie' had introduced the world-famous duet of Wooster and Jeeves, a case might be made that no writer in history, perhaps not even Shakespeare, W. of Warwickshire, has ever, within one calendar year, spawned as many as three immortal characters. In christening Wooster's valet, Wodehouse who, in more blissful days at Dulwich College, opened the first eleven bowling and once dismissed the great Kenneth Hutchings, must have read of the death on the Western Front of Percy Jeeves, a Yorkshire discard who, by 1913, had established himself as one of the stars of the Warwickshire side. In the following year he was chosen for the Players against the Gentlemen, performing so well that no less influential a judge than Pelham Warner predicted that before long Percy Jeeves would be bowling for England. A month later the Great War began, Jeeves went into the Royal Warwickshires and never played first-class cricket again. Wisden says of him that 'he was very popular among his brother players'. Like his namesake.

IN the year 1886, when the death of Gordon was on everyone's lips; when gold was discovered beneath the Transvaal dust; when Joey Chamberlain and Aston Villa were twin gods in Birmingham—William Ansell secured a lease of land from the Calthorpe Estate in Edgbaston, for the use of the Warwickshire County Cricket Club, which had been formed two years previously. Those were the spacious days when cricket *was* what it used to be. Overarm bowling had been cautiously permitted, but you only had four deliveries in an over. Cricket was luxurious and simple, relaxed and leisurely, fast and furious; cricket was as straightforward and paradoxical as it is today.

In 1894 the club was admitted to first-class status. In those days, when the players sat down to luncheon, there was salmon—for the amateurs, and cod—for the professionals. One of the early professionals was Jack Shilton, a left-arm bowler with a fast yorker. He was a Yorkshireman and 'a bit of a card'. Once, when a member asked him whom he considered the greatest bowler in England, he replied modestly, 'It isn't for me to say, sir!' Another member requested his services at the nets. He bowled his fastest and best for an hour, the member thanked him, and presented him with—

twopence! Jack Shilton's comment on this incident is not recorded. Visiting professionals were boarded at hotels, the amateurs as guests at private houses. When Yorkshire came over in 1896, Lord Hawke, F. S. Jackson and F. W. Milligan stayed with G. H. Cartland (a great name in Warwickshire cricket). This was the famous occasion when Yorkshire batted for two days and made the record score for a county of 887. Cartland's revenge on the second day was swift and terrible—he knocked off the amateurs' champagne—had Lord Hawke known that such an effective form of sanctions was to be introduced, he might well have declared with a mere 700 on the board!

In 1898, Joe Manton, a good club cricketer (he was later to become a great headmaster), who had learnt the game at King Edward's, Birmingham, found himself at The Oval deputising as captain for H. W. Bainbridge. Walking in to bat, he was greeted by Tom Richardson—'Full toss on the leg side, sir!' Joe Manton missed it. Tom Richardson obligingly bowled him another full toss, which was hit for four. Then he edged a single. His next ball was Joe Manton's last in county cricket.

1902 saw the first Test Match at Edgbaston and the Australians were all out for 36. Warwickshire's 'Dick' Lilley was playing for England. But the wet summer meant a disastrous season. £1,500 had been spent on building a new stand, and introducing other improvements. Warwickshire's share for the Australian tour was £750, and the county faced the first of many financial crises.

The hot blazing summer of 1911 marked the meteoric rise to fame of Frank Rowbotham Foster. Offered the captaincy at the age of 22, he had accepted with hesitation: half-way through the season the side was bottom but one in the championship table, then came victory after victory: all depended on the last game, against Northamptonshire—and Warwickshire were champion county: never previously had they been higher than fifth. Foster's personal share was 1,459 runs and 124 wickets. Septimus Kinneir topped the batting averages, and Frank Field took 128 wickets: the Warwickshire team—C. S. Baker, C. Charlesworth, F. E. Field, F. R. Foster, W. C. Hands, S. P. Kinneir, A. A. Lilley, J. H. Parsons, W. G. Quaife, S. Santall, E. J. Smith, F. G. Stephens. Mr. Punch celebrated the occasion with a cartoon in which Shakespeare—who himself had a birth qualification for the county—greets Foster with the quotation 'Warwick, thou art worthy!' to which the latter replies, 'Tell Kent from me she hath lost.' *Wisden* spoke highly of F. R. Foster, commenting: 'Not since W. G. Grace in the early days of the Gloucestershire XI has so young a captain been such a match-winning force on the county side. Foster was always getting runs, always taking wickets, and, over and above all this, he proved himself a truly inspiring leader.' At the end of the season A. A. (Dick) Lilley retired, having served the county for twenty-four years: he had claimed 626 victims for Warwickshire, and no fewer than 84 against the Australians.

Foster himself had comparatively poor seasons in the next two years, but in 1914 he was back in form, scoring 1,396 runs and taking 117 wickets. He made his highest score, 305 not out, against Worcestershire, putting on 166 with E. J. Smith in seventy minutes. He was injured in a motor cycle accident, and his cricket career was tragically terminated at the age of twenty-five.

Another brilliant and all too brief career was that of Percy Jeeves, a fast-medium right-arm bowler, with a great deal of 'life' off the pitch, and an enormous zest for the game. Percy Jeeves only played for two seasons. He took a hundred wickets in 1913, his first full season. Many people believed that he had a great Test Match career in front of him: he was killed in action in 1916, at the age of twenty-eight.

Incidentally, it was very interesting to learn recently from Mr. P. G. Wodehouse that the latter got the name for his inimitable butler as a direct result of seeing Percy Jeeves playing for Warwickshire versus Gloucestershire at Cheltenham in 1913. 'I suppose that Jeeves's bowling must have impressed me,' he writes, 'for I remembered him in 1916 when I was in New York and starting the Jeeves and Bertie saga.'

After the war, Warwickshire, like all the other counties, had to start again. The Hon. F. S. G. Calthorpe captained the side from 1920 to 1929. He and Harry Howell shouldered most of the bowling, W. G. Quaife occasionally chipping in with his artful slows—the majority of the fielders spread round the boundary! The effortless grace of Calthorpe's curving run up to the crease was something quite unforgettable; at the other end, Birmingham's own Harry Howell laboured with valiant gusto. They had their day of glory when they skittled out Hampshire for 15 runs in 53 balls—but Fate wasn't always so kind to them!

In 1930 R. E. S. Wyatt became captain: before the outbreak of the second war he had received almost every honour that the game has to offer. In 1928 he had become the first Warwickshire player to score 2,000 runs for the county. A fine fielder, he achieved a fantastic swing with the new ball. J. H. (Danny) Mayer, perhaps the greatest English bowler who never represented his country, had taken over from Harry Howell—and once got both Hobbs and Sandham out in the first over of the game. Derek Foster, Wyatt and George Paine gave him support, but often the bowling lacked penetration. The batting at its best was superlative. Apart from Wyatt, there was J. H. Parsons (now the Rev. Canon J. H. Parsons), who played both for the Players and for the Gentlemen, and who once hit four sixes in succession; 'Tiger' Smith and Arthur Croom, who were consistent; Reggie Santall, who once scored 173 before lunch; Calthorpe, tantalisingly brilliant; the classical Len Bates; the prolific Norman Kilner; and the famous, diminutive Willie Quaife, who scored 71 centuries, the last of them at the age of fifty-six. The best example of the amazing heights that batting could reach occurred in 1925: set 392 to win in four hours against Sussex, Warwickshire scored the runs, for the loss of one wicket, in three hours and a quarter, Smith (139 not out), Parsons (124) and Calthorpe (109 not out) were the batsmen concerned.

In 1932 Eric Hollies, and in 1934 H. E. (Tom) Dollery, started playing for the county: by 1939 they were established members of a promising side, now led by Peter Cranmer. They were three young players who should have been at their peak between 1939 and 1945: history decreed otherwise.

In 1946, as in 1919, it was a case of starting again. The side was fortunate in having Peter Cranmer available as captain. In 1948 Eric Hollies bowled twice against the redoubtable Bradman and got him out twice. The next year Tom Dollery became Warwickshire's first professional captain. Writing in *Wisden* (1950) M. F. K. Fraser referred to the committee's confidence that the Championship would be won 'in the near future'.

And in 1951 they did it. As was the case forty years before, they were inspired by an enterprising captain with a tremendous flair for tactics. Tom Dollery had the intuition necessary in generalship: he had the intuition of the gambler who wins. His timing of declarations was splendid; he would give seemingly innocent runs away to the opposition, who were thus lured to destruction. He was remarkably sensitive to atmosphere: on going into the dressing room in the morning he could often sense which of his bowlers was likely to command success. In addition, he himself was one of the greatest No. 5 batsmen the game has ever known, with a truly remarkable capacity for playing to the needs of a particular game. One piece of good fortune attended him—this all-professional team went through the season without injury.

He had some fine bowlers. Once, C. B. Harris of Nottinghamshire, going in to face Pritchard's express deliveries, passing the alert array of Warwickshire slip fielders, greeted them unforgettably—'Good morning, fellow workers!' And Eric Hollies, wreathed in sweaters and smiles, would mutter gleefully when called on: 'What they get off me they've got to earn!' Pritchard and Grove were more than effective as opening bowlers; Hollies took 145 wickets; Weeks fought, and eventually won, a fascinating duel with Denis Compton at Lord's, whilst Townsend, says *Wisden*, 'often came to the rescue by breaking an awkward stand'. Of the batsmen, Dollery, Spooner—later to keep wicket for England—Gardner, Ord and Wolton all reached their thousand runs. A factor that contributed to the side's success was the brilliant close in fielding, especially that of Spooner, Townsend at slip, Dollery—of course!—and Gardner.

A cricket writer referred to Warwickshire as 'this extraordinary team of ordinary cricketers'—though anyone who could believe Dollery and Hollies to be ordinary cricketers could believe anything. Dollery himself said: 'You will see many better cricket teams, but I doubt if you will see a keener one. And I know that there never has been a more loyal one, not only to the club but to the captain.' The champions of 1951 were as follows: H. E. Dollery, F. C. Gardner, C. W. Grove, R. E. Hitchcock, W. E. Hollies, J. S. Ord, T. L. Pritchard, R. T. Spooner, A. Townsend, R. T. Weeks, A. V. Wolton, Donald Taylor.

It would be invidious to try to compare the relative merits of the two championship sides, but it should be said that two entirely different scoring systems were in operation. In 1911 a percentage method was employed; Somerset played only sixteen matches, Lancashire and Surrey thirty—Warwickshire played twenty matches, but they didn't play either Kent or

Middlesex who came second and third. In 1951 all the counties played 28 matches, 12 points being awarded for a win, and 4 for first-innings lead: Warwickshire played Yorkshire, their nearest rivals, twice—and won both matches.

1952–56 were years of transition. The county's most exciting game during this period was the epic encounter with the Australians, played immediately before the Final Test in 1953. Set 165 to win in two hours, fifty minutes, the Australians were only too thankful to survive with 53 for five, scored in 59 overs, Lindsay Hassett protecting even Keith Miller from the wiles of Eric Hollies! The old order changed. Dollery (1955) and Hollies (1957) retired. Hamlet without the Prince was perhaps a faint possibility; Warwickshire without Dollery and Hollies seemed inconceivable. Leslie Deakins wrote of the latter: 'We at Edgbaston will always remember him in the mind's eye as we saw him in his great days when the ritual never varied—the removal of the cap, the sweater, the marking of the run, the reflected pleasure in the feel of the ball, the easy run, the smooth action, and that unexpectedly vicious follow through.' His tally of victims was 2,323: one of his greatest achievements was when he took all ten wickets against Nottinghamshire without the help of a fielder.

A new era began in 1957, when Michael Smith took over the leadership of a young and talented side. New names were appearing on the score cards—Horner, Bannister, Ibadulla, Abberley, Amiss, David Brown, Cartwright, Jameson, the last of the Richardsons, Alan Smith—the fourth Warwickshire player to keep wicket for England—W. J. Stewart.

Michael Smith proved himself a captain in the accepted tradition. He set a splendid example in the field, snapping up catches within a yard of the bat, and scoring 2,000 runs in his first season for the county. The side would do anything for Michael Smith, with his apparently casual approach to the game, his dry sense of fun and his ability to command respect by example. It was a thousand pities that in his decade of captaincy the team never quite pulled off the Championship that they so richly deserved.

In his first two years as captain, the side achieved mediocre results, but in 1959 they finished fourth—and very nearly won the title. 'Michael Smith fired the side with his own enthusiasm for real and purposeful cricket', says the Annual Report (1959), 'and backed by his magnificent personal achievements which made him the first player in the country to aggregate over 3,000 runs for ten years, the team as a whole responded splendidly.' Seven players scored twenty centuries between them; during the season 100 sixes were hit; including 17 by W. J. Stewart in one match against Lancashire: all over the country cricket crowds flocked to see Warwickshire play.

1960 was a disappointing season, chiefly because of disappointing weather; but Horner and Ibadulla had an unbroken first-wicket stand of 377 against Surrey. In the next year the team did a little better, finishing twelfth compared with fifteenth.

The years 1962–67 were probably Warwickshire's best six consecutive seasons since the Club was formed. In 1962 the team finished third, missing the Championship by the narrowest of margins; Cartwright performed the 'double'—the first player for the county to do so since F. R. Foster—M. J. K. Smith, Stewart and Ibadulla all scored 2,000 runs; Bannister, Cartwright and Wright took 100 wickets; A. C. Smith had 78 victims behind the stumps. M. J. K. Smith made 48 catches, including 6 in one innings against Leicestershire.

In 1963 the team finished fifth; about mid-August there was an outside chance of winning the title, but the last three matches were lost to the rain, rather than the opposition. The advent of R. W. Barber to the side—on his day the most exciting batsman in England—was a great acquisition.

In 1964 Warwickshire made a glorious challenge both for the Championship and for the Gillette Cup. The Championship soon resolved itself into a struggle for supremacy with Worcestershire, the latter eventually drawing away by mid-August. R. V. Webster's analysis in the match against Yorkshire needs no comment:

O.	M.	R.	W.
12.4	7	6	7

Against the Australians R. W. Barber batted splendidly to score a century before lunch. The county reached the final of the Gillette Cup competition but came to grief against Sussex, when N. I. Thomson bowled excellently in the humid morning atmosphere. The next year produced a mild relapse, the team finishing eleventh; and losing by 20 runs to Yorkshire in the semi-final of the Gillette Cup. Rain seemed to follow Warwickshire everywhere. Asked by an interviewer to explain the county's relatively low position, Michael Smith replied with justification that you can't win matches if you can't get on to the field.

In 1966 the team finished sixth. The highlight here was a three-wicket victory in a low-scoring match against Yorkshire at Hull. In this year Warwickshire won the Gillette Cup, thanks to enterprising batting and a splendid battery of seam bowlers. Victories against Glamorgan, Gloucestershire and Somerset were followed by the defeat of Worcestershire in the final. Accurate bowling (Cartwright three for 16 in 12 overs) and a brilliant catch by Ibadulla to dismiss Graveney confined Worcestershire to 155 in 60 overs: victory was achieved fairly comfortably by 5 wickets. In a superbly played challenge match against the West Indies, the latter scored 257 for four at five runs an over. Warwickshire batted bravely, Barber scoring 63 and Amiss 76, losing in the end by 19 runs.

In 1967 Warwickshire were once again foiled by the weather in the early part of the season, and in the Gillette Cup the team lost a rain-ridden match to Somerset. Better results were achieved in the sunshine, the team eventually finishing tenth. Amiss was second in the batting averages, Cartwright third in the bowling averages. The team included seven players who have represented their country in Test Matches—and the famous Lance Gibbs will be available this year.

Running more or less parallel to Michael Smith's captaincy has been the remarkable development of the Supporters' Club, with the result that

Warwickshire, long accustomed to struggling from one financial crisis to another, now have no money problems. With a membership of 700,000 paying a shilling a week, the Supporters' Club has spent £750,000 on the redevelopment of the Edgbaston ground as a Test Match centre; including—putting first things first—the completion of an Indoor Cricket School. The organising geniuses behind all this are Mr. and Mrs. David Blakemore.

No survey of Warwickshire cricket would be complete without reference to H. W. Bainbridge, L. C. Docker, C. A. F. Hastilow and Edmund King, stalwarts who between them have notched nearly two centuries of service to the Club, as players and as administrators; Lt.-General Sir Oliver Leese, Bt., the President of the Club, is the only man with Warwickshire associations to have become President of the M.C.C.

The county has been fortunate in having three outstanding secretaries, passionately devoted to the game in general and to the Club in particular; and three great groundsmen—John Bates, Ted Leyland and Bernard Flack, who have made Edgbaston what Colin Cowdrey has called one of the three best cricket grounds in the world. George Austin 'scored' every run for the two Championship sides. Sydney Santall, bowler, coach, cricket historian, served the Club valiantly for fifty years. E. J. Smith—the incomparable 'Tiger'—played in the Championship team of 1911, and coached the Championship team of 1951. Now, at eighty-one, he still helps the versatile Derief Taylor—who came from Jamaica as a player and remained as a coach—at the Indoor Cricket School. 'The gatemen are beginning to know me, now!' says Tiger with a Falstaffian chuckle, and with that characteristic wicked twinkle in his eye.

Michael Smith—the only Warwickshire player to have been appointed M.C.C. captain in Australia—has, alas, retired. We can rest assured that his successor, Alan Smith, will live up to the county tradition—that of playing cricket as it should be played.

You can do worse.

EPILOGUE

With the 1968 edition of Wisden there closes an era which had lasted ever since the spread of the game two hundred years before, a period in which the troubles of cricket, large though they may have loomed at the time, can be seen in retrospect to have been little ones. Even the great row over Bodyline had its roots in something quaintly parochial, differing interpretations of the laws of the game. Bitter though it was, that argument was a purely cricketing one in the sense that all the disputatious spirits who involved themselves were animated by what happened on the field. Through the 1960s, new problems seemed to be taking on subtly unfamiliar and vaguely ominous aspects. Falling attendances and financial crises, the embracing of sponsorship, the acceptance of the one-day game as an economic expedient, all these nightmares had their effect on the changing face of the English game. But still the problems of cricket were cricket problems although the abolition of the distinction between Amateurs and Professionals was a belated reflection of profound social changes taking place in English life.

But thus far administrators had succeeded, if not in keeping politics out of cricket, at any rate concealing its presence there. The events of the 1968 season, reported in the 1969 Almanack, finally flung the game into the very forefront of world politics, splashing cricket all over the front page, splitting the nation down the middle. The old order, by which anything awkward or ugly was either swept under the carpet or muffled in euphemism, was about to be blown apart once and for all. The compilers of the 1968 edition would have been incredulous had anyone suggested to them that the next time they produced an edition of Wisden, the landscape would be an unfamiliar and frightening one. Cricket, so far from keeping itself out of politics, was about to *become* politics.